Social Work

Series Editor

Richard Hugman, School of Social Sciences, University of New South Wales, Sydney, NSW, Australia

The MRW in Social Work enables social work practitioners, policy makers and academics across the world to access in-depth, authoritative literature and cutting-edge research into professional practice, ethics, practice-based research methods and policy in the field. Grounding practice and policy in systematic theories and principles, it covers all specialties in the field including children and families, older adults, mental health, people with disabilities, domestic and gendered violence, intercultural practice, sexuality, international social work and community development. Drawing on a strong scientific basis, it offers reviews and analyses of key social issues, policy frameworks and practice methods, including counseling, casework, family therapy, groupwork, community work, community development, social development and social policy practice.

Dorothee Hölscher · Richard Hugman ·
Donna McAuliffe
Editors

Social Work Theory and Ethics

Ideas in Practice

With 17 Figures and 6 Tables

Editors
Dorothee Hölscher
School of Nursing, Midwifery and
Social Work
The University of Queensland
St Lucia, Brisbane, QLD, Australia

Richard Hugman
School of Social Sciences
University of New South Wales
Sydney, NSW, Australia

Donna McAuliffe
School of Health Sciences and Social Work
Griffith University
Logan, QLD, Australia

Social Work
ISBN 978-981-19-1014-2   ISBN 978-981-19-1015-9 (eBook)
https://doi.org/10.1007/978-981-19-1015-9

© Springer Nature Singapore Pte Ltd. 2023
This work is subject to copyright. All rights are solely and exclusively licensed by the Publisher, whether the whole or part of the material is concerned, specifically the rights of translation, reprinting, reuse of illustrations, recitation, broadcasting, reproduction on microfilms or in any other physical way, and transmission or information storage and retrieval, electronic adaptation, computer software, or by similar or dissimilar methodology now known or hereafter developed.
The use of general descriptive names, registered names, trademarks, service marks, etc. in this publication does not imply, even in the absence of a specific statement, that such names are exempt from the relevant protective laws and regulations and therefore free for general use.
The publisher, the authors, and the editors are safe to assume that the advice and information in this book are believed to be true and accurate at the date of publication. Neither the publisher nor the authors or the editors give a warranty, expressed or implied, with respect to the material contained herein or for any errors or omissions that may have been made. The publisher remains neutral with regard to jurisdictional claims in published maps and institutional affiliations.

This Springer imprint is published by the registered company Springer Nature Singapore Pte Ltd.
The registered company address is: 152 Beach Road, #21-01/04 Gateway East, Singapore 189721, Singapore

Series Preface

Professional social work now exists in over 90 countries. From its early origins in the later part of the 1800s, it has sought to develop a strong scientific basis, grounding practice and policy in systematic theories and principles. Today, as social work grows in all parts of the world, its body of knowledge about social issues, practices to address these and relevant policy frameworks is expanding rapidly. Consequently, keeping up to date on such knowledge is increasingly challenging for practitioners, policy makers and academics in the field. This series makes research-based knowledge available for everyone who has an interest in maintaining their grasp of the discipline by bringing together leading social work scholars, practitioners and policy makers to examine contemporary evidence on various aspects of the field. In this way, it provides an authoritative range of voices from which everyone in the profession may gain a deeper understanding grounded in evidence.

As it has expanded, social work has developed many areas of specialty, each of which now has its own body of knowledge that constitutes a sub-field of the profession as a whole. The Major Research Works in Social Work series addresses the need for up-to-date, authoritative, extensive reviews and analyses of knowledge in a range of areas of social work. Edited by significant contributors in each aspect of specialty, these volumes offer in-depth discussion of the specific practices and issues of policy and the organisation of relevant services. By taking this approach, it is possible to ensure appropriate coverage of the range of specialties and also at the same time to provide sufficient depth of analysis and discussion of key ideas.

As a profession, social work can be understood in a number of ways. First, there are fields of practice. These include children and families, older adults, mental health, people with disabilities, domestic and gendered violence, inter-cultural practice, sexuality and international social work. Second, methods of practice also define areas of knowledge in social work. These include counselling, casework and case management, family therapy, groupwork, community work and community development, social development, social policy practice. Third, there are overarching issues that contribute to social work knowledge and theory, including professional ethics, practice-based research methods, policy studies. These are examples indicative of the range, rather than forming a definitive list, and point to the way in which a series may enable both breadth and depth to be addressed. At the same time, they point to the extensive coverage that is relevant to the broad social work field.

Although much of the tradition of social work research and analysis came originally from those countries that experienced early industrialisation (the 'global North'), given the worldwide growth of social work, the editorial approach for this series also aims to be global in its focus. Volume editors and contributors are drawn purposefully from around the world and they in turn are expected to take a world-wide view of ensuring that the current evidence and analysis is presented. In addition to established leaders in the field with identification of the emerging leaders of the future whose work is seen as cutting edge.

This series will develop by selecting major themes across fields of practice, methods of practice and over-arching issues. Future titles will be added to the initial five areas, reflecting the breadth of the social work profession. At the same time, because Springer Major Research Works are 'living' publications, able to be updated, the continuing development of the profession will be reflected in analysis and discussion that grows with the field through publication of revised chapters as further evidence and analysis becomes available.

As Editor-in-Chief, I acknowledge the commitment and insights of the editors to each specific volume. Their expertise and hard work enable this series to pursue its overall goal. As one of the editors of this present volume, I wish to acknowledge and thank my two co-editors, Dorothee Hölscher and Donna McAuliffe, for their collegiality, perceptiveness, judgement and hard work. I also thank our Publishing Editor at Springer Nature, Dr. Mokshika Gaur, for her vision, enthusiasm and support, and other colleagues at Springer Nature who have assisted in the process of creating these volumes.

Emeritus Professor of Social Work Richard Hugman PhD
University of New South Wales, Australia
Series Editor, Springer Nature Major Research
Works Social Work Series
March 2023

Volume Preface

This reference work uniquely brings together the complementary dimensions of social work theory with each other and with ethical research and scholarship in the field. Thus, it presents an analysis of the ideas of social work in a way that enables connections between them to be identified and explored.

Much of the existing social work literature addresses questions of theory and ethics separately so that a distinction is created between them. However, the differences between these categories of thought can be somewhat arbitrary. This volume goes beyond this simple separation of categories. Although it recognises that questions of theory and ethics may be addressed distinctly, the connections between them can be made evident and drawn out by analysing them alongside each other. Moreover, ethical issues are currently emerging at a global scale, which present new and previously hard-to-imagine challenges and which require a theoretical re-grounding of social work and a re-consideration of the range of theories to which they may connect. In this way, social work contributes to wider debates through the advancement of its own perspectives and knowledge gained through practice and the ethics that inform all aspects of social work.

Social work's use and development of theory can be understood in two complementary ways. First, theory from the social sciences and other disciplines can be applied for social work; second, considered, systematic examinations of practice have enabled theory to be developed out of social work. These different approaches are often referred to as theory for practice and practice theory. The advancement of social work theory occurs often through the interplay between research and scholarship across these two dimensions. Similarly, social work ethics draw on values and principles that have their roots in philosophical inquiry while also involving the applied analysis of the particular issues and challenges with which social workers engage, and of their practices in doing so. These 4 categories of social work theorising and ethical thought – theory for social work, social work practice theory, social work values and principles, and ethical issues and challenges – provide the 4 sections into which the 24 substantive chapters that make up this volume are divided.

Across these sections, this volume connects social work theory and ethical questions using four conceptual arcs. There are, firstly, those chapters, which place the human at the centre of social work's primary mandate. Then, there are those chapters which critically engage with the person/structure interface where many of social work's theoretical and ethical conundrums arise. Thirdly, there are a number of chapters which are concerned specifically with the effects of colonialism and the mainstreaming of previously marginalised traditions within social work. Finally, forming a fourth arc, there is a set of chapters, which provide thought-provoking contributions that de-centre the human and consider its complex multispecies relationships.

This volume brings together 36 authors from 5 continents and draws on decades of social work theorising and ethics. Each chapter provides an account of the treatment of its topic in social work scholarship; relates its topic to the nature and purpose of social work; and provides its authors' analysis of key elements, presenting their own argument about what is significant in the topic at hand. Together, the authors demonstrate how well-placed social work is to respond to the complex challenges and increasingly intersecting crises, to which human activity has given rise but which also always also contain openings and possibilities for a more just and caring world. *Social Work Theory and Ethics* is an essential reference book for social work students, academics, researchers, practitioners, and policymakers.

Brisbane, Australia   Dorothee Hölscher
Sydney, Australia   Richard Hugman
Logan, Australia   Donna McAuliffe
March 2023

Contents

Part I Introduction 1

1 Theory and Ethics: Defining the Field 3
   Richard Hugman, Dorothee Hölscher, and Donna McAuliffe

Part II Theories for Social Work 15

2 Psychological and Clinical Theories 17
   Herman Hay Ming Lo

3 Systems Theory and Social Work 39
   Jan V. Wirth and Heiko Kleve

4 Revisiting Critical Theory 61
   Edgar Marthinsen

5 Postmodern Theory in Practice: Narrative Practice in
   Social Work 79
   Catrina Brown

6 Colonisation, Post-colonialism and Decolonisation 101
   Susan Green

7 Post-anthropocentric Social Work 121
   Karen Bell

Part III Social Work Practice Theory 141

8 Person-Centred Approaches to Social Work Practice 143
   Adrian D. van Breda

9 Problem-Solving Theory: The Task-Centred Model 169
   Blanca M. Ramos and Randall L. Stetson

10 Anti-oppressive Social Work Practice Theory 189
   Donna Baines and Hannah Kia

11 **Caring Justice:** *The Global Rise of Feminist Practice Theory* 209
Tina Maschi, Smita Dewan, Sandra G. Turner, and Padma Christie

12 **Developmental and Community-Based Social Work** 229
Janestic Mwende Twikirize

13 **Indigenous Knowledge and Social Work Crossing the Paths for Intervention** 251
Allucia Lulu Shokane and Mogomme Alpheus Masoga

14 **Environmental Social Work** 267
Margaret Alston

Part IV Social Work Values and Principles 287

15 **Social Work, Human Rights, and Ethics** 289
Sharlene Nipperess

16 **Social Justice and Social Work** 311
Neil Thompson and Paul Stepney

17 **Virtues, Social Work and Social Service Organizations** 331
Eleni Papouli

18 **An Ethic of Care: Contributions to Social Work Practice** 349
Donna McAuliffe

19 **Reconfiguring Social Work Ethics with Posthuman and Post-anthropocentric Imaginaries** 367
Vivienne Bozalek and Dorothee Hölscher

20 **Ethical Pluralism and Social Work** 397
Richard Hugman

Part V Ethical Issues and Challenges in Social Work 419

21 **The Ethical Challenge of Populism in Social Work** 421
Dorothee Hölscher and Derek Clifford

22 **Critical Social Work and Ethics: Working with Asylum Seekers in Australia** 445
Kim Robinson

23 **Emerging Ethical Voices in Social Work** 463
Ming-Sum Tsui, Ruby Chien-Ju Pai, Peace Yuh Ju Wong, and Cheong-Hay Chu

24	**Social Work in Extremis: Human Rights, Necropolitics, and Post-human Onto-ethics**	479
	Goetz Ottmann and Iris Silva Brito	
25	**Emerging Futures and Technology Ethics**	499
	Melanie Sage and Gina Griffin	

Part VI Conclusion **517**

26	**The Ideas of Social Work Practice**	519
	Dorothee Hölscher, Donna McAuliffe, and Richard Hugman	

Index 533

About the Editors

Dr. Dorothee Hölscher is a social work lecturer in the School of Nursing Midwifery and Social Work at The University of Queensland in Australia and a research associate with the Department of Social Work and Criminology at the University of Pretoria in South Africa. Previously, she worked at Griffith University (Australia) and the Universities of KwaZulu Natal and the Witwatersrand (South Africa). Currently, she serves on the editorial board of the journal *Ethics and Social Welfare* (ESW).

Dorothee began her social work education in Germany, followed by the completion of a Master of Social Science (*cum laude*) and a PhD (by publication) in South Africa. Her practice experience comprises social work with refugees and other cross-border migrants, community development, and child protection.

Dorothee's research areas are applied ethics (with a focus on justice) in higher education and social work practice, anti-oppressive social work theory, and social work with migrants and culturally and linguistically diverse communities. Having participated as co-investigator in four international research projects at the intersection of higher education and social justice, Dorothee's research skill set comprises a wide range of qualitative and post-qualitative methodologies. To date, she published 1 monograph and over 39 edited collections, book chapters, and scholarly articles, serves as a reviewer for 8 local and international journals, and presents regularly at local and international conferences.

Richard Hugman, PhD, is an emeritus professor of Social Work in the School of Social Sciences (SoSS) at the University of New South Wales, Australia. He has practised, taught, and researched social work in Australia and the UK. He has also worked as an independent consultant, most notably for UNICEF Vietnam (from 2004 to 2022). Richard's work has variously focused on professional ethics, social development, refugees and forced migration, mental health, and social work with issues of late life. He has published widely in these areas, as well as being an editor or member of editorial boards of several major social work journals. In addition, Richard was the ethics commissioner of the International Federation of Social Workers (2008–2014) and a member of the 'expert panel' which drafted the 2004 international statement on ethics for social work. He was a Foundation Fellow of the Australian College of Social Work.

Donna McAuliffe is a professor and academic lead for Social Work in the School of Health Sciences and Social Work, Griffith University, Australia. Donna completed her PhD on ethical dilemmas in social work practice at the University of Queensland in 2000 after many years of practice in mental health, legal social work, community development, and social policy. Her primary focus area of teaching and research is professional and applied ethics, and she has developed a well-known model of ethical decision-making that is widely used in social work education. Donna is the sole author of the second edition text, *Interprofessional Ethics: Collaboration in the Social, Health and Human Services* published by Cambridge University Press. She is also the lead co-author of the 7th edition text, *The Road to Social Work and Human Service Practice*, published by Cengage. She has a longstanding commitment to Editorial Boards of journals, including *Ethics and Social Welfare*, *International Social Work*, and *International Journal of Social Work Values and Ethics*. She regularly reviews for a number of other national and international journals. Donna has been actively involved in revisions of the Australian social work Code of Ethics and is a Life Member of the Australian Association of Social Workers. She is also a Senior Fellow of the Higher Education Academy.

Contributors

Margaret Alston Social Work, University of Newcastle, Newcastle, NSW, Australia

Monash University, Melbourne, VIC, Australia

Donna Baines School of Social Work, University of British Columbia, Vancouver, Canada

Karen Bell School of Social Work and Arts, Charles Sturt University, Wagga Wagga, NSW, Australia

Vivienne Bozalek Women's and Gender Studies, University of the Western Cape, Cape Town, South Africa

Centre for Higher Education Research, Teaching and Learning (CHERTL), Rhodes University, Eastern Cape, South Africa

Iris Silva Brito Australian College of Applied Professions (ACAP), Discipline of Social Work, Melbourne, Australia

Catrina Brown School of Social Work, Dalhousie University, Halifax, NS, Canada

Padma Christie Graduate School of Social Service, Fordham University, New York, NY, USA

Cheong-Hay Chu Felizberta Lo Padilla Tong School of Social Sciences, Caritas Institute of Higher Education, Hong Kong, Hong Kong

Derek Clifford Formerly, Liverpool John Moores University, Liverpool, UK

Smita Dewan New York City College of Technology, City University of New York, New York, NY, USA

Susan Green SIAS, Charles Sturt University, Wagga Wagga, NSW, Australia

Gina Griffin James A Haley Veterans Administration, Tampa, FL, USA

Dorothee Hölscher School of Nursing, Midwifery & Social Work, The University of Queensland, St Lucia Brisbane, QLD, Australia

Department of Social Work & Criminology, University of Pretoria, Pretoria, South Africa

Richard Hugman School of Social Sciences, University of New South Wales, Sydney, NSW, Australia

Hannah Kia School of Social Work, University of British Columbia, Vancouver, Canada

Heiko Kleve Stiftungslehrstuhl für Organisation und Entwicklung von Unternehmerfamilien, University Witten/Herdecke, Witten, Germany

Herman Hay Ming Lo Department of Applied Social Sciences, Hong Kong Polytechnic University, Hung Hom, Hong Kong

Edgar Marthinsen Department of Social Work, Norwegian University of Technology and Science, NTNU, Trondheim, Norway

Tina Maschi Fordham University, New York, NY, USA

Mogomme Alpheus Masoga Faculty of Humanities and Social Sciences, University of Zululand, KwaDlagezwa, South Africa

Donna McAuliffe School of Health Sciences and Social Work, Griffith University, Logan, QLD, Australia

Sharlene Nipperess School of Global Urban and Social Studies, RMIT University, Melbourne, VIC, Australia

Goetz Ottmann School of Social Work, Federation University Australia, Berwick, VIC, Australia

Ruby Chien-Ju Pai Department of Guidance and Counselling, National Changhua University of Education, Changhua, Taiwan

Eleni Papouli University of West Attica, Athens, Greece

Blanca M. Ramos State University of New York at Albany, Albany, NY, USA

Kim Robinson School of Health & Social Development, Faculty of Health, Deakin University, Geelong, VIC, Australia

Melanie Sage University at Buffalo School of Social Work, New York, NY, USA

Allucia Lulu Shokane Department of Social Work, Faculty of Humanities and Social Sciences, University of Zululand, KwaDlagezwa, South Africa

Paul Stepney Tampere University, Tampere, Finland

Randall L. Stetson State University of New York at Oswego, Oswego, NY, USA

Neil Thompson Avenue Consulting and visiting professor at the Open University, Wrexham, UK

Ming-Sum Tsui Felizberta Lo Padilla Tong School of Social Sciences, Caritas Institute of Higher Education, Hong Kong, Hong Kong

Sandra G. Turner Graduate School of Social Service, Fordham University, New York, NY, USA

Janestic Mwende Twikirize Makerere University, Kampala, Uganda

Adrian D. van Breda Department of Social Work and Community Development, University of Johannesburg, Johannesburg, South Africa

Jan V. Wirth Hochschule Düsseldorf, Düsseldorf, Germany

Peace Yuh Ju Wong Department of Social Work, National University of Singapore, Singapore, Singapore

Part I
Introduction

Theory and Ethics: Defining the Field

Richard Hugman, Dorothee Hölscher, and Donna McAuliffe

Contents

Introduction	4
Theory	5
The Development of Theory in Social Work	6
Ethics	8
The Growth and Relevance of Ethics in Social Work	9
Theory and Ethics as the 'Ideas of Social Work'	11
Conclusion	12
References	13

Abstract

As well as being a set of practices, social work is also comprised of diverse ideas about the social issues and personal problems in which those practices intervene. This introductory chapter presents a review of the two major types of ideas of social work: theory and ethics. Two forms of theory are identified, namely 'theory for practice' (that is, theories developed in separate areas of inquiry that are brought to the concerns of social work) and 'practice theory' (that is, theories that are developed from the conscious and systematic reflection on practice). The chapter then looks at ethics, first in the ethical principles that have their origins outside social work, and then in critical analysis of specific ethical issues that are

---

R. Hugman (✉)
School of Social Sciences, University of New South Wales, Sydney, NSW, Australia
e-mail: r.hugman@unsw.edu.au

D. Hölscher
School of Nursing, Midwifery and Social Work, University of Queensland, St. Lucia, Australia
e-mail: d.holscher@uq.edu.au

D. McAuliffe
School of Health Sciences and Social Work, Griffith University, Logan, QLD, Australia
e-mail: d.mcauliffe@griffith.edu.au

encountered in practice, including those now emerging. In this sense, both types of ideas have aspects that are brought into and those that are developed within social work. There is also an interplay between social work theory and ethics, with some common themes that reflect the focus of social workers on the origins of the structural issues and personal problems with which social workers intervene and ways to address such issues and problems. In this way, bringing theory and ethics together as 'the ideas of social work' reveals the continuities between the ways in which sense is made of questions concerning the what, how and why of social work.

Keywords

Social work · Theory · Ethics · Practice - Profession

Introduction

All professional practices are grounded in ideas. This is so whether the practice in question is the early medicine of Hippocrates (circa 460–375 BCE) or the most up to date quantum electronics (Simmons 2002). Even before social work was recognized as a distinct area of human activity, what might be termed proto-social-work was developed from various sets of ideas about social issues and personal problems, their causes and possible resolution (Payne 2005). These ideas not only addressed the nature of such issues and problems but also the social actions that might be undertaken goals and purposes and about the ways in which they might effectively be undertaken. As social work has professionalized the body of ideas that inform and define its areas of knowledge and practice have developed, through critical reflection and research.

The sets of ideas that have come to define social work can be regarded as two related but distinct types. The first of these concern concepts that explain the world: theory. In a professional practice field such as social work, theory may be regarded as a systematic body of explanations of the (social) world that not only inform an understanding of the concern of the profession (in this case social issues and personal problems) but also at the same time indicate actions that might be undertaken to address these.

The second set of ideas relates to consideration of what is good and right in the goals of social work and the means of achieving them: ethics. Like theory, these ideas are explanatory, but their focus is on the values that are expressed through different practices. For example, it may be that a particular action could be successful in resolving a particular social issue or personal problem, but consideration must also be given to whether that action can be considered good or right in terms of the moral values of the profession and the wider society.

Grasping the ideas that inform social work is vital if we are to understand, critique, and further develop the profession. Both theory and ethics are embedded in the practices of social work, not only informing what social workers do but actually constituting the very nature of the profession in all its various aspects. These two sets of ideas are the focus of this volume.

Theory

A theory is a systematic explanation of the way in which phenomena occur. As this applies to human behaviour and society, theories are explanations of the ways in which people think and act and of the social relations and structures that form the context of their lives. In a world dominated by a scientific worldview, theories may be expected to be based on rigorously examined evidence.

A series of studies in the UK in the early 1980s argued that there was little indication of social workers integrating theory in their work (Parsloe 1981). In the context of a major, rapid development in the professionalization of social work in that country, Parsloe's research was concerned with how this process could be enhanced and what needed to be done to make it more robust in dealing with the tasks that had been assigned to it. Others were perhaps less committed to social work as a profession. One critic even claimed that social work should be seen as 'a theory*less* practice' (Bailey 1980, emphasis added). For Bailey, this led to the conclusion that social work was unlikely to develop further as a profession, even that it would be better seen as a set of administrative practices that ought to be prescribed by legal and political processes. Others, such as Brewer and Lait (1980) argued that social work had a place within the professions, but because it did not have a clear body of theory that was tested scientifically only in so far as it was directed and supervised by a profession that did. In their conclusion this should be psychiatry (although they restricted this to behaviourist and pharmacological psychiatry and explicitly excluded psychotherapy). Unlike Parsloe, who thought that a body of theory could be developed, both Bailey and Brewer and Lait concluded that this was at best unlikely and probably impossible.

Against this negative view, Curnock and Hardiker (1979) and Hardiker and Barker (1981) proposed a way of understanding different types of theory that *are* evident in social work. They identified two forms of theory. The first of these is 'theory for practice', in which the theories of the wider social sciences are brought to bear on social work issues and practices (such as from psychology, sociology, anthropology, political science, economics, and so on; bio-medical theory might also be added to this list). The second form is 'practice theory', which is generated by systematic consideration of social work actions and their outcomes. The distinction between these types made clearer the way in which social workers did engage with theory, even if individual practitioners did not report this as 'use of theory'. Hardiker and her colleagues pointed to the ways, in the many other countries in which social work was professionalizing, it was already grounded in theory, even if that theory did not necessarily conform to the very scientific model asserted by critics such as Brewer and Lait. Indeed, it is noticeable that this debate occurred specifically in the

UK, in the aftermath of a major change in the organization of social work and where social work was mostly provided through government agencies and, hence, already subject to the sort of legal and political direction suggested by Bailey.

The Development of Theory in Social Work

In the intervening decades there has been a significant growth in the extent to which a concern with the ideas that inform social work are analysed, debated and applied. For example, Howe (1987) and Payne (1990) demonstrated that social work draws on a very wide range of theories, also providing evidence of their use in practice. Indeed, in recent years there has been an expansion in the range of such analyses, supporting Howe's and Payne's argument (such as Trevithick 2012, Gray and Webb 2013, Healy 2014, Chenoweth and McAuliffe 2020).

The ongoing debates about theory in social work have tended to diverge around two sub-themes. The first of these can be understood as a type of 'chicken-and-egg' argument about which comes first. Is theory derived from academic research in the bio-psycho-social sciences and then applied to social issues and personal problems? Alternatively, is theory developed out of critical reflection on what makes sense in practice experience? This debate continues, even though it is now several decades since Hardiker and her colleagues (1979, 1981) pointed out that both forms of theorizing are central to social work. The distinction between them is helpful for consideration of any theoretical statement, but this is not an 'either-or' question. Recognition of the value of both types of theory has been helpful as social work has professionalized over the last 40 years and continues to be so. (Indeed, a similar argument appears as part of the contribution by Wirth and Kleve in this present volume.)

This 'both-and' approach to theory is clearly evident in Payne's (2021) continued review of modern social work theory. From a smaller coverage in the first edition in 1990, the most recent iteration now addresses 15 areas of theory relevant to social work, as well as a more extensive discussion of theory and its relationship with practice, including the theory for practice and practice theory distinction that has been noted here. These theories include both micro and macro perspectives on the understanding of the (social) world and on the practice orientations of social work. Howe's later work (2014) has a similar broad focus across different types of theory. This inclusive view of theory in relation to the various approaches taken in social work appears to the present authors to be the most appropriate way to view both social work and the theory that informs it (compare with Hugman 2009, Chenoweth and McAuliffe 2020). Although, appropriately, there are now many discussions of specific theories related to particular aspects of social work practice, or to distinct practices, any review of research and scholarship on the nature of theory in social work and the overall relationship of theory and practice ought to be inclusive.

In the specific areas of practice and their associated theories considerable progress has been made in recent decades. It was not correct to argue in the late 1970s that there was no theory used in social work. Examples include the casework theory of

Reid and his colleagues (1969, 1972), which was itself grounded in systems theory, or the community social work of Leonard (1975). However, it was probably the case that most social workers did not recognize these ideas explicitly as *theory*.

As noted above, greater awareness of theory in social work has led to a diverse range of ideas. One approach is to examine a particular element of personal experience and social life. For example, some theories are concerned with individual human functioning, with clear links to psychology in behavioural models, especially cognitive-behavioural theory, and in psychodynamic theory. There are also theories that focus on the individual level but are social and structural in nature, such as the task-centred theory noted above, crisis intervention, narrative, humanistic (including existential), and spiritual ideas (Trevithick 2012; Healy 2014; Howe 2014; Chenoweth and McAuliffe 2020; Payne 2021). Another broad set of theories can be seen in what might be understood as social-critical approaches, such as anti-discriminatory, feminist, anti-racist and multicultural, and ecological theories (Trevithick 2012; Healy 2014; Howe 2014; Chenoweth and McAuliffe 2020; Payne 2021). Cutting across these distinctions other theories can be seen to operate. These include strengths and solution focused practice, empowerment and advocacy, and critical practice. Although a distinction revolving around micro and macro focused practices might be assumed (such as between casework and community development), there is a great deal of influence from all these theories on micro level practice, for example, in feminist counselling or the use of strengths-based ideas in casework. Conversely, macro level practices such as social and community development are unlikely to be areas where psychologically informed theories are found. However, this is not an absolute distinction, as evidenced by recent research in trauma theory, from which the implications for both micro and macro level practices are currently being developed (Levenson 2017; Goelitz 2021).

In this present volume, reviews and discussion of developments in social work theories are presented in two parts (groups of chapters). The first of these (Part II) considers theories that are derived from distinct areas of academic or other research inquiry, under the notion of 'theory for social work' (to use Hardiker et al.'s term). These include psychological and clinical theory, narrative theory, decolonial theory, systems theory, critical theory, and post-humanist theory. The next part brings together chapters on person-centred practice, problem-solving practice (including task-centred social work), feminist theory, Indigenous theory, anti-oppressive practice, and environmental social work. The thread linking these discussions is that of 'practice theory' (to employ a widely used term). The range of theories included here is not exhaustive, but rather seeks to take key forms of theory as it is relevant for social work, ensuring coverage across individual and collective human experience, so drawing on various disciplinary backgrounds. In some instances, the relevance of theory for micro level practice is dominant, others are clearly macro level in focus; however, in other areas, theories are not so simply contained in one particular level, so that strengths-based ideas, and empowerment and advocacy, are seen to inform both micro and macro theories and practices, for example.

Greater emphasis on theory in the social work curriculum as well as in everyday practice has assisted social work in several ways. First, it has encouraged social workers to be more conscious of the bases for their actions, so that they are able to increase their competence. Second, consequently, it has enabled social work to be more effective and to demonstrate its effectiveness to others. Third, arising from the interplay between the first and second factors, theoretical awareness and sophistication has enhanced the ability of social workers to be ethically accountable for their practice. The capacity to explain the reasons informing choices of actions to service users and to other professions helps others to be able to make use of social work intervention and to work together with the social worker. In particular, this strengthens the agency of service users, which is not only practically helpful but also promotes the ethical dimensions of social work practice (compare with IFSW/IASSW 2018). In this sense there is a strong connection between the two sets of ideas: theory and ethics.

Ethics

Ethics can be understood as the intentional reflection on moral values. That is, ethics concerns deliberation on what is good and bad, or right and wrong in human thought and action. The concern with ethics can be seen over several thousand years and is present in all cultures, in the form of lore, law, religion and philosophy. Examples that continue to have great influence in the twenty-first century include the ideas of the classical Greek thinkers (such as Socrates, Plato and Aristotle) and ancient Chinese teachers (such as Confucius) as well as the traditions embedded in African and other Indigenous cultures.

As a consequence of the processes of modernization, colonialism, and globalization, ethical principles prevailing in many parts of the world are derived from the European traditions. These, in turn, have arisen from the developments of classical Greek philosophy, mediated through mediaeval Christianity, the Enlightenment and the rise of positivistic science (MacIntyre 1998). However, as the world is rapidly changing, this dominance is shifting, so that ethical systems from Africa and Asia increasingly are becoming more prominent in international discourse, along with the emergence of ethical principles and values from Indigenous cultures in various parts of the world.

Ethical ideas can be seen to operate at three levels: meta-ethics; normative ethics; descriptive ethics (Banks 2020 p. 5). The first of these, meta-ethics, refers to the nature of morality in general terms. For example, debates about notions such as 'good' or 'right' or how ethical judgements might be made constitute this level. Second, normative ethics is seen in consideration of particular moral questions and problems. For example, thinking about the right course of action in a given situation, and which principles should be brought to bear on it, and expression of the normative level. Third, the idea of descriptive ethics refers to portrayals or analysis of what ethical decisions and actions have applied in any given situation. For example, asking what judgements were made and why is a form of descriptive ethics. In popular use, the term 'ethics' usually is not differentiated between these levels, but in philosophy, the natural and social sciences, and in professional practice, it is important to recognize how this term is being applied. Indeed, it is often the case that even in these more specific contexts that 'ethical' is frequently used instead of the terms 'good' or 'right' (as in saying that a person 'is ethical', meaning that they are a good person). However, more correctly, ethics refers to the process of conscious deliberation about moral values – that is, it applies to a process of human activity – and it is used in this way throughout the present volume. Nevertheless, although the discourse of professional ethics may refer to meta-ethics in order to establish the basis of its deliberations, it largely is concerned with normative and descriptive ethical questions.

Ethics has become a much more important aspect of professional life over the last 100 years. It can even be said that by the latter part of the twentieth century ethics had become a key aspect of occupational claims to professionalism (Hugman 1991, 2005; McAuliffe 2021). That is, in order to be able to assume the status of a profession, with the associated assumptions of independent governance and accountability, any occupation is expected to be able to articulate an explicit statement of ethical commitments. Thus, professional status derives not only from distinct areas of knowledge and skill, but also to having an ethical dimension that is core to the nature of that occupation. Yet, at the same time, knowledge and skill are part of this process. Reasons for the importance of ethics in the professions can be explained from the increasing knowledge base of such occupations that relate not only to aspects of human life, in terms of what people do and the social context in which they do it, but to human beings themselves, physically, psychologically, culturally, spiritually, and so on. These capacities carry with them considerable social power to act in ways that either promote or act against the well-being and interest of others. Therefore, these occupations carry a very high level of responsibility, to those who use or receive their services and the wider society.

One example of this can be seen in the case of medicine. At times during the twentieth century medical practitioners and researchers acted in ways that were harmful to others, such as in conducting experiments on people that led to death or permanent impairment, in conditions where those people lacked power to resist. As a consequence, clear ethical protocols for conduct in medicine have been developed, such as the Declaration of Helsinki (WMA 1969). Similar statements of ethical principles have been made in relation to other health professions, as well as fields such as education and law (McAuliffe 2021). An example of a core principle in each of these statements is that of human rights that are held by every member of society, together with associated duties and responsibilities of members of professions to uphold and promote such rights. Social work is clearly as bound by these principles as any other human service occupation.

The Growth and Relevance of Ethics in Social Work

Compared to the earlier stages of its development, in recent decades social work has seen a rapid growth in the explicit attention that is paid to ethics as an important aspect of its professionalism. Several analyses have pointed to this development and sought to articulate particular ways to understand the forms that social work professional ethics has taken in recent years (for example see Hugman 2005, Bowles et al. 2006, Congress et al. 2009, Reamer 2013, Banks 2020). Various explanations are offered as to why social work has produced so much research and writing on ethics in recent years. For Reamer (2013), it is a reflection of professional maturation. In contrast, Banks (2020) emphasizes the contested nature of social work, both within any one country but also between countries and regions around the world, as the source of interest in ethics. What these two statements about social work share is the sense that the rapidly growing attention to ethics arises from the relationship between the purposes of social work and the means by which social workers seek to achieve those purposes.

Part of the literature on ethics in social work addresses the interplay between meta-ethics and normative ethics, as these are defined above. Particular attention has been paid to the principles of human rights and of social justice (Lundy 2004; Ife 2013). These two approaches have their roots, respectively, in the moral philosophies of deontology (the ethics of moral duty to principle) and Utilitarianism (the ethics of just consequences). They are also normative, in that they provide the framework in which social work ethics has been discussed internationally (IFSW/IASSW 2018). However, there appears often to be a tendency to see these two major principles as the totality of social work ethics. Against this, more recent writing has identified virtue ethics (the ethics of character) as relevant to social work and to a more complete view of the normative ethical terrain on which social work is continuing to develop (McBeath and Webb 2002; Banks and Gallagher 2009; Papouli 2018; Hugman et al. 2021). Moreover, although this work is still to be undertaken, the inclusion of virtue ethics in social work's focus opens up possibilities of moving beyond the dominance of European philosophical roots (Hugman 2013).

Other newer developments in moral philosophy can also be seen in social work, including the feminist ethics of care (Barnes et al. 2015; Shaw 2018), anti-discriminatory ethics (Clifford and Burke 2009), and environmental ethics (Gray and Coates 2012; Dominelli 2014). These areas draw, in different ways, on the integration of insights from the three major approaches of deontological, utilitarian, and virtue ethics, while at the same time offering new insights that seek to guide social work theory and practice in response to changes in the broader social context. Other areas of ethical inquiry have begun even to question the humanist assumptions that underpin dominant paradigms. This too is beginning to be seen as a possible area of social work consideration. The chapters in Part IV of this present volume review and discuss key ethical principles ad approaches of these kinds. In turn they address human rights, social justice, virtue, ethics of care, ethical pluralism, post-human(ist), and post-anthropocentric ethics. Taken together, these chapters point to the way in which ethical debate is not static, but rather constantly develops, as the chapters on care, pluralism, post-humanism, and post-anthropocentrism demonstrate that the boundaries between the classic distinctions of duty (to principle), consequences, and character are more fluid than traditional debates allow.

To some extent, these new approaches to ethics also bridge normative and descriptive ethics. Consequently, in recent years, social work has also much more explicitly begun to consider applied areas of ethical inquiry. These include questions of the ways in which social work is affected by and can respond to technological change, extreme social and political conditions (such as war and civil disorder), displaced populations (refugees and asylum seekers), emergent non-European ethical voices, and resurgent populism and authoritarianism in politics. Part V of this present volume address these concerns in turn. While the established concerns with rights, justice, and virtue continue to be centrally relevant to such discussions, the relationships between these principles and their implications for social work are shown to be contingent on historical circumstances. It is not that the values of human rights, social justice, or virtuous character are less relevant – certainly they cannot be abandoned – but rather that they must constantly be rethought and brought afresh to understanding social work's goals and methods.

Theory and Ethics as the 'Ideas of Social Work'

A review of the chapters on theory and on ethics reveals that there are some ideas that bridge the two broad areas that are the concern of this volume. That is, the same concerns can be seen in both theory and in ethics. These address critical questions about the nature of the social world and human relationships, especially as these relate to social divisions, discrimination and oppression, and social power. In particular, the themes of feminism, anti-racism and decolonization, environmentalism and the relationship between humanity, other species and the physical world are all evident in both theorizing and ethical debate. Much of the social work literature addresses questions of theory and ethics separately, so that the body of thought that is represented in social work scholarship and research creates a distinction between them. Separation of these themes is certainly not always easy and is frequently not appropriate; the differences between these categories of thought can be somewhat arbitrary. For example, feminist theory and feminist ethics are often interlinked, as can be environmental theory and ethics, or post-structural and postmodern theory and ethics. Feminist theory may also be expressed in the ethics of care, environmental ethics, and post-humanist and post-anthropocentric ethics; and so on. This volume seeks to go beyond this simple separation of categories. Although it recognizes that questions of theory and ethics may be addressed distinctly, the connections between them can be made evident and drawn out by analysing them in diverse ways. Thus, this present volume is not structured in terms of a neat and obvious parallel of topics between the various parts.

Similarly, social work ethics draws on principles and concepts that have their roots in philosophical inquiry and also involve applied analysis in the particular issues with which social workers engage and their practices in doing so. In this way social work contributes to wider debates through advancement of its own perspectives and knowledge gained through practice. In other words, ethical inquiry not only is informed by theoretical developments, but in turn may contribute to furthering theoretical inquiry. Thus, there is a cyclical relationship between the two areas of ideas. This volume offers a unique approach by bringing together the complementary dimensions of theory with each other and at the same time with ethical research and scholarship. In this way it presents an analysis of the diverse ideas of social work in a way that enables connections between them to be identified and explored.

As the notion of practice theory suggests, social work not only involves the application of ideas in practice, but also involves a process in which ideas are generated from the experience of practice. Thinking and doing occur in a dynamic relationship where each informs the other. So, not only is there an interplay between theory and ethics, but both also involve the interaction between thinking and doing. For some analysts, to this twofold relationship, other dimensions should also be added, including being, feeling (affect) and skills. This is most clear in feminist theory and ethics, the ethics of care, through the assertion that human life is always contextually situated and that it involves four elements: head (thinking); heart (feeling); hands (skills); and feet (practice/action). In particular, this way of understanding ideas counters the dominant concern with a distinction between 'fact' and 'value' that is characteristic of the modernist or scientific era in which social work has developed as a profession. Postmodern and post-structuralist theory and ethics, and environmental perspectives also take a multi-dimensional approach that does not separate these elements and is not confined to a binary construct, such as 'theory/ethics' or 'ideas/practice'. In some of these debates, the notion of spirituality is also re-emerging as an area of concern (for example, see Gray and Coates 2012, Hugman 2013). Although this is not addressed as a distinct theme in the present volume, it is relevant to aspects of culture, and environment, so is evident in the chapters that are concerned with those issues.

While the integration of these different dimensions can be seen most clearly in Parts III and V of this present volume, it also underpins the discussions of theories and principles in Parts II and IV. In other words, the relationship between theory and practice, theory and ethics, and ethics and practice is complex and multi-dimensional (compare with: Howe 2014, Banks 2020). Any attempt to capture this complexity will, therefore, be partial at best, as it involves the representation of phenomena that are intangible, even though they are very powerful, and whose relationships are not fixed. So, in order to focus the discussion, the structure and content of this volume is guided by the overarching notion of 'ideas' as a starting point to consider social work across the wide range of issues, commitments, and practices on which it is constructed.

Conclusion

In order to take responsibility for the development of social work, it is vital that the ideas that form one key dimension of the profession (together with feelings, skills, and actions) are explicitly reviewed. Although it is important to know how to undertake social work, it is also essential to understand how practitioners know *what* they might do, *how* to do these things, and *why* these things might be better than other courses of action. In social work inquiry, such questions are largely divided into two. First, theory is concerned with thinking about questions of what might be done and how it might be accomplished. Second, ethics is concerned with questions of why some courses action might be better than others, not simply on technical or practical grounds but more importantly on the basis of the moral values that are expressed in choice about thinking and acting.

This introductory chapter has introduced key areas of inquiry into the specific themes of social work they do and ethics. In doing so, it has also argued for connections between them, so that the common roots of many theories and ethical principles can be identified and considered. Furthermore, the division between fact and value as characteristic of two separate types of knowledge or thought has been challenged as it is apparent in social work through the ideas expressed in the most recent critical inquiry. What is apparent in the chapters of this volume is that social work does not only receive ideas from the wider society, including research and practice communities as well as service users, but also speaks to those other communities. Overall, theory and ethics are conversations between people in the present and over time – we both communicate with our contemporaries, and we listen to those from the past and speak to those of the future that is yet to happen. The chapters in this present volume both record and contribute to these conversations. In so doing they point to the ideas that form a central element not only in understanding but also in doing social work.

References

Bailey J (1980) Ideas and intervention. Routledge & Kegan Paul, London
Banks S (2020) Ethics and values in social work, 5th edn. Red Globe Press, London
Banks S, Gallagher A (2009) Ethics in professional life: virtues for health and social care. Palgrave Macmillan, Basingstoke
Barnes M, Brannelly T, Ward L, Ward N (eds) (2015) Ethics of care: critical advances in international perspective. Policy Press, Bristol
Bowles W, Collingridge M, Curry S, Valentine B (2006) Ethical practice in social work: an applied approach. Allen & Unwin, Crow's Nest
Brewer C, Lait J (1980) Can social work survive? Temple Smith, London
Chenoweth L, McAuliffe D (2020) The road to social work and human services, 6th edn. Cengage, Southbank
Clifford D, Burke B (2009) Anti-oppressive ethics and values in social work. Palgrave Macmillan, Basingstoke
Congress E, Black P, Strom-Gottfried (eds) (2009) Teaching social work ethics and values. Council on Social Work Education, Alexandria
Curnock K, Hardiker P (1979) Towards practice theory. Routledge & Kegan Paul, London
Dominelli L (2014) Green social work: from environmental crises to environmental justice. Polity Press, Cambridge
Goelitz A (2021) From trauma to healing: a social worker's guide to working with survivors. Routledge, New York
Gray M, Coates J (2012) Environmental ethics for social work. Int J Soc Wel 21(3):239–247

Gray M, Webb S (eds) (2013) Social work theories and methods. Sage, Thousand Oaks
Hardiker P, Barker M (1981) Theories of practice in social work. Academic Press, New York
Healy K (2014) Social work theories in context. Palgrave Macmillan, Basingstoke
Howe D (1987) An introduction to social work theory. Wildwood House, Aldershot
Howe D (2014) The compleat social worker. Palgrave Macmillan, Basingstoke
Hugman R (1991) Power in caring professions. Macmillan, London
Hugman R (2005) New approaches in ethics for the caring professions. Palgrave Macmillan, Basingstoke
Hugman R (2009) But is it social work? Some reflections on mistaken identities. Brit J Soc Wk 39(6):1138–1153
Hugman R (2013) Culture, values and ethics in social work. Routledge, London
Hugman R, Pawar M, Anscombe AW, Wheeler A (2021) Virtue ethics in social work practice. Routledge, London
Ife J (2013) Human rights and social work: towards rights-based practice. Cambridge University Press, Port Melbourne
International Federation of Social Workers/International Association of Schools of Social Work (IFSW/IASSW) (2018) Global statement of social work ethical principles. Downloaded from https://www.ifsw.org/global-social-work-statement-of-ethical-principles/. on 18 April 2022
Leonard P (1975) The sociology of community action. University of Keele, Keele
Levenson J (2017) Trauma-informed social work practice. Soc Work 62(2):105–113
Lundy C (2004) Social work and social justice. Broadview Press, Calgary
MacIntyre A (1998) A short history of ethics, 2nd edn. Routledge, London and New York
McAuliffe D (2021) Interprofessional ethics: collaboration in the social, health and human services, 2nd edn. Cambridge University Press, Cambridge, MA
McBeath G, Webb SA (2002) Virtue ethics and social work: on being lucky, realistic, and not doing your duty. Brit J Soc Wk 32(8):1015–1036
Papouli E (2018) Aristotle's virtue ethics as a conceptual framework for the study and practice of social work in modern times. Eur J Soc Wk 22(6):921–934
Parsloe P (1981) Social services area teams. George Allen & Unwin, London
Payne M (1990) Modern social work theory, 1st edn. Macmillan, London
Payne M (2005) The origins of social work: continuity and change. Palgrave Macmillan, Basingstoke
Payne M (2021) Modern social work theory, 5th edn. Red Globe Press, London
Reamer FG (2013) Social work values and ethics, 4th edn. Columbia University Press, New York
Reid W, Epstein L (1972) Task-centered casework. Columbia University Press, New York
Reid W, Shyne AW (1969) Brief and extended casework. Columbia University Press, New York
Shaw J (2018) Homines curans and the social work imaginary: post-liberalism and the ethics of care. Brit J Soc Wk 49(1):183–197
Simmons MY (2002) Nanotechnology, small things, big science. Chapman and Hall, London
Trevithick P (2012) Social work skills and knowledge. Open University Press, New York
World Medical Association (WMA) (1969) The declaration of Helsinki, as amended 2004. World Medical Association, Ferney-Voltaire

Part II

Theories for Social Work

Psychological and Clinical Theories 2

Herman Hay Ming Lo

Contents

Introduction: Applying Psychological and Clinical Theories in Social Work Practice	18
Self-Knowledge and Interpersonal Communication for Helping	19
Supporting Individuals' Mental Health	19
Responding to Social Care Needs across the Lifespan	20
Advancing Practice in a Complicated Society	20
Psychodynamic Theory and Social Work Practice	20
Humanistic Theories and Social Work Practice	22
Cognitive Behavioural Theories and Social Work Practice	23
Postmodern Theories and Social Work Practice	24
Psychological Theories in Relating to Objectives of Social Work Practice	25
Mindfulness as a Psychological Theory	26
Is Mindfulness Compatible with Social Work Objectives?	27
Adaptation of Mindfulness-Based Programs in Social Care	28
Developing the Practice Knowledge in Applying Mindfulness in Family Social Work Practice	30
Ethical Issues and Trauma-Informed Practice in Delivering a Mindfulness Program	32
Benefits of Mindfulness in Social Workers' Professional Practice and Development	33
Conclusion	34
References	34

Abstract

Psychological and clinical theories are one of the major sources of knowledge in social work practice. The first part of this chapter provides a critical review of four psychological theories — psychodynamic, humanistic, cognitive behavioural and postmodern theories — and their application in social work practice. The

---

H. H. M. Lo (✉)
Department of Applied Social Sciences, Hong Kong Polytechnic University, Hung Hom, Hong Kong
e-mail: herman.lo@polyu.edu.hk

© Springer Nature Singapore Pte Ltd. 2023
D. Hölscher et al. (eds.), *Social Work Theory and Ethics*, Social Work,
https://doi.org/10.1007/978-981-19-1015-9_2

theories' relevance to social work objectives and their strengths and limitations are discussed. The second part of the chapter considers mindfulness as a newly emerging psychological and clinical theory. A review of its philosophical underpinnings and relation to major social work objectives is provided. Using mindfulness as an exemplar, the author demonstrates how psychological theory can be applied and adapted in the process of social work program planning and practice. The design of mindfulness-based programs for children and parents in social work programs is introduced, with a discussion of practice knowledge, ethical issues and trauma-informed practice using mindfulness. Finally, the benefits of learning and practicing mindfulness for social work practitioners are discussed. The conclusion of the chapter is that social workers should spend more effort to reflect and adapt the use of psychological and clinical theories in practice. The benefits of mindfulness in empowering the lives of clients and practitioners and its impact the social work profession should be reviewed and promoted.

Keywords

Psychological and clinical theories · Psychodynamics theory · Humanistic theory · Cognitive behavioural theory · Postmodern theory · Mindfulness-based programme

Introduction: Applying Psychological and Clinical Theories in Social Work Practice

Psychology, as the science of mind and behaviour, offers various approaches and theoretical orientations from which to study the individual. The disciplines of psychology and social work have been closely aligned since the 1920s. Psychology is fundamental to understanding all aspects of human life and, as such, it informs the development and daily practice of the social work profession (Nicolson et al. 2006). Psychological theories and ideas offer social work practitioners a language and strategies for putting humanistic values and goals into practice.

Psychological theories have contributed to several dimensions of social work practice, including the application of interpersonal and communication skills, understanding the signs and needs of individuals impacted by health and mental health issues, identifying changes and needs across the human life span, and designing supportive interventions according to these analyses. Social workers continue to reflect on the relevance of theories generated from psychology and clinical practice and to advance knowledge by analysing theories, conducting practice research in specific service contexts and contributing to the development of new theories (Healy 2005; Nicolson et al. 2006). We explain these four aspects of application in the following sections.

Self-Knowledge and Interpersonal Communication for Helping

Most social workers spend their time talking and listening to clients and colleagues. As the profession is inspired by psychological theories, they should be able to understand themselves, including their own drives and impulses, before they can truly accept the bright and dark sides of clients. Self-awareness, self-understanding and self-care are the keys to developing effective working relationships in practice (Nicolson et al. 2006).

Psychological theories further provide knowledge for social workers to gather information and conduct effective assessments on the issues faced by individuals and families. Individual qualities necessary for helping others include empathy, respect and genuineness. Verbal and non-verbal communication skills such as listening, questioning, paraphrasing, summarizing, appropriate facial expression, posture, voice and physical proximity are borrowed from interviewing skills in counselling psychology (Cournoyer 2016; Egan 2013).

Psychological theories of group dynamics largely influence the development of social work practice, especially groupwork practice. Social psychology studies on the factors that influence people's interactions apply in counselling psychology and inform groupwork skills such as understanding the stages of group development, setting norms, leading groups, drawing out passive members and cutting off dominant members. Such groupwork skills inform social work practice with individuals, families, teams and communities (Trevithick 2008).

Supporting Individuals' Mental Health

A significant proportion of service users report common mental health disorders such as mood and anxiety disorders, whereas others have more serious disorders such as schizophrenia. The field of abnormal psychology provides an understanding of various aspects of these mental health issues, including the role of individual characteristics of people in recovery, the components of treatment, the specific practice context, and intervention and prevention procedures, which is useful in supporting people in recovery and their family caregivers (Long et al. 2007). Practitioners should not rely on reflection, intuition and practice experience, and all judgments and interventions should be grounded in relevant knowledge from psychology and clinical disciplines.

The roles of social workers with statutory responsibilities such as child protection, criminal justice and mental health recovery are critical. Practitioners need guidelines on how to conduct assessments, and to make judgments and recommendations about how trustworthy or mentally stable their clients are, or how well they can cope on their own. Clinical work includes procedures and skills for conducting risk assessments, care planning and crisis management, which should be guided by psychological theories and related scientific evidence (Nicolson et al. 2006).

Responding to Social Care Needs across the Lifespan

Developmental or lifespan psychology provides important knowledge about human development from cradle to grave. A social worker's assessment of a child should explore his or her developmental needs, the parents' capacity, and family and environmental factors with reference to specific psychological theories, including attachment theory and systems and ecological theory (Spray and Jowett 2011). Psychological theories of late life suggest that there is a progressive disengagement from social relationships, but successful aging emphasizes the potential benefits of maintaining and enhancing positive activity and social engagement. Psychological theories can provide a framework for social workers to promote the strengths of individuals during the aging process (Payne and Reith-Hall 2019).

Advancing Practice in a Complicated Society

Uncertain and complex environments pose a particular challenge for social workers because they make it impossible to predict or control individuals' behaviours with precision. Practitioners often need to evaluate and apply psychological theories and research findings in a specific context. For example, there has been an on-going debate about the preference between residential care and care by natural birth parents who consistently abuse or neglect their children. In response to this challenge, social workers in child protection services developed a risk assessment and structural decision-making tool and evaluated its validity using a rigorous research process including scale validation, outcome evaluation and data analysis (Shlonsky and Wagner 2005).

Payne and Reith-Hall (2019) suggested that social workers should develop theories about their roles in making interpersonal, social and political changes; their positions in relation to other professions within the policy, legal and organizational contexts in which they practice, and their positions in relation to debates arising from political and cultural issues. Psychological theories need to be reviewed against the values and objectives of social work practice. In the following sections, four major psychological and clinical theories are selected for review and their strengths and limitations in social work practice are evaluated.

Psychodynamic Theory and Social Work Practice

Psychodynamic theory has been widely applied as a therapeutic approach since the 1920s, with the ideas of Sigmund Freud and others such as Adler and Jung providing the emerging social work profession with a practice model that could guide practitioners to change individuals' behaviours (Noble 2019). Mary Richmond (1922) made adaptations to psychodynamic theory and developed the psychosocial casework model in her classic work, *Social Diagnosis*. Although it has been largely replaced by other approaches in recent decades, some of its principles and insights are still relevant for professional practice.

Freud emphasized the role of the unconsciousness in people's behaviour. According to his personality theory, the id is the source of the basic drive to survive, the superego is the conscious public self that develops moral principles based on what is socially acceptable, and the ego is the part of the self that seeks to understand and manage the environment and mediates between the id and the superego. Individuals may not be fully aware of the unconscious and conscious interactions between the id, the ego, and the superego. People develop defence mechanisms to protect themselves from anxiety and from being overwhelmed by impulses and threats. Common defences include denial (acting as though an event or experience has not happened), repression (suppressing memories of bad experiences and unacceptable desires), projection (perceiving someone else as having one's own emotional state) and displacement (directing a negative emotion from its original source to a less threatening recipient). According to psychodynamic theory, our unconscious thoughts are dynamic and our behaviour in adulthood is influenced by our early development, even if we are unaware of it. Freud also emphasized the importance of transference, whereby a service user transfers emotions generated in past relationships onto the professional.

Psychodynamic theory has influenced social work practice as it helps social workers understand how people react to their social environment and their transference to social workers. The theory had a strong impact on Bowlby's attachment theory and Erickson's stages of development theory, both of which affirm social workers' roles in safeguarding the interests of children and their families. Traditional interventions based on psychodynamic theory tend to be non-directive and clients are expected to lead the therapeutic direction. The therapist facilitates the emergence of insight when the client experiences the unfolding of hidden thoughts and feelings. Problem behaviours caused by repressed inner conflicts can be understood and gradually resolved.

Prior to the 1960s, most social work theory was based on psychodynamic ideas, now called psychosocial theory. Informed by psychosocial theory, the social worker provides a psychosocial diagnosis based on an exploration of the person-in-the-environment. Although the social worker sets the form and direction of help, self-determination and the helping process are emphasized. The role of the social worker is to improve the client's capacity for coping (Payne 2014). Earlier psychoanalytic therapists applied techniques such as free association, in which clients are encouraged to say whatever comes to mind and report any feelings and thoughts that arise. Dream analysis is used to uncover unconscious processes and offer insights into unresolved problems. The analysis and interpretation of transference facilitate clients to express what is buried in their unconscious mind (Corey 2016). More supportive techniques have been promoted in recent decades including exploration (helping the client to interpret and understand behaviour and events), venting (allowing the expression of emotions so that the client can move on from their feelings and act rationally again), clarification (reflecting on how the environment has affected the client, exploring behavioural patterns and how they have been developed, and exploring the possibilities for better adaptation), and sustainment (improving the client's self-esteem and confidence by showing understanding and trust in the client's ability to make progress) and they have been integrated into social workers' generic practice (Brandell 2010).

Apart from those in private practice, many social workers may feel a time pressure to delve into clients' pasts and spend lengthy periods facilitating the emergence of insights using a non-directive approach (Payne 2014). Maclean and Harrison (2015) also made an interesting comment that the exploration of sexual fantasies, particularly in relation to clients' parents, may put social workers in a vulnerable position due to their child protection responsibilities.

Humanistic Theories and Social Work Practice

The humanistic theories, particularly the principles of Carl Rogers's person-centered approach, has influenced social work practice for several decades. They focus on self-actualization and empowerment and are strongly committed to the values of equality and respect, and the importance of non-directive and non-judgmental in helping. Rogers viewed the therapist as an active listener and emphasized the use of empathy and genuineness, with a focus on the 'here-and-now' rather than on the exploration of the client's history. In his classic work, *On Becoming a Person* (1961), he emphasized openness to experience, trust in one's experience, an internal locus of evaluation and the willingness to be involved in the therapeutic process. With little emphasis on problem-solving or diagnosis, the goal of the therapeutic process is to achieve a greater degree of independence and integration, and to assist clients in their personal growth so that they can better cope with their current and future problems. According to Roger's humanistic theory, the core components of helping lie in a practitioner's accurate reflection of the client's feelings, the quality of the therapeutic relationship, and a strong connection with the client. Based on these principles, variations in humanistic theories have been developed, such as person-centered expressive arts therapy, which integrates person-centered therapy with art therapy (Rogers 2016), and the focusing approach, which integrates the awareness of bodily senses and attention in psychotherapy (Gendlin 1998).

Recently, social workers have contributed to the evolution of humanistic theories. Payne (2014) drew a link between the self in humanistic theory and spirituality, as a shared exploration between our own existence and the existence of others in relation to us. Inspired by Eastern thought from traditional Chinese medicine, Daoist, and Buddhist teachings, Lee and colleagues (2009) developed an innovative approach called integrative body–mind–spirit social work that addresses the needs arising from health and mental health conditions. The approach fosters well-being by imparting knowledge and skills to help restore a dynamic equilibrium among the body, mind, and spirit. It combines the use of bodily techniques for reducing physical symptoms, such as qi-gong movement, and mind techniques such as meditation and breathing exercises with spiritual components such as meaning making, psychoeducation on suffering, drawing, and reflective journal writing.

The efficacy of integrative body-mind-spirit social work has been evaluated in a range of health issues such as women undergoing in vitro fertilization, cancer patients, and sleep disturbance.

Brown (2006) explored shame as one of the most primitive and universal human emotions in the context of a competitive and materialistic culture, and proposed shame resilience theory for dealing with shame and its impact. Strategies to cultivate shame resilience include recognizing and accepting personal vulnerability, contextualizing by raising awareness of social and cultural expectations, normalizing by formulating empathic relationships and facilitating reaching out to others, and demystifying by speaking about shame and developing the emotional competence to share and discuss it (Brown 2015). It is interesting to note that Brown has been stepping out of the interview room and expanding the impact of her theory by providing public education through multimedia such as self-help books, podcasts and her well-known TED talks.

Cognitive Behavioural Theories and Social Work Practice

Cognitive behavioural therapy (CBT) is an overarching term that encompasses various behavioural and cognitive theories for working with individuals, groups, couples and families. Beck (2011) outlines several basic features with the central feature of a problem conceptualization in cognitive terms. Others include the emphasis of a sound therapeutic alliance, the collaboration and active participation from the client and therapist. CBT is time-limited and takes place in structured sessions that are goal-oriented, problem-focused and present-oriented. In CBT, the role of the therapist is to teach clients how to recognize, assess and respond to their thoughts, and make good use of cognitive, behavioural, and affective strategies. Thus, it educates clients about their problems and teaches them strategies to help prevent relapse.

The ABCDEF model proposed by Ellis (1962) in his Rational Emotive Therapy, one of the major approaches in CBT, provides a structural overview of many CBT intervention. The client is taught to reflect on the Activating experience (A), their Beliefs (B) about themself and about A, and the emotional and behavioural Consequences (C) of those beliefs. After exploring these beliefs, the intervention further guides the client to Dispute (D) the beliefs and question whether they are rational, and to replace them with Effective rational beliefs (E). Finally, the client describes the Feelings (F) impacted by the new beliefs. The aim of CBT is to support the person in understanding the impact of their thoughts and then test them against events in their own world. Many CBT therapists offer homework through which the client learns to apply the new approach to their daily life.

CBT offers a range of practical tools for social workers who practice in the areas of mental health, substance use disorders and other forms of clinical practice. CBT has been adapted for specific contexts relating to social work practice such as abused children, grief, trauma and for different cultural or sexual minority groups (Craig et al. 2013; Ng and Wong 2018; Ronen and Freeman 2007). CBT is a treatment option that is efficient, brief and supported by extensive research and empirical evidence (Hofmann et al. 2012). However, social workers should be aware of certain limitations, such as its less favourable outcomes among people with physical complaints, strained family relationships, or rigidity in thinking and attitudes (Lo et al. 2011). Concern has also been raised about its preoccupation with efficiency and personal changes, with insufficient attention to social and political dynamics such as the limited client options in service delivery as well as the inequalities and marginalization of the client's external environment (Rasmussen 2018).

Postmodern Theories and Social Work Practice

Narrative theory, the strengths-based model, and solution-focused therapy share a forward-looking perspective and reject problem-solving as the focus of intervention. They are all influenced by postmodern and social constructionist ideas that are concerned with how power relations are expressed, and their founders are from a social work background (Payne 2014).

According to narrative theory, service users' lives are constrained by the harmful narratives that have been generated about them. A diagnosis that was originally developed to help the person can eventually imprison them. There are four key principles of narrative theory that focus on the narratives that shape service users' lives (Healy 2005). First, its practitioners seek to challenge harmful narratives and transform those that construct our lives. Second, it emphasizes that the person is not the problem, and the person should be separated from the problem through externalizing conversations. Third, narrative theory aims to reconstruct the dominant narratives, which emphasize pathology, into narratives that highlight and support the client's capacities. Finally, people can co-construct a narrative through and with the community. Strategies should be developed to build a supportive and life-affirming community around the service user.

The strengths-based model promotes a new perspective that emphasizes possibilities rather than problems, options rather than constraints, and wellness rather than sickness. It aims to develop positive outcomes in areas such as quality of life, achievement, sense of competency, life satisfaction and empowerment. Compared with narrative theory, the strengths-based model provides a relatively concrete framework for assessment and intervention, addressing areas such as current strengths, desires and aspirations, past strengths in daily living, assets, employment, education or specialized knowledge, supportive relationships, wellness and health, and leisure. The roles of spirituality and culture in supporting personal life are recognized (Rapp and Goscha 2011). Originally developed for people recovering from psychiatric illness, the application of the strengths-based model has been extended to various social work target populations such as ex-offenders, substance abusers and older adults (Saleeby 2013).

Solution-focused therapy, or solution-focused brief therapy (SFBT), emerged from the discovery that people who come to therapy usually have exceptions from their problems. Therapists from the SFBT approach focus on investigating what their clients had been done that have created change and amplifying it. SFBT offers a streamlined and unified approach that can apply to many issues and problems for social work practice: these are, exploring the outcome the client hopes for, eliciting a detailed description of how the outcome can be realized, and tracking the client's progress toward realizing the outcome. In SFBT, an understanding of the client's history is not necessary for change and questions are used to guide clients to talk about their resources and open up possibilities for change. It also offers helpful techniques for interviewing, such as miracle questions (inviting clients to describe a problem-free future in detail) and scaling questions (using grading to construct the client's understanding of their concerns and solutions). SFBT emphasizes clients' motivation to seek help and further develop skills to expand its application to involuntary clients in social work practice, such as individuals in probation and child protection services (Shennan 2019).

A major criticism of postmodern theories is that they lack research support and evidence. As social workers play a role in maintaining social order in statutory practice, they may encounter ethical dilemmas with postmodern theories that focus on the positive. Postmodern theories may be inadequate for reducing problems among service users that could be harmful to themselves and others. Furthermore, these approaches have a narrow focus of change and do not address inequalities in the societal context (Healy 2005; Payne 2014). Overall, however, such theories provide helpful guidance for social workers who intend to empower their users according to professional core values such as respect and faith in their capacity to change.

Psychological Theories in Relating to Objectives of Social Work Practice

We have reviewed four major psychological and clinical theories, each with its own philosophical and theoretical perspectives on human nature and social issues. When we apply these psychological theories in practice, it is necessary to examine the extent to which they are compatible with the values and objectives of social work. According to Payne (2014), there are three major social work objectives that represent the basic principles of how social work practice can contribute to society: empowerment, problem solving and social change. It should be emphasized that these objectives are three ideal-types and social work practice are often an integrating of these objectives and they are not exclusive.

The first social work objective is based on empowerment and views social work as seeking the highest level of well-being for individuals, groups and communities by promoting and facilitating growth and self-fulfilment. Practitioners help clients to gain power over their feelings and way of life, enabling them to overcome their suffering and disadvantage. The empowerment orientation emphasizes the importance of helping people by developing their skills and personal relationships without imposing diagnoses and standardized procedures for change. The second objective is based on a problem-solving perspective and emphasizes social work as a profession for maintaining social order and supporting people during transitions and difficult periods. The role of social work practitioners is to help people acknowledge their responsibility to cope with their problems and support them to make necessary adjustments. The third objective is based on the social change perspective, in which the aim of social work practice is to seek cooperation and mutual support in society so that the most oppressed and disadvantaged people can gain power over their lives. To free people from oppression due to age, gender, class, ethnicity or spiritual beliefs, sexual preferences and membership of non-dominant groups, social work practice should be transformational so that clients can gain the power and resources to promote more egalitarian relationships in society (Noble 2019).

Given the extensive range of psychological theories, it is impossible to introduce them all in one chapter. Social work practitioners should have a broad understanding of these ideas and examine how they are applicable to our professional practice. Overall, psychological and clinical theories place more emphasis on the objectives of problem-solving and empowerment with relatively less attention on social change. With an overview of the objectives and orientations of different theories, social workers can apply them selectively (by selecting a theory to use with a particular service user or in a practice context) and eclectically (by taking ideas from several theories and integrating them to produce an approach that suits the agency, the capacities and preferences of the practitioner and individual clients) (Payne 2014).

Mindfulness as a Psychological Theory

Mindfulness is defined as paying attention to the present moment non-judgmentally (Kabat-Zinn 2013; Segal et al. 2013). Mindfulness originates from Eastern traditions and its recent popularity in Western psychology is largely due to the development and widespread application of two standardized mindfulness-based programs (MBPs): mindfulness-based stress reduction (MBSR) and mindfulness-based cognitive therapy (MBCT) (Kabat-Zinn 2013; Segal et al. 2013). MBPs integrate traditional mindfulness practice with contemporary psychological knowledge to improve psychological functioning and well-being.

Clients who participate in an MBP can strengthen their competence in coping with stress through the integration of programmed mindfulness exercises with psychoeducation on stress coping and specific health issues. Most MBPs consist of group-based learning and participants are offered a range of formal and informal mindfulness practices, including body scan, mindful stretching, mindfulness of breath, mindfulness of sounds and thoughts, and mindfulness of other daily routines such as walking and eating (Kabat-Zinn 2013; Segal et al. 2013).

A growing body of robust evidence from randomized controlled trials has demonstrated that MBPs are effective in improving a range of clinical and non-clinical psychological outcomes, including anxiety, risk of relapse for depression, stress, chronic pain, quality of life and other psychological symptoms in patients with chronic conditions (Gu et al. 2015). That review further proposed four possible mechanisms of change through MBPs, including learning mindfulness skills, reducing repetitive thinking, promoting self-compassion and decreasing cognitive and emotional reactivity (Gu et al. 2015).

Mindfulness has become one of the most frequently used psychological theories in recent years (Norcross et al. 2013). As social work is one of the major professions that applies psychotherapy and counselling theories in practice, interest in mindfulness in the social work context has long been recognized (Birnbaum and Birnbaum 2008; Hick 2009; Temme and Kopak 2016).

Is Mindfulness Compatible with Social Work Objectives?

Mindfulness is a unique approach with its own philosophical and theoretical orientation and it is important to examine whether it is compatible with the values and objectives of social work. As discussed earlier, social work has three major objectives, representing three basic principles for how social work practice can contribute to the greater society based on empowerment, problem-solving and social change (Payne 2014). Here, we investigate the extent to which mindfulness aligns with these social work objectives.

Mindfulness is consistent with empowerment in that it is non-judgmental about human experience. In a mindfulness-based eating program, for example, clients with eating disorders can learn to manage their thoughts, feelings and behaviours in relation to eating and develop a non-judgmental awareness of their patterns of disordered eating. Clients can find an internal space for self-compassion, an intention to face their sources of emotional distress and experience an empowering process of change. The themes of self-resilience and self-care are cultivated by attending to one's own physical, emotional and social needs (Beccia et al. 2020).

The position of mindfulness in relation to the second objective, problem-solving, is less clear, although it has been widely used in psychotherapy and clinical practice. Such issue was explicitly discussed by the founders of MBCT when they originally integrated CBT, a psychological approach that provides structured problem-solving procedures with mindfulness. MBCT de-emphasizes the problem-solving (or 'fixing') mode and teaches people how to manage difficult experiences that often lead to internal struggles with thoughts and emotions. Instead of promoting strategies for temporary relief, mindfulness allows people to observe their experiences just as they are, a process that is often referred to as radical acceptance (Segal et al. 2013). The use of embodiment to approach mind–body experiences with curiosity and a non-judgmental stance is promoted. During the class inquiry between the instructor and participants, an open-ended questioning technique that does not offer answers to problems is used to facilitate awareness and insights. In other words, problem solving is the by-product of an empowering process.

Finally, the relevance of mindfulness to the third objective, social change, is open to debate, as most psychological and clinical theories may have limited relevance to this dimension. However, mindfulness has promoted changes to social institutions such as education, multi-cultural practice and green social work, and has other policy implications that promote social change (Crews and Besthorn 2016). For example, members of an all-party parliamentary group in the United Kingdom who practice mindfulness have formed projects that can develop policy recommendations for government and provide a forum for discussion in parliament on the role of mindfulness and its implementation in public policy (Report by the Mindfulness All-Party Parliamentary Group 2015). Initiatives and social entrepreneurship have also been set up by individuals practicing mindfulness and such effort shows that mindfulness can also have a transformational impact on social change (Schmid and Aiken 2021).

Adaptation of Mindfulness-Based Programs in Social Care

In this section, we further discuss the first two objectives of social work practice in terms of the development of procedures and action steps for applying mindfulness. Application of mindfulness in parenting and family intervention is selected as an exemplar, as parents and families are a major service target in social work practice.

The idea of mindful parenting, first proposed by Jon Kabat-Zinn and Myla Kabat-Zinn (2013), which is defined as the ability to intentionally and non-judgmentally pay attention to children and parenting in the present moment. It is an on-going process through which parents can develop greater awareness of a child's unique nature, feelings and needs, a stronger ability to be present and listen with full attention, recognize and accept things as they are in each moment, whether pleasant or unpleasant, recognize their own reactive impulses, and learn to respond more appropriately and imaginatively with greater clarity and kindness (Kabat-Zinn and Kabat-Zinn 2021). An increasing number of studies have found that mindful parenting can benefit both parents and children. A recent study found that mindful parenting can be assessed in four dimensions: compassion for the child, non-judgmental acceptance in parenting, emotional awareness in parenting and listening with full attention (Lo et al. 2018). For parents, mindful parenting is associated with less parenting stress, better mental health, higher levels of positive parenting practices and better collaborative parenting (Bögels et al. 2014; Gouveia et al. 2016). For children, mindful parenting is associated with better well-being, including physical, emotional, mental, social and behavioural aspects, and less psychopathology, including internalizing and externalizing problems (Geurtzen et al. 2015; Parent et al. 2016; Turpyn and Chaplin 2016).

A recent meta-analysis suggested that MBPs for parents significantly reduce parenting stress and psychopathological symptoms, and have a positive influence on children's development, psychological functioning, and overall quality of life (Burgdorf et al. 2019). Another randomized controlled study of a family-based MBP reported that after the 9-h program, children showed increase in morning cortisol levels and decrease in diurnal cortisol slopes, and parents displayed decrease in evening cortisol levels compared with the control group counterparts. These findings suggest that a brief MBP for families can benefit both parents' and children's neuroendocrine functioning (Ho et al. 2020).

Unlike MBSR and MBCT for general adult populations, there is no standardized program for parents and families in social work practice. Some social workers and allied health professionals have gradually modified MBPs for clinical populations to create a new program structure for parents and families. Fraser and Galinsky (2010) described a five-stage program adaptation model. The first step involves selecting problem and program theories. Social work practice mostly targets families that are disadvantaged due to age, health, disability, poverty, race, ethnicity, or sexual orientation (Sue et al. 2016). Family stress theory was originally developed to facilitate understanding of the stress encountered by economically disadvantaged families. Financial pressures such as unemployment and low incomes increase parenting stress and parental depression, which in turn affect marital quality and parenting practices. This process has negative impacts on family functioning, child mental health and behavioural problems (Conger et al. 2010). Family stress theory may be further expanded to families facing other external sources of disadvantages. MBPs are therefore selected to promote acceptance and approach strategies in coping with family stress.

The second step is to specify the program structures and processes. Two benchmark MBPs, MBSR and MBCT, last for 20–26 h depending on whether day retreats are included. An MBP for parents called Mindful Parenting has been developed by clinical psychologists (Bögels and Restifo 2014), which lasts for nine 3-h session. One benefit of having a longer session is that parents have adequate time for in-class practice and dialogues with instructors and fellow participants, as in MBSR and MBCT programs. The program does not include a day retreat because parents are often preoccupied with household tasks and responsibilities and may find it challenging to arrange the time to attend a day retreat. Some studies choose to modify the structure of mindful parenting programs. For example, for children with ADHD or ASD and their parents, there is an MBP called MYMind with a different protocol that lasts for nine 1.5-h sessions (de Bruin et al. 2015; Chan et al. 2018). The parent mindfulness training program is a brief version of the original mindful parenting course developed by Bogels and Restifo (2014). Shorter programs allow both parents and children to participate in parallel groups in the same time slots, which offers greater convenience for logistic arrangements and program implementation. A brief program is also consistent with the low-intensity public health intervention approach, which is more cost-effective for the health and social care system. Moreover, considering the age appropriateness of mindfulness practice, a single mindfulness practice should be less than 10 min for school age children and the whole session can be around 30 min to 1.5 h. Social work practitioners, service operators and policy makers should consider the pros and cons of different program designs and select a program structure that best suits the client.

The third step is to refine and confirm the program's efficacy. Given the short history of applying mindfulness to parents and families, practitioners and researchers should make joint efforts to generate evidence of efficacy in this emerging field. To investigate the feasibility of a brief MBP for parents, a protocol for a six-session, 9-h MBP for parents of preschool children with developmental disability was developed by social workers and psychologists. A randomized, waitlist-controlled trial was conducted and parents reported improvements in parental stress, depression and parent–child dysfunctional interaction (Lo et al. 2017). It serves as a template for different family-based interventions for social work practice.

The fourth step is to apply the same protocol to different social work practice settings. The above-mentioned brief parent MBP (Lo et al. 2017) was integrated with a child mindfulness program by Snel (2014) and formulated two protocols for children with ADHD symptomology and economically disadvantaged families and their parents (Lo et al. 2019, 2020). Empirical studies provided initial evidence that a parallel MBP for young children and parents can improve children's attention and behaviour problems and reduce parenting stress. Recently, there is another attempt to modify the mindful parenting program and to develop a four-session program for parents of adolescents following social unrest during the COVID-19 pandemic (Lo et al. 2022). Significant improvements in family functioning among parents who reported at least low levels of depressive symptoms at pretest were found after the program, compared with the counterparts. More studies in different social work practice settings are needed to strengthen the evidence base of social work practice for parents and families facing challenges.

The last step involves disseminating the program findings and materials. In view of the demand for services by families and the growing number of social worker practitioners applying mindfulness in advancing practice, different levels of professional sharing and training to disseminate findings should be organized so that social work frontline practitioners can apply different mindfulness programs across practice settings (Fraser and Galinsky 2010). We further discuss the issue of knowledge and competence in teaching mindfulness in social work practice in later sections.

Developing the Practice Knowledge in Applying Mindfulness in Family Social Work Practice

It is important to acknowledge that both social work practice and mindfulness training are knowledge-based practices and social workers should acquire these knowledge so that they can translate different theories into practice (Trevithick 2008). Many social workers are familiar with the problem-solving approach, which involves defining the problem, designing the intervention and evaluating the outcomes.

However, as suggested by the social work objective of an empowering approach and the principles of mindfulness, implementing an MBP requires a different mindset from that required to delivering a program based on problem-solving approach such as parent behaviour training. It is important to emphasize that instructors of MBPs for parents do not offer specific child discipline techniques (Bögels and Restifo 2014). An MBP instructor leads a program for parents by being present as parents who struggle to parent well and do not have the answers in parenting issues. Practitioners can help by joining together with the parents in mindfulness practice and sharing their own suffering as human beings. Parents are supported to observe their own limits and to bring awareness and acceptance to themselves, not to react emotionally but to respond to their children with conscious choices (Bögels and Restifo 2014).

A few adaptations have been made to our MBPs for parents so that clients can benefit from drawing the relevance of mindfulness practice to their parenting. The mindful eating practice, as the first mindfulness practice scheduled in many MBPs, has a special meaning for parents. After parents have experienced the use of five senses to observe their moment-to-moment experiences in a mindful eating practice in the class, the mindfulness instructor will invite the parents to observe their children using the same qualities as they eat the raisin in a home assignment (Bögels and Restifo 2014). Many parents commented that after being inspired by the mindful eating exercise, they learned to see their children as a whole, instead of focusing on their problem behaviours or their own expectations of them. It also gave the parents a new perspective on relationships as they learnt to see their own children with a more open mind. For parents of younger children, mindful eating became a more interesting ritual at home. Some parents reported that their children loved being a junior mindfulness teacher at home and led the family members to hold, see, touch, smell and taste the food step-by-step. Children are empowered and parents are reminded to let go of their expectations of and control over their children (Lo et al. 2022).

The ice cube exercise is one of the most popular mindfulness exercises among children (Greenland 2016). It is a mindfulness game that allows MBP participants to observe their reactions to an unpleasant experience. Children learn to sit still and observe how they react when an ice cube is placed in their hand. To provide a safe environment for the participants to learn from the practice, we allow different options such as choosing a small or big ice cube, holding one or two pieces in the hand, placing a paper towel under the ice cube to reduce the intensity of the experience, changing the position of the ice in the hand, or transferring the ice cube from one hand to the other to take a break from the unpleasant experience. The ice cube exercise was originally a practice designed for pregnant mothers who are expected to apply mindfulness in coping with the intense pain in delivery (Bardacke 2012) but we find the exercise is suitable to all parents and family caregivers. Many parents described how, as the painful sensations emerged and faded away, they felt enlightened and became more mindful about their emotional reactivity in daily life. It is a particularly helpful exercise in a brief MBP for parents. Because a session of a brief MBP for parents normally lasts only 1.5 hours, there is not enough time for them to do a 30- or 40-minutes sitting practice to experience how mindfulness practice provides opportunities to explore ways to manage unpleasant experiences. The ice cube activity provides an alternative way to observe their reaction to an unpleasant experience in a safe and timely way. We once witnessed a parent who chose to hold two ice cubes in her hand, but violently threw them on the floor after less than 15 seconds. At the end of the program, she recognized that it was her most memorable experience of the program, and she became more aware of the impact of unpleasant experiences and her emotional reaction to them.

Ethical Issues and Trauma-Informed Practice in Delivering a Mindfulness Program

As a growing number of studies emphasize the positive effects of mindfulness, it is also important to uphold the principle of doing no harm and to consider professional ethics in the application of mindfulness. This is a challenging issue for social work practitioners as we reach out to clients with complex life issues. Richards and Bergin (2007) provided four important counter-indicators that practitioners should bear in mind in the application of spirituality-related interventions: clients who have indicated that they do not want to participate in a spiritual-oriented intervention; clients who are delusional or psychotic; clients who seek professional help for problems that are unrelated to spiritual issues; and clients who are minors and for whom consent from parents or guardians has not been solicited. Most MBPs have clear guidelines about conducting a briefing session or intake interview prior to the program. However, many social workers apply mindfulness as part of a brief program, and it may not be realistic to conduct a separate session to provide all necessary information and to screen participants before the commencement of the MBP.

In these situations, it should be remembered that for ethical practice, a practitioner should provide brief and adequate information about mindfulness at the beginning of the program. Clients should have the opportunity to ask for clarifications and raise questions about their concerns, and there should be adequate time and space to decide whether they feel they are suitable to participate in an MBP. Both MBSR and MBCT programs have clearly indicated criteria that exclude people with active symptoms of psychosis, recurrent suicidal ideation, current addiction to drugs or alcohol or in early recovery, or who have experienced a recent loss (Koerbel and Meleo-Meyer 2019; Segal et al. 2013). MBPs with multiple sessions should follow the same rules and clients should be given individual attention as they may not be comfortable discussing these issues in a group session.

In addition to the general principle of applying mindfulness safely, concern has been raised in trauma-informed practice in recent years (Levenson 2017). Social workers frequently encounter clients with a history of trauma, who have been affected by a physical or psychological threat to themselves or others that they reacted to with helplessness and fear (American Psychiatric Association 2013). Trauma experiences take many forms, usually involving an unexpected event outside a person's control such as criminal victimization, a serious traffic accident, natural disaster, war, or exposure to community or family violence. A population-based study that surveyed over 17,000 adults in the United States health system found that 64% of them reported at least one type of childhood maltreatment or household dysfunction, and 13% reported four or more (Centers for Disease Control and Prevention 2013). It is likely that the prevalence of adverse childhood experiences is even higher among poor, disadvantaged, clinical and criminal populations within our practice recipients (Levenson 2017).

In the past decade, professionals have developed a deeper understanding of trauma and have become more sensitive in adapting their practice to better support clients experiencing post-traumatic stress. The key principles for working with people impacted by trauma include safety (helping clients to feel calm, comfortable, respected and secure in their relationships with professionals), trust (helping clients to anticipate what is expected of them and what they can expect from the social worker by eliminating ambiguity and vagueness), choice (allowing clients to make decisions with a sense of control over their recovery), collaboration (building a genuine alliance in recovery, especially in cases of possible resistance due to activation of past authority figures) and empowerment (using a strengths-based approach and rebuilding a sense of efficacy and hopefulness) (Levenson 2017).

Mindfulness is a double-edged sword for trauma survivors. On the one hand, it can promote self-regulation by regulating attention and emotions and promoting bodily awareness, which can increase the capacity to integrate trauma with survivors' present lives. On the other hand, while practicing mindfulness, people are likely to reexperience the traumatic stimuli and may feel overwhelmed as such experiences dominate their field of awareness. Mindfulness can end up triggering traumatic symptoms and clients may feel discouraged, desperate and even blame themselves for their hopelessness (Treleaven 2018).

In view of its possible impact on people practicing mindfulness, there are some important reminders for professionals who offer MBPs. Mindfulness is not a one size fits all therapy and some people may not respond well to mindfulness practice. Some people mistakenly think that it is their fault for not able to benefit from mindfulness and end up struggling with their negative experiences in the midst of shame and isolation. Practitioners may not know when someone in the class is struggling with post-traumatic stress. While certain instructions in mindfulness practice facilitate people to explore their limits and expand their levels of acceptance toward unpleasant experiences, clients may have a sense of obligation to follow the instructions and believe they have failed to follow the good intentions of the mindfulness instructor. Therefore, when mindfulness is offered, clients should be prepared for a range of experiences, both pleasant and unpleasant, and should be reassured that these experiences are not related to their personal effort. Moreover, clients should be enabled to explore their personal anchors of attention among possible options, including locating the sensation of breath in the nose, chest, or abdomen, their hands, their feet on the floor, or their buttocks on a chair or a cushion, that can help to cultivate concentration and stabilize attention (Treleaven 2018). Clients should be reminded repeatedly that they should not hesitate to consult their mindfulness teacher about their experiences relating to practice after class.

Benefits of Mindfulness in Social Workers' Professional Practice and Development

Mindfulness is much more than a method that can be applied in social work practice (Wong 2019); it also has important and invaluable implications for our professional lives. Mindfulness can enhance practitioners' self-care, cultivate presence in the therapeutic relationship and deepen self-awareness and critical reflection.

In a recent study the benefits of social work and other social care professionals enrolled in a mindfulness elective course as part of their curriculum was investigated (Lo et al. 2021). Students who completed the MBSR program showed greater improvements in perceived efficacy and vigour, and significant reductions in physical distress, total job burnout, emotional exhaustion and depersonalization of clients, compared with the control group. Just as clients under stress can benefit from an MBP, social work students and social work practitioners can benefit and grow in similar ways. A recent review suggested three possible mechanisms by which MBP can influence physical health through biological pathways (including the promotion of stress regulation and reduction of stress reactivity in the brain), psychological pathways (including attention regulation and acceptance) and health behaviour pathways (including reduction of addictive behaviours and promotion of a healthy diet, sleep and related behaviours) (Crewell et al. 2019). These health outcomes and theory suggest that mindfulness should be promoted for social workers to improve their resilience to cope with challenges in their professional practice.

Overall, participating in an MBP not only increases social workers' knowledge and skills for helping people but also enhances their competency and efficacy, which can impact the overall quality of helping. The superior effect of MBSR compared with active control groups suggests that MBSR or similar programs should be promoted for social work education and professional development.

Conclusion

This chapter provides an overview of the application of psychological and clinical theories in social work practice. The first part reviews four major theories and their implications for our profession. This is followed by a critical discussion of how mindfulness can contribute to advancing social work practice. Due to the uniqueness of the social work profession in serving disadvantaged groups, specific mindfulness-based practice knowledge and skills should be generated to facilitate its adaptation. More effort is recommended to investigate and explain how psychological and clinical theories, including mindfulness, can be applied to our clients. As social workers, we can make use of mindfulness first by experiencing how it nurtures our lives through personal practice and then by applying it to different contexts and issues in professional practice.

References

American Psychiatric Association (2013) Diagnostic and Statistical Manual of Mental Disorders, fifth edition. the author

Bardacke N (2012) Mindful birthing: training the mind, body, and heart for childbirth and beyond. Harper Collins

Beccia AL, Ruf A, Druker S, Ludwig VU, Brewer JA (2020) Women's experiences with a mindful eating program for binge and emotional eating: a qualitative investigation into the process of change. The journal of alternative and complementary medicine 26(10):937–944

Beck J (2011) Cognitive behaviour therapy: basics and beyond, 2nd edn. New York, Guilford

Birnbaum L, Birnbaum A (2008) Mindful social work: from theory to practice. J Religion Spiritual Soc Work 27:87–104

Bögels SM, Restifo K (2014) Mindful parenting: a guide for mental health practitioners. Springer, New York

Bögels SM, Hellemans J, Van Deursen S, Römer M, van der Meulen R (2014) Mindful parenting in mental health care: effects on parental and child psychopathology, parental stress, parenting, coparenting, and marital functioning. Mindfulness 5:536–551. https://doi.org/10.1007/s12671-013-0209-7

Brandell JR (Ed.). (2010) Theory & practice in clinical social work. Sage

Brown B (2006) Shame resilience theory: a grounded theory study on women and shame. Fam Soc 87:43–52

Brown B (2015) Daring greatly: how the courage to be vulnerable transforms the way we live, love, parent, and lead. Penguin

Burgdorf V, Szabó M, Abbott MJ (2019) The effect of mindfulness interventions for parents on parenting stress and youth psychological outcomes: a systematic review and meta-analysis. Front Psychol 10:1336. https://doi.org/10.3389/fpsyg.2019.01336

Centers for Disease Control and Prevention (2013) Adverse childhood experiences study: prevalence of individual adverse childhood experiences. Retrieved from http://www.cdc.gov/ace/prevalence.htm

Chan SKC, Zhang D, Bögels SM, Chan CS, Lai KYC, Lo HHM, ... Wong SYS (2018) Effects of a mindfulness-based intervention (MYmind) for children with ADHD and their parents: protocol for a randomised controlled trial. BMJ open 8(11):e022514

Conger RD, Conger KJ, Martin MJ (2010) Socioeconomic status, family processes, and individual development. J Marriage Fam 72(3):685–704

Corey G (2016) Theory and practice of counseling and psychotherapy, Enhanced. Cengage Learning

Cournoyer BR (2016). The social work skills workbook. Cengage Learning

Craig SL, Austin A, Alessi E (2013) Gay affirmative cognitive behavioral therapy for sexual minority youth: A clinical adaptation. Clin Soci Work J 41(3):258–266

Crewell JD, Lindsay EK, Villalba DK, Chin B (2019) Mindfulness training and physical health: mechanisms and outcomes. Psychosom Med 81:224–232

Crews D, Besthorn FH (2016) Ecosocialwork and transformed consciousness: reflections on eco-mindfulness engagement with the silence of the natural world. Journal of Religion & Spirituality in Social Work: Social Thought 35(1–2):91–107

de Bruin EI, Blom R, Smit FMA, van Steensel FJA, Bögels SM (2015) MYmind: mindfulness training for youngsters with autism spectrum disorders and their parents. Autism 19:906–914

Egan G (2013) The skilled helper: a problem-management and opportunity-development approach to helping. Cengage Learning

Ellis A (1962) Reason and emotion in psychotherapy. Lyle Stuart

Fraser MW, Galinsky MJ (2010) Steps in intervention research: designing and developing social programs. Res Soc Work Pract 20:459–466

Gendlin ET (1998) Focusing-oriented psychotherapy: a manual of the experiential method. Guilford Press

Geurtzen N, Scholte RH, Engels RC, Tak YR, van Zundert RM (2015) Association between mindful parenting and adolescents' internalizing problems: non-judgmental acceptance of parenting as core element. J Child Fam Stud 24(4):1117–1128

Gouveia MJ, Carona C, Canavarro MC, Moreira H (2016) Self-compassion and dispositional mindfulness are associated with parenting styles and parenting stress: The mediating role of mindful parenting. Mindfulness 7(3):700–712

Greenland SK (2016) Mindful games: sharing mindfulness and meditation with children, teens, and families. Shambhala Publications

Gu J, Strauss C, Bond R, Cavanagh K (2015) How do mindfulness-based cognitive therapy and mindfulness-based stress reduction improve mental health and wellbeing? A systematic review and meta-analysis of mediation studies. Clin Psychol Rev 37:1–12

Healy K (2005) Social work theories in context: creating frameworks for practice, 2nd edn. Palgrave Macmillan, Basingstoke

Hick S (2009) Mindfulness and social work. Lyceum Books, Chicago

Hofmann SG, Asnaani A, Vonk IJ, Sawyer AT, Fang A (2012) The efficacy of cognitive behavioral therapy: A review of meta-analyses. Cognitive therapy and research 36(5):427–440.

Ho RTH, Lo HHM, Leung TCT, Choi CW (2020) Effects of a mindfulness-based intervention on diurnal cortisol pattern in disadvantaged families: a randomized controlled trial. Psychoneuroendocrinology. https://doi.org/10.1016/j.psyneuen.2020.104696

Kabat-Zinn J (2013) Full catastrophe living: using the wisdom of your body and mind to face stress, pain, and illness (revised and updated ed.). Bantam Books, New York

Kabat-Zinn M, Kabat-Zinn J (1997) Everyday blessings: the inner work of mindful parenting. Hachette, New York

Kabat-Zinn M, Kabat-Zinn J (2021) Mindful parenting: perspectives on the heart of the matter. Mindfulness. https://doi.org/10.1007/s12671-020-01564-7

Koerbel L, Meleo-Meyer F (2019) Mindfulness-based stress reduction (MBSR) curriculum and teaching guide. Brown University Mindfulness Center, Providence, Rhode Island

Levenson J (2017) Trauma-informed social work practice. Soc Work 62:105–113

Lo HHM, Epstein I, Ng SM, Chan CLW, Kwan HCSF (2011) When cognitive behavioral group therapy works and when it doesn't?: clinical data mining on good and poor CBGT outcomes for depression and anxiety among Hong Kong Chinese. Soc Work Ment Health 9:456–472

Lo HHM, Chan SKC, Szeto MP, Chan CYH, Choi CW (2017) A feasibility study of a brief mindfulness-based program for parents of children with developmental disabilities. Mindfulness 8:1665–1673

Lo HHM, Yeung JWK, Duncan LG, Chan SKC, Szeto MP, Ma Y, Siu AFY, Choi CW, Chow KW, Ng SM (2018) Validating of the interpersonal mindfulness in parenting scale in Hong Kong Chinese. Mindfulness 9:1390–1401

Lo HHM, Wong JYH, Wong SWL, Wong SYS, Choi CW, Ho RTH, Fong RW, Snel E (2019) Applying mindfulness to benefit economically disadvantaged families: a randomized controlled trial. Res Soc Work Pract 29:753–765

Lo HHM, Wong SWL, Wong JYH, Yeung JWK, Snel E, Wong SYS (2020) The effects of family-based mindfulness intervention in ADHD symptomology in young children and their parents: a randomized control trial. J Atten Disord 24:667–680. https://doi.org/10.1177/1087054717743330

Lo HHM, Ngai S, Yam K (2021) Effects of mindfulness-based stress reduction on health and social care education: a non-randomized controlled study. Mindfulness. https://doi.org/10.1007/s12671-021-01663-z

Lo HHM, Lau ENS, Tam CHL, Ngai SW, Chan SHW, Leung FH, Wong ET, Wong EWWY, Wong GOC, Cho, WC, Tsang AWK, Singh NN (2022) A mindfulness-based support program for parents of adolescents following social unrest in Hong Kong. Mindfulness 13:248–261

Long KJ, Homesley L, Wodarski JS (2007) The role for social workers in the managed health care system: a model for evidence-based practice. In: Thyer B, Wodarski JS (eds) Social work in mental health: an evidence-based approach. Wiley, Hoboken, pp 527–543

Maclean S, Harrison R (2015) Social work theory: a straightforward guide for practice educators and placement supervisors. Kirwin Maclean Associates

Ng TK, Wong DFK. (2018) The efficacy of cognitive behavioral therapy for Chinese people: A meta-analysis. Australian & New Zealand Journal of Psychiatry 52(7):620–637

Nicolson P, Bayne R, Owen J (2006) Applied psychology for social workers, 3rd edn. Palgrave Macmillan, London

Noble C (2019) Psychological and counselling theory in social work: a critical overview. In: Payne M, Reith-Hall E (eds) The Routledge handbook of social work theory. Routledge, Abingdon, pp 28–40

Norcross JC, Pfund RA, Prochaska JO (2013) Psychotherapy in 2022: a Delphi poll on its future. Prof Psychol Res Pract 44:363–370

Parent J, McKee LG, Rough JN, Forehand R (2016) The association of parent mindfulness with parenting and youth psychopathology across three developmental stages. J Abnorm Child Psychol 44:191–202

Payne M (2014) Modern social work theory, 4th edition. Palgrave Macmillan, Basingstoke

Payne M, Reith-Hall E (2019) Social work theory, knowledge and practice. In: Payne M, Reith-Hall E (eds) The Routledge handbook of social work theory. Routledge, Abingdon, pp 7–17

Rapp CA, Goscha RJ (2011) The strengths model: a recovery-oriented approach to mental health services, 3rd edn. Oxford University Press, New York

Rasmussen B (2018) A critical examination of CBT in clinical social work practice. Clin Soc Work J 46:165–173

Report by the Mindfulness All-Party Parliamentary Group (MAPPG) (2015) Mindful nation UK. Available online https://www.themindfulnessinitiative.org/Handlers/Download.ashx?IDMF=1af56392-4cf1-4550-bdd1-72e809fa627a

Richards PS, Bergin AE (2007) A spiritual strategy for counseling and psychotherapy, 2nd edn. American Psychological Association, Washington, DC

Richmond ME (1922) What is social case work?. Russell Sage Foundation

Rogers N (2016) Person-centered expressive arts therapy: a path to wholeness. In: Approaches to art therapy (pp. 230–248). Routledge

Ronen T, Freeman (eds) (2007) Cognitive behavior therapy in clinical social work practice. Springer, New York

Saleebey D (2013) The strengths perspective in social work practice. Pearson, Upper Saddle River

Schmid B, Aiken GT (2021) Transformative mindfulness: the role of mind-body practices in community-based activism. Cult Geogr 28:3–17

Segal ZV, Teasdale JD, Williams JMG (2013) Mindfulness-based cognitive therapy for depression, 2nd edn. Guilford, New York

Shennan G (2019) Solution-focused practice in social work. In: Payne M, Reith-Hall E (eds) The Routledge handbook of social work theory. Routledge, Abingdon, pp 224–235

Shlonsky A, Wagner D (2005) The next step: integrating actuarial risk assessment and clinical judgment into an evidence-based practice framework in CPS case management. Child Youth Serv Rev 27:409–427

Snel E (2014) Mindfulness matters: mindfulness for children, ages: 5–8. Trainer's handbook 1. The Academy for Mindful Teaching, Amsterdam

Spray C, Jowett B (2011) Social work practice with children and families. Sage

Sue DW, Rasheed MN, Rasheed JM (2016) Multicultural social work practice: a competency-based approach to diversity and social justice, 2nd edn. Wiley, Hoboken

Temme LJ, Kopak AM (2016) Maximizing recovery through the promotion of mindfulness and spirituality. J Religion Spiritual Soc Work 35:41–56

Treleaven DA (2018) Trauma-sensitive mindfulness: practices for safe and transformative healing. W.W. Norton, New York

Trevithick P (2008) Revisiting the knowledge base of social work: a framework for practice. Br J Soc Work 38:1212–1237

Turpyn CC, Chaplin TM (2016) Mindful parenting and parents' emotion expression: effects on adolescent risk behaviors. Mindfulness 7(1):246–254

Wong RY (2019) Mindfulness and social work. In: Payne M, Reith-Hall E (eds) The Routledge handbook of social work theory. Routledge, Abingdon, pp 256–267

Systems Theory and Social Work

Jan V. Wirth and Heiko Kleve

Contents

Introduction	40
Social Change Through Differentiation	42
Today's Person: From Individual to the Dividual	46
Dealing with Complexity: Systems and Environment	47
Social Work Between Society and the Individual	48
Life Conduct as Socio-individual Ambivalence	50
Inclusion and Exclusion	52
Conclusion	56
References	57

Abstract

This chapter discusses the theorising of social work in the field of systems theory. In particular, it takes Niklas Luhmann's biopsychosocial systems theory as the starting point. Luhmann's transdisciplinary theory has been widely received in the German-speaking world. For social work, which is placed in a relationship of tension between society and the individual, systems theory seems to be well suited, as it can deal with contradictions, paradoxes and ambivalences. In our contribution, we explain the crucial theoretical figures that seem particularly useful for an application in social work. In doing so, social work is linked to the problem of 'conduct of life' (in German: Lebensführung). The conduct of life,

---

J. V. Wirth (✉)
Hochschule Düsseldorf, Düsseldorf, Germany
e-mail: jan.wirth@hs-duesseldorf.de

H. Kleve
Stiftungslehrstuhl für Organisation und Entwicklung von Unternehmerfamilien, University Witten/Herdecke, Witten, Germany
e-mail: heiko.kleve@uni-wh.de

© Springer Nature Singapore Pte Ltd. 2023
D. Hölscher et al. (eds.), *Social Work Theory and Ethics*, Social Work,
https://doi.org/10.1007/978-981-19-1015-9_3

like social work, is crucially dependent on how it is possible to unfold contradictions and ambivalences and to work with them constructively in an appreciated manner.

Keywords

Systems theory · Social work · Epistemology · Luhmann · Social change · Constructivism · Life conduct · Contradiction · Ambivalence · Inclusion · Exclusion

Introduction

Systems theory is currently one of the most important paradigms in the scientific discourse of social work. Its applicability extends at many levels of interaction as an extremely diverse consulting concept, from bodies conducting organisational development to wider applications in society in the context of the enduring question of the social function of social work.

However, there is no single systems theory, but many very different and even incompatible systems theories. Their common feature is merely an interest in the relationship between part and whole and reciprocal interactions between systems and the environment. Even in the question of what should be understood as a system, the different systems theory approaches diverge widely. Historically, in social work discourse, socio-ecological approaches have enjoyed considerable popularity. These, too, are partly fed by basic assumptions of systems theory (see Lewin 1969; Bronfenbrenner 1979; and Germain and Gitterman 1983, 1999) However, in this chapter, they are not taken into account.

In terms of the philosophical question of how cognition (*Erkennen*) is possible, positions range from ontological realism (Obrecht 2001; Staub-Bernasconi 1995) to operative constructivism (Luhmann 1984) or radical constructivism (Kleve 2010). Ontological realism sees the world and everything in it as 'being' (*Seiend*) and clearly recognisable through scientific or logical means. Radical constructivism, in contrast, claims that the world is constructed in different ways – through perceiving, thinking or speaking. We will return to this notion below.

The scientific connection between social science systems theories and social work has existed since the 1960s–1970s. Gordon Hearn wrote in 1958 about new publications on general systems theory as a "fortunate accident":

> These scientists were contending that all forms of animate matter, including individuals, groups, and communities, together with various forms of inanimate matter could be regarded as systems; that, as such, they had certain common properties; and that eventually the laws governing their functioning would be known. (Hearn 1958, p. 5)

As early as the 1950s, in the context of the School of Welfare of the University of California, Berkeley, it was demanded:

that a researcher ought to make explicit at the outset the philosophical base from which he (*sic*) approaches his theory domain [...]. (Hearn 1958, p. 5)

This remark is noteworthy insofar as, to this day, prominent theories of social work are developed without their philosophical underlying assumptions made explicit (Thiersch 1986; 2006; Böhnisch 1994).

This can lead to learners or social work practitioners being unable to distinguish between different categories of theory formation. Back in 2013, as part of the discourse on the formation of social work theory, we proposed a distinction between theories *about* social work, theories *in* social work and theories *of* social work (Kleve and Wirth 2009/2013).

Theories *about* social work come, for example, from sociology, social psychology or social policy. Theories *in* social work can be, for example, communication models such as the Pragmatic Communications Axioms of the so-called Palo Alto School (Watzlawick et al. 1967; 1972) or the very well-known "Four-ear model of communication" (Thun 1981; 2010).

Theories *of* social work include, for example, life-world-oriented social work (Thiersch et al. 2005, 2012), the theory of coping with life (Böhnisch 1994), systemic-ontological social work (Obrecht 2005; Staub-Bernasconi 2007) and systemic social work (Hosemann and Geiling 2013; Kleve and Wirth 2009/2013). The last two theoretical perspectives embody the contrast between realism and constructivism in the systemic theorising mentioned above.

In the following, we will explain the newer constructivist system theory according to Kleve and Wirth (Wirth and Kleve 2019; Wirth and Kleve 2020). This approach, entitled *Life Conduct and the Postmodern World*, addresses the question of life conduct as a social phenomenon and the potential for social work to act in relation to it, as elaborated in systems theory. This conception of the person and society is predominantly based on the insights and work of the newer systems theory according to Niklas Luhmann.

Luhmann worked on a theory of society from the 1960s until his death in 1998. In so doing, he provided one of the most complex and voluminous theoretical structures of a widely respected systems theory. Although Luhmann was a sociologist, his work has a strong philosophical background and its widely interdisciplinary results range from a theory of society including organisations to a theory of interaction or communication between social and psychological systems (Berg/Schmidt 2000).

It was, therefore, to be expected that Luhmann's systems theory work would also permeate social work to advance its theoretical profiling. The initial spark for this was his essay on *Forms of helping in the changing social conditions* (Luhmann 1973). This essay is used as a starting point to explain the basic assumptions of Luhmann's systems theory, which are essential for social work. A complete representation or reconstruction of its development is not possible here, due to lack of space. Rather, the aim of our chapter is to sharpen systems theory for real-life problems and to articulate the need for reflection in social work, both as a science and profession.

Social Change Through Differentiation

Luhmann analyses help as a mode of interpersonal needs compensation against the background of three different forms of social differentiation during the social evolution of humanity.

In the so-called 'segmentary differentiated' society, also described as the tribal society, help occurred within the segment (the tribe) with each other and for each other in reciprocity and as a matter of course. Everyday life was characterised by unforeseeable catastrophes, such as drought, wars and epidemics. Each member of society could equally face a similar situation, in which help had to be provided immediately, irrespective of circumstances and without strategic calculations.

In the so-called 'stratificatory differentiated' society, also known as the corporative society, a hierarchy of social structures and positions led to unequal life situations that could not be easily compared with each other. As a rule, the large farmer was not dependent on any material or financial compensation from socially lower positions such as serfs, migrant workers, etc. The reciprocity of life situations and the so-called reciprocity of aid was broken. Social help now took place from top to bottom, as with the often religiously motivated alms by which the donor aimed to secure her or his place in the hereafter.

At the same time, however, social – mostly ecclesiastical – aid developed for those who could not be cared for by their family or relatives: the old, the sick, the insane or the orphaned. For these groups, specialised help institutions such as the Hospitals (places of shelter) developed. The urban or municipal welfare developing from this represents the beginning of another new form of differentiation – functional differentiation – the emergence of which coincides approximately with mechanisation, the beginning of book printing, the founding of universities, industrialisation and the emergence of today's sciences.

The form of differentiation in today's highly organised and – in socio-cultural terms – pluralistic society corresponds to functional differentiation. This does not mean – especially in global society – that segmentary or stratificatory forms of differentiation have become obsolete or disappeared. Tribes, castes, estates and classes – all these can still be observed.

Rather, systems theory holds that social development is primarily governed by functional differentiation, because the inclusion of as large a part of the population as possible in the various subsystems of society is generally prioritised. This vision of society finds its expression in the so-called 'postulate of full inclusion': everyone should be able to attend school, receive an education, find employment, start a family, have the right to health care and practice a religion of choice.

Functional differentiation is the hallmark of modernity. A society governed by functional differentiation is characterised by the fact that the social whole is increasingly differentiated horizontally into different functional areas. According to Luhmann, these functional areas are organised as social systems, each with its own logic and internal rules (codes and subcodes). As functional systems, they each assume different functions and services for society as a whole.

Modern systems theory, following the research results of Luhmann, generally assumes the existence of the following functional systems (Roth and Schütz 2015) (Fig. 1).

However, when we speak of 'existence', 'facts' or 'being present' in the context of the system theory in question here, we are dealing with phenomena, and connections between them, that are constructed by social or psychic systems in communication and with the use of symbols.

These constructions of the world and reality, their impact on the conduct of life as well as their interpretation for social work practice can be attributed to constructivism as an epistemological approach. The constructivism of the 1960s and 1970s is based on the results and works of Gregory Bateson, Paul Watzlawick, Ernst von Glasersfeld and, in particular, Heinz von Foerster and Humberto Maturana among many others (Bateson 1979; 1984; Glasersfeld 1995; 1997; Foerster 1981/1984; Foerster 1992; Maturana and Varela 1973/2004).

Constructivism, according to Falko von Ameln (2004), is a current of thought:

> That feeds from and feeds back on a multitude of basic assumptions from different individual disciplines – from biology to philosophy, from pedagogy to neurophysiology, and from cybernetics to linguistics. The unifying bracket between the various constructivist approaches is not a common theoretical problem, but a basic epistemological conviction that can be summarised as follows:
> 1. What we experience as our reality is not a passive image of reality but the result of an active cognitive effort.
> 2. Since we do not have any instrument outside our cognitive possibilities to check the validity of our cognition, we cannot make any assured statements about the correspondence between subjective reality and objective reality. (Ameln 2004, p. 3)

Radical constructivism in the style of Humberto Maturana (2002) and Heinz von Foerster (1992) and social constructivism as developed by Kenneth Gergen (1999; 2002) have been applied in social work since the 1990s together with Luhmann's systems theory model of society. Important in this respect are a large number of works by Heinz J. Kersting, Heiko Kleve, Albert Scherr and, most recently, Jan V Wirth (Vogel and Kaiser 1997; Kleve 1996; Scherr 2000; Wirth 2014) among many others, which have generated many somewhat critical resonances in the research discourses on social work (e.g. Staub-Bernasconi 2000).

As mentioned above, three different types of constructivism can be distinguished: firstly, radical constructivism with its focus on individual cognition; secondly, social constructivism with its focus on language and, thirdly, system-theoretical constructivism with its focus on communication.

System-theoretical constructivism, according to Niklas Luhmann, strictly distinguishes biological, psychological and social systems in its specific internal operations. Accordingly, it is described, not only by Luhmann himself, as "operative constructivism" (Lambers 2014; Lambers 2010). While radical constructivism, in Luhmann's opinion, hardly differs from subjective idealism, the term 'operative constructivism' is preferable to 'radical constructivism', indicating, in Luhmann's words, a change of reference (reference perspective) from a time-honoured subject to

System	Code	Medium	Program*	Function
Political System	government/opposition	power	ideology	limitation
Economy	payment/non-payment	money	price	distribution
Science	true/untrue	truth	theory	verification
Art	innovative/imitative	style	fashion	creation
Religion	immanent/transcendent	faith	confession	revelation
Legal System	lawful/unlawful	norm	law	standardization
Sport	success/failure	achievement	goal	mobilization
Health System	ill/healthy	illness	diagnosis	restoration**
Education	placeable/unplaceable	vita	curriculum	formation
Mass Media	informative/non-informative	medium	topic	multiplication

Fig. 1 Function systems of society (Roth/Schütz 2015, p. 24)

an "empirically observable, operationally closed, self-differentiated system" (quoted by Pfeifer-Schaupp 1995, 1997).

Here, it must be emphasised that, since its beginnings in England, the USA or Germany, professional social work has always taken the overall circumstances – society, the family, the life situation – into consideration. Pedagogy at the time of Pestalozzi was already aware that not only do people create circumstances, but also that circumstances create people (quoted by Wulf 2004, p. 34).

However, the application of modern systems theory is not exhausted in a pragmatic view of the supposed whole or the interactions between society and the individual, nor even in a socio-ecological view of the relationship between organisms and the social environment. For a so-called systemic work, i.e. the practical application of systems theory to social work, a whole series of characteristics have become condensed. First, we must ask how the emergence of a system actually occurs.

The answer to the above question is that they occur by observation. Without observing, nothing can be specified as a system. Without observers, there is no observation. By 'observer', we mean a system that is able to distinguish and organise itself in such a way that it can again connect to these distinctions (observations). Biological, psychical and social systems have this capacity for self-organisation (Maturana 1982).

In contrast to biological systems, social and psychical systems use meaning (Sinn) as their basis. Systems of meaning are of central importance for systemic social work and may include systems of pairs, siblings, a family, group, team, organisation, a subsystem – such as the state as a functional system of national society, or global society – the "total communication that can be reached for each other" (Luhmann 1997/1998, p. 36).

Systems theory suggests that meaning is a basic concept for social work. Meaning is determined by Luhmann phenomenologically, in the distinction between reality and potentiality:

> Meaning appears in the form of a surplus of references to other possibilities of experiencing and acting. (Luhmann 1984, p. 93)

For the concept of meaning, reality only becomes meaningful through the horizon of potentiality. Every reality is merely a selection from the realm of the possible and therefore always refers to a potentiality (Stäheli 2000, p. 66). Luhmann emphasises:

> That there is always something else as well - be it indeterminate, be it determinate, be it necessary or undeniable, be it merely possible or doubtful, be it natural or artificial. (1984, p. 93)

Every processing of meaning thus generates a value (reality) and a counter-value (possibility) with constantly changing selections and signs. The generation of meaning and significance is always directed towards producing the ability to act and security for the preservation of a life's accomplishments or the conduct of life.

Only systems of meaning are able to connect respectively to their own selections (observations) or to negate the connection to previous selections. Only thus does the difference between actuality (reality) and potentiality (possibility) emerge. Reality can be negated; possibilities are sought. Thus, the difference releases psychic movement and physical energy to design alternative realities, which in turn offer new possibilities to connect.

Attempts to flee from the world of reality into the world of possibilities are particularly expected in difficult life situations. Mental health, however, collapses when the difference between reality and possibility recedes:

> when the sense of reality of the person in question disappears, when he (*sic*) is no longer able to distinguish what happens in his fantasies and what happens independently of them. (Elias and Scotson 1965; 2006, p. 40)

Today's Person: From Individual to the Dividual

'Psychical systems' denote the psyches or consciousnesses of (in)dividuals. This notation is used to indicate that, according to systems theory, a human being is not 'individual' (indivisible), but 'dividual' (divisible), since the bodies of individuals (matter) cannot enter into communication with different social systems (for example voice messages, pictures, videos, sculptures); matter and body remain external to any communication.

The biological system of the body of the human being does not operate via communicative-linguistic messages, but via cell metabolism and electrochemical impulse rates. Just as no thoughts leave or transcend the psychical system, or communicate the social system, biological operations are not able to operate outside their own system. This is crucial for systems theory: the operation of one system can only ever connect to its own operations, not to operations outside the system. Attention to these system boundaries is therefore crucial in being able to describe phenomena of the coupling between different systems in theoretically precise way.

Humans participate in the communication of social systems only in the form that their psychical system (consciousness or thoughts) is structurally (via expectations) or operatively (via language) coupled to the social systems – or not. Looking at the participation (inclusion) or non-participation (exclusion) of individuals in different social subsystems of society, the question and problem of coupling or non-coupling to maintain the conduct of life becomes important not only for those concerned. This is also highly relevant for social work. We will return to this issue later.

By making distinctions as system operations, the system designs itself as distinct from its environment. The system emerges, generates itself and reproduces itself in its own way.

A family, for example, creates and sustains its 'holistic existence' in this system-theoretical perspective by the fact that its members mutually recognise each other as part of the family and relate to each other through communication with each other that does not include members of other families. These communications create a shared identity as a family, team or society, and this identity secures the boundary between system and environment. Social work may enter the family's space, but the professional social work does not become part of the family. However, there may be too rigid a coupling between the family and social work, which may deactivate the self-help forces of the family. Social work, then, is symbiotically, but without merging with it, part of the family, when the family can no longer organise its own daily, household, health care or leisure activities without external help.

Again, to put it more abstractly: a system is thus constructed and reproduced in the long run by making – and because it makes – a distinction between system and environment in its own way. Whether the distinction between system and environment is applied within the system or outside does not matter initially. The prerequisite is that there is an observer who divides the world around them, and of which they are a part, between 'system' and 'environment' (*Umwelt*). Under observation, the system reintroduces the distinction between system and environment within itself.

Dealing with Complexity: Systems and Environment

It goes without saying that an observer who aims to divide the world between systems and environment will immediately find an unmanageable mixture of systems, subsystems and their environments.

Working systemically – whether in counselling, therapy or education – means using the distinction between system and environment to analyse life situations and needs for help, as well as to design ways of helping. In particular, social systems are distinguished from their environment in social work, insofar as social work has to differ from medicine (organisms) and psychology (psyches) in creating identities.

Not all social systems will be alike. Rather, the attentive observer will discover that global society and social intercourse have quite different system formations. The functional systems of society have already been mentioned, to which we can add organisations, families, couples or volatile systems of interaction.

Despite similarities in self-organisation or self-reproduction, different system formations follow different forms. For this very reason, it is interesting to explore whether, in social work, there is a particular mechanism by which systems couple with their environment or social systems – whether as a functional system, organisation or family – access individuals in their communications.

In this respect, the distinction between inclusion and exclusion suggests itself. This distinction raises the important question of the extent to which social systems continue, i.e. open or close, boundaries and possibilities of access and participation (or non-access or non-participation). At least theoretically, it is advantageous for the conduct of life if sufficient options are included in various subsystems of society in an individually self-determined manner.

Consequently, a complex of different interlocking and interrelated distinctions is at the centre of today's way of life and related social work. Luhmann's system theory offers a valuable observation apparatus here. However, Luhmann, as a sociologist, had other epistemological interests than social work: he had set himself the task of designing a theory of society that could capture precisely the complexity and variety of social evolution.

This systems theory operates in practical terms like an observer in the lookout, or crow's nest, of a ship. It is not primarily interested in the hardships and sufferings of the oarsmen in the bowels of the ship but, rather, soberly analyses social systems in their structures and processes, such as their formal organisation, the control of their operational processes, internal handling or processing of disturbances.

Social Work Between Society and the Individual

Social work, in contrast, is constantly active in the tension between society and the individual. According to ethical codes, it is committed to social change as well as to human well-being (International Federation of Social Workers 2021). The systems theory devised by Luhmann, a sociologist, can paradoxically not be used easily in social work. The most important element here seems to be to use not only social systems but also psychical system contexts as dual reference points. Only then can circular interactions and interdependencies be perceived and considered.

In short, this systems theory of social work is not only about social evolution and social theory, but about the question of the conduct of life of individuals, families or groups and society as a whole and about corresponding social professional possibilities for action (prevention, intervention and so on). However, since the one (society) is not possible without the other (the individual), the reference problem of social work would also have to be determined differently from the one-sided approach in the sense of an either/or, as in the case of social problems versus individual problems.

Since the emergence of the scientific foundations of social work, various theoretical proposals have been made with regard to its reference problem (Lambers 2020). These range from "individual failures in the community" (Scherpner 1962; 1974) to "coping with life" (Böhnisch 1994), "life-world and everyday orientation" (Thiersch 1986; 2006) to "social problems" (Staub-Bernasconi 2007) or a radical critique of capitalist society as a whole (Khella 1974).

In particular, the life-world and everyday orientation of social work, which is largely based on the work of Hans Thiersch, has become a widespread theoretical and action concept in the fields of social work action and institutions over the last 30 years (loc. cit.). This theoretical concept cannot be explained in detail here, but the important element is that it focuses on two central distinctions: on the one hand, the distinction between system and life-world according to Jürgen Habermas (Habermas 1981; 1995a, b) and, on the other hand, the ambiguity of everyday life (Lefebvre 1968; 1972) in the sense of critical theory.

These distinctions not only unlock valuable spaces for reflection but also reveal the ambivalences and paradoxes that social work, especially as a profession, fundamentally and inevitably has to address. It is obvious that the recognition of ambivalence and paradoxes is at odds with the idea of an objectivist, unambiguous and contradiction-free theorising of social work.

Besides Heiko Kleve (2007), Fritz Schütze (1992) has notably highlighted the paradoxes of professional action in an influential way:

> In the application of professional analysis and action procedures to the concrete project or case problem, paradoxes of professional action occur again and again, that is difficulties and dilemmas in the work process that cannot be resolved or circumvented, and in which the professional thus becomes entangled by necessity. (Schütze 1992, p. 137)

For the processing and reflection of contradictions, ambivalences and paradoxes in social work, Luhmann's system theory seems particularly suitable, assuming that knowledge and identity are constituted through negation (Spinoza, Hegel) and difference (Derrida 1972).

In this respect, this systems theory does not ask what people are, but how social communication makes people what they are for each other: boss, lover, politician, criminal, youth, case-worker, teacher, immigrant, racist, old, poor, helpless or effective helper. All the distinctions thus raised, however, are not just different as such; inherent in every distinction is the potential to develop into ambivalence via the asymmetrical attribution of value.

Hegel termed precisely this moment of the emergence of a contradiction an 'antithesis'. Karl Marx, in his materialist theory of history, developed – to put it simply – the distinction between two classes, the capitalists and the workers, and elaborated it as a class conflict. Sigmund Freud's psychoanalysis highlights the distinction between the conscious and unconscious as significant for understanding mental movements. Selective school systems, as in Germany, organise learning processes and careers according to a distinction between those who are capable of learning and those who are not: capable/incapable. Conservative politics emphasise – just one arbitrary example of many – the difference between homosexual and heterosexual in contrast to liberal views. Science insists on truth in the negation of the possible falsity of its knowledge, etc.

Forming real barriers, a multitude of distinctions cut through society and the life courses of individuals as well as through the spaces of theorising, action and reflection of social work. The task of social work would then be to recognise and resymmetrise these one-sided and destructively entrenched ambivalences and to make them accessible again to shared judgement for benefits in education, counselling, therapy, etc.

In recent years, the present authors have published a number of pieces that place the appropriate or successful handling of ambivalences at the centre of professional competencies in social work (Wirth and Kleve 2012, 2019, 2020). Accordingly, life conduct (Lebensführung), our proposal for a new formulation of the problem of reference of social work, is not a clearly determinable, unquestionably acceptable and unilaterally controllable case of designing and realising one's own individual life but can be described only as an ambivalence of social and individual possibilities, abilities and willingness to participate or not participate. Accordingly, it is not a matter of developing one's own definition of life in the sense of a good or happy life

(Nussbaum 1988/1999) or possibly obligating others in a paternalistic way. This would be tantamount to erasing ambivalence.

Instead, it is precisely the recognition of ambivalence that is important, because only ambivalence, as a moment of uncertainty, of being open, pausing, allows for deeper reflection on important life decisions. For, if it is already clear which side of the distinction should be accepted, social work is no longer a profession aimed at enabling self-determination, but an instrument for stabilising possibly socially unjust living conditions.

Life Conduct as Socio-individual Ambivalence

It is particularly true today that life conduct can no longer be pigeonholed; it is not possible to describe it in just one way or category – it is characterised precisely by being neither a purely individual nor a purely social fact.

We are not omnipotent captains of our own life design, nor is our way of life determined entirely by social conditions. It is neither possible to simply continue to live in the traditions and social order of our ancestors, nor to pursue our own way of life, rational to us, without question or alternative.

The communications and interactions in a variously differentiated society are characterised by the fact that any thesis is immediately accompanied by a counter-thesis. No description of reality and no life plan based on it are so sustainable that they do not at the same time strengthen the plausibility of the counter-thesis: rigid order entails spaces of disorder, rationality the desire for irrationality, pluralisation uniformity and intentions unintended effects. According to the philosopher Wolfgang Welsch, we cannot discuss a single outstanding phenomenon of our time without at the same time placing another reading alongside it (Welsch 1987, 2002). In other words, "ambivalence is the least we have to reckon with in contemporary world relations" (Welsch 1987, 2002; Kleve 2007).

If we apply systems theory as a matter of reciprocal coupling to systems that are operationally closed to one another, it seems plausible that the conduct of life is not unilaterally controllable.

This non-controllability introduces another important feature of systems, according to the systems theory used here. In the discussion of social work as well as that of pedagogy, the so-called "technology deficit" plays a prominent role (Luhmann 1990/2004; Luhmann/Schorr 1982).

The technology deficit refers to the impossibility of transferring an operationally closed system from system state 'A' to system state 'B' safely and predictably. Accordingly, enlightenment, teaching and education do not mean filling an empty vessel with information or messages; in terms of systems theory, they mean designing communication, interaction and learning processes in such a way that they can at best stimulate, but not instruct, their subjects to discover for themselves new possibilities of acting, feeling and recognising and to link them in interactive processes to new skills and competencies.

The language course for immigrants, the seminar for students, the local youth centre, the residential group for people with disabilities, etc. are, therefore, not to be designed as impositions, obligations or even a form of paternalism, but offered in such a way that they are perceived, described and, thus, evaluated as meaningful, appropriate and useful from the perspective of their recipients.

Meaningful in this context means that they reveal opportunities that people pursue for good reasons. Appropriate means that the offers are linked to the current requirements of life and the skills of the recipients in terms of subject matter, space and time. Useful means that the offers are perceived as useful by their recipients because they make something possible that would not otherwise have come about.

With the theoretical lens of systems theory, it is the task of life conduct to constructively shape contradictions, transitions and paradoxes. A way of life can be described from 'discrepant' to 'divided' because – in a multi-differentiated society – we constantly have to address ambiguities, contrasts, incompatibilities and divisions. The way of life of society and its individuals is continuously splitting: distinctions such as old/young, woman/man, poor/rich, residents/immigrants, healthy/sick, etc. become divisions and incompatibilities if they solidify themselves as differences, and limit or even block our possibilities for action in advance.

A classic problem of incompatibility is seen, for example, in the reconciliation of work and family life. This incompatibility is based on the incompatible needs of constant care (of children) and professional mobility. Unless a home office is involved, a different space is added: the family lives in A, the company is in B.

Space locations, that is places, can only be occupied once. The subject of the socially and socially produced, and thus changeable, incompatibility of permanence (in the family) and mobility (in professional life) fills books and magazine shelves. However, even expert advice does not provide childcare; it can only stimulate and, at best, enable people to contribute selected information or knowledge and to make decisions on this basis. This fragility of life, its wholeness broken into more and more individual distinction complexes, such as belonging/not belonging, cannot be escaped. The transition from distinctions into incompatibilities and divisions (and vice versa) is fluid. It is not the solidification or absence of distinctions that can become problematic, but how they are addressed. Some of these demarcations are only temporary; others are helpful in the long term.

Take the distinction of I and You. Children who grow up in families that do not allow for I-They or I-You distinctions are trapped in an amorphous 'we', prevented from building their own identity, self-worth and corresponding self-efficacy. These experiences and processes are variously described in the contexts of counselling and psychotherapy (Cierpka 1996, 2008).

The difference between the 'other' and 'I' must be incorporated into the system, arranging the interactions raised with the split for a meaningful, mobile and stable coupling. This is a prerequisite for successful individual development into a socially integrated individual. How are we responsible for our actions and their consequences, and how are others responsible for them?

The answer to this question is related to how we, together with others, draw the boundaries between ourselves and the relevant others. It is clear that we expand our possibilities for action when we see ourselves as responsible, when we assume that it is only from ourselves that the power of change can emanate.

Life conduct is constantly faced with the challenge of addressing contradictions, divisions and transitions constructively. Constructive means regarding the obstacles that appear as developmental tasks, which – again a task of counselling – favour the elaboration of abilities and resources.

This task can be accomplished less and less in isolation as an individual. Rather, it is a social task, that is the task of networks such as friends, parents, families, work groups and teams, in which individuals support each other in integrating different perspectives in a way that is both fact- and relationship-oriented. This mutual giving and taking are sometimes not seen as balanced, as each one of us knows from our own experience.

Moreover, there is no way to control or even direct the communication from one side (Wirth/Kleve 2012). There is no possibility or ability to predetermine or directly target the experience and behaviour of the other interaction partner at specific content (see above on the technology deficit). Individual life conduct faces the paradoxical task of being expected to achieve something by itself that cannot be achieved without others and third parties.

Whether the conduct of life has a happy, good or successful outcome is not examined in systems theory, which is not concerned with value judgements. Rather, it soberly tries to observe the observations of the observers (people, professionals, scientists). How do they manage to construct their world(s) without at the same time seeing the blind spots that their observation generates?

An especially important characteristic of the application of systems theory in social work is, therefore, creating situations and settings in which it is possible to switch from unreflective observation (first-order observation) to observation of the observer (second-order observation) (Luhmann 1984). Such situations may take the form of counselling sessions, collegial counselling or supervision, but also professional conferences, in other words any situation in which we allow ourselves to reflect on the fact that there could also be other interpretations and related possibilities for action.

Inclusion and Exclusion

In practical terms, the application of the system-theoretical distinction between inclusion and exclusion is interesting in terms of society, a way of life bound to participation or non-participation and related social work:

> Inclusion (and correspondingly exclusion) can only refer to the way in which people are designated, that is, considered relevant, in the context of communication. (Luhmann 2005, p. 229)

The system-theoretical form of 'inclusion/exclusion' is generally (cf. Farzin 2006, p. 11), depending on the systems- or society-theoretical context, either:

(a) About the relationship between mental and social systems, or
(b) Between the individual and society, and finally
(c) About themselves in their quality as difference, which raises the question of the properties of inclusive or exclusive communications in the different kinds of social systems

> Both psychical and social systems are conceived in systems theory as autopoietic (self-generating), that is, as systems consisting of and linking only elements that do not occur outside the system. (Maturana 2000, p. 106)

For social systems, these elements are communications. No communication is possible outside social systems, and each communication links to a previous one. Psychical systems operate on the basis of consciousness, with thoughts as basic elements, relating to themselves.

Thus, the unity of the system is ensured by the accomplishment of operations which, in turn, link to their own accomplished operations. From this operative and self-referential concept of system in the sense of autopoiesis results in the difference-theoretical version of system identity. The system is the unity of the difference of system and environment, which has to be observed and updated again and again in its self-execution. This gives rise to multiple possible system-environment differences, since systems cannot observe each other except as environments, and each as a different environment:

> The choice of a system reference simultaneously designates the system that draws its own boundaries and thus itself divides the world into system and environment. (Luhmann 2005, p. 157)

For social work, this is consequential and instructive in several ways: each mental and social system must be understood as a respective individual system that constructs environmental perspectives in its own way. The talk of people as 'generic beings' loses its plausibility when systems represent environments for each other, and indeed a different environment for each other. This radically individualistic orientation of systems theory is highly congruent with the individualisation of case-based processing necessary in social work. Thus, in social work, it is important to connect to the different life histories and life situations of those involved and to generate appropriate help and resources in relation to them.

The concept of community – and the mythologies associated with it – also dissolve in the separation of social and psychological systems. According to Luhmann (1984, p. 297ff), community can no longer be understood as a "fusion of psychical and social systems", but as the possibility and ability of social systems to calculate or count back on the consciousness of the participants, or the understanding and production of consciousness in communication.

In a society governed by functional differentiation, the position of an individual in the social structure is no longer predetermined by birth, status or household affiliation, as in feudal society. The conversion of the social order to various subsystems, which claim sole competence to solve certain social problems, has far-reaching consequences for the individual. Integration into the subsystems is situational and no longer permanent:

> The individual can no longer belong to one and only one subsystem. She can engage professionally/professionally in the economic system, in the legal system, in politics, in the education system, and so on; but she cannot live alone in a functional system. However, since society is nothing more than the totality of its internal system/environmental conditions and cannot occur again in itself as a whole, it no longer offers the individual a place where he can exist as a 'social being'. He can only live outside of society, only reproduce himself as a system of his own kind in the environment of society, whereby for him society is a necessary environment for this. The individual can no longer be defined by inclusion, but only by exclusion. (Luhmann 1993, p. 158; own translation)

The uniqueness of the person, important as that is, is no longer determined by inclusion, as a holistic and complete integration of a person into a subsystem, but by exclusion:

> [...] exclusion individuality thus reacts to the demands that a functionally differentiated society places on the psychic systems in its environment. The individual must be able to adapt to a wide variety of social expectations and role requirements in a context-sensitive manner, and at the same time, he must qualify himself as the addressee of expectations. While in corporative society the general characteristics of the peasant, the nobleman or the cleric were the decisive factor for what could be expected of the persons concerned in the context of communication, now impersonal roles and the individuality of the person take their place and determine what is to be expected and what is not. (Farzin 2006, p. 29; own translation)

Social work now has work within a system-theoretical perspective with individuals, regardless of whether they feel individual:

> The in-dividuum is defined by divisibility. It needs a musical self for the job, a patient self for the family. What he has left for himself is the problem of his identity. (Luhmann 1993, p. 223)

The profession of social work thus comes as a network-shaped, decentralised, organised institution of the welfare state, which – in accordance with legal requirements – helps individuals either to meet urgent, functional and context-related behavioural requirements or to develop alternative patterns of inclusion. As a "representative" communication, it includes individuals and their families in order to:

- Support them in their inclusion (as in therapy support)
- Support renewed inclusion (as in the search for work) or

- Be able to manage their exclusion (as in aid for the homeless) (Bommes and Scherr 2000, 2012)

Social work aims to observe problematic inclusion patterns in the life conduct of modern society as early as possible and to design concepts to react to them, such as 'early help' immediately after birth, 'debt counselling' in companies with low wages or 'social counselling' in refugee shelters.

The peculiarity in the application of the system-theoretical distinction of inclusion and exclusion now lies in the fact that:

> the side of exclusion cannot be marked communicatively without the exclusion being converted into inclusion. (Farzin 2006, p. 107)

The most important consequence of this orientation is that space-bound definitions of exclusion and inclusion cannot be maintained. Spaces of inclusion and exclusion are, therefore, not topographical or geographical places to which we can go and then, as it were, look exclusion in the eye. Inclusion and exclusion are communicative differences and system-internal attributions at different levels of interaction, organisation and functional systems, each generating different forms of exclusion.

As an example, with regard to interaction systems, exclusion is the normal case. It would be nonsensical to assign about six billion potentially excluded persons to each interaction system. Regarding non-membership in organisations, it would also be nonsensical to define a general problem. The question is rather the graded criteria and categories used by organisations to recruit their personnel and allow some people to become members but not others (see the proportion of women in leadership positions, for example). It is undisputed that everyone in modern society should be allowed to participate in all functional systems (postulate of full inclusion). Mass exclusions, social exclusions and impoverishment in modern society have their causes both structurally and operationally in the solidification of structures as well as symbolic practices.

Social work oriented towards systems theory is, therefore, concerned with compensating for or reversing social exclusion (in the form of single or multiple sub-systemic exclusion) by explicitly including service-users as individuals in the interactions, mediating and enabling inclusion in organisations and helping to articulate or realise claims to participation in the various subsystems of society.

Social work that is based on the standards of the 'constructivist systems theory' explained here must refrain from contributing linear, mono-causal explanations. Communication, whether in the family, in a team or in parliament, depends on an understanding of the reciprocity and circularity of what happens: communication is a dance that requires at least two people or parties. It functions by assuring the participation of psychical systems in its own continuation. Of course, communication can also be terminated by social work. Outside help should necessarily be followed again by self-help.

If possible, exclusion should not be an irreversible decision without alternative possibilities of inclusion, because this would be tantamount to explicit entrenched and persistent exclusion, which would contradict the code of values of social work in an unacceptable way. After all, social work represents the last safety net of the modern social and welfare state for the lives of many individuals and families who are unable to meet the complex and contradictory behavioural demands of the subsystems.

However, it is not considered to be a foregone conclusion, and it is the task of social work, in fact, not hastily to create one-sided or linear constructions of problems when faced with a mix of structural and behavioural causes of problems. Was it the crisis in the car industry or the depression caused by divorce that caused the client's unemployment? We argue that this is not at all important in social work, which has to understand itself as part of the whole in its particular function and its own ambivalent identity between the established subsystems of society.

While linearity means the sequence of cause and effect, circularity means recognising the interrelation of cause and effect, in which certain behaviours are integrated in a circular context and must be understood as a whole. Whether certain factors are cause or effect, and whether this is of any importance for the help offered is not, at least initially, to be assessed within social work but within the client (system). This can – if desired – be accompanied by a professional assessment.

Circularity also means looking at the whole in its interdependent parts, identifying any room for manoeuvre in terms of perspective, allowing for contradictions and criticism, understanding back and forth as part of the process and, last but not least, integrating the hopes and anticipations of those involved in recurring communication processes.

Conclusion

Social work, then, is not to be confused with politics (we decide), justice (we judge) or medicine (we heal). If, with the help of systems theory, the autonomy of systems is taken seriously, social work would be a matter of connecting to the client's problem construction and opening up spaces for reflection and action in which clients move towards valued and shared goals for good reasons.

Systems theory, we conclude, offers a multifaceted yet precise tool for analysing social change, change in organisations, inclusion and exclusion in society and, not least, structures and changes how to conduct our lives in our complex society. With systems theory, social work can empower itself to embrace the autonomy of systems and develop appropriate approaches. With the recognition of ambivalence, opening spaces for reflection becomes a professional necessity. Finally, the 'observation of the observers' provides social work with the appropriate inventory to stimulate and evaluate reflection processes.

References

Ameln Fv (2004) Konstruktivismus. Francke, Tübingen
Berg Hd/Schmidt JFK (Hrsg.) (2000) Rezeption und Reflexion. Zur Resonanz der Systemtheorie Niklas Luhmanns außerhalb der Soziologie. Suhrkamp, Frankfurt am Main
Bateson G (1979; 1984) Geist und Natur. Eine notwendige Einheit, 4. Aufl. Suhrkamp, Frankfurt am Main
Böhnisch L (1994) Gespaltene Normalität. Lebensbewältigung und Sozialpädagogik an den Grenzen der Wohlfahrtsgesellschaft. Juventa, Weinheim
Bommes, M, Scherr A (2000/2012) Soziologie der sozialen Arbeit: eine Einführung in Formen und Funktionen organisierter Hilfe, 2. Aufl. Juventa, München
Bronfenbrenner U (1979) Die Ökologie menschlicher Entwicklung. Klett-Cotta, Stuttgart
Cierpka, M (Hrsg.) (1996; 2008) Handbuch der Familiendiagnostik. Springer, Heidelberg
Derrida J (1972) Die Schrift und die Differenz. Suhrkamp, Frankfurt am Main
Elias N, Scotson JL (1965/2006) Etablierte und Außenseiter. Suhrkamp, Frankfurt am Main
Farzin S (2006) Inklusion/Exklusion. Entwicklungen und Probleme einer systemtheoretischen Unterscheidung. transcript, Bielefeld
Gergen KJ (1999; 2002) Konstruierte Wirklichkeiten: eine Hinführung zum sozialen Konstruktionismus. Kohlhammer, Stuttgart
Germain CB/Gitterman A (1983; 1999) Praktische Sozialarbeit. Das "Life Model" der sozialen Arbeit (first published in 1980 in English). Original title: the life model of social work practice (1996), 3rd edn, fully revised. Enke, Stuttgart
Habermas J (1981; 1995) Theorie des kommunikativen Handelns Bd. 1. Handlungsrationalität und gesellschaftliche Rationalisierung. Suhrkamp, Frankfurt/Main
Habermas, J (1981; 1995) Theorie des kommunikativen Handelns Band 2. Zur Kritik der funktionalistischen Vernunft. Suhrkamp, Frankfurt/Main
Hearn G (1958) Theory building in social work. Oxford University Press, London
Hosemann W, Geiling W (2013) Einführung in die systemische soziale Arbeit. Mit 5 Tabellen. Reinhardt, München u.a.
International Association of Social Workers (IFSW) (2021) „Erklärung der globalen Sozialarbeit zu ethischen Grundsätzen". https://www.ifsw.org/global-social-work-statement-of-ethical-principles/
Khella K (1974) Theorie und Praxis der Sozialarbeit und Sozialpädagogik, Band 1. Einführung, Hamburg
Kleve H (1996) Konstruktivismus und Soziale Arbeit. Die konstruktivistische Wirklichkeitsauffassung und ihre Bedeutung für die Sozialarbeit/Sozialpädagogik und Supervision. Kersting, Aachen
Kleve H (2007) Postmoderne Sozialarbeit. Ein systemtheoretisch-konstruktivistischer Beitrag zur Sozialarbeitswissenschaft. Springer VS, Wiesbaden
Kleve H (2010) Konstruktivismus und Soziale Arbeit. Einführung in Grundlagen der systemisch-konstruktivistischen Theorie und Praxis. Springer VS, Wiesbaden
Kleve H/Wirth JV (2009; 2013) Die Praxis der Sozialarbeitswissenschaft. Eine Einführung, 3. Aufl. Schneider Verlag Hohengehren, Baltmannsweiler
Lambers H (2010) Systemtheoretische Grundlagen Sozialer Arbeit. Budrich, Opladen
Lambers H (2014) Reflexionsgrundlagen Sozialer Arbeit. Eine systemtheoretische Einführung. Beltz Juventa, Weinheim
Lambers H (2020) Theorien der Sozialen Arbeit. Ein Kompendium und Vergleich, 5. überarbeitete Aufl
Lefebvre H (1968; 1972) Das Alltagsleben in der modernen Welt. Suhrkamp, Frankfurt/Main
Lewin K (1969) Grundzüge der topologischen Psychologie. Hans Huber, Bern, Stuttgart, Wien
Luhmann N (1973) Formen des Helfens im Wandel gesellschaftlicher Bedingungen. In: Otto H-U, Schneider S (Hrsg.) Gesellschaftliche Perspektiven der Sozialarbeit 1 – Kritische Texte zur Sozialarbeit und Sozialpädagogik. Luchterhand, Neuwied, Darmstadt. S. 21–44.

Luhmann N/Schorr KE (1979; 1999) Reflexionsprobleme im Erziehungssystem. Suhrkamp, Frankfurt/Main

Luhmann N (1984) Soziale Systeme. Grundriss einer allgemeinen Theorie. Suhrkamp, Frankfurt am Main

Luhmann N (1990; 2004) Das Erkenntnisprogramm des Konstruktivismus und die unbekannt bleibende Realität. In Luhmann, N (Hrsg.) Soziologische Aufklärung 5. Konstruktivistische Perspektiven. VS, Wiesbaden, p. 31–57

Luhmann N (1993) Gesellschaftsstruktur und Semantik. Studien zur Wissenssoziologie der modernen Gesellschaft, Bd. 3. Suhrkamp, Frankfurt am Main

Luhmann, N (1994/2005) Inklusion und Exklusion. In Luhmann, N (Hrsg.) Soziologische Aufklärung 6. Die Soziologie und der Mensch. VS, Wiesbaden, p. 226–51

Luhmann N (1997/1998) Die Gesellschaft der Gesellschaft. Suhrkamp, Frankfurt am Main

Maturana HR (1982) Erkennen: die Organisation und Verkörperung von Wirklichkeit – ausgewählte Arbeiten zur biologistischen Epistemologie. Vieweg, Braunschweig

Maturana HR/Varela FJ (1984; 2005) Der Baum der Erkenntnis. Die biologischen Wurzeln des menschlichen Erkennens. Goldmann, München

Maturana HR (2002) Biologie der Realität. Suhrkamp, Frankfurt am Main

Maturana HR, Varela, FJ (1973/2004) De máquinas y seres vivos. Autopoiesis: la organización de lo vivo. Santiago de Chile: Editorial Universitaria, Grupo Editorial Lumen.

Nussbaum MC (1988/1999) Gerechtigkeit oder Das gute Leben. Suhrkamp, Frankfurt/Main

Obrecht W (2001) Das Systemtheoretische Paradigma der Disziplin und der Profession der Sozialen Arbeit. Eine transdisziplinäre Antwort auf das Problem der Fragmentierung des professionellen Wissens und die unvollständige Professionalisierung der Sozialen Arbeit. Zürcher Fachhochschule, Hochschule für Soziale Arbeit, Zürich

Obrecht W (2005) Ontologischer, sozialwissenschaftlicher und sozialarbeitswisssenschaftlicher Systemismus – Ein integratives Paradigma der Sozialen Arbeit. In: Hollstein-Brinkmann H, Staub-Bernasconi S (Hrsg.) Systemtheorien im Vergleich. Was leisten Systemtheorien für die soziale Arbeit?. VS, Wiesbaden, S. 93–172

Pfeifer-Schaupp H-U (1995; 1997) Jenseits der Familientherapie. Systemische Konzepte in der sozialen Arbeit, 2. Aufl. Lambertus, Freiburg im Breisgau

Roth S, Schütz A (2015) Ten systems: toward a canon of function systems. In: Cybernetics and human knowing, H. 4, S. 11–31 (auch online unter https://papers.ssrn.com/sol3/papers.cfm?abstract_id=2508950)

Scherpner H (1962; 1974) Theorie der Fürsorge. Vandenhoeck & Ruprecht, Göttingen

Scherr A (2000) Luhmanns Systemtheorie als soziologisches Angebot an Reflexionstheorien der Sozialen Arbeit. In: de Berg H, Schmidt JFK (Hrsg.) Rezeption und Reflexion. Zur Resonanz der Systemtheorie Niklas Luhmanns außerhalb der Soziologie. Suhrkamp, Frankfurt am Main, S. 440–468

Schütze F (1992) Sozialarbeit als "bescheidene" Profession. In Dewe, B/Ferchhoff, W/Radtke, FO (Hrsg.) Erziehen als Profession: zur Logik professionellen Handelns in pädagogischen Feldern. Leske u.Budrich, Opladen, p. 132–170

Stäheli U (2000) Sinnzusammenbrüche. Eine dekonstruktive Lektüre von Niklas Luhmanns Systemtheorie. Velbrück Wissenschaft, Weilerswist

Staub-Bernasconi S (1995) Systemtheorie, soziale Probleme und Soziale Arbeit. Lokal, national, international – oder: Vom Ende der Bescheidenheit. Haupt, Bern

Staub-Bernasconi S (2000) Machtblindheit und Machtvollkommenheit Luhmannscher Theorie. In: Merten R (Hrsg.) Systemtheorie Sozialer Arbeit. Neue Ansätze und veränderte Perspektiven. VS Verlag für Sozialwissenschaften, Wiesbaden, S. 225–242

Staub-Bernasconi S (2007) Soziale Arbeit als Handlungswissenschaft. Systemtheoretische Grundlagen und professionelle Praxis – ein Lehrbuch. Haupt, Bern

Thiersch H (1986; 2006) Die Erfahrung der Wirklichkeit. Perspektiven einer alltagsorientierten Sozialpädagogik. 2., ergänzte Auflage. Juventa, Weinheim

Thiersch H/Grunwald K, Köngeter S (2005; 2012) Lebensweltorientierte Soziale Arbeit. In: Thole W (Hrsg.) Grundriss Soziale Arbeit – Ein einführendes Handbuch. 4. überarb. und aktualisierte Aufl. VS, Wiesbaden, S. 175–196

Vogel H-C, Kaiser J (Hrsg.) (1997) Neue Anforderungsprofile in der Sozialen Arbeit. Probleme – Projekte – Perspektiven. Kersting, Aachen

von Foerster H (1981/1984) Observing systems, 2nd edn. Intersystems Publications, Seaside

von Foerster H (1992) Ethics and second-order cybernetics. In: Cybernetics & human knowing 1, H. 1. pp 9–19

von Glasersfeld E (1995; 1997) Radikaler Konstruktivismus – Ideen, Ergebnisse, Probleme. Suhrkamp, Frankfurt am Main

von Thun FS (1981; 2010) Störungen und Klärungen. Allgemeine Psychologie der Kommunikation, 48. Aufl., Orig.-Ausg. Rowohlt, Reinbek bei Hamburg

Watzlawick P, Beavin JH, Jackson DD. (1967; 1972) Menschliche Kommunikation. Formen, Störungen, Paradoxien. 3., unveränd. Aufl. Huber, Bern

Welsch W (1987; 2002) Unsere postmoderne Moderne. Akademie, Berlin

Wirth JV/Kleve H (Hrsg.) (2012, 2022) Lexikon des systemischen Arbeitens. Grundbegriffe der systemischen Praxis, Methodik und Theorie. 2. Auflage. Carl-Auer, Heidelberg

Wirth JV (2014) Die Lebensführung der Gesellschaft. Grundriss einer allgemeinen Theorie. Springer Research, Heidelberg

Wirth JV, Kleve H (2019) Die Ermöglichungsprofession. 69 Leuchtfeuer für systemisches Arbeiten. Carl-Auer, Heidelberg

Wirth, JV, Kleve H (2020) Von der gespaltenen zur verbundenen Lebensführung. Systemische Wege für das alltägliche Leben. Vandenhoeck & Ruprecht, Göttingen

Wulf C (2004) Anthropologie. Geschichte, Kultur, Philosophie. Rowohlt, Reinbek bei Hamburg

Revisiting Critical Theory

Edgar Marthinsen

Contents

Introduction 61
The Heritage of the Frankfurt School 63
The Mind and Language 64
From Negative Dialectic to Symbolic Power 68
Critical Theory: A Critique of an Unjust World 70
Critical Theory and Social Work Practice 73
A Future for Critical Theory 75
References 76

Abstract

The important role of critical thinkers in modern societies ultimately rests on their critical position in relation to mechanisms of domination and analysis of hierarchies of power. It also rests on challenges to the institutionalised abuse of power as the cause of vast inequalities and injustice.

(Grey and Webb 2013 p. 99)

Keywords

Critical theory · Social work

Introduction

Grey and Webb (2013) refer to Bourdieu's three types of professional: the critical intellectual, the professional expert and the servant to the Prince. Critical often relates to questioning power, which is a core social phenomenon in social work,

E. Marthinsen (✉)
Department of Social Work, Norwegian University of Technology and Science, NTNU, Trondheim, Norway
e-mail: edgar.marthinsen@ntnu.no

but the concept also refers to questioning of our perceptions in general – not only to power. This text develops an understanding of critical theory and how it may enlighten our minds and give ideas for action. It also refers to some of the rich literature on Critical Social Work which has its own discourse on this theme.

What is it in critical theory that makes it critical? The notion of critical relates to the concept radical as well as reflexivity. Critique may be considered as a normative stance and may operate in the discourse of politics on all sides, but Agger (2013 p. 5) argues that *the role of Critical social theory is to raise consciousness about present oppression and to demonstrate the possibility of a qualitatively different future society*. A postmodern stance may refer to critique as questioning the interpretation as such. A radical stance may refer to all shades of politics pushing towards extremes depending on different perspectives. Critical theory may open the movement towards new ways of understanding, new ideologies and life and living – and some of these ways may be regarded as radical since the change is thorough and groundbreaking, maybe altering power relations and values. In my view critical theory should be regarded as normative and usually take a stance against inequality, exploitation and suppression and promotes equality, justice and fairness. As an epistemic social science position, it is also critical in the sense that it promotes a search for enlightenment and insight into complex problems. Complexity theory and critical realism may support critical social analysis, but this text does not elaborate these possibilities.

We usually consider critical theory as the work of the Frankfurt school established in 1923 and continued after WW2. Social injustice and inequality were evident during the early twentieth century and the class struggle increased with a growing organisation of the working class and the emergence of revolutionary forces and political parties fronting socialism and social democracy enabled by expanding voting rights (Piketty 2020). I acknowledge this context of the Frankfurt school, but argue for a more generic idea of the concept of critical. We may depart from the human condition that promotes solidarity and empathy as we encounter burdens, tragedies, inequality, and poverty – we are curious to understand the world and our lives and destines and may aim to improve and change. Part of the riddle is that some still tend to split the world into winners and losers and bother little with the burdens produced. A just and decent society is the concern of many others than just critical Marxists, but without the ideology of a non-capitalist society. A just society with human rights, equality and an outspoken ethics of decency and respect is a hallmark of communitarian philosophy and theory. John Rawls, Charles Taylor, Amartyra Sen, Martha Nussbaum, Avishai Margalit and many others may be counted in defending a just society. I will mention some of these as they contribute to a critical sense and theorising. *Theorizing refers to the active attempts of human agents to make sense of and or explain some aspect of social reality* (Thorpe 2019). Critical theorists and communitarians may share many of the same ideas of a just and decent world and worldview but may disagree on the politics of moving towards and envision other futures. My position is that Social Work can only relate to and be part of larger movements, a profession is not capable of changing the world or to play a major role, but we may act as homo politicus and show an integrity and front some strong values. We may contribute to creating – in a Heideggerian sense – a mood for a just society that is decent and does not humiliate its citizens (Heidegger 1993, 1999, 2000; Margalit 1998). Garret (2021) argues that social work and its values as presented in the international social work association are threatened by neo liberal policy to an extent that we have to develop a dissenting social work based on critical theory and resistance. In any sense, critical theory may be regarded as an important tool for developing social work.

The Heritage of the Frankfurt School

Important contributors of the early Frankfurt school were Löwenthal, Grossman, Pollock, Horkheimer, Adorno, Fromm, Benjamin, Marcuse and later Habermas and others. Their hallmark idea was a Marxist critique of capitalism regarding society as based on the forces of production and the emergence of a class structure (Granter 2019). Hegel's idea of dialectic materialism was part of the theoretical foundation in Marx and Engels work. Hegel believed in the positive spirit of modernity – that the world moved forward in leaps as far as reason and development was concerned. Marx primary critique intended to create awareness on the real and symbolic exploitation of workers and the negative influence of capitalism on social life. In their struggle to understand the horrors of Hitler's Nazism, Adorno reinterpreted Hegel's dialectics to explain how enlightenment retracted to myths rather than leading to a continuous struggle for reason, freedom and emancipation. This *negative dialectic* could explain how the world not necessarily always becomes a better place. In this sense Nazism became an antithesis to a rational modernity.

The Frankfurt school relied on earlier theory and ideas we may regard as belonging to a wider understanding of phenomenology, hermeneutics and social constructionism with history and language as important contributors to the central task of interpretation. Piketty (2020 p. 7) insists that the realm of ideas, the political-ideological sphere is truly autonomous and does not regard the relations of production as determinous. Such a view allows alternative critical positions without the narrow Marxist premise of master and slave. Marx developed his ideas based on historical knowledge, historicity, necessary to recognise oppression and develop ideas of emancipation. Hegel as well as Kant plays an important role in developing critical theory with their work on mind and society – which people like Marx and Engels had access to. Streeck, who wrote *How Will Capitalism End?* (2016), regards his work as an alternative perspective and argues that concerning theory it may be hard to say where non-Marxism ends and where Marxism begins (Streeck 2014).

Husserl and Heidegger contributed heavily to what we today may regard as critical theory often embedded in categories like phenomenology and hermeneutics. The theorising of socialisation, language and interpretation based on the social and historical context plays an important role in critical theory. The dominant discourse of science and social science up to the 1960s were realist and positivist. Agger (2013 p. 29) argues that the positivist stance still plays an important role in sociology in the USA and that this positioning departs from the sociology where social work is a part of the discourse. The positivist stance emphasises causal explanation and purports not to be political or engage in advocacy where critical theorist *emphasise historicity, the susceptibility of social data to be viewed in the light of their possible transformation* (Agger 2013 p. 25). The interpretive and subjective stance returned in the 1960s with Berger and Luckman, Foucault and was later followed by a new social constructivist and post-modern critique of modernity and positivism. Postmodernism evolving as a critique of modernity during the last part of twentieth century saw the rise of a communitarian theorising of society with a strong ethical positioning focusing on civil rights and liberty (Rawls 1971; Nussbaum 2004). The discourse of post-modernism in the social sciences also related to social work. Social work writers like Leonard claimed post-modernism should be linked to Marxism to enable emancipation, and Healy and Fook used the concept of critical postmodernism (Pease 2013). In my view postmodernism is related to the language turn and neo-Aristotelian philosophy moving further into the art of interpretation through a revival of phenomenology and hermeneutics as mentioned above. We may regard Gadamer and Ricoeur as contributing to the hermeneutics of tradition while Habermas, Foucault and Bourdieu focus on interests and power games. Generic language interpretation is central to all these. Agger (2013) suggests interpretive theories try to understand social action on the level of the meanings that people attach to it and do not intend to produce social laws. In opposition to critical theory, they do not attempt to mobilise social activism. In *Truth and Method* Gadamer (1960–1992) emphasised the importance of presuppositions and the need for fusion of horizons of understanding in dialogue and reading text. Foucault's idea of the de-centred mind in *Le mots et le choses* (1966) allowed for understanding of the multiplicity we experience among humans trying to conceive the world through language and life. Polanyi (2001) thorough historically founded critique of market society from the 1940s insists that capitalism is always embedded. Heidegger's existential thinking in *Being and Time* from 1927 was advanced by Sartre in his *Being and Nothingness* (1943). Bourdieu (1991) also refers to Heidegger and this work is continued by Wacquant, Boltanski and Chiapello as well as Taylor, Fraser, Nussbaum and more directly linked to the Frankfurt school, Benhabib and Honneth. (I will elaborate on some of these later.) Inequality, ideas of justice, respect and recognition as well as participation may be playing a stronger role in critical theory today than earlier. Neoliberalism, governmentality and consumerism may have replaced some of the focus on capitalism and mode of production as such. A returning question in critical theory is how we are determined by language, historical materialism and to what extent we are free to act and think. The space of possibility is easier to explore in radical and critical theory than positivist thinking.

The Mind and Language

There is a crack in everything, and that is where the light comes in – Leonard Cohen's poesy strikes the chord of critical theory. It is about new ways of seeing.

Curiosity is a central drive in social research and our minds are set to explore the world. Social theories correspond to and are embedded in language theory, and since critical theory is set to challenge what may seem evident and search for other explanations, interpretation and communication becomes crucial. Thinking does not necessarily produce new truths; it may as well develop new myths.

Critical theory may be applied in designs searching for facts and opinions and perspectives and the critical is part of the worldview of the researcher. All worldviews may contain and conceal their own myths that may later be challenged through new perspectives and ideas. Bonemark (2020) argues that the horizon is always there, regarding every position as just a step towards broader understanding – always leaving space for new discoveries and ideas of the world. In this sense only relying on Marx strong emphasis on historical materialism may lead astray as much as you would by leaning heavily on concepts like homo economicus in the neoliberal dogma – rational choice theory or exchange theory. Bonemark uses the metaphor of the wall being built and written on, hiding the view of the horizon where you may move towards new discoveries. The horizon of understanding is also used by Gadamer to depict the position from where you interpret the world. He introduced the notion of prejudice in accordance with Heidegger's concept of geworfenheit – understanding or reading of signs and messages as they are conceptualised by tradition. Ricoeur developed this further with his idea of the hermeneutics of suspicion – to interpret the deeper or underlying meaning – the *deep structure* of language (versus the surface structure – the words or text not undergoing any further interpretation). Although none of these writers are regarded as critical theorists, their methodological input may be essential to critical theorising and the encounter between social work and the citizens.

In his breakthrough work on *Being and Time*, Heidegger (1926/1993) explores the world and language as poetic – a position inherited from the German poet Hölderlin. He argues that our understanding of language is based upon socialisation to accept meanings communicated in the social, given meanings that are offered or thrown (geworfen) upon us in the social. We live with the things and connect to the world through language. We learn what a dog is, a horse and a hammer, mothers and brothers. But he also asks the question of *what makes* a hammer, a dog and other suppositions. Critical theory tends to exchange the noun with the verb largely based on his thinking. The hammering, the clientmaking and the mothermaking are processes where we learn to use words on similar things and situations and settings. Just using the words as presented without thinking and reasoning makes us *das man*. We may become obedient and manage, but we do not question the world. A social worker is in this sense made into the servant of the Prince. Böe (2017) quotes Taylor on his idea of communication enabled through communion where we relate emotionally to the world and others and share. He argues that *language cannot be generated from within; it can only come to the child from her milieu – although once it is mastered, innovation becomes possible* (Taylor 2016 p. 55). Feminists like Smith and Fraser use critical theory to question gendering as well as mothering to reveal tradition and power embedded in language. MeToo is a good example of how innovative communication reveals and opens critique of a field of power.

For critique to enter the mind we must think, question the world as it appears and the way we conceptualise it. Arendt (1978) who reinterprets Hegel, Husserl and

Heidegger's work in *The Life of the Mind* argues that thinking requires us to be *in the now* – being present in order to enable the gap between the past and future to open up. This gap only opens in reflection where the matter is absent – the past has disappeared, and the future is not yet there. *Reflection draws these absent 'regions' into the mind's presence* (Arendt 1978 p. 206).

During the rise of the Nazi in hindsight we may reflect on the situation for reason. The modern era carried an optimistic view of science's ability to reveal all God's secrets – the God-trip of the modern age. A secular age was expected to result in a scientific worldview, but ideology and myths returned to the scene, and we seem unable to bridge the gap – with xenophobia, fake news and conspiratory ideas flourishing in social media (Taylor 2007). Hitler's *Mein Kampf* drew heavily on racism enabled by the idea of evolution but ignored a not yet discovered DNA of humanity as a totally mixed race. The idea of 'Übermensh' was a foul interpretation of a poet – Nietzsche. The socialist alternative suffered heavy losses in France, Germany and Spain. A democratic socialist like Gramsci did not fare well among communists and ended up in Mussolini's prison. Socialism as it developed ignored the entire sphere of political deliberation (Honneth 2017). Gramsci's idea of the supremacy of a social group is still relevant as it manifests itself through domination and intellectual and moral leadership (Garrett 2021). Garrett insists Gramsci's thinking is important to evolve a dissenting social work through promoting critical ideas and actions in practice.

In 1933 Freud discussed Marxism and the determining influence which is exerted by the economic conditions of humanity upon their intellectual, ethical and artistic reaction. He argued that

> it cannot be assumed that economic motives are the only ones which determine the behaviour of men (*sic*) in society... we must not forget that the mass of mankind, subjected though they are to economic necessities, are borne on by a process of cultural development – some call it civilisation – which is no doubt influenced by all the other factors, but is equally certainly independent of them in its origin; it is comparable to an organic process, and is quite capable of itself having an effect upon the other factors. It displaces the aims of the instincts and causes men to rebel against what has hitherto been tolerable; and, moreover, the progressive strengthening of the scientific spirit seems to be an essential part of it. If anyone were in a position to show in detail how these different factors – the general human instinctual disposition, its racial variations and its cultural modifications – behave under the influence of varying social organisation, professional activities and methods of subsistence, how these factors inhibit or aid one another – if, I say, anyone could show this, then he would not only have improved Marxism but would have made it into a true social science (Freud 1933).

Freud continues the argument for a scientific worldview:

> A Weltanschauung (Worldview) based upon science has, apart from the emphasis it lays upon the real world, essentially negative characteristics, such as that it limits itself to truth and rejects illusions. Those of our fellowmen who are dissatisfied with this state of things and who desire something more for their momentary peace of mind may look for it where they can find it. We shall not blame them for doing so; but we cannot help them and cannot change our own way of thinking on their account.

The unscientific escape from a scientific worldview is relevant to critical theory, since much of theorising about people and society is based on (reflexive) thinking and is in its sense normative and subjective both regarding the view and analysis of the past as well as the protention of ideas (to hold on to hope and maybe utopian ideas about futures). Freud attend to the same interpretation as Arendt in the sense that his psychoanalysis remembers and reinterprets the past, reflects upon how it may have altered and influences our lives, enabling us to be set free and rethink the influence the past should be allowed to play on our futures. This is the healing that psychoanalysis enables – just the same idea as we may allow for critical theory. We find the same enlightenment idea in Fanon (1967) as well as in Freire's (1974) work, to raise a critical consciousness about our lives and society in order to set ourselves free based on questioning power and interest. Garrett (2021) puts forth four themes from Fanon that are important to social work. First the worlds social work operates in may give rise to reasonable anger that rightly canalised may generate new and progressive political possibilities. Second, Fanon's work may help practitioners and educators to attain better understanding of dynamics of colonisation and decolonisation. Social work may sometimes have reinforced the colonial project. Third he enhances the importance of fanons opposition to situating individuals in categories which classify, dominate and demean. Fanon use the concept of 'antennae' to detect racialisation – an antennae Garret think social workers should adopt. Social workers should be able to see how individuals are emptied of substance forced into categories. Fourth Garret argues that Fanon's theorising may be used to pivot the need to instil democracy and to promote anticolonial and non-racial universalism.

Bourdieu use the notion of *socio-analysis* inspired by Freud's perspective on the mind. Socio-analysis enables the social theorist *to avoid being the toy of social forces* (Bourdieu and Wacquant 1992 p. 183) – or the servant to the Prince? Huston (2019) refers to Bourdieu on how our reflexivity may be channelled in two directions to avoid the taken-for-granted assumptions. One is *to reflect on our personal values, attitudes and perceptions and how they shape our actions*. The other area is to reveal *the influence of the field in which social workers perform their professional duties* (Huston 2019 p. 108). If we keep the Marxist position in mind, *socialism involves not only critique but also a political practice that aims to transform capitalism into an alternative form of society based on the promotion of human welfare* (Moth 2020 p. 5). Hägglund (2020) argues that critical analysis, like Fanon or Fraser who argue for redistribution without transcending capitalism, come short of socialism since the idea of profit is not necessarily replaced by human freedom as the paramount goal. Our spirituality has to rely on a secular belief as social, historically positioned beings who are able to question and change the way of the world. Hägglund regards capitalism as a historically positioned life form, not a natural cause. As humans we have to change our minds – which puts the responsibility in agency. Social work agency should to a larger extent lean on virtues like recognition rather than positive knowledge as such (Mcbeath and Webb 2002; Marthinsen and Skjefstad 2011).

The historical epistemology of Bourdieu is a version of social constructionism where agency (our personal worldview, our trajectory through life) and structure (background, the basis or the system world) enable us to position each of us in time and place. He has expanded the understanding of materialism in the Marxist tradition and developed a (critical?) theory of how we adapt to life through and evolving *habitus* (a way of living, thinking and acting partly without knowing – presuppositions or doxa). We are enabled to deconstruct the *symbolic capital* at play in the *social fields* we operate within. Bourdieu (1999) uses three forms of symbolic capital: economic, cultural and social. All these have symbolic values in the social, and thus social capital includes the other forms. The idea is that all distinctions we develop in the social also express values that we categorise and sort in hierarchies that objectify the symbolic power. This is mirrored with an opposing set of negative symbolic capital (or burdens) expressed as the least attractive among those distinctions, and which often lie at the bottom of the value hierarchies (Marthinsen 2003). Lacking access to resources and always ending up with the short straw leaves one in a burdened position, which is true for many of those labelled 'marginalised'. Disrespect, shame and humiliation may appear, rather than respect, honour and success. Bourdieu's idea of the economic mind is based on the ontological premise is that we fetish our environments and actions (see also Derrida 1994 *the spectres of Marx*). The tendency to structure our world not based on exchange value rather than use value is regarded as a social and relational phenomenon creating a social economy. The socio-analysis may enable us to reveal the *distinctions* that we hold as attractive at a certain time in history. These distinctions are valued based on the meaning given in a social field where actors over time have come to agree and support the value ascribed to the certain phenomenon, act or object. The symbolic capital attached to the distinctive object may change over time and new habituses develop – some objects may increase in value while other are devalued. These connotations are purely social and relational but may also operate within the economic sphere as such with prices set based on market value. The social market and the economy may in some sense correspond.

From Negative Dialectic to Symbolic Power

Bourdieu (1999) developed the concept of practical sense and used it in his deconstruction of the phenomenon of symbolic power. The power embedded in language and our social fields where we are often not aware of the norms and signs history and struggle have created – they have transformed into doxa and may be revealed only through a deeper analysis of context and history. In our struggle to make ourselves reasonable we try to do things right, to be in the comfort zone or just be straight. Not so different from Heidegger's *das Man*. These historical structures were untangled during post-modernism, and Bourdieu and his colleague at Ecole de France, Foucault, both have contributed to unmasking of symbolic power, hegemonic discourses and governmentality. Both contribute to a critical gaze with their theorising and concepts, but can we regard them as critical theorist? Bourdieu developed a historical epistemology where Marxism was part of the canon used. Foucault (2004) refuted Marxism, partly due to its lack of theorising the role of the state, which was important in his critique of power, but still contributed to a critical gaze. In Bourdieu's work *On the state* (2014) he alters Weber's understanding of the state from having the *monopoly of legitimate violence* to *legitimate physical and symbolic power*. According to Durkheim he argues that the state is the foundation of the logical and moral conformity of the social world. He continues to argue that Marxism is only concerned with how the state becomes an apparatus to benefit the dominant and does not pay attention to the actual structure and mechanisms deemed to produce its foundation. *The state is the name that we give to the hidden, invisible principles of the social order, and at the same time of both physical and symbolic domination, likewise of physical and symbolic violence.* A common function of the state is thus to produce and canonise social classifications (Bourdieu 2014 pp. 3–9). The state is not a bloc, but it is a field of power. In this sense one of critical social works tasks may be to question such illusory realities that are collectively validated by consensus – symbolic valuing of people.

The Marxist Leninism and Maoism of the 1960 and 1970s did not appeal much to a democratic mind – made worse by the totalitarian development in the Soviet Union, China and Cambodia. The West still stuck to ideas of freedom, brotherhood and justice. What emerged would rather be a return of capitalist domination through neoliberalisation. Critical theorist like Brown (2015) use Foucault's 1978–79 lectures on neoliberalism in her own analysis of the undoing of democratic arenas. Foucault's revelation of the new formation of society that would later come to dominate Europe and the World is regarded as extraordinary. His ideas of the formation of the state, its governance and the power exerted on the subjects have become an important discourse in the social sciences.

The election of Regan and Thatcher in the years following Foucault's lectures and the worldwide expansion of neoliberal ideas forged a new discourse of neoliberalisation and New Public Management which now has inspired a new critique of capitalism and a return of the discourse on democratic socialism – which I regard as some of the new critical theory.

If we return to background knowledge, the semiotic theorising of the sign by Saussure at the turn of the century heightened the awareness of the scholastic fallacy (Bourdieu 1999) – saying the word is like the World. The sign refers to something – the signified. But it has a signifier – a person with a language and a historised lifeworld which also contains myths (Barthes 1957/1999). These may be hidden from view and consciousness or act as Bourdieu call doxa. Eco advanced the semiotic model with a new layer by adding culture to establish a context for the sign as well as the signifier and the myth. Advancing critical theory to develop an eye for these embedded meanings into signs is crucial. That will allow for the deep structure of the text to evolve and be hypothesised.

The concept of ideology adds to this complex. Piketty (2020 p. 3) *use 'ideology' in a positive and constructive sense to refer to a set of* a priori *plausible ideas and discourses describing how society should be structured. An ideology has social, economic, and political dimensions. It is an attempt to respond to a broad set of questions concerning the desirable or ideal organization of society. Given the complexity of the issues, it should be obvious that no ideology can ever command full and total assent: ideological conflict and disagreement are inherent in the very notion of ideology.*

All this may be contained in an advanced understanding of the concept of worldview – that which develop through our own existence – to live to death (Heidegger). The worldview will have the same problem at the sign, that we may have difficulties exploring and advancing a clear understanding of what it contains, and it is always in flux. Habermas contributed to our struggle for understanding and explanation of communication. He worked for a while with Adorno and later replaced Horkheimer as professor in Frankfurt. Kalleberg (1999) regards Habermas as a 'West-Marxist' due to the separation of Europe in West and East at that time. His political ambition for a modern society is to create a community of freedom and equality – which makes his idea of dialectics align with Hegel, not the negative dialectic of Adorno. Influences by Mead and others, Habermas (1968, 1990) argue we become human through the social interplay with significant others. Our identities and thinking develop in the social. What do we do with speaking? We listen to reason and act according to our moral and ethics. Meaning what we express is to make a claim for truth – a truthclaim. Idealism and ideology enter our communication through our expressions. Our world consists of three realities, an objective world, a social world and a subjective world. Three types of speech acts are produced; we *establish facts* and explain them, *assessments* where social conditions are accepted or refuted, and the third is *self-presentation* where we express our own feelings, attitudes and opinions. Our communication may express will to communicate, to front our interests or just be strategic. These categories may serve our analysis as we aim to reflect and develop critique. As many others he elaborates on the idea of agency and structure and developed the concepts of lifeworld and systems world to identify the forces structuring ourselves and our lives. Lack of balance regarding freedom and equality evolve where at least one cultural element in a tradition is denied expression, if one sphere of values lack integration or one sphere ends up dominate all others. These are situations we may find in many everyday lives around the world today. We have recent movements as Black Lives Matter, MeToo, Attack, LGBT and feminism in general – all fighting for the right to express themselves and having a just cause. In the critical sense we also see negative dialectics creating new myths to support ideas like those hailed by Daesh/IS and fundamental religious groups denying the very idea of freedom with totalitarian views rather than democracy.

The concept of worldview and the role of language and interpretation may lead us into some of the core ideas needed to understand and theorise critique.

Critical Theory: A Critique of an Unjust World

Honneth is regarded as a follower of Habermas and has developed his ideas further. In some sense he aligns with many of those we have categorised as communitarians focusing on ethical aspects of life and society. His framework for interpreting social struggles is a normative account of the claims being raised in these struggles (Honneth 1995). Honneth situates his project within the tradition that emphasises the struggle for establishment of relations of mutual recognition as a precondition for self-realisation. This means that the conditions for individual self-realisation are inter-subjective, and he stresses the importance of social relationships to the development and maintenance of a person's identity. Central to the theory is his account of self-confidence, self-respect and self-esteem, which he calls 'practical relations-to-self'. These are beliefs about one's self or emotional states, and they involve a dynamic process in which individuals come to experience themselves as having a certain status as well as being a responsible agent and a valued contributor to shared projects. According to Honneth we struggle for recognition of the value we ascribe to ourselves according to different forms of social communities. Social struggles are often motivated by the experience of being denied these conditions for identity formation, and Honneth refers to this as disrespect. There are three forms of relations of recognition: primary relationships with love and self-confidence; legal relations with rights and self-respect; and third, community of value with solidarity and self-esteem. His three forms of disrespect are: violation of the body, denial of rights and denigration of ways of life. Basic self-confidence has to do with one's ability to express needs and desires without fear of being abandoned as a result. Love, being an element in recognition, means a confirmation of independence guided by care. Everyone has needs and emotions, and these needs and emotions must be granted recognition by others, with those who grant recognition similarly being recognised in return. Honneth is challenged by Fraser who claims that his model has to include the right to express yourself, to voice in a democratic setting. In some sense she seems more aligned with the Marxist and feminist approaches expressing the need to promote a more just redistribution of power and resources (Fraser and Honneth 2003).

Benhabib (1986), a critical theorist herself, claims Habermas replaced the instrumental reason with communicative rationality. He follows Mead that 'I' is possible only in 'we' that exists with language in active community with the other. We have the ability and will to a reflexive distant position where we may listen to the arguments of others and attempt to understand their views. This enables a weak deontology (a secular view) where norms are legitimated by their arguments seeking support (truth claims). Habermas' idea is that an extensive democratisation will enable participation to such an extent that public life may operate in a distributive fair manner. Habermas recommend we dethrone some of the experts and allow for the citizen herself to argue. This is to some extent similar to communitarian views presented by Rawls – for example his theory of justice and the ignorant position as the locus of a normative justice (Rawls 1971). The ignorant position is to imagine that the lawmaker does not know what position in or what society he may have to live – the law or rule should be universal and just for all. The major difference between communitarians and critical theorist remains the Marxist-based critique of capitalism and the idea that no fairness or freedom may be established within capitalism. In such a view social democracies and welfare states can only limit the damage of capitalism, not solve the problem (Hägglund 2020).

Seeing exchange value as being more important than use value may be regarded as a human trait, competition and greed regarded as almost embedded in our genetic imprint. Elaborating on his concept of practical sense, Bourdieu (1999 p. 59) argued that we are situated within a relational field where we cannot avoid becoming aware of ourselves, that we should stand out and play out our distinctive traits – we play the games within the 'social' regulated by hierarchies of taste and preferences. Taylor (1995) operates with the notion of strong and weak values, and where strong values represent principles and preferences, we do not usually negotiate but see as fundamental. Weak values may be regarded as taste where we allow for differences of a range of possibilities. While Bourdieu saw these mechanisms primarily as human and social traits, within a neoliberal framework these social mechanisms are transformed to operate within a market where everything becomes commodified. Social and cultural capital as commodities transforms into resources that also count for economic accumulation. Our everyday experience as consumers has become commodified to such an extent that everything operates on a market model. Boltanski and Chiapello (2007: 10–11) argue that

> The spirit of capitalism is precisely the set of beliefs associated with the capitalist order that helps to justify this order and, by legitimating them, to sustain forms of action and predispositions compatible with it. These justifications, whether general or practical, local or global, expressed in terms of virtue or justice, support the performance of more or less unpleasant tasks and, more generally, adhesion to a lifestyle conductive to the capitalist order... we may indeed speak of a dominant ideology...

The common trait was to succumb to market mechanism and the recommodification of many areas of life that had been kept out of markets, such as education, health and social care. It also led to turning areas of public interest and shared values into business, like transport, power supply and infrastructure as such. Hemerijck (2013) argued that the foundations created for social citizenship during the twentieth century are still resisting neoliberalisation to such an extent that they remain a strong political force within our democratic systems. This created the space for so-called Third Way politics (Giddens 1994, 2001). Negotiations are thus still an important trait within our political systems, reducing the ability to maximise profits. Since people also make up a huge market, this cannot be ignored and must be regarded as a counter force in the globalisation of market and politics. Values have also turned into a major commodity with significant symbolic power influencing the distribution of symbolic power – for example, the growth of green power literally as well as real.

Democratic socialism and social democracy are founded on the central ideas of redistribution and acknowledgement of differentiated capabilities among men, women and groups of people – requiring systems of sharing and shared responsibility for long-term goals (Honneth 2017). Just as 'Man' must be tamed by common laws and shared systems of values regarded as just among the majority of people, we have to regulate capital and its inherent finance systems. Today we are witnessing proofs of increasing inequality once again when it comes to ownership and access to wealth (Piketty 2014, 2020).

Critical Theory and Social Work Practice

In S*ocial Work futures – Crossing Boundaries, Transforming Practice,* Adams et al. (2005) use the concept of *criticality* as a mode to contribute to alternative discourses. Critical thinking may be regarded as a way of looking at the agenda, language, context and content of our experiences (op.cit. 2005 p. 11). Five ways of thinking add a critical element.

- Being reflexive, to identify the taken-for-granted
- Contextualising, social relations and policy where practice takes place
- Problematising, how policy and law inform us
- Being self-critical, to have our own and others actions troubled
- Engaging with transformation, to identify barriers and divisions leading to oppression and try to move beyond.

The authors compare social work to creative musicians and how performance may be enhanced as we are aware of our own values and prejudices. Reflexivity and awareness thus become a crucial competence in acting out a critical practice. In her chapter on social work research, Dominelli argues that two of the purposes of research are to elucidate depth and complexities in practice and to enhance critical reflection. Practitioners and researchers should engage more in developing client's well-being. The focus on transformation in social work raises the need for a heightened ethical awareness and this also counts for research. Thus, the need for participation and cocreation became appearent, along with accountability to service users, and Dominelli calls for involving service users as full partners in research.

The concept of reflection and reflexivity often coincide with critical thinking. Among many other authors in Social Work White et al. (2006) have discussed how practitioners, educators and researchers may develop the competence to 'see what they do not see'. Hidden, tacit or taken-for-granted aspects need exploring. Referring to Bourdieu *subjects do not, strictly speaking, know what they are doing that what they do has more meaning than they know* (op.cit.xiv). Taylor (2013) distinguishes between reflective practice and critically reflective practice. She applies the concept of 'confessional tales' to describe reflective practice which she claims not to consider the complex social, historical and politically influenced reality. Critically reflective practice should make a political commitment to social justice. In her view reflective and critically reflective practice shares some common traits. Both perspectives view practice as *messy and indeterminate rather than orderly and linear* (Taylor 2013 p. 85). Both regard knowledge coming from practice and dealing with complex problems as important as knowledge produced outside practice. Both are attuned to reflection-on-action. For critical reflection it is important to keep necessary distance to from practice to obtain a critical position. It rejects individualism and political neutrality. She states that *critical reflective practice sees individual selves as produced in interaction with others – social selves...* (Taylor 2013 p. 86). Critically reflective practice questions the notions of care and help, and the helping relationship itself as a form of possible domination. To explore the multitude of practices the way in which reality is constituted in discourse has to be examined. This is where critical social theory comes to the fore and she refers to Foucault's idea of discourse as *practices which systematically form the objects of which they speak…* and she concludes – *Examining the politics of representation lies at the heart of critical reflective practice* (Taylor 2013 p. 87). She refers to the micro-politics of power played out in social interactions and through texts. Taylor positions critically reflective practice between ambitions for social change reached for in radical social work and change at the individual level reached for in reflective practice. In her conclusion she refers to Rossiter (2007) and claims that *the core function of critically reflective practice should be to interrogate ambivalence and contradiction not simply for its own sake, but in order to accomplish social justice work in the routines of practice* (Taylor 2013 p. 93). The interrogative mode is the aspiration and different voices and different modes of representation should prevail to accomplish social justice in helping. The following questions are suggested for critically reflective practice:

- *Making the 'case': How is the service users constituted in different modes of representation?*
- *How does power operate through the presentation of 'facts' and modes of representation?*
- *What is obscured or denied expression by the various modes of representation? Whose story or stories are denied expression, and what are the effects of this?*
- *How has this category of 'concern' been (re)constructed over time in the policy area?*
- *What orthodoxies are underpinning or shaping professional discourses?*
- *What possibilities of change emerge from this analysis?* (Taylor 2013 p. 94).

Another important link to critical social work is feminist theory and its implication on social work practice since the 1970s. Gender inequality is linked to systems of domination like class, race/ethnicity and sexuality. The mode of feminism is to achieve women's liberation (Valentich 1996). Humphries (2005) mentions feminism as one of many epistemologies for critical research in social work. Orme (1998 p. 224) argued that *feminist approaches have provided substantive critiques of all social work activity.* Her idea was that feminism should not only be about women and the attempt to empower them but seek to address the conditions of oppression in general – *to challenge and transform policy, practice and the organisation of the service delivery which constrains people in gender-specific roles or oppresses them by the inappropriate exercise of power* (op.cit. p. 227). In this interpretation critical social science and feminism merge in a normative stance towards inequality and injustice.

Skeggs (1997) has applied both Bourdieu's toolbox on symbolic capital and feminist theory in her work with class and gender. Her work was motivated politically to create space for the experiences and language to enable empowerment and respect based on their situated knowledge and the reflexivity produced by the research involvement.

A Future for Critical Theory

Any cultural field exerts censorship through its structure (Bourdieu 1991), and the world today is quite different from a century ago when Critical Theory developed. If the aim of critical theory is to emancipate and enable authentic free ways of living, we must revolt against a resignated, inauthentic existence of the self-governed economic man. Heidegger's concept of *das Man* (one) means life is reduced to being loyal to power and structure and just being 'common' or average, where exploitation or deceit is not opposed. That is the opposite of a critical stance questioning power and interests and exploring new ideas and ideologies to living and life. This is in line with the idea of the early Frankfurt school where a critical perspective seeks social transformation as form of justice, equality and emancipation (Webb 2017 in Granter 2019). My idea is that critical theory must relate to ongoing history and social theory in development. If Horkheimer would have access to Bourdieu's theorising on symbolic capital, he could have elaborated on his notion of 'good connections' as social and cultural capital needed to be positioned for a post or to have a standing in the social (field). We may stand on the shoulders of both and all others who have contributed to the toolbox we may call critical theory today.

Critical social work takes a perspective which rejects many contemporary social arrangements and regards itself as part of a progressive political project (Gray and Webb 2013). Through acts of resistance and interruption they have to imagine new futures and new ways of thinking and acting (op.cit.). The authors of *A New Politics for Social Work* refer to Fraser's version of critical theory where she promotes the concept 'parity of participation'. This is meant to alleviate the inequalities of class structure. We find this move to some extent in the evolving discourse on relational welfare and in the concept of co-creation, although often rather as empowerment than radical emancipation. The need for sufficient equality of power and wealth are seldom available or the means of communication may not be at hand. Pease (2013) argues that empowerment is appropriated and reshaped as individual self-promotion and co-opted into the neoliberal agenda of self-interested citizens. He continues with the negative dialectic that anti-oppressive and anti-discriminatory practice has failed. Rather we see a change of language, behaviour and attitudes rather than the material conditions.

Garrett concludes his book on dissenting social work with a view of a future where social work is an outward facing activity keen to expand the politics of engagement and progressive coalition building with user and other social movements. Second, dissenting social work may contribute to distinctive form of critical praxis where the concept of Fanon's antennae for building special relationships. Third, it may provide a new knowledge project and a different type of analytical lens to view the practices and maybe generate new insights and deconstruct uncritical mainstream conceptions of 'social problems' (Garrett 2021 p. 227).

Mechanisms of domination and hierarchies of power remain on the agenda alongside innovative use of language for the critical intellectual. The future of critical or critical reflective social work is imagined by many social work authors as central to theoretical development. The political perspective expands the horizon to a lot of the ongoing discussion on justice and fairness, respect and a decent society. Fighting neoliberalism/capitalism is a part of this struggle, but in practical social work critical theory it is also about supporting and developing the empowering and liberation of the individual and families in everyday life. The role of critical social theory is also to support the belief in a better world and to build confidence in keeping up the struggle.

References

Adams R, Dominelli L, Payne M (2005) Social work futures – crossing boundaries, Transforming Practice. Palgrave Macmillan. Transforming Practice
Agger B (2013) Critical Social Theories. Oxford University press
Arendt H (1978) The life of the mind. Harcourt Brace
Barthes R (1957/1999) Mytologier. Fakkel, Oslo (Mythologies, 1957, Editions de Seuil)
Benhabib S (1986) Critique, norm and utopia. Columbia University Press
Böe S (2017) Språkdyret. Agora nr 4, 16–1, 17. pp 349–355
Boltanski L, Chiapello E (2007) The new spirit of capitalism. Verso
Bonemark J (2020) Horisonten finns alltid kvar. Om det bortglömda omdömet. Volante
Bourdieu P (1991) The political ontology of Martin Heidegger. Stanford University Press
Bourdieu P (1999) Praktiskt förnuft. Bidrag till en handlingsteori. Daidalos
Bourdieu P (2014) On the state. Lectures at the college de France 1989–1992. Polity
Bourdieu P, Wacquant L (1992) An invitation to reflexive sociology. University of Chicago Press, Chicago
Brown W (2015) Undoing the demos. Neoliberalism's Stealth Revolution. Zone Books
Derrida J (1994) Specters of Marx, the state of the debt, the work of mourning, & the new international. Routledge
Fanon F (1967) Jordens fordømte. Pax
Foucault M (1966) Les mots et les choses: Une archéologie des sciences humaines. Éditions Gallimard
Foucault M (2004) The birth of biopolitics: lectures at the college de France, 1978–79. Ed. M. Snellart. Picador
Fraser N, Honneth A (2003) Redistribution or recognition: a political-philosophical exchange. Verso
Freire P (1974) De undertryktes pedagogikk. Gyldendal
Freud S (1933) Lecture XXXV. A philosophy of life. New introductory lectures on psycho-analysis. Publ. Hogarth Press. Downloaded 20210320 https://www.marxists.org/reference/subject/philosophy/works/at/freud.htm (1932)
Gadamer HG (1960–1992) Truth and method, 2nd edn, New York
Garrett PM (2021) Dissenting social work, critical theory, resistance and the pandemic. Routledge, London/New York
Giddens A (1994) Beyond left and right. Polity Press, Cambridge
Giddens A (2001) The global third way debate. Polity Press, Cambridge
Granter E (2019) Critical theory and critical social work. In: Webb S (ed) The Routledge handbook of critical social work. Routledge
Gray M, Webb SA (2013) The new politics of social work. Palgrave Macmillan
Habermas J (1968) Vitenskap som ideologi. Fakkel
Habermas J (1990) Kommunikativt handlande – texter om språk, rationalitet och samhälle. Daidalos
Hägglund M (2020) Vårt enda liv. Volante, Stockholm (orig. This Life – Secular Faith and Spiritual Freedom 2019)

Heidegger M (1993) Varat och tiden. Del 1 og Del 2 Daidalos First published 1927: Sein und Zeit. (Erste Hälfte.) In: Jahrbuch für Philosophie und phänomenologische Forschung. Band 8, 1927, S. 1–438
Heidegger M (1999) Vad er metafysikk. Det lille forlag
Heidegger M (2000) Sproget og ordet. Hans Reitzels forlag
Hemerijck A (2013) Changing welfare states. Oxford University Press
Honneth A (1995) The Struggle for Recognition: The Moral Grammar of Social Conflicts, Polity Press, Cambridge
Honneth A (2017) The idea of socialism. Polity press
Humphries B (2005) From margin to centre: shifting the emphasis of social work research. Cpt. 20. In: Adams R, Dominelli L, Payne M (eds) Social work futures – crossing boundaries, transforming practice. Palgrave Macmillan
Huston S (2019) Extending Bourdieu for critical social work. In: Webb S (ed) The Routledge handbook of critical social work. Routledge
Kalleberg R (1999) Moderne samfunns utfordringer. In: Habermas J (ed) Kraften i de bedre argumenter. Ad notam, Gyldendal
Margalit A (1998) Det anständiga samhället. Daidalos
*Marthinsen E (2003) Symbolsk kapital og symbolske byrder i et senmoderne barnevern. NTNU phd theses
*Marthinsen E, Skjefstad N (2011) Recognition as a virtue in social work practice. Eur J Soc Work 14:(2):195–212
Mcbeath G, Webb SA (2002) Virtue ethics and social work: being lucky, realistic and not doing ones duty. Br J Soc Work 32(8):1015–1036
Moth R (2020) Socialism. In: Pollock S, Parkinson K, Cummins I (eds) Social work and society. Political and Ideological Perspectives. Policy Press
Nussbaum MC (2004) Hiding from humanity: disgust, shame, and the law. Princeton University Press, Princeton
Orme J (1998) Feminist social work. Cpt. 18. In: Adams R, Dominelli L, Payne M (eds) Social work – themes, issues and critical debates. Macmillan
Pease BA (2013) History of Critical and Radical Social Work. In: Gray M, Webb SA (eds) The new politics of social work. Palgrave Macmillan
Piketty T (2014) Capital in the Twenty-First Century. Harvard University Press
Piketty T (2020) Capital and ideology. The Belknap Press of Harvard University Press
Polanyi K (2001) The great transformations. Beacon Press, Boston
Rawls J (1971) A theory of justice. The Belknap Press of Harvard University Press, Cambridge, MA
Skeggs B (1997) Formations of class and gender. Becoming Respectable. Sage
Streeck W (2014) Buying Time. The Delayed Crisis of Democratic Capitalism. Verso
Streeck W (2016) How will capitalism end? Essays of a Failing System. Verso
Taylor C (1995) Identitet, frihet och gemenskap. Daidalos
Taylor C (2007) A Secular Age. Belknap Press of Harvard University Press, Cambridge, MA
Taylor C (2013) Critically Reflective Practice. Chp. 5. In: Gray M, Webb SA (eds) The new politics of social work. Palgrave Macmillan
Taylor C (2016) The language animal. The Full Shape of the Human Linguistic Ability. Harvard University Press, Cambridge
Thorpe C (2019) Reimagining social theory for social work. In: Webb S (ed) The Routledge handbook of critical social work. Routledge
Valentich M (1996) Feminist Theory and Social Work Practice. Chp. 12. In: Turner FJ (ed) Social work treatment – interlocking theoretical approaches. The Free Press, New York
White S, Fook J, Gardner F (2006) Critical reflection in health and social care. Open University Press
*some of the text on Honneth and on Neoliberalisation are rewritten from these two papers

Postmodern Theory in Practice: Narrative Practice in Social Work

5

Catrina Brown

Contents

Introduction	80
Narrative Therapy Epistemology: Disrupting Conceptual Practices of Power	81
Knowledge, Power and Discourse	81
The Subject	84
Experience	85
The Politics of Emotion	85
Stories	86
Counternarratives as Resistance	87
Feminist Narrative Therapy	89
Therapeutic Alliance	90
Counterviewing the Dangers of Trauma Talk and Dominant Discourses of Coping	90
Scaffolding Questions	92
Exploring the Effects or Influence of Trauma	93
Influence on Trauma	93
Depression: Influence of Trauma	94
Making Sense of the Coping	94
Leah's Influence on Depression and Trauma	94
Leah's Influence *on* Trauma through Drinking	95
Creating Alternative or Counterstories	95
Narrative Therapy, Mental Health and Addiction Policy	96
Conclusion	97
References	97

Abstract

Rooted in postmodernism and social constructionism, narrative theory as applied to social work bridges the gap between clinical work and social justice theory. This chapter discusses the relationship between narrative therapy, social justice and social work practice. A narrative approach focuses on the interpretation and

---

C. Brown (✉)
School of Social Work, Dalhousie University, Halifax, NS, Canada
e-mail: catrina.brown@dal.ca

© Springer Nature Singapore Pte Ltd. 2023
D. Hölscher et al. (eds.), *Social Work Theory and Ethics*, Social Work,
https://doi.org/10.1007/978-981-19-1015-9_5

meaning people ascribe to their experiences through their identities, lives and problem stories. Counterviewing problem stories enables the nurturance of counterstories that disrupt and challenge the unhelpful influence of dominant social discourses which reinforce social inequity and oppression in people's lives. Counternarratives resist the discursive mechanisms of power within stories and disrupt their hegemony. The postmodern influence on narrative therapy is seen in White and Epston's (Narrative means to therapeutic ends. W.W. Norton, New York, 1990) interpretation of Foucault's approach to knowledge, power, subjectivity and discourse which provides central underlying assumptions in the creation of narrative therapy and its dual processes of deconstructing problem stories and reconstructing preferred counternarratives. I will explore the theoretical foundations of narrative work and provide a mental health case example to demonstrate how stories can be deconstructed through counterviewing and how preferred counternarratives can be facilitated.

Keywords

Narrative therapy · Social justice · Social work · Postmodernism

Introduction

Narrative therapy is a social justice-based approach to social work practice, rooted in postmodernism and social constructionism. As applied to social work, narrative theory bridges the gap that often exists between clinical work and social justice theory. I argue in this chapter that narrative therapy offers social work a clinical way to address the gap between critical theory and social justice based social work (Baines 2017; Brown 2017; Brown and MacDonald 2020). Located within a critical rather than a traditional therapeutic framework, narrative therapy is on the side of social justice and social change. I will argue that although the application of a narrative approach has been surprisingly limited in social work, the underlying epistemology of narrative therapy and the practice of discursive resistance through counterstorying offers a unique contribution to the field of social work theory and practice (Baldwin 2013; McKenzie-Mohr and Lafrance 2017). A significant number of social work scholars/practitioners continue to advance this approach (Baldwin 2013; Beres 2014; Brown and Augusta-Scott 2007; Freedman and Combs 1996; Madigan and Law 1998; Morgan 2000; White and Epston 1990).

The postmodern influence on narrative therapy is seen in White and Epston's (1990) interpretation of Foucault's approach to knowledge, power, subjectivity and discourse which provides central underlying assumptions in the creation of narrative therapy. This influence can be seen in the focus in narrative therapy process on the deconstruction or unpacking and contextualization of how people's stories have been constructed over time and in the reconstruction or creation of people's preferred counternarratives. The person(s) seeking therapy and the therapist work collaboratively in this process and both seen as partial knowers rather than neutral participants. At the same time the therapist is reflexively aware of their social and institutional power within the relationship.

In a narrative approach the focus is on the meaning making process which is viewed as both social and political. Counterviewing solicits counterstories that disrupt and challenge unhelpful dominant social discourses which reinforce social inequity and oppression. Counternarratives resist the discursive power mechanisms within stories and disrupt their hegemony. This chapter explores the theoretical foundations of narrative work, and then provides a case example to demonstrate how these ideas can be applied in practice. Through Leah's case study and her trauma experiences, I illustrate the deconstruction of stories through counterviewing and the creation of preferred counternarratives.

In order for mental health to be understood as not just an issue of individual distress but as an issue of social justice, the profession of social work must concentrate on ways to view individual problems within a social and cultural context. This means adopting a collaborative, contextual, non-pathologizing, holistic bio-psycho-social approach which firmly interrogates the authority and limitations of the biomedical disease model.

Narrative Therapy Epistemology: Disrupting Conceptual Practices of Power

Knowledge, Power and Discourse

Narrative therapy has emerged in recent years as an approach which is highly compatible with social justice principles. Indeed, it was Michael White from Australia and David Epston from Canada (White and Epston 1990) who were the initial creators of this approach. It has been described as postmodernism in practice largely drawing on the work of political philosopher Michel Foucault (1964, 1980a, b, 1984, 1991, 1995). Through engaging with issues of power and knowledge narrative therapy moves beyond traditional psychological/psychiatric systems-based approaches to family work (Flaskas and Humphreys 1993). To appreciate the unique contribution this makes to the field of social work, it is necessary to understand the underlying epistemology of narrative therapy. Specifically, narrative therapy translates and operationalizes Foucault's analysis of knowledge, power, subjectivity and discourse into clinical practice.

The postmodern influence on narrative therapy is seen most pointedly in White and Epston's (1990) interpretation of knowledge, power, subjectivity and discursive resistance. The Enlightenment enterprise, and with it, modernist notions of the pursuit of absolute truth through reason and science is abandoned as a fiction. In short, postmodernism rejects the premises of modernism and its promise of a linear progression of social life. Within postmodernism, reality is fluid and multiple, ever changing. Importantly, the objectivist idea that there is one knowable universal truth that can be discovered through science and reason is rejected (Leonard 1997; Nicholson 1990). However, postmodernism has risked shutting down not just conventional truth claims, but those of social critique as well, emphasizing instead a focus on the local rather than generalized critiques of the power structures of society such of those in particular of Karl Marx whose views had been the foundation of significant social critique and radical social work (Leonard 1997; Marx 1978). While postmodernism's interest in interrogating and rejecting foundational or grounding ideas offers the value of deconstruction and analysis it can also have the effect, intended or not, of producing 'anemic' social critique and visions for alternative visions of society (Flax 1990). It has been noted by feminist critics that this had the effect of shutting down the critical analyses and voices of those marginalized and oppressed, such as those of Black women just as these voices were emerging (hooks 1990). Postmodernism was critiqued for how its relativism restricted possibilities for social change. Bordo (1990) and Haraway (1988) both argued that postmodern fluidity and multiplicity dangerously creates views that have no accountability or responsibility. Bordo describes postmodern relativism:

> [it] may slip into its own fantasy of escape from human locatedness – by supposing the critic can become wholly protean by adopting endlessly shifting seemingly inexhaustible vantage points; none of which are owned by either the critic or the author of the text under examination (1990, p. 42)....Deconstructionist readings that enact this protean fantasy are continually slip-sliding away through paradox, inversion, self-subversion....they often present themselves as having it any way they want. They refuse to assume a shape for which they must take responsibility (p. 44).

Similarly, Haraway argues that relativism like objectivism is a god trick – promising a view from everywhere and nowhere simultaneously:

> Relativism is a way of being nowhere while claiming to be everywhere equally. The equality of positioning is a denial of responsibility and critical inquiry. Relativism is the perfect mirror twin or totalization of the ideologies of objectivity; both deny the stakes in location, embodiment and partial perspective; both make it impossible to see well. Relativism and totalization are both god tricks promising vision from everywhere and nowhere equally and fully (1988 p. 584).

In the end, critics observed the ironic similarity between modernism and postmodernism and their overlapping desire to avoid positionality. Feminist postmodernism, through a commitment to social justice, alternatively seeks to offer a hybrid of postmodern deconstruction and interrogation, while also advocating positionality and visions for change refusing to adopt the dangerous limitations of the endlessly fluid 'anything goes' stance. Like feminist postmodernism, narrative therapy is a social justice approach on the side of social change which engages in unpacking individuals' stories within the context of dominant social discourses and normative mechanisms of power (Brown 2003, 2007a, b, c, d, 2020).

Following the work of White (2001) in particular, narrative therapy is anti-objectivism and anti-foundationalism, and therefore, rejects socially constructed, essentialist and totalizing notions of truth about both the self and society. Reflecting postmodern philosophy, narrative therapy is deconstructive and rejects these modernist premises as well as the either/or binaries that have tended or organize notions of truth and are reflected for instance in the social construction of categories such as gender, race, class, sexual orientation, ability and age. Discursive analysis is central to narrative therapy as it explores how both individual and social stories are constituted (Brown and Augusta-Scott 2007; McKenzie-Mohr and Lafrance 2014). Indeed, individual stories are always seen as social, and as such, there is no single author. Socially constructed dominant discourses of for instance health, mental health, addiction, beauty, fitness, success, sex and love often shape the stories people have of their lives and their identities in ways that are unhelpful and often pivotal to their suffering. As the creation and transmission of dominant stories in culture is a complex social process, restorying requires moving past surface readings (Shotter 1993). A narrative approach to stories explores how they are socially organized and how they can be reconstructed to create thicker descriptions of people's experiences (Geertz 1986).

Narrative positionality alongside post-positivist epistemology is further linked to the anthropological approaches of the social and cultural storying of experience (Bruner 1986, 1987; Geertz 1986). Narrative therapy weaves together an understanding of the relationship between knowledge, power, subjectivity and experience through therapeutic processes which deconstruct and reconstruct clients' stories. The relationship between knowledge and truth as conceptualized by Foucault is central to not only social justice, but narrative therapy itself: "We are subjected to the production of truth through power and we cannot exercise power except through the production of truth" (Foucault 1980b, p. 93). Knowledge and power are viewed as inseparable whereby "a domain of knowledge is a domain of power, and a domain of power is a domain of knowledge" (White and Epston 1990 p. 22). For Foucault (1972), knowledge and power are joined through discourses which are social "practices that systematically form the objects of which they speak" (p. 49). Following Foucault, White and Epston (1990 p. 19) argue that "We are subject to power through the normalizing 'truths' that shape our lives and relationships". However, while power and knowledge imply each other they cannot be reduced to each other, as knowledge is not simply an instrument of power. Challenges to dominant discourse can therefore be created. The production of transformative critical knowledge disturbs or disrupts normalizing truths, as does the narrative process of unpacking and resisting the influence of dominant discourse on people's lives. The reflexivity necessary for social justice based social work challenges both what we think we know and our practices (Chambone 1999; Fook 2016). Therapy is then a political activity which challenges the normalizing truths that constitute people's lives and critically uncovers techniques of power that subjugate persons to a dominant ideology (Foucault 1980a; White 1994). Social justice, narrative therapy and social work are joined by discursive resistance (McKenzie-Mohr and Lafrance 2017).

A social constructionist epistemology which holds that all ideas and knowledges are created by people through social processes over time shapes narrative therapy, leading to an emphasis on interpretation and meaning making in people's stories. For Berger and Luckmann (1967 p. 23) what is defined as real is real in its consequences. They state, "The reality of everyday life is taken for granted *as* reality". Even though socially constructed, ideas become embedded as if they are real, taking on a life of their own with significant and powerful effects. We can see this in internalized negative identity conclusions people have about themselves. When dominant social views are unquestioned and treated as absolute truth, other perspectives and interpretations are often invisibilized and delegitimized. This essentializing prejudice is what Fricker (2010) refers to as a form of epistemic injustice.

Within a constructionist paradigm, as societies create knowledge and meaning there is no one absolute objective universal truth. People are both producers of and produced by this knowledge (Berger and Luckmann 1967; Marx 1978). All knowledge is relational as meaning arises within the context of social interaction. Embedded within this context, knowledge is neither private nor universal. Working in tandem, postmodernism and constructionism maintain there are multiple social realities and that knowledge is tied to power. Within narrative therapy, all meaning is interpretative. The interpretations and understandings attached to events/things and how we talk about them allow for connections between people. Like knowledge, meaning is always partial, always situated. However, while influenced by postmodernism, narrative therapy does not surrender to a relativist endless fluidity and multiplicity (Bordo 1990) and holds onto the importance of positionality more often associated with modernism, in order to sustain a commitment to the ethics of social justice (Weinberg 2020).

Grounded in this view, narrative therapy reflexively deconstructs the negative influence of stories on people's lives and encourages clients to take a position against this influence (Morgan 2000). Gergen (1999) suggests social constructionism opens ".... new spaces of possibility for creating the future.....we begin to locate alternative visions of knowledge, truth, and the self" (p. 5). Power is organized and reinforced through discourse including therapeutic discourse (Chambone et al. 1999). As an emancipatory practice committed to social justice, narrative therapy is necessarily rooted in emancipatory epistemology. This means that narrative therapy avoids reifying concepts or categories which are central ingredients in dominant discourses of power, knowledge, subjectivity and experience. Instead, we need to attend to the way conceptual practices and interpretations may reify or challenge dominant stories (Smith 1990). In narrative therapy, the counterstorying process unpacks and resists the discursive construction of problem stories. This includes rejecting the construction of binary social categories (body/mind; emotion/cognition; individual/social) which are often evident in dominant social discourse. I will explore how some of these central concepts influenced by postmodernism are deployed in narrative therapy.

The Subject

In addition to Foucault's analysis of knowledge, power and discourse, his understanding of the subject influences narrative therapy. Foucault does not separate his analysis of power from that of individuals. A postmodern and constructionist view of the subject holds that the self does not escape social influence. Our naturalized asocial notions of the self as pregiven and individually created are abandoned and it is recognized that essentialized notions of self are problematically separated from power and therefore social influence (Brown 2020, 2021). Adopting a non-essentialist and fully social approach to the subject "requires humans to confront how power is implicit in our very subjectivity, that which people wish to honor and privilege as individual, private and outside the social" (Brown and Augusta-Scott 2007, p. xxi). Gergen (1999) refers to the 'shaky scaffold of the self' (p. 6) which is based on dualist notions of the reality of the 'world out there' and the reality of the mind 'in here' (p. 8). From a postmodern lens there is no autonomous, discoverable, authentic or real self (White 2001). There is not one single story of the self and there are many possible understandings. The self becomes the person or persons our stories demand.

Experience

The concept of 'experience' and the idea that clients are 'experts' of their own lives has been central to empowerment based social work practice, often used as a way to challenge the idea of the all-knowing expert therapist. Narrative therapy offers an alternative and non-essentialized approach to centring the importance of experience through unpacking how stories of experience are socially constructed and organized over time (Brown and Augusta-Scott 2007). As such experience stories do not represent an absolute uncontested truth. Stories about experiences, including experiences of self and identity, are not only interpretive, they are always partial (Haraway 1988). From this view, narrative therapy asserts there are no experts, and that both client and therapist can only bring partial knowledge to the conversation and the unpacking of unhelpful stories. The client and therapist work collaboratively to deconstruct and reconstruct unhelpful stories (Brown and Augusta-Scott 2018). Scott (1992) observes that stories of experience are an interpretation in need of an interpretation.

The Politics of Emotion

Emotion is in the grip of culture and not subjectively innocent (Ahmed 2004a, b; Brown 2019 p. 158). "Emotional life is at the center of subjectivity, inseparable from our interpretation of the world and dominant social discourse" (Brown 2014 p. 179). Emotion is therefore not outside of culture and meaning and is a central ingredient in the discursive construction of stories. Emotion is often a pivotal entry point in narrative therapy. Getting to the heart of people's emotional experiences (i.e., sadness, grief, loss, love, fear, anger, happiness), through narrative exploration allows for a fully embodied uncovering of the discursive construction and meaning of stories. For instance, the emotional responses to trauma and abuse are fully discursive, moving back and forth between what may appear like 'simply' emotional experience and its discursive construction. When the emotional is joined with cognitive content and social context we can engage the personal is political approach. For instance, the social and subsequent individual demand today for emotional self-management creates acceptable boundaries of adequate self-regulation including how we speak of distress or discontent. Ahmed urges us to ask what do emotions do as a cultural practice (Ahmed 2004a, b)? The dominant cultural discourse of self-management shapes the expectations and performance of emotion management. Self-management and self-surveillance is structured by dichotomized either/or assumptions in policing the self, including, good/bad, in control/out of control, good enough/not good enough, powerful/powerless, being productive/unproductive. This emotional self-management schema allows little if any room for stepping out of line in a neoliberal culture.

Encoded feeling talk is 'known and familiar' and often appears as metaphors in our thinking processes (Brown 2014 p. 175). For instance, in women's struggles with their bodies and eating 'disorders' the socially constructed meaning of fatness and thinness become metaphors. 'Experience near' language reflects people's own understanding of feeling fat which is equated with feeling bad, unattractive and out control. In contrast, feeling thin is associated with feeling good, attractive and in control (Brown 2014; McKenzie-Mohr and Lafrance 2014 p. 7; White 2007). Encoded speech ties feeling life with social life, and provide rich material for a deeper unpacking of their discursive construction.

Stories

We live storied lives with each other. These stories shape our lives and constitute or create our identities. Drawing on White (2001) "our stories do not simply represent us or reflect back, like a mirror, a discernable reality; instead, our stories are active –they constitute us" (Brown and Augusta-Scott 2007 p. xix). Stories are a form of discourse; the discursive way in which we organize, account for, give meaning to and understand the circumstances and events in our lives. Meaning is derived through structuring experience into stories. Through narratives we construct meaning in everyday life which forms, informs and re-forms our views of reality. Stories are often messy, full of contradictions and gaps. There are many ways to tell a story – for instance through body language, facial expressions, tone of voice, silence, pauses, or through other things such as coping strategies, art, music or film. Stories can only ever be incomplete or partial, as no one story can capture the full complexity of events. The construction of narratives is a selective process about which information to include and much goes untold or is only partially spoken. Stories are pregnant with the 'yet to be spoken'. Practitioners need to be aware of the partiality of stories, the dangers of telling them, and notice impediments to telling or hearing a story. Both the telling and hearing of stories are important – co-occurring and mutually reinforcing. As these moments are always hermeneutic or interpretive, there can be no neutral stories, no neutral hearing of stories.

Stories emerge in social, cultural, political, economic and historical contexts (White 2001, 2007). Stories are never simply individual as we construct stories through culturally available discourses and social contexts of meaning (Brown and Augusta-Scott 2007). Negative and often oppressive stories of identity emerge in these contexts of knowledge and power. People often internalize dominant ideas or discourse as though they were absolute truths. These dominant discourses then shape people's stories. These stories are often unhelpful and injurious ('rape is sex', 'you are to blame') and can often be seen through discourses of self-management, self-regulation, self-correction and self-surveillance especially under the discursive influence of neoliberalism (Brown 2014, 2020; Foucault 1980a). People discipline themselves through these normalizing practices of self, shaping and trying to control how they are seen and thereby valued by others.

Narrative therapy explores what people's stories do in their lives (Frank 2010) and views stories as critical spaces for producing counter knowledges (McKenzie-Mohr and Lafrance 2014). From a narrative perspective, all stories need to be told, deconstructed, reconstructed not simply heard (White 2001). Therefore, narrative therapy emphasizes moving past problematically reifying the problem story through a repetitive process of simply telling and retelling a story. The work of therapy often involves unpacking the meaning and construction of unhelpful stories (i.e., 'I am worthless', 'I am stupid') and producing counterstories or alternative/preferred stories. Narrative therapy recognizes that stories offer endless meanings and multiple interpretation to be explored through mutual inquiry. Stories are not static; they are 'perpetually in motion' (DeVault 2014). People are not simply products of our stories or the culture in which stories emerge, but active co-creators of ourselves through our stories. As people's stories typically involve both agency and resistance: "The therapeutic approach is one of possibility, of hope, enabling the rewriting and subsequent reliving of one"s lives through more helpful stories' (Brown and Augusta-Scott 2007 p. xx).

Counternarratives as Resistance

Dominant stories are ironically both 'omnipresent and yet often invisible' (McKenzie-Mohr and Lafrance 2014 p. 5) as they are typically taken for granted as truth. Ormond maintains (2001 pp. 7–8): "The master narrative finds its niche and function in society by clothing itself within the protection of a cloak of invisibility. It is the role of the counter-story to rip off this cloak and reveal the politics at work". These dominant stories are highly influential, often producing negative effects and damaged identities (White 2001). Butler (1997) argues that forcing experience into such discourses produces injurious speech. The injurious speech of dominant social discourse constrains women's speech – for instance, in the case of sexualized violence, 'you caused the violence' or 'it wasn't as bad as you say it was', or 'it did not really happen' (Butler 1997; Madigan 2003). There is little foundation in dominant culture for women to tell their stories of trauma. *Tightrope talk* refers to the way women make meaning of their experiences when the dominant frameworks within culture fail them (McKenzie-Mohr and Lafrance's (2011). It is into this vacuum that there is a pressing need to create counterstories.

Given this, McKenzie-Mohr and Lafrance (2014) ask us to consider from a therapeutic perspective how the 'goodness' of stories for people's lives can we assessed and how we can listen for their preferred stories, suggesting "[b]etter stories, then, are those that reveal, resist, and recast such forms of oppression.... their power is in their ability to contest taken for granted and oppressive 'truths' set forth by master narratives" (2014 p. 192). Narrative therapy resists injustice and oppression through disrupting and subverting dominant discourses or master narratives through counterstorying with new resistant story lines. It takes as a starting point awareness of the relationship between power and knowledge in dominant social discourse and that people's stories very often reflect weakly formed resistant discourses. Like story telling itself, discursive resistance is often hesitant and partial, whereby double listening is needed to help us notice and support the resistance in people's talk (Brown 2014; Morgan 2000; White 2000). Discursive resistance is often conceptualized in terms of counternarratives, counter discourses or counterstories which challenge or disrupt hegemonic framing as social realities (McKenzie-Mohr and Lafrance 2014). Social workers can support people's "acts of narrative resistance through exploring the effects of people's narratives on their lives, their links to power and their potential for harm" (McKenzie-Mohr and Lafrance 2017 p. 189). As resistance, counternarratives 'talk back' to injurious master narratives (189).

Feminist narrative approaches to social work practice can challenge the unhelpful discursive shaping of women's intersectional experiences and help to create more helpful, less oppressive and preferred counterstories which challenge the ways that dominant discourse renders invisible the social and political context of people's suffering and struggles as the focus remains on the individual (see Brown 2019). The frameworks available for women to make meaning of their experiences are often injurious for them, while reinforcing the dominant biomedical paradigm and continuing to decontextualize them through centring on individual disease and pathology.

Neoliberal dominant discourses shape the conceptualization of mental health today (Brown et al. 2021). Specifically, alongside fiscal restraint and the reduction of services is the responsibilization of the individual for their own well-being and recovery (Liebenberg et al. 2013) through self-management and the centring of all mental health problems within a biomedical model (Brown 2014, 2021). These discourses co-exist within the oppressive discursive context of racism, sexism, homophobia and neoliberal capitalist economic restraint (Morrow and Weisser 2012).

The prevailing biomedical disease-based dominant social discourse on mental health in the Western world is presented and taken up as inherently legitimate. Often injurious, this discourse is individualized, decontextualized and pathologized and clients themselves regularly frame their own stories within the limitations of these discourses (Madigan 1998, 2003). The taken for granted authority of the *DSM-5* in mental health work is a central ingredient in the dominant bio-medical model in mental health service provision (Strong 2012) and offers the 'lure of legitimacy' (Lafrance and McKenzie-Mohr 2013). Cermele et al. (2001) demonstrate clear biases related to race and gender in the application of the *DSM-5*. Arguably, a commitment to social justice-based therapy should always interrogate the authority and legitimacy of dominant mental health discourse and practices. Both feminist and narrative therapies have operationalized the critical theorization of mental health problems as simultaneously individual, social and political through clearly articulated critical clinical practices (Brown and MacDonald 2020). Mental health needs to be recognized as a social justice issue:

> Absent from this official story are perspectives and forms of evidence that start with an analysis of power and consider the social, political, cultural, and economic production of mental health problems and solutions. Absent too are the diverse voices of experience psychiatric survivors and those who have lived with various forms of social marginalization and (not unrelated) emotional suffering.... (Morrow and Malcoe 2017 p. 6)

Unlike other therapeutic approaches such as brief solution focused or cognitive behaviour therapy, the clinical practice of narrative therapy is consistent with its postmodern and social constructionist view of knowledge and the hermeneutic meaning making process. Narrative therapy emphasizes the meaning-making process in understanding how people's dominant problem-saturated stories have been constructed by social processes, ideas and individuals over time. Narrative therapy is, therefore, interested in the history and influence of problem stories on people's lives and in creating counterstories which resist this influence.

Feminist Narrative Therapy

Feminist narrative therapy is positioned on the side of women, and attentive to issues of power, safety and control in its collaborative approach. The feminist narrative lens used here draws upon feminist trauma work and its significant contribution to working with sexualized violence (Brown 2004, 2013, 2018, 2020; Burstow 2003; Herman Lewis 2015; Tseris 2013; Webster and Dunn 2005). Avoiding revictimization or retraumatization involves creating an environment that is emotionally safe, where she is believed, respected and in control. Research has shown how common it is for women who have dealt with complex and often lifelong experiences of trauma and abuse to be labelled, pathologized and often diagnosed with various problems including 'borderline personality disorder' (Herman Lewis 2015; Brown 2004, 2020; Cermele et al. 2001; Marecek and Gavey 2013; Tseris 2013; Ussher 2010). Frequently psychiatrized, diagnosed and prescribed medication, women often receive very little support for their history of trauma.

> Case Example
> Leah is a 50-year divorced woman with grown children and works as a veterinary assistant. Through her life she has struggled with depression and alcohol use subsequent to a childhood of significant trauma. She experienced sexual abuse by her father beginning at age 9 and physical abuse by her mother from early childhood until she was a teen. These experiences left her believing that she was not valued or loved and that people could not be trusted. She has struggled through her life with feeling lonely, depressed and worthless. She uses alcohol as a way to numb these feelings. She initially sought therapy to talk about her worry that her drinking was out of control and could jeopardize her employment. While she

limits her drinking to evening and weekends, she finds her drinking is becoming more difficult to control. Leah's story is not uncommon. The pathway of sexualized and physical trauma leading to depression and low self-worth and subsequent efforts to self-medicate is well supported in the research literature (Larkin et al. 2014).

Therapeutic Alliance

The therapeutic alliance is central to collaborative therapeutic approaches such as feminist and narrative therapy, and is particularly important when trauma experiences shape the person's story. A therapeutic alliance is critical when relational injury is present which is often an effect of child abuse where the child learns to expect that people will always let them down. Through a strong therapeutic alliance women can experience someone who does not betray or abuse them, but who is on her side. The therapist's position of respect and compassion towards her ongoing struggles with her trauma history and her corresponding strategies for coping reinforces the significance of her story. As with any client, working with Leah first involves establishing rapport and being clear about how you approach working with the effects of trauma. In-depth conversations of her trauma history and its impact using a collaborative non-pathologizing approach will allow for the *counterviewing* and counterstorying of her problem story. The co-occurrence of trauma, depression and substance use is common. We will explore how her coping strategies make sense and we will employ a harm reduction approach for her alcohol use concerns (Brown and Stewart 2021).

As feminist narrative practitioners, we unpack her self-blame, sense of worthlessness and pathologization in her story. We listen carefully and respectfully to her disclosures and understand the need for skilled and adequate follow through. Most children reach adulthood with their abuse secret intact and its traumatic effects unexplored or shared often spending years in treatment for an alcohol use problem, or depression with the impact of trauma unaddressed. Practitioners can have strong emotional reactions to trauma stories and need to deal with their own issues, or responses. Feminist therapy has argued that we need to use our own reactions and emotions as they provide important information in collaborative work. We need to be cautious not to censor the woman's story or her reactions due to our own fears, anxieties or anger. Some topics may make a practitioner uncomfortable, but we cannot shut down or discourage what we have a hard time hearing. Women need to believe that the practitioner working with them can handle their story – if she is to risk the dangers of being vulnerable; of speaking.

Counterviewing the Dangers of Trauma Talk and Dominant Discourses of Coping

Trauma work requires an appreciation of the dangers of speaking in a culture in which violence against women and children often continues to be *normalized and minimized*. These constraining discourses are *inadequate and incongruent* with women's experiences (McKenzie-Mohr and Lafrance 2011, 2014). Women reveal this *incongruence* in their efforts to story their experiences. Telling trauma stories may also be experienced as dangerous as they trigger uncomfortable/painful emotions, fear of disclosure, of being blamed or not believed, of being judged or thought less of, of the perpetrator and shame, guilt and/or lack of trust. Together these dangers shape the story telling. Self-protection, caution and self-surveillance may render invisible, or disqualify aspects of the story. Trauma stories often involve telling without telling, especially when dangerous. Foucault (2001) points out that the risk involved and the consequences of speaking out through telling stories are not equal.

The telling of trauma stories may be partial, incomplete, uncertain, tentative, selective contradictory, full of gaps or merely hinted at – they may be stories in the making. It is common for stories to be told in pieces or indirectly; we need to expect this. And women need to be able to tell their stories however they can. By showing we hear, through acknowledging what is being said, partially said and not said, we open up the possibility of the story unfolding rather than encouraging it to retreat. Double-listening opens spaces and possibilities for telling the trauma story and our responses to the trauma story, can then validate the trauma experience and also provide us with opportunities to uncover the skills and knowledges embedded within the coping strategies that the client developed to cope, survive and perhaps resist the traumatic experiences when they were happening. We need to recognize how difficult processes of change are and how creative coping strategies often are and how they become habituated and embedded beyond the trauma crisis. As practitioners we bear witness, serve as allies and as advocates while helping to contain the sometimes deep and overwhelming aspects of telling the story.

It is important to explore the constraints and dangers of telling a trauma story. In listening beyond the words, "[we] can challenge the dominant discourse and work toward the development of alternative and more helpful narratives" (DeVault 1990 p. 52). As people are multi-storied, double-listening means we listen for both the explicit and implicit aspects of stories. Explicit stories are often surface stories or thin descriptions and problem saturated. We listen for these *absent but implicit* stories to facilitate movement from problem-saturated identities to a greater sense of agency, power and choice (Morgan 2000; White 2004). We need to ask questions that allow for elaboration and recognition without pushing and that do not inadvertently silence her or exacerbate her uncertainty.

Counterviewing questions are helpful in unpacking the stories Leah tells about herself (Madigan 2003). We focus on externalizing the abuse and trauma and the effects on Leah. Externalizing conversations make the abuse or trauma the problem not Leah (White and Epston 1990). Externalizing problem stories and negative identities contextualizes and depathologizes how Leah copes with the effects of trauma and violence. I objectify abuse by turning it into an object – 'the abuse'. This narrative approach addresses the history and influence of the abuse on Leah's life, and moves to explore how Leah has also influenced the dominant story at times by living outside its effects.

Through counterviewing conversations we can create counterstories to the unhelpful dominant stories that emerged from the history of violence and trauma and from the dominant social discourses on gender, violence, mental health and addiction and larger society that has normalized violence and abuse against women and children. It is no surprise then that telling trauma stories often involves significant uncertainty, minimization and self-blame alongside apparent contradiction and gaps (Brown 2013). The feminist narrative practitioner working with women's trauma stories needs to be comfortable with uncertainty and partial telling. Women do not come to therapy with their trauma stories and coping all worked out.

Leah describes her drinking as a way of coping, by numbing her pain. When Leah begins to drink she describes often feeling very anxious, lonely and sad. These feelings are replaced by numbness as the drinking progresses. She often focuses on feeling she is not good enough, that she is unlovable and that she will always be alone. There is no point trying to have relationships as she has learned people will just hurt her. She feels unable to control her drinking and oscillates between the story that she is an 'addict' with a 'disease' and that she is coping to deal with the painful effects of abuse and trauma. Exploring her drinking is blocked by the internalized idea that any reason for using a coping strategy is just an excuse. She does not believe she deserves these efforts at minimizing her pain and finding some comfort. She is critical of her use of alcohol as it feels out of control. Overall, she expresses very little compassion for herself.

It makes sense that Leah feels these ways and that these feelings reflect her dominant story in connection to her abuse experiences. As the negative identity conclusions about herself and others interfere with her life, it is important to counterview these stories together. In the counterviewing process, each question and therapeutic response is an entry point to a more elaborated conversation.

A feminist narrative approach will adopt the stance that coping strategies make sense and that they serve as an entry point to exploring what the client is coping with and to the deconstruction of unhelpful dominant stories. Leah initially sought therapy to address her drinking behaviour. It makes sense that Leah has had to discover ways to cope with her traumatic abusive experience. Rather than pathologize these coping efforts, her thoughts and feelings are unpacked and situated within the context of where they emerged. Engaging in this exploration is itself a *unique outcome* – a time when Leah is able to be outside the problem story, as it is likely rare for Leah, like for many abused women, to show herself some compassion and it demonstrates the beginning of recognizing the importance of her experience and her responses to trauma.

Scaffolding Questions

Scaffolding questions can provide a map for moving through the dominant story and the effects of this story on Leah (White 2007). These questions are intended to provide direction for counterviewing the negative unhelpful stories Leah tells about herself. This narrative approach addresses how the dominant story has influenced Leah's life, and moves to explore how Leah has also influenced the dominant story at times by living outside its effects. We explore the many ways she has had influence over the negative impact of the trauma *often through her efforts at coping*.

With these sample counterviewing questions we can explore that it was difficult to live with the abuse and that it was too much for a small child to deal with. Counterviewing allows us to unpack how the abuse was unfair and that her feelings and needs were disregarded by the people who were supposed to take care of her and the abuse made her feel sad and bad about herself. It also allows us to unpack that and the adults who chose to harm her were to blame. Overall, we explore the effects of the abuse.

Exploring the Effects or Influence of Trauma

- Does it make sense to you that the abuse you experienced has had an effect on you?
- How did the abuse make you feel about yourself?
- Do you think the abuse that happened to you as a child was fair?
- Thinking about it now, were you capable of protecting yourself from the abuse as a child?
- What difference would it have made to you if someone would have stood up for you?
- Who do you think was to blame for the abuse?
- What difference would it have made to you if you had not experienced the abuse?

The following counterviewing questions explore unique outcomes related to trauma. Rather than how the trauma influenced her we explore how she was able to have influence over the trauma.

Influence on Trauma

- How have you coped with the abuse?
- How did you cope as a child?
- How do you cope now?
- Who knows this about you?
- How did you find ways to help yourself deal with the abuse?
- As an adult what do you think it took for little Leah to come up with that?
- Did you ever feel that you did not deserve to be treated in this way?
- Can you remember a time that you felt safe as a child?
- What was different about this time?
- Are there times you feel safe now?
- Are there any times you felt loved as a child?
- Are there times you feel loved now?

- Can you remember any times you felt you could trust people as a child?
- Are there times you trust people now?

Depression: Influence of Trauma

As Leah has told me that she has struggled with depression as a result of her childhood experiences abuse I ask these questions:

- When did you first notice feeling depression in your life?
- How did the abuse make you feel sad?
- Tell me about the depression? What does it feel like?
- How has the depression affected your life, relationships, work, etc.?
- How has the abuse made you feel about yourself?
- How has the abuse made you feel about others?

We explore her experiences of depression and how they may be connected to trauma. We also explore how she copes with depression subsequent to trauma through her use of alcohol. By exploring her coping we simultaneously explore both the influence of trauma – *the need to cope* – and her influence over the trauma – *that she copes* (Brown 2020). In this process, we need to reframe 'symptoms' as 'coping skills' and avoid viewing trauma as a disorder, but instead as 'a reaction to a kind of wound' (Burstow 2003 p. 1302). As practitioners, we need to avoid pathologizing the very behaviours that have helped people to survive (Burstow 2003).

Making Sense of the Coping

Counterviewing of the central discourses shaping Leah's efforts at coping with trauma means we begin from the assumption that Leah is not 'mentally ill' or an 'addict'. Rather we take the stance this makes sense. We explore how her coping efforts have helped her survive while also having some negative consequences. Through her coping efforts Leah is trying to take care of herself. This is a *unique outcome* central to the development of a counterstory.

Leah's Influence on Depression and Trauma

- How do you cope with the depression?
- What do you need at these times?
- How are you able to get on with thing you have to do?
- Can you think of a time that the depression was not there?
- What was different about this time?
- How did this feel different?
- How were you able to have this influence over the depression?

- How did it feel to have this influence?
- What helped you at those times to have less or no depression in your life?
- Who else noticed this?
- What would you need to be able to continue on in this direction?

In the process of thickening potential alternative stories it is important to identify supports for the new emerging storyline. 'Re-membering' is a way for people to explore who has a positive influence and negative influence in their life, and whose influence is important to elevate (Russell and Carey 2002). Building the emerging preferred story into the future creates a sense of possibility.

We explore the ways she has influenced the negative impact of the trauma often through *influencing the effects* or negative impact of the abuse. Counterviewing coping through drinking allows us to see that these are times she is trying to take care of and nurture herself, and reduce her pain. We can build on the importance of her taking care of her own emotional needs and the development of self-compassion in living her life. With these next questions we begin to explore the history and influence of the abuse and trauma on Leah and her influence on them.

Leah's Influence *on* Trauma through Drinking

- You have also described drinking as a way of coping?
- Can you tell me about that?
- How do you feel before you begin drinking?
- Are there ways you find drinking unhelpful?
- How does it help you?
- How do you feel during drinking?
- How do you feel after drinking?

Many sparkling moments emerge which allow Leah to counterview the trauma and its effects, and to fashion preferred stories about herself. Our initial conversations of her alcohol use move into conversations about coping with depression which intersects with her traumatic experiences. We explore the connections or pathway between trauma, depression and her use of alcohol. We discuss what works and does not work, what helps and what does not help. We move back and forth between these themes and thus thicken her emerging alternative story. The questions counterview assumptions she has about herself that contribute to unhelpful, negative identity conclusions (White 2001).

Creating Alternative or Counterstories

By unpacking coping with drinking we can explore the deep emotional wounds that arose from the abuse Leah experienced and acknowledge her resourcefulness. Coping behaviours form an entry point to exploring the effects of trauma on Leah through connecting how they are ways to deal with sadness, emptiness and loneliness. These feelings are explored as outcomes of the abuse and the dominant stories she tells about herself and others. By talking about coping strategies rather than pathology, Leah is able to talk about the abuse both directly and indirectly.

In creating a counterstory with Leah, we shift from the disease model to a feminist narrative lens which gives value to the meaning of her coping efforts. By disrupting and deconstructing dominant stories and negative identity conclusions we create the platform for an alternative more helpful counterstory. We have simultaneously explored both the influence of trauma and her influence over the trauma through exploring her coping. Her problem story emerged from the context of trauma and her emerging counterstory challenges her conclusions that she is unlovable, not good enough, and people can never be trusted. She replaces the self-censure of a lack of control and willpower with a self-caring appreciation that her use of alcohol was an effort to takecare of herself by numbing the pain and depression that arose from the trauma. Her counterstory maintains the belief she does deserves to be loved and treated well through a growing sense of self-compassion and a strong therapeutic alliance with her social worker. If Leah is able to hold onto this counterstory and find an audience of support, it will thicken or strengthen over time.

Narrative Therapy, Mental Health and Addiction Policy

International research has argued that social work identity is in a state of crisis with a prevailing sense of moral despair when expected to comply with the combined systemic demands of bio-medicalism and neoliberalism (Brown 2021; Brown et al. 2021; Spolander et al. 2014). Today, taken together bio-medicalism and neoliberalism limits how social workers are able to practice often creating moral distress. The dominance of the biomedical paradigm makes it difficult to assert an alternative and distinctly unique social work paradigm. Professional autonomy and respect is denied when social work must comply with the biomedical and psychological models of other professions (Brown et al. 2021; Hyslop 2018; Rossiter and Heron 2011). More, now than ever, social work needs to assert its professional paradigm and ethical commitment to social justice for mental health practices that ensure individuals are not pathologized, and that their struggles are placed in historical, social and cultural contexts (Brown and MacDonald 2020). Social work needs to treat mental health and substance use as social justice issues through advocating for policies and associated funding to support a critical clinical approach. Taken together, shifts in public policy and institutional policy practices towards social justice in mental health will challenge the dominant biomedical model, allow a broader scope of practice that allows for a bio-psycho-social approach, that abandons the efficiency versus caring ethos of the fiscal constraints which determine treatment modalities, number of sessions, and fails to address the social determinants of mental health in a preventative manner (Baines et al. 2019; Brown et al. 2021; Pease and Nipperess 2016). Government and institutional policies which shape mental health and substance use service delivery need to consult with diverse communities rather than making detached decisions from 'above' and ensure greater diverse representation among service providers.

Conclusion

Narrative therapy is a social justice-based approach to social work practice. Rooted in postmodernism and social constructionism, narrative theory as applied to social work bridges the gap that often exists between clinical work and social justice theory. A narrative approach explores the construction and meaning of stories which shape people's lives. The meaning making process is viewed as social and political and a process of counterviewing helps to create counterstories that often disrupt and resist unhelpful dominant social discourses which reinforce social inequity and oppression. This chapter explored the epistemological and theoretical foundations of narrative work and provided a case example to demonstrate the deconstruction process of stories through counterviewing and the creation of counternarratives emphasizing the importance of double listening and appreciating the dangers of speech. While often pathologized, we need to make sense of coping behaviour which has often helped people to survive.

I have argued that it is imperative for social work to intentionally address and integrate theoretical underpinnings that contribute to a social justice-based approach to clinical social work and to acknowledge mental health as a social justice issue. A commitment to social justice is a pivotal social work value and must be translated in all parts of our practice. The illustration of scaffolding counterviewing questions for therapeutic conversation provides a map but will differ in each conversation. Narrative therapy, social justice and social work converge through discursive resistance.

References

Ahmed S (2004a) The cultural politics of emotion. Edinburgh University Press, Edinburgh

Ahmed S (2004b) Affective economies. Social Text 79 22(2):117–139

Baines D (2017) Doing anti-oppressive practice. In: Social justice social work. Fernwood Press, Black Point

Baines D, Bennett B, Goodwin S, Rawsthorne M (eds) (2019) Working across difference. Social work, social policy, and social justice. Red Globe Press, pp 247–260

Baldwin C (2013) Narrative therapy: theory and application. Bristol University Press, Bristol

Beres L (2014) The narrative practitioner. Red Globe Press, New York

Berger P, Luckmann T (1967) The social construction of reality: a treatise in the sociology of knowledge. Anchor Books, New York

Bordo S (1990) Feminism, postmodernism, and gender skepticism. In: Nicholson L (ed) Feminism/Postmodernism. Routledge, New York, pp 133–156

Brown L (2004) Feminist paradigms of trauma treatment. Psychother Theory Res Pract Train 41(4): 464–471

Brown C (2013) Women's narratives of trauma: (Re)storying uncertainty, minimization and self-blame. Narrat Works 3(1):1–30

Brown C (2014) Untangling emotional threads, self-management discourse and women's body talk. In: LaFrance M, McKenzie-Mohr S (eds) Women voicing resistance. Discursive and narrative explorations. Routledge, New York, pp 174–190

Brown C (2017) Critical clinical practice: creating counterstories through feminist narrative therapy. In: Baines D (ed) Doing anti-oppressive practice: building transformative, politicized social work, 3rd edn. Fernwood Press, Toronto, pp 212–232

Brown C (2018) The dangers of trauma talk: counterstorying co-occurring strategies for coping with trauma. J Syst Ther 37(3):42–60

Brown C (2019) Speaking of women's depression and the politics of emotion. Affilia J Women Soc Work 34(2):151–169

Brown C (2020) Feminist narrative therapy and complex trauma: critical clinical work with women diagnosed as "borderline". In: Brown C, MacDonald J (eds) Critical clinical social work: counterstorying for social justice. Canadian Scholars Press, Toronto, pp 82–109

Brown C (2021) Critical clinical social work and the neoliberal constraints on social justice in mental health. Res Soc Work Pract:1–9. https://doi.org/10.1177/1049731520984531

Brown C, Augusta-Scott T (eds) (2007) Narrative therapy. Making meaning, making lives. Sage, Thousand Oaks

Brown C, Augusta-Scott T (2018) Reimagining the intersection of gender, knowledge and power in collaborative therapeutic conversations with women and eating disorders and men who use violence. In: Audet C, Pare D (eds) Social justice and narrative therapy. Routledge, New York, pp 143–158

Brown C, MacDonald J (2020) Critical clinical social work: counterstorying for social justice. Canadian Scholars Press, Toronto

Brown C, Stewart SH (2021) Harm reduction for women in treatment for alcohol use problems: exploring the impact of dominant addiction discourse. Qual Health Res 31(1):54–69. https://doi.org/10.1177/1049732320954396396

Brown C, Johnstone M, Ross N (2021) Repositioning social work practice in mental health and health equity in Nova Scotia. Nova Scotia College of Social Workers

Bruner E (1986) Experience and its expressions. In: Turner V, Bruner E (eds) The anthropology of experience: 3–30. Chicago University of Illinois Press

Bruner J (1987) Life as narrative. Soc Res 54:1–17

Burstow B (2003) Toward a radical understanding of trauma and trauma work. Violence Against Women 19:1293–1317

Butler J (1997) Excitable speech: a politics of the performative. Routledge, New York

Cermele J, Daniels S, Anderson K (2001) Defining normal: constructions of race and gender in the DSM-IV casebook. Fem Psychol 11(2):229–247

Chambone A (1999) Foucault's approach: making the familiar visible. In: Chambone A, Irving A, Epstein L (eds) Reading foucault for social work. Columbia University Press, New York

Chambone A, Irving A, Epstein L (eds) (1999) Reading Foucault for social work. Columbia University Press, New York, pp 51–81

DeVault M (1990) Talking and listening from women's standpoint: feminist strategies for interviewing and analysis. Soc Probl 37(1):96–116

DeVault M (2014) Language and stories in motion. In: LaFrance M, McKenzie-Mohr S (eds) Women voicing resistance. Discursive and narrative explorations. Routledge, New York, pp 16–28

Flaskas C, Humphreys C (1993) Theorizing about power: intersecting the ideas of Foucault with the problem of power in family therapy. Fam Process 32(1):35–47

Fook J (2016) Social work: a critical approach to practice, 3rd edn. Sage, London

Foucault M (1964) Madness and civilization. Vintage Books, New York

Foucault M (1980a) The history of sexuality Vol 1. An introduction. New York, Vintage

Foucault M (1980b) Power/knowledge: selected interviews and other writings 1972–1977. Patheon, New York

Foucault M (1984) In: Rabinow P (ed) The Foucault reader. Pantheon Books, New York
Foucault M (1991) Politics and the study of discourse. In: Burchell G, Gorden C, Miller P (eds) The Foucault effect, studies in governmentality. Harverster, London, pp 53–72
Foucault M (1995) Strategies of power. In: Anderson W (ed) The truth about the truth: De- and reconfusing the postmodern world. Tarcher/Putnam, New York, pp 40–45
Frank AW (2010) Letting stories breathe: a socio-narratology. University of Chicago Press, Chicago
Freedman J, Combs G (1996) Narrative therapy and the social construction of preferred identities. W.W. Norton, New York
Fricker M (2010) Epistemic justice. Power and the ethics of knowing. Oxford University Press, Oxford
Geertz C (1986) Making experience, authoring selves. In: Turner VW, Bruner E (eds) The anthropology of experience. University of Illinois Press, Chicago, pp 373–380
Gergen K (1999) Traditions in trouble. In an invitation to social construction. Sage, Thousand Oaks
Haraway D (1988) Situated knowledges: the science question in feminism and the privilege of partial perspective. Fem Stud 14((3), Fall):575–599
Herman Lewis J (2015) Trauma and recovery. The aftermath of violence- from domestic abuse to political terror, 2nd edn. Basic Books, New York
hooks b (1990) Postmodern blackness. Postmod Cult 1(1). https://doi.org/10.1353/pmc.1990.0004
Hyslop I (2018) Neoliberalism and social work identity. Eur J Soc Work 21(1):20–31
Lafrance M, McKenzie-Mohr S (2013) The DSM and its lure of legitimacy. Fem Psychol 23(1):119–140
Larkin H, Felitti V, Anda R (2014) Social work and adverse childhood experiences research: implications for practice and health policy. Soc Work Public Health 29(1):1–16. https://doi.org/10.1080/19371918.2011.619433
Leonard P (1997) Postmodern welfare. Reconstructing an emancipatory project. Sage, Thousand Oaks
Liebenberg L, Ungar M, Ikeda J (2013) Neo-liberalism and responsibilisation in the discourse of social service workers. Br J Soc Work 45(3):1006–1021
Madigan S (2003) Counterviewing injurious speech acts: destabilising eight conversational habits of highly effective problems. J Narrat Ther Commun Work 1:43–59
Madigan S, Law I (eds) (1998) Praxis. Situating discourse, feminism and politics in narrative therapies. Cardigan Press, Vancouver, pp 207–230
Marecek J, Gavey N (2013) DSM-5 and beyond: a critical feminist engagement with psychodiagnosis. Fem Psychol 23(1):3–9
Marx K (1978) The German ideology. In: Tucker R (ed) The Marx Engels reader. Norton, New York, pp 146–200
McKenzie-Mohr S, Lafrance M (2011) Telling stories without the words: "Tightrope talk" in women's accounts of coming to live well after rape or depression. Fem Psychol 21(1):49–73
McKenzie-Mohr S, Lafrance M (eds) (2014) Women voicing resistance. Discursive and narrative explorations. Routledge, New York
McKenzie-Mohr S, Lafrance M (2017) Narrative resistance in social work research and practice: counter-storying in the pursuit of social justice. Qual Soc Work 16(2):189–205
Morgan A (2000) What is narrative therapy? Dulwich Centre Publications, Adelaide
Morrow M, Malcoe H (2017) Introduction. Science, social injustice, and mental health. In: Morrow M, Malcoe LH (eds) Critical inquiries for social justice in mental health. University of Toronto Press, Toronto, pp 3–30
Morrow M, Weisser J (2012) Towards a social justice framework for mental health recovery. Stud Soc Justice 6(1):27–43
Nicholson L (ed) (1990) Feminism/postmdoernism. Routledge: New York
Ormond A (2001) Voice of Maori youth: the other side of silence. In: Fine M, Harris AM (eds) Under the covers: theorizing the politics of counter stories. Lawrence & Wishart, London, pp 49–60

Pease B, Nipperess S (2016) Doing critical social work in the neoliberal context: working on the contradictions. In: Pease B, Goldingay S, Hosken N, Nipperess S (eds) Doing critical social work. Transformative practices for social justice. Allen and Unwin, pp 3–24

Rossiter A, Heron B (2011) Neoliberalism, competencies, and the devaluing of social work practice. Canadian Soc Work Rev/Revue canadienne de service social 28(2):305–309

Russell S, Carey M (2002) Re-membering: responding to commonly asked questions. Int J Narrat Ther Commun Work 3:23–31

Scott J (1992) Experience. In: Butler J, Scott J (eds) Feminists theorize the political. Routledge, New York, pp 22–40

Shotter J (1993) Cultural politics of everyday life. Social constructionism, rhetoric and knowing of the third kind. University of Toronto Press, Toronto

Smith D (1990) The conceptual practices of power. A feminist sociology of knowledge. University of Toronto Press, Toronto

Spolander G et al (2014) The implications of neoliberalism for social work: reflections from a six-country international research collaboration. Int Soc Work 57(4):301–312

Strong T (2012) Talking about the DSM-V. Int J Narrat Ther Commun Work 2:54–64

Tseris E (2013) Trauma theory without feminism? Evaluating contemporary understandings of traumatized women. Affilia: J Women Soc Work 28(2):153–164. https://doi.org/10.1177/0886109913485707

Ussher J (2010) Are we bio-medicalizing women's misery? A critical review of women's higher rates of reported depression. Fem Psychol 20(1):9–35

Weinberg M (2020) Critical clinical ethics. In: Brown C, MacDonald J (eds) Critical clinical social work: counterstorying for social justice. Canadian Scholars Press, Toronto, pp 59–79

White M (1994) The politics of therapy: putting to rest the illusion of neutrality. Dulwich Centre:1–4

White M (2001) Narrative practice and the unpacking of identity conclusions. Gecko: J Deconstruct Narrat Ideas Ther Pract 1:28–55

White M (2007) Maps of narrative practice. W.W. Norton, New York

White M, Epston D (1990) Narrative means to therapeutic ends. W.W. Norton, New York

Colonisation, Post-colonialism and Decolonisation

6

Susan Green

Contents

Introduction	102
Colonisation	104
Post-colonial Theory	106
Decolonisation	109
Implications for Social Work	111
My Perspective as a Wiradyuri yinaa (Woman)	114
Conclusion	117
References	118

Abstract

Social justice and human rights are key foundations for the practice of social work, and most social work profession organisations around the world call on their members to advocate for the most disadvantage and marginalized within society. Colonisation has impacted negatively upon many people from around the globe and none more so that Indigenous peoples. The impact of colonisation has been ongoing and continues today. Therefore, social workers have a responsibility to know, understand how colonisation continues to impact upon Indigenous people and to work alongside Indigenous people to dismantle the structures that create inequality today. In developing an understanding of colonisation, it is also important to understand the debates around post-colonialism and decolonisation. This chapter highlights some of the debates and also argues that it is important to decolonise before there is any possibility of living in a post-colonial world.

S. Green (✉)
SIAS, Charles Sturt University, Wagga Wagga, NSW, Australia
e-mail: sugreen@csu.edu.au

© Springer Nature Singapore Pte Ltd. 2023
D. Hölscher et al. (eds.), *Social Work Theory and Ethics*, Social Work,
https://doi.org/10.1007/978-981-19-1015-9_7

Keywords

Colonisation · Decolonisation · Post-colonialism · Indigenous peoples · Wiradyuri

Introduction

This chapter will discuss post-colonial theories and decolonisation as they apply to social work. To commence this discussion, it is essential to firstly consider what colonisation is. The chapter also looks at the discussions and debates around post-colonial theory before moving onto decolonisation. It then moves on to look at how this relates and impacts upon social work theory and practice with a discussion on the need to decolonise social work theory and practice before concluding with a perspective of a Wiradyuri (Indigenous) social worker within Australia.

It is an important protocol for Wiradyuri people and for many other Indigenous peoples around the world to commence any meeting or discussion with an introduction to who they are and what their purpose is within that meeting or discussion, and thus this chapter will start with an introduction to who I am.

Yuwindhu Dyudyan Garbargarbar, Galari Wiradyuri yinaa, Biira-gu-bu Yilaaydya-gu-bu Yuluwidya-gu-bu garingun, Bala-dhu ngama Yandru-gu-bu Danyal-gu-bu Yalidya-gu-bu. Bala-dhu gunhinarrum-bu badhiin-bu galingabangbur-guliyagu. Baladhu Girramaa Marramaldhaany. Ngadhu yalmambili Wiradyuri-dyi gari-dyi.

My name is Susan Green, Galari (Lachlan river clan), Wiradyuri (nation) woman, grand-daughter to Vera, Eliza and Louisa and mother to Andrew, Daniel and Alicia, and grandmother to their children. I am a social worker. I teach Wiradyuri truth.

The invasion of my Country, Wiradyuri Country, commenced in 1813, some 25 years after Captain Arthur Philip and the first fleet arrived in Sydney Cove, and around 4 years after that 'white' men arrived on my clan's land in Euabalong, western New South Wales, Australia. My family has seen the incursions of Europeans and their animals from quite early after the first 'explorers' arrived, with many of my family working on the local pastoral station and later on the railway line that passes through the town. Today, the town is very small with only a pub (hotel) and houses. There is no longer any other services, such as the school my grandmother and her siblings attended, the post office has closed, there are no shops and many of my clan have moved to larger towns in search of employment and education or were removed as children under the Assimilation Policy and other child removal practices (HREOC 1997). Colonisation has deeply affected my Ngurambang (Country) with mining and farming as well as removal of people from their Country (land). The impact upon Ngurambang, not only due to the environmental damage but also the stealing of children, the force removals off Ngurambang, the force moving onto Ngurambang of people from other places and the stopping of cultural practices and speaking of language, has created displacement not only physically but also culturally. However, Wiradyuri are walan (strong), and we continue to protect our land and culture and fight to make sure it does not die. A harder battle is to fight against the environmental destruction of our Ngurambang by those seeking to exploit her resources. Today we (Wiradyuri) learn, teach and speak our language, practice our culture and fight to protect the mother (our earth), and we are continuing to pass on our knowledge to the future generations.

As a Wiradyuri social worker and as a granddaughter, daughter, mother and grandmother, I have the responsibility to look after our buyaa (law/lore), giilang-bilang (stories) and giira (future). I am in a direct relationship with everything that exists and therefore have a responsibility to everything that exists. As a Wiradyuri person I know that nothing has never existed and that nothing will ever cease to exist, so there is at no point of time that my responsibilities and accountability have never existed and will never cease to exist. In the context of being a social worker and in this chapter, I have a responsibility to share with you the knowledge that I hold about colonisation and the impact it has had for us all. It is important that we be gari-garra (true) and maram-bul (correct, good, right) in our words, our intentions and our actions. From this positioning, I speak (or write) as a Wiradyuri woman, mother, grandmother and a social worker. Thus I have the responsibility to share my thoughts on how we can decolonise and move forward personally and professionally.

The International Federation of Social Workers (IFSW) states that its core mandates include:

> ... promoting social change, social development, social cohesion, and the empowerment and liberation of people. (IFSW 2021).

Further to this, the IFSW also states that:

> ... social work is informed not only by specific practice environments and Western theories, but also by indigenous knowledges. Part of the legacy of colonialism is that Western theories and knowledges have been exclusively valorised, and indigenous knowledges have been devalued, discounted, and hegemonised by Western theories and knowledge. The ... definition attempts to halt and reverse that process by acknowledging that Indigenous peoples in each region, country or area carry their own values, ways of knowing, ways of transmitting their knowledges, and have made invaluable contributions to science. Social work seeks to redress historic Western scientific colonialism and hegemony by listening to and learning from Indigenous peoples around the world. In this way social work knowledges will be co-created and informed by Indigenous peoples, and more appropriately practiced not only in local environments but also internationally. (ISWF 2021)

These statements by the IFSW clearly outline that social workers as a whole and across the globe have a responsibility for addressing the legacies of colonisation that have impacted upon Indigenous peoples regardless of where they originate from or where they are currently residing. Further to this, the IFSW acknowledges the importance of Indigenous knowledges, and that social work knowledges (theories and practices) need to incorporate Indigenous knowledges. I would argue that social work knowledges need to do more than incorporate Indigenous knowledges but rather need to be grounded in the Indigenous knowledges of the Indigenous peoples on which social work and the organisations where the social workers are being educated, trained and employed are based. However, to get to the point of discussing the implications for social work, we must first understand just what colonisation is and how it has occurred.

Colonisation

Colonisation was occurring long before British colonisation and what is termed 'modern colonisation', of which Britain is a part of, commenced in the 1500s with the Portuguese and the Spanish (Lima 2016; Engerman 2012). However, this chapter will focus on British colonisation due to the author's location being in Australia and being directly impacted upon by British colonisation. There are two main categories of colonisation, exploitative and settler. Exploitative colonisation is where the resources and wealth of a country that is being colonised were/are being exported to the coloniser or colonising country (Wolfe 1999). Those resources include food, minerals, animals and labour. The labour was provided through slavery, and slavery occurred both within the colonised country and was exported to other countries. People who were forced into slavery were sold and traded in the same way as the food, minerals and animals were. The coloniser sets up an administration to oversee its activities and to control the people whose country is being colonised. The administration was often backed up with military force to ensure that any resistance is stopped or prevented in the first place. Many exploitative colonies are today classified as 'third world countries' (Wolfe 1999).

Settler colonisation is similar in every aspect to exploitative colonisation but involves the transfer (migration) of people from the colonising country such as 'settlers' and in many cases convicts. The coloniser declares sovereignty over the colonised country and eventually that sovereignty is handed over to the descents of the original colonisers (Green 2014). America and Australia are two examples (there are many others, such as Canada and New Zealand) of settler colonies. The British attempted on two occasions to establish a permanent colony in Roanoke Island (off coast of North Carolina), the first in 1584 and the second in 1587, both ending disastrously (Rowse 1955). However, Britain then went on to establish 13 separate colonies within the Americas during the seventeenth and eighteenth centuries, commencing at Jamestown in 1607 (Taylor 2002). These colonies were known as the United Colonies and in 1776 became the Unites States of America (Taylor 2002). The colonies of America are an interesting example of a settler colony in that there are Indigenous peoples whose lands were invaded and colonised, the descendants of convicts, free settlers and the colonisers, as well as the descents of the people who were forced as slaves to go to America. Further to this America also became a colonising country, colonising other countries such as Hawaii in 1898 (Merry 2000). Furthermore, America took over the control of what had been Spanish colonies, including Cuba, Puerto Rico, Guam and Philippines following the Spanish-American war in 1898 (Smith 1994).

Australia is another British settler colony with the British invading in 1788 through the arrival of the first fleet, despite the fact that the British took possession in 1770 under the guise of Terra Nullius, a land belonging to no one (Green 2014). The early part of Australian colonisation was based around the transportation of convicts and the colony of New South Wales was formed in 1788, followed by Western Australia in 1825, South Australia in 1836, Port Philip (now Victoria) in 1851 and Queensland and Tasmania in 1859 (Rimer 1973). Originally the states of the Northern Territory and Australian Capital Territory were part of the colony of New South Wales. Australia became a federated country in 1901 (Grimshaw 2008). Similar to America, Australia had Britain declare its sovereignty and then hand that sovereignty over to the descendants of the original colonisers. The two countries are also similar in that their populations today are made up of the descendants of Indigenous peoples, convicts, settlers, slaves and those who have since migrated.

An interesting contrast between America and Australia is the acknowledgement of their involvement in slavery and the recognition of the descendants of whose arrival in the colonies was due to slavery. Whilst America recognises people who are the descendants of those who were slaves, Australia has a hidden history of slavery with even the current Prime Minister (at the time of writing) denying slavery occurred within the country (Koslowski 2020). Furthermore, the population of people who are descended from those forced to migrate to America is significantly higher than in Australia. People from the South Sea Islands were brought to Australia as slaves in the 1860s (Higginbotham 2017). Higginbotham (2017) estimates that as many as 62,000 people were forcibly brought from the South Sea Islands as slaves. Australia stopped importing slaves in 1901 following pressure from the British anti-slavery movement and Australia government order that South Sea Islanders be repatriated back to the South Sea Islands. The government legislated through The Pacific Island Labourers Act of 1901 that ordered the deportation of many of the 10,000 slaves or what they termed 'indentured labourers' (Higginbotham 2017). However, some descendants of those people brought to Australia as slaves have remained in Australia and today demand recognition (Higginbotham 2017).

Another noteworthy contrast between America and Australia is the roles of both countries within colonisation. As noted above, America went onto to also become a coloniser. Australia whilst not directly being a coloniser has a direct link in the colonisation of New Zealand. Within Captain Arthur Philips' instructions, the Islands adjunct to the east coast of Australian were included as part of the Colony of New South Wales, with a declaration being made in 1840 that formally extended the Colony of New South Wales to include New Zealand following the Treaty of Waitangi (Williams 1985). However, by 1841, New Zealand ceased to be part of the colony of New South Wales following the enactment of The Charter for Erecting the Colony of New Zealand (Simpson 2012).

An important comparison between exploitative colonies and settler colonies is that many exploitative colonies are today what is termed as 'third world countries' or 'developing countries, whilst many settler colonies are part of what is termed 'first world countries' or 'developed countries'. Despite the 'first world' status of these so-called 'developed' countries, Indigenous peoples are in general the most disadvantaged and marginalised populations within those countries today. In addition, those descendants of the people who were brought to settler colonies as slaves still experience high rates of discrimination and marginalisation as well. However, the same cannot be said about the descendants of convict populations, who very quickly were absorbed into the settler population and over time any negative connotation associated with having a convict history has disappeared. The history of colonisation and the current status of colonisation must be considered when examining the current socio-economic status within a country and also the status of particular groups of people. We need to ask how has colonisation impacted upon people, how has it created particular sets of circumstances for different groups of people and what does this mean for how social workers work to overcome the disadvantage and marginalisation without our societies today? As well, we need to consider the role of social work within colonisation and what responsibilities social workers have for addressing the problems that have come from colonisation? Furthermore, this leads us to consider the terminology we use for where we are currently situated within colonial history and the consequences of that terminology for how we see ourselves and the impact upon our current societies.

Post-colonial Theory

It is argued that post-colonial theory is a body of work that provides us with ways of understanding the impact of European colonial rule throughout the period of the eighteenth to twentieth century (Gandhi 1998; Sawant 2011). It is claimed that post-colonial theory is important, because it provides a space for those deemed to be 'colonised' to have a voice and to address the imbalance between those who are colonised and those who colonise. Bhabha explains that post-colonial studies developed from colonial experiences and provides a voice for those that have been disadvantaged by colonisation (1994). The rise of post-colonial theory began with the writings of theorist such as Fanon (1952, 1959, 1961), Freire (1972) and Said (1978) who all focused on providing the voice of the 'colonised' and speaking back to the 'coloniser'. However, exactly what is post-colonial theory and whether it can be generalised across all locations and times where European colonisation has taken place and across the different types of colonies are highly contentious.

There has been continuous work since the 1950s that forms post-colonial theory and the debates around colonialism and post-colonialism. Gandhi discusses how post-colonial theory has become a "meeting point and a battle ground for a variety of disciplines and theories" (1998 p. 3). Part of the debate about post-colonial theory is what Adesanmi see as an issue around the "geographical and institutional location of those who produce the knowledges which tend to be privileged as post-colonial" (2003 p. 177). Adesanmi is writing about concerns regarding the absence of African voices within post-colonial studies and goes on to quote Dirlik who states that post-colonial theory

> ... is intended, therefore, to achieve an authentic globalization of cultural discourses by extension globally of the intellectual concerns and orientations originating at the central sites of Euro-American cultural criticism and by introduction into the latter of voices and subjectivities from the margins of earlier political and ideological colonialism (2003 p. 178).

However, Zeleza (2006) argues that whilst it might be seen that African scholars are 'ambivalent or utterly hostile' towards post-colonial theory, they were still writing about decolonisation and the 'destruction and deconstruction of European hegemony'. Thus, rather than concluding that there is an absence of African voices within post-colonial studies, it should be seen that they are rejecting the notion of post-colonial as they are focused on decolonising their reality of imperialism and colonisation or what is termed as neo-colonisation. African writers such as Thiong'o (1992) argue that imperialism through neo-colonialism continues on in the 'economic, political, military, cultural and psychological consequences' throughout the world. On the other hand, another more recent African writer, Ndlovu-Gatsheni (2013) talks about a 'post-colonial neocolonized world', but whilst using the term post-colonial, he essentially continues to agree with Thiong'o that African is still dominated by the 'West' and this domination continues to impact on all aspects of African existence. So, whilst Ndlovu-Gastsheni uses the word post-colonial, he does not suggest that colonisation is something that is 'post' or in other words in the past, but rather a continuing active process that continues to dominate those who have been colonised. This is also argued by other writers whose lands and lives have experienced imperialism and colonisation such as Rao (2000) in India, Trees and Nyoongah (1993) in Australia and Mignolo (1997) in Argentina.

Another area of debate that has formed around post-colonial theory is about the term 'post-colonial' itself. Hall (in Mishra and Hodge 2005 p. 377) stated that:

> ... postcolonial is not the end of colonisation. It is after a certain kind of colonialism, after a certain moment of high imperialism and colonial occupation-in the wake of it, in the show of it, inflected by it-it is what it is because something else has happened before, but it is also something new.

Hall's claims to what post-colonial means, fits within what Sawant argues, which is that post-colonial studies are based on the premise that "the postcolonial means the period beginning with national independence in contrast to the colonial rule" (2011 p. 130). This would indicate that those colonies that are 'exploitive colonies' are the focus of post-colonial theory. Spivak and Said also both argued that the ongoing effects of colonialism continues well after the return to self-governance to the former colonies (Carey and Silverstein 2020 p. 3). Sawant highlights the difficulties with claiming a former colony as post-colonial by focusing on countries such as Nigeria and India which can be claimed to be post-colonial as they have obtained formal independence and freedom from Britain whilst also arguing that neo-colonialism is present due to colonialism still ruling the psychology of those countries and the people (2011 p. 130). However, there is a need to consider if post-colonial means decolonised and what exactly is decolonisation, which is discussed in the next section.

If post-colonial theory seems problematic for those former 'exploitative colonies', the issues are only heightened in so-called 'settler colonies', which are no longer seen as colonies, but as independent nation states. However, they lack the formal removal of the colonial power, but saw a transfer of power from the original colonisers to the descendants of the colonisers, whilst still using the same governing and administrative structures. Childs and Williams point out that one of the issues with claims of post-colonialism is that colonialism is persistent and that European control is still very present (1997 p. 5).

Post-colonial theorists who consider settler colonies such as Ashcroft, Griffiths and Tiffin explain that they use:

> ... the term "post-colonial". ... to cover all the cultures affected by the imperial process from the moment of colonization to the present day (Carey and Silverstein 2020 p. 3)

However, critics of this approach including McClintock who states that post-colonial theory is unable to account for the 'power differential between the colonisers and the colonised' and Wolfe who argues post-colonial theory generally has a "... monolithic, and generally unexamined, notion of colonialism" (Carey and Silverstein 2020 p. 4). Further when considering the application of post-colonial theory to settler colonies, Wolfe explains that the original theorists (such as Fanon, Freire, Hall and Said) were speaking from the position of being from exploitative rather than settler colonies and that post-colonial theory fails to acknowledge the fundamental differences between the two (Carey and Silverstein 2020 p. 4; Gandhi 1998). Roy further articulates the issues around this generalisation as:

> ... such claims of universalization of a theory that misreads historical difference as empirical variation, are part and parcel of a theory culture that reproduces Eurocentrism (2015 p. 205)

Roy concerns about post-colonial theory are also voiced by Childs and Williams who have a concern that post-colonial theory is by intellectuals who might be complicit with the coloniser (1997 p. 15). This concern is also voiced by Mignolo (1993 p. 131) who is concerned that colonial and post-colonial studies run the risk of "... exportation of theories, and internal (cultural) colonialism ...". A further concern is articulated by Araeen who argues that whilst post-colonial theory is supposed to be challenging "... dominant assumptions", it "has in fact reinforced those assumptions" (2000). There is a growing concern that post-colonial theory no longer is giving voice to the voiceless but rather has been an intellectual pursuit that sits separately to the lived realities of those who have been or are being colonised. Thus, the risk for post-colonial theory is that it is or it is becoming a tool of ongoing oppression and colonisation by creating an invisibility to the current realities of colonisation. Childs and Williams believe that there is a divide between those who are "'obvious[ly]' post-colonial" and where post-colonial status is unsettled by the continuing presence of 'white settlers' (1997 pp. 12–13). The presence of 'white settlers' would also account for the descendants of the original 'white settlers'. However, despite the differences between 'exploitative' and 'settler' colonies, colonisation still appears to be a very real and current day reality whether it be psychological as claimed by Sawant (2011) or through the ongoing occupation of Indigenous lands and a continuing colonial social relationship (Wolfe 1999). Therefore, it could be argued that it is not possible to even consider being post-colonial until decolonisation has occurred.

Decolonisation

Discussions about decolonisation can be seen as being linked to the decline in the British Empire's control over its colonies, or former colonies. Hopkins (2017) offers an understanding of decolonisation by stating that there have been two waves of decolonisation; the first with the creation of independent states within the Americans in the late eighteenth century and the second following World War 2 which resulted in a number of new states in Africa and Asia. However, Hopkins does not appear to have settler-colonies (with the exception of the Americas) within this understanding and whilst he does mention them, it is as "the old colonies of white settlement" (Hopkins 2017 p. 734). It would appear that whilst there is a recognition of the colonisation of those 'colonies of white settlement', there also appears to be an acceptance of them as now European nation states rather than colonised countries that have displaced Indigenous peoples or the positioning of Indigenous peoples within those so-called 'new' nation states.

Much like post-colonial studies, there are many debates around what is decolonisation and who or what should be decolonised. Many of these arguments mirror those of post-colonial theory. There are concerns about the voices of those who have been 'colonised' being lost in intellectual claims to the space, the impact at the time of colonisation, as well as the different types of colonisations and how all of these factors play out in decolonial theories. An interesting argument about who speaks within this space of decolonisation is presented when Moosavi warns about the pitfalls of 'intellectual decolonisation' within academia, and said that there is a difference between the 'global North' and the 'global South' whilst also arguing there is a risk of the 'global North' could actually enact 'intellectual colonisation' rather than dismantling it by ignoring the perspectives of the 'global South' (2020 p. 334). This argument is not focused on the rights of the 'colonised' to speak, but rather upon academics and the focus shifts from the 'colonisers' and the 'colonised' to the 'global North' and 'global South'. Moosavi concludes the article by stating that "... each decolonial scholar must ask themselves whether our decolonisation efforts are merely tokenistic ..." (2020 p. 350). Thus, as colonialism cannot been seen as just being about invasions, occupation and taking of resources, decolonisation cannot just be seen as the creation of a new nation state or shifting the governance and socio-economic structures but must also be the decolonisation of minds and bodies (Battiste in Wright 2001 p. 58). For Hack (2019 p. 832), decolonisation must not only be about building a new nation state but must be about building something new and distinct from the 'colonial inheritance' that is grounded in the language and culture of those who have experienced colonisation of their lands and being. In considering the role of language for decolonisation, Hall (1997) offer some interesting insights, in claiming that language and culture are linked and that they are linked to identity, belonging and knowledge. This illustrates the point that decolonisation cannot just be about the creation of a new (or replacement of) nation state but also must be able the minds of those colonised. However, Wright (2001 pp. 58–59) warns us that decolonisation is more about the 'coloniser' than the 'colonised' as it is more than just about mind and bodies, but also about the dominant power structures of the coloniser. So, it is important to look at decolonisation as being about the deconstruction of colonial power structures, the production of knowledge and the minds of both the 'colonised' and the 'coloniser'. These power structures, knowledge production and mindsets exist at every level within our societies. As articulated by Tuhiwai Smith, decolonisation is more than just handing back the governance of a country but it is also "... a long term process involving bureaucratic, cultural, linguistic, and psychological divesting of colonial power" (2012 p. 175). Thus, decolonisation needs to start with the individual, in decolonising their minds and hearts and move into the professions who then can advocate to governments to change the ways in which our societies keep perpetrating colonisation and colonialism.

Decolonisation is not just about Indigenous peoples, but about all people, as everyone is affected by colonisation, either benefitting from or being disadvantaged by the legacies and ongoing structures of colonisation. It also is not just in one time period or geographical location. Thus, the processes of decolonisation cannot be the same for all but need to be localised. There are many different aspects and justifications for colonisation, and in understanding the experiences and impact of colonisation upon different groups, it is important to consider the different ways in which colonisation has been implemented and the results of colonisation in different places and upon different groups of people. Foucault's work on power and coloniality has been criticised for failing to address the role of the 'West' as in geolocation as well as the role of capitalism in colonisation (Castro-Gomez 2021). Others have been concerned that the role of patriarchy has been overlooked both in terms as its role in colonisation and also its role in analysing colonial power structures (Spencer-Wood 2016). Quigano (2008), using the Latin American experience, defines coloniality as power relationships between race, class and gender. Further, Quigano also argues that race is a key element of coloniality and that coloniality is built upon hierarchies of race that still exist today (Udha 2021). Thus, the key role that race played and continues to play in colonisation and in all other areas of colonisation, including capitalism, cannot be ignored. Ashiagbor (2021 pp. 515–516) uses the term 'racial capitalism', which is argued to be directly link to slavery which in turn is linked to colonisation. Colonisation has impacted heavily upon Indigenous peoples in every aspect of their lives and that colonisation continues on and permeates every aspect of the lived experiences of Indigenous peoples.

Colonialism and the resulting neoliberal economic societies which for the most part we live within have at their bases the exploitation of natural resources (Pyles 2016). The exploitation of natural resources results not only in the inequality, oppression and disadvantage of Indigenous peoples but also impacts upon the living conditions of all people. Furthermore, so-called 'natural disasters' that the world is now living with are a direct result of the exploitation of natural resources. Globally we are living with the impact of climate change which has resulted in droughts, floods, fires, famine and disease. All of these are directly attributable to the way in which we currently live and the impact that we have upon the earth. Decolonisation must be focused on dismantling a global society that exists on the exploitation of 'natural resources' and of people and so focus upon ways of sustainable living, and based upon the knowledges and practices of the Indigenous peoples of each country and by country, meaning Indigenous Countries, not modern-day nation states that have been formed out of colonisation. Indigenous knowledges are local knowledges that can address how we should and must live in order to achieve social and environmental justice – in short, we must decolonise the way we think, feel and act. We must decolonise our present in order to live in a decolonised future. To do this, we must understand our past and tell the truth of what has happened and why. We must disrupt the silences that allow colonialism to continue to thrive in all its forms.

Implications for Social Work

As quoted in the introduction, the core mandate of social work is about social change, development, cohesion and the empowerment and liberation of people. Given that we live in a world that has been deeply impacted upon by colonisation and that people are still living with the effects of colonisation, then the social work profession has a responsibility to address the legacies and ongoing effects of colonisation. As argued within the section on post-colonial theory, colonisation has not ended and therefore social workers have a role in ending the ongoing colonisation that is continuing to disadvantage and marginalise people throughout the world. Further to this, social work as a profession needs to also examine its own roles within colonial practices and colonisation of particularly Indigenous people in order to decolonise as a profession.

Choate (2019) calls on social work:

> ... not only address its historical and current role in the colonisation ... but also deconstruct its practices.

Whilst there are many who have written and attempted to address the issues of colonisation and colonialism within social work theory and practice, social work practice continues to be embedded within colonialism (Fortier and Wong 2019; Libesman and Briskman 2018). Despite the growth of the social work profession across the global, theories and practices of social work are still grounded in Western theories and practices (Osei-Hwedie and Rankopo 2009; Gair et al. 2013; McNabb 2019). Hence social work has played a pivotal role in exacerbating the 'oppression and dispossession' of Indigenous people (Green and Baldry 2008). The IFSW clearly states (as outlined in the introduction) that social work acknowledges the part Western knowledges and theories have played in colonisation and the damage they have cause. Hence, those very same knowledges and theories have underpinned social work knowledge, theory and practice. Furthermore, social work acknowledges the importance of developing and reviewing knowledge, theory and practice.

Research is important to social work in order further develop the profession's knowledge and theory base, to provide evidence for particular fields of practice as well as highlighting areas that need resources and interventions, that research of based in Western methodologies and methods is still colonial. Rowe et al. (2015 p. 298) in their discussion on social work research argue that by using 'Indigenous knowledges, methodologies, and approaches to social work', it results in making visible how inadequate Western knowledges are when non-Indigenous researchers conduct research with Indigenous people. What is gained from research then in turns informs social work education and training which then produces social workers and their practice. Hence the very structures that formed the profession in turn reproduce the profession and so on. So basically, what we have is a profession that has been formed by the same structures that has produced and used colonialism to oppress people throughout the world and in turn has produced disadvantaged and marginalisation. However, that very same profession aspires to change societal structures in order to stop and prevent disadvantage and marginalisation.

The challenge here is how to stop and/or prevent something using the very thing that caused this problem in the first place. It is not possible unless you change what you use or, in the case of social work as a profession, you change the very foundations of your theory and practice. This sounds like a massive job to arrive at something completely new. However, it does not need something completely new, as Indigenous knowledges, theories and practices have existed since the beginning of time and Indigenous peoples have understood how to live well within their environment (social and natural). The biggest part of the job is changing the relationships between the profession and Indigenous peoples. It is essential to acknowledge that Indigenous people are not only clients of the social work profession, but there are many social workers who are Indigenous themselves. Indigenous social workers have been central to the acknowledgement of the need to decolonise social work theories and practices (Green and Bennett 2018). Thus, there is a basis for the individuals who make up the profession, social workers, to gain fundamental understandings of how to decolonise themselves and their practices and to work within a way that peruse justice for all.

However, there is not a single Indigenous knowledge, theory and practice that the international social work profession can grab and implement throughout the world or even based on a nation-by-nation bases. Indigenous people are very diverse, not just globally but within nations. Further to this whilst colonialism is rooted in the same ideologies, the initial invasions and many of the resulting practices have differed over time and location, even within the same nations. Thus, the ways to decolonise also need to differ and be developed at the local area. In fact, by working with Indigenous people at their local level, using local knowledges, theories and practices is in fact part of the process of decolonisation (Green and Bennett 2018; Choate 2019). It is important that social work education starts the process of decolonisation with the acknowledgement that colonisation is an ongoing process that continues to impact upon people and communities (Dumbrill and Green 2008).

However, it is important to move beyond acknowledgements and ensuring that social work education and training also decolonises both itself and its process. Frequently words and terms become catchphrases which everyone agrees are important but there is no shared understanding of what they mean or how to enact them. Decolonisation risks becoming another in a long line of phrases used when speaking about human rights and social justice. Tuck and Yang warn us that if decolonisation becomes just another metaphor, it actually "kills the very possibility of decolonization" (2012 p. 3). They further argue that decolonisation cannot be grafted onto other frameworks or discourses even if they are about rights and justice. This means that decolonisation and Indigenous knowledges are not something that can be picked up and used outside of their context. You cannot simply use one form of Indigenous knowledge and apply it to all Indigenous context nor can you seek to decolonise in one location and apply the same methods across all locations. However, the thinking and actions that are responsible for colonisation are all based in and on the same ideologies and thus decolonisation has the same starting point in disrupting those ideologies.

In addition, colonisation is also built upon global relationships (Tuck and Yang 2012). Hence, we must think and act globally and locally at the same time but being careful not to apply a 'one size fits all' thinking or model. McNabb (2019) calls on the regulatory bodies of social work, both globally and locally, to create ways in which social work education is developed to allow for decolonising practices. An essential step in decolonising is to ensure that social work education and training is developed using localised materials and that the curriculum and teaching methods fits the "local contexts against the long history of colonial and racial oppression" (Qalinge and van Breda 2017). However, working to decolonise social work education and training is only one part of the picture.

Whilst social work education and training is the starting point for social work practice, we have to ensure that social workers are able to practice and work within organisations that allow for them to advocate for decolonisation whilst not practicing in a way that is embedded within colonialism. As Pyles (2016) reminds us, we are still living in a world that is based in a neoliberal economic system, which has grown out of colonisation. The societal structures and thus governments, bureaucracies and organisations where social workers are employed are also embedded in coloniality. However, we have now reached another 'chicken and egg' type of scenario. How do we decolonise the places where social workers practice, in order to allow social workers to advocate and work towards decolonisation, when the call is for social workers to decolonise our societal structures that are embedded within the workplaces to begin with? This dilemma is also located within the very places that educate and train social workers, such as universities and within our professional bodies as well. Therefore, decolonisation is a personal and a professional process that has to occur alongside one and other, and social work must decolonise as a professional practice at the same time as social workers must decolonise as individuals and as a collective. One of the difficulties we face at this time is that whilst there has been a focus on decolonising social work education and training, it has been assumed that this would also transform social work practice. It is important that we start considering how we decolonise the very structures and places where social workers are employed and engaged to ensure that social workers are not working in isolation whilst trying to decolonise their workplaces and practices.

In many ways this chapter has raises many questions and provided very few answers. However, I do not make any apologises for this. Decolonisation is a process, not a single act, in the same way that colonisation has been a process and was/is not a single act. It is a journey that we must take and to ensure that we do this right, so as not to continue the marginalisation of people and of environment. Neither person nor environment can continue to be exploited if we are to ensure the sustainability of our lives here on earth. The only answer I can give you here that I know is true is that social work must take responsibility for working alongside Indigenous people to disrupt the ideologies and spaces that allow colonialism to continue to flourish and to work alongside Indigenous people to achieve decolonisation for us all. It is not a journey that anyone can travel alone because we are tied up in one way or another with colonialism and thus together, we must dismantle it.

My Perspective as a Wiradyuri yinaa (Woman)

This section is written from the perspective of a Wiradyuri woman who is also a social worker with many years of social work practice and also as a social work educator. Currently I do not formally write within a social work position. However, I believe that the work that I am currently doing still firmly sits within the field of social work practice. I am currently the course director for the Graduate Certificate of Wiradjuri Language, Culture and Heritage at a large regional university that sits on the lands (Country) of my people, the Wiradyuri people. The course is a partnership between Wiradyuri Elders and Charles Sturt University. It has won a number of national and international awards for the work that it does in the restoration and revitalisation of Wiradyuri language and in ensuring that Wiradyuri people have access to their language. The purpose for restoration our language in the words of Senior Elder, Dr. Uncle Stan Grant is that "We are rebuilding our language to heal the people" (2022). In rebuilding our language and healing the people, we are strengthening our culture and also healing country. For me as a social worker, this is the essence of social work practice and fits with both the Australian and the International Social Work Code of Ethics, mentioned earlier in this chapter. Furthermore, I am the Aboriginal and Torres Strait Islander Board Director on the Australian Association of Social Work, an elected position, that allows me to directly engage with the direction and aspirations of the profession of Social Work within Australia.

I started this chapter with an introduction to me that positioned myself and my views to assist the reader in understanding my perspective as the author of the chapter. In this section, I will share with you more about my perspective and how that is part of the process of decolonisation. However, before we start on that, I must firstly explain to you, the reader, about some terminology that I have used within this chapter and why. You might have noticed a slippage between using the terms 'colonised' and 'Indigenous people', which some might have found that confusing or annoying. However, I think it is important to use the language that those writing about colonisation, post-colonial and decolonisation have been and are using. For me, there is a link between colonisation and post-colonial theory in that the discourses are embedded within colonialism. Yes, I do acknowledge that people have been impacted differently depending upon whether they were part of the colonising group or those who were being colonised. However, it really isn't that simple. As all people are affected by colonialism, it is as much psychological as it is structural, so colonialism infects our minds and this allows the structures to go unchallenged or become normalised and accepted (Sayyid 2015; Bulhan 2015).

Furthermore, whilst I believe our minds can be infected with colonialism, our bodies can be imprisoned but not be colonised. The way I explain this is to consider a bird in a cage. Does the bird become the cage or is the bird imprisoned within the cage? I think most people would say the bird is still a bird and it does not become the cage – they are two separate things. Now when the door of the cage is opened the bird has a choice, it can either fly away or it can stay in the cage. If a bird has been in the cage for long enough, it frequently stays in the cage, or it might leave briefly and return in order to be fed and watered. The bird might feel that its captor is its protector and friend, as the one who provides for it, and maybe the bird likes the cage that has been provided for it and no longer see itself as being captured. However, this still does not make the bird the cage, but rather the bird accepts its situation and may even feel comfortable in it. People are much like the bird. Colonisation is our cage, we are trapped and dependent upon our captors; our cage might be quite comfortable or more comfortable than the unknown. It might be thought that in order to decolonise, we are walking into the unknown, to the strange and possibly threatening but this is not the case. What is known is that Indigenous people lived sustainably for a very long time. Whilst at times this might be disputed, the fact that it is for much longer than colonisation cannot be denied. To live sustainably will mean that we have to change the way we live. However, as we continue onwards, the reality of our current lives cannot provide us with a false sense of security anymore. We must act and act fast, and we do not need to produce new knowledges or practices but to return to what worked for a very long time, tens of thousands of years if not hundreds of thousands of years.

For me that knowledge is embedded within the Wiradyuri cosmology (Grant and Rudder 2014), which is the foundation for everything Wiradyuri. I must clearly and firmly state at this point, that Wiradyuri cosmology is only one of the many Indigenous Cosmologies that exist within the world and whilst I share this with you, it is not possible to take it and transplant it in another location. To attempt to do so firstly takes it out of context and then it is no longer what holds its meaning and secondly it becomes colonialism; you must engage with the Indigenous people within your location to learn their cosmology, but again if you are not an Indigenous person or an Indigenous people from another area, you cannot just take this knowledge and re-present it and take control of it. The Wiradyuri cosmology or foundations for all of Wiradyuri life and being is holistic, and whilst when we explain the cosmology, we break it down into five parts, and none of these parts exist within the others or as a single part. In much the same way as we talk about our body, we might speak about a particular part of our body, but it is not separate to the rest of our body. There is also no order in which the parts of the cosmology nor significance being more or less for any parts. Each part is interconnected to all other parts and in speaking about one part, you are speaking about the whole. I will talk about the cosmology in the way that most makes sense for me, but this does not mean it will make sense for another Wiradyuri person in this way or even for you the reader, it just does for me and the way my mind works.

In the Wiradyuri cosmology, relationships are the bases for everything, as everything is in relationship with all else, people to people, people to animals, people to land, animals to land, water to people, water to sky, sky to people and so on. Relationship also exists over time, the past to the present and the future, the future to the present and the past, the present to the past and the future and so on. Relationships are something that are not new or newly formed; they have always existed. I have a relationship with you that not only now exists through you reading what I have written, I have a relationship with you before even though we might not have ever had any connection that we are aware of. I have a relationship with my ancestors and they with me; I have a relationship with my future descendants and they already have that relationship with me. At no point does anything never exist and at no point does it ever ceases to exist – it is always in existence, whether we know it or not, whether we can see it or not, it still exists.

Relationships gives us our identities and we can only understand and know ourselves and each other through those identities. Identities are different depending upon where we are at a particular point of time and what our relationship is with who or what we are with. Country makes me human and my belonging to it makes me Wiradyuri. I am a mother through my relationship with my children; I am a grandmother through my relationship with my grandchildren; I am a daughter to my father and a granddaughter to my grandmothers. My grandmothers are still my grandmothers despite one dying 55 years before I was born and the other dying when I was in my mid-20s. My ancestors are still my grandmothers and grandfathers no matter when they walked the earth as humans and I will still be a grandmother to generations to come after I no longer inhabit a human body. I will still exist; I will still have those relationships that give me my identities.

Our identities and relationships then form our focus. Our focus is what gives us structure and determines what we believe and what we see as reality and as important. Our focus also determines the nature of our relationships and which identities we give priority over others, and it shapes what we see as important. For me, my identity as Wiradyuri shapes and forms my focus, which in turns shapes and informs my actions. Actions are the outward workings of our relationships, identities and focus. How we act with one person will be very different to who we act with another, and the time and place will also determine our relationships, our identities and our actions. All actions have a reaction or consequence, and as Wiradyuri, we do not believe anything ever changes but transforms, and this transformation informs our relationships, identities, focus and actions, and thus it continues over time and space.

Another way to explain this is that when you are born, you did not just begin to exist. You existed inside your mother as she carried you, your body existed in the eggs that you mother hold in her body which also existed in her mother's body as the eggs your mother carried already existed within the egg that formed her body. Thus, your existence was always there, within the bodies of your ancestor grandmothers. However, your body is just the physical shell that carries you and the core of who you are is not seen but exists inside. Some people call this 'spirits' and this is the English word that Wiradyuri also use today. However, the spirits are our ancestors and they are also our future generations. So, when you are formed in your mothers' body, your spirit enters the human body being formed. You are born into the world as a baby and as you grow you transform from a baby, to a toddler, to a child and if you live long enough to an elderly person, before your body dies and you transform back to the spirit world. The core of who you are never changes, it always remains. This also can be used to consider the whole notion of 'colonised peoples', colonisation did not change the person but rather transformed the world in which we live and as we are in a constant state of transformation, moving back and forth in our relationships, identities, focus and actions that in turn results in transformation. Thus, for me, colonisation is an action that came about through the focus of certain groups of men who wanted to dominate and exploit the earth and its people and those actions created a relationship of domination and subservience which can be transformed by bringing back balance to those relationships between people and between people and Country.

Wiradyuri have a phrase, Yindyamarra Winhanganha, whose understanding can be gained through the words. Yindyamarra means respect, honour, be polite, do slowly and be gentle (Grant and Rudder 2010 p. 485). This word lets us know how we should behave and live. As well if you break down the word and look at the 'marra', it is an action to make or cause something to happen (Grant and Rudder 2010 p. 405), which clearly tells us that you have to act in order to have or give respect, and it is not just something that occurs. Windhanganha means to know, think and remember (Grant and Rudder 2010 p. 469), which tells us that we do know how to be respectful, we just have to remember what we already know. Yindyamarra Windhanganha tell us that we have to slow down, show respect and live gently within the world and with each other. In order to decolonise, we must follow Yindyamarra Winhanganha in all our relationships with all else and in all our actions – the way in which we live.

As outlined at the start of this chapter, the International Federation of Social Work clearly outlines that social work and thus social workers must "... listen to and learn from Indigenous people around the world ..." (2021) in order to decolonise social work practice at both the local and international levels.

Conclusion

We currently live in a world that is in crisis and a growing crisis that threatens every aspect of our lives. This crisis did not simply occur but was created out of the way in which we live today. Our lives today are a direct result of the colonisation that has occurred over the last four centuries and the earth has been terribly harmed through this. Whilst colonisation has occurred in different ways at different times and places, the harm is the same, and we must act to not only stop further harm but to allow the world to heal. Social work is mandated as a profession to work alongside Indigenous people to take up the challenge of disrupting the colonialism that is embed globally within our societal structures and to work towards decolonising our world. There are many Indigenous social workers across the globe, but it is not their responsibility to always be the ones speaking out about colonialism or working to deconstruct the colonial structures that are embedded within social work theory and practice. It is important that non-Indigenous social workers and the social work profession take on decolonisation as its priority in order to address the social inequalities and injustices around the globe. However, in order to decolonise, social work must also work to actively decolonise the professional through the decolonisation of its practitioners and its own structures and practices. We cannot live in a post-colonial world until we have first decolonised.

References

Adesanmi P (2003) Africa, India and the Postcolonial: Notes Towards a Praxis of Infliction. Arena Journal (21):173–196. https://search.informit.org/doi/10.3316/informit.240930986172681

Araeen R (2000) A new beginning. Beyond postcolonial cultural theory and identity politics. Third Text 14(50):3–20

Ashiagbor D (2021) Race and colonialism in the construction of labour markets and precarity. Ind Law J 5(4):506–531

Bhabha HK (1994) The location of culture. Routledge, London

Bulhan H (2015) Stages of colonialism in Africa: from occupation of land to occupation of being. J Soc Polit Psychol 3(1):239

Carey J, Silverstein B (2020) Thinking with and beyond settler colonial studies: new histories after the postcolonial. Postcolonial Stud 23(1):1–20

Castro-Gomez S (2021) Michel Foucault and the coloniality of power. Cultural Studies. https://www-tandfonline-com.ezproxy.csu.edu.au/doi/full/10.1080/09502386.2021.2004435. Accessed 02 Feb 2022

Childs P, Williams P (1997) An introduction to post-colonial theory. Prentice Hall, London

Choate PW (2019) The call to decolonise: social work's challenge for working with Indigenous peoples. Br J Soc Work 49:1081–1099

Dumbrill GC, Green J (2008) Indigenous knowledge in the social work academy. Soc Work Educ 27(5):489–503

Engerman SL (2012) Colonisation and development. Econ Hist Dev Reg 27(1):28–40

Fanon F (1952) Black skin, white masks. Plato Press, Manchester

Fanon F (1959) A dying colonialism. Grove Books, New York

Fanon F (1961) The wretched of the Earth. Grove Books, New York

Fortier C, Wong EH (2019) The settler colonialism of social work and the social work of settler colonialism. Settler Colonial Stud 9(4):437

Freire P (1972) Pedagogy of the oppressed. Herder and Herder, New York

Gair S, Miles D, Thomson J (2013) Reconciling Indigenous and non-Indigenous knowledges in social work education: action and legitimacy. J Soc Work Educ 41(2):179

Gandhi L (1998) Postcolonial theory: a critical introduction. Allen & Unwin, New York

Grant S (2022) Personal communication. 19th January 2022. Narrandera NSW

Grant S, Rudder J (2010) A New Wiradjuri Dictionary. Restoration House, Wagga Wagga
Grant S, Rudder J (2014) A grammar of Wiradjuri language. Restoration House, Wagga Wagga
Green S (2014) The history of Aboriginal welfare in the colony of NSW. 1788–1856. University of New South Wales. Unpublished thesis
Green S, Baldry E (2008) Building Indigenous Australian social work. Aust Soc Work 61(4):389–402
Green S, Bennett B (2018) Wayanha: a decolonised social work. Aust Soc Work 71(3):261–264
Grimshaw P (2008) Federation as a turning point in Australian history. Aust Hist Stud 33(118):25
Hack K (2019) Unfinished decolonisation and globalisation. Decolonisation and globalisation. J Imperial Commonw Hist 47(5):818–850
Hall S (1997) The work of representation. Chapter 1. In: Hall S (ed) Representation. Cultural representations and signifying practices. The Open University, London
Higghinbotham W (2017) Blackbirding: Australia's history of luring, tricking and kidnapping South Sea Islanders. ABC News. https://www.abc.net.au/news/2017-09-17/blackbirding-australias-history-of-kidnapping-pacific-islanders/8860754. Accessed 17 Feb 2021
Hopkins AG (2017) Globalisation and decolonisation. J Imperial Commonw Hist 45(5):729–745
HREOC (1997) Bringing them home. Report of the national inquiry into the separation of Aboriginal and Torres Strait Islander children from their families. Commonwealth of Australia
International Federation of Social Workers (2021) Global definition of social work. https://wwwifsworg/what-is-social-work/global-definition-of-social-work/. Accessed 21 Apr 2021
Koslowski M (2020) 'It's just denial': Bruce Pascoe, labor condemn PM's 'no slavery in Australia' claim. The Sydney Morning Herald. https://www.smh.com.au/politics/federal/it-s-just-denial-bruce-pascoe-labor-condemn-pm-s-no-slavery-in-australia-claim-20200611-p551jo.html. Accessed 26 Apr 2021
Libesman T, Briskman L (2018) Indigenous Australians: continuity of colonialism in law and social work. In: Rice S, Day A, Briskman L (eds) Social work in the shadow of law, 5th edn. The Federation Press
Lima LFS (2016) Between the new and the old world: Ilberian prophecies and imperial projects in the colonisation of the early modern Spanish and Portuguese Americas. In: Crome A (ed) Prophecy and eschatology in the transatlantic world, 1550–1800. Christianities in the trans-Atlantic world, 1500–1800. Palgrave Macmillan, London
McNabb D (2019) Decolonising social work education in Aotearoa New Zealand. Adv Soc Work Welf Educ 21(1):35–50
Merry SE (2000) Colonizing Hawai'i. The cultural power of law. Princeton University Press, Princeton
Mignolo WD (1993) Colonial and postcolonial discourse: cultural critique or academic colonialism? Lat Am Res Rev 28(3):120–134
Mignolo WD (1997) Coloniality is far from over, and so must be decolonity. Afterall 43:39–45
Mishra V, Hodge B (2005) What was postcolonialism? N Lit Hist 36:375–402
Moosavi L (2020) The decolonial bandwagon and the dangers of intellectual decolonisation. Int Rev Sociol 30(2):332–354
Ndlovu-Gatsheni (2013) Coloniality of Power in Postcolonial Africa. Myths of Decolonization. Council for Development of Social Science Research in Africa. Angle Canal. ISBN: 978-2-86978-578-6
Osei-Hwedie, Rankopo (2009) Developing culturally relevant social work education in Africa: the case of Botswana. In: Coates J, Gray M (eds) Indigenous social work around the world. Routledge, London
Pyles L (2016) Decolonising disaster social world: environmental justice and community participation. Br J Soc Work 47(3):630–647
Qalinge L, van Breda AD (2017) Decolonising social work in South Africa. Report on the 2017 social work conference held at OR Tambo Conference Centre from 8–11 October 2017. Association of South African Social Work Education Institutions, Johannesburg. S Afr J Soc Work Soc Dev 30(1). https://upjournals.co.za/index.php/SWPR. Accessed 1 May 2021

Quigano A (2008) Coloniality of power, eurocentrism and Latin America. In: Morana M, Dussel E, Jauregui CA (eds) Coloniality at large: Latin America and the postcolonial debate. Duke University Press, Durham, pp 181–224

Rao N (2000) "Neocolonialism" or "Globalization"?: postcolonial theory and the demands of political economy. Interdiscip Lit Stud 1(2):165–184

Rimer PJ (1973) The search for spatial regularities in the development of Australian seaports 1861–1961/2. Chapter 5. In: Hoyle BS (ed) Transport and development. Macmillan, London

Rowse AL (1955) American Colonisation. In: The Expansion of Elizabethan England. Palgrave Macmillan, London. https://doi.org/10.1057/9780230597136_6

Rowe S, Baldry E, Earles W (2015) Decolonising social work research: learning from critical Indigenous approaches. Aust Soc Work 68(3):296

Roy A (2015) Who's afraid of postcolonial theory? Int J Urban Reg Res. https://onlinelibrary-wiley-com.ezproxy.csu.edu.au/doi/abs/10.1111/1468-2427.12274. Accessed 20 Apr 2021

Said E (1978) Orientalism. Routledge & Kegan Paul, London

Sawant D (2011) Perspectives on post-colonial theory: Said, Spivak and Bhabha. Lit Endeavour 2:129–135

Sayyid S (2015) Colonialism is a state of mind. In theory, opinion. Washing Post. https://www.washingtonpost.com/news/in-theory/wp/2015/11/13/colonialism-is-a-state-of-mind/. Accessed 12 Dec 2021

Simpson T (2012) The immigrants: the great migration from Britain to New Zealand 1830–1890. Penguin Random House, Auckland

Smith J (1994) The Spanish-American War 1895–1902. Conflict in the Caribbean and the Pacific. Routledge, London

Spencer-Wood S (2016) Feminist theorizing of patriarchal colonialism, power, dynamics, and social agency materialized in colonial institutions. Int J Hist Archaeol 20(3):477–491

Taylor A (2002) American colonies: the settling of North America. The penguin history of the United States, vol 1. https://books.google.com.au/books?hl=en&lr=&id=-wY5FQBSH7UC&oi=fnd&pg=PT10&dq=American+colonies:+The+settling+of+North+America&ots=G1SHRM4l9O&sig=OtMegYWIEtWtEa3JHvh9GtqD-rA&redir_esc=y#v=onepage&q=American%20colonies%3A%20The%20settling%20of%20North%20America&f=false. Accessed 1 May 2021

Thiong'o NW (1992) Decolonising the mind: the politics of language in African literature. Currey, J. U Heinemann, N H, London

Trees K, Nyoongah M (1993) Postcolonialism: yet another colonial strategy? e-Spania 1(36):264–265

Tuck E, Yang KW (2012) Decolonization is not a metaphor. Decolonization: Indigeneity Educ Soc 1(1):1–40

Tuhiwai Smith L (2012) Decolonising methodologies: research and Indigenous peoples, 2nd edn. Zed Books, London

Udha H (2021) Coloniality of power and international students experience: what are the ethical responsibilities of social work and human educators? Ethics Soc Welf 15(1):84–99

Williams DV (1985) The annexation of New Zealand to New South Wales in 1840: what of the treaty of Waitangi? Aust J Law Soc 2:41–55

Wolfe P (1999) Settler colonialism and the transformation of anthropology. The politics and poetics of an ethnographic event. Cassell, London

Wright S (2001) International human rights, decolonisation and globalisation. Becoming human. Routledge, London

Zeleza PT (2006) The troubled encounter between postcolonialism and African history. J Can Hist Assoc 17(2):89–129

Post-anthropocentric Social Work

Transformative Philosophy for Contemporary Theory and Practice

Karen Bell

Contents

Introduction	122
The Global Context of Contemporary Social Work	122
The Anthropocene and Mainstream Social Work	124
Post-anthropocentric Transformation	127
Post-anthropocentric Social Work	127
Transformative Processes, Challenges, and Implications	130
Some Further Considerations for Post-anthropocentric Social Work	134
Chapter Summary and Conclusion	136
References	137

Abstract

Social work, as a profession and as an academic discipline, is based on principles of respect for diversity, equity, beneficence, non-maleficence, and collective responsibility. Through critical reflection on systems of structural oppression, social work aims to resist oppression through transformative action and to work for sustainable improvements to wellbeing and justice for all. From an affirmative, creative, and hopeful stance, this chapter explores post-anthropocentrism and posthumanism as transformative paradigms for evolving contemporary social work. Before engaging with these paradigms, the modernist, anthropocentric foundations of conventional mainstream social work are considered in the context of persistent global inequities and injustices. A rationale for the transformation of social work is then articulated as the foundation for a reimagined future for the evolving profession, beyond the Anthropocene. Using relational ethics as a compass, key aspects of transformative social work are conceptualised drawing from post-anthropocentric and critical posthumanist theory. To close the chapter,

K. Bell (✉)
School of Social Work and Arts, Charles Sturt University, Wagga Wagga, NSW, Australia
e-mail: kbell@csu.edu.au

some broader implications are explored including the possibilities as well as challenges for post-anthropocentric social work in the twenty-first century.

Keywords

Post-anthropocentric theory · Posthumanist · Transformative social work paradigm · Ecosocial work · Philosophy of social work · Relational ethics

Introduction

As articulated in the International Federation of Social Workers' (IFSW) *Global Agenda for Social Work and Social Development* (Truell and Jones 2020), contemporary social work aims to address inequality and injustice, to respectfully engage with Indigenous knowledges, and work towards environmental sustainability for all. To achieve these unifying, emancipatory aims, the profession must continue to critically reflect on and further develop its philosophical base to ensure its foundations are fit for such transformative practice. As many have argued, social work must challenge itself and transcend theories and practices that are at odds with these emancipatory aims. Specifically, the profession needs to evolve beyond over-reliance on paradigms founded on hierarchies, divisiveness, disembodiment, and dominance to ensure that social work is characterised more often as a catalyst for social change and less often as an agent of social control (Bell 2012; Bozalek and Pease 2021; Chigangaidze et al. 2022; Clarke 2021).

To explore the possibilities for transformative social work practice in the twenty-first century, this chapter begins by describing some of the major global challenges facing us all and outlining how these challenges have largely emerged from the anthropocentric paradigm. Key features of the anthropocentric paradigm are then discussed, and dominant forms of social work are located as a product of the Anthropocene. Considering the impacts of the Anthropocene's intersecting systems of oppression, and in light of the profession's core values, the case for the evolution of social work towards post-anthropocentric theory and practice is presented. Transformative processes are also articulated along with some of the potential challenges, opportunities, and implications of post-anthropocentric transformation in social work.

It is important to note that this chapter is written by an author located on the unceded land of the Australian First Nations Wiradjuri people, and to acknowledge and pay respect to the wisdom of Elders past, present and future.

The Global Context of Contemporary Social Work

At the time of writing this chapter, political volatility, disinformation, and violent conflicts within and between nation states continue to escalate across the planet (Amnesty International 2022). These human-induced social disasters occur against a backdrop of intensifying human-induced environmental disasters and pervasive global warming – creating an "omnicrisis" (Nissen and Scheyett 2021 p. 5). The COVID-19 pandemic, despite initial expressions of togetherness and 'building back better', has exacerbated inequality and instability rather than systematically reducing it (Amnesty International 2022 p. ix). As an illustration of the "grotesque manifestation of inequality", during the first 2 years of the pandemic, it is reported that 99% of humanity experienced a decline in income, whereas the world's ten wealthiest individuals – all of them male – experienced a doubling of their already extreme fortunes (Oxfam 2022 as cited in Ioakimidis and Maglajlic 2022 p. 605). What can be done to disrupt this "heteropatriarchal capitalist status quo" (Hamilton et al. 2021 p. 237)? It is not an overstatement to claim that humankind has brought itself to brink of destruction – there are big problems on this small blue planet.

In a report by the Intergovernmental Panel on Climate Change (IPCC 2022 p. 6), climate change and its impacts on ecosystems, biodiversity and human society are described as "increasingly severe, interconnected and often irreversible". Further, the IPCC report highlights the need to mobilise multidisciplinary knowledge from the natural, ecological, social and economic sciences as well as Indigenous and local knowledge, to build a future in which equity, justice and health can flourish – human health, ecosystem health and planetary health.

The social work profession's commitment to the global aims of the United Nations' (UN) Sustainable Development Goals (SDGs; UN 2015) is described by the International Federation of Social Workers (IFSW 2021). The IFSW identifies three intersecting foci for transformative change – social, economic, and ecological – and the ways in which they align with the profession's collective commitment to act for justice, diversity, and equity for all (IFSW 2014, 2021). However, it must also be noted that progress on achieving sustainable, socially just outcomes is threatened by escalating crises and widening global inequities, which in turn have been further exacerbated by the COVID-19 pandemic (Hujo and Kempf 2021). These "dire effects of anthropogenic processes on the planet" (Noble 2021 p. 95) highlight pre-existing inequalities in human society and the urgent need for pacific, relational approaches for the good of all. As Truell (2022 p. 19) states, "with climate change, the failing global economy, increased military actions and a worldwide pandemic, it is again time for the profession to promote change based on our longstanding and tested ethics and values".

Through everyday social work practice, social workers are well aware of the brutal, multifaceted local and global impacts of inequality on individuals, groups, and communities and the need for social work to work be part of a community of professions tackling inequalities (Ioakimidis and Maglajlic 2022). Due to the breadth of the social work domain, the profession has the capacity to contribute to multidisciplinary efforts towards global health, justice, and equity.

The pressing need for transformational change does, however, raise challenges for social work. The profession must continue to work for structural change to address intersecting, compound risks and concurrently, the profession must engage in "futures thinking" to accelerate the evolution of "thinking, practices and capabilities" for transdisciplinary, equity-centred practice (Nissen and Scheyett 2021 p. 6).

A predominantly "business as usual approach" will only keep us all on the same destructive trajectory.

The profession of social work is typically enacted within contexts dominated by neoliberal discourse, under-resourced welfare service systems and increasingly market-oriented, privatised models of service provision (McGregor 2021). Considering the complexities of the contexts in which social work practice occurs and the different levels of social work engagement, the profession is well-positioned to contribute to multidimensional, creative efforts for change. However, to achieve this the profession needs an accommodating, flexible paradigm for creative, critically reflective theory and practice (McGregor 2021).

Before considering some of the transformative possibilities for post-anthropocentric social work, it is important to explore the modernist, anthropocentric foundations of mainstream social work in more detail and in particular, the fundamental limitations of anthropocentrism and humanism. Through greater awareness of these limitations and linearities, the possibilities for innovation, flexibility, and creativity open-up as a basis for future social work, beyond the Anthropocene.

The Anthropocene and Mainstream Social Work

Dominant forms of conventional social work emerged from modernist Euro-Western, industrialised contexts – a "narrow ancestry" of "Western colonial ontology" (Clarke 2021 p. 2). This period of existence characterised by the "overwhelming influence of humans (read: man) upon the earth", the "uneven hand of capitalism and ... environmental disasters" has also been described as the Anthropocene (Noble 2021 pp. 100–101). The Anthropocene is a term representing a geological era through which the Earth's ecological balance has become increasingly directly regulated by humans (Braidotti 2013).

Anthropocentrism and humanism are central pillars of the modernist paradigm. Anthropocentric ontology positions humans at the supreme centre of all existence and foregrounds human interests above all else (Braidotti 2013). Anthropocentrism constructs humans as exceptional and entitled – as the dominant species in relation to the natural environment and to all other living non-human beings (Braidotti 2019). Within this paradigm, ethical value is human-centred while non-human living things and the physical environment do not necessarily have intrinsic value – any value ascribed to non-human living things and the environment is ascribed by humans with reference to human interests (Kopnina et al. 2018). This central "binary division of nature and society" also ontologically positions humans at the epicentre of existence, as individual, independent subjects focused on competition and dominance over all else (Haraway 2016 p. 50). This construction is problematic because it undermines relationality and the intrinsic interconnectedness and interdependence of all living and non-living things – that is humans, non-human living things and the physical environment (Noble 2021).

Anthropocentrism is grounded in liberal humanism which likewise constructs humans as autonomous, self-determining individuals and as "nature's most precious subject" (Webb 2021 p. 19). An important aspect of humanist discourse is that it also privileges some categories of humans over others, with male humans – especially white, Western, able-bodied males who align with hegemonic heterosexual masculine ideals – as the "universal human" at the top of the hierarchy of unearned privilege (Pease 2021 p. 108). Within this gendered, racialized species hierarchy, all "others" are positioned in relation to the "supreme ontological entitlement" of the hegemonic male, and "others" are seen to be negatively different (Braidotti 2013 p. 68). Further, this divisive patriarchal order is a tool of governance that situates hegemonic males as disembodied and independent, in a position of masculinist mastery over subordinate 'other' humans, non-human living things and the natural environment (Braidotti 2013; Hamilton et al. 2021; Plumwood 1994).

The constant interplay between anthropocentrism and humanism sustains a series of entangled, mutually reinforcing binaries between humans and the natural environment, as well as hierarchical dichotomies between categorised humans. Hierarchical dualisms such as male-female, mind-body, culture-nature, white-non-white, able-disabled (and others) form a "polarised logic of Western thought" and are "the backbone" of the epistemology of the modernist paradigm (Noble 2021 p. 100). These anthropocentric and humanist ontologies are the foundations of inequitable socio-political and economic systems, cultural practices and the privileged access to resources afforded to those in dominant positions. As such, anthropocentrism and humanism are at the heart of sexism, racism, able-ism, colonialism, and other persistent forms of oppression; they have "colonised our imagination" regarding alternative worldviews, philosophies, and transformative practices (Noble 2021 p. 102).

The embeddedness of anthropocentric views often makes it difficult to imagine other ways of being and other possibilities as cultural practices, historical accounts, knowledge-creation, and languages (etcetera) reflect and reinforce anthropocentrism. As Blackstock notes, this colonisation of imagination not only impacts on creative capacities, it also "substantially interferes" with our ability to break through the "white noise barrier" making it difficult at times to "see negative outcomes resulting directly or indirectly from our works" (Blackstock 2009 p. 28).

Within the Anthropocene, the dominant socio-cultural, political context is characterised by a social contract based on explicit and implicit rights and obligations between governments and citizens including accountability and the rule of law, legitimacy, social security, and social order (Hujo and Kempf 2021). The anthropocentric framing of this social contract means that the natural environment is rendered invisible; there is no inherent obligation to protect the planet's finite resources and the natural systems of which humans are a part. The ideals underpinning the rights and obligations of the liberal-humanist social contract have also been consistently eroded by anthropocentrism's intersecting systems of oppression and hierarchical androcentric social ordering resulting in racism, sexism, colonialism, able-ism, other forms of discrimination, unearned privilege, and disconnectedness from the natural environment. This hierarchical social order has resulted in an uneven distribution of material wealth, evidenced by persistent wage disparities and embedded advantages of some over others and the entrenched marginalisation of Indigenous knowledge and practices (Hujo and Kempf 2021).

The provision of public welfare services as an enactment of the traditional, modernist social contract has also been steadily unravelling since the 1980s as neo-liberalism gained traction. This has resulted in increased reliance on market mechanisms over communal mechanisms and universal models of practice in health, education, and welfare. Globalisation, debt crises, entrenched inequality, and austerity policies have exacerbated this shift. In addition, through a range of unsustainable practices the natural environment is in a state of devastation, due to rampant consumption, over-production, unrelenting extraction of the planet's finite resources, pollution, dispossession, and failure to protect biodiversity (Hujo and Kempf 2021). Braidotti (2019 p. 42) describes the inherent unsustainability of anthropocentrism as a "toxic habit" of "eating up the future" – of depleting the ecosystem in which we all co-exist (Braidotti 2013). Likewise, Kopnina et al. (2018 p. 123) identify anthropocentrism as a profoundly demeaning paradigm, lacking capacity to lead us into a sustainable future and as "clearly a significant driver of ecocide and environmental crisis ... without considering that humanity is (in the end) fully dependent on nature".

Despite its inherent hierarchies and significant limitations, the anthropocentric paradigm remains as a pervasive presence permeating the dominant discourse of conventional social work theory and practice (Bell 2012; Clarke 2021; Coates and Gray 2018). This implicates the profession as part of these anthropocentric practices, raising major challenges for social work in relation to its transformative aspirations (Pease and Bozalek 2021; Ross et al. 2021). To address this, social work must continue to engage in a "collective professional shift" if it is to move beyond the status quo, learn from and ultimately transcend its complicity in practices of state-sanctioned social control, settler colonialism, and Euro-centric norms (Morgenshtern et al. 2022 p. 2). Social work needs to "decolonize the single-story narrative of the profession" through better understanding of localised knowledge and Indigenous knowledge (Clarke 2021 p. 5). The profession must also actively attend to its evolving philosophy and conceptual foundations to ensure they are consistent with the profession's commitment to justice, peace, sustainability and equity. An underexplored, prevailing paradigm founded on the inherent injustices, dominance, linearity, and inequities of anthropocentrism is plainly incongruent with the profession's radical aspirations.

The dominance of anthropocentric thinking and modernism as reference points for conventional social work also reinforces the over-reliance on individualised practice and obscures the focus on structural issues, placing it at odds with core professional values of contemporary global social work, such as relationality, respect, equity, and justice (Chigangaidze 2022; Jaswal and Kshetrimayum 2022; Krings et al. 2020). Given the complexity of the contemporary global context of social work practice, there is a persuasive rationale for a collective paradigmatic shift to ensure the profession's radical aims align with its philosophical foundations.

Post-anthropocentric Transformation

Before focusing on the transformative possibilities of the post-anthropocentric paradigm for contemporary social work, it is useful to consider the meaning of transformation itself and what distinguishes change as transformational as opposed to merely superficial, or cosmetic change. At the broad societal level, the three main drivers for transformative, post anthropocentric change are escalating global inequalities, the climate crisis, and increasingly unstable political systems (Hujo and Kempf 2021). Transformative approaches aim to achieve radically different outcomes; they aim to address the root causes of inequality, poverty, and unsustainability, whereas cosmetic change temporarily ameliorates the symptoms of underlying oppression without an explicit focus on underlying factors that generate and reproduce inequities. Thus, transformative approaches inspire hope "for breaking vicious cycles of inequality and oppression – people, the environment, the whole planet" by addressing the drivers of oppression rather than engaging in "endless palliative, patchwork and ad hoc approaches" (United Nations Research Institute for Social Development – UNRISD 2016 pp. 32–34). Transformation requires individual effort as well as collective effort – it is achieved through multilevel action for change at political, institutional, social, practical and conceptual levels. Transformation is not necessarily a smooth, linear path but rather a more nuanced, often patchy effort moving at varying speeds at various times.

The UNRISD (2016 p. 266) guidelines for transformative change highlight the need for a paradigm shift towards post-anthropocentrism to make the economy work for society as a whole and not mostly for a privileged few. The UNRISD argues that the focus of human effort should be on "planetary health and sustainability" and not on competition and profit to serve a privileged minority. To achieve this, it is necessary to reverse the existing anthropocentric hierarchy that positions economic concerns above social and environmental imperatives and promote meaningful participation and empowerment. Policy frameworks and paradigms for practice designed through a post-anthropocentric paradigm, using an ecosocial lens, have the capacity to position equity and justice as central reference points underpinning innovative approaches to global challenges. The discipline of social work is well-placed to increase the momentum of its movement towards transformative change and to consciously reorientate theory and practice in alignment with post-anthropocentric ideals, explored below in more detail.

Post-anthropocentric Social Work

Ontologically, the post-anthropocentric paradigm links all humans to all other living things and to the natural environment recognising the entanglements, dynamism and fluidity of interconnectedness. Thus, humans are situated not as an exceptional, transcendent category, but rather as embodied, embedded entities in symbiosis with other species and the natural environment in mutual co-existence and interdependence (Braidotti 2013). Post-anthropocentric thinking also disrupts the myth of human exceptionalism – the anthropocentric ontological positioning of humans as independent from and in-charge of the natural environment and all other species. Rather, from a post-anthropocentric perspective, humans are viewed ontologically as one species within an interconnected web of multispecies living in coexistence on this planet (Pease and Bozalek 2021). Post-anthropocentric thought is also a powerful tool in the process of transformation because of its capacity to deconstruct the man-made myth that all forms of life and the material world exist to serve market economies and human interests (Webb 2021).

Another salient feature of the post-anthropocentric paradigm is its disruption of humanist hierarchies that position some categories of humans above others. Critical posthumanism rejects the dualist construction of "the human man as if it was humanity itself", as if "he" was the universal reference point for humankind with supremacy over females, non-conforming males, and "others", as well as his mastery of the planet (Pease 2021 p. 109). This "unmasking of patriarchy" in all its forms is central to the transformative effort as patriarchal power is a stubborn system of oppression that intersects and reinforces other systems of oppression (Bell 2021 p. 59).

Drawing on post-anthropocentric and posthumanist thinking, a transformative philosophy for contemporary social work is based on relational ontologies of equality, interdependence, embodiment, and interconnectedness. As many ancient and ongoing Indigenous knowledge traditions centre on relationality and interspecies ecojustice, there is much richness to nurture the post-anthropocentric social work paradigm. Some examples of non-anthropocentric knowledge systems based explicitly on eco-centric communitarian foundations include Ubuntology – "seeing oneself through others" (Chigangaidze et al. 2022 p. 1; Chigangaidze 2022), Eco-swaraj – ecological democracy (Hindi/South Asian), and Sumak Kawsay – harmonious living (Quechua/Latin American), as well as a range of First Nations' ancient and ongoing Indigenous knowledges (Bennett and Green 2019; Desai 2022).

Communitarian approaches based on reciprocity and complementarity – between individuals, communities, and material locations – have the capacity for participatory "bottom-up, radical re-imagining" (Desai 2022 p. 1). However, as these knowledge systems have been largely marginalised by anthropocentrism, great care must be taken as part of the transformative effort to engage respectfully to ensure that neo-colonial practices and cultural appropriation are not perpetuated. It is also important recognise that even in non-dominant communitarian paradigms, some communities and groups can still be marginalised and "not accorded the same respect and equity as dominant groups" and that non-dominant worldviews are also dynamic and evolving (Desai 2022 p. 1). As always, a respectful, critically engaged, systematically eclectic approach is warranted to encourage the development of coherent theory-building for practice.

Other major sources of complementary theory emerge as particularly influential in building a rich, flexible, post-anthropocentric paradigm for social work. These theories and bodies of work include feminism and ecofeminism, ecosocial work theory, and relational ethics. Noble (2021) provides a detailed account of the longstanding feminist critiques of exceptionalism and male dominance. Valuable contributions to post-anthropocentric thinking have also emerged from feminist studies of science (for example, Code 1991; Harding 2009; Plumwood 1994) especially in relation to the gendered nature of knowledge-production, the 'neutral' scientific subject, epistemic agency, mastery, and the need for ecological thinking based on co-operation and interdependence. Plumwood (1994) and others have exposed the illusion of objectivity claimed by dominant forms of Western positivist science, arguing that rather than being unbound by material concerns of embodiment and physical location, Western modernism is imbued with the gendered concerns of the privileged hegemonic male subject. And while it may be argued that many positive developments have emerged from the modernist paradigm, the constraints of the paradigm were never *necessary* for the purposes of anthropo*genic* knowledge-creation and advancement. Indeed, the pace and quality of scientific knowledge-creation has been hindered by the anthropo*centric* paradigm as the talents and valuable knowledge of many have been marginalised by the privileged few. In this respect, notions of merit and fairness have been undermined as legitimate bearers of knowledge have been actively marginalised or excluded entirely from recognised processes of knowledge-creation.

Feminist studies of science encourage us to imagine a different scenario in which 'good science' is produced (rather than partial, hegemonic, 'bad science'). With equality, diversity, and co-operation as central to the creation of rich knowledge, the ideas and talents of many are not overlooked or ignored or actively excluded from processes of knowledge creation. Formerly marginalised people are not denied epistemic agency as legitimate bearers of knowledge resulting in richer, more diverse knowledge for the benefit of all (Code 1991; Harding 2009; Plumwood 1994).

Noble (2021) also describes the emergence of ecofeminism in the 1960s–1970s and notes how it expanded the feminist critique of capitalism, militarism, and nuclearisation by foregrounding the natural environment and adding a multispecies perspective to concerns for planetary wellbeing. Ecofeminism brings into focus how the conventional gender binary (male-female) underpins entrenched patterns of cumulative advantage and disadvantage. Ecofeminist theory also explores the intersectionality of gender oppression, environmental degradation, and poverty. Some foundational ecofeminist theorists who linked patriarchy, ecological destruction, and social injustice include Francoise d'Eaubonne, Rachel Carson, Karen Warren, Greta Gaard and Lori Gruen, and Vandana Shiva (Bell et al. 2019). Ecofeminism explores how anthropocentric thinking – especially hierarchical binaries – produces and reproduces intersecting systems of oppression. This multi-dimensional approach continues to offer a great deal of conceptual power to social work theory and practice, including collectivist approaches to address marginalisation and work for transformative, sustainable change for just outcomes.

Ecosocial work perspectives also draw on core post-anthropocentric concepts including the intrinsic interdependence of ecological and social concerns, and the interconnectedness of humans and all living things with the natural environment (Boetto 2017; Gray and Coates 2012; Heinsch 2012). As in ecofeminism, social justice concerns are explicitly located within an expanded view of the environment to include the natural environment as well as socio-political and cultural concerns (Besthorn 2003; Molyneux 2010). As ecosocial work gains traction in mainstream social work discourse, so too does the need for the profession to articulate a comprehensive post-anthropocentric philosophy to underpin ecosocial theory and practice.

Other post-anthropocentric concepts of importance in the philosophy of transformative post-anthropocentric social work include the centrality of affirmative relationships, relational ethics, and the ethics of peace, nonviolence, and love (Haraway 2016; Ross et al. 2021). Affirmative relationships based on respect, equity, and justice are critical to the collective, transformative effort. The collective, collaborative nature of post-anthropocentric thinking helps us to undo "thinking as usual" – it underpins an affirmative stance, rendering individualist, competitive thinking as, ideally, ultimately unthinkable (Haraway 2016 p. 44).

Central to the vision of critical posthumanist, post-anthropocentric transformation are principles of practice including working with those marginalised by systems of oppression, valuing experiential knowledge, working for transformative, sustainable justice (Braidotti 2019). The profession of social work is well-placed as an important contributor to post-anthropocentric change given that longstanding descriptions of the social work domain typically include the profession's ability to work at ground level with marginalised individuals, groups, and communities for socially just outcomes and systemic change.

Transformative Processes, Challenges, and Implications

Processes of transformation are inherently dynamic and continuous as we carefully consider the limitations (and possibilities) of the anthropocentric paradigm in relation to conventional social work and the possibilities (and limitations) of a post-anthropocentric paradigm for contemporary social work. As we engage in this careful consideration, it is important to focus on particular aspects of and types of oppression – so that we can see how the parts are contextualised within the whole series of intersecting, mutually reinforcing systems of oppression. Thus, transformation typically requires a systematic, transdisciplinary approach, and the creative deployment of knowledge from a wide range of sources to form a coherent framework for transformative theory and practice (Braidotti 2019; IPCC 2022). "Creative visionaries", "radical imagination and inventive practices" – and not "game over cynicism" – are the needed for the profession to "stay with the trouble" and reach its potential as a movement for justice and equity (Haraway 2018 p. 105).

Along with new imaginaries, Desai (2022) and Hujo and Kempf (2021) advocate for there to be a re-envisioned ecosocial contract – a contract that centralises human equality and social protection and one that recognises the intrinsic interdependence of all to the Earth. An ecosocial contract framed by post-anthropocentrism is a solid basis for recognizing and addressing the underlying causes of environmental destruction, racial injustice, and gender oppression. Further, the ecosocial contract promotes just transitions through multidisciplinary alliances, a spirit of unity, and new forms of solidarity to promote inclusion and equity. Within the reimagined social contract, non-human living beings and ecosystems are positioned as fundamental to adaptation, mitigation and climate resilient futures (IPCC 2022). Thus, the principles underpinning a transformational social contact support: distributive justice – the allocation of intergenerational burdens and benefits among individuals, communities and nations; procedural justice – participatory decision-making for shared futures; and respect – engagement, fairness, and diversity (IPCC 2022). This re-envisioned ecosocial contract aligns with social work values, purpose and skills, and would be the reference point for framing new approaches to welfare provision within health and welfare systems capable of integrated, holistic practice.

A critical process of transformative change involves recognition of the ultimate futility of anthropocentrism – the deconstruction of anthropocentrism and humanism. Braidotti (2019 p. 31) describes how this ongoing process of deconstruction is the foundation for making a "qualitative leap to become a supra discipline" with the capacity for transdisciplinary practice, based on the systematic gathering of a range of knowledge to inform theory and practice and guided by a relational core.

Guided by the profession's core values and overtly relational ethics, social workers are generally adept at drawing on a range of transdisciplinary knowledge to underpin their multidimensional practice. Social workers have the skills to work with marginalised groups as well as working within and between pockets of resistance – between individuals, organisations and institutions – to make connections, to forge new alliances and mobilise others in the collective effort of transformation. These integrative capacities are the basis of an ideal skillset enabling the profession to "nurture wisdom in the soil of injustice" (Fine 2012 p. 15).

Post-anthropocentric and critical posthumanist theorists have invoked various imagery to describe such processes of transformation, including that of composting to develop a "nutrient rich basis for future growth" and sustainability, and tentacular thinking (Hamilton and Neimanis 2018 p. 501). Hamilton and Neimanis' (2018) notion of tentacular thinking describes the curious, non-linear, creative process of gathering ideas for composting into rich paradigm framework for post-anthropocentric practice. Here, composting and tentacular thinking not only refer to the use of a range of knowledge from multidisciplinary sources, but also how this creative curation needs to be done with care to ensure that all ingredients reflect post-anthropocentric and posthumanist relational, collectivist principles.

In light of the global context and the realities of the Anthropocene, movement towards a post-anthropocentric perspective is essential to the ongoing relevance of social work. An important element in the paradigm framework for contemporary social work, the post-anthropocentric perspective disrupts the anthropocentric view of humans as the central, dominant species in a species hierarchy. As a basis for making meaningful contributions to the collective effort of transformative change, social work can maintain the momentum in moving its dominant theory, as well as its practices, beyond the anthropocentric inequities and the constraints of "dualistic frameworks that dichotomise the social and the natural" (Bozalek and Pease 2021 p. 1). The transformation of social work theory and practice must therefore be holistic, dynamic, and intersectional to enhance the profession's capacity for action as we disentangle interlocking systems of power and oppression.

The complexities of 'undoing' the intersecting systems of oppression, transformation should also be seen as "an ongoing and evolutionary process" rather than as a neat, one-off event with a clear beginning and end. Likewise, transformative paradigms are not like positivist rules to be applied, but rather more like flexible "scaffolding" to be "stretched, adapted and revised as needed by creative and intelligent practitioners, service users, educators and policy makers around the globe" as a basis for coherent theory-building for professional practice (McGregor 2021 p. 2125).

As argued by McGregor (2021), the paradigm framework for transformative contemporary social work must have the capacity to situate social work in its local and global contexts and it should also have the capacity to frame decolonised and decolonising practice methodologies. In addition, the paradigm framework for contemporary practice should identify core social work knowledge and be sufficiently flexible to enable imaginative, reflexive professional practice.

McGregor (2021 p. 2120) also emphasises the dynamic nature of knowledge and encourages the avoidance of "over-simplified dichotomies" urging instead critical engagement with underpinning assumptions, contextual and causal factors, professional role, and actions to ameliorate social inequality. This fluid interplay between knowledge and the context of professional practice highlights the importance of the social work skillset. A particular strength of social work is its capacity to draw on a variety of knowledge sources as we work to address the complexities of practice. The profession's commitment to lifelong learning along with its capacity for interdisciplinary practice are key features of social work's multifaceted professional identity (Moorhead 2021). Reinforcement of these professional strengths would not only enhance the profession's collective identity but would also foreground the profession as a valuable contributor to post-anthropocentric transformation.

Expanding further on McGregor's (2021) paradigm framework for social work, the features of a post-anthropocentric paradigm for contemporary social work theory and practice should position the profession as:

- Contextual and situational – as a dynamic "work in progress", not as fixed, rule driven and benign. The social work paradigm should be flexible enough to account for locality and capable of accommodating contemporary issues of "time, space and place" (pp. 2115, 2121).
- Decolonised and decolonising – to be epistemologically open to, to value and respectfully learn from non-dominant, diverse sources of knowledge so as to decrease the dominance of Western perspectives.
- A global profession – capable of identifying "what is core to the form and nature of social work knowledge" – to articulate a clearer definition of global social work informed by research, evidence and experience (pp. 2122).
- Creative and flexible – as a basis for theory-informed practice methods through innovation and professional judgement guided by relational, transformative purposes.

Building on the paradigm framework for evolving social work, Ioakimidis and Maglajlic (2022 pp. 606–607) refer to the IFSW (2022) *Integrated Actions for Change* and Truell (2022) to describe six focal points for transformative post-anthropocentric social work theory and practice, and broader social change:

1. Economics – advocating for a fundamental shift from market-based assumptions and measures to sustainability-based models for wellbeing.
2. Environment – continuing to move towards an Indigenous eco-philosophy of respectful co-existence, including renewable energy sources, and away from rampant exploitation of finite resources.
3. Nationalism – moving away from "national introspection" to meaningful global citizenship, fairness and shared futures.
4. Business – moving away from models based on competitive market domination to sustainable cooperative approaches focusing on fair trade, social and environmental outcomes.
5. Work – towards recognition of all work as valuable (including care work), ensuring fair remuneration and decent working conditions for all.
6. State responsibility – shifting from reactive spending on public infrastructure to proactive investment in public wellbeing.

The comprehensive nature of this framework for post-anthropocentric transformative change raises many challenges. In relation to economic transformation and nationalist concerns, how can those who benefit most from anthropocentrism be convinced to truly engage in paradigmatic change – "what will be required to decentre anthropocentric masculinity" (Pease 2021 p. 110)? How can global citizenship be centralised as necessary for sustainable, shared futures? What can be done to undo thinking as usual and what can be done to move us beyond anthropocentric business-as-usual? How can we move beyond being paralysed by the enormity of the transformative task? How might social work sustain its transformative efforts and ensure holistic approaches to change and avoid fragmentation of effort? How does the profession ensure that the rhetoric of change is more than cosmetic? And, while the case for transformation is persuasive there is also "a narrowing window of opportunity" to implement sustainable change (IPCC 2022 p. 33). Given the urgency of global issues, and given the care needed for careful, considered transformation, can we work quickly enough for a just world?

While there are no neat, easy answers to these questions, it is argued that the divisive hierarchies between humans, the natural environment, and other living things all effectively reproduce intersecting systems of oppression that if left unchallenged, will be ultimately catastrophic (Pease and Bozalek 2021). If the divisive hierarchies persist, so too will systems of oppression. Action is needed and all constructive efforts towards transformative change count, whether little or large. Knowing that even relatively small 'wins' and modest gains contribute to momentum for change, in some way at least helps to sustain our efforts towards transformation.

The UNRISD (2016) identifies some common obstacles to transformative change, including the risk of change being fragmented rather than a holistic effort, and mismatches between the rhetoric of transformation and concrete actions. These obstacles potentially result in cosmetic change at best and the reinforcement of underlying anthropocentrism at worst. For example, when transformative policies are at odds with overarching conservative policy settings and actions, the result could be uneven policy settings with some progressive ideas being loosely attached to otherwise dominant conservative, conventional ideology. As described by Catney and Doyle (2011 p. 188) this presents a gossamer thin veil of change, but essentially maintains inequities as new maps of oppression are inscribed onto old maps "this time wearing a green cloak".

As social workers build new affirmative partnerships and activist coalitions for change, an interdisciplinary orientation and interdisciplinary scholarship are critical (Noble 2021). The breadth of the social work domain underpins the profession's capacity to make "the process of future-building a democratic, expansive, and equity-centred proposition" (Nissen and Scheyett 2021, p. 5). This can be gradually achieved through working to break down barriers to knowledge-sharing and engaging in sustained efforts to enable multidisciplinary sources of knowledge to combine as a collective power for transformation towards common goals of health – human health, the health of non-human living beings, and a healthy planet (IPCC 2022).

In new partnership-building, there must also be care attention to any pre-existing, ongoing power imbalances. Careful partnership-building based on respectful knowledge exchange and shared futures will enhance the potential for genuinely transformative, new partnerships to flourish, reducing the likelihood of old patterns of oppression being mapped onto new initiatives and partnerships.

Some Further Considerations for Post-anthropocentric Social Work

The goals of achieving sustainable futures and climate justice are best served by post-anthropocentric ethics (Webb 2021). However, as the post-anthropocentric paradigm decentres humans and broadens the focus to the interconnectedness of all living things, how does this impact on the traditional domain of social work practice? How can we justify a shift in focus to multispecies ecosocial justice without first addressing oppression amongst humans based on sex, gender, race, class, ability, etc.? What does 'thinking beyond the human' mean for social work (Webb 2021)?

These important considerations can at least be partially addressed by returning to some of the central tenets of post-anthropocentric thought – in particular, the concepts of interdependence and interconnectedness. From a transformed post-anthropocentric perspective, humans are not positioned as separate to all other things and likewise, the wellbeing of all is interconnected and inseparable. Given this ontology, having concern for human welfare remains legitimate, if human interests are not positioned as supreme to all else. Likewise, a concern for human welfare would also only become problematic if human wellbeing is privileged as if it were a linear precondition for more comprehensive concern for broader ecological justice. As argued by Kopnina et al. (2018 p. 117), if multispecies eco-justice is positioned as secondary to human-centred social justice, "in all likelihood, it will never be achieved". Rather, within the post-anthropocentric paradigm, all living things and the natural environment have intrinsic ethical value as part of the interdependent web of connectivity. In this way, post-anthropocentrism positions social justice as inseparable from and intertwined with eco-justice and it recognises that human needs can be addressed without diminishing the interests of others and without environmental degradation (Kopnina et al. 2018). Thus, emancipatory action with any one part of the whole is intrinsically linked with the shared futures of the whole and social work becomes part of the collective effort of post-anthropocentric transformation. The holistic approach to justice also underpins a consciously broadened frame of reference for participatory social work action and a flattening-out of the false dichotomy between social work clients and social workers, working in partnership (McGregor 2021).

The holistic approach to equity and the movement towards a post-dualist, post-binary world should not however be a basis for erasing the longstanding and ongoing intersectional effects of the Anthropocene, such as sexism, racism, able-ism, ageism, and the like. Post-anthropocentric thinking enables a 'qualitative shift' in thinking so that it is possible to recognise and trace the interconnections between destructive anthropocentric hierarchies, adverse environmental outcomes and multiple forms of discrimination, disempowerment, and disadvantage, bringing them into sharp focus (Braidotti 2013 p. 89). Transformative actions to address the wide-ranging deleterious effects of anthropocentrism must be multifaceted, comprehensive and non-linear to systematically address intersecting systems of oppression. Again, through actions little and large, collective responsibility for transformative change can add momentum post-anthropocentric change.

Relational ethics as a central core of post-anthropocentric social work also centralises care as a matter for all. Relational ethics shifts care out of the place it currently occupies in the anthropocentric private sphere, breaking down the false dichotomy between private and public concerns. The collective care agenda moves care work into the interconnected, interdependent post-anthropocentric open. At a policy level, foregrounding a care agenda would be the basis for the allocation of public resources to care, for re-balancing the care workload and for constructing an expansive form of care encompassing humans, all living things and the biosphere (Esquivel and Kaufman 2017).

The equitable relational positioning of humans in the post-Anthropocene also brings the notion of 'universal human rights' into focus. The dominant anthropocentric construction of human rights is arguably an anthropocentric, settler-colonialist construction and is not necessarily shared by marginalised Indigenous worldviews and ancient wisdom (Morgenshtern et al. 2022). A transformed construction of rights as multispecies eco-justice is distinct from the conventional construction of human rights in that it is based on interdependence and relationality, as distinct from anthropocentric individualism, competition, divisive binaries, and exceptionalism. Desai (2022) reminds us of the potential of formerly marginalised communitarian concepts to inform the evolution of post-anthropocentric social work based on relational ontology. She highlights the importance of ensuring a comprehensive reimagining of social work theory and practice, including terminology to reflect relationality between human and non-human and living and non-living entities as we work to transform eco-social, economic and political institutions.

Chapter Summary and Conclusion

This chapter has outlined how dominant forms of Euro-Western social work have emerged from an anthropocentric paradigm. Anthropocentrism has been explored with a focus on how exceptionalism and humanism form a series of hierarchical dualisms which produce and reproduce intersecting systems of oppression. The major limitations of anthropocentrism have been considered, including how the paradigm marginalises some forms of knowledge as well as some categories of people as holders and creators of legitimate knowledge, creating a self-sustaining system based on division, competition and partial knowledge. The constraints of anthropocentric thinking render it as ultimately incapable of leading us to a sustainable, equitable, peaceful future. It has been argued that the social work profession's commitments equity and justice are at odds with anthropocentrism and to achieve emancipatory aims, there must be sustained focus on transformative approaches in social work theory and practice otherwise, we remain stuck within self-perpetuating systems of oppression.

The key features of a post-anthropocentric paradigm for social work have been presented, including its ontology, epistemology, and methodology. Ontologically, post-anthropocentric social work is characterised by the interconnectedness, interdependence and relationality of all material and non-material entities. Epistemologically, post-anthropocentric social work values rich sources of diverse knowledge, including the embodied, experiential knowledge of previously marginalised entities and knowledge traditions. Methodologically, democratised, co-constructive participatory approaches and respectful partnerships are consistent with post-anthropocentric thinking. These foundations underpin the major methods of post-anthropocentric social work practice, including transdisciplinary practice and affirmative partnership-building for collective action. In addition, some of the processes, challenges, and implications of transformative practice beyond the Anthropocene have been outlined.

As a foundation for ongoing transformative action to take us into the post-Anthropocene, the profession must continue to evolve and further develop a coherent philosophy consistent with its values and professional purpose. The profession must also sustain – or ideally accelerate – its collective and intentional resistance to the divisive logics of anthropocentrism. Anthropocentrism is the predominant basis for the parlous state of world as we all face the effects of global warming, environmental degradation, and largely unabated human violence in all its forms. And yet hope for transformative change remains – a hope in human capacity for change, so that we can all work in various ways and to varying degrees to address the damage caused by anthropocentrism. Social work can continue to evolve and to work in respectful, affirmative, and creative ways as we add to the movement towards a sustainable, equitable shared future for all in the post-Anthropocene.

References

Amnesty International (2022) Amnesty International Report 2021/22: global analysis and regional overviews. https://amnesty.org. Accessed 31 Mar 2022

Bell K (2012) Towards a post-conventional philosophical base for social work. Br J Soc Work 42(3):408–423

Bell K (2021) A philosophy of social work beyond the anthropocene. In: Bozalek V, Pease B (eds) Post-anthropocentric social work: critical posthuman and new materialist perspectives. Routledge, London, pp 58–67

Bell K, Kime K, Boetto H (2019) Gender, environmental degradation and eco-feminism. In: Rinkel M, Powers M (eds) Social work promoting community and environmental sustainability: a workbook for social work practitioners and educators, vol 3. International Federation of Social Work (IFSW), Rheinfelden, pp 117–137. https://www.ifsw.org/product/books/social-work-promoting-community-and-environmental-sustainability-volume-3/. Accessed 31 Mar 2022

Bennett B, Green S (eds) (2019) Our voices: Aboriginal social work. Red Globe Press, London

Besthorn F (2003) Radical ecologisms: insights for educating social workers in ecological activism and social justice. Crit Soc Work 3(1):66–107

Blackstock C (2009) The occasional evil of angels: learning from the experiences of Aboriginal people and social work. First Peoples Child Fam Rev 4(1):28–37

Boetto H (2017) A transformative eco-social work model: challenging modernist assumptions in social work. Br J Soc Work 47(1):48–67

Bozalek V, Pease B (eds) (2021) Post-anthropocentric social work: critical posthuman and new materialist perspectives. Routledge, London

Braidotti R (2013) The posthuman. Polity Press, Cambridge, UK

Braidotti R (2019) A theoretical framework for the critical posthumanities. Theory Cult Soc 36(6): 31–61

Catney P, Doyle T (2011) The welfare of now and the green (post) politics of the future. Crit Soc Policy 31(2):174–193

Chigangaidze R (2022) Environmental social work through the African philosophy of Ubuntu: a conceptual analysis. Int Soc Work. https://doi.org/10.1177/00208728211073382

Chigangaidze R, Mafa I, Simango T, Mudehwe E (2022) Establishing the relevance of the Ubuntu philosophy in social work practice: inspired by the Ubuntu World Social Work Day, 2021 celebrations and the IFSW and IASSW's (2014) Global Definition of Social Work. Int Soc Work. https://doi.org/10.1177/00208728221078374

Clarke K (2021) Reimagining social work ancestry: toward epistemic decolonisation. Affilia. https://doi.org/10.1177/08861099211051326

Coates J, Gray M (2018) Domestication or transformation? Transitioning to the ecosocial. Can Soc Work 20(1):50–71

Code L (1991) What can she know? Feminist theory and the construction of knowledge. Cornell University Press, Ithaca

Desai M (2022) Going beyond the social: communitarian imaginaries as inspirations for rethinking the eco-social contract? Transformative social policy: translating social policy into policy and practice. United Nations Research Institute for Social Development (UNRISD), issue brief 12, April 2022. Retrieved from https://www.unrisd.org/en/library/publications/going-beyond-the-social-communitarian-imaginaries-as-inspirations-for-rethinking-the-eco-social-cont. Accessed 24 Apr 2022

Esquivel V, Kaufman A, (2017) Innovations in care: new concepts, new actions, new policies. Friedrich Ebert Stiftung Study. Retrieved via UNRISD 13282.pdf (fes.de). Accessed 24 Apr 2022

Fine M (2012) Troubling calls for evidence: A critical race, class and gender analysis of whole evidence counts. Feminism and Psychology 22(1):3–19

Gray M, Coates J (2012) Environmental ethics for social work: social work's responsibility to the non-human world. Int J Soc Welf 21:239–247

Hamilton J, Neimanis A (2018) Composting feminisms and environmental humanities. Environ Humanit 10(2):501–527

Hamilton J, Zettel T, Neimanis A (2021) Feminist infrastructure for better weathering. Aust Fem Stud 36:237–259

Haraway D (2016) Staying with the trouble: making kin in the Chthulucene. Duke University Press, Durham

Haraway D (2018) Staying with the trouble for multispecies environmental justice (author response). Dialogues Hum Geogr 8(1):102–105

Harding S (2009) Standpoint theories: productively controversial. Hypatia 24(4):192–200

Heinsch M (2012) Getting down to Earth: finding a place for nature in social work practice. Int J Soc Welf 21:309–318

Hujo K, Kempf I (2021) Joining up the dots between social and climate justice: time for a new eco-social contract. UNRISD think piece series, the time is now! Why we need a new eco-social contract for a just and green world. United Nations Research Institute for Social Development (UNRISD). Retrieved from https://www.unrisd.org. Accessed 11 Apr 2022

IFSW (2014) Global definition of social work. https://www.ifsw.org/what-is-social-work/global-definition-of-social-work/. Accessed 16 Apr 2022

IFSW (2021) Social work and the UN SDGs. https://www.ifsw.org/social-work-and-the-united-nations-sustainable-development-goals-sdgs/. Accessed 16 Apr 2022

Intergovernmental Panel on Climate Change (IPCC) (2022) Climate change 2022: impacts, adaptation and vulnerability – summary for policymakers. IPCC working group 2 contribution to the sixth assessment report of the IPCC. WMO, UNEP. https://report.ipcc.ch/ar6wg2/pdf/IPCC_AR6_WGII_FinalDraft_FullReport.pdf. Accessed 1 Apr 2022

International Federation of Social Workers (IFSW) (2022) Integrated actions for change. https://www.ifsw.org/co-building-a-new-eco-social-world-leaving-no-one-behind-peoples-summit/ and https://newecosocialworld.com

Ioakimidis V, Maglajlic R (2022) Global inequality, failed systems and the need for a paradigm shift. Br J Soc Work 52(2):605–608. https://doi.org/10.1093/bjsw/bcac018

Jaswal S, Kshetrimayum M (2022) A review of Indigenous social work around the world: concepts, debates and challenges. Int Soc Work. https://doi.org/10.1177/00208728211073851

Kopnina H, Washington H, Taylor B, Piccolo J (2018) Anthropocentrism: more than just a misunderstood problem. J Agric Environ Ethics 31:109–127

Krings A, Victor BG, Mathias J et al (2020) Environmental social work in the disciplinary literature, 1991–2015. Int Soc Work 63(3):275–290

McGregor C (2021) A paradigm framework for social theory for early 21st century practice. Br J Soc Work 49:2112–2129

Molyneux R (2010) The practical realities of ecosocial work: a review of the literature. Crit Soc Work 11(2):61–69

Moorhead B (2021) Sustaining professional identity during the initial post-qualification period: implications for retention strategies. Int Soc Work 64(6):1009–1021

Morgenshtern M, Schmid J, Yu N (2022) Interrogating settler social work with Indigenous persons in Canada. J Soc Work. https://doi.org/10.1177/14680173211056823

Nissen L, Scheyett A (2021) Pandemics, economic systems, and the future of social work (editorial). Soc Work 67(1):5–7

Noble C (2021) Ecofeminism to feminist materialism: implications for anthropocene feminist social work. In: Bozalek V, Pease B (eds) Post-anthropocentric social work: critical posthuman and new materialist perspectives. Routledge, New York, pp 95–107

Pease B (2021) Fostering non-anthropocentric vulnerability in men: challenging the autonomous masculine subject in social work. In: Bozalek V, Pease B (eds) Post-anthropocentric social work: critical posthuman and new materialist perspectives. Routledge, New York, pp 108–120

Pease B, Bozalek V (2021) Towards post-anthropocentric social work. In: Bozalek V, Pease B (eds) Post-anthropocentric social work: critical posthuman and new materialist perspectives. Routledge, New York, pp 1–16

Plumwood V (1994) Feminism and the mastery of nature. Routledge, New York

Ross A, Bennett B, Menyweather N (2021) Towards a critical posthumanist social work: transspecies ethics of ecological justice, nonviolence and love. In: Bozalek V, Pease B (eds) Post-anthropocentric social work: critical posthuman and new materialist perspectives. Routledge, New York, pp 175–187

Truell R (2022) The importance of social work ethics and values at a time of global change. Int J Soc Work Values Ethics 19(1):18–19

Truell R, Jones D (2020) The global agenda for social work and social development: extending the influence of social work. International Federation of Social Workers (IFSW). https://www.ifsw.org/wp-content/uploads/ifsw-cdn/assets/ifsw_24848-10.pdf. Accessed 30 Mar 2022

United Nations (2015) Transforming our world: the 2030 agenda for sustainable development. https://sdgs.un.org/2030agenda. Accessed 30 Mar 2022

United Nations Research Institute for Social Development (UNRISD) (2016) Policy innovations for transformative change: implementing the 2030 agenda for sustainable development – flagship report, 2016. Policy innovations for transformative change: implementing the 2030 Agenda for sustainable development | Publications | UNRISD. Accessed 30 Mar 2022

Webb S (2021) What comes after the subject? Towards a critical posthumanist social work. In: Bozalek V, Pease B (eds) Post-anthropocentric social work: critical posthuman and new materialist perspectives. Routledge, New York, pp 19–31

Part III

Social Work Practice Theory

Person-Centred Approaches to Social Work Practice

Adrian D. van Breda

Contents

Introduction	144
Locating Person-Centred Approaches Within the Social Work Agenda	146
Person-Centred Social Work Practice Approaches	147
Task-Centred Social Work	148
Strengths-Based Social Work	149
Relational Social Work	152
Narrative Therapy	154
Prominent Person-Centred Theories Drawn from Other Professions	156
Person-Centred Therapy	157
Cognitive Behavioural Therapy	158
Mindfulness-Based Interventions	158
Psychodynamic Therapy	159
Motivational Interviewing	159
Key Elements of Person-Centred Social Work Practice	160
Conclusion	162
References	162

Abstract

This chapter addresses social work practice approaches (or theories and models) that focus on facilitating change in the person, rather than change in social environment, for example. The author notes that in many countries social workers gravitate towards individual, person-centred social work. These person-centred approaches to social work, however, are not oblivious to the environments surrounding individuals. The author argues strongly that person-centred practice does and must take cognisance of the social environment, though this is made complex by social work's reliance on practice models drawn from other

---

A. D. van Breda (✉)
Department of Social Work and Community Development, University of Johannesburg, Johannesburg, South Africa
e-mail: avanbreda@uj.ac.za

professions, notably psychology. In light of this, four practice approaches developed by and conceptualised within social work receive thorough attention: task-centred social work, strengths-based social work (including the strengths perspective), relational social work and narrative therapy (with mention of solution-focused brief therapy). In addition, the chapter also addresses five practice approaches that do not emanate from social work, but are used extensively by social workers, viz. person-centred therapy, cognitive behavioural therapy, mindfulness-based interventions, psychodynamic therapy and motivational interviewing. The author draws not only on classical writings and contemporary summaries of these approaches, but also cutting-edge social work research on each of the approaches. The chapter concludes with a call to social workers to ensure the location of person-centred practice approaches within the broader social, systemic and structural environments around persons.

Keywords

Case work · Person-centred social work · Task-centred social work · Strengths-based social work · Relational social work · Narrative therapy

Introduction

The profession of social work has, since its inception, centred on the person as its primary object of change. While this has evolved and changed over time, the enduring focus on the individual person remains. It is rooted, perhaps, in the early writings of Mary Richmond (1922, pp. 98–99): "social case work consists of those processes which develop personality [i.e. the person] through adjustments consciously effected, individual by individual, between men [sic] and their social environment". Richmond's fundamental focus on a person-centred approach to social work persists to the present day. For example, the benefits of group work have recently been described almost entirely as individual benefits, such as "mutual aid" and "testing new behaviours" (Kirst-Ashman and Hull 2018, p. 104), confirming the title of a classic group work text, *Individual change through small groups* (Sundel et al. 1985).

Despite the pervasiveness of this perspective, a person-centred approach to social work is not a cohesive body of scholarly thought, in the way that anti-oppressive social work, green social work, feminist social work and developmental social work may be. Indeed, readers may primarily associate the term person-centred approach with Carl Rogers' (1951) seminal client-centred therapy, which later became known as the person-centred approach (Joseph and Murphy 2013). In the context of this chapter, however, 'person-centred' is used more broadly to refer to those practice theories or models that focus on the person as the primary target of change. In this context, therefore, a person-centred approach to social work comprises a rather

8 Person-Centred Approaches to Social Work Practice

varied collection of theories and models. For example, both psychoanalysis and task-centred social work qualify as person-centred approaches to social work, though they have little in common theoretically and practically.

Person-centred approaches to social work practice draw not only on practice models developed by social workers, but also those developed by psychologists and other professions. Cognitive behavioural therapy is a good example – it is one of the most widely used practice models by social workers yet is not a social work practice model. There has, furthermore, been relatively little investment in the development of practice models by social workers. Nevertheless, there are several important practice models developed by social workers, which enjoy focused attention in this chapter.

This chapter aims to review recent scholarship regarding a range of social work and non-social work practice approaches, theories or models that are commonly used by social workers. To accomplish this, I conducted several scans of publications on various approaches using Google Scholar. Scholar, rather than one or more of the numerous academic databases (such as EBSCOhost), was preferred, because of its inclusion of a wider range of academic publications than a single database would and because of its inclusion of grey literature (e.g., dissertations, theses and research reports) and books. While this chapter does not constitute a systematic review of literature on the practice approaches described (the sheer number of available publications would have made this impossible), it provides nonetheless a sufficiently comprehensive overview of recent studies to inform a considered critique of each approach.

Even though person-centred approaches to social work practice are prominent in contemporary social work education and practice, this chapter argues that such approaches risk falling short of social work's wider commitment to environmental, structural and systemic change, captured particularly in the person-in-environment approach (Weiss-Gal 2008). Arguably, social work practice that ignores the environment is not social work at all. Thus, person-centred approaches, while important and prominent in social work practice, cannot be the only approaches used and person-centred approaches that lend themselves to a more inclusive consideration of the environment as well as the person are argued to be better aligned with the social work profession and discipline.

The chapter opens with a critical reflection on focusing on the person or individual in social work, giving attention to the importance and place of the environment in such approaches. A total of nine practice approaches are discussed and critically reviewed within an understanding of social work aims and values: four prominent approaches developed by social workers and five developed by other professions but used extensively by social workers. A brief synthesis of key elements that constitute a valid person-centred social work practice approach is presented, in light of the critical reflections in the previous two sections. The chapter closes with a brief reflection on learning about person-centred social work practice, particularly the need to consider the social environment.

Locating Person-Centred Approaches Within the Social Work Agenda

Social work's focus on the individual as the primary target of change extends back to the earliest days, particularly in the writing of Mary Richmond. It was subsequently significantly influenced by psychoanalytic theory, which shaped most (though not all) social work thinking in the USA and perhaps globally until the 1960s (Healy 2014; McNutt 2013). Since then, social workers have drawn on a wider range of practice theories from other professions, of which psychoanalysis is just one. There has also been a significant increase in macro practice, with its focus on systemic and structural change, rather than on changing the person or helping individuals to adapt to dysfunctional environments.

In parallel to this increased focus on macro change, there has been a resurgence of interest in the person-in-environment (PiE) (Weiss-Gal 2008). This concept also dates to Mary Richmond, who centred on the individual as the target of change but saw the impetus for that change being in relation to the person's social environment, which she goes on to define as including not only social relationships, but everything around a person that impacts them, including the physical environment and national conditions. However, Richmond's focus on the PiE often devolved into a focus on individual change. She viewed social group work, social reform (what we would now call community work or community development) and social research as ultimately impacting the person (Richmond 1922, pp. 223–224). This focus on the individual is evident also in Richmond's earliest writings, where she says, "It is impossible to treat the individual poor man [sic] without affecting the condition of his fellows [sic] for better or worse, and it is impossible to deal with social conditions without affecting the units that compose society", and goes on to say, "I shall [in this book] dwell particularly upon individual service" (Richmond 1899, p. 6).

In the history of social work, therefore, we see an ambivalence in the focus on person and environment. While the conceptual tools were there for inclusive, holistic social work practice – that is, the concept of PiE – the practice of social work all too often devolved into person-centred change. This continues today. Pritzker and Applewhite (2015) and Rothman and Mizrahi (2014), for example, note that around 90% of Masters of Social Work students in the US focus on micro or advanced generalist practice, rather than macro or policy practice. A study in South Africa similarly found that most social workers and most programme time were invested in casework and remedial services, despite 15 years of a developmental social welfare approach (Patel and Hochfeld 2012). Similar situations are reported elsewhere in the world, such as England (Higgins 2015), Australia (Ablett and Morley 2016) and India (Dash 2017), with critical and radical voices at the margins. By contrast, Latin America appears to be a region where this emphasis on micro and remedial social work is not predominant (Brito and Ottmann 2019).

This apparent preference for person-centred approaches may be rooted in broader discourses in society and in social work and social welfare (Healy 2014). Discourses are broad narratives that shape how we perceive and interact with the world. They in turn shape theory and people's theoretical preferences and practices. Healy (2014) observes the dominance of a biomedical discourse, which emphasises disease, diagnosis and professional cure; neoclassical economics and new public management discourses, which, along with neoliberalism, tend to privatise social problems and their solutions; and psychological discourses, which tend to emphasise personal problems and individuals as change targets. These discourses, often lying outside of our conscious awareness, influence thinking and behaving by individual practitioners, managers, organisation, funders and nations. The result may be a tendency to focus excessively on the person and inadequately on the environment (including broader social systems and structures, and the natural and built environments).

In more recent years, the growing emphasis on the environment, systems and structures, including shifts in discourse towards sociological, citizen rights and environmental discourses (Healy 2014), has led some to be highly critical of social work interventions targeting individuals. For example, Midgley and Conley (2010, p. xvi) state that:

> developmental social workers do not place much emphasis on therapeutic counselling ... [and are] critical of interventions that maintain clients in an ongoing, maintenance relationship with service providers ... although they recognize that counselling can be helpful, they are critical of its central role in social work today.

This view is held because the major problems that negatively impact the lives of most people are structural and systemic, not personal, and as much as person-centred interventions may assist such people cope with these adversities or even improve their own situation, they will not change the situations themselves. For this, systems-oriented, critical, radical, decolonial and developmental approaches to practice are needed – themes that are addressed elsewhere in this book.

In this chapter, therefore, it is argued that even when social work practice has a person-centred approach, genuine and active consideration of the multisystemic environment is essential for the practice to qualify as 'social work'. Furthermore, while person-centred social work may be an important and necessary approach to social work, it cannot be the only one. A more inclusive, generalist approach to practice, that gives priority to addressing the challenges facing most people, is essential.

Person-Centred Social Work Practice Approaches

Social workers have developed several important and enduring practice approaches. Helen Perlman's (1957) social casework model, which drew on the problem-solving model prominent at that time in social work and other disciplines, such as Dewey's work in education (Sarfaraz and Ishrat 2012), was an influential model until recent times. A key value of her model was that it focused on developing the problem-solving capacities of people, so that they could solve not only their presenting problem, but also future problems. In this section, four practice approaches developed by social workers are presented, viz. task-centred social work, strengths-based social work, relational social work and narrative therapy (which also includes mention of solution-focused brief therapy). Each model is critiqued on the extent to which it constitutes a person-centred social work practice approach.

Task-Centred Social Work

Task-centred social work was developed by social workers Laura Epstein and William J. Reid (1972). It emerged out of several ideas that had been growing in popularity in the 1960s (Fortune and Reid 2017). John Dewey's systematic, rational and action-oriented approaches to problem solving were influential and combined with Helen Perlman's (1957) *Social casework: A problem-solving approach*, which also adopted a problem-solving approach to social work. Studt's (1968) work on the centrality of clients undertaking tasks to address their concerns was influential, as was Reid and Shyne's (1969) research which showed that brief therapies were as effective as long-term therapies. This model is thus based less on theory than it is on empirical evidence of what works.

Task-centred social work has several assumptions (Fortune and Reid 2017). Problems are constructed as temporary breakdowns in problem solving and coping capacities, rather than problems of the personality. Change is seen as resulting from the clients acting, rather than talking, expressing feelings or working through past traumas. While a positive helping relationship is deemed necessary, it is not the agent of change. The relationship requires both support and challenge for change to occur. The change that is sought is located not within the person, but rather at the point of interface between the person and their environment, that is on "problems-in-living" (Fortune and Reid 2017, p. 533).

Task-centred social work uses a highly structured and systematic procedure, clearly set out in Fortune and Reid (2017, p. 537). The work starts with the identification, assessment and prioritisation of the client's concerns, within their social contexts, and the development of an initial small, achievable task to be performed by the client after the first session. Thereafter, each session starts with a review of tasks performed since the previous session and identifying and removing obstacles to task performance. This is followed by the task planning and implementation sequence, where tasks as selected, contracted and planned. Time is spent facilitating client motivation for the task, identifying and removing anticipated obstacles, and detailed planning and practising. This systematic and detailed work is based on research showing that "the more time spent doing task planning, the more likely tasks are to be successful and that problems will be improved" (Fortune and Reid 2017, p. 539).

While task-centred social work was highly popular some decades ago, this appears to have waned over time and there is no longer much scholarly focus on the model. A Google Scholar search for the terms 'social work' and 'task-centred' (or 'task-centered') over the past 10 years generated approximately 2000 hits – the second lowest number of hits of all the models presented in the chapter. Moreover, task-centred social work seldom appeared in the title of studies, and most texts addressing task-centred social work were textbooks on social work practice models.

Nevertheless, task-centred social work does continue to be used for person-centred work with individuals, groups and communities (Marsh and Doel 2005; Tolson et al. 2003) around the world (Fortune et al. 2010). A recent survey of clinical social workers in South Africa, for example, found that 19% use task-centred social work (Van Breda and Addinall 2021). This may owe to the accessibility of the task-centred practice model, which is highly proceduralised, practical and specific. Furthermore, it targets discrete measurable outcomes, which may fit well with neoliberal agendas (Harms Smith 2017).

Task-centred social work with individuals has been successfully used with involuntary clients (Rooney 2018). Task-centred social work has also been used in work with groups. For example, Goeke et al. (2011) report using the task planning and implementation sequence in a feminist-informed peer mentoring group for junior female academics. The authors found the use of the model helpful and that it aligned well with feminist principles of cooperation, caring and non-hierarchical relationships. Another study (Verma and Chaudhury 2017) used task-centred group work for people with schizophrenia and found that the intervention produced positive mental health change compared with a no-treatment control group. Another study reported on a task-centred approach to providing support to older persons aimed at promoting well-being and mental health (Chapin et al. 2012), which found participants to evidence reduced symptoms of depression and improved health and functioning.

Task-centred social work is clearly person-centred in its approach, aiming to improve the well-being and functioning of persons. Its focus on identifying and removing obstacles, however, which are often in the environment, lends itself to being a PiE practice model. Clients are encouraged to change not just their own behaviour, but also to identify environmental factors that impede their flourishing. The client, together with the social worker, and potentially other key persons and systems in the client's world, may be mobilised to effect systemic and structural change, thus constituting a person-centred social work practice approach.

Strengths-Based Social Work

Strengths-based social work appears to be the most prominent social work practice approach currently. A Google Scholar search for the terms 'social work' and 'strengths based' or 'strengths perspective' over the past 10 years generated approximately 20,000 hits. Van Breda and Addinall's (2021) survey of clinical social workers in South Africa found that 38% of participants reported using the strengths perspective – seventh most frequent on a list of 29 practice models. While the strengths perspective is today most closely associated with Dennis Saleebey, thanks to his book on the topic (first published in 1992), the term goes back an additional few years to Weick et al. (1989). These authors bemoaned the pervasive focus on deficits and pathology in social work, and called for a greater emphasis on strengths: "A strengths perspective rests on an appreciation of the positive attributes and capabilities that people express and on the ways in which individual and social resources can be developed and sustained" (p. 352). Based on this 'strengths perspective' – which is a perspective or way of looking at, perceiving, making sense of and ultimately acting upon the world, comparable to the notion of 'discourses' (Healy 2014) – they mapped out preliminary ideas for a 'strengths-based practice'. The strengths perspective and strengths-based practice model have since burgeoned and become almost foundational to social work (Price et al. 2020), in that it is hard to imagine an acceptable form of social work that is deficit based rather than strengths based.

The strengths perspective fosters a paradigm shift from a deficit to a strengths or resilience perspective (Van Breda 2019d). Strengths, then, focus not so much on people's problems or challenges (though usually does not ignore them), but rather identifies and mobilises indigenous and local protective factors or resilience processes. Resilience, which is the theoretical framework explicitly or implicitly underlying the strengths perspective (Van Breda 2019c; Zimmerman 2013), can be defined as "the multilevel processes that systems engage in to obtain better-than-expected outcomes in the face or wake of adversity" (Van Breda 2018b, p. 4). While resilience theory historically (and still to an extent today) has focused on the psychological resilience of individuals rising above environmental adversity, contemporary approaches to resilience, notably social-ecological (Ungar 2012) and multisystemic resilience (Theron and Van Breda 2021; Ungar and Theron 2020), emphasise the resilience of systems around people, in interaction with each other, that explain more variation in individual outcomes than psychological resilience – in short, a PiE construction of resilience (Van Breda 2018b).

What the strengths perspective does not offer, compared with task-centred social work, for example, is a singular or primary model of practice. Task-centred social work offers a kind of manual or recipe for practice, which looks similar across authors (e.g., Ramos and Tolson 2008, compared with Fortune and Reid 2017). The strengths-based approach does not. One recent studied identified 17 different practice models under the umbrella of strengths-based, including asset-based community development, appreciative inquiry, motivational interviewing, narrative approaches, person-centred approaches (i.e., Rogerian), and solution-focused therapy (Price et al. 2020). Most of these practice models are stand-alone models that fall within a broad family of strengths-based, resilience-aligned models.

As good a strengths model as any is proposed by Rapp and Goscha (2011), in which a phased model is presented: engagement and relationship building; assessment of personal and environmental strengths across seven life domains; collaborative personal planning to achieve the client's goals through tasks; acquiring the resources required to implement the plan from the environment, with particular attention to building networks of supportive community relationships; ongoing monitoring and enabling of "self-efficacy, community integration, and recovery" (p. 69); and gradual disengagement from professional support. This model is useful in its strong focus on strengths, its use of a familiar planned change process (Kirst-Ashman and Hull 2018) and having substantial book chapters on each of the phases. There are, however, many other texts that offer overarching strengths-based practice guidelines and models (e.g., Pomeroy and Garcia 2017).

The strengths perspective has been widely applied to a wide range of life challenges and client demographics at case, group and community work levels. For example, recent strengths-based studies have been conducted with young people with intellectual disabilities or mental health concerns (Crous et al. 2021), older persons (Nelson-Becker et al. 2020; Rajeev and Jeena 2020), social work supervisees (Engelbrecht 2021), suicide prevention among Indigenous Australians (Dudgeon et al. 2020), Indigenous youth (Njeze et al. 2020), child maltreatment (Diaz et al. 2021), offender recidivism (Donnelly 2021), positive parenting (Katsama 2022), and so on. These studies showed the benefit of the strengths-based practices to personal (e.g., personal growth), social (e.g., support systems, spirituality, cultural identity), systemic (e.g., housing, voluntary organisation, school-based programmes, work training) and structural (e.g., racism, poverty) domains.

A number of strengths-based assessment tools have also been developed, such as the Youth Ecological Resilience Scale (Van Breda 2017), the Perceived Organisational Support for Strength Use (Keenan and Mostert 2013), the Military Social Health Index and Military Resilience Assessment Protocol (Van Breda 2011), and the Protective Factors for Reducing Juvenile Reoffending tool (Barnes-Lee 2020). These tools target not only psychological or individual strengths, but also relational and environmental strengths and resources, aligned with contemporary resilience theory (Van Breda 2018b).

Despite the substantial body of writing and the widespread uptake of strengths-based practices, there is surprisingly little evidence in support of it producing good outcomes. A recent systematic review on "on the effectiveness and the implementation of different strengths-based approaches within adult social work in the UK" identified over 5000 studies, not one of which met the criterion for their effectiveness question, viz. "outcomes could be directly related to people's individual outcomes or outcomes at the level of families or communities" (Price et al. 2020, p. 3), and only 15 met the criteria for the implementation question, only "six of which were assessed as 'good quality'" (p. 4).

Notwithstanding the concerns about the lack of outcome data, the strengths perspective is a social work practice model located the PiE interface. While historically, and still currently (Garrett 2016), the strengths perspective, and the related resilience theory, has often individualised both challenges and strengths of clients, aligned to neo-liberal discourses, they still have ample potential and frequently are focused on strengths and resilience resources not only in individuals, but in the multiple layers of the ecosystem (Van Breda 2019b). The strengths perspective is less marred by its individualisation of clients and more by its tendency to not challenge, and thereby to tacitly support, systemic adversity and oppression (Garrett 2016). A strengths perspective that does more to recognise and challenge social injustice in the social environment would be better aligned with social work values.

Relational Social Work

Relational social work is an increasingly recognised social work practice approach. It may be contested whether it was developed or appropriated by social workers. Regardless, there is now a coherent body of practice theory termed 'relational social work', though not as prolific as the other three approaches covered in this section. A Google Scholar search for 'relational social work' over the past 10 years yielded about 600 publications, while in the South African survey of clinical social workers, 9% of participants reported using relational social work (Van Breda and Addinall 2021).

The focus on relationships in social work practice perhaps dates back to the PiE principle discussed previously, which emerged at the origins of social work. PiE does not imply considering both people and environments – if that were so, the term would be better written 'person and environment'. The use of the preposition 'in' and the use of hyphens to tie the three words into a compound word imply that there is a singular focus on the interface between people and their environments (Van Breda 2018a). The 'in' in PiE thus becomes the most conceptually loaded word – it infers the liminal space between people and their environments as being the primary focus of social work practice: neither the person, nor the environment, but rather the interface between them. In psychodynamic terms, this is termed the 'third space' (Miehls 2017, p. 432).

Relational social work reinterprets what could be meant by "person-centred approaches" to social work, in that the focus is neither on the client nor on the social worker with their arsenal of theory and techniques, but rather on the relationship itself, or more precisely, a range of relationships within the individual, in the consulting room and in the broader society. Relational social work appears to date back to the 1990s (Ornstein and Ganzer 2005), though its roots go back several decades before that.

The psychodynamic approach to relational social work (Tosone 2004; Tosone and Gelman 2017) is rooted in psychoanalysis, particularly object relations theory and practice, which shifted focus from one person (the client) to two persons (the client in a range of other relationships) (Miehls 2017). Indeed, the word 'relations' in object relations foregrounds the shift in focus from Freud's emphasis on instinctual drives and tensions to Klein's emphasis on actual relationships and internalised objects (Lemma 2016), followed by others, such as Kernberg, Winnicott, Kohut, and Sullivan (Borden 2000; Miehls 2017). Drawing on this foundation, Tosone and others emphasise the centrality of the internal object relations within the client, the therapeutic relationship between the client and worker, and the plethora of personal and institutional relationships between the client and their environment. Tosone (2004, p. 481) thus defines relational social work as "the practice of using the therapeutic relationship as the principal vehicle to effect change in the client's systemic functioning referring to the inherent interconnection of the intrapsychic, interpersonal and larger community systems".

Extending from this premise, relational social work in the broad frame advanced by Tosone emphasises the centrality of the intrapersonal network of internalised relationships, rooted in actual relationships with early caregivers and subsequent individuals in one's life world (Winter 2019). In addition, external contemporary relationships between the client and people in their social environment are highly significant for the social worker. Beyond merely interpersonal relationships, a relational social work approach considers also the social context, including societal structures, with which a person interfaces. Turney (2012) argues that these structures can be particularly important for involuntary clients, for example in child protection services.

Relational social work emphasises the mutuality between people in a relationship (Miehls 2017), which others have referred to as interactional (Van Breda 2018a). The mutual or interactional consideration of relationships raises issues of relational dynamics, including power and control, which are central themes in social work. For this reason, both feminist and critical race theorists have contributed to relational social work (Miehls 2017). Drawing on social constructionism, relational social workers critically engage with the ways society constructs human sexuality, gender, race, age, ethnicity, unemployment, etc. so that the relational interactions between persons and social constructs are made visible and questioned.

The professional relationship between social worker and client also comes under scrutiny, with a far greater awareness of the power, assumptions and potential privileges of the worker. The worker becomes a real human and not merely a professional service provider, who can make mistakes, have blind spots and biases, all of which can become material that impinges on practice, and conversely, material that can be worked on in practice (Miehls 2017).

To translate relational social work towards practice implications, Rosenberger (2014) makes several suggestions, including: the importance of empathic attunement; recognising the mutual and bidirectional nature of the helping relationship; the co-construction rather than prescription of meaning; adopting an inquiring position of not knowing; affirming client strengths; and engaging with the client's culture, social context and politics.

Relational social work's emphasis on the centrality of relationship resonates with African constructions of social work based on ubuntu philosophy (this term appears in different forms in different languages across the continent). Ubuntu can be translated as, "a person is a person through other people" (Van Breda 2019a, p. 439), and most simply implies mutual aid and solidarity. Tusasiirwe (2021, p. 175) shows that ubuntu harmonises well with relational social work in its emphasis on "interconnectedness, collectivism, solidarity, caring for and about others, and the environment". But the concept goes far deeper to show that the quality of relationality lies at the foundation of almost all human experience. In his paper on the theorisation of ubuntu for social work, Van Breda (2019a) maps out how ubuntu speaks to social work ethics, sustainable development and ecospirituality. There is thus considerable potential for the enrichment of relational social work, by drawing on Indigenous constructs of relationality from Africa and other Indigenous communities.

Although the importance of the professional relationship is accepted by almost all social workers, relational social work extends this basic understanding of the primacy of the helping relationship to attend also to the client's historical relationships with others, current relationships with the social worker and current relationships with others in their social environment, and an appreciation of the diverse, complex and power-laden nature of many interpersonal relations. In this way, relational social work has a strong PiE focus – the client is understood to be part of large and complex networks of relationships in their time and space environments. If change in the environment is to be accomplished in this therapeutic approach, it will be by shifting the client's relationship to others in their environment. This could emerge from an understanding of the power and other dynamics of these relationships and learning to position oneself differently in relation to others.

Narrative Therapy

Narrative therapy is the last practice model originated by social workers that will be considered in this chapter. It was pioneered by Michael White, together with David Epston, Australian and New Zealand social workers respectively. They began developing and writing their thinking about alternative approaches to social work practice in the early 1980s. Much of White's seminal writings are in the form of relatively brief, practice-oriented articles published by the Dulwich Centre, which they founded in 1983. It has since become a highly popular therapeutic approach, used not only by social workers, but also by psychologists (Olthof 2018), pastoral counsellors (Lee 2017) and others. A Google Scholar search for 'narrative therapy' and 'social work' over the past 10 years generated over 6000 hits. In South Africa, a quarter of clinical social workers surveyed reported using narrative therapy (Van Breda and Addinall 2021). Solution-focused brief therapy, which has some similarities to narrative therapy, generated 10,000 hits on Google Scholar and was reported to be used by a third of social workers in the South African survey.

Frank (2018, p. 555) argues that White's narrative therapy is quite distinctly *not* psychological. White's critique of psychology and psychiatry are, indeed, quite scathing. Instead, White draws on the likes of Bateson's interpretive method, Goffman's analogy, Foucault's focus on knowledge and power, Ricoeur's work on postmodernism (discussed elsewhere in this book), Derrida's deconstruction and post-structuralism (Payne 2006). These are "sociologists, anthropologists and philosophers" (Frank 2018, p. 555) who reflect deeply on the roots of power, oppression and control in society, through narrative, and how deconstructive and subversive narrative can begin to wrest power back from the powerful. This is much more aligned with radical and critical social work (discussed elsewhere in this book) than with task centred or strengths-based social work.

Power is arguably central to narrative therapy (Brown 2003; White 1992). Narrative therapy views all human problems as being rooted in the construction and misuse of power by self, others and systems. It is the way the world is constructed through discourse that enables oppressive and socially unjust life experiences, which leads to personal and family problems that are brought to social workers for assistance. Narrative therapy, as written about by White and his colleagues, is about recognising and deconstructing these power-laden narratives or discourses. "In this way, treatment can nurture ... an emancipatory narrative" (Ungar 2001, p. 61). The tone of this approach is quite different from the task-centred focus on activities a client can do to overcome obstacles and reach desired goals and the strengths perspective's focus on mobilising resources in the PiE to facilitate well-being and social functioning.

While narrative therapy bears a close resemblance to the solution-focused brief therapy of social workers Steve de Shazer and Insoo Kim Berg (De Shazer and Berg 1988; De Shazer and Dolan 2007) – the focus on solutions, the centrality of unique outcomes or exceptions, the optimistic playfulness – narrative therapy has a far deeper and more serious, perhaps even darker foundation, centred on an appreciation for the ways powerful people and discourses oppress and harm others. There are two key points here: first, both narrative and solution-focused brief therapies are social work practice models, developed by social workers – we should not allow them to be co-opted by other professions as their own; second, narrative therapy (unlike solution-focused brief therapy) has deep roots in social work's commitment to social justice and human dignity.

Narrative therapy (Van Breda 2019d; White 2007) starts with the gathering of the client's problem saturated story, during which the social worker seeks to personify the problem by giving it a name, which continues with extensive use of externalising language which seeks to separate the problem out of the person. This form of externalising conversation continues throughout the therapy. All the while, the therapist considers the broad socio-political context of the issue at hand, and how factors like race, class, gender and age might influence the client's problem and world. Relative influence questioning about the problem's influence on the person is followed by the relative influence of the person on the problem, leading to the excavation of unique outcomes – bits of narrative that disappear because they do not fit within the dominant power-laden narrative of the problem. One unique outcome leads to another, and through a process of weaving these outcomes together with the client-assigned meaning of the outcomes (the landscapes of action and identity respectively) a re-authoring conversation emerges, in which the client generates a new, rich, power-filled and agential narrative about their life. In addition to this overall process, narrative practitioners also make use of documents, other members of the client's life world, letter writing and engagement with people's ancestors (White and Epston 1990).

Narrative therapy has been effectively used in various ways with a range of groups and problems, including feminist narrative therapy with complex trauma (Brown 2020), couples facing cancer (Rajaei et al. 2020), children with developmental disabilities (Baldiwala and Kanakia 2021), vulnerable children and young people (Nyirinkwaya 2020), older persons (Bayram and Artan 2020), men who perpetrate domestic violence (Wendt et al. 2020), homelessness (Mills 2021), and loss and grief (Yousuf-Abramson 2021). In all these examples, narrative therapy was found to be useful, and in all but the last example, substantial attention was given to the presentation of and work with power and empowerment.

Because of narrative therapy's roots in critical theory, it is well suited not only to therapeutic work on personal problems, but also to facilitated work that, while still person-centred, addresses the person within broader contexts of oppression and injustice (Brown 2003; Riessman and Quinney 2005; Van Breda 2019d). McKenzie-Mohr and Lafrance (2017) extend this impetus by constructing the notion of 'narrative resistance' as a way of constructing counternarratives that compete with oppressive, power-laden and limiting 'master narratives'. In this way, narrative therapy has strong decolonial or post-colonial practice potential (these are discussed elsewhere in this book).

Butler (2017), for example, writes about using narrative therapy as an Aboriginal person. He critically observes that the narratives of Aboriginal people in Australia tend to be deficit- and damage-centred and told by non-Aboriginal people. These third-person, thin stories become dominant narratives, for both non-Aboriginal and Aboriginal people. Using narrative therapy methods in consciousness-raising groups, Butler invites Aboriginal groups to set aside the thin narratives and to begin telling their own narratives, including narratives of colonisation, dispossession and genocide, to deconstruct third-person narratives, and to make sense of and embrace their own thick narratives. White et al. (2013) report effectively implementing similar processes among women from Myanmar.

In related ways, Strauven (2020) drew on the narrative therapy techniques of witnessing and definitional ceremonies in her work with refugees in Australia, which was then witnessed and written about by an academic, and then subsequently further witnessed by those who read and engaged with his writing. This example of resistance to dominant power discourses is a person-centred use of a social work practice approach with deep roots in social justice.

Narrative therapy has been used primarily to effect person-centred change, more than social or systemic change. It is thus primarily a person-centred approach to social work practice. However, in contrast to the previous social work practice models, and solution-focused therapy with which it has much in common, narrative therapy gives substantial attention to issues of power, oppression, justice and transformation, and deliberately locates oppression not only within the individual or family, but also within the broader systems of society. While narrative therapy's light-hearted methods can lead it to being used as little more than a set of creative expressive arts techniques and storytelling (e.g., Malchiodi 2008), when White's original theorising of narrative therapy is taken seriously, it becomes a powerful and socially disruptive therapeutic process, with capacity to be used to facilitate systemic change.

Prominent Person-Centred Theories Drawn from Other Professions

While social work is an autonomous profession, it overlaps in various ways with other professions, including psychology and family therapy. As a result, social workers have frequently drawn on practice theories and models developed in other professions and used them either as is or adapted them formally or informally to align with social work's identity, values and principles. These theories will not be discussed in great detail, but because of their frequent use by social workers and their prominence in the many social work books on practice theories (e.g., Bolton et al. 2021; Brandell 2020; Payne and Reith-Hall 2019; Turner 2017; Walsh 2014), it seems important to mention some of them and how they are being used by social workers. The selected five approaches should be considered as exemplars of the numerous therapies available. (See also ▶ Chap. 2, "Psychological and Clinical Theories".)

This section will show that all these therapies (person-centred, cognitive behavioural, mindfulness-based, psychodynamic and motivational) are person-centred, in that they work to develop the individual's insight, coping skills, readiness to change, sense of self, awareness of self, and well-being. However, while they are not disengaged from the world around the client, little to no attention is given to facilitating change in the client's social environment, even through the client. Consequently, they cannot easily be considered 'social work' interventions, unless there is greater investment on the part of the social worker to translate therapeutic gains into environmental changes.

Person-Centred Therapy

A Google Scholar search for person- or client-, –centred or -centered social work generated almost 49,000 hits. However, this search was complicated by the non-Rogerian use of the term 'person centred' to mean any kind of service that puts the person first (rather than the institutional mandate, rules, procedures, etc.). This is captured in the following titles, "Providing person-centred care to older people with intellectual disabilities during the COVID-19 pandemic" (Thalen et al. 2021) and "Person-centred approaches to social work with older people" (Sieminski 2020), neither of which cites Carl Rogers nor makes any reference to person-centred therapy. It thus likely that the actual research on Rogerian therapy is far less and would require a very rigorous process of sourcing relevant literature. Nevertheless, almost half (41%) of the South African clinical social workers surveyed indicated that they used the person-centred approach (Van Breda and Addinall 2021).

Person-centred therapy was developed by psychologist, Carl Rogers (1951). It is a non-directive therapeutic approach that places the client central in the therapeutic process. Roger's core conditions – genuineness or congruency, unconditional positive regard and empathy – and his values – respect, individualisation, self-determination and confidentiality (Mbedzi 2019) – have been widely adopted as (arguably) foundational to all therapeutic work in social work (Egan 2014). The approach has also been applied to other methods of social work, including community work (Schenck et al. 2010).

In addition to the relational underpinnings of person-centred practice are Rogers' 19 propositions, which constitute his theory of personality and behaviour (Rogers 1951). Rogers' nineth proposition refers to a person's "interaction with the environment and . . . with others" connoting a PiE perspective (Rogers 1951, p. 498). However, in the rest of the propositions, the focus is less on the environment (as an external fact) and more on the 'field' which refers rather to the person's experience of the environment. Proposition 2 states (Rogers 1951, p. 484), "The organism reacts to the field as it is experienced and perceived. This perceptual field is, for the individual, 'reality'". Thus, while Rogers recognised the external world, his understanding of people and thus his therapy focuses on their experience of the world.

Cognitive Behavioural Therapy

Cognitive behavioural therapy (CBT) is frequently used by social workers. A Google Scholar search over the past 10 years for 'cognitive behavioural therapy' and 'social work' generated 27,000 hits. Four thousands of these hits were for trauma-focused CBT (TF-CBT). In the South African survey of clinical social workers, CBT was the second most frequently used model (by 46% of participants), second only to grief counselling (at 48%) (Van Breda and Addinall 2021). Furthermore, 40% of participants reported using trauma counselling (including TF-CBT).

CBT appears to be a popular practice model because it is structured, clear and tangible, produces rapid results, including quick relief from distressing symptoms. In a neo-liberal, managed care context, which applies increasingly to much of the world, brief interventions that are effective at reducing troublesome symptoms are much in demand (Ingram 2019; Rabeyron 2019). Others, however, have lauded the alignment between CBT values and social work values (González-Prendes and Brisebois 2012).

CBT and TF-CBT do appear to be highly effective, particularly in the context of narrowly constructed randomised clinical trials, and also to have good sustainability over time (Chipalo 2021). While some reviewers raise questions about the qualitative experience of participants, the appropriateness of treatment for context and so on, they remain persuaded by the statistics about CBT's efficacy and cost-effectiveness (Holtzhausen et al. 2016). CBT is also frequently used in the global South, where it often generates positive results (Murray et al. 2015). CBT thus remains widely used by social workers for various psychosocial challenges and with various vulnerable or marginalised groups.

Mindfulness-Based Interventions

Mindfulness interventions have gained popularity recently. A Google Scholar search generated 19,000 hits, while in the South African survey of clinical social workers, 25% reported using mindfulness in their clinical practice (Van Breda and Addinall 2021). Mindfulness practices emerge from several eastern philosophical and spiritual traditions, especially Buddhism (Tan and Keng 2020). Since around the 1960s, mindfulness and other Buddhist practices have gained increasing interest in the West and in therapeutic practice. Mindfulness has since influenced other practice models, such as mindfulness-based cognitive therapy, dialectical behaviour therapy and acceptance and commitment therapy (Tan and Keng 2020).

Mindfulness comprises a set of techniques to facilitate "paying attention to the experiences in the present moment in an open, intentional, and nonjudgmental manner" (Tan and Keng 2020, p. 312). Techniques include walking meditation, body scan exercises, breathing techniques and yoga, which are practiced regularly. These focus on the person's inner experience and cultivate internal resources to manage their problems and stress.

Studies, including systematic reviews, have shown mindfulness-based interventions to be effective. For example, a systematic review of studies on youth with anxiety found mindfulness to reduce anxiety symptoms (Borquist-Conlon et al. 2019). Interestingly, many of the recent publications on mindfulness and social work have focused on the use of mindfulness by social workers and student social workers for themselves, rather than for their clients (Beer et al. 2019; Feize et al. 2021; Warren and Chappell Deckert 2019). In addition to these, there are numerous studies on the use of mindfulness with a wide range of client groups, and in both case and group work contexts.

Psychodynamic Therapy

Psychodynamic therapy has been alluded to previously under relational social work, which is largely social work's adaptation of psychodynamic practice. Nevertheless, while there were only about 600 Google Scholar hits for relational social work, there were about 16,000 hits for psychodynamic therapy and social work over the past 10 years. Moreover, in the South African survey of clinical social workers, 46% of participants reported using psychodynamic therapy, with small numbers using psychoanalytic therapy (14%), object relations therapy (13%), and analytical psychotherapy (6%) (Van Breda and Addinall 2021).

Research on psychodynamic therapy tends to focus on specific clients groups or problems or particular psychodynamic themes, such as countertransference (Van Breda and Feller 2014), the social worker as wounded healer (Macfarlane 2020), therapist distance (Egozi et al. 2021) and complex PTSD (Levi 2020). In addition to this body of publications, psychodynamic literature also gives attention to some of the more critical issues in contemporary society, for example, issues of race and racism, both in the world and in the interactions between client and worker (Stevenson 2020), LGBT issues among Arab clients and workers (Qushua and Ostler 2020), diversity and power (Lee and Rasmussen 2019) and mass incarceration (Kita 2019).

Motivational Interviewing

Motivational interviewing is a popular practice model, generating 15,000 hits when paired with 'social work' on Google Scholar and reported by 14% of clinical social workers in the South African survey (Van Breda and Addinall 2021). Motivational interviewing was developed by psychologists William Miller and Stephen Rollnick. Motivation interviewing is a highly relevant and useful practice theory for social workers, given our extensive work with people abusing substances and with reluctant clients who are court-ordered for services. The developers found that confrontational approaches, which were popular at a time, elicited resistance from clients and were counterproductive to engaging clients in treatment processes. Instead, motivation can be facilitated by an empathic listening style, talks about change and resolution of ambivalence about change (Rollnick and Allison 2004). Three key concepts in motivational interviewing are readiness for change, which can be linked to the transtheoretical or stages of change model (Prochaska et al. 1992); ambivalence regarding the losses associated with change, even when change is desired; and resistance, which is the reluctance to change in response to the worker's pressure or cajoling.

Hohman's (2021) second edition of *Motivational Interviewing in Social Work Practice* is perhaps a key text on this model, providing in-depth information on the various strategies and techniques that comprise the model. The book also addresses motivational interviewing in relation to critical race theory. Motivational interviewing has been used to promote COVID-19 contact tracing (Hohman et al. 2021), and engage people at risk of sex trafficking (Gerassi and Esbensen 2020), families in child welfare services (Hall et al. 2019), and youth aging out of alternative care (Richmond and Borden 2020).

Key Elements of Person-Centred Social Work Practice

This chapter has identified several tensions in the person-centred approaches used in social work. There is an ambivalence in the profession regarding the person and the environment, with a tendency to bifurcate these into separate practice approaches (micro and macro) and insufficient attempts to incorporate the person-in-environment integration into person-centred approaches (see section "Locating Person-Centred Approaches Within the Social Work Agenda"). The person-centred practice approaches drawn from psychologists (person-centred therapy, cognitive behavioural therapy, mindfulness-based interventions, psychodynamic therapy and motivational interviewing, among others) (see section "Prominent Person-Centred Theories Drawn from Other Professions") tend largely to neglect the environment in favour of the person, resulting in practice approaches that primarily target personal change. I say, "tend largely", because these therapies do not entirely ignore the environment – psychodynamic and attachment theories, for example, give strong recognition to the world out there and back then (Jacobs 2006), both of which are located in the external world and important to psychodynamic practice. Nevertheless, the overwhelming emphasis remains on personal change.

The person-centred practice approaches developed by social workers (task-centred, strengths-based and relational social work, and narrative therapy, among others) (see section "Person-Centred Social Work Practice Approaches") focus also primarily on the person, since they are intended to be person-centred approaches.

However, they give more recognition to the need to make changes in the environment. Task-centred social work, for example, identifies environmental obstacles that impede the client's progress and seek ways to remove such obstacles. Strengths-based social work identifies and leverages resources in the social environment to the benefit of the client, so that client growth is not a result only of personal effort, but also ecological mobilisation. Relational social work centres on the therapeutic relationship but gives considerable attention to the role of external relationships, past and present, in the therapeutic work. And narrative therapy is deeply rooted in concepts of power and oppression, deliberately focuses the practitioner on justice and transformation, actively incorporates the social ecology into the counselling space, and can be used to facilitate decolonial and anti-oppressive change processes.

These critiques raise the important question of what constitutes a coherent person-centred social work practice approach. It is one thing to critique existing models; it is another to articulate what it is that person-centred social work approaches should be striving to achieve. This final section thus attempts, briefly, to conceptualise what constitutes a coherent person-centred social work practice model or theory. It draws from the preceding sections to identify some general principles or assumptions shared across the various models presented.

First, a social work practice approach is ideally designed by a social worker, rather than adopted or adapted from a model designed by another professional. Social work has a particular set of values, identity markers and priorities that differentiate it from other professions. We have a distinctive professional identity that has its roots in the history of our profession and how it is has evolved over time. This identity is not the same as that of other professions. A practice approach developed by social workers is, hopefully, more likely to embrace the professional values and priorities stated in the global definition of social work (IASSW 2014).

Second, a person-centred approach to practice places the person first. The individual in front of us (or the family, group or community) is our priority and primary focus. This is what makes the social work practice approach person-centred. There is, in some contexts, such as in the global South where I am based, a sense of shame in centring social work on a person, given the massive needs at the macro level. However, focusing on the person does not diminish or disregard the needs of the community or society; it just means focusing for now on this person and helping this person change their life.

Third, a person-centred approach to social work practice must bear in mind the multiple layers of systems and structures around a person, and the ways they enable or hinder the person's journey through life towards well-being and accomplishment. Improving the lived experience of this person requires not only personal change but also environmental change. Such change could be actioned by the client, or the social worker or some other social worker or person; but a person-centred social work practice approach must incorporate initiatives to address the environment, when salient.

Fourth, a person-centred approach to social work practice must recognise that these systems are often powerful and oppressive. They may limit, hinder, diminish and harm the person. Changing the environment may involve challenging people and systems with power. This change is thus not neutral, but political, and may require the social worker and person to engage powerfully with the environment.

I suggest that it is the combination of all four of these elements that makes a practice model or theory a person-centred social work approach. Of all the models presented in this chapter, Michael White's narrative therapy most fully meets these criteria.

Conclusion

Notwithstanding a groundswell of interest in social work addressing and dismantling the macro, systemic and structural issues that are prime contributors to the difficulties faced by most of the world's population, there remains within social work an enduring interest in and commitment to social work practice directed at individual change. While it may be tempting to put this down to social workers being enamoured with psychology, the person-centred practice models that social workers have generated (e.g., problem-solving, task-centred, strengths-based, narrative, solution-focused and relational) have significant weight and have been taken up (and sometimes even annexed) by other professions. These models universally consider the PiE, by emphasising the importance of people's context, and in some cases (notably narrative therapy) sharply critique society's power structures and systems. While person-centred approaches do not directly aim to change these systems, they do often help people recognise and dissent with them and perhaps even challenge and subvert them. Clinical social work participants in the South African study referred to in this chapter (Van Breda and Addinall 2021) argued strongly that clinical or person-centred social work does make a significant contribution to addressing developmental and decolonial issues in South Africa, through a focus on the person.

Nevertheless, the development of social work scholarship concerning person-centred practice theories and models should give greater consideration to the socio-political environment surrounding clients, to the power issues inherent in these systems and the ways that such models could contribute to shifting these macro patterns. A recent example of this is Van Breda's (2018c) attempt to develop a social casework model rooted in and aligned with developmental social work priorities. All social work, whether person-centred or radical, should be mindful of and address the macro systems that subject and limit the flourishing of individual people. After all, that is what makes social work social work.

References

Ablett P, Morley C (2016) Towards a history of critical traditions in Australian social work. Soc Altern 35(4):7–13. https://doi.org/10.3316/ielapa.872114663499986

Baldiwala J, Kanakia T (2021) Using narrative therapy with children experiencing developmental disabilities and their families in India: a qualitative study. J Child Health Care. https://doi.org/10.1177/13674935211014739. (Online first)

Barnes-Lee AR (2020) Development of protective factors for reducing juvenile reoffending: a strengths-based approach to risk assessment. Crim Justice Behav 47(11):1371–1389. https://doi.org/10.1177/0093854820949601

Bayram Y, Artan T (2020) This is not all your life but the pieces you talked about your life: the narrative therapy with the elderly. Turk J Appl Soc Work 3(1):45–58

Beer OWJ, Phillips R, Stepney L, Quinn CR (2019) The feasibility of mindfulness training to reduce stress among social workers: a conceptual paper. Br J Soc Work 50(1):243–263. https://doi.org/10.1093/bjsw/bcz104

Bolton KW, Hall JC, Lehmann P (2021) Theoretical perspectives for direct social work practice: a generalist-eclectic approach, 4th edn. Springer, New York

Borden W (2000) The relational paradigm in contemporary psychoanalysis: toward a psychodynamically informed social work perspective. Soc Serv Rev 74(3):352–379. https://doi.org/10.1086/516409

Borquist-Conlon DS, Maynard BR, Brendel KE, Farina ASJ (2019) Mindfulness-based interventions for youth with anxiety: a systematic review and meta-analysis. Res Soc Work Pract 29(2):195–205. https://doi.org/10.1177/1049731516684961

Brandell JR (ed) (2020) Theory and practice in clinical social work, 3rd edn. Sage, Thousand Oaks

Brito IS, Ottmann G (2019) Refractory interventions: the incubation of rival epistemologies in the margins of Brazilian social work. In: Tascón SM, Ife J (eds) Disrupting whiteness in social work. Routledge, London, pp 139–155

Brown C (2003) Narrative therapy: reifying or challenging dominant discourse. In: Shera W (ed) Emerging perspectives on anti-oppressive practice. Canadian Scholars, Toronto, pp 223–246

Brown C (2020) Feminist narrative therapy and complex trauma: critical clinical work with women diagnosed as "borderline". In: Brown C, Macdonald JE (eds) Critical clinical social work: counterstorying for social justice. Canadian Scholars, Toronto, pp 82–109

Butler J (2017) Who's your mob? Aboriginal mapping: beginning with the strong story. Int J Narrat Ther Community Work 3:22–26

Chapin RK, Sergeant JF, Landry S, Leedahl SN, Rachlin R, Koenig T et al (2012) Reclaiming joy: pilot evaluation of a mental health peer support program for older adults who receive medicaid. Gerontologist 53(2):345–352. https://doi.org/10.1093/geront/gns120

Chipalo E (2021) Is trauma focused-cognitive behavioral therapy (TF-CBT) effective in reducing trauma symptoms among traumatized refugee children? A systematic review. J Child Adolesc Trauma 14:545–558. https://doi.org/10.1007/s40653-021-00370-0

Crous G, Montserrat C, Balaban A (2021) Young people leaving care with intellectual disabilities or mental health problems: strengths and weaknesses in their transitions. Soc Work Soc 18(3):1–19

Dash BM (2017) Revisiting eight decades of social work education in India. Asian Soc Work Policy Rev 11(1):66–75. https://doi.org/10.1111/aswp.12114

De Shazer S, Berg IK (1988) Constructing solutions. Family Therapy Networker, September/October, pp 42–43

De Shazer S, Dolan Y (2007) More than miracles: the state of the art of solution-focused brief therapy. Haworth, Binghamton

Diaz MJ, Wolfersteig W, Moreland D, Yoder G, Dustman P, Harthun ML (2021) Teaching youth to resist abuse: evaluation of a strengths-based child maltreatment curriculum for high school students. J Child Adolesc Trauma 14(1):141–149. https://doi.org/10.1007/s40653-020-00304-2

Donnelly J (2021) Rethinking reentry: a look at how risk-based approaches limit reentry success, and a case for why strengths-based approaches may better reduce recidivism. Masters thesis, University of Pittsburgh, Pittsburgh

Dudgeon P, Bray A, Walker R (2020) Self-determination and strengths-based Aboriginal and Torres Strait Islander suicide prevention: an emerging evidence-based approach. In: Page AC, Stritzke WGK (eds) Alternatives to suicide. Academic Press, London, pp 237–256

Egan G (2014) The skilled helper: a problem-management and opportunity-development approach to helping, 10th edn. Brooks/Cole, Cengage Learning, Belmont

Egozi S, Tishby O, Wiseman H (2021) Changes in clients and therapists experiences of therapeutic distance during psychodynamic therapy. J Clin Psychol 77(4):910–926. https://doi.org/10.1002/jclp.23077

Engelbrecht L (2021) Strengths-based supervision. In: O'Donoghue K, Engelbrecht L (eds) The Routledge international handbook of social work supervision. Routledge, Abingdon

Feize L, Faver C, Gorabi V (2021) Employing experiential learning as a tool to teach Mindfulness Cognitive Behavioral Therapy (MCBT) to Latino social work graduate students. J Teach Soc Work 41(1):16–41. https://doi.org/10.1080/08841233.2020.1846668

Fortune AE, Reid WJ (2017) Task-centered social work. In: Turner FJ (ed) Social work treatment: interlocking theoretical approaches, 6th edn. Oxford University Press, New York, pp 532–552

Fortune AE, McCallion P, Briar-Lawson K (eds) (2010) Social work practice research for the twenty-first century. Columbia University Press, New York

Frank AW (2018) What is narrative therapy and how can it help health humanities? J Med Humanit 39(4):553–563. https://doi.org/10.1007/s10912-018-9507-3

Garrett PM (2016) Questioning tales of "ordinary magic": "resilience" and neo-liberal reasoning. Br J Soc Work 46(7):1909–1925. https://doi.org/10.1093/bjsw/bcv017

Gerassi LB, Esbensen K (2020) Motivational interviewing with individuals at risk of sex trafficking. J Soc Work. https://doi.org/10.1177/1468017320919856

Goeke J, Klein EJ, Garcia-Reid P, Birnbaum AS, Brown TL, Degennaro D (2011) Deepening roots: building a task-centered peer mentoring community. Fem Form 23(1):212–234

González-Prendes AA, Brisebois K (2012) Cognitive-behavioral therapy and social work values: a critical analysis. J Soc Work Values Ethics 9(2):21–33

Hall MT, Sears J, Walton MT (2019) Motivational interviewing in child welfare services: a systematic review. Child Maltreat 25(3):263–276. https://doi.org/10.1177/1077559519893471

Harms Smith L (2017) "Blaming-the-poor": strengths and development discourses which obfuscate neo-liberal and individualist ideologies. Int Soc Work 60(2):336–350. https://doi.org/10.1177/0020872815594218

Healy K (2014) Social work theories in context: creating frameworks for practice, 2nd edn. Macmillan International Higher Education, New York

Higgins M (2015) The struggle for the soul of social work in England. Soc Work Educ 34(1):4–16. https://doi.org/10.1080/02615479.2014.946898

Hohman M (2021) Motivational interviewing in social work practice, 2nd edn. Guilford Publications, New York

Hohman M, McMaster F, Woodruff SI (2021) Contact tracing for COVID-19: the use of motivational interviewing and the role of social work. Clin Soc Work J 48:419–428. https://doi.org/10.1007/s10615-021-00802-2

Holtzhausen L, Ross A, Perry R (2016) Working on trauma: a systematic review of TF-CBT work with child survivors of sexual abuse. Soc Work 52(4):511–524. https://doi.org/10.15270/52-2-528

IASSW (2014). Global definition of social work. https://www.iassw-aiets.org/global-definition-of-social-work-review-of-the-global-definition/

Ingram N (2019) Suicide and neoliberalism: an imminent critique of cognitive-behavioral therapy. Paper presented at the Seaver College research and scholarly achievement symposium, Malibu

Jacobs M (2006) The presenting past: the core of psychodynamic counselling and therapy, 3rd edn. Open University Press, Maidenhead

Joseph S, Murphy D (2013) Person-centered approach, positive psychology, and relational helping: building bridges. J Humanist Psychol 53(1):26–51. https://doi.org/10.1177/0022167812436426

Katsama I (2022) Promoting positive parenting: a group social work intervention in a workplace setting. J Soc Work Pract 36(1):57–71. https://doi.org/10.1080/02650533.2021.1926223

Keenan EM, Mostert K (2013) Perceived organisational support for strengths use: the factorial validity and reliability of a new scale in the banking industry. SA J Ind Psychol 39(1):1–12. https://doi.org/10.4102/sajip.v39i1.1052

Kirst-Ashman KK, Hull GH (2018) Understanding generalist practice, 8th edn. Brooks/Cole, Cengage Learning, Belmont

Kita E (2019) "They hate me now but where was everyone when I needed them?": mass incarceration, projective identification, and social work praxis. Psychoanal Soc Work 26(1):25–49. https://doi.org/10.1080/15228878.2019.1584118

Lee H (2017) Narrative therapy for pastoral theology, care, and counseling. Korean J Christ Stud (？ 국기독교신 h논총) 105:247–268

Lee E, Rasmussen B (2019) Psychoanalysis, socioanalysis, and social work: psychodynamic contributions to understanding diversity, power, and institutions in social work practice. Smith Coll Stud Soc Work 89(2):83–90. https://doi.org/10.1080/00377317.2019.1686873

Lemma A (2016) Introduction to the practice of psychoanalytic psychotherapy, 2nd edn. Wiley, Chichester

Levi O (2020) The role of hope in psychodynamic therapy (PDT) for complex PTSD (C-PTSD). J Soc Work Pract 34(3):237–248. https://doi.org/10.1080/02650533.2019.1648246

Macfarlane S (2020) The radical potential of Carl Jung's wounded healer for social work education. In: Morley C, Ablett P, Noble C, Cowden S (eds) The Routledge handbook of critical pedagogies for social work. Routledge, London, pp 322–332

Malchiodi CA (ed) (2008) Creative interventions with traumatized children. Guilford, New York

Marsh P, Doel M (2005) The task-centred book. Routledge, Abingdon

Mbedzi P (2019) Person-centred. In: Van Breda AD, Sekudu J (eds) Theories for decolonial social work practice in South Africa. Oxford University Press South Africa, Cape Town, pp 198–221

McKenzie-Mohr S, Lafrance MN (2017) Narrative resistance in social work research and practice: counter-storying in the pursuit of social justice. Qual Soc Work 16(2):189–205. https://doi.org/10.1177/1473325016657866

McNutt JG (2013) Social work practice: history and evolution. In: Franklin C (ed) Encyclopedia of social work. National Association of Social Workers Press/Oxford University Press, New York

Midgley J, Conley A (2010) Introduction. In: Midgley J, Conley A (eds) Developmental social work and social development: theories and skills for developmental social work. Oxford University Press, New York, pp xiii–xx

Miehls D (2017) Relational theory and social work treatment. In: Turner FJ (ed) Social work treatment: interlocking theoretical approaches, 6th edn. Oxford University Press, New York, pp 428–440

Mills J (2021) Retelling stories of resilience as a counterplot to homelessness: a narrative approach in the context of intensive team-based housing support services. Soc Work Policy Stud Soc Just Pract Theory 4(1):1–17

Murray LK, Skavenski S, Kane JC, Mayeya J, Dorsey S, Cohen JA et al (2015) Effectiveness of trauma-focused cognitive behavioral therapy among trauma-affected children in Lusaka, Zambia: a randomized clinical trial. JAMA Pediatr 169(8):761–769. https://doi.org/10.1001/jamapediatrics.2015.0580

Nelson-Becker H, Lloyd L, Milne A, Perry E, Ray M, Richards S et al (2020) Strengths-based social work with older people: a UK perspective. In: Mendenhall AN (ed) Rooted in strengths: celebrating the strengths perspective in social work. University of Kansas Libraries, Lawrence, pp 327–346

Njeze C, Bird-Naytowhow K, Pearl T, Hatala AR (2020) Intersectionality of resilience: a strengths-based case study approach with Indigenous youth in an urban Canadian context. Qual Health Res 30(13):2001–2018. https://doi.org/10.1177/1049732320940702

Nyirinkwaya S (2020) Games, activities and narrative practice: enabling sparks to emerge in conversations with children and young people who have experienced hard times. Int J Narrat Ther Community Work 1:34–45

Olthof J (2018) Handbook of narrative psychotherapy for children, adults, and families: theory and practice. Routledge, New York

Ornstein ED, Ganzer C (2005) Relational social work: a model for the future. Fam Soc 86(4):565–572. https://doi.org/10.1606/1044-3894.3462

Patel L, Hochfeld T (2012) Developmental social work in South Africa: translating policy into practice. Int Soc Work 56(5):690–704. https://doi.org/10.1177/0020872812444481

Payne M (2006) Narrative therapy: an introduction for counsellors, 2nd edn. Sage, London

Payne M, Reith-Hall E (eds) (2019) The Routledge handbook of social work theory. Routledge, London

Perlman HH (1957) Social casework: a problem-solving process. University of Chicago Press, Chicago

Pomeroy EC, Garcia RB (2017) Direct practice skills for evidence-based social work: a strengths-based text and workbook. Springer, New York

Price A, Ahuja L, Bramwell C, Briscoe S, Shaw L, Nunns M et al (2020) Research evidence on different strengths-based approaches within adult social work: a systematic review. NIHR Health Services and Delivery Research topic report

Pritzker S, Applewhite SR (2015) Going "macro": exploring the careers of macro practitioners. Soc Work 60(3):191–199. https://doi.org/10.1093/sw/swv019

Prochaska JO, DiClemente CC, Norcross JC (1992) In search of how people change: applications to addictive behaviors. Am Psychol 47(9):1102–1114

Qushua N, Ostler T (2020) Creating a safe therapeutic space through naming: psychodynamic work with traditional Arab LGBT clients. J Soc Work Pract 34(2):125–137. https://doi.org/10.1080/02650533.2018.1478395

Rabeyron T (2019) From neoliberalism to the cognitive-behavioural tsunami in Great Britain. Rech Psychanal 2:112a–134a

Rajaei A, Brimhall AS, Jensen JF, Schwartz AJ, Torres ET (2020) Striving to thrive: a qualitative study on fostering a relational perspective through narrative therapy in couples facing cancer. Am J Fam Ther 49(4):392–408. https://doi.org/10.1080/01926187.2020.1820402

Rajeev S, Jeena A (2020) Strengths perspective in working with elderly. Indian J Gerontol 34(3):377–393

Ramos BM, Tolson ER (2008) The task-centered model. In: Coady N, Lehmann P (eds) Theoretical perspectives for direct social work practice: a generalist-eclectic approach, 2nd edn. Springer, New York, pp 275–295

Rapp CA, Goscha RJ (2011) The strengths model: a recovery-oriented approach to mental health services, 3rd edn. Oxford University Press, Oxford, UK

Reid WJ, Epstein L (1972) Task-centered casework. Columbia University Press, New York

Reid WJ, Shyne AW (1969) Brief and extended casework. Columbia University Press, New York

Richmond ME (1899) Friendly visiting among the poor: a handbook for charity workers. Macmillan, London

Richmond ME (1922) What is social case work? An introductory description. Russell Sage Foundation, New York

Richmond A, Borden LM (2020) Motivational interviewing: an approach to support youth aging out of foster care. J Soc Work. https://doi.org/10.1177/1468017320920176

Riessman CK, Quinney L (2005) Narrative in social work: a critical review. Qual Soc Work 4(4):391–412. https://doi.org/10.1177/1473325005058643

Rogers CR (1951) Client-centered therapy: its current practice, implications, and theory. Constable, London

Rollnick S, Allison J (2004) Motivational interviewing. In: Heather N, Stockwell T (eds) The essential handbook of treatment and prevention of alcohol problems. Wiley, Southern Gate, pp 105–115

Rooney R (2018) Task-centered intervention with involuntary clients. In: Rooney R, Mirick R, G. (eds) Strategies for work with involuntary clients, 3rd edn. Columbia University Press, New York, pp 248–297

Rosenberger JB (2014) Orientation to and validation of relational diversity practice. In: Rosenberger JB (ed) Relational social work practice with diverse populations. Springer, New York, pp 13–30

Rothman J, Mizrahi T (2014) Balancing micro and macro practice: a challenge for social work. Soc Work 59(1):91–93. https://doi.org/10.1093/sw/swt067

Saleebey D (ed) (1992) The strengths perspective in social work practice. Longman, New York City

Sarfaraz FF, Ishrat SS (2012) Social case work as a problem solving process: an introduction. J Soc Sci Humanit 51(2):235–247

Schenck R, Nel H, Louw H (2010) Introduction to participatory community practice. Unisa Press, Pretoria

Sieminski S (2020) Person-centred approaches to social work with older people. In: Seden J, Matthews S, McCormick M, Alun M (eds) Professional development in social work: complex issues in practice. Routledge, London, pp 118–125

Stevenson S (2020) A racist attack managing complex relationships with traumatised service users: a psychodynamic approach. J Soc Work Pract 34(3):225–235. https://doi.org/10.1080/02650533.2019.1648247

Strauven S (2020) A politics of witnessing: definitional ceremony as social justice work in academia. Int Rev Qual Res. https://doi.org/10.1177/1940844720968203

Studt E (1968) Social work theory and implications for the practice of methods. Soc Work Educ Report 16:22–46

Sundel M, Glasser P, Sarri R, Vinter R (1985) Individual change through small groups, 2nd edn. Free Press, New York

Tan SY, Keng S-L (2020) Application of mindfulness-based approaches in the context of social work. In: Ow R, Poon AWC (eds) Mental health and social work. Springer, Singapore, pp 311–329

Thalen M, van Oorsouw WM, Volkers KM, Frielink N, Embregts PJ (2021) Providing person-centred care to older people with intellectual disabilities during the COVID-19 pandemic: experiences of direct support workers. Int J Dev Disabil:1–7. https://doi.org/10.1080/20473869.2021.2019921

Theron LC, Van Breda AD (2021) Multisystemic enablers of sub-Saharan child and youth resilience to maltreatment. Child Abuse Negl 119(2):105083. https://doi.org/10.1016/j.chiabu.2021.105083

Tolson ER, Reid WJ, Garvin CD, Garvin C (2003) Generalist practice: a task-centered practice, 2nd edn. Columbia University Press, New York

Tosone C (2004) Relational social work: honoring the tradition. Smith Coll Stud Soc Work 74(3):475–487. https://doi.org/10.1080/00377310409517730

Tosone C, Gelman CR (2017) Relational social work: a contemporary psychosocial perspective on practice. In: Turner FJ (ed) Social work treatment: interlocking theoretical approaches, 6th edn. Oxford University Press, New York, pp 420–427

Turner FJ (2017) Social work treatment: interlocking theoretical approaches, 6th edn. Oxford University Press, New York

Turney D (2012) A relationship-based approach to engaging involuntary clients: the contribution of recognition theory. Child Fam Soc Work 17(2):149–159. https://doi.org/10.1111/j.1365-2206.2012.00830.x

Tusasiirwe S (2021) Social workers navigating a colonial bureaucratic system while also re-kindling Obuntu-led relational social work in Uganda. In: Boulet J, Linette H (eds) Practical and political approaches to recontextualizing social work. IGI Global, Hershey, pp 175–191

Ungar M (2001) Constructing narratives of resilience with high-risk youth. J Syst Ther 20(2):58–73

Ungar M (2012) Social ecologies and their contribution to resilience. In: Ungar M (ed) The social ecology of resilience: a handbook of theory and practice. Springer, New York, pp 13–31

Ungar M, Theron L (2020) Resilience and mental health: how multisystemic processes contribute to positive outcomes. Lancet Psychiatry 7(5):441–448. https://doi.org/10.1016/S2215-0366(19)30434-1

Van Breda AD (2011) Resilience assessments in social work: the case of the SA Department of Defence. Soc Work 47(1):1–14. https://doi.org/10.15270/47-1-139

Van Breda AD (2017) The Youth Ecological-Resilience Scale: a partial validation. Res Soc Work Pract 27(2):248–257. https://doi.org/10.1177/1049731516651731

Van Breda AD (2018a) "We are who we are through other people": the interactional foundation of the resilience of youth leaving care in South Africa Professorial Inaugural Lecture

Van Breda AD (2018b) A critical review of resilience theory and its relevance for social work. Soc Work 54(1):1–18. https://doi.org/10.15270/54-1-611

Van Breda AD (2018c) Developmental social case work: a process model. Int Soc Work 61(1):66–78. https://doi.org/10.1177/0020872815603786

Van Breda AD (2019a) Developing the concept of Ubuntu as African theory for social work practice. Soc Work 55(4):439–450. https://doi.org/10.15270/55-4-762

Van Breda AD (2019b) Reclaiming resilience for social work: a reply to Garrett. Br J Soc Work 49(1):272–276. https://doi.org/10.1093/bjsw/bcy010

Van Breda AD (2019c) Resilience. In: Van Breda AD, Sekudu J (eds) Theories for decolonial social work practice in South Africa. Oxford University Press South Africa, Cape Town, pp 120–139

Van Breda AD (2019d) Strengths-based. In: Van Breda AD, Sekudu J (eds) Theories for decolonial social work practice in South Africa. Oxford University Press South Africa, Cape Town, pp 243–261

Van Breda AD, Addinall RM (2021) State of clinical social work in South Africa. Clin Soc Work J 49(3):299–311. https://doi.org/10.1007/s10615-020-00761-0

Van Breda AD, Feller T (2014) Social work students' experience and management of countertransference. Soc Work 50(4):469–484. https://doi.org/10.15270/50-4-386

Verma P, Chaudhury S (2017) Efficacy of task centered group work intervention in schizophrenia patients. J Psychiatry 4:1–4. https://doi.org/10.4172/2378-5756.1000413

Walsh J (2014) Theories for direct social work practice, 3rd edn. Cengage, Belmont

Warren S, Chappell Deckert J (2019) Contemplative practices for self-care in the social work classroom. Soc Work 65(1):11–20. https://doi.org/10.1093/sw/swz039

Weick A, Rapp C, Sullivan WP, Kisthardt W (1989) A strengths perspective for social work practice. Soc Work 34(4):350–354. https://doi.org/10.1093/sw/34.4.350

Weiss-Gal I (2008) The person-in-environment approach: professional ideology and practice of social workers in Israel. Soc Work 53(1):65–75. https://doi.org/10.1093/sw/53.1.65

Wendt S, Buchanan F, Dolman C, Moss D (2020) Engagement: narrative ways of working with men when domestic violence is noticed in couple counselling. J Soc Work 20(2):234–256. https://doi.org/10.1177/1468017318794253

White M (1992) Deconstruction and therapy. In: Epston D, White M (eds) Experience, contradiction, narrative and imagination. Dulwich Centre, Adelaide, pp 109–151

White M (2007) Maps of narrative practice. W. W. Norton, London

White M, Epston D (1990) Narrative means to therapeutic ends. W. W. Norton, New York

White C, Denborough D, van Zuijlen M (2013) Narrative responses to human rights abuses. Dulwich Centre Foundation, Adelaide

Winter K (2019) Relational social work. In: Payne M, Reith-Hall E (eds) The Routledge handbook of social work theory. Routledge, London, pp 151–159

Yousuf-Abramson S (2021) Worden's tasks of mourning through a social work lens. J Soc Work Pract 35(4):367–379. https://doi.org/10.1080/02650533.2020.1843146

Zimmerman MA (2013) Resiliency theory: a strengths-based approach to research and practice for adolescent health. Health Educ Behav 40(4):381–383. https://doi.org/10.1177/1090198113493782

Problem-Solving Theory: The Task-Centred Model

9

Blanca M. Ramos and Randall L. Stetson

Contents

Introduction	170
Problem-Solving Theory and Social Work	170
Brief Overview of the Crisis Intervention Model	171
The Task-Centred Model	173
General Overview	173
Historical Development	174
Key Principles and Constructs	175
Basic Structural Characteristics	177
A Generalist Practice Framework	177
Diversity, Social Justice, Multiculturalism	178
Application Procedures and Techniques	179
Critique and Future Direction	184
Conclusion	185
References	185

Abstract

This chapter examines the task-centred model to illustrate the application of problem-solving theory for social work intervention. First, it provides a brief description of the problem-solving model. Its historical development and key principles and concepts are presented. Next, the chapter offers a general overview of the crisis intervention model. The task-centred model and crisis intervention share principles and methods drawn from problem-solving theory. The remainder of the chapter focuses on the task-centred model. It reviews its historical background, viability as a framework for social work generalist practice, as well as its

B. M. Ramos (✉)
State University of New York at Albany, Albany, NY, USA
e-mail: bramos@albany.edu

R. L. Stetson
State University of New York at Oswego, Oswego, NY, USA
e-mail: randall.stetson@oswego.edu

© Springer Nature Singapore Pte Ltd. 2023
D. Hölscher et al. (eds.), *Social Work Theory and Ethics*, Social Work,
https://doi.org/10.1007/978-981-19-1015-9_9

applicability with diverse client populations and across cultural settings. The structured steps that guide task-centred implementation throughout the helping process are described. A brief critical review of the model's strengths and limitations is provided. The chapter concludes with a brief summary and some closing thoughts.

Keywords

Problem-solving theory · Task-centered model · Task-centered practice · Generalist social work practice · Crisis intervention · Multiculturalism

Introduction

This chapter focuses on the task-centred model (Reid and Epstein 1972) as a prime example of the major influence problem-solving theory has exerted in the practice of social work. First, as background for understanding the development of the task-centred model, the chapter offers a brief account of the historical development of the problem-solving model (Perlman 1957) and describes its key underlying principles and concepts. Next, the chapter provides a general overview of the crisis intervention model. At times, the literature presents crisis intervention together with the task-centred model highlighting their shared principles and methods, which are drawn primarily from the problem-solving approach. The remainder of the chapter examines the task-centred model in greater detail. It discusses the model as a viable framework for social work generalist practice as well as its applicability in practice with diverse client populations and across cultural settings. The structured steps that guide task-centred implementation throughout the helping process are presented. A brief critical review of the model's strengths and limitations is provided. The chapter concludes with a brief summary and some closing thoughts.

Problem-Solving Theory and Social Work

The notion of problem solving is at the core of several theoretical frameworks across disciplines, but the nature of the problems, methods, and resolution strategies are more discipline specific. In social work, problem-solving theories have informed the development and evolution of social work practice throughout the history of the profession. Since the beginning, a main focus of social work has been the resolution or amelioration of problems at both the individual and societal levels (Brieland 1977).

Early social work pioneers such as Mary Richmond (1861–1928) and Jane Addams (1860–1935) sought to address or 'solve' the problems of their times, even though social work was in its infancy and did not have yet a clearly defined approach for the delivery of services. Problem-solving in that earlier context was more akin to what D'Zurilla and Goldfried (1971) refer to as effectively responding to an issue (Nezu et al. 2012). Social work's initial description of a systematic approach to resolving client problems was first delineated in the Milford Conference report titled *Special Case Work: Generic and Specific* published in 1929. This report outlined specific steps and procedures for the problem-solving process as key components of a proposed unified generic approach to service delivery (Schatz et al. 1990). To some extent, this report laid the groundwork for the development of the social work problem-solving model by Helen Perlman (1957).

Perlman's problem-solving model was rooted in psychodynamic ego psychology theory (Coady and Lehmann 2016). Perlman, a social work scholar in the Chicago School of Social Service Administration, had been formally trained in the Freudian Diagnostic school of casework, and was strongly influenced by the Functional school of thought that emerged at the University of Pennsylvania. Perlman's model integrated ideas from the two dominant schools of thought of that era. It applied psychodynamic theory through the scientific process of study, diagnosis, and treatment while incorporating the functional emphasis on breaking down problems into manageable subcomponents, focusing on the present, and building a working relationship that supports clients' growth (Coady and Lehmann 2016). Perlman described social work casework as "a series of problem-solving operations carried on within a meaningful relationship. The end of this process is contained in its means: to so influence the client-person that he develops effectiveness in coping with his problems..." (Perlman 1957, p. 5). Since it was first introduced, the problem-solving model has been implemented with different populations and client systems, and with a vast array of psychosocial problems (see Malouff et al. 2007; Nezu et al. 2012).

Perlman's landmark problem-solving model is a cornerstone of social work practice today. Notably, its main theoretical assumptions have contributed greatly to the development of the generalist perspective, a conceptual framework that underlies most contemporary social work education and practice (Coady and Lehmann 2016). The systematic application of a generic problem-solving process that can be applied to ameliorate client difficulties and a focus of intervention on problems of living rather than on clients' personality issues are at the root of the generalist perspective.

The problem-solving model has also informed the development of some prominent intervention frameworks for social work practice, namely the crisis intervention and task-centred models. The remainder of the chapter provides a brief overview of crisis intervention and a more in-depth description of the task-centred practice model.

Brief Overview of the Crisis Intervention Model

Crisis intervention is a short-term practice model that offers immediate assistance for clients experiencing a state of crisis. During a state of crisis, a person feels overwhelmed and has difficulty coping with the acute distress generated by a stressful, traumatic, or catastrophic event (Roberts 2005). The goals of crisis intervention include alleviating clients' immediate pressure and restoring their problem-solving abilities to at least a pre-crisis level of functioning (Poal 1990). Crisis intervention practice has evolved over time and is implemented in seven stages following a clearly delineated step-by-step set of directives (Regehr 2017; Roberts 2005). Crisis intervention has been implemented with multiple client populations, in various settings, and with individuals, families, groups, and communities. Roberts (2005) compiled a comprehensive edited volume that describes the application of crisis intervention with client populations deemed at risk of experiencing a state of crisis due to the nature of the precipitating event.

The crisis intervention model has roots in psychodynamic ego psychology and some of its principles are drawn from cognitive-behavioural theory (Coady and Lehmann 2016). At the same time, most of its basic assumptions and methods are similar to those of the problem-solving approach. For example, according to Payne (2014), a focus of crisis intervention is to address clearly identifiable problems and embolden clients' active efforts to solve them. Regehr (2017) states that crisis interventions are intended to help clients mobilize their own strengths and resources to resolve an immediate problem (Regehr 2017; Roberts 2005). For Roberts (2005) the ultimate goal of crisis intervention is to bolster or help re-establish clients' available problem-solving abilities. Consistent with key principles underlying the problem-solving perspective, experiencing a state of crisis is a normal occurrence as part of life and usually a person's ability to effectively problem-solve is only temporarily compromised. Crisis intervention practice methods also rest on a planned, structured, systematic approach.

Throughout the developmental history of this model, the literature often presents crisis intervention as a multi-professional perspective that brings together psychiatry, psychology, and social work, reflecting the contribution of these professions (Payne 2014). Crisis intervention traces its origins to the work of Erich Lindemann and Gerald Capland in the field of psychiatry. Lindeman's initial definition of crisis and its accompanying symptoms were introduced in 1944, prompting the development of crisis theory. Based on his well-known study on grief reactions, he concluded that acute grief is a normal reaction manifested through a series of clearly delineated symptoms (Poal 1990). In the 1960s, Copland expanded the definition of crisis and introduced the notion of homeostasis for its conceptualization. His work with immigrant families after World War II led him to view a crisis as a person's reaction to an imbalance between the severity of a perceived threat and the resources available to address it. Effective treatment would restore a person's equilibrium or homeostatic state (Poal 1990). Several theorists from the fields of psychiatry and psychology subsequently built upon these initial formulations to further develop and refine crisis theory.

In 1957, Capland invited social workers to contribute to the development of crisis theory and its application in the practice setting. He especially recognized that social workers had the knowledge and expertise required to effectively identify and incorporate environmental factors into treatment (Regehr 2017). Social work scholars and practitioners who joined this multidisciplinary effort made critical contributions to the development of the crisis theory model. For example, Parad (1965) emphasized that a person's perception of a precipitating event is what determines if it is a crisis or not. The event must be perceived as an overwhelming problem that the person cannot resolve with the resources already in place. Parad and Capland (1960) applied crisis intervention to social work practice with families.

Among other social work contributions, Strickler (1965) identified key similarities and differences between crisis intervention and social casework, including some related to the problem-solving process and approach (Regehr 2017). Naomi Golan et al. (1969) set forth procedures to guide social workers in the application of crisis intervention in a mental health hospital, procedures that closely resemble those currently used by social work practitioners in emergency settings. Initial efforts to evaluate the effectiveness of crisis intervention in social work practice were reported by Parad and Parad (1968), Duckword (1967), and Morris (1968) who conducted studies in child guidance clinics and social welfare agencies (Regehr 2017).

Crisis intervention is widely used in contemporary social work. For example, social workers in mental health hospitals, homelessness and domestic violence shelters, suicide prevention centres, hospice care, emergency departments, and child welfare intake units among others use crisis intervention as a primary strategy in their practice (Regehr 2017). Furthermore, social workers are likely to encounter clients in a state of crisis in every practice setting and across client populations at any point in time. This is particularly the case now when we are in the midst of the COVID-19 pandemic, one of the worst deadly, catastrophic events of our times. Its traumatic consequences have undoubtedly precipitated a state of crisis for millions of people around the world, and its insidious effects continue at the present time.

The Task-Centred Model

General Overview

The task-centred model is a problem-solving, empirically based, short-term practice model. It was developed by social work educators Bill Reid and Laura Epstein (1972) and was intended for practice with various client populations, including clients from historically oppressed, diverse backgrounds. An underlying premise of the task-centred model is that life circumstances inevitably present social and psychological challenges, or problems, and everyone is inherently capable of resolving them. Task-centred practice supports clients' efforts to actively solve problems as they define them, through tasks. Respect for the clients' rights to self-determination is central in task-centred practice. The task-centred model offers a framework for generalist practice. Its underlying principles, structural characteristics, and theoretical underpinnings align with those of a generalist practice perspective. The task-centred model has been the subject of more than 200 published articles, books, and dissertations in at least ten languages and implemented in different parts of the world (Fortune and Reid 2011; Reid and Ramos 2002; Rooney 2010).

Historical Development

Origins and Historical Context

The origins of the task-centred model are rooted in the empirical practice movement that gathered momentum during the 1950s and 1960s in the United States (Fortune 2012). The movement, led by social work scholars interested in research-oriented interventions, was spurred by a growing concern surrounding the empirical rigor of the then-dominant psychodynamic methods of social work casework. Several faculty members at the Columbia University School of Social Work recognized the need for interventions that could demonstrate effectiveness based on empirical evidence (Fortune 2012). These US colleagues and some prominent European researchers contributed to the development of evidence-based social work practice and influenced the development of the task-centred model.

According to Fortune (2012), the early beginnings of the empirical practice movement coincided with the appearance of the more research-friendly behavioural models that were emerging in the mid-1960s. At first, the social work community criticized the behavioural models as being too restrictive. Eventually, behavioural theory began to influence social work thought and curricula in various schools of social work across the country until it became the dominant form of empirical practice in the 1970s and 1980s. The empirical practice movement had a lasting effect on social work by introducing the notion of the practitioner as a key member of the research team, which enhanced the development of the task-centred model (Fortune 2012).

Faculty members Bill Reid and Laura Epstein developed the task-centred model with their graduate students at the University of Chicago School of Social Service Administration in the late 1960s to early 1970s (Fortune 2012). During that time, Reid was director of the Center of Social Casework Research at the Community Service Society of New York. It was there that he and his colleague Ann Shyne designed research studies comparing different types of casework interventions, the results of which would serve as the impetus for developing the task-centred model. Several students of Reid and Epstein who were involved in developing the task-centred model have maintained an interest in the task-centred model throughout the years and continue to publish book chapters and journal articles on the topic. During the task-centred model's development, Reid and Epstein were influenced by several theoretical models and patterns of thought circulating at the time, both integrating and expanding on them through several empirical studies.

Empirical Orientation

The task-centred model was developed using an empirical Research and Development (R&D) approach. This approach guided the development and maturation of the task-centred model by testing interventions, assessing results, refining the interventions, testing them again, and then repeating the cycle with new clients and new problems (Fortune et al. 2022; Fortune 2012). In the task-centred model, theories and methods with empirical support and data-driven intervention decisions are utilized whenever possible (Fortune et al. 2022).

Short Term

The brevity of the task-centred model is built on research evidence demonstrating the effective use of brief treatment. Reid and Shyne's CSS study in New York (1969) found that time-limited treatment was just as effective as its open-ended counterpart such as psychodynamic treatment. Further studies continued to support these initial findings and, in some cases, demonstrated that time-limited treatment was more effective (e.g., Hoyt 2000). Furthermore, studies supporting the use of brief treatment showed that the largest gains in the helping process occur in the early sessions (e.g., Hubble et al. 1999). Time-limited treatment also partly addresses the issue of early termination or client 'drop out'. According to several research findings, many clients terminate treatment prematurely (e.g., Garfield 1994). Early termination can be attributed to several causes that undermine client engagement and motivation. Strean (1968) found that the lack of congruence between client and worker about the focus of treatment leads to early dropout, which the task-centred model addresses by partnering with clients to focus on issues of concern to the client.

Demonstrated Effectiveness

The effectiveness of the task-centred model has been demonstrated empirically with a growing number of populations, settings, and cultures over the past five decades. This includes interventions involving the aging population, clients struggling with mental health issues, school-age children displaying academic and behavioural concerns, clients involved with the child welfare system including those in foster care, underage parents, clients with healthcare concerns, siblings who display aggressive behaviours, mandated and involuntary clients, high-risk youth, persons with diabetes, and family members of persons with AIDS (Fortune et al. 2022). The findings of these, and many more, support the effectiveness of the task-centred model (Fortune 2012; Rooney 2010). In addition, an earlier meta-analysis found a greater average effect size for the task-centred model when compared to other generalist approaches (Gorey et al. 1998).

Key Principles and Constructs

Several interrelated theoretical principles underlie the task-centred model. These are drawn primarily from Perlman's (1957) problem-solving paradigm. Studt's (1968) emphasis on the use of tasks during treatment, Hollis' (1970) psychosocial approach to treatment, and Parad's (1958) seminal work on crisis intervention exerted an important influence on its development (Payne 2014). Conceptual premises and intervention strategies drawn from ecosystems, strengths, and empowerment perspectives also guide task-centred practice (Ramos and Tolson 2016).

In task-centred practice, assumptions about the nature and source of problems clients are likely to experience and clients' ability to address or solve these problems are closely tied to the central premises of the problem-solving model (Perlman 1957). Problems are viewed as inevitable challenges in daily living and involve both individual and social factors. At the same time, clients are viewed as active problem-solvers who are intrinsically capable of addressing and/or solving the psychosocial problems they might encounter. Task-centred intervention supports clients' efforts to solve problems when their independent problem-solving efforts have been unsuccessful. As Perlman pointed out, effective problem-solving, whether in everyday life or professional helping, consists of similar processes (Coady and Lehmann 2016).

Task-centred intervention rests on the general principle that problem-solving action through tasks is an effective strategy for change. Studt (1968) described tasks as clearly defined activities, underscoring the benefits of incorporating the use of tasks in social work practice intervention. Furthermore, in task-centred practice, clients conduct tasks that are congruent with the strengths and empowerment perspective. For example, tasks are designed building on clients' strengths by drawing from their own internal and external resources. Similarly, clients are placed at the centre of the helping process and viewed as the primary agents of change, fostering client empowerment (Ramos and Garvin 2003). Clients are in charge of identifying, defining, and prioritizing the problems they choose to address. Successful experiences carrying out tasks can reinforce clients' belief in their own competence, which in turn, can increase their sense of self-efficacy and serve as a source of motivation for change (Ramos and Tolson 2016).

The task-centred model is grounded in the assumption that clients are essentially woven into the fabric of their various interconnected environmental systems. Ecosystems theory views human problems, social conditions, and living situations as interrelated. People's lives are invariably influenced by the reciprocal exchange that takes place with the multiple systems with which they interact (Coady and Lehmann 2016). Hollis's (1970) pioneering work on social casework called for practitioners to take into account both the psychological and social aspects of a client's life as these interact with each other. Intervention strategies incorporate personal and professional representatives from the client's various networks, facilitating multilevel linkages and interconnectedness (Ramos and Tolson 2016). Task-centred practice incorporates clients' micro, mezzo, and macro-environmental factors in the identification and contextualization of presenting problems.

The task-centred model recognizes the importance of a good client-practitioner relationship. This assertion is closely aligned with psychodynamic principles and the problem-solving approach (Hollis 1970; Perlman 1957). In task-centred practice, this relationship is built based on an egalitarian approach. Practitioners and clients work collaboratively as partners, with clients holding the power to choose the course of action and practitioners supporting their change effort (Ramos and Tolson 2016).

A key structural component of the task-centred model is planned brevity, a basic tenet of the crisis intervention approach. Parad (1958) called for the use of short-term interventions in practice with clients undergoing crisis situations. He stressed that problems in living could be resolved more effectively if addressed swiftly (Fortune 2012; Parad 1966).

Basic Structural Characteristics

The task-centred model is generally defined by the following characteristics:

Client Centred. Clients are placed at the centre of the change process. Practitioners demonstrate unconditional positive regard for clients.

Client Empowerment. The client rather than the practitioner is the primary agent of change. Clients hold the power to determine the focus of the intervention and the course of action. Respect for a client's right to self-determination throughout the change process is pivotal.

Egalitarian Client-Practitioner Relationship. The relational stance is highly collaborative and egalitarian. Clients and practitioners work together as partners within a non-hierarchical power structure.

Empirically Based. An integrative approach grounded on research-based theories and practice models. Integrates several compatible theoretical assumptions and practice methods.

Empirical Orientation. Emphasis on empirically supported theories and methods. Hypotheses about clients' behaviours and situations are to be based on factual information. Includes research procedures that facilitate data collection and outcome evaluation.

Multi-systemic Application. The model is readily applicable across systems. Specific guidelines on how to apply task-centred practice with individuals, families, groups, communities, and organizations have been developed.

Problem Solving Actions. Well-defined problem-solving structure supports clients' efforts to actively solve problems, through tasks. A flexible set of procedures and techniques are adapted to the client's distinctive situation.

Planned Brevity. Short-term, time-limited interventions of 6–12 weekly sessions during a period of 4 months. Length of time can be extended to accommodate a client's particular situation.

Eclecticism. Does not hold rigidly to any theory or approach. Practitioners draw from a range of complementary theories and practice models based on the client's personal characteristics and environmental milieu, to increase intervention effectiveness.

Ancillaries. Supplementary material comprised of directives, forms, and evaluation tools is readily available. These include the Task Planning and Implementation Sequence which provides a number of structured activities that guide intervention.

A Generalist Practice Framework

The task-centred model offers a framework suitable for generalist practice (Tolson et al. 2003). Its underlying principles, structural characteristics, methods, and theoretical assumptions are compatible with generalist approaches. For example, generalist practitioners conduct multi-level assessments and multi-method interventions, utilize practice methods and skills that are transferable across all levels of the human system, and engage in activities beyond direct practice such as working towards just social policies and conducting and applying research (Miley et al. 2017).

In task-centred practice, target problems are identified, contextualized, and addressed, taking into consideration environmental influences at the micro, mezzo, and macro levels. The inclusion of collaterals, who are representatives of various client systems, facilitates multilevel linkages and interconnectedness. Since the task-centred model is theoretically open, practitioners draw from various theories and practice models, depending on a client's specific situation, target problem, and tasks. Practitioners have opportunities to devise and implement tasks that focus on clients' advocacy and policy change. The task-centred model incorporates research strategies that facilitate data collection and outcome evaluation within a practitioner's own practice (Ramos and Tolson 2016).

A defining characteristic of generalist approaches, problem-solving, has been at the centre of the task-centred model since its inception. Similarly, the development of a good client-practitioner relationship is critically important. Clients and practitioners work collaboratively identifying and transforming a problem into a task or set of tasks. Task-centred practice's commitment to diversity and difference and guidelines for multilevel intervention across fields of practice are also consistent with generalist practice (Ramos and Tolson 2016).

Diversity, Social Justice, Multiculturalism

Task-centred practice is applicable in practice with racially, culturally, and ethnically diverse clients. In the United States, it has been applied in practice with clients from African American, Asian, and Latin American ethnic groups. The task-centred model's theoretical assumptions and practice strategies align closely with the concepts of culture, powerlessness, oppression, and injustice. Its basic principles are generally cross-culturally applicable and its flexible methods and techniques can be easily modified (Ramos and Garvin 2003).

First, task-centred practice's emphasis on clients' environmental contexts, which include culture, is congruent with the notion that culture can differentially shape the nature of a client's psychosocial challenges, help-seeking practices, and problem-solving preferences. In task-centred practice, clients play a central role in defining problems and tasks, thus, relevant culture-specific variables can be incorporated freely. Practitioners communicate respect, acceptance, and unconditional positive regard for the clients' guiding cultural value system. The potential ensuing experiences of cultural affirmation, acceptance, and reassurance could be beneficial for culturally and ethnically diverse clients, particularly immigrants and refugees whose lives are often marked by xenophobia, stereotyping, and cultural oppression.

Second, empowerment, the cornerstone of the task-centred model, is critical in practice with clients who experience oppression, unequal treatment, and limited access to resources. Clients in socioeconomically disadvantaged positions, who are totally capable of resolving immediate problems, may feel disempowered against overwhelming oppressive environments that can block effective problem-solving abilities.

Task-centred practice's empowering strategies that place clients at the centre of the change process as primary agents of change and strategies that aim to increase clients' self-efficacy through task competence can be particularly meaningful. Similarly, contextualizing the identified problems helps determine their environmental sources including poverty, oppression, racism, injustice, and other power structures. Clients and practitioners collaboratively devise tasks that build on clients' internal and external resources, but clients have the final word with practitioners promoting and respecting clients' right to self-determination at all times (Ramos and Tolson 2016).

In cross-cultural practice, sometimes the task-centred model's methods and techniques may need to be modified or communicated sensitively to accommodate different cultural values and world views. For example, task-centred practice's highly structured, time-limited approach may work very well with clients from some Northern European and East Asian cultures, but it may not always be a good fit for clients from Native American and Latino American ethnic groups. Adaptations to the task-centred model need to be client-specific and should consider acculturation levels, individual preferences, and within cultural group diversity. Similarly, an overemphasis on an egalitarian practitioner-client relationship may not be advisable with clients from some Eastern cultures who may prefer a more directive, practitioner-led approach. For a more thorough discussion on the application of the task-centred model with racially, culturally, and ethnically diverse clients, see Ramos and Garvin (2003).

The task-centred model has been adopted in different cultural settings around the world. Beyond the United States, the model has reached 13 countries where it has been applied at individual, family, and group levels. For example, task-centred has had a long-time presence in social work education, practice, and research in the United Kingdom (Marsh 2010), the Netherlands (Jagt and Jagt 2010), Australia (Trotter 2010), and Hong Kong (Lo 2010). In these countries, the model has become part of the curriculum in social work education and in-service trainings are conducted with social work practitioners in agency and community settings (Marsh and Doel 2005; Jagt and Jagt 2010). Task-centred practice has been applied and tested with children and family systems, clients with developmental disabilities, and clients in the child protection and criminal justice systems among others (Fortune et al. 2010; Ramos and Tolson 2016).

The original English version of the task-centred model has been translated into several languages including Chinese, German, Korean, Dutch, Japanese, Norwegian, Spanish, and Catalan (Fortune et al. 2010; Reid and Ramos 2002; Ramos and Tolson 2016). In some countries, the model was applied with some modifications. For instance, in Korea it was adapted to fit Korean cultural and systemic realities (Huh and Koh 2010). In Germany, on the other hand, task-centred practice fits well with German culture and did not require modifications (Naleppa 2010).

Application Procedures and Techniques

The implementation of task-centred practice is organized into three discrete phases that mirror closely a generalist practice helping process: initial, middle, and termination. Although these phases are presented in a linear, sequential order, their activities are not limited to a specific phase and are often repeated throughout the change process. These procedures can be used with individual and multiple-client systems with relevant modifications.

Task-Centred Practice with Individual Client Systems

The main activities and procedures for practice with individual clients are synthesized below. Reid (1992) and Tolson et al. (2003) describe them more extensively. Ramos and Tolson (2016) and Fortune and colleagues (2022) use case scenarios to illustrate more comprehensively task-centred practice's step-by-step application.

Initial Phase

This phase involves activities related to engagement, assessment, goal setting, and contracting. The first step during engagement is to share basic information about the practitioner, agency setting, and referral source. The task-centred model's general assumptions and procedures are discussed emphasizing its client-focused and time-limited characteristics which could potentially increase clients' motivation. An important goal of engagement is to begin developing an effective working relationship. Practitioners are expected to be empathic, warm, genuine, non-judgmental, and most importantly, respectful of the clients' right to self-determination. The connection ensues from working collaboratively in a problem-solving process and helps build an effective practitioner-client relationship.

Assessment is guided by an Ecosystems framework where micro, mezzo, and macro factors are considered. Information is gathered primarily to identify, prioritize, and specify target problems. To identify target problems, practitioners ask clients to describe the psychosocial challenges they want to address and generate an inclusive list. Sometimes clients do not readily identify problems and it may be necessary to engage in a problem search by reviewing the various areas of the clients' life. Next, clients prioritize the problems in the list and select those they want to target first. Practitioners may suggest potential target problems explaining their rationale, but clients must make the final decision. It is recommended not to focus on more than three target problems simultaneously.

Problem specification entails a detailed exploration of the target problems as clients experience them. Clients describe how the problems are manifested and their frequency, severity, and duration. This enables practitioners to individualize interventions and to monitor changes over time. Monitoring change helps assess intervention effectiveness and informs decisions as to whether adjustments are needed. Incorporating this evaluative component is an important step in task-centred practice. The task-centred model's systemic assessment yields information on the contextual factors that shape target problems and helps to identify potential collaterals, the personal and professional connections in a client's life. When problems are contextualized, clients are able to recognize structurally based influences at the root of the target problems.

The final activities in this initial phase include establishing goals, setting time limits and contracting. Goals are determined by the client based on the chosen target problems. The practitioner helps to articulate the goals in measurable terms based on the quantifiable information gathered during problem specification. Setting time limits jointly and at this early stage is imperative. Time limits could be as brief as one session but usually range from 6 to 12 sessions. Practitioners should provide the rationale behind the brevity of task-centred practice. Contracting is usually a verbal agreement. Contracts describe explicitly the target problems, goals, client and practitioner roles, and number and frequency of sessions. The length of a contract can be extended when a client who is actively working to address target problems needs additional time.

Middle Phase

The focus of this phase is on intervention. It centres around tasks, the primary mechanism to address target problems. Depending on the situation, clients complete tasks in-session or outside the session. Completing tasks outside the session is preferable as it gives them the opportunity to take action in the real-life setting where problems are embedded. In-session tasks are primarily used in family and group practice. Practitioners complete tasks on some occasions such as when clients are not able to carry out them and to advocate for structural changes and on the clients' behalf in multi-systemic interactions (Ramos and Tolson 2016).

The Task Planning and Implementation Sequence (TPIS) provides specific, structured activities to guide task-centred practice intervention. TPIS includes detailed activities designed to generate, summarize, and simulate tasks; plan task implementation; identify obstacles to task completion; establish tasks' rationale and elicit clients' agreement to complete them; and review task accomplishment and problem change (Tolson et al. 2003). These activities are the essence of the intervention in task-centred practice and are briefly described below.

Although the sequence in which the TPIS activities are accomplished is flexible, generating tasks at the beginning is highly recommended. Here, the practitioner and the client jointly compile a list of potential tasks, the more the better. Together, they evaluate the advantages and disadvantages of each task on the list based on the client's personal strengths and environmental resources. Clients select their preferred tasks and are asked if they are willing to attempt them. As with target problems, the ultimate decision in selecting tasks rests with the client (Ramos and Tolson 2016).

Once the tasks are selected, the implementation details are planned. Decisions about logistics and other factors that could contribute to successful task completion are carefully made. Potential obstacles are identified and the ways to overcome them are discussed. Clients are encouraged to believe they are capable of carrying out even the most challenging tasks. Practitioners and clients review the rationale behind task completion, highlighting how this could help address the target problem and, at the same time, strengthen the client's problem-solving skills. Incentives, or concrete client rewards to recognize task completion, are important. These could be provided by the client, practitioner, or collaterals (Ramos and Tolson 2016).

Task simulation involves rehearsing the task. Clients have the opportunity to practice the task and practitioners offer constructive observations that could enhance client's success. Practitioners, with strong client input, provide a verbal summary of the tasks that clients have selected and agreed to carry out before the next session. Depending on the particular situation, the client could present the summary (Ramos and Tolson 2016). Clients are asked to confirm the accuracy of the summary and their willingness to complete the tasks. An optional written summary and a task review schedule form are offered to remind clients between sessions.

TPIS also includes activities designed to review task accomplishment and problem change. A 4-point scale is available to rate both task accomplishment and problem review. Practitioners praise clients when tasks are implemented. Information gathered for the problem specification during the initial phase can serve as the basis for problem review. For tasks that are not implemented or do not have the intended effect, clients and practitioners identify the obstacles that might have interfered. Tasks can be adjusted or change accordingly. When tasks consistently are not performed, the target problems are re-evaluated to determine if these are still the problems the client wants to change. At each session, clients and practitioners discuss the number of sessions that have already taken place and the number that still remain. Time limits can be renegotiated providing the client has been carrying out tasks and problem resolution is likely to occur in a specified period of time (Ramos and Tolson 2016).

Termination Phase
Termination takes place during the last session. Practitioners and clients discuss termination regularly as they review the goals and number of sessions remaining to accomplish them. In this phase, practitioners and clients engage in the following activities: conduct a final review of the target problems, devise strategies for enhancing or maintaining gains, examine the problem-solving process, and discuss thoughts and feelings related to termination. Practitioners praise clients' accomplishments generously.

Task-Centred Practice with Group and Family Systems
This section provides a brief overview of key procedures and methods that characterize task-centred practice with groups and family systems. The focus is on how these differ from those outlined for practice with individual clients. Tolson et al. (2003) provide detailed descriptions on the use of task-centred practice with these mezzo-level client systems.

Family Systems
In task-centred practice, a family unit is defined as two or more persons living together regardless of marital status or internal living arrangements. Target problems, and the tasks devised to address them, consider the following internal family dimensions: alliances, beliefs and worldviews, boundaries, closeness, conflictual relationships, communication patterns, control, flexibility, intrusiveness, and problem-solving skills. These dimensions were drawn from various theoretical assumptions about family functioning including structural family theory, attribution, communication, and family problem-solving theories (Dohert 1981; Watzlawick et al. 1967; Nichols and Schwartz 2001), cognitive behavioural approaches (Dattilio

1998), and theories of reciprocity and exchange (Ruben 1998). As is the case in practice with individual clients, target problems and devised tasks are always considered within a family's external environmental and multi-systemic contexts (Tolson et al. 2003).

In practice with families, sometimes the processes of determining target problems and devising tasks may not be as smooth and straightforward. Each family member's identified problem must be considered, and when the identified problems differ, prioritizing and reaching an agreement as a family could be difficult. In these situations, practitioners facilitate discussions that help clients recognize those problems in the list whose resolution would benefit the family as a whole. A useful strategy is to review each problem listed and ask whether it affects one or more than one family member and whether its resolution requires a change in a family member (Ramos and Tolson 2016).

Tasks may be completed in and outside sessions by the practitioner, individual family members, and family members jointly. Ideally, all family members should attend sessions together. Yet, it is not required that all family members attend all the sessions. Task-centred practice is a flexible practice approach designed to support families to address a broad range of problems across a wide variety of practice settings (Fortune et al. 2022).

Task-Centred Practice with Groups

In task-centred practice, a group is defined as two or more unrelated persons assembled to address together similar types of psychosocial problems. These groups could be naturally or deliberately formed. Task-centred practice with groups builds on the general principles and processes of group work. Practitioners draw from a range of theories to gain an understanding of their group dynamics and identity effective interventions. Cognitive behavioural, learning, role, ego psychology, and ecosystem theories may inform task-centred practice with groups and family systems. The task-centred model's procedures and techniques supplement basic group work so practitioners' familiarity with small group theory may make it more amenable to empirical testing (Tolson et al. 2003; Ramos and Tolson 2016).

A main thrust of task-centred group work is to develop a collaborative environment of inclusion where members support each other in their problem-solving efforts and practitioners provide the structure, facilitate interactions, and implement the task-centred model efficiently and effectively. Group members meet together for every session and supplemental individual sessions are arranged when needed. Holding individual sessions with each potential group member to jointly discuss their interest and willingness to participate in group work, and in that particular group, is highly recommended (Ramos and Tolson 2016). Practitioners could use this opportunity to address questions, highlight the benefits of group work and most importantly, acknowledge, and validate related concerns, doubts, and fears potential members may be experiencing. This strategy can enhance potential members' motivation and willingness to participate.

Throughout the change process, group members learn to use the problem-solving method and strengthen their ability to give and receive feedback as well as to talk and listen to one another empathically. Ultimately, group members help each other to identity target problems and explore appropriate tasks to address them (Ramos and Tolson 2016).

Critique and Future Direction

The task-centred model has made important contributions to the practice of social work including its active problem-solving empirical orientation, brevity, and emphasis on placing the client at the centre of the change process. It is highly structured, aligns closely with the generalist practice perspective, builds on clients' strengths, and incorporates the social work values of self-determination and unconditional positive regard. Its focus on client empowerment, flexibility, and attention to environmental contexts makes task-centred practice a viable model for practice with racially, culturally, and ethnically diverse clients, and for international social work. In essence, task-centred practice could be viewed as a meta-model that exemplifies how a social work practice model could be construed (Rooney 2010).

The task-centred model may be difficult to implement with clients who, due to cognitive limitations and/or environmental factors, are not able to identify problems and/or carry out tasks. This model may not be a good choice for clients who are not highly motivated to address the presenting problem. Yet, in some cases, empowering strategies may help increase a client's motivation level. Similarly, a highly structured, brief intervention approach may be optimal for some clients and problem areas, but not for others. Depending on the specific situation, these methods can be adapted accordingly. Such could be the case, for example, when the model is applied cross culturally. Nevertheless, the task-centred model can be used widely for most types of problems and with most client populations (Ramos and Tolson 2016).

The vast number of publications that have focused on the task-centred model attest to the widespread impact and prominent place this well-established model has achieved in the United States and other parts of the world. These include several books that describe the model in great detail authored by the original social work scholars and practitioners who developed it, research articles that report controlled intervention and explanatory studies, dissertations, and publications that describe task-centred practice with specific client populations. A chapter describing the task-centred model has been invariably included in the major social work practice theory textbooks commonly adopted in social work education.

Since its inception, the task-centred model was conceptualized as an open, pluralistic practice model that would continue to evolve in response to ongoing research and to advancements in knowledge and technology compatible with its basic principles (Fortune 2012). Thus, it is an inclusive model with wide applicability cross-culturally and across individuals, families, groups, organizations, and communities. More empirical testing, refinement, and effective practice application of the task-centred model will enhance outcomes for many populations (Ramos and Tolson 2016).

Conclusion

This chapter examined the task-centred model (Reid and Epstein 1972) to illustrate the significant impact of problem-solving theory in social work practice. General overviews of the problem-solving and crisis intervention models were presented. The chapter provided a comprehensive overview of the task-centred model.

Social work has a long history as a problem-solving profession. This has implications for domains beyond the direct provision of client services. For example, some organizations and institutions struggle with systemic problems associated with culture, climate, turnover, new practice models, and race equity and decolonization. Problem-solving strategies to address such systemic problems could include some of the same practices used with individuals, families, and groups. Thus, one of the challenges for twenty-first century practice is the adaptation of problem-solving models to larger systems. Action teams, functioning and empowered to be change agents, can potentially be developed to be organizational and systemic problem solve.

References

Brieland D (1977) Historical overview. Soc Work 22(5):341–346. http://www.jstor.org.libezproxy2.syr.edu/stable/23712810

Coady N, Lehmann P (2016) The problem-solving model: a framework for integrating the science and art of practice. In: Lehmann P, Coady N (eds) Theoretical perspectives for direct social work practice: a generalist-eclectic approach, 3rd edn. Springer

D'Zurilla TJ, Goldfried MR (1971) Problem solving and behavior modification. J Abnorm Psychol 78(1):107–126. https://doi.org/10.1037/h0031360

Dattilio F (1998) Cognitive behavioral therapy. In: Dattilio M (ed) Case studies in couple and family therapy: systems and cognitive perspectives. Guilford, New York, pp 62–82

Dohert W (1981) Cognitive processes in intimate conflicts: extending attribution theory. Am J Fam Ther 9:3–12

Duckword G (1967) A project in crisis intervention. Soc Casework 48(4):227–231

Fortune AE (2012) Development of the task-centered model. In: Rzepnicki TL, McCracken SG, Briggs HE (eds) From task-centered social work to evidence-based and integrative practice: reflections on history and implementation. Oxford University Press, pp 15–39

Fortune AE, Reid WJ (2011) Task-centered social work. In: Turner F (ed) Social work treatment: interlocking theoretical approaches, 6th edn. Oxford University Press, New York, pp 513–532

Fortune AE, McCallion P, Briar-Lawson K (Eds.) (2010) Social work practice research for the 21st century. New York: Columbia University Press

Fortune AE, Ramos BM, Reid WJ (2022) Task-Centered practice. In: Lisa Rapp-McCall, Kevin Corcoran & Albert R. Roberts, (eds.), Social workers' desk reference, 4th edn Oxford University Press, New York

Fortune AE, Ramos BM, Reid WJ (2022) Task-Centered Practice. In: Lisa Rapp-McCall, Kevin Corcoran, Albert R Roberts, (Eds.). Social Workers' Desk Reference, 4th edition. New York: Oxford University Press

Garfield SL (1994) Research on client variables in psychotherapy. In: Bergin A, Garfield S (eds) Handbook of psychotherapy and behavior change, 4th edn. Wiley, New York, pp 190–228

Golan N, Carey H, Hyttinnen E (1969) The emerging role of the social worker in the psychiatric emergency service. Community Ment Health J 5(1):55–61

Gorey KM, Thyer BA, Pawfuck DE (1998) Differential effectiveness of prevalent social work practice models: a meta-analysis. Soc Work 43:269–278

Hollis F (1970) The psychosocial approach to the practice of casework. In: Theories of social casework. University of Chicago Press, pp 33–75

Hoyt MF (2000) Some stories are better than others: doing what works in brief therapy and managed care. Brunner/Mazel, Philadelphia

Hubble M, Duncan B, Miller S (1999) Introduction. In: Hubble M, Duncan B, Miller S (eds) The heart and soul of change: what works in therapy. American Psychological Association, Washington, DC

Huh NS, Koh YS (2010) Task-centered practice in South Korea. In: Fortune AE, McCallion P, Briar-Lawson K (eds) Social work practice research for the 21st century. Columbia University Press, New York, pp 235–239

Jagt N, Jagt L (2010) Task-centered practice in the Netherlands. In: Fortune AE, McCallion P, Briar-Lawson K (eds) Social work practice research for the 21st century. Columbia University Press, New York, pp 208–212

Lo TW (2010) Task-centered practice in Hong Kong. In: Fortune AE, McCallion P, Briar-Lawson K (eds) Social work practice research for the 21st century. Columbia University Press, New York, pp 240–244

Malouff JM, Thorsteinsson EB, Schutte NS (2007) The efficacy of problem-solving therapy in reducing mental and physical health problems: a meta-analysis. Clin Psychol Rev 27(1):46–57

Marsh P (2010) Task-centered practice in Great Britain. In: Fortune AE, McCallion P, Briar-Lawson K (eds) Social work practice research for the 21st century. Columbia University Press, New York, pp 203–2007

Marsh P, Doel M (2005) The task-centred book. Routledge, Abingdon/New York

Miley K, O'Melia M, DuBois (2017) Generalist social work practice: an empowering approach. Allyn & Bacon, Boston

Morris B (1968) Crisis intervention in a public welfare agency. Soc Casework 49(10):612–617

Naleppa M (2010) Task-centered practice in Germany. In: Fortune AE, McCallion P, Briar-Lawson K (eds) Social work practice research for the 21st century. Columbia University Press, New York, pp 213–216

Nezu AM, Nezu CM, D'Zurilla T (2012) Problem-solving therapy: a treatment manual. Springer

Nichols M, Schwartz R (2001) Family therapy. Allyn and Bacon, Needham Heights

Parad HJ (1958) Ego psychology and dynamic casework. Family Association of America, New York

Parad H (1965) Preventive casework: problems and implications. In: Parad H (ed) Crisis intervention: selected readings. Family Service Association of America, New York

Parad H (1966) The use of time-limited crisis interventions in community mental health programming. Soc Serv Rev 40(3):275–282

Parad H, Capland G (1960) A framework for studying families in crisis. Soc Work 5(3):3–15

Parad H, Parad G (1968) A study of crisis oriented planned short-term treatment. Soc Casework 49 (6):346–355

Payne M (2014) Modern social work theory, 3rd edn. Palgrave Macmillan, Basingstoke

Perlman HH (1957) Social casework: a problem-solving process. University of Chicago Press, Chicago

Poal P (1990) Introduction to the theory and practice of crisis intervention. Quadernos Psicol 10: 121–140

Ramos BM, Garvin C (2003) Task centered treatment with culturally diverse populations. In: Tolson E, Reid W, Garvin C (eds) Generalist practice: a task centered approach, pp. Columbia University Press, New York, pp 441–463

Ramos B, Tolson E (2016) The task-centered model. In: Lehmann P, Coady N (eds) Theoretical perspectives for direct social work practice: a generalist-eclectic approach, 3rd edn. Springer

Regehr C (2017) Crisis theory and social work treatment. In: Turner F (ed) Social work treatment: interlocking theoretical approaches. Oxford University Press

Reid WJ (1992) Task strategies: an empirical approach to social work practice. Columbia University Press, New York

Reid WJ, Epstein L (eds) (1972) Task-centered casework. Columbia University Press, New York

Reid W, Ramos B (2002) Intervención "Centrada en la Tarea", un Modelo de Práctica de Trabajo Social. Rev Treball Soc 168:6–22

Reid WJ, Shyne AW (1969) Brief and extended casework. Columbia University Press, New York

Roberts A (2005) Bridging the past and present to the future of crisis intervention and case management. In: Roberts A (ed) Crisis intervention handbook: assessment, treatment, and research, 3rd edn. Oxford University Press

Rooney RH (2010) Task-centered practice in the United States. In: Fortune AE, McCallion P, Briar-Lawson K (eds) Social work practice research for the 21st century. Columbia University Press, New York, pp 195–202

Ruben D (1998) Social exchange theory: dynamics of a system governing the dysfunctional family and guide to assessment. J Contemp Psychother 8(3):307–325

Schatz MS, Jenkins LE, Sheafor BW (1990) Milford redefined: a model of initial and advanced generalist social work [Article]. J Soc Work Educ 26(3):217–231. https://doi.org/10.1080/10437797.1990.10672154

Strean HS (1968) Some reactions of case workers to the war on poverty. J Contemp Psychother 1:43–48

Strickler M (1965) Applying crisis theory in a community clinic. Soc Casework 46:150–154

Studt E (1968) Social work theory and implication for the practice of methods. Soc Work Educ Report 16:22–46

Tolson R, Reid W, Garvin C (2003) Generalist practice: a task-centered approach, 2nd edn. Columbia University Press, New York

Trotter C (2010) Task-centred practice in Australia. In Fortune AE, McCallion P, Briar-Lawson K (Eds.), Social work practice research for the 21st century, 235–239. New York: Columbia University Press

Watzlawick P, Bervin J, Jackson D (1967) Pragmatics of human communication. W.W. Norton, New York

Anti-oppressive Social Work Practice Theory

Activist Social Justice Social Work

Donna Baines and Hannah Kia

Contents

Introduction	190
Background and Core Themes of AOP Theory and Practice	191
Seven Core AOP Themes	192
Expanding AOP Theory and Practices	198
Capacity to Advocate	198
Capacity to Mobilize Colleagues and Others Around Positive Action	199
Critical Ally-Ship	199
Critical Attunement	200
Cultural Safety and Cultural Humility	201
Areas for Further Development	202
Mutual, Reflexive Dialogue Between Indigenous Social Work and AOP	202
LGBTQI+ Social Work	203
BLM, Defund the Police and Social Work's Relationship to the State, Coercion and Control	203
Conclusions	204
References	205

Abstract

In this chapter on anti-oppressive theory and practice (AOP), we ask what knowledge, theory, ethics and skills (practices) are necessary in order for social work not to be complicit or active in the kinds of state-linked atrocities that have headlined in many nations in the recent past. We argue that critical and AOP theories provide a way to end social work's participation in 'horrible histories' such as those denounced by Black Lives Matter and other anti-oppressive initiatives, by firmly grounding practice in critical, social justice-based knowledges and theories. We argue further that AOP theories and knowledge map onto critical engaged, reflexive, activist practices that can build ongoing social justice and

D. Baines (✉) · H. Kia
School of Social Work, University of British Columbia, Vancouver, Canada
e-mail: dbaines@mail.ubc.ca; hannah.kia@ubc.ca

© Springer Nature Singapore Pte Ltd. 2023
D. Hölscher et al. (eds.), *Social Work Theory and Ethics*, Social Work,
https://doi.org/10.1007/978-981-19-1015-9_10

equity. These processes include: critical social analysis; advocacy; building capacity to mobilize colleagues and service users around positive and progressive action; critical ally-ship; critical attunement; and cultural humility and cultural safety. The chapter also identifies areas for further development including mutual dialogic development of practice and theory between Indigenous social work and AOP (including reconciliation and decolonization); LGBTQI+ social work; and social work's relationship to the state, coercion, control and the challenges posed by Black Lives Matter and campaigns to defund the police. We conclude by emphasizing AOP's capacity to provide the critical knowledges, theories and practices to intervene decisively on the side of equity and social justice.

Keywords

Critical ally-ship · Critical attunement · Critical reflexivity · Cultural humility and cultural safety · Decolonization · Relationship to the state

Introduction

Ioakamidis and Trimikliniotis (2020) argue that social work is dogged by "histories of complicity, or at least acquiescence, in acts of state violence and institutionalised oppression" (p. 1890) including fascist, colonial and white supremist governments and causes. In the current context of Black and Indigenous challenges to the racism, militarization and violence of police forces around the world, social work once again faces the need to explore its links to state coercion and control, and its compliance with carceral approaches to social problems (Klufts 2020; NASW 2020). Another contemporary example of social work's involvement in institutionalized oppression can be seen in British Columbia (Canada) where this chapter is being written and where the government recently commissioned an inquiry into systemic racism against Indigenous peoples in the health care system (Turpel-Lafond 2020). The report substantiates that "widespread racism has long been known by many within the health care system, including those in positions of authority, and is widely acknowledged by many who work in the system" (Turpel-Lafond 2020, p. 6). The report also confirms that regulated, licensed, highly educated social workers and other professionals were active or complicit in these transgressions resulting in "a range of negative impacts, harm, and even death" (Lafond-Turpel 2020, p. 6). None of the professionals, including social workers, seemed to have the skills, knowledge, theory or capacity to halt or interrupt this travesty. These disturbing contemporary revelations lead us to ask the rhetorical question of how did social work go so wrong. The chapter will ask what knowledge, theory, ethics and skills (practices) are necessary in order for social work (and other professions) not to be complicit or active in these and similar atrocities.

In this chapter, it is argued that critical and anti-oppressive practice (AOP) theories provide a way to end participation in 'horrible histories' by firmly grounding social work practice in critical, social justice-based knowledges and theories.

It will be argued further that AOP theories and knowledge map onto critical engaged, reflexive, activist practices that have the potential to build ongoing social justice and equity. The processes discussed include: critical social analysis; advocacy; building capacity to mobilize colleagues and service users around positive and progressive action; critical ally-ship; critical attunement; and cultural humility and cultural safety.

Using social work's complicities in oppressive histories as a general exemplar and backdrop to our analysis, this chapter advances an argument for emancipatory social work based in AOP. Drawing on a rich AOP literature, the chapter begins by reviewing the seven core themes of AOP theory and elaborates the critical practices noted above and their potential for social justice-enhancing social work. The chapter then identifies areas for further theoretical and practice development including mutual dialogic development of practice and theory between Indigenous social work and AOP (including reconciliation and decolonization); LGBTQI+ social work; and social work's relationship to the state and the challenges posed by Black Lives Matter and campaigns to defund the police. The chapter concludes by emphasizing AOP's capacity to provide the critical knowledges, theories and practices to intervene decisively on the side of equity and social justice.

Background and Core Themes of AOP Theory and Practice

As a historical phenomenon, social work is often argued to have developed during mid-nineteenth century Victorian UK as a reaction to the mass poverty and inequities of industrial capitalism (Ehrenreich 2014; Mullaly 2010; Abramovitz 2000). In the UK and some of its colonies, Charitable Organizations Societies, headed by men, hired middle-class women to work as "friendly visitors" or early social workers, providing putatively uplifting lectures on morality, hygiene and living good, Christian lives to those living in privation and distress (Mendes 2005). Occasionally they provided concrete resources such as food or clothing but only to those deemed to be the "worthy" poor, or those thought not to be morally flawed, slothful or otherwise responsible for their own poverty (Abramovitz 2000).

These charitable interventions failed to analyse or even identify capitalism as a system that exploited the poor and generated misery while simultaneously providing wealth and luxury to the privileged classes (Kennedy Kish et al. 2017; Withorn 1984). Dominelli (2012) argues that as such social work was a tool of the elites (p. 328), primarily used to suppress rising socialist and social democratic organizing and unrest among the working poor and impoverished people. This tradition of band-aid and pejorative social work that distracts from the need to mobilize for comprehensive social change continues today in the form of interventions that pathologize and divide service users into 'worthy' and 'unworthy' categories, and provide a subsistence level of support while leaving untouched the larger social systems that generate and profit from social inequities and injustices.

However, as Iokamidis and Trimikliniotis (2020) argue, "a radical kernel within social work existed since the inception of the profession" (p. 1890). They argue further that "this legacy deserves more recognition and celebration as it captures social work's long-standing commitment to social justice values" (p. 1890). AOP is part of this historical and contemporary radical kernel. Finding its early roots in a pragmatic synthesis and application of Marxist, feminist, anti-racist, structuralist social work (Kennedy Kish et al. 2017; Morgaine and Capous-Desyllas 2020; Mullaly 2010), AOP continues to develop in the face of changing social conditions and the deep seated local and global social, political and economic problems facing humanity today.

AOP is an intersectional, multi-strand analysis. Drawing on the work of Black feminists (Combahee River Collective 1977; Hill Collins and Bilge 2016; Carbado et al. 2013; Crenshaw 1989), AOP uses the concept of intersectionality (Baines 2017; Dominelli and Campling 2002) which argues that oppressive forces never operate in complete isolation from each other. Instead, they form complex and constantly changing web of oppressions depending on the context and the people involved. AOP recognizes that multiple social relations such as race, class, gender, ableism and homophobia shape everyday lived-experience, and that social injustice and inequity take place at the intersection of numerous social forces such as class, race, gender, (dis)ability and colonialism. These forces work to privilege some, while simultaneously marginalizing those targeted by systems of oppression.

Recent AOP literature asserts the importance of re-storying or using counter narratives, as a tool to empower those who hold marginalized positions in society's structures and who may have adopted negative storylines about themselves (Brown and McDonald 2020; Hulko et al. 2019). Though mainstream social work focuses on the individual as the primary and often exclusive site for intervention and change, as will be expanded upon below, AOP offers a strong counter narrative arguing that analysis and intervention must focus on the individual (micro), the organizational level (meso) and the larger social structures that hold oppressions in place and benefit from them (macro) (Baines 2017; Ferguson et al. 2018; Kennedy Kish et al. 2017; Parada and Wehbi 2017). The ultimate goal of AOP theory and practice is the emergence of social systems and social relations based on equity, fairness and social justice or the emancipation of all people from oppression and inequity (Baines 2017; Kennedy Kish et al. 2017; Morgaine and Capous-Desyllas 2020).

Seven Core AOP Themes

As part of the discussion of each of the seven core themes of AOP, this chapter returns to the question asked above, namely, what knowledge, theory, ethics and skills (practices) are necessary in order for social work (and other professions) to not to become complicit or active "in acts of state violence and institutionalised oppression" (Iokamidis and Trimikliniotis 2020, p. 1890).

Strategic, Pragmatic, Heterodox Social Justice Theory and Practice
Anti-oppressive social work is committed to fairness, equity and social justice (Mullaly 2010; Rush and Keenan 2014; Morgaine and Capous-Desyllas 2020;

Cocker and Hafford-Letchfield 2014). It actively embraces a pragmatic, heterodox, intersectional approach because it offers the maximum potential for strategically interweaving the strengths of many critical traditions, including Marxism, post-structuralism, anti-racism, feminism, intersectionality, post modernism, post colonialism, queer theory, social (dis)ability theory, sanism and mad studies, green, human rights and other historical and emerging traditions based in struggles for human rights, equity and social justice. This heterodox approach affords a comprehensive, yet pragmatic approach to critiquing multiple, constantly changing, complex oppressive systems and ushering in justice and equality-oriented practices and social change (Carbado et al. 2013; Collins and Bilge 2015). By not committing itself to a single theory or model, AOP does not rigidly define its boundaries or exclude other critical perspectives. Instead, it draws in knowledges, theories and practices from a broad array of critical traditions, and in the process, AOP refines and extends them to best meet the social needs and pressing problems facing social work in its many contexts and challenges.

Though some would argue that at the level of epistemology and ontology, modernist and post-modernist/post-structuralist perspectives cannot be integrated, AOP sees the ultimate test of theory to be at the level of practice and melds diverse and seemingly disparate theories into a frequently changing and dynamic whole (Baines 2017; Mullaly 2010). A contemporary application of heterodoxy can be found in new work bridging trauma-informed social work and anti-oppressive approaches to practice. Feminist scholars have historically (and validly) highlighted the pathologizing and thus depoliticizing potential of trauma-informed approaches that focus exclusively on the body as the target of medicalized intervention, particularly among trauma survivors who are women (Tseris 2013; Wilkin and Hillock 2015). They have validly cautioned social service providers against using body-centred approaches that ignore the structural and social conditions underlying the experiences of trauma survivors, including intersectional violence, as these serve to reinforce the systems of oppressions at play (Tseris 2013). Recently, despite apparent incompatibilities between feminist and body-centred trauma-informed approaches, critical scholars and practitioners have (re)conceptualized approaches to trauma work that attend to the somatic (physiological) effects of trauma, while also accounting for the broader structural context of oppression that constructs the realities of traumatic experience (Johnson 2015; Menakem 2017; Wilkin and Hillock 2015). A particularly innovative approach includes the work of Resmaa Menakem (2017), who has described the leveraging of group-based somatic practices, including mindfulness through collective singing, rhythmic clapping, and drumming, to engage in healing and resistance against the trauma that white body supremacy has historically inflicted on Black bodies and communities in the United States.

As a core AOP theme, the openness of heterodoxy ensures that theory and practice are constantly interacting with new knowledges, lived experience and emerging ideas. Rooted in and constantly intermingling with the best of other critical theories, heterodoxy acts as an accountability mechanism, keeping theory and practice from becoming stale, inflexible or complacent. Basing this heterodoxy in critical theory means that AOP remains closely tethered to social justice projects and thus provides firm boundaries to prevent slippage into complicity or active involvement in state, institutionalized or social oppression.

Macro-, Meso- and Micro-Social Relations Generate Oppression

The term 'social relations' refers to the activities, policies, practices, cultures, politics and economics that dynamically interact, conflict and interweave to generate the conditions under which we live and make choices about our lives (Baines and Sharma 2021). Though we are often led to believe that the rich make good decisions and work very hard for their wealth while the poor make bad decisions and are frequently lazy, people's lives are shaped by complicated social relations and the limited 'choices' most people have within constrained contexts. In short, our everyday lives are organized by social, political and economic forces that shape our lived experience and sense of options, but these wholly social relations are areas in which we can undertake and should undertake action to expand social equity and justice (Ferguson et al. 2018; Morgaine and Capous-Desyllas 2020; Parada and Wehbi 2017).

Macro-level social relations are often referred to as larger social structures, social forces, social institutions and social processes. They include: capitalism; governments and their economic, social, financial and international polices; religious and cultural institutions; and international trade and financial bodies (Ife 2012; Kennedy Kish et al. 2017; Mullaly 2010). Meso-level social relations refer to policies, culture and practices at the level of organizations such as social service agencies and the continuously shifting lines between government funders, employers, employees, service users and the wider community (Barnoff 2017; Ramsundarsingh and Shier 2017). Micro-level social relations include social norms, everyday practices, values, identities and so-called common sense (Brown and MacDonald 2020; Smith 2017; Pease et al. 2020). Together, these micro-, meso- and macro-level social forces sustain the unearned privilege and oppression that shape lived experiences, "intersecting with each other at numerous points, creating a total system of oppression" (Mullaly 1997, p. 105), privilege and opportunities for resistance and change (Collins and Bilge 2015). Examples of intersecting macro/meso/micro melded social relations that are particularly important in social work practice include those pertaining to race, class, gender, (dis)ability, sexual orientation, age and colonialism, among others (Baines et al. 2019; Pease et al. 2020), though as Yuval-Davis (2006) notes, we can never fully list the totality of intersecting oppressions and privileges.

This core AOP theme provides a strong critical framing based in addressing inequities and injustices at multiple levels of society, rather than exclusively or even predominantly at the level of the individual. Analyses that focus exclusively on the individual have a tendency to blame and pathologize those seeking support. Blaming and pathologizing make it easier to dehumanize and marginalize populations and to participate in state, institutionalized and relational oppression and violence. This core theme anchors AOP to critical social analysis, critical knowledges, theories, ethics and skills (practices) aimed at resisting 'acts of state violence and institutionalised oppression' rather than quietly or actively acquiescing to them.

Assist Individuals While Simultaneously Seeking to Transform Society

Dovetailing with the macro, meso and micro analysis discussed above, rather than an exclusive emphasis on changing individuals, AOP works with individuals to meet their needs, whenever possible in participatory ways, while simultaneously holding space to challenge and transform those forces within society that benefit from and perpetuate inequity and oppression (Brown and McDonald 2020; Massaquoi 2017). Similar to the core AOP themes above, this theme links the demanding work of everyday direct intervention to larger themes of social change and transformation. As such it means that practitioners are less likely to get lost in the rushed, nitty gritty of providing short term, depoliticized surface solutions and more likely to remain aware of and active in efforts large and small to build far reaching social justice-based change.

Social Work Is Not a Neutral, Caring Profession, but an Active Political Process

As noted above, social work emerged from at least two distinct roots: conventional approaches focused on adjusting the individual to better fit society; and more radical approaches focused on adjusting society to better meet the needs of all people (Kennedy Kish et al. 2017; Morgaine and Capous-Desyllas 2020; Pease et al. 2020). These trends continue today with some social work approaches concentrating on how to use therapy or individual behaviour change to assist individuals in adapting to the neoliberal world. In contrast, the AOP-based critical clinical approach analyses how social relations shape everyday experiences of oppression and/or privilege, and how to resist them helpfully and healthfully. AOP social workers work closely with service users to explore the painful and harmful impacts of social relations on lived experience and to re-story their lives in more constructive and empowering ways (Brown and MacDonald 2020).

Social work is very much about politics or power relations and how they operate at the intersection of the family, the community, the market and the government (Tascon and Ife 2019). As such, it is about small 'p' politics or struggles over resources, affirming identities, and who has a voice on the issues that shape our lives. AOP critical clinical approaches explore the many ways that social work practice and everyday struggles are about how power is distributed in the world, and who can access and use power with ease, as well as how various groups are systemically and personally disadvantaged by sexist, racist, hetero- and cis-normative, ageist and ableist social storylines (Brown and MacDonald 2020; Hulko et al. 2019; Kia et al. 2021). Approaches that are more conventional view social work as apolitical, remaking it as a neutral profession and a skills-based, technical form of work undertaken by well-educated, kindly people (Fook 2016; Pease et al. 2020). AOP and other critical approaches note that social work is and has always been a series of intense, ongoing political struggles over what privileges, services and resources will be provided, to whom, by whom, in what amount and to what end (Kennedy Kish et al. 2017). Politicizing social work makes it easier to identify practices of power, particularly misuses of power, and to take ameliorative action. It also aids in the development of critical social analysis, which can be liberatory for workers and service users alike.

This core theme brings the issues of power and power relations to the surface of the social work endeavour and calls upon AOP social workers to wield their power consciously and conscientiously in the service of those who are oppressed and marginalized. This theme represents a method that AOP practitioners can use to identify the play of politics (power) in their workplaces and social worlds, and through this process, remain accountable to social justice and equity rather than inadvertently becoming complicit or active in state, social and institutionalized oppression.

Self-Reflexive Practice and Ongoing Social Analysis

While many professions undertake reflexivity to improve their practice, most focus exclusively on the micro level of how to improve outcomes in a specific situation. For example, teachers reflect on how to reach students who may be struggling with course content. Real estate agents reflect on how to get a higher price on their next sale. In contrast, AOP social workers critically reflect on the role of micro level interactions, along with relevant meso and macro social relations, in shaping the lived experiences and possibilities for transformative change and resistance in any given practice example (Massaquoi 2017).

This means that AOP social workers are attentive to their social, cultural, political and economic environments and policies, and engage in a practice of constructive criticism vis-à-vis their own and others' connections to oppressive as well as emancipatory practices and systems within these contexts. By examining their own location and actions within the complex web of power relations, social workers can recognize social work practice as a set of power practices and can more effectively address social problems by politicizing them. It is this multi-level critical reflection that allows the process to have transformative potential (Fook and Askeland 2007) and provides a fertile ground for social workers to use their lived experiences to develop and refine theory, knowledge and practice (Morley et al. 2017; Tascon and Ife 2019).

Critical reflexivity is a central, critical social work practice and provides a strong mechanism through which to reflect on, analyse and build resistance to state, social and institutionalized violence, and oppression. This core AOP theme provides the theoretical base for the development of critical knowledge and practice embedded in the lived experience of practitioners and service users, and interpreted and deepened iteratively through the interplay with larger social contexts and relations. Finally, critical reflexivity provides a way for social workers to maintain a degree of independence and relative autonomy from state, institutional and social discourses and practices, and thus preserve a space in which to maintain social justice ethics, practices and critiques, and to build individual and collective resistance.

Participatory Approaches Between Practitioners and Service Users

Though more conventional approaches position the social worker as the expert, AOP social workers focus instead on sharing power and expertise by drawing on the lived experience and knowledge of service users and communities with respect to the structural and social conditions and challenges they face. AOP practitioners work with, and actively partner/ally with service users and communities to find participatory solutions to individual pain and suffering and to challenge the social relations that benefit from and perpetuate them. Service users are not viewed as only as victims and survivors of oppression, but also as agentic people who have much to contribute to policies, programs and evaluation plans. Service users' lived experiences can offer important insights and energy for them to challenge oppression against themselves and others, and social workers can partner and critically ally themselves by catalysing and facilitating these processes.

This core theme grounds AOP in the lived experience of those using social work supports and in inclusive, participatory processes aimed at providing voice for those less heard in society and often in mainstream social work. The egalitarian sensibility of this core theme is strengthened and amplified in the other core themes emphasizing social work as a political process that operates simultaneously at the micro-, meso- and macro levels to expand possibilities for social justice. This theme potentiates a valuable counterbalance to state, social and institutional discourses and practices that discount and silence the voices of marginalized people, making it easier to victimize and oppress them.

Theoretical and Practical Development Must Be Based on the Struggles and Needs of Those Who Are Oppressed and Marginalized

Social work knowledge and practice must be grounded in the lives of those who are marginalized and oppressed. Linked to this, they must seek more equitable ways to distribute wealth, resources in general, access to affirming identities and the means to participate fully in society (this builds on Fraser's 2010 formulation of social justice). Social work needs to be assessed in relation to this critical anchoring in social justice struggles in order to ensure that we are building lasting change and not unintentionally reproducing various kinds of oppression (for further elaboration of these concepts, see the discussion of BLM, defund the police and social work's relationship to the state, coercion and control below). As one of social work's early social justice activists and theorists, Bertha Capen Reynolds, asserted, "Social work exists to serve [marginalised] people ... If it serves other classes who have other purposes, it becomes too dishonest to be capable of either theoretical or practical development" (Meyer 1973, p. 173).

As part of larger processes grounding AOP social work in struggles for equity and fairness, AOP social work needs to build allies and work with social causes and movements. Social work ethics state that social workers should be involved in advocacy, social policy change and activism (IFSW 2012). It is not an optional aspect of ethical practice but a core feature. However, even the most activist social workers cannot resolve larger social, economic and political problems on their own. They must join with other groups to organize and mobilize people to make larger scale, transformative changes at multiple levels of society. This core theme affords AOP a way to be accountable to those most marginalized and made vulnerable in this society, and to work collectively with social movements and organizations to counter actions that extend state, institutionalized and social oppression and violence.

Expanding AOP Theory and Practices

As noted above, the seven core AOP themes map onto critical social work practices that can advance social justice at the micro-, meso- and macro levels, and have the potential to guide social workers away from active support for or complicity in state, institutional and social violence and oppression. Obviously many other social work skills such as critical social analysis, politicizing everyday practice, sharing power, counter and re-storying, communication, case planning, counselling and psychosocial assessments are also integral parts of AOP social work practice. However, history as well as the current context of BLM and COVID unrest and protest point to the need for theory, knowledge and practice that severs the links between social work and participation in institutional racism, sexism, colonialism, ableism, etc. and in their place generates inclusive, fair and equity-inducing practice. For example, in light of social work's historical and ongoing complicity with police violence (Jacobs et al. 2020), and recent calls to defund the police by the BLM (Klufts 2020), social work is well positioned to develop emancipatory praxis that reflects a stronger commitment to anti-oppression and unwavering support for comprehensive social change. In Canada and elsewhere, police shootings happen with alarming frequency during wellness checks, or home visits from police at the request of family members of people who are struggling with mental health issues. Rather than take over this role as police are asked to leave it and become 'soft cops' within a systemically oppressive system, social work can be part of a fundamental rethinking of this role and work with lived experience to ground these services firmly in the community and in AOP. All seven of the aforementioned core themes underlie the practices discussed below. This section of the chapter identifies and analyses practices that can prevent the abuses documented in British Columbia and elsewhere including: the capacity to advocate; capacity to mobilize; critical ally-ship; critical attunement; and cultural safety and cultural humility.

Capacity to Advocate

As noted above, advocacy, social policy change and activism (IFSW 2012) are central aspects of social work codes of ethics and, therefore, are intended to be central aspects of social work practice. Though advocacy has been discouraged or diminished in neoliberalized social service workplaces (Maddison and Carson 2017), these social justice-engaged practices are not merely an optional aspect of ethical social work practice but remain a core feature. Most social workers work within complex organizations and on a daily basis engage with complex policies and interpersonal relationships. Effective advocacy generally involves drawing on these relationships and the workers' familiarity with workplace policies to build support for a cause, practice or policy change. Though advocacy can be effective in quiet ways such as one-on-one conversations, it sometimes requires the mobilization of opinion and the building of consensus, collaboration and coalition with colleagues, service users, communities and social change groups.

AOP encourages the development and refinement of advocacy skills and participatory social analysis as a way to educate, engage and politicize one's self, colleagues, service users and allies in meaningful social justice-based social change at the micro-, meso- and macro levels. In the context of state, social and institutional violence and oppression, self-reflexive advocacy can be a means through which social workers, social service users and allies can identify and redistribute flows of power within organizations and challenge and change inequitable practices and policies in large and small ways (Cox et al. 2017).

Capacity to Mobilize Colleagues and Others Around Positive Action

Though social workers frequently work within multi-disciplinary teams, they do not always feel confident in their capacities to motivate social action from others, and to build the consensus necessary to mobilize for social change or to challenge oppressive practices and work culture. In part this is because the interdisciplinary team approaches used in most organizations focus on cost-effectiveness and short term, carefully quantified allotments of standardized service rather than open-ended, social justice-engaged, participatory empowerment and capacity building (Baines 2017). Like advocacy, the skills associated with mobilizing colleagues and communities fit neatly with the commitment to social justice required of social workers by their codes of ethics (Spencer et al. 2017). In the context of neoliberalism's focus on easily quantifiable and measurable interventions, the open-ended, hard to measure, social justice practices such as activism, advocacy and community development are increasingly marginal within the institutional landscape of social work practice (Rawsthorne and Howard 2019), and as such may be viewed with scepticism by other professionals. However, they are an important skill set rooted in participation, power sharing and social change and as such are obvious tools for those seeking to build AOP for social work practice that is firmly rooted in the pursuit of social justice. Mobilization practices are also spaces in which social workers can draw on their group work and communication skills to re-story workplace discourses that may be limiting or oppressive, and gently or directly challenge oppressive practices.

Critical Ally-Ship

From the perspective of AOP, collaborative alliances between practitioners and service users are not just desirable, they are essential in order for social justice social work interventions to be meaningful and sustainable. As Bennett et al. (2021) note, to work as an ally, one must act in solidarity with those who are marginalized, exploited and subjugated. In other words, AOP must work in solidarity and ally-ship with those experiencing historical and/or contemporary state, social and institutional violence and oppression.

Bennett et al. (2021) argue further that simple ally-ship is not enough given the structural inequities present in Australia and globally, and the growing social tensions underlying the COVID-19 pandemic. They assert that the focus in social work education should involve the development of a strong allegiance with disadvantaged communities and include a commitment to undertake decisive actions to redress the entrenched colonial, capitalist, systemic and structural inequities that continue to oppress many and provide unearned privilege and advantage to others (Bennett et al. 2021). Bennett et al. (2021) provide the following actions social workers might undertake in critical ally-ship: (1) through critical reflexivity, acknowledge your biases; (2) educate yourself before you engage; (3) understand that systemic racism goes beyond police brutality to the systems in which social workers are employed; (4) target racism, speak up against racism, and involve yourself in projects, campaigns and actions challenging racism and oppression; and (5) make critical ally-ship and allegiance a research, policy and practice change priority.

A growing literature suggests that rather than ally, words such as 'accomplice' or 'co-conspirator' more usefully identify the risk-taking and rule-breaking and require working for meaningful change alongside those structurally oppressed (Clemens 2017; McKenzie and Balasubramanian 2014). Many in AOP use the term critical ally-ship (Nixon 2019; Yomantas 2020) to emphasize ally-ship's link to critical social work theory and practice, and to differentiate it from its increasingly corporatized and depoliticized use in mainstream discourse. Critical ally-ship emphasizes the need for critical reflexivity on individual practice and positionality, highlighting the continuous connection between action and analysis. Finally, critical ally-ship focuses on building strategies and tactics for ongoing solidarity with Black, Indigenous and People Of Colour and their struggles and through this active, dynamic engagement, develop ways to progress towards greater racial equity and social justice (Bennett et al. 2021).

Critical Attunement

Historically, attunement has been conceptualized by social service practitioners, including some social workers, as the "full, clear, non-anxious, and warm validating observation" of service users, which ideally occurs in unison with the practitioner's own moment-to-moment awareness of themselves (Barrett and Fish 2014, p. 57). Often, this term is used to describe the deep and genuine empathic connection that is sought in relationships between social service practitioners and service users (Barrett and Fish 2014). Past conceptions of attunement have often failed to account for the structural and social conditions that construct and shape the transitory micro-level interactions of social workers and social service users, and have thus rightfully received criticism for lacking emancipatory potential (Gatzambide 2014). Accordingly, scholars have called for approaches to attunement that require practitioners to cultivate moment-to-moment attention to the structural and social forces often influencing interpersonal dynamics with service users, instead of focusing on the minutiae of these exchanges (Chang et al. 2020; Gatzambide 2014).

Critical attunement is defined in practice as an attempt, among social workers engaged at micro, meso and macro levels, to cultivate empathic relationships that feel safe and genuine for service users, and that actively invite service users to educate practitioners about the social forces shaping their relationships with social work. As Chang et al. (2020) have argued, practitioners must remain empathically open to receiving criticism and feedback in moments of conflict (or 'rupture') with service users, and to use these windows of interaction to develop critical consciousness as it relates both to inequities in power affecting the relationship, and to broader systems of oppression. Social workers must then work to repair these ruptures in relationship by affirming service users' experiences, and to recommit to anti-oppression by engaging in activism that disrupts the social forces (e.g., racism and misogyny) and structures (e.g., institutional policies) originally underlying the 'rupture' between the practitioner and service user. Although critical attunement may, on the surface, appear exclusively relevant for social workers engaging with service users in direct practice, all social workers interfacing with marginalized communities at any level require this approach for ethical and equitable engagement.

Cultural Safety and Cultural Humility

Several approaches have been employed to engage constructively with diversity including cultural sensitivity, cultural competence, cultural safety and cultural humility. The recent report on anti-Indigenous racism in health in British Columbia recommends the latter two and they are discussed here (Turpel-Lafond 2020). While well intentioned and sometimes linked to AOP approaches (Danso 2018), cultural sensitivity and cultural competence have been comprehensively critiqued for: being narrow and tokenistic; lacking an analysis of power and privilege (Beagan 2015); adopting a singular focus on race and ethnicity rather than other axes of culture and social location (Fernando and Bennett 2019); and acting as a laundry list to memorize and a form of new racism (Pon 2009).

In contrast, cultural safety represents a paradigmatic shift that situates service users as those who decide whether the professional relationship feels culturally safe (Linette 2014). In this case, understandings of 'culture' are drawn from social movements of marginalized people and include, but are not limited to collectives that are differentiated on the basis of sexuality, gender, age, religion, (dis)ability, Indigeneity, race, ethnicity and so forth (Linette 2014). Rather than memorizing a list of possible unchanging characteristics for various social groups, workers learn to deconstruct pre-existing and often stereotypical notions of culture and develop ways to indicate mutual respect, openness and willingness to listen, and a shared acknowledgement of the unique identity of others (Skellett 2012).

Similarly, cultural humility does not view 'culture' as monolithic or unchanging. Instead, it focuses on recognizing the operation of power in everyday life and draws on an intersectional analysis to understand multiple perspectives as they relate to interlocking social locations (Bennett and Gates 2021). Like AOP, cultural humility involves critical reflexivity and engages with complex questions in order to build transformative perspectives of various cultures (understood in the broadest sense) and social locations (Fisher-Borne et al. 2015). Reflecting the paradigm shift noted above, both these practices redistribute power and affirming identities from the institution to the service user and thus provide a challenge and preventive mechanism to institutional, state and social oppression.

Areas for Further Development

This section identifies and analyses areas that in the current context require further elaboration and development from AOP scholars and practitioners. It includes mutual, reflexive dialogue between Indigenous social work and AOP; LGBTQI+ social work; and BLM, defunding the police and social work's relationship to the state, coercion and control.

Mutual, Reflexive Dialogue Between Indigenous Social Work and AOP

Though AOP theory is a heterodox, umbrella theory and Indigenous knowledges, anti-colonialism and anti-racism are central aspects of AOP theory, more can and should be done to foreground the centrality of Indigenous issues and unresolved injustices against Indigenous peoples in Canada, the USA, Australia and the postcolonial world. Indigenous perspectives have often paralleled AOP theorizing, presenting an important worldview, but at the periphery of the largely Westernized social work endeavour (Bennett and Green 2019; Walter et al. 2011). In their classic article, Green and Baldry (2008) argue that while Indigenous social work theory prioritizes decolonization for Indigenous and non-Indigenous people, AOP and Indigenous social work share common goals including: self-determination (though they note that Indigenous social work emphasizes individual and collective self-determination); interdependence; reciprocity; obligation; and emancipation. Despite a significant synchronicity at the level of theory, Rowe et al. (2015) argue that in order to achieve positive outcomes for Indigenous peoples, research and practice undertaken by non-Indigenous peoples requires a paradigmatic shift, exposing colonizing and racist assumptions underpinning praxis (also Sinclair 2016). One method to build this paradigmatic shift is for Indigenous and non-Indigenous social work scholars and practitioners to draw on deep critical reflexivity (Morley et al. 2017; Morley 2021) to expose and explore the processes and practices of ongoing colonialism, whiteness and racism in mainstream and AOP social work. Critical reflexive engagement can generate new social justice practices, theory and dialogue. This project should not be a mere blending of Indigenous and AOP but an extension and deepening of each and their shared ground.

LGBTQI+ Social Work

In recent decades, social work scholars and practitioners have increasingly drawn attention to the experiences, issues and priorities of lesbian, gay, bisexual, transgender, queer, intersex and other sexual and gender minority communities (LGBTQI+) as relevant areas of attention for social workers and, more broadly, for social justice work (Dentato 2017; Gezinski 2009; O'Neill et al. 2015). Much of this work has been concerned with addressing the structural and social context of those in these groups, which is characterized by systemic exposure to oppressive social forces that include (but are not limited to) homophobia, transphobia, heterosexism and cis-normativity (Dentato 2017; Todd 2015). In recent years, the focus has been on recognizing and accounting for intersectional differences within the 'LGBTQI+' umbrella along dimensions such as gender, race, ability and class (O'Neill et al. 2015). For example, trans individuals are known to experience significant mental health inequities relative to cisgender (non-trans) sexual minorities by virtue of their heightened susceptibility to violence (Su et al. 2016), and racialized sexual and gender minorities distinctively encounter the intersecting effects of racism and anti-LGBTQI+ oppression (Ghabrial 2017). In addition, some scholars have drawn attention to the salience of poverty in LGBTQI+ communities as a relevant site for social justice work, particularly given dominant myths of 'gay affluence' that have led many in positions of power to neglect issues of economic injustice among sexual and gender minorities (Kia et al. 2020).

Anti-oppressive social workers need to be proactive in learning about the intersectionally varied experiences, issues and priorities of LGBTQI+ groups, and to practice critical reflexivity in relation to their interactions with these communities. Critical attunement, critical ally-ship and cultural safety and humility are particularly important in this work with LGBTQI+ groups and individuals. In order to ensure that AOP social workers remain cognizant of – and responsive to – the social conditions of these groups as these change with time, they will need to proactively and consistently engage with the AOP and critical literature as well as with service users, activism, critical community-based literature and grassroots coalition-building.

BLM, Defund the Police and Social Work's Relationship to the State, Coercion and Control

In various eras, debates have raged through social work as to whether social workers are angels of mercy or agents of the coercive state (Kennedy Kish et al. 2017; Withorn 1998). The reality is that social workers are neither, but further work needs to be done to clarify this complicated and contradictory relationship to the state. The government is the single biggest funder of social programs and employs a large number of human service workers both directly (in public services) or indirectly (by funding non-profits and for-profits). Some years ago, a group in the UK coined the phrase "in and against the state" to depict the tensions that many social justice social workers experience as employees of the state or state funded organizations (working within) while decisively critiquing government policy and practice and demanding the government lead decisive social justice action to reverse inequity and address harms (working against) (London-Edinburgh Return Group 1980).

Clarifying social work's convoluted relationship to the state has become more critical in the context of BLM and calls to demilitarize and defund the police (Klufts 2020; NSCSW 2020; NASW 2020). While social work's opposition to racism and police violence is essential, caution needs to be exerted as social work is increasingly asked to take on roles previously held by police or to work closely with police on tasks such as wellness checks and domestic violence calls. Unless these roles are fundamentally restructured, social work risks taking on aspects of policing and extending racist and coercive relations further into the lives of marginalized people. Ironically, the largely female social worker profession is likely to do this work for lower pay and with less status than police while unintentionally expanding a murky mandate of social control into the community and limiting solutions to social problems to policing, criminalization and imprisonment. Employing the term 'carceral social work', a growing literature critiques social work's close links to the coercive and policing aspects of society and urges a social work to fundamentally rethink the current willingness to step into spaces and services saturated with contradictions to our participatory and social justice mandates (Jacobs et al. 2020; Richie and Martensen 2020). AOP social workers already have the critical skills and theory to develop alternative, social justice-based, participatory responses to the issues currently addressed by carceral approaches; however, without deep links to marginalized communities, adequate funding and resources from governments and autonomy from the police, even the best of these efforts is likely to have more than a token impact, underscoring the ongoing dilemmas of working in and against the state.

Conclusions

This chapter first identified some of the harms that social work has participated in historically and in the current context. It then asked what knowledge, theory, ethics and skills (practices) are necessary in order for social work (and other professions) not to be complicit or active in these and similar atrocities. The chapter presented a strong argument that AOP theories and knowledge map onto critically engaged, reflexive, activist practices that have the potential to build ongoing social justice and equity, and to challenge systemic and interpersonal oppression in its many forms. Ross (2017) draws on AOP to theorize that social work resistance and activism should be understood as a broad tent that involves many ways to push back individually and collectively at policies and practices that harm people and rob them of their hope and dignity. As part of this project of resistance and dignity, AOP knowledge, theory and practice are part of larger processes of resisting oppression and transforming social work and larger social life in more socially just and equitable ways. These processes, both within and beyond the profession, are especially salient at this point in time, given the many visible and pressing calls for far reaching social change and social justice.

References

Abramovitz, M. (2000). Under attack, fighting back: Women and welfare in the United States. New York City: NYU Press.

Baines D, Sharma A (2021) Anti-oppressive practice. Social justice social work. In: Shaikh S, LeFrançois B, Macías T (eds) Social work theory & praxis. Fernwood Publishing, Halifax

Baines D, Bennett B, Goodwin S, Rawsthorne M (2019) Working across difference. Social work, social policy and social justice. Macmillan International Higher Education, London

Baines, D (2017) "Anti-Oppressive Practice: Roots, Theory, Tensions." In Donna Baines (ed.). Doing Anti-Oppressive Practice: Social Justice Social Work (3rd ed.). Halifax: Fernwood

Barnoff, L (2017) Business as Usual. Doing Anti-Oppressive Organizational Change. In Donna Baines (ed.), Doing Anti-Oppressive Practice: Social Justice Social Work (3rd ed.). Halifax: Fernwood

Barrett M, Fish L (2014) Ethical attunement. In: Treating complex trauma: a relational blueprint for collaboration and change. Routledge, London, pp 57–66

Beagan B (2015) Approaches to culture and diversity: a critical synthesis of occupational therapy literature. Can J Occup Ther 82(5):272–282

Bennett B, & Green S (Eds.). (2019). Our voices: Aboriginal social work. London: Macmillan International Higher Education

Brown, C., & MacDonald, J. E. (Eds.). (2020). Critical clinical social work: Counterstorying for social justice. Toronto: Canadian Scholars' Press

Carbado, D, Crenshaw, K, Mays, V and Tomlinson, B (2013) "Intersectionality: Mapping the Movements of a Theory." Du Bois Review: Social Science Research on Race 10, 2

Chang D, Dunn J, Omidi M (2020) A critical-cultural-relational approach to rupture resolution: a case illustration with a cross-racial dyad. J Clin Psychol. https://doi.org/10.1002/jclp.23080

Clemens C (2017) Ally or accomplice? The language of activism. Teaching Tolerance. https://www.tolerance.org/magazine/ally-or-accomplice-the-language-of-activism

Cocker C, Hafford-Letchfield T (eds) (2014) Rethinking anti-discriminatory and anti-oppressive theories for social work practice. Palgrave Macmillan, London

Combahee River Collective (1977) The Combahee River collective statement. Blackpast, South Carolina. https://www.blackpast.org/african-american-history/combahee-river-collective-statement-1977/. Accessed 31 Jan 2021

Cox L, Tice C, Long D (2017) Introduction to social work: an advocacy-based profession. Sage, Newbury Park

Collins, P H and Bilge, S (2016) Intersectionality. Hoboken, New Jersey: John Wiley and Sons

Crenshaw, K (1989) "Demarginalizing the Intersection of Race and Sex: A Black Feminist Critique of Antidiscrimination Doctrine, Feminist Theory and Antiracist Politics." University of Chicago Legal Forum 1

Danso R (2018) Cultural competence and cultural humility: a critical reflection on key cultural diversity concepts. J Soc Work 18(4):410–430

Dentato M (2017) Social work practice with the LGBTQ community: the intersection of history, health, mental health, and policy factors. Oxford University Press, Oxford

Dominelli L (2012) Anti-Oppressive. In: The SAGE handbook of social work. Sage, London, pp 328–339

Dominelli L, Campling J (2002) Anti-oppressive social work theory and practice. Macmillan International Higher Education, London

Ehrenreich J (2014) The altruistic imagination: a history of social work and social policy in the United States. Cornell University Press, Ithaca

Ferguson, I., Ioakimidis, V., & Lavalette, M. (2018). Global social work in a political context: Radical perspectives. London: Policy Press.

Fernando T, Bennett B (2019) Creating a culturally safe space when teaching Aboriginal content in social work: a scoping review. Aust Soc Work 72(1):47–61

Fisher-Borne M, Cain J, Martin S (2015) From mastery to accountability: cultural humility as an alternative to cultural competence. Soc Work Educ 34(2):165–181

Fook, J., & Askeland, G. A. (2007). Challenges of critical reflection:'Nothing ventured, nothing gained'. Social work education, 26(5):520–533

Fook J (2016) Social work: a critical approach to practice. Sage, London

Gates T G, Bennett B, & Baines D (2021). Strengthening critical allyship in social work education: Opportunities in the context of# BlackLivesMatter and COVID-19. Social Work Education, 1–17.

Gatzambide D (2014) Addressing cultural impasses with rupture resolution strategies: a proposal and recommendations. Prof Psychol Res Pract 43(3):183–189

Gezinski L (2009) Addressing sexual minority issues in social work education: a curriculum framework. Adv Soc Work 10(1):103–113

Ghabrial M (2017) "Trying to figure out where we belong": narratives of racialized sexual minorities on community, identity, discrimination, and health. Sex Res Soc Policy 14:42–55

Hulko, W, Brotman, S, Stern, L, & Ferrer, I (2019). Gerontological social work in action: Anti-oppressive practice with older adults, their families, and communities. London: Routledge

IFSW 2012. "Statement of Ethical Principles, International Federation of Social Workers."

Ife J (2012) Human rights and social work: towards rights-based practice. Cambridge University Press, Cambridge, UK

Jacobs L, Kim M, Whitfield D, Gartner R, Panichelli M, Kattari S, Mountz S (2020) Defund the police: moving towards an anti-Carceral social work. J Progress Hum Serv 32 (1):1–26

Johnson R (2015) Grasping and transforming the embodied experience of oppression. Int Body Psychother J 14(1):80–95

Kia H, Robinson M, MacKay J, Ross L (2020) Poverty in lesbian, gay, bisexual, transgender, queer, and two-spirit (LGBTQ2S+) populations in Canada: an intersectional review of the literature. J Poverty Soc Justice 28(1):21–54. https://doi.org/10.1332/175982719X15687180682342

Kia, H., MacKinnon, K.R. & Coulombe, A. (2021). Where Is the "T"? Centering Trans Experiences in Social Work Curricula Addressing LGBTQ+ Issues. Journal of Social work Education. https://doi.org/10.1080/10437797.2021.1969302

Klufts J (2020) Statement: Social Work Response and Recommendations on Police Reforms. https://www.naswma.org/news/516947/Statement-Social-Work-Response-and-Recommendations-on-Police-Reforms.htm. Accessed 31 Dec 2020

Lenette, C. (2014). Teaching cultural diversity in first year human services and social work: The impetus for embedding a cultural safety framework. A practice report. Student Success, 5(1), 117

Ioakimidis, V. & Trimikliniotis, N. 2020. 'Making sense of social work's troubled past: Professional identity, collective memory and the quest for historical justice', The British Journal of Social Work, 50(6), 1890–1908

London Edinburgh Weekend Return Group. 1980. "In and against the state". London: Pluto Press

Maddison S, Carson A (2017) Civil voices: researching not-for-profit advocacy. Pro Bono Australia and Human Rights Law Centre, Canberra

McKenzie M, Balasubramanian J (2014) Black girl dangerous. BGD Press, Oakland

Menakem R (2017) My grandmother's hands: racialized trauma and the pathway to mending our hearts and bodies. Central Recovery Press, Yorkdale

Mendes P (2005) The history of social work in Australia: a critical literature review. Aust Soc Work 58(2):121–131

Meyer, Carol H 1973. "Purposes and Boundaries–Casework Fifty Years Later." Social Casework 54, 5

Morley C, Macfarlane S, Ablett P (2017) The neoliberal colonisation of social work education: a critical analysis and practices for resistance. Adv Soc Work Welfare Educ 19(2):25–40

Morley C, & O'bree C (2021). Critical Reflection: An Imperative Skill for Social Work Practice in Neoliberal Organisations?. Social sciences, 10(3):97

Morgaine, K. and Capous-Desyllas, M. (2015). Anti-oppressive social work practice: Putting theory into action. Newbury Park, CA: Sage

Massaquoi, N (2017) Crossing Boundaries: Radicalizing Social Work Practice and Education.In Donna Baines (ed.), Doing Anti-Oppressive Practice: Social Justice Social Work (3rd ed.). Halifax: Fernwood

Mullaly, B 1997. "Structural Social Work. Ideology, Theory and Practice". Toronto: Oxford University Press

Mullaly R (2010) Challenging oppression and confronting privilege: a critical social work approach. Oxford University Press, Oxford

NASW (2020) NASW seeks to dismantle racist policing. https://www.socialworkers.org/News/News-Releases/ID/2205/NASW-Seeks-to-Dismantle-Racist-Policing. Accessed 31 Dec 2020

Nixon S (2019) The coin model of privilege and critical allyship: implications for health. BMC Public Health 19(1):1637

NSCSW (2020) Black lives matter: dismantling white supremacy in social work. https://nscsw.org/dismantling-white-supremacy/. Accessed 31 Dec 2020

O'Neill B, Swan T, Mulé N (2015) LGBTQ people and social work: intersectional perspectives. Canadian Scholars' Press, Toronto

Parada, H and Wehbi, S 2017. Reimagining anti-oppression social work practice. Toronto: Canadian Scholars

Pease B, Allan J, & Briskman L (2020). Critical social work: Theories and practices for a socially just world. London: Routledge

Pon G (2009) Cultural competency as new racism: an ontology of forgetting. J Progress Hum Serv 20(1):59–71

Ramsundarsingh, S, & Shier, M L (2017). Anti-oppressive organisational dynamics in the social services: A literature review. British Journal of Social Work, 47(8):2308–2327

Rawsthorne M, Howard A (2019) Everyday community practice. Allen and Unwin, Melbourne

Richie B, Martensen K (2020) Resisting carcerality, embracing abolition: implications for feminist social work practice. Affilia 35(1):12–16

Ross M (2017) Social work activism within neoliberalism: a big tent approach.? In: Baines D (ed) Doing anti-oppressive practice: social justice social work, 3rd edn. Fernwood, Halifax, pp 304–320

Rowe S, Baldry E, & Earles W (2015). Decolonising social work research: Learning from critical Indigenous approaches. Australian Social Work, 68(3):296–308

Rush, M, & Keenan, M (2014). The social politics of social work: Antioppressive social work dilemmas in twenty-first-century welfare regimes. British Journal of Social Work, 44(6):1436–1453

Sinclair R. (2016). The Indigenous child removal system in Canada: An examination of legal decision-making and racial bias. First Peoples Child & Family Review. 11(2):8–18

Skellett L (2012) Cultural awareness and cultural safety. Australian Pharmacist 31(5):382–385

Smith, K. (2017) "Occupied Spaces: Unmapping Standardized Assessments." In Donna Baines (ed.), Doing Anti-Oppressive Practice: Social Justice Social Work (3rd ed.). Halifax: Fernwood

Spencer E, Gough J, Massing D (2017) Progressive, critical, anti-oppressive social work: ethical action. Oxford University Press, Toronto

Su D, Irwin J, Fisher C, Ramos A, Kelley M, Mendoza D, Coleman J (2016) Mental health disparities within the LGBT population: a comparison between transgender and nontransgender individuals. Transgender Health 1(1):12–20. https://doi.org/10.1089/trgh.2015.0001

Tascon S, Ife J (2019) Disrupting whiteness in social work. Routledge, London

Todd S (2015) Social work and sexual and gender diversity: celebrating human diversity. In: Hick S, Stokes J (eds) Social work practice in Canada: an introduction. Thompson Educational Press, Toronto, pp 298–325

Tseris E (2013) Trauma theory without feminism? Evaluating contemporary understandings of traumatized women. Affilia 28(2):153–164. https://doi.org/10.1177/0886109913485707

Turpel-Lafond ME (2020) In plain sight. Addressing Indigenous-specific racism and discrimination in B.C. health care. Government of British Columbia, Victoria. https://engage.gov.bc.ca/app/uploads/sites/613/2020/11/In-Plain-Sight-Full-Report.pdf

Walter M, Taylor S, & Habibis D (2011). How white is social work in Australia?. Australian Social Work, 64(1):6–19

Wilkin L, Hillock S (2015) Enhancing MSW students' efficacy in working with trauma, violence, and oppression: an integrated feminist-trauma framework for social work education. Fem Teach 24(3):184–206. https://doi.org/10.5406/femteacher.24.3.0184

Withorn, A (1984). Serving the people: Social services and social change. New York City: Columbia University Press

Withorn, A (1998). No Win… Facing the Ethical Perils of Welfare Reform. Families in Society, 79 (3), 277–287

Yomantas E (2020) Decolonizing knowledge and fostering critical allyship. In: Parson L, Ozaki CC (eds) Teaching and learning for social justice and equity in higher education. Palgrave Macmillan, London, pp 303–328

Yuval-Davis N (2006) Intersectionality and feminist politics. Eur J Women's Stud 13(3):193–209

Caring Justice: *The Global Rise of Feminist Practice Theory*

11

Tina Maschi, Smita Dewan, Sandra G. Turner, and Padma Christie

Contents

Objectives	210
Introduction	210
Foundations of Feminist Theory and Practice	211
Social Workers and Empowerment	212
The Evolution of Diversity in Feminist Theories	216
Intersectionality Theory	216
Black Feminism	217
Feminist Environmental Justice Theory	217
Migrant Women and Feminist Theory	218
Indigenous Feminist Theory	218
Feminist Relational Social Work Practice	219
Caring Justice Framework: An Integrated Gender-Based Paradigm	221
Summary and Conclusion	226
References	227

Abstract

This chapter provides an in-depth exploration of feminist practice theory, especially as related to social work practice. Grounded in women's 'herstory' we map the global evolution of thought across a diversity of feminist perspectives and practices. Directly following, we draw from and build upon insights from feminist practice theory about its core values and principles, concepts, propositions,

---

T. Maschi (✉)
Fordham University, New York, NY, USA
e-mail: tmaschi@fordham.edu

S. Dewan
New York City College of Technology, City University of New York, New York, NY, USA
e-mail: sdewan@citytech.cuny.edu

S. G. Turner · P. Christie
Graduate School of Social Service, Fordham University, New York, NY, USA
e-mail: sturner@fordham.edu; pchristie3@fordham.edu

© Springer Nature Singapore Pte Ltd. 2023
D. Hölscher et al. (eds.), *Social Work Theory and Ethics*, Social Work,
https://doi.org/10.1007/978-981-19-1015-9_11

theories of change, and practice techniques. To this end, we describe how feminist thought and practice have evolved over time by conducting an integrative analysis using feminist practice theories for problem formulation (e.g., patriarchal 'imprisonment', powerlessness, domination/subordination, victimization/criminalization, gender, race, violence, and other inequalities). We also present a caring justice framework that includes solution focused practice strategies for women and girls of all ages.

Keywords

Feminist practice theory · Caring justice · Theories of change

Objectives

The objectives of this chapter are to:

- Describe the evolution and diversity of feminist theories.
- Provide an overview of the values, and central concept, and theories of change, and practice techniques.
- Conduct an integrative analysis of problem definitions and suggesting solution focused strategies.
- Articulate the diversity of feminist theories: We do an integrative analysis of the concepts and values underlining the theories and introduce an integrating theoretical model of caring justice.

Introduction

As we write this chapter, 'modern' social work practice is navigating a very complex environment with the COVID-19 pandemic, racial, gender based, environmental and other injustices. These confluences of events have elevated the health and social disparities that have 'plagued' people across the globe on the basis of racial/ethnic, gender, class, sexual and neuro divsersities and divisions. We are now at a critical crossroad at which we assert that existing thought has failed to adequately identify the roots of the problems as well as sustainable solutions to achieving peace, justice, equality/equity for people of all ages across the globe.

This is also a call to social work to respond to this crisis as an opportunity to fulfil our collective purpose and mission as defined by the International Federation of Social Workers as a:

> "Practice-based profession and an academic discipline that facilitates social change and development, social cohesion, and the empowerment and liberation of people. Principles of social justice, human rights, collective responsibility and respect for diversities are central to social work. Underpinned by theories of social work, social sciences, humanities and

indigenous knowledge, social work engages people and structures to address life challenges and enhance wellbeing".

Feminist values are clearly reflected in social work principles. The key principles of social work as laid out by the International Federation of Social Work clearly demonstrate how they are consonant with feminist values. The following principles are especially indicative of feminist values: inherent dignity of humanity, promoting human rights, promoting social justice (i.e., challenging discrimination and institutional oppression, respect for diversity, access to equitable resources, challenging unjust policies and practices, building solidarity), promoting the right to self-determination, promoting the right to participation, treating people as whole persons, and working with professional integrity.

Implicitly and explicitly, social work empowerment is at the core of feminist theory (Turner and Maschi 2015). Empowerment as a concept is well positioned in the preamble of the National Association of Social Workers (NASW) *Code of Ethics*, which states: "The primary mission of the social work profession is to enhance human well-being and help meet the basic human needs of all people, with particular attention to the needs and empowerment of people who are vulnerable, oppressed, and living in poverty" (NASW 2017, p. 1). In this statement, empowerment can be understood as a fundamental goal that social workers pursue when the theory of empowerment is put into practice.

Foundations of Feminist Theory and Practice

In this segment, we explore and contemplate historical and emerging feminist theories, perspectives, and praxis, and the movement towards gender integration and justice. These theories support the notion that vertical systemic (hierarchical patriarchy) imbalances favour and advantage the privileged or dominant groups (e.g., white males and the wealthy) as compared to less privileged or subordinate groups (e.g., females whose majority and minority statuses vary by race, class, gender conformity, sexual orientation, and/or geographic and social location). Systemic imbalances of power create and maintain continuing conflicts for the less powerful resulting in a fragmented social service system that perpetuates existing inequalities. Consequently, women and non-majorities continue to have less access to power, resources, and services and are at a heightened risk of victimization and oppression in the home, community, and systems of care (Crenshaw 1991; Jordan 2010; Turner and Maschi 2015).

In our discussion of feminist theory, we weave in critical intersectional theories. These theories also often account for race and intersectionality and multilevel anti-oppressive practices such as the *4-level model of oppression* model (Mullaly and West 2017). Moreover, these theories assert that the underlying condition or 'problem focus' in need of a transmutation is oppression and disempowerment in which marginalized groups and societies, oppression based on gender, race, class, and other intersectional identities heighten the risk of disempowerment, trauma, abuse, and health and justice disparities. The five faces of oppression are: exploitation, marginalization, powerlessness, cultural imperialism, violence (Young 1990; see Figs. 1 and 2), to which, Maschi and Morgen (2020) suggest, should be added the additional faces of voicelessness and criminalization. According to these perspectives, the perpetuation of violence and abuse and overall crime are rooted in the patriarchal system that includes characteristics such as hierarchical vertical domination, control, and abuse of authority and oppression (Maschi and Morgen 2020; Turner and Maschi 2015; Young 1990).

The good news is that once this problem of 'gender and intersectional oppression' is diagnosed, we can use various feminist theories, including the caring justice framework to create a solution focused action plan. As detailed later in the chapter, the aim is to restructure the system from a fear-based hierarchy and violent society to a more creative, compassionate, fair, equal society. Towards this end, we also propose to use a solution focused language and approach. It is important to note that although described as the 'problem' of sexism and other forms of oppression (the problem we don't want), we do so to be able to engage readers in the language they are currently familiar with in order to shift them to a more positive focused health, equality, and well-being for humanity, the earth, and all living beings (a state we do want).

Social Workers and Empowerment

As a profession, social work has been dominated by historically 'disempowered' groups and often been referred to as one of lower rungs of health professions (Maschi and Baer 2013). Based on recent research, the 'feminization' of social work and the 'call to social work' has mostly been answered by women followed by minorities of diverse gender and sexual identities (Turner and Maschi 2015). In the USA, for example, a report by the 2017 Council on Social Work Education (CSWE) Report found that out of approximately 400,000 practicing social workers, 4 out of 5 social workers were female (83%). The authors projected that women are more likely to continue to dominate the profession given that the majority (84%) of current students were also female (Salsberg et al. 2017).

Current social work and interprofessional educational standards, which have incorporated values of feminist theory and practice within their policies, are promising for opening an avenue for the elevation of feminist theory and practice. For example, the most recent Educational Policy and Accreditation Standards (EPAS) by the United States-based Council on Social Work Education (Competency 3; CSWE 2015) underscores that social workers should engage in human rights and social justice practice. The Australian social work education standards also require that social work curriculum includes feminist social work. The Canadian Association for Social Work Education also stresses the need to focus on social justice (CASWE 2021). Social workers also understand the forms and mechanisms of oppression and discrimination and recognize the extent to which a culture's structures and values, including social, economic, political, and cultural exclusions, may oppress, marginalize, alienate, or create privilege and power. It is in response to this awareness that feminist social work has much to offer.

Another opportunity for feminist theorizing in social work curricula is the human rights and social justice competency because it underscores knowledge (e.g., theory), values (e.g., ethics, attitudes and beliefs), and skills (e.g., multilevel practice strategies) that social workers are expected to understand and then apply in practice. Social workers across the globe understand the interconnections between oppression and human rights violations. They are most equipped to apply theories of human needs, justice, and multilevel practice strategies to best ensure justice, equality, and human rights. Most entities overseeing social work education incorporate rights and justice-based content in the curriculum in varying forms and include recommendations for the use of skills self-awareness and critical thinking. We highlight feminist thought in this chapter for multi-level social work to demonstrate how it serves to enhance practice (Salsberg et al. 2017).

The current state of world chaos and emergence of complex global and local social problems has exposed the inability of traditional feminist theorizing to develop solutions. Feminist theorists now recognize the need for a shift in perspective by attempting to develop newer ways of thinking about old problems. This has occurred through an emergence of issue-based feminism such as eco-feminism, black feminism or migrant feminism. Another way this takes place is through the development of an innovative theorizing by introducing a new framework, i.e., the Caring Justice framework.

To better equip social workers this chapter intentionally highlights feminist practice theory from its 'ancient' to modern times. Grounded in women's 'herstory' we first map the global evolution of feminist thought across a diversity of feminist perspectives and practices including emerging integrated gender theories. We then spotlight feminist core values and principles, concepts, propositions, theories of change, and multilevel practice techniques for transformative personal social ecological change. Thereafter, we discuss how the application of feminist theory in social work has evolved according to the local and global issues that social workers address. We focus on three major recent social movements of racial justice, i.e., Black Lives Matter movement, gender justice, i.e., Me Too movement and environmental justice where women have led many efforts to address the needs of their families and communities. Each of these three movements will be examined using a feminist theoretical framework. We then conduct an integrative analysis using feminist practice theories for problem formulation (e.g., patriarchal 'imprisonment', powerlessness (domination/subordination)/ victimization/criminalization, gender, race, and other inequalities, violence, and comprised well-being). We conclude with solution focused practice strategies and application of theory in practice (e.g., empowerment, gender and intersectional equality, peace, and holistic well-being) with examples relevant to women and girls of all ages, backgrounds and their families, and local and global communities.

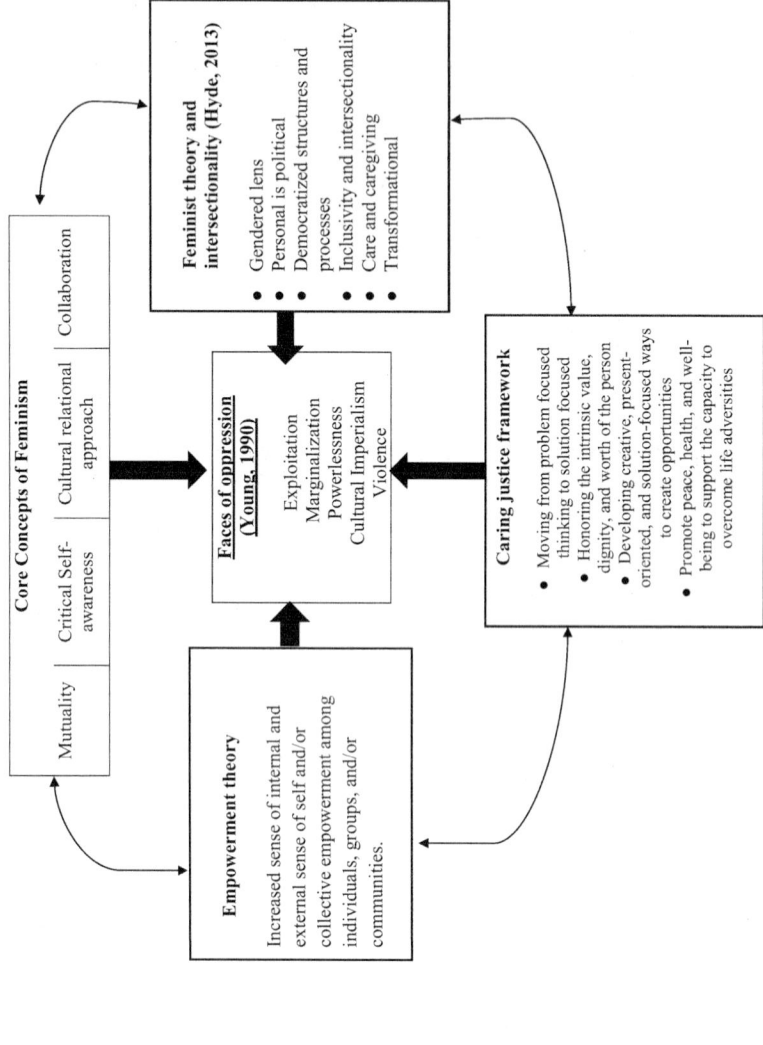

Fig. 1 Feminist theorizing and oppression

Fig. 2 Caring justice framework

This conceptual model illustrates the pathways to dismantle, release, and/or transform internalized (e.g., homophobia, xenophobia etc.) and externalized oppression (e.g., marginalization, discrimination, and victimization, and criminalization) in which individuals, groups, and/or communities use a conscious practice of unconditional living to boost confidence and motivation that fosters liberation, empowerment, and well-being. Through this conscious practice, the promotion of personal, relational, and mass liberation, empowerment, and well-being for oppressed individuals and groups, such as LGBTQIA+ and their families and communities, can be advanced locally and globally.

The Evolution of Diversity in Feminist Theories

Various authors have highlighted the chronological order of feminist responses to the existing social issues addressed at the time. For example, the first wave of feminism focused on women's suffrage and legal rights around property ownership, and the second wave which was directly following the civil rights movement during the 1960s to 1980s focused on a range of issues, particularly violence against women, reproductive rights, equal rights, and equity legislation. Feminism in the third and fourth waves which are identified as those from 1990s to 2013 and to the present addressed individual self-expression, promotion of diversity, intersectionality, reproductive rights, and sexual harassment. The third wave of feminism is marked by activism against workplace sexual harassment that was direct result of the Anita Hill case (Swigonski and Raheim 2011) and the emergence of the concept of "intersectionality" coined by Crenshaw (1991), to highlight ways in which different forms of oppression based on gender and race intersect. One unique characteristic of a distinct fourth-wave feminism is the use of internet and online technology for political activism (Day and Wray 2018). While the four waves are not demarcated in a chronological order, they have some utility in explaining the evolution of the theories.

A variety of perspectives of feminism also identify the primary causes of inequality and oppression of women differently. For example, the liberal perspective of feminism considers that sex role stereotyping and/or structural barriers are the main causes of inequality and oppression of women. The radical perspective of feminism on the other hand posits that white male supremacy and cultural patriarchy are the primary causes of inequality and oppression. Other feminist perspectives are the (a) socialist perspective that considers the intersection of gender and class including disparities resulting from labour markets and economic structures; (b) cultural perspective that recognizes the denial and repression of women's ability to nurture; and (c) the womanist perspective that states that the intersection of race and gender leads to inequality and oppression of women (Hyde 2013).

Intersectionality Theory

Crenshaw (1991) developed Intersectionality theory which is founded on the principle of the importance of examining the multiple identities of people. She discussed how people who share one identity characteristic such as gender may be doubly discriminated against if they are also black or native American, and perhaps have more privilege if they are both women and white. The concept of intersectionality shows how important it is to look at discrimination and oppression using multiple lenses. The #Me Too Movement was founded in 2016, and many feel that the oppressive experiences of Black, disabled, and queer women have often been marginalized in the movement (Garza 2020). The movement often overlooks that minority cisgender and transgender women are discriminated against differently when the focus is just on men as the abusers and women as victims. Sometimes what is happening is that cisgender women as well as men are the ones harassing transgender women. Mehrotra (2010) suggests that intersectionality theorizing must go beyond the usual triumvirate of US racial, class, and gender-based oppressions to include postcolonial, queer, and transnational feminist theorizing.

Black Feminism

The evolution of feminist theories within social work practice is in keeping with the socio-political developments in the USA and around the world. Practice that is informed by feminist theories advocates for approaches that take into consideration gender and power at the centre of the therapeutic process (Dunkerley 2017). For example, there have been numerous efforts to include a black feminist framework into social work education and practice. This perspective recognizes that Black women's reality must be seen from a positive standpoint, moving away from perspectives that are based on racist-patriarchal constructs and helps to forge a greater understanding of their strengths, resilience, and struggles. Another important contribution of the black feminist theory is its assertion that social work practice must take into account the historically traumatic experiences of Black communities, including slavery and its aftermath. Historical trauma refers to the cumulative emotional and psychological wounding over the lifespan and across generations, emanating from massive group trauma, which may be experienced by individuals, families, and communities as historical unresolved grief (Brave Heart et al. 2011).

The feminist movement has not adequately acknowledged that it has been primarily spearheaded by white women and does not recognize and encompass the contributions of Black women (Walker 1983; Gaard 2010). In addressing the lack of representation and recognition of the experiences of Black women, Black feminists have created more diverse narratives, specifically intersectionality, which focuses on the intersections of race, class, gender, and sexuality, emphasizing that only focusing on gender oppression marginalizes the experience of women of colour (Crenshaw 1991).

Feminist Environmental Justice Theory

In addition to Black feminism, another emerging and evolving theory is the feminist environmental justice theory, also known as eco-feminism. Within the social work publications, eco-feminism is also emerging as eco-social work which focuses specifically on issues related to disaster response or recovery, access to natural resources and food security (Bell 2019). The term eco-feminism (Francoise d'Eaubone in 1974, in Bell 2019) was coined to illustrate the potential of women for bringing about an ecological revolution to guarantee human survival. Eco-feminism is therefore a theory and movement for social change that combines ecological principles with principles of feminist theory. This theory comes with its own criticisms and debates, but in the context of its application to social work practice, this theory requires us to use a social justice logic to understand the interconnectedness focus of the model that suggests that the struggles against oppressive, systemic forces that denigrate nature are also intertwined with the struggles against all forces that oppress humans. The oppression that keeps realization of a dynamic, harmonious human/nature relationship out of consciousness is connected to other forms of human oppression including economic exploitation, racism, sexism, and patriarchy. Though human oppression and oppression of nature appear to exist in separate forms, struggle against any one in isolation cannot be effective.

Migrant Women and Feminist Theory

Another area of social work practice where feminist theory is still evolving is in its application to practice with migrant and/or immigrant women. Within migration studies, migration theorists have recognized a need to include gender into any analysis of migration, especially to explain the predominance of women in certain types of migratory labour flows, the conditions under which women migrate, the reasons why women become transnational migrants, enter into trafficking channels or seek refugee resettlement (Boyd and Grieco 2003). Answering these questions through migration theories that are informed by feminist theories is important for the social work profession as well which ultimately serves the multiple and complex needs of these populations. The call for incorporating gender in migration theories has been a direct consequence of the feminist movement. When feminist theory is applied to migration, it helps social workers understand how patriarchy which gives preferential access to the resources to men, affects women's ability to migrate, how it shapes the migration experience and how it impacts the women's experience in their final destination. Feminist theories also help social workers understand how the migration experience might impact the interpersonal relationships of the women within their families and communities of their final destination.

Indigenous Feminist Theory

Indigenous or Aboriginal feminists, in solidarity with other women of colour and 'Third world' women, have felt alienated by what they view as a 'Western' feminist movement that has either marginalized them or not accurately represented their experiences and interests especially as these relate to their experiences with colonialism (Sunseri 2000). This branch of feminism highlights that one of the worst direct outcomes of patriarchy and colonization is experienced by Indigenous women. Currently, Indigenous women are among the most deeply marginalized groups in the world, especially in 'Western' countries where, relative to other groups, they are over-represented in the worst social indices of poverty, health, education, and unemployment (Makere Stewart-Harawira 2007). Indigenous feminists stress the important role of women and femininity in those pre-colonial Indigenous societies which were gynocentric. Application of Indigenous feminist theorizing in social work practice is still in its infancy.

Feminist Relational Social Work Practice

Empowerment is an antidote to oppression, and feminism and empowerment as a theory and process incorporates a human rights and social justice approach to practice. Feminist theory focuses on the centrality of gender when examining the effects of oppression and domination and has as its core the belief that women of all classes and races are oppressed differently than men (Collins 1991; DeBeauvoir 1957; Hamilton et al. 2019). It is also important to emphasize that women of colour have been and still are oppressed differently than white women (Gaard 2010).

Feminist theory has much in common with oppression and empowerment theories. Feminism emphasizes the importance of the social, political and economic structures that shape human societies and stresses that a focus on gender is essential when analysing the effects of domination, power, and powerlessness in our society. There are four core concepts of feminist theory: (1) mutuality, (2) critical self-awareness, (3) cultural-relational awareness, and (4) collaboration (Turner and Maschi 2015). When working directly with clients, feminist and empowerment theories are useful in guiding social workers to help clients claim their power, build self-confidence, and self-esteem as they engage in mutual, non-hierarchical relationships (Crenshaw 1991; Jordan 2010). Those who espouse feminist theory and principles believe that the inferior status of women is derived from unequal political, economic, and social power relations. For proof of this perhaps, one need not look any further than the difficulty women face getting elected to high office or becoming a CEO or celebrated authors and scientists. Although oppression and empowerment theories and a human rights perspective are considered mainstream in social work, feminist theory and gender issues have yet to have a prominent place in social work curricula (Hafford-Letchfield et al. 2014).

Jordan et al. (1991) developed a relational model of practice, in which practitioners develop mutual, collaborative relationships with their clients. They do not work as outside observers attempting to understand what the other person is dealing with or has experienced. Social workers who practice from a feminist theoretical perspective let themselves be seen by their clients, and the relationship itself is often the vehicle to foster strength and self-esteem (Turner 2001). Feminist social work practice extends strengths-based practice. The practitioner must be relational and open to new ways of knowing and understanding (Hyde 2013). A study of feminist interventions in Canada found that feminist models of working with clients are effective in supporting mutual client-worker strategies to change larger system targets. Feminist interventions enable clients to engage in examining structures and processes that are rooted in patriarchal systems and values. They have proven to be more effective than those based on other models of practice, such as CBT and psychodynamic approaches (Gorey et al. 2002) which focus on individual change.

As stated earlier, in feminist theory, there are four core concepts: (1) mutuality, (2) critical self-awareness, (3) cultural-relational approach, and (4) collaboration. When working directly with clients, feminist and empowerment theories and practice are useful in guiding social workers to help clients claim their power, build self-confidence, and self-esteem as they engage in mutual, non-hierarchical relationships (Crenshaw 1991; Jordan 2010). Mutual relationships based on a cultural-relational approach and collaboration help to build critical self-awareness and self confidence and self-esteem.

Additionally, social workers have ethical responsibilities to respect and promote clients' rights to self-determination, pursuit of life purpose, and goals which are core elements of the empowerment process. Social workers generally serve individuals and groups who vary by race/ethnicity, gender identity, sexual orientation, immigration, criminal justice history, physical or mental abilities, and age. Access to power, privileges, services, and justice is often influenced by individuals' social identities or social locations (e.g., being a Caucasian abled-bodied heterosexual male compared to being an African American lesbian with a physical and mental disability female). Therefore, at the broader societal level, social workers also have an ethical responsibility to increase choice and opportunities for community, collective, and political empowerment, especially among vulnerable individuals and groups. By applying the principles of a feminist perspective, both the social worker and the client are able to challenge oppressive social and institutional processes that impact their well-being.

Interestingly, while empowerment practice is almost synonymous with social work practice in general and more specifically with feminist social work practice, its meaning and application remains somewhat elusive and a matter of debate. In fact, interpretations of empowerment differ on whether empowerment is a philosophy, theory, or a practice model (Gutierrez and Lewis 1999). In addition, there is no consensus among scholars on a single, all-encompassing definition or conceptualization of empowerment (Speer and Peterson 2000). Despite these differences, empowerment has continued to capture the altruistic imagination of social workers. Empowerment as a theory for direct social work practice at individual, group, community, and political levels is a staple in many social work texts that promote a generalist model of social work (Allen-Meares and Garvin 2000; Robbins et al. 2012).

Therefore, it is important in any discussion of empowerment to address the many 'faces' of empowerment since as a concept it varies in meaning and is defined and operationalized in varied ways (Cattaneo and Chapman 2010). For example, empowerment is described as a perspective or philosophy guided by principles of social justice, such as inclusivity, equality, and an understanding of oppression. This description is closely related to empowerment as an ideal condition, a process, and a way of acting in carrying out social work roles. Common processes that social workers engage in when applying an empowerment perspective include sharing power, consciousness raising, collaboration, and partnership. These practice approaches and techniques are very similar to those that feminist social work practitioners have engaged in explicitly since the 1980s when the concept of mutuality was introduced and developed (Carr 2003; Jordan 2010; Hyde 2013; Turner and Maschi 2015).

Lastly, as an outcome, empowerment is operationalized as an increase in power in intrapersonal, interpersonal, and community realms. At the intrapersonal level with individuals, this outcome often includes an increase in perceived competency and self-efficacy, or the ability to experience competence in one's life (Carr 2003; Bandura 1982). Increased self-efficacy, viewed as increased power, then translates into an increased ability to influence events in one's life, interpersonally in one's relationships and in the socio-political sphere. An outcome of building empowerment would be an increased sense of internal and external sense of self and/or collective empowerment among individuals, groups, and/or communities. There also is a psychological and emotional component. For example, individuals may experience a positive shift in one's internal thoughts and emotions that they then can use to reframe their external relationships with others and their environment. The individual, group, or collective that participates in this process is perceived as becoming stronger or more empowered and more able to influence their inner and outer worlds. They do so by engaging in practice, such as critical reflection and psychological transformation, group and community participation, capacity building, and knowledge and skill attainment. Empowerment social work practice is much like the feminist approach which operates within a human rights and social justice framework with the goal of building a more compassionate world. The work is both clinical and community oriented (Lee 2001; Turner and Maschi 2015).

Caring Justice Framework: An Integrated Gender-Based Paradigm

The Caring Justice framework is an emerging framework that aligns with feminist principles (Maschi and Morgen 2020). It can be applied as a solution to societal unsolved problems that involve complex systems, such as violence, crime, and health and justice disparities that intersect with the political, social, economic, health systems, and local and global systems. This perspective aligns with and

Table 1 Caring justice: Different levels of recognizing and responding to the plight and suffering of others

Sympathy	Thought	Recognition of experience of 'suffering'
Empathy	Thought + emotion-action (not necessarily with action)	Recognition and vicariously experiencing the thoughts and emotions not necessarily with action
Compassion/ unconditional love	Thought + emotion + nonjudgemental + action	Recognition and experiencing the thoughts, emotions, and experience without judgement, and acting.

Other terms use radical empathy (Wilkerson 2020), radical forgiveness, and transformative empathy. Wilkerson (2020) states that we need to practice "radical empathy" (or transformative), which is going beyond putting yourself in another's shoes to understand another person's experience from their perspective

Table 2 From problem focused to solution-focused thinking and approaches *Caring Justice Roadmap*

Problem Focused	Solution Focused
Fear-Based Thinking (Survival Mode, Contraction)	Creative Thinking (Creative and Expansive)
Problem-focused	Solution-focused and mission-driven
Trauma/stressed/crisis	Resilient; crisis as opportunity
Negative/pessimistic/stressed	Mutuality
Dualistic/binary thinking	Relational
Linear thinking only,	Relaxed, creative, positive, optimistic
Deductive thinking predominant	Unity/collective (I/we) systems thinking
Ego-driven and intellectual only focus	Linear and systems thinking
Self-preservation	Circular/deductive and inductive thinking
Self-focused (ego-centric)	Heart driven, emotional, compassionate
Self-cantered or either-or impulsive	Group-focused
fear-based decision-making	Open-minded
Closed minded	Collective centred decision-making (for the highest good of all; sustainable)
Irratinoal biased	
Judgmental	Positive thoughts and emotions
Competitive	Fair and non-judgmental, compassionate caring
Power over vertical	Horizontal power within/power with model
Hierarchy/domination	Non-judgmental
Control-focused	Collaboration/partnerships
Criticizes/discriminates	Honours diversity and difference
Does not honour diversity and difference	Grass roots participation; bottoms up approach
Top-down partial decision-making	

complements feminist and human rights perspectives. It intentionally does so by moving from problem focused (negative) thinking to solution focused (positive) thinking to focus on the ideal. For example, if we don't want violence, injustice, and health disparities, it allows for the creation of the ideal narrative to work towards what we do want as individuals and/or as a collective. This framework allows for a new visualization of how to achieve peace, justice, and health for all if human and natural rights are valued and practiced. These values and principles include but are not limited to: honouring the intrinsic value, dignity, and worth of the person and developing creative, present-oriented, and solution-focused ways to create opportunities for care and justice through ethics, principles, and guidelines that promote peace, health, and well-being of individuals, families, groups, and communities to support the capacity to overcome life adversities and become stronger- not only surviving, but also thriving (see Tables 1, 2, and 3 and Fig. 3 in the appendix; Meadows 2008; Maschi and Morgen 2020).

From an integrated outlook, the caring justice perspective is guided by a new way of thinking and being. Based on Einstein's 'you can't solve the problem with the same level of thinking that created the problem' quote, caring justice identifies the problem and moves into solution-focused thinking. The Caring Justice framework helps to identify fear-based negative thinking and change to solution focused positive thinking for assessment realizing peaceful, safe, and healthy individuals, groups, and communities. For example, the dominance of problem focused thinking

Table 3 Caring justice: From problem to creative solution Focus-part 1: Example identified issues/problems

Levels of Assessment and Intervention	Problem Focus	Solution Focus
Cultural level: Transmitted through cultural, community, and mass media systems	Negative fear-based media messages (me vs you thinking) about women and people of colour. The issue focus (e.g., showing continuous violence on TV; fear-based strategies about the spread of illnesses and no focus on recovery, adverse portrayal of women in the media, lack of coverage of black women killed by police violence compared to black men) Lack of truth and reconciliation racial health discussions for those harmed and those who harmed (to read more see: https://theconversation.com/do-truth-and-reconciliation-commissions-heal-divided-nations-109925)	Collective and media outlets practice a compassionate/gender integration caring justice partnership society and culture using mass media; watch positive gender, race, etc... Programming on TV or no TV; support and frequent alternative mass media programs; positive and inclusive programming for people of all gender, race, and sexual identities Truth, healing, and transformation discussions using solution-focused approaches
Structural/institutional level: Transmission through social policies and institutions	Reactionary social action; engage policy campaigns that focus on what we don't want; campaigns that use double negatives, such as end injustice, community violence, gun violence, or end starvation; end poverty, one side only perspective campaigns Collective phraseology-how we discuss and develop goals and indicators of change Economic and business systems- competitive and hierarchal Hierarchical models/power over	Contemplative reflexive social action; engage in positive policy campaigns of what we do want and inclusive of multiple perspectives; revise campaigns that use double negatives, such as end community violence or gun violence, and positively reframe them to what we do want (e.g., the compassionate and peaceful community campaign; the equality agenda; food at every table; prosperity everything, caring justice worldwide) Partnership models power within/power with SDGS Further develop collaborations and cooperative businesses; also use barters and good exchange (food co-ops time banks, microfinancing)

(continued)

Table 3 (continued)

Levels of Assessment and Intervention	Problem Focus	Solution Focus
Personal level: Transmitted through everyday relationships	Uses negative phraseology and disrespectful verbal and non-verbal behaviours; describe people derogatorily, disrespectfully, or by a label; does not use humanizing language or engage in abusive behaviours in personal and professional settings	Use new phraseology and respectful verbal and non-verbal behaviours In personal life- tell loved ones you love them; learn conflict resolutions In practice- call people by their first names as opposed to their diagnoses; if needed, rephrase the description: a person in a recovery program
Internal level: Impact of other levels on the psychological, emotional, and overall Well-being of individuals	Person who engages in self-criticism negative emotions and other internalized oppressive beliefs practices, shift from a negative mindset to a positive emotional state	Promote self-directed wellness, shift to a positive mindset and emotional state, self-empowerment, peer-led individual and group support, community connections
Research and evaluation: Exploratory, intervention, participatory research, and diverse perspectives	No research on the topic; research abuses- no participatory research; findings not available for public consumption Rational focused science; lack of diverse perspectives; control of research and funding by outside parties and experts without the lived experience or situation; all stakeholders not involved	Research from diverse perspectives and ways of knowing Use for self and public awareness, prevention, assessment, intervention, advocacy, policy development, and reform Use of qualitative, quantitative, mixed methods, participatory, and emerging methods (evaluation of assessment interventions at all levels) Engage key stakeholders in research, especially as the researchers and not just the 'researched' Grassroots, community-based led research initiatives that engage all key stakeholders in identifying the problem(s) and solutions
Rule of law and the environment	Use of human made Laws for the rule of law for peace, justice, health	Living in accordance with natural law for human and natural world sustainable peace, justice, and health

that favours the negative, binary or dualistic, hierarchy, competition conflict, and domination will lead to negative processes and outcomes and repetitions of tragedies. Examples include the repetition and patterning of global pandemics, political

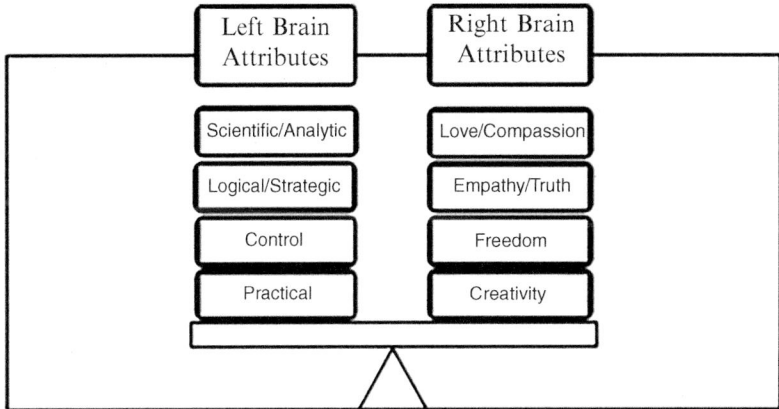

Fig. 3 Integrated 'Caring Justice' Self

violence, mass violence and genocide, global war and conflict, and climate change. In comparison, a solution focused perspective that favours the positive, I/We unity thinking (interconnectedness), holistic circular thinking, cooperation, peace and calmness, and equality leads to sustainable solutions and intervention designs fuelled by peace, understanding, compassion, justice, and equality. Examples of public health and safety problems outline the differences between a problem focused and solution focused perspective and how this impacts the ability to deliver peaceful, healthy, and just outcomes (see Maschi et al. 2021 for additional information).

The Caring Justice framework unconditionally addresses 'inner love, justice, and peace' and right and left-brain integration for all genders (Maschi and Morgen 2020). Persons and inner and external environments embody aspects of 'caring' or 'compassion' and are feminine and nurturing principles as well as masculine aspects (e.g., protection, balance and truth, order, rationality, structure, and rule of law). The system is in balance and leans towards equality. Additionally, the caring justice framework is solution-focused, and strengths-resilience based. It reflects the balance and integration of the right (feminine) and left (masculine) sides of the brain that inform different ways of thinking, feeling, and behaving (Maschi and Morgen 2020). This framework posits that finding peace within can occur by individuals taking responsibility for healing their inner wounded masculine and feminine and get back into a state of unconditional love (for self and others) and balance. As individuals become integrated and whole again, we can begin to cocreate loving kindness relationships, communities, and the global natural world that flourish.

The core concepts and drivers embodied in the caring justice framework are 'care' and 'justice'. These are two core aspects for the health functioning of a complex system, such as the human body as well as a local to global community. In order to survive and thrive, two key aspects are care (e.g., emotional and instrumental care) and justice (e.g., balance homeostasis). In the caring justice perspective, 'caring' refers to emotional and behavioural aspects that include unconditional love, empathy, compassion, authenticity, treating others with dignity and respect, acknowledgment of the worthiness and wellness of self and others, prudent optimism, and unity in the form of inner and outer relational interconnections, and being of service to others. The core aspects of justice are represented by ideals of truth, rationality, balance, order, harmony, morality, and equity/equality. In the model the critical drive is the presence of care that reaches a level of unconditionality in the form unconditional love that supersedes sympathy and empathy.

This conceptual model illustrates the pathways to dismantle, release, and/or transform internalized (e.g., homophobia, xenophobia, etc.) and externalized oppression (e.g., marginalization, discrimination, victimization, and criminalization) in which individuals, groups and/or communities use a conscious practice of unconditional living to boost confidence and motivation that fosters liberation, empowerment, and well-being. Through this conscious practice, the promotion of personal, relational, and mass liberation, empowerment, and well-being for oppressed individuals and groups, such as LGBTQIA+ and their families and communities can be advanced locally and globally.

The caring justice framework can also be utilized to examine global indicators of peace, justice, inclusion, and health. Using United Nations Data Tracking for the Sustainable Development Goals (Sachs et al. 2020), we posit that countries with higher scores on the indices of peace would also report higher levels of health and well-being, gender equality, and reduction in inequalities.

Summary and Conclusion

This chapter explored feminist practice theory, especially as relates to a rapidly evolving social work practice. The global evolution of thought across a diversity of feminist perspectives and practices has generally focused on core principles that integrate women's ways of knowing, especially related to care, equality, process oriented and holistic thinking, and respect for relationship to the others as well as the earth. Feminist informed interventions apply these core values and theories of change that often honour the individual in the context of the whole. We provided the readers with a historical journey of the feminist thought and practice 'train' over time by conducting an integrative analysis. We outlined how feminist practice theories have been used for problem formulation (e.g., patriarchal 'imprisonment', powerlessness, domination/subordination, victimization/criminalisation, gender, race, and other inequalities, violence, and compromised well-being). We also offer caring justice framework focused practice strategies (e.g., empowerment, gender and intersectional equality, peace, and holistic well-being) for women and girls of all ages and their families and communities.

References

Allen-Meares P, Garvin CD (2000) The handbook of social work direct practice. Sage Publications, Los Angeles

Bandura A (1982) Self-efficacy mechanism in human agency. Am Psychol 37(2):122–147. https://doi.org/10.1037/0003-066X.37.2.122

Bell K (2019) Australian social work transforming social work for environmental justice: theory, practice, and education. Aust Soc Work 72:242–244. https://doi.org/10.1080/0312407X.2019.1569080

Boyd M, Grieco E (2003) Women and migration: incorporating gender into international migration theory. Retrieved from http://incedes.org.gt/master/boydgriecodiez

Brave Heart MY, Chase J, Elkins J, Altschul DB (2011) Historical trauma among Indigenous peoples of the Americas: concepts, research, and clinical considerations. J Psychoactive Drugs 43(4):282–290. https://doi.org/10.1080/02791072.2011.628913

Carr ES (2003) Rethinking empowerment theory using a feminist lens: the importance of process. Affilia 18(8):8–20

CASWE (2021) Canadian social work education standards, 2021. Retrieved from https://caswe-acfts.ca/wp-content/uploads/2021/08/EPAS-2021-1.pdf

Cattaneo LB, Chapman AR (2010) The process of empowerment: a model for use in research and practice. Am Psychol 65(7):646–659. https://doi.org/10.1037/a0018854

Collins P (1991) Black feminist thought. Routledge, New York

Council on Social Work Education (2015) Educational policy and accreditation standards for baccalaureate and master's social work programs. Alexandria, VA

Crenshaw K (1991) Mapping the margins: intersectionality, identity politics, and violence against women of color. Stanford Law Rev 43:1241–1299

Day K, Wray R (2018) Fourth-wave feminism and postfeminism: successes and failures. Transform: J Radical Left 4:113–137

DeBeauvoir S (1957) The second sex. Alfred A. Knopf, New York

Dunkerley S (2017) Mothers matter: a feminist perspective on child welfare-involved women. J Fam Soc Work 20(3):251–265. https://doi.org/10.1080/10522158.2017.1322163

Gaard G (2010) New directions for ecofeminism: toward a more feminist ecocriticism. Interdisciplinary studies in literature and environment. Oxford University Press

Garza A (2020) The purpose of power: how we come together when we fall apart. One World

Gorey KM, Daly C, Richter NL, Gleason DR, McCallum MJA (2002) The effectiveness of feminist social work methods: an integrative review. J Soc Serv Res 29(1):37–55

Gutierrez LM, Lewis EA (1999) Empowering women of color. Columbia University Press, New York

Hafford-Letchfield T, Lambley S, Spolander G (2014) Inclusive leadership in social work and social care. Policy Press, Bristo

Hamilton LT, Armstrong EA, Seeley JL, Armstrong EM (2019) Hegemonic femininities and intersectional domination. Sociol Theory 37(4):315–341. https://doi.org/10.1177/0735275119888248

Hyde C (2013) Feminist social work practice. Retrieved from https://doi.org/10.1093/acrefore/9780199975839.013.151

Jordan J (2010) Relational-cultural therapy. American Psychological Association, Washington, DC

Jordan J, Kaplan A, Miller JB, Stiver I, Surrey J (1991) Women's growth in connection: writings from the stone Center. Guilford Press, New York

Lee JAB (2001) The empowerment approach to social work practice. Columbia University Press, New York

Makere Stewart-Harawira (2007) Practicing Indigenous feminism: resistance to imperialism. Zed Books. Available at SSRN: https://ssrn.com/abstract=2828271

Maschi T, Baer J (2013) The heterogeneity of the world assumptions of older adults in prison: do differing worldviews have a mental health effect? Traumatology 19(1):65–72. https://doi.org/10.1177/1534765612443294

Maschi T, Morgen K (2020) Aging behind prison walls: studies in trauma and resilience. Columbia University Press, New York. Retrieved April 9, 2021, from http://www.jstor.org/stable/10.7312/masc18258

Maschi T, Rios J, Kaye A (2021) Co-constructing community: visualizing and realizing a 2020 vision of care and justice in social work. (online) Naswinstitute.inreachce.com. Available at: https://naswinstitute.inreachce.com/Details/Information/db957917-a663-467b-904e-888a6b0ad128. Accessed 9 Apr 2021

Meadows DH (2008) Thinking in systems: a primer. Chelsea Green, White River Junction

Mehrotra G (2010) Toward a continuum of intersectionality theorizing for feminist social work scholarship. Affilia 25(4):417–430. https://doi.org/10.1177/0886109910384190

Mullaly B, West J (2017) Challenging oppression and confronting privilege, 3rd edn. Oxford University Press, Don Mills

National Association of Social Workers (2017) Code of ethics of the National Association of Social Workers. https://www.socialworkers.org/About/Ethics/Code-of-Ethics/Code-of-Ethics-English

Robbins SP, Chatterjee P, Canda ER (2012) Contemporary human behavior theory: a critical perspective for social work. Media Production Services Unit, Manitoba Education

Sachs J, Schmidt-Taub G, Kroll C, Lafortune G, Fuller G, Woelm F (2020) The sustainable development goals and COVID-19. Sustainable development report 2020. Cambridge University Press, Cambridge

Salsberg E, Quigley L, Mehfoud N, Acquaviva KD, Wyche K, Silwa S (2017) Profile of the social work workforce. Retrieved from https://hsrc.himmelfarb.gwu.edu/sphhs_policy_workforce_facpubs/16

Speer PW, Peterson NA (2000) Psychometric properties of an empowerment scale: testing cognitive, emotional, and behavioral domains. Soc Work Res 24(2):109–118. https://doi.org/10.1093/swr/24.2.109

Sunseri L (2000) Moving beyond the feminism versus national dichotomy: an anti-colonial feminist perspective on Aboriginal liberation struggles. Can Women Stud 20(2):143–148

Swigonski ME, Raheim S (2011) Feminist contributions to understanding Women's lives and the social environment. Affilia: J Women Soc Work 26(1):10–21. https://doi-org.avoserv2.library.fordham.edu/10.1177/0886109910392517

Turner S (2001) Resiliency and social work practice: three case studies. Fam Soc 82(5):441–448

Turner S, Maschi T (2015) Feminist and empowerment theory and social work practice. J Soc Work Pract 29(2):151–162

Walker A (1983) In search of our mothers' gardens: womanist prose. Harcourt Brace Jovanovich, San Diego

Wilkerson I (2020) Caste. Random House, New York

Young IM (1990) Justice and the politics of difference. Princeton University Press, Princeton

Developmental and Community-Based Social Work

12

Janestic Mwende Twikirize

Contents

Introduction	230
The Conceptual Evolution of Developmental Social Work	231
Conceptualising Developmental Social Work	233
Links to Developmental Social Welfare	234
Social Development as a Framework for Developmental Social Work	235
Developmental Social Work and Community Development	237
Key Features of Developmental Social Work	239
Skills for Developmental Social Work Practice	242
Developmental Social Work's Link to the Nature and Purpose of Social Work	242
Challenges to Adoption of Developmental Social Work	244
Conclusion: Future Outlook for Developmental Social Work	246
References	247

Abstract

Developmental social work is part and parcel of mainstream social work that emphasises use of investment strategies to meet the material needs of individuals and groups and the adoption of practice interventions that lead to progressive, sustainable social change. It is predominantly macro-level practice with most interventions targeted at community level, as well as engaging with societal systems, structures and institutions to address the root causes of oppression, exploitation and vulnerability. It is inspired by the broader field of social development and closely interlinked with community development and developmental social welfare. Developmental social work reclaims social work's primary mission of liberating people from poverty, vulnerability and oppression. It is also squarely fitting into social work's current orientation towards promoting social

---

J. M. Twikirize (✉)
Makerere University, Kampala, Uganda
e-mail: janestic.twikirize@mak.ac.ug

© Springer Nature Singapore Pte Ltd. 2023
D. Hölscher et al. (eds.), *Social Work Theory and Ethics*, Social Work,
https://doi.org/10.1007/978-981-19-1015-9_13

change and social cohesion, human rights, social justice and equality. Although predominantly researched, theorised and practiced in the global South, particularly in Africa, developmental social work is deemed relevant in contexts of the global North.

Keywords

Developmental Social Work · Social Development · Community development · Social welfare · Africa

Introduction

For several decades, there have been calls by social work scholars (Midgley 1995, 2001; Midgley and Conley 2010; Patel 2005; Patel and Hochfeld 2012; Lombard 2008; Lombard and Wairire 2010; Spitzer et al. 2014; Gray and Simpson 1998; Gray 2002; van Breda 2015; Mupedziswa 2001) to move towards a developmental model of social work especially in countries of the global South. This call has been sanctioned by a growing dissatisfaction with the traditional approaches to social work practice which have mostly been perceived as remedial. The remedial model, which is commonly associated with psychotherapeutic social work as conceived and practiced in countries of the global North, is deemed inadequate to tackle deep-rooted systemic and structural problems of poverty and deprivation, social inequality and oppression, which are widespread across many countries. One of the core arguments is that social work should transcend its residual maintenance roles and actively contribute to national development while at the same time liberating people from poverty and deprivation and affording them more freedoms (Midgley 1995; Midgley and Conley 2010; Gray and Simpson 1998; Anderson et al. 1994). The predominant argument in the literature is that the mission and purpose of social work has always been change oriented; but along the way, a lot of focus was placed on psychotherapeutic as well as other forms of maintenance and remedial roles at the expense of promoting sustainable change. This also meant that community practice which provides greater opportunity for developmental social work interventions has tended to be side-lined as a method of social work in several countries especially in the global North (Midgley 2010b). Hence, there is a general recognition of the need to promote a model of social work that makes it a visibly significant contributor to national development. This model of social work is also believed to contribute towards more sustainable social change in accordance with the mission and goal of the social work profession.

Developmental social work is inspired by the broader field of social development; has strong links to community development; and has at the same time been intertwined with a related construct of developmental social welfare. Although mostly popular in the global South, developmental social work is deemed relevant as well in the more developed countries of the global North due to its strong focus on equality, social justice and human rights (Midgley and Conley 2010; Hugman 2016).

In this chapter, an attempt is made to deconstruct developmental social work as presented in contemporary literature, highlighting its theoretical underpinnings, principles, key features and practice skills, as well as its links to mainstream social work. A brief commentary on the relationship between developmental social work and community development is made as most developmental social work interventions take place through community practice. The chapter begins with the historical evolution of developmental social work in the global South, also highlighting its conceptualisation in the literature. The next sub-sections present an overview of social development as a framework for developmental social work, followed by the links between developmental social work and community development. This is followed by a discussion of the key features as well as skillsets associated with developmental social work practice. A brief discussion on how developmental social work links to the nature and purpose of the social work profession is then provided. The chapter concludes with a highlight of the main challenges in the adoption of developmental social work as well as its outlook.

The Conceptual Evolution of Developmental Social Work

Developmental social work is presented in the literature as an evolving approach to practice which represents a paradigm shift requiring that social work's institutionalised ways of operating be modified due to the need to cause real improvements in people's lives as individuals and as a collective (Midgley and Conley 2010). The evolution of developmental social work as both a concept and approach arose out of the dissatisfaction with remedial social work and its limitations in contributing to long-term changes in community life and overall national development. Whilst acknowledging the strong inspiration and influence of the field of social development on developmental social work, authors such as Midgley (2010b) contend that developmental social work has its roots in the debates that have characterised the very nature of social work since its inception. Having been motivated by poverty and its correlates that were offshoots from the industrial revolution in Europe and America, social work's mandate had a strong focus on addressing poverty, social inequality and other forms of vulnerability (Midgley 2010b). This in essence was a mission to promote social change, as doing otherwise would be to misrepresent the profession's goal and purpose. In their provocatively titled book, *Unfaithful Angels: How Social Work Has Abandoned Its Mission*, Specht and Courtney (1994) accuse social workers of abandoning their original mission of liberating people from poverty and destitution and instead focusing on psychotherapy, which according to the authors, ignores critical concerns of the community. Thus, by promoting developmental social work, there is no deviation from mainstream social work, but rather a reclaiming of the formative mission of social work. According to Midgley (2010b), the challenge has been in divergent views on how to achieve the goal of liberating people from poverty and oppression. Whilst some firmly choose individualised clinical social work, others choose group and community organising approaches, while still others believe in the institutionalised approach that centres expanded government social services and income maintenance programmes as the core of social work and social welfare (Midgley 2001). It is the wide criticism of social work's disproportionate focus on individualised psychotherapeutic approach that has given rise to developmental social work, which in a way represents a transition to concepts around social change, development and integration.

In Africa, the remedial model of social work introduced by the colonial government largely lacked a developmental focus and rather aimed to provide remedial welfare (IASSW 1974 cited in Asamoah 1994), although there were at the same time efforts to promote community development. Between mid-1960s and early 1980s, the Association of Social Work Education in Africa (ASWEA) held a series of conferences and seminars to refocus social work to be more relevant in Africa by addressing the development challenges of poverty, deprivation, rural and community development. They argued for and directed efforts towards adoption of more developmental approaches in both education and practice (ASWEA 1973). A conference of social work educators held in Addis Ababa, Ethiopia, noted that the mandate of the emerging social work profession transcended "the remedial roles of alleviating, curing or preventing social evils to more importantly promote active participation in development" (Yimam 1976, p. 19). In fact, there was an idea that "an end to be put on social work as social welfare and instead emphasise its role in national development" (Yimam 1976, p. 20). Social workers, according to ASWEA, were expected to develop the capacity of citizens for full and meaningful participation in national development besides supporting them to adjust to the ever-changing environments. Addressing social and economic inequalities, rural-urban differentials in development, unemployment and underemployment, poverty and deprivation, community development and empowerment were considered as critical social work roles in developmental welfare. This discourse has been sustained mostly by social work scholars in Southern Africa and gradually across different countries in the global South (Midgley 1995, 2001; Midgley and Conley 2010; Patel 2005; Patel and Hochfeld 2012; Lombard 2008; Lombard and Wairire 2010; Spitzer et al. 2014; Gray and Simpson 1998; Gray 2002; van Breda 2015; Mupedziswa 2001). Specifically, in South Africa, developmental social work gained theoretical traction in response to the country's post-Apartheid *White Paper on Social Welfare* (1997), which proposed adoption of developmental social welfare and social development as the main model for social services (Lombard 2008). Later, in East Africa, a consortium of universities undertook a project between 2012 and 2018 to strengthen professional social work to contribute to social development more effectively (Spitzer and Twikirize 2014; Twikirize and Spitzer 2019) thus reflecting efforts to promote a developmental model of social work across the region.

Scholars from other parts of the global South have made similar arguments in efforts to promote developmental social work. For example, Bose (1992 cited in Midgley 2001, p. 28) highlighted the inappropriateness of the remedial models of social work in India that focused on the individual and family rather than addressing the systemic and structural issues of poverty and social inequality.

Conceptualising Developmental Social Work

Although no standard definition currently exists for developmental social work, several authors offer useful descriptions to shape its conceptualisation. Gray (2002, p. 13) describes developmental social work as "a type of social work that affirms the profession's commitment to poverty alleviation and social inclusion, recognises the link between social and economic development, and construes welfare as an investment in human capital rather than a drain on limited resources." Patel (2005, pp. 206–207) defines developmental social work as the "practical and appropriate application of social development knowledge, skills and values to social work processes to enhance the well-being of individuals, families, households, groups, organizations and communities in their social context". Patel's definition is linked to that offered by Midgley and Conley (2010) who conceptualise developmental social work as the application of the theory, principles and values of social development to social work, mostly at a macro level. Lombard and Wairire (2010, p. 100) borrow ideas from different authors to characterise developmental social work as 'an integrated, holistic approach to social work that recognises and responds to the interconnections between the person and the environment; links micro and macro practice; and utilises strength-based and non-discriminatory models, approaches and interventions, and partnerships to promote social and economic inclusion and well-being'. These definitions highlight both the nature, approach and goals of developmental social work, especially centring it on adoption of macro-level, reformist interventions to contribute towards social and economic progress.

Community level interventions lie at the centre of developmental social work. In fact, Gray et al. (2017a, p. 2) categorically state that developmental social work "means basically shifting from casework to community development as a major intervention strategy". Despite this macro-level focus, developmental social work does not totally discard case work or other micro-meso level interventions (Midgley and Conley 2010; Patel and Hochfeld 2012; Hugman 2016; van Breda 2015). Hugman (2016) contends that social work with individuals, groups, families, communities and at the national level can be developmental social work. van Breda (2015) provides a process model for developmental case work, while Midgley and Conley (2010) provide case examples of developmental social work innovations across different practice fields including childcare services and other would be remedial-oriented fields. Developmental social work, however, emphasises distinct practice modalities that emphasise use of tangible social investment strategies including, for example, promotion of gainful employment, assets and livelihoods development, microfinance and savings and credit schemes, and adult literacy (Midgley 2010b). These predominantly economic interventions take place across the continuum of micro–macro level and potentially enhance people's capacities and their participation in development (Midgley and Conley 2010; Patel and Hochfeld 2012; Hugman 2016; van Breda 2015).

Developmental social work adopts an eco-systems approach where interventions cut across the micro-meso-macro levels involving local, national, and global systems (Gray 2002). Hence the person, the environment, and the dynamic interactions between them is central to this practice (Patel 2005). This approach is important in addressing structural and systemic challenges of poverty, inequality, and social injustice. In line with this eco-systemic thinking, Estes (1997) identifies four roles associated with developmental social work, namely, (1) Provision of personal social services to people in distress, for example orphans and vulnerable children, refugees, and people living in extreme poverty, (2) Organisational efforts to help poor and marginalised people to confront and remove sources of their oppression, (3) Institutional building, including building new institutions and strengthening existing ones to make them more responsive to the needs of the people, and (4) Directly contributing to accelerating the pace of macro-level social development as well as promoting adherence to internationally guaranteed human rights. This description places developmental social work in conformity with the original mission and purpose of social work at its multi-level and multi-dimensional approaches.

Links to Developmental Social Welfare

Because social work professionals are primarily engaged with delivering social welfare services, developmental social work has at the same time been linked to the construct of 'developmental social welfare'. Developmental social welfare is perceived as a model of social welfare that, rather than being consumption-oriented and diverting resources from economic development, has the potential to contribute to social and economic development through enlisting the active participation of the welfare service beneficiaries into the productive economy. It challenges models that promote dependency and aims to promote self-reliance among service users. This perspective of social welfare emphasises the need for social services to go beyond addressing immediate needs of people and focus on realising larger social and economic changes in the environment to prevent future disruptions in people's functioning and promote quality of life more sustainably (Anderson et al. 1994). It emphasises change, partnership, justice, and the development of human potential in place of condescension, passive provision, segregation and negative labelling of individuals and groups (United Nations 1986 cited in Noyoo 2014). Five critical features for developmental social welfare can be identified from the literature, namely, an emphasis on rights-based approaches (where development and access to an income is a right rather than a favour), interrelation between social and economic development, democracy and participation, social welfare pluralism (where not only the state but civil society and communities play a role in social welfare) and reconciling the micro-macro divide where social welfare organisations provide generalist, holistic services that meet diverse needs of clients across the different systems (Patel and Hochfeld 2012; van Breda 2015; Mbecke 2016). Developmental social work is conceptualised as the delivery mechanism for developmental social welfare within the social development framework.

Social Development as a Framework for Developmental Social Work

Developmental social work is intricately linked to the field of social development and yet the two are not synonymous. Social development is a much broader multi-disciplinary field where social work plays a role (Midgley 1995, 2010b). The relationship between the two fields is that of interdependence and mutuality. Hugman (2016) perceives social development as a distinct approach to social work. This was earlier qualified by Midgley (2001) and Midgley and Conley (2010) who refer to social development as the developmental perspective in social work while inversely referring to developmental social work as the social development approach to social work. Hence, social development provides the framework and basic principles for developmental social work practice while the social work profession more concretely contributes to social development through developmental social work.

One of the most popular definitions of social development is offered by Midgley (1995, 2001) who conceptualises it as a process of planned social change designed to promote the well-being of the population as a whole within the context of a dynamic multifaceted development process. Midgley (1995, 2001) identifies several defining features of social development:

- It is a dynamic process (as opposed to static addressing of immediate need).
- It is progressive (intended to promote steady improvements).
- It is multifaceted (integrates social, cultural, economic, political, environmental and other factors).
- It is interventionist (requires action in the form of programs, plans and projects).
- It is productivist (contributes to economic growth and development).
- It is universalist (considers the population as a whole).
- It is community-oriented (even when addressing individual needs).
- It aims to promote wellbeing (see also Hugman 2016; Pawar 2014).

Social development is concerned with promoting people-centred development through investment in human capital development as well as creation of an enabling environment where people's needs and aspirations are sustainably met. Pawar (2014, p. 4) bases on the definitions by different authors to characterise social development as "about systematically introducing a planned (sometimes radical) change process, releasing human potential, transforming people's determination, reorganizing and reorientating structures and strengthening the capacity of people and their institutions to meet human needs". It is a systematic process that seeks to harmonise social and economic development goals and to link social services to economic development in a dynamic way to improve wellbeing. In this process, social goals are not subsidiary to but equal in status with economic development goals (Pawar 2014). Estes (1997, p. 4) identifies the value base for social development, which is accordingly shared across the social work profession, as "respect for the unity of life on earth, the minimization of violence, the satisfaction of basic human needs, the primacy of human dignity, the retention of diversity and pluralism and, the need for universal participation in the process of attaining worldwide social transformation". More precisely, as a people-centred approach, social development is underpinned by ideals of social justice and equity, human rights and dignity, participation and democracy, and sustainability and peace (Hugman 2016). As an approach, it should positively address social disadvantage, exclusion and inequality (Hall 1990 cited in Anderson et al. 1994).

In developing countries, social development is mostly concerned with poverty eradication as well as provision of quality social services including health, education, safe water and sanitation, environmental health, food security and nutrition (Gray 2002; Lombard 2008; Mbecke 2016). As a framework for practice, social development requires that social workers become aware and comfortable working with the economic, political, and technological aspects of development (Hugman 2016).

From a social development perspective, economic development should benefit the whole population while social welfare interventions should positively contribute to economic development. As an approach, it was intended to lessen emphasis on remedial social welfare and redesign it to entail community-based interventions which facilitate acquisition of skills and engagement in projects that could lead to concrete transformations in society. In this way individuals could be equipped to be active participants in the development process rather than passive recipients of welfare services and goods. The commonly cited 1995 World Summit on Social Development (Copenhagen Declaration) bolstered social development as the more relevant model of development through which poverty, unemployment and social inequality could be tackled (Lombard 2008; Midgley 1995; Midgley and Conley 2010). These goals were later picked up in the Millennium Development Goals and their successor Sustainable Development Goals, all of which place social and human development at the centre. The World Bank (2004) views social development not only as a way of tackling poverty through context specific social change but also a means to making development more effective. Social development also draws on Amartya Sen's capabilities approach which emphasises people's freedom and 'functionings' (Sen 1999; Midgley 2010b). These ideas and concepts are in turn underscored in developmental social work where the emphasis is on enhancement of people's capacity and confidence to take charge of the issues that affect their lives and to actively participate in the development process and community life. Specific actions associated with social development at individual and community levels include among others, community education, conscientisation and empowerment, advocacy, capacity building, organising, and grassroots research (Midgley 1995). At the community level social development encompasses community development, social action and promotion of participation (Midgley 1995; Hugman 2016).

It is these principles and concepts that provide a structure for developmental social work practice. As a framework for developmental social work, social development demands that social workers more actively engage with macro-level tasks related to social policy and planning, social administration, programme evaluation and community organisation (Anderson et al. 1994; Midgley 1995; Hugman 2016). Social workers must also be comfortable working with multi-disciplinary teams since promoting sustainable social change demands multi-sectoral strategies and diverse skillsets. The community provides the milieu for social development and most developmental social work practice. This makes the two fields interwoven with another construct of community development.

Developmental Social Work and Community Development

There is a very thin line between developmental social work and community development especially in some countries of the global South where social workers mostly work at the community level to address poverty and related problems. However, not all community practice by social workers is necessarily developmental as some organising activities may not be aimed at progressive change especially in people's economic wellbeing. Developmental social work is mostly implemented through community development projects which emphasise social investment and social enterprises that should lead to tangible services to the community members (Midgley and Conley 2010). Thus, when compared to other approaches such as psychotherapeutic social work, community development is the most strongly associated with developmental social work practice (Midgley and Conley 2010). According to Hugman (2016) the easiest way to distinguish between community development and social development is to perceive the latter as providing the overarching framework for community development (as it does for developmental social work). Both community development and social development are characterised as macro-level practices, concerned with structures, systems and processes rather than direct work with individuals and families only (Hugman 2016). Hugman (2016), however, argues against this dichotomy between micro- and macro level practice or direct and indirect practice, stating that practitioners within the so-called macro-level practices such as community development and social development must be capable of working with individuals and groups to effect changes at a personal level, which have the potential to contribute to collective development goals.

Historically, the notion of community development was inspired by the desire to promote integrated development through use of local resources and grassroots participation (Swanepoel and De Beer 2011). It involves collective action by community members to address problems that confront them and promote change that is meaningful to them. They do this through mobilisation of resources available within the community and/or working in partnership with external collaborators including local governments and civil society organisations (Staples 2016). Gray (1996 cited in Gray 2009, p. 78) describes community development as "an intervention strategy, a way in which services are rendered". She goes ahead to describe this strategy as "a democratic, grassroots or bottom-up, humanistic, people-centred approach that emphasises the participation and involvement of local people in all aspects of development and their empowerment through, among other things, education, conscientisation, awareness raising, capacity building, community action and community organising" (Gray 2009, p. 78). Staples (2016) characterises community development as involving participants in constructive activities and processes to produce improvements, opportunities, structures, goods, and services that increase the quality of life, build individual and collective capacities and enhance social solidarity. Hence, collective identity and action are prioritized in community development.

Other key features associated with community development include, an integrated approach, collective action, an orientation towards perceived and actual needs of the community, specific goals and objectives for every action, grassroots action, local assets and democracy (Swanepoel and De Beer 2011). Other key characteristics include self-help and cooperation, resource redistribution, mass education aimed at conscientization, as well as capacity development (Estes 1997). Community development is also important to the larger processes of social and economic change. Generic roles of community development practitioners include educational (e.g., awareness raising), facilitative (e.g., group facilitation, mediation, negotiation), representational (e.g., advocacy, networking, resource finding) and technical roles [(e.g., financial control, management, research, technology) (Ife 2013 cited in Hugman 2016, p. 119)].

Community-based interventions have been expanded through decentralised service delivery systems as well as the work of non-governmental organisations (NGOs) and community based civil society organisations in many countries of the global South. Many government poverty reduction strategies have adopted community-based programmes that involve a range of interventions such as youth livelihood programmes, women enterprise development programmes, which require working with different segments of the community to enhance social and economic progress. In this sense, community development is part and parcel of the democratisation process. Quite often though, these programmes are determined from the central governments and handed down to the communities through the local governments. Conversely, NGOs tend to engage more closely with the local communities to facilitate active participation and decision-making in the social development process; although undue influence through preconceived problem-solving models is not uncommon (Twikirize 2017). In several African countries where there is lack of strong state welfare systems, social workers are mostly employed in the non-governmental sector and they are at the forefront of working with communities to design and implement several livelihood development projects.

Similar to developmental social work, community development is predicated upon recognition and enhancement of people's strengths and upholds democratic ideals of equality, social justice and participation in decision-making (Swanepoel and De Beer 2011). Developmental social workers work with communities to identify pressing issues, collaboratively set goals and organise to implement specific interventions that are change-oriented and aim to lead to tangible improvements in people's lives.

Key Features of Developmental Social Work

Several traits and features of developmental social work have been elaborated in the literature. The main interlinked features are presented below:

Developmental social work is change oriented. Implied in this change is progress. Midgley (2010b) relates this change to both micro and macro levels; at micro level, the change is perceived in terms of personal growth while at the macrolevel, collective improvements should lead to better integration, community functioning, equality and social justice as well as tangible improvements in people's standards of living. This explains developmental social work's conceptualisation within the social development framework.

Social investment strategies are a core ingredient of developmental social work. A key role in promoting social change is poverty alleviation since most other problems that confront social work clients especially in the global South revolve around lack of necessities for decent living. Because of this, social investment strategies and productivist interventions are a core ingredient for developmental social work (Midgley and Conley 2010). Social investment comprises interventions targeted at meeting the material needs of social work clients and facilitating their full integration into the social and economic development processes. Human capital investments through education and skills training, micro enterprises, micro-credit, asset building and social capital development are critical (Midgley and Conley 2010). Hence, developmental social workers are social entrepreneurs (Gray 2002). Social entrepreneurship involves use of business principles and logic in a novel way that creates social value and specifically, to improve the situation of segments of the population that are excluded, marginalised or suffering (Saebi et al. 2018a, b). As social entrepreneurs, developmental social workers pursue the dual mission of innovating for social and economic goals within communities and play critical roles in ensuring that even the most vulnerable individuals, families and groups at the grassroots level participate in innovative processes, in line with core professional principles of empowerment, participation, social justice and social inclusion (Spitzer and Twikirize 2021). Interventions can include, for example, establishment of a community day care centre or community based agricultural advisory services that assist rural subsistence farmers to improve their productivity.

Developmental social work underscores notions of strengths, empowerment and capacity building. These are seen as necessary means through which social change can be achieved (Midgley 2010b). An underlying assumption of the strength's perspective is that every person has inherent ability to guide personal and social transformation if the environment is conducive. Thus, developmental social workers focus on the strengths, capacities, resources and potential that client systems present rather than being preoccupied with deficits (Midgley 2010b; Gray 2002, 2009; Gray et al. 2017a). They also desist from labelling clients as necessarily oppressed and exploited, which automatically sows feelings of disempowerment (Gray 2002). Instead, they view client systems as partners and appreciate the inner personal and communal resources that have helped them to survive the situations they are in and then together forge ways of making sustainable improvements. Strengths are also linked to resilience theory which is concerned with ways in which people and systems respond to, recover from, overcome and often thrive in the wake of adversity (Saleebey 1996; van Breda 2015). Social workers' roles include facilitating removal of obstacles that stand in the way of clients' progress whether these obstacles are personal or within the environment and building people's capacity for more sustainable progress (Gray 2002).

Developmental social work is committed to the promotion of human rights, equality and social justice. Developmental social work affirms the commitment of the social work profession to social justice and human rights and to the eradication of poverty and inequality (Lombard 2014; Lombard and Wairire 2010). Human rights are premised on the intrinsic value and dignity of every individual (Staub-Bernasconi 2012). They go hand in hand with equality and social justice (Lombard and Twikirize 2014; Wronka 2012). A human rights perspective emphasises the fact that every citizen has a right to development and to participate in the process of development. Therefore, promotion of equitable social structures which can provide people with greater security and development while upholding their dignity (United Nations 1994) is a critical element of developmental social work. This human right perspective provides a strong basis for "an assertive practice that seeks to realise the social justice goals of social workers, in whatever setting" (Ife 2012, p. 6 cited in Lombard and Twikirize 2014, p. 47).

Social justice is one of the defining principles of social work (Hölscher 2012; IASSW, ICSW and IFSW 2012; Lombard 2014). Social justice and injustice are often maintained through political, social and cultural systems, structures and institutions of society and they are manifested in relationships between members of society as individuals, families, communities and populations (Jordan 2013). Hölscher (2012) rightly argues that the presence of social injustice anywhere exacerbates processes and cements structures of social exclusion, thus hampering the furtherance of human rights both within and across societies. Developmental social workers engage with different elements at the micro-meso and macro levels to promote just relations and directly challenge injustice through, for example, speaking out against forms of oppression and exploitation and ensuring that their own actions and decisions are fair and promote equal opportunities for all.

Developmental social work upholds principles of participation and self-determination. Clients have a right not only to participate in decisions and actions that affect their lives but also access services that meet their needs and aspirations (Midgley and Conley 2010; Gray and Simpson 1998). This contrasts with the conservative approaches where the professional acts as an expert who prescribes solutions. As argued by Nyirenda (1976 cited in Anderson et al. 1994, p. 84) social workers must not see themselves as privileged and removed from society, "…but as ordinary members of the society ready to use their newly-acquired knowledge and skill in the service of that society". They therefore must uphold the ethic of self-determination as well as participation by individuals and communities.

Developmental social work emphasises the concept of integration rather than isolation and institutionalisation. Clients should be supported to live as part and parcel of community rather than be isolated. Midgley and Conley (2010) contend that such integration is desirable and requires heavy investments in housing, education facilities, transport, and cultural and recreational facilities among other essential services.

Developmental social work embraces political participation and activism. Rather than shy away from politics, developmental social workers are expected to become active participants in political processes including agitating and advocating for issues of peace, democratic governance, equality and social justice (Gray 2002; Midgley 2010b). According to Gray (2002) social workers' pursuit of social justice inevitably makes their work political. Similarly, their engagement in policy is a political process aimed to ensure that clients have access to services and resources. Developmental social work's emphasis on political participation is premised on the fact that politics and governance affect all facets of ordinary life and the issues that ordinary people are confronted with. Unfortunately, quite often, social workers are preoccupied with trying to right the wrongs generated from poor politics and governance. Political activism requires grassroots action as well as macrolevel engagement by social workers to ensure that proper policies are being designed and implemented, social injustices are confronted and addressed, and that people enjoy their freedoms and rights as citizens.

Developmental social work involves consultation and partnership development. Whether working directly with community members or through organisations, developmental social workers consult with different stakeholders to clarify goals, strategies and approaches. Gray (2002) notes that while the consultative process at the international level might require the social worker to operate as an expert, at the local level, the social worker needs to pay full attention to the experience and knowledge of participants who best know their own capacities and strengths. This is aligned with the indigenisation and decoloniality philosophy. Similarly, building and working in partnerships with likeminded organisations and stakeholders is important in mobilising resources, sharing ideas and enhancing synergy to better achieve objectives of developmental social work. This requires establishing strong coordination mechanisms through which different players harmonise their goals and interventions to avoid duplication and resource wastage.

Developmental social workers use assets-based community development: Assets-based community development operates from a strengths perspective where the social worker engages communities in a collaborative process to unleash their potential. Midgely (2010, p. 18) observes that developmental social workers are less in offices and mostly up and about in interacting with clients in their natural community environments "to secure resources, access networks, and establish local projects". Ultimately the goal is to solve problems and achieve progress but in a manner that acknowledges existing resources. Asset building and capabilities go hand in hand. While assets are perceived in terms of physical and financial resources, capabilities are inherent and allow individuals to make good use of the assets. Assets may also include good health, education, belonging, leadership, relations of trust and values. The expansion of assets and capabilities enables marginalised populations to participate in, negotiate with, influence, control and hold accountable the institutions that affect their lives (World Bank 2005). Supporting people to acquire economic assets is crucial in liberating people from poverty.

Other features associated with developmental social work include its orientation towards participatory action research, use of facilitative group work, as well as having an international awareness (Gray 2002; Midgley 2010b), traits that are embraced in conventional social work. Participatory research gives voice to the people, acknowledging that they know what is best for their welfare and could find solutions if conditions are made favourable for their full participation (Gray 2002). Facilitative group work is the common means through which communities are organised and projects are undertaken. Finally, regarding international awareness, Midgley (2010b) argues that developmental social workers are open to innovations being utilized elsewhere and how these can inform practice in other settings without necessarily compromising contextual relevance. Hence, whilst strongly associated with Indigenous and decolonial perspectives, developmental social work does not close out everything foreign if it is adaptable and relevant to bolster desired social change.

Skills for Developmental Social Work Practice

Most of the skills required for developmental social work practice are not any different from conventional social work skills, save for the fact that they are applied in a slightly different setting to achieve different goals. Skills in establishing and maintaining relationships with client systems, communication, advocacy, mediation and negotiation, partnership and networking, resource mobilisation, decision-making, group facilitation and leadership skills are all important for developmental social workers (Midgley and Conley 2010; Hugman 2016). Relationship skills are, for example, essential in gaining entry into the community and maintaining effective relationships with the different stakeholders. Due to an emphasis on social investment strategies that tackle poverty and promote economic empowerment, social workers must have skills in resource mobilisation, project planning and management, and use of innovative methods to promote sustainable income generating activities.

Developmental Social Work's Link to the Nature and Purpose of Social Work

Historically the mission of the social work profession is to liberate people from suffering through addressing obstacles at the personal and environmental levels. Social work's core mandates include promoting social change, social development, social cohesion and the empowerment and liberation of people (IASSW 2014). Its main roles involve remedial, maintenance, prevention and social change functions (Midgley 2010b). As argued by Midgley (2010b), whilst there is no contention about the purpose and goal of the social work profession, the challenge lies in the pathways to the achievement of the stated goals. The predominant model of social work has mostly focused on remedial and maintenance functions that are often statutory, while developmental social work strives to promote long-term sustainable social changes especially targeted at making the structures, systems, and institutions more responsive to the needs and aspirations of the community members particularly the material needs. It also aims to minimize dependency and to instead build people's capacity to actively participate in the development process and community life.

The current global definition of social work adopts the developmental approach to social work as reproduced below.

> Social work is a practice-based profession and an academic discipline that promotes social change and development, social cohesion, and the empowerment and liberation of people. Principles of social justice, human rights, collective responsibility and respect for diversities are central to social work. Underpinned by theories of social work, social sciences, humanities and indigenous knowledges, social work engages people and structures to address life challenges and enhance wellbeing. (IASSW 2014, p. 1)

The commentary accompanying the definition states that the social change function is "driven by the need to challenge and change those structural conditions that contribute to marginalization, social exclusion and oppression" (IASSW 2014, p. 1). This requires moving beyond reactionary responses to problems, to interventions that lead to significant and sustainable improvements in people's wellbeing and in the wider social conditions (Midgley and Conley 2010, p. 4). Other key concepts used in the definition including social cohesion, empowerment, social justice, human rights and collective responsibility strongly resonate with developmental social work, and so does the emphasis that social work engages both people and structures. The development of movements and networks such as the Social Work Action Network (SWAN) that emphasise the advancement of radical social work to challenge social injustice and the structural barriers to people's welfare (SWAN 2021) further attest to the intention to promote sustainable changes in the way society functions. Developmental social work contributes directly towards these goals and aspirations.

Social work is concerned primarily with the vulnerable and the poor and, as argued by Lombard (2008), it must accept its share of responsibility in addressing inequality and poverty by promoting the rights of poor people to social and economic development. Indeed, the development of social work as a profession was inspired by the need to liberate people from poverty. Hugman (2016, p. 5) contends that "Social work has either been ignorant of the way in which its professional concerns have an economic dimension, and so has failed to engage with economic matters, or has at least failed to understand that human need has a material basis". Developmental social work attempts to reclaim this cutting edge for social work so that it effectively fulfils its mission to support the poor and vulnerable groups in society.

In terms of its principles, developmental social work maintains a strong emphasis on client self-determination which is a core principle in social work right from its inception. It also recognises that clients have strengths and personal resources but that these need to be augmented with public resources for full productivity and social functioning. Social work has been presented as a human rights profession that concerns itself with promotion of social justice and equality (IASSW 2014; Lombard 2014; Lombard and Twikirize 2014). Developmental social workers aim to promote structures and institutions that are equitable, and which uphold human rights and social justice. They engage in advocacy and other macro-level actions to contribute toward these goals.

The person-in-environment perspective has been at the centre of social work since its infancy. This approach views the individual and his or her multiple environments as a dynamic, interactive system, in which each component simultaneously affects and is affected by the other (Hare 2016). Based on this approach, the social work profession seeks to resolve issues at the micro-level by enhancing individual functioning while at the same time seeking to modify the environment to become more responsive to the needs of the individual. The latter is the social change function and involves development of pro-poor policies, promotion of social justice and equality and challenging oppressive systems. Developmental social work is consistent with this approach as it is underpinned by an eco-systemic approach. However, whilst traditional social work models have disproportionately laid emphasis on enhancing individual adaptability to the environment, developmental social work focuses on achieving social reform through addressing structural and systemic issues that generate most of the challenges that individuals face (Midgley 2010b). Hence, rather than only preoccupy themselves with managing the adverse effects of unjust economic policies, developmental social workers aim to understand and engage with these processes and build the capacity of individuals and groups to effectively participate in the development process.

Challenges to Adoption of Developmental Social Work

Despite its allure, developmental social work must overcome several challenges for it to be fully established. Some of these relate to issues such as clearly defining social work's mandate within the broader field of social development and maintaining a clear identity within multidisciplinary teams; limited resource allocations for concrete social services; nature of social work training and curricula; nature of social service agencies, as well as absence of regulations and clear guidelines (Manyama 2018; Lombard and Wairire 2010; Midgley and Conley 2010; Hugman 2016).

Adoption of developmental social work has been shrouded by concerns about social workers losing their professional identity as primarily focused on social welfare services, which despite some theoretical expressions in policy, have tended to remain remedial. Social workers find their identity when delivering clearly delineated statutory social welfare services. As developmental social workers operating in the wider social development field, there is the fear of getting lost in the crowd due to failure to clearly craft out their niche and the specialized skills that social workers bring to the field. Hence questions arise on what it is that social workers do in the field of social development that could not be done by several other professionals in that field. Lombard and Wairire (2010) suggest that for social work to position itself as a role player in social development, it needs to be formally recognised as a profession and regulated so that its mandate and roles are noticeably clear.

The approach has been criticised for its uncritical emphasis on economic undertones including social enterprises and investment strategies, which closely align it to a neoliberal agenda (Midgley and Conley 2010). At the same time, the approach is seen as not radical enough since despite its claim on social change, in practice developmental social workers engage less with structural injustice and exclusion based on issues such as identity and race and therefore it may not be as emancipatory and transformational as it promises.

An overemphasis on developmental social work also runs the risk of condescending case work and other practice domains where remedial approaches are inevitable and where developmental approaches may not always be clear cut. Hence social work professionals engaged in such practices might begin to feel that they do not contribute as much to social wellbeing even when they do. Some scholars such as van Breda (2018) have attempted to develop a conceptual model for a developmental case work, which is a positive step. However, in most cases, social workers' innovative capacity in adopting a developmental approach is challenged by the heavy caseloads within statutory roles such as in child protection case management. When there are not enough social workers in the formal system, the temptation is to concentrate on the more streamlined roles that use conventional case management approaches rather than social change-oriented interventions.

There is also the challenge of limited resource allocations to the social development sector in most countries. And yet to effectively practice from a developmental perspective requires sustainable funding, logistics, personnel and other investments (Midgley and Conley 2010). To provide tangible goods and services takes national budget commitments. Most community level interventions that are currently supported by social workers are run through civil society organisations and tend to be projectized and donor driven. This threatens their sustainability and can sometimes lack genuine bottom-up community engagement due to the influence of the donors and development partners.

Finally, for developmental social work practice to take root, there must be radical shifts in education to make it relevant to the preferred model of practice. Although there has been progress with re-orientation of social work education towards this goal especially in sub-Saharan Africa (Hugman 2016; Spitzer and Twikirize 2014; Twikirize and Spitzer 2019; Mupedziswa 2001; Gray et al. 2017b), there is need to strengthen this focus. It is impossible to train and orient future social work professionals from a traditional psychotherapeutic perspective and then expect them to effectively adopt a developmental approach in practice. A good example can be drawn from the 1970s social work education in Africa where the Association of Social Work Education in Africa undertook a project to collect, analyse and disseminate case studies on social development for purposes of indigenising and adopting a developmental approach in social work education (ASWEA 1973). The social work curriculum should be emancipatory, transformational and radical and adequately prepare students for macro-level, structural practice (Midgley 2010b). Mupedziswa (2001) suggests a framework for assessing and reorienting social work education through curriculum and non-curriculum related activities. Curriculum-related aspects include ongoing curriculum review to align training to emerging needs of a country, relevant field placements, use of relevant developmental concepts, progressive delivery methods that emphasise classroom interaction and ensuring the relevance of student projects and assignments. Extra-curricular activities include generation and use of Indigenous materials, local research, networking with other institutions, localisation of staff complement, relevant graduate employment patterns and meaningful contributions by staff towards local social policy. This and other innovative methods should ensure that social work graduates are adequately prepared for adoption of developmental approaches in practice.

Conclusion: Future Outlook for Developmental Social Work

This chapter has presented developmental social work as part and parcel of mainstream social work. It neither contradicts nor compromises the nature and purpose of social work whose calling is to promote change or social stability, whichever will be liberating for people living in difficult situations, and to promote more equal and just societies where everyone enjoys their human rights and has their needs and aspirations met. Although predominantly macro-level in outlook, developmental social work is applicable across the different domains of social work, with interventions potentially targeting individuals and families, communities and society. Its strong link with the field of social development requires that social work practitioners pay attention to the material needs of clients and to both the social and economic goals, as well as to systems, structures and institutions. The challenge is to position social work not just as an agent of consumption-oriented social welfare services but also an active contributor to development. Social development is not just a framework but also one of the stated goals for the social work profession. Developmental social work thus becomes a privileged model to achieving core social work goals. As argued by Lombard (2014), it does challenge social work to reclaim its social reform function.

In the past decade, there have been significant strides towards a wider adoption of developmental social work especially in Africa, spurred on by developments in indigenisation and decolonisation of social work to make a relevant and significant contribution to social development. Further, in many countries of the global South, where a reasonable number of social work professionals work with communities, it is relatively easier to adopt the developmental model especially as they engage families and groups in interventions to tackle poverty. An extensive study on social work conducted in East Africa (Spitzer and Twikirize 2014), illustrates the increasing adoption of developmental social work and its positive outlook. Spitzer and Twikirize reported from this study, that social workers in this region are already engaged in various activities that support a developmental perspective including, for example, facilitating the formation and functioning of micro-saving and micro-credit schemes within communities, assisting poor households to start income-generating activities, supporting youths in vocational skills training programmes and supporting vulnerable children to enrol and complete school. All these are done through community-based projects. However, stronger engagement with other macro-level interventions such as policy practice, advocacy, research, programme and project evaluation are needed to further strengthen developmental social work.

Based on the generalist education curricula offered in most schools of social work, developing skills for developmental social work practice should not be difficult. In fact, Gray (2002) contends that social workers already have the knowledge, skills and value framework needed to take on the challenge of developmental social work and what is needed is to be more open and embrace developmental social work. Systematic adjustments in the curricula and most importantly social work pedagogy to give stronger focus on developmental social work concepts, approaches and methods is important in developing skills and influencing mindsets. The updated Global standards for social work education and training underscore this view by reiterating the need to prepare students to understand the interconnectedness of practice at all levels – individual, family, group, organization and community to help them become "critical, ethical and competent practitioners" (IASSW, ICSW and IFSW 2020, p. 1).

Developmental social work is firmly reflected in the Global Agenda for Social Work and Social Development, first launched in 2012, where the three global social work organisations committed to "supporting, influencing, and enabling *structures and systems that positively address the root causes of oppression and inequality*" (IASSW, ICSW and IFSW 2012, p. 1 emphasis added). The new agenda 2020–2030 is even more explicit with its overarching 10-year theme of "co-building inclusive social transformation" (IFSW, ICSW and IASSW 2012). The first two themes of the agenda are, 'Ubuntu: strengthening social solidarity and global interconnectedness' and 'Co-building a New Eco-Social World: Leaving No One Behind'. Through this agenda, social workers across the world commit among others to "...promoting people's active role in leading sustainable development" and to "working together to co-design and co-build thriving communities and societies for people and the environment" (IFSW, ICSW and IASSW 2012, p. 1). The themes, commitments and concepts in this agenda place developmental perspectives at the heart of social work education and practice in the next decade. Hence, developmental social work no doubt has a positive outlook as not just preferred but definitely a more effective model of social work.

References

Anderson SC, Wilson MK, Katembula-Mwansa L, Osei-Hwedie K (1994) Empowerment and social work education and practice in Africa. J Soc Dev Afr 9(2):71–86

Asamoah Y (1994) Challenges to social work around the world: Africa. Center for International Social Work: inaugural conference. University of Connecticut, School of Social Work,

Connecticut. https://opencommons.uconn.edu/cgi/viewcontent.cgi?article=1002& context=sw_intlconf. Accessed 30 Apr 2021

ASWEA (1973) Case studies of social development in Africa. Association of Social Work Education in Africa-Information Centre, Addis Ababa

Estes RJ (1997) Social work, social development, and community welfare centers in international perspective. Int Soc Work 40(1):43–55

Gray M (2002) Developmental social work: a 'strengths' praxis for social development. Soc Dev Issues 24(1):4–14

Gray M (2009) Theories of social work practice. In: Nicholas L, Rautenbach J, Maistry M (eds) Introduction to social work. Juta, Cape Town, pp 75–98

Gray M, Simpson B (1998) Developmental social work education: a field example. Int Soc Work 41(2):227–237

Gray M, Agllias K, Mupedziswa R, Mugumbate J (2017a) The expansion of developmental social work in southern and East Africa: opportunities and challenges for social work field programmes. Int Soc Work 61(6):974–987

Gray M, Agllias K, Mupedziswa R, Mugumbate J (2017b) The role of social work field education programmes in the transmission of developmental social work knowledge in southern and East Africa. Soc Work Educ 36(6):623–635

Hare I (2016) Defining social work for the 21st century. Int Soc Work 47(3):407–424

Hölscher D (2012) Social justice. In L. L. Lyne M. Healy and R (Ed.), Handbook of International Social Work. Human Rights, Development, and the Global Profession. New York: Oxford University Press, p 44–54

Hugman R (2016) Social development in social work. Practices and principles. Routledge, New York

IASSW (2014) Global definition of social work. Retrieved from https://www.iasswaiets.org/global-definition-of-social-work-review-of-the-global-definition/. On 31.03.2022

IASSW, ICSW and IFSW (2012) Global agenda. International Association of Schools of Social Work International Council on Social Welfare, International Federation of Social Workers. http://cdn.ifsw.org/assets/globalagenda2012.pdf. Accessed 06 May 2021

IASSW, ICSW and IFSW (2020) 2020 to 2030 global agenda for social work and social development framework: 'co-building inclusive social transformation'. https://www.ifsw.org/2020-to-2030-global-agenda-for-social-work-and-social-development-framework-co-building-inclusive-social-transformation/. Accessed 06 May 2021

IFSW, ICSW and IASSW (2012) Global agenda. International Association of Schools of Social Work International Council on Social Welfare, International Federation of Social Workers. Retrieved from http://cdn.ifsw.org/assets/globalagenda2012.pdf. Accessed 06 May 2021

Jordan B (2013) Social justice. In: Worsley A, Mann T, Olsen A, Mason-Whitehead E (eds) Key concepts in social work practice. SAGE, London, pp 242–245

Lombard A (2008) The implementation of the white paper for social welfare: a ten-year review. The Social Work Practitioner-Researcher/Die Maatskaplikewerk Navorser-Praktisyn 20(2):154–173

Lombard A (2014) A developmental perspective in social work theory and practice. In: Spitzer H, Twikirize JM, Gachunga GW (eds) Professional social work in Africa: towards social development, poverty reduction and gender equality. Fountain, Kampala, pp 43–55

Lombard A, Twikirize JM (2014) Promoting social and economic equality: social workers' contribution to social justice and social development in South Africa and Uganda. Int Soc Work 57(4):313–325

Lombard A, Wairire GG (2010) Developmental social work in South Africa and Kenya: some lessons for Africa. The Social Work Practitioner-Researcher/Die Maatskaplikewerk Navorser-Praktisyn (Special Issue) 98–111

Manyama W (2018) Where is developmental social work as social work practice method in Tanzania? The case of Dar es Salaam Region. Int J Soc Work 5(2):43–57

Mbecke P (2016) Developmental social work: a derailed post-apartheid development approach in South Africa. International Journal of Economics and Management Engineering 10(9): 3197–3204

Midgley J (1995) Social development: the developmental perspective in social work. SAGE, London

Midgley J (2001) Issues in international social work: resolving critical debates in the profession. J Soc Work 1(1):21–25

Midgley J (2010a) The theory and practice of developmental social work. In: Midgley J, Conley A (eds) Social work and social development: theories and skills for developmental social work. Oxford University Press, New York, pp 3–29

Midgley J (2010b) Community practice and developmental social work. In: Midgley J, Conley A (eds) Social work and social development. Theories and skills for developmental social work. Oxford University Press, New York

Midgley J, Conley A (2010) Social work and social development: theories and skills for developmental social work. Oxford University Press, New York

Mupedziswa R (2001) The quest for relevance: towards a conceptual model of developmental social work education and training in Africa. Int Soc Work 44(3):285–300

Noyoo N (2014) Introduction to the concepts of social development. Presentation at the Fachhochschule Erfurt University of Applied Sciences – Summer School, Germany, 28. Retrieved from: https://www.academia.edu/8368353/Introduction_to_the_concepts_of_social_development. Accessed 06 May 2021

Patel L (2005) Social welfare and social development. Oxford University Press, Cape Town

Patel L, Hochfeld T (2012) Developmental social work in South Africa: translating policy into practice. Int Soc Work 56(5):690–704

Pawar M (2014) Social work practice with local communities in developing countries. SAGE Open 4(2). https://doi.org/10.1177/2158244014538640

Saebi T, Foss NJ, Linder S (2018a) Social entrepreneurship research: past achievements and future promises. J Manag 45(1):70–95

Saebi T, Foss NJ, Linder S (2018b) Social entrepreneurship research: past achievements and future promises. Journal of Management 45(1):70–95

Saleebey D (1996) The strengths perspective in social work practice: extensions and cautions. Soc Work 41(3):296–305

Sen A (1999) Development as freedom. Anchor, New York

Social Action Network (2021) Social Action Network. Available at: https://socialworkfuture.org/. Accessed 05 May 2021

Specht H, Courtney ME (1994) Unfaithful Angels: how social work has abondoned its mission. NewYork. The Free Press

Spitzer H, Twikirize JM (2014) A vision for social work in East Africa. In: Spitzer H, Twikirize JM, Gachunga GW (eds) Professional social work in Africa: towards social development, poverty reduction and gender equality. Fountain, Kampala, pp 373–384

Spitzer H, Twikirize J (2021) Social innovations in rural communities in Africa's Great Lakes region. A social work perspective. J Rural Stud. https://doi.org/10.1016/j.jrurstud.2021.10.013

Spitzer H, Twikirize JM, Gachunga GW (eds) (2014) Professional social work in East Africa: towards social development, poverty reduction and gender equality. Fountain, Kampala

Staples L (2016) Roots to power; a manual for grassroots organizing, 3rd edn. Praeger, Santa Barbara

Staub-Bernasconi S (2012) Human rights and their relevance for social work as theory and practice. In: Healy L, Link RJ (eds) Handbook of international social work. Human rights, development and the global profession. Oxford, New York, pp 30–36

Swanepoel H, De Beer F (2011) Community development. Breaking the cycle of poverty, 5th edn. Juta, Landsowne

Twikirize JM (2017) Social work practice in the NGO sector in Uganda and Kenya. Opportunities and challenges. In: Gray M (ed) The handbook of social work and social development in Africa. Routledge, New York/London, pp 367–381

Twikirize JM, Spitzer H (eds) (2019) Social work practice in Africa: Indigenous and innovative approaches. Fountain, Kampala

United Nations (1994) Human rights and social work. A manual for schools of social work and the social work profession. Professional training series 1. Centre for Human Rights, Geneva

Van Breda A (2015) Developmental social case work: a process model. Int Soc Work 61(1):66–78

World Bank (2004) Social development in World Bank operations: results and way forward. World Bank, Washington, DC

World Bank (2005) Measuring empowerment: cross-disciplinary perspectives. World Bank, Washington, DC

Wronka J (2012) Overview of human rights: the UN conventions and machinery. In: Healy LM, Link RJ (eds) Handbook of international social work. Human rights, development, and the global profession. Oxford University Press, New York

Yimam A (ed) (1976) Proceedings of the 3rd conference of the Association of Social Work Education in Africa held in Adis Ababa, 1976. ASWEA information Centre

Indigenous Knowledge and Social Work Crossing the Paths for Intervention

13

Allucia Lulu Shokane and Mogomme Alpheus Masoga

Contents

Introduction	252
Indigenous Social Work Practice	253
Establishing the Context for Indigenous Knowledge	255
Afro-Sensed Approach	258
Indigenous Knowledge Systems in Social Work	259
Indigenous Models of Social Work Practice	260
Conclusion	263
References	264

Abstract

Looking at the field of social work from the perspective of Indigenous knowledge is an interesting enterprise. With this chapter, the authors wish to achieve recognition for Indigenous knowledge as both critical and substantial for intervening in the decolonisation of social work studies that is currently underway. Decolonisation is a process through which those pained and hurt by colonialisation are enabled to voice or express their worldviews, narratives, and stories for analysis, education, research, governance, etc. in their own way. The field of Indigenous knowledge has gained traction, and many scholars have started to embrace its importance in their research and teaching and learning. The chapter considers the field of Indigenous knowledge with the aim of advancing social work practice, teaching, and research. The authors define both fields and demonstrate how these fields could benefit from crossing paths for the

---

A. L. Shokane (✉)
Department of Social Work, Faculty of Humanities and Social Sciences, University of Zululand, KwaDlagezwa, South Africa
e-mail: ShokaneA@unizulu.ac.za

M. A. Masoga
Faculty of Humanities and Social Sciences, University of Zululand, KwaDlagezwa, South Africa
e-mail: MasogaM@unizulu.ac.za

© Springer Nature Singapore Pte Ltd. 2023
D. Hölscher et al. (eds.), *Social Work Theory and Ethics*, Social Work,
https://doi.org/10.1007/978-981-19-1015-9_14

advancement of the social sciences with reference to appropriate examples taken from actual lived experiences. For this purpose, the authors used the Afro-sensed approach, which was developed within the Indigenous knowledge paradigm of reflection and enquiry. The authors explain their stance on the use of the Afro-sensed approach and perspective in this case. The Afro-sensed approach argues that African contexts and spaces present unique opportunities in the discourse of knowledge development. While the authors acknowledge the nomothetic characteristics of knowledge, they also realise the importance of its idiographic perspective. In this case, a balance is struck between universal and specific aspects of knowledge development.

Keywords

Indigenous knowledge · Indigenous social work · Decolonisation · Afro-sensed · Culture

Introduction

This chapter contributes to the discourse on Indigenous knowledge and social work interventions, specifically in the African context. Indigenous knowledge is elucidated as knowledge that is "owned by local people in their specific communities and passed on from generation to generation and this type of knowledge could be from people who lives in rural or urban areas" (Masoga 2017). Therefore, Indigenous knowledge refers to the particular values, beliefs, rituals, traditions, and environmental relationships that exist in an Indigenous community. In this context, Indigenous community is a community that practices Indigenous ways of knowing as part of its culture or way of life of people in a specific community. Indigenous knowledge is developed and exists in a particular community. Suggestively, "this Indigenous knowledge is related to the survival of the Indigenous community, in general or specific fields, such as protection and use of the local environment, enhancing food security, especially during periods of stress" (Shokane and Masoga 2021; Fouche et al. 2021).

Generally, the social work profession has been practiced for many years in Africa, though it is still very reliant on models and literature that were developed in and are borrowed from the West. Consequently, Western models have been criticised by scholars for their failure to address the unique social issues and problems experienced by the majority of Africans in Indigenous communities. The challenges facing social work practice are widely known; it is a profession that has been dominated by Western models, frameworks, and philosophies, to the detriment of the vulnerable populations that the profession strives to serve. Social workers, especially in Africa, are encouraged to move away from models that rely only on Western frameworks and philosophies. The oppressive nature of these 'educational' regimes has now been recognised, and the value inherent in Indigenous knowledge is being increasingly understood (Dumbrill and Green 2008, p. 490). The social work profession is well placed to deal with *issues of social justice, inequity, and structural oppression.* In South Africa, colonialism is purportedly to involve four stages: (i) unofficial colonisation by Black people from the North; (ii) official colonisation from the South, by the Dutch East India Company (VOC); (iii) official colonisation by Great Britain; and (iv) internal colonisation from 1961 to 1994, by White Afrikaners (Oliver and Oliver 2017 p. 4–8). Therefore, Hart (2009) argues that anti-colonialism is complex, and must address and "de-legitimize" political, historical, social, and economic structures rooted in Eurocentric ideology. Furthermore, anti-colonialism, in this context,

> seeks to reaffirm Indigenous knowledge and culture, establish Indigenous control over Indigenous national territories, protect Indigenous lands from environmental destruction and develop education opportunities that are anti colonial in their political orientation and firmly rooted in traditions of Indigenous nations (Hart 2009, p. 32).

It is noteworthy that the authors have adopted a postcolonial and anti-colonial social work approach to writing this chapter, while striving to decolonise the social work profession through Indigenous approaches. In the context of decolonising the social work profession, Gray et al. (2013, p. 7) endorse the significant need to

> acknowledge its complicity and cease social work participation in colonizing projects, openly condemn the past and continuing effects of colonialism, collaborate with Indigenous Peoples to engage in decolonising activities against public and private colonizing projects, and seek to remove the often-subtle vestiges of colonisation from theory to practice.

During colonisation and at the introduction of formal professional services, these social systems and approaches were widely ignored, or even suppressed. In the postindependence period, when social work began to emerge as formal professional services, it relied almost exclusively on Western sciences and methods, instead of building on local knowledge and practices. It is, therefore, essential to dismantle all forms of oppression, and to reject discrimination against knowledge, skills, values, beliefs, and habits that were forced on people in Indigenous communities. In this context, the understanding and application of a decolonisation approach must focus on reconnecting to Indigenous ways of knowing, being, and doing, to provide a solid foundation for Indigenous social work practice. From this background, it is worth mentioning the positionality of the authors as Indigenous knowledge researchers and to the extent of activism. The authors have spent the greater part of their academic lives writing and addressing challenges facing the Indigenous scholarship. Their participation in the field has been endorsed by the communities they have been working with.

Indigenous Social Work Practice

Social work educators and professionals are, therefore, urged to examine new methods of social work practice through diverse theories, concepts, beliefs, values, practices, behaviours, policies, and realities that may not be familiar, but which ultimately meet the needs of the diverse people the profession represents (Faruque and Ahmed 2013, p. 63). In reality, Indigenous culture-specific forms of knowledge for helping, coping, resilience building, and problem-solving are still not embraced and are underrepresented in contemporary social work education, theory, practice, and policy in many countries, including social work on the African continent.

Various Indigenous and non-Indigenous social workers and scholars such as Twikirize and Spitzer (2019), Shokane and Masoga (2018), Shava and Manyike (2018), Gray et al. (2013), Olaleye (2013), Mwansa (2010), Thabede (2008), and St-Denis and Walsh (2017) are actively engaged in decolonising social work education and practice and conducting research from anti-colonial and postcolonial frameworks. However, a gap still exists regarding Indigenous social work literature that is developed by African social scientists and professionals, and the authors of this chapter are of the view that there is a gap that must be bridged by social work practice that supports theory and models built from Indigenous knowledge systems. In this regard, the necessity of embracing Indigenous knowledge in the social work profession was evidently recognised by the International Federation of Social Workers (IFSW) and the International Association of Schools of Social Workers (IASSW) (2014) in their global definition of social work in 2014, as

> a practice-based profession and an academic discipline that promotes social change and development, social cohesion, and the empowerment and liberation of people. Principles of social justice, human rights, collective responsibility and respect for diversities are central to social work. Underpinned by theories of social work, social sciences, humanities and Indigenous knowledge, social work engages people and structures to address life challenges and enhance wellbeing.

It is against this backdrop that social scientists, including social workers, are urged to embrace Afrocentric and Afro-sensed models that are based on Indigenous knowledge systems, community-based interventions, and local values and practices (Masoga and Shokane 2019, p. 4; Shava 2013; Mwansa 2010, p. 11). Accordingly, the authors' main drive was to accelerate the indigenisation of social work and striving to bringing social justice and restore the worth and dignity of people in Indigenous communities, in line with the global definition of social work.

Suggestively, the objective of this chapter is to present an interdisciplinary approach that links Indigenous knowledge and social work for practitioners working in Indigenous communities to intervene appropriately. The position of this chapter is that social work and Indigenous knowledge can be incorporated to intervene in psychosocial support practices, such as reunification services, not only for the wellbeing of children, but also for families and the Indigenous community as a whole. In addition, this contribution aims to address and develop social consciousness of the indigenisation agenda in social work that the authors have contributed to for some time now.

Though the authors are writing from the context of South Africa, their scholarship contribution is relevant beyond the South Africa's shores. This relevance stems from several areas. Firstly, language and languaging which the authors are conversant with. Secondly, the etic and emic (insider and outsider perspective) privileges they had in terms of having access to the local communities that we engaged with. The above two areas should not at all suggest that they have remained uncritical of the data and context of the research within which the research was based. In this case, the authors were able to apply critical thinking and appreciation of the phenomena in the process of doing this research.

Therefore, the chapter will discuss how contributing to these debates through an Indigenous perspective can contribute to much-needed social change. For a case in point, indigenisation is concerned with the "appropriateness of theories and practice, as well as values, norms, and philosophies which underlie practice" (Osei-Hwedie 1996). This contribution also adds to the voices of various indigenisation authors' writings which are often on the topics of the redress of the historical injustices of the past, and colonialism – their interest is in line with the striving by the social work profession to ensure application of ethical principles and principles of social justice, equality, and respect for human dignity (Osei-Hwedie 1996; Thabede 2008; Mwansa 2010). Equality, in this regard, includes accepting other people's cultures and Indigenous knowledge. It is essential for social services professionals to appreciate and embrace the sociocultural beliefs of people (Thabede 2008). For social work practice, it implies an openness and respect for and humility in relation to other cultures. Cultural humility is described by Isaacson (2014) as openness to other cultures, and the ability to be self-reflective and self-critical regarding inter- or cross-cultural interactions. It is a captivating idea that the matter of the dissenting voice could be applicable here, to dismantle the colonial pillars of social work practice, education, and research. In point of fact, scholars such as Dumbrill and Green (2008, p. 489) emphasised that the "disruption is crucial because, despite a commitment to diversity and inclusion, most social work academies continue to teach from a Eurocentric perspective in a manner that perpetuates the colonisation of not only Indigenous people and knowledges", but all other knowledge of people that falls outside the dominant European paradigm. As scholars in Indigenous knowledge studies, the authors strive to contribute to the discourse on Indigenous knowledge and social work.

Establishing the Context for Indigenous Knowledge

Indigenous knowledge is wisdom of people grounded in their local customs, culture, and beliefs, and is often contrasted with scientific epistemology associated with Western cultures (Breidlid 2009). Scientific epistemology has been linked to class and patriarchy (Campbell and Wasco 2000) and colonialism (Rugege 2003), thereby reifying historical trauma. Devaluation of Indigenous knowledge combines with structural oppression and bias to marginalise and exclude community members, social workers, and learners who do not easily identify with Western scientific ways of knowing. Thus, not only are the people's ways of knowing shut out of education, but the wisdom contained within Indigenous knowledge is lost. In most cases, Indigenous knowledge is identified as local, and it is often created within communities (Masoga 2017). Indigenous knowledge is being distinguished as:

> transgenerational, transmitted from generation to generation orally (through narratives, stories/folklore, songs and poetry), visually (through arts, such as 'bushmen' paintings, writings, craft, cultural rituals and dance), practically (through doing and the artefacts associated with practice) and spiritually (through dreams and visions from the ancestors) (Shava and Manyike 2018, p. 36).

Indigenous cultures have unwritten societal rules, which are transferred from generation to generation through word of mouth. Since much of Indigenous knowledge, especially Africa's traditional knowledge, is presented in an oral form, and not documented, it is disposed to extermination or being sent to obscurity. Shokane and Masoga (2018) affirm that, as a consequence of colonialism and apartheid in South Africa, Indigenous knowledge in Africa has remained unacknowledged, disparaged, and subjugated by Western theories and knowledge. Consequently, education in South Africa has been exposed to the harsh realities of colonisation and apartheid. The authors have seen an exigence on the scholarship of Indigenous knowledge, especially as a result of student movements such as #fees must fall and calls for the decolonisation of the curriculum. It has been revealed that some of Africa's development was disturbed by colonisation, and it has been claimed that much of the way things are done or practiced in Africa has been affected by colonialism; nevertheless, some systems of African origin have persisted and are still employed by Africans for solving their social and economic problems, including earning their livelihoods. What this means is that Africa has gone through various stages of governance, which, according to Rugege (2003), can be classified into the precolonial phase, the colonial phase, and the postindependence phase.

It is recognised that "Africa has a long history of traditional problem-solving systems and approaches that go back to the precolonial era". In the precolonial phase, problems were solved through traditional leaders, who considered the care and welfare of their people by providing them with land for agriculture and grazing to meet their subsistence needs. Additionally, the welfare and well-being of all who were destitute and orphaned were provided for. In the colonial phase, Rugege (2003) contends further, powers were taken over from traditional leadership and communities by the colonial state and, later, in South Africa, by the apartheid state, thus weakening the role of traditional leaders and institutions that govern African people. Furthermore, the postindependence phase is characterised by the post-1994 democratic dispensation, and a new Constitution for the Republic of South Africa (Act No. 108 of 1996), specifically, Section 30, which promotes respect for cultural rights.

The use of Indigenous knowledge is essential for reinforcing these traditional beliefs systems. This knowledge is purported to bring pleasure and reinforce tradition and belief systems. The authors of this chapter agree with Shava and Manyike (2018) and Masoga (2017) that the main structures of Indigenous knowledge include people, space and context, culture, language, knowledge, and practices that are dynamic. The main structures of Indigenous knowledge can be expounded as follows:

- **People**: People are regarded as the Indigenous holders of traditions, customs, and beliefs, specific to an Indigenous community. Peoples have an intimate knowledge of the environment, treating it as endowed with human moods and emotions. For social work the focus is on helping people to reach their full potential – young and old in all spheres of life, and whether vulnerable, oppressed, or marginalised.
- **Space**: Traditional Indigenous knowledge is located in a sacred space related to community practice of Indigenous knowledge holders. If the social work profession is to work *within* Indigenous knowledge systems, work must be done *with* Indigenous individuals, families, and communities. This work includes working with Indigenous knowledge holders who are recognised in that particular community.
- **Context**: Social work interventions have to encourage people to use their local, specific context and traditional knowledge – knowledge systems as knowledge and technologies around communities, which are Indigenous to a particular space and context (Masoga 2017). It is significant to also understand the gender issues, especially the role of women in the particular community. For an example, if a female social worker is wearing pants and this is not appreciated, then she cannot intervene in family disputes or address community gatherings who are based in the rural context.
- **Sociocultural** and religious **motifs**: This refers to the local knowledge that is unique to a given culture or society. Indigenous knowledge includes and takes consideration of various cultures, customs, beliefs, and traditions. The social work profession has a moral obligation and duty to respect people's cultures. As most South African communities have strong beliefs and traditional practices, these should be observed in social work intervention with communities.
- **Language**: The use of Indigenous knowledge can promote and preserve the use of the languages of local people in communities. In the case of South Africa, 11 official languages (Afrikaans, English, IsiNdebele, Sepedi, Sesotho, IsiSwati, Xitsonga, Setswana, Tshivenda, IsiXhosa, and IsiZulu) must be considered. It is essential for a social work practitioner to learn other people's languages in the community where they serve. Local Indigenous language and knowledge can be applied in cases of storytelling and learning the communication patterns of a particular community. An example in case is the use of Indigenous languages in South Africa can assist to promote community heritage and culture. As Ngũgĩ wa Thiong'o (1986, p. 75) explains, language has a dual character: it serves as a means of communication and a carrier of culture. It is, therefore, essential for social workers working with Indigenous communities to learn local languages.
- **Knowledge**: Knowledge refers to the traditional Indigenous knowledge of the people that has been in existence in local communities for ages, which is grounded in oral traditions, and seldom documented.
- **Practices**: Traditional Indigenous and healing practices, such as acknowledging rituals and ancestral beliefs that promote traditional healing practices of Indigenous communities. Traditional-Indigenous healing knowledge and practices involve the knowledge and skills that local communities have been using over the years for healing and survival. Puckree et al. (2002) and Truter (2007) found that most Indigenous South Africans consult Indigenous traditional healers for

various psychosocial problems, to a greater extent than Western-trained healers. Embracing Indigenous thinking and practice does not mean doing this without critically evaluating their strengths and weaknesses. In fact, Indigenous communities have a critical relationship with their practices and knowledge reservoirs. What is required is the ability to see how this is done within the community.

Outstanding examples of structures for problem-solving and helping within Indigenous systems of knowledge and practice are those of family and kinship systems, mutual aid groups, and other forms of reciprocity, solidarity, and alliance. This is the basis for Ubuntu and Indigenous knowledge. Ubuntu here refers to communal assistance and support. The common expression is: I am because we are. The individual cannot be alone or survive alone. Like the proverb: the one who eats alone dies alone (for further details, see section "Indigenous Models of Social Work Practice" below). Twikirize and Spitzer (2019) appeal to social workers to understand social values in a given knowledge and cultural space, and to incorporate that into their professional practice. The knowledge form could be used for solving problems related to kinship and ties of marriage, whether traditional or religious, and even family structures established as a result of cohabitation. An argument is made for social workers to make strides in taking advantage of the knowledge at peoples' disposal and utilise that for the betterment of the population. It becomes critical that when all the Indigenous intervention options have been exhausted, other social work services are sought as a measure of last resort.

Therefore, this chapter strives to guide the social worker and practitioner, in both the social sciences and human service professions, through an *indigenised* research process. The term indigenised refers to a deliberate acknowledgement of local community expressions, worldviews, and ontological frames. This process allows communities among whom social workers are intervening and conducting research to have their say in these intervention efforts and any process of doing research. The main learning objective is to encourage human and social sciences researchers to engage in African epistemological-ontological debates, without resistance, and to develop the ability to use a culturally appropriate lens in the African context to examine how Indigenous social work practices could serve as a resource for deriving alternative care and support strategies.

Afro-Sensed Approach

It is therefore, in this case, imperative for the authors to explain their stance on the use of the Afro-sensed approach and perspective to understand Indigenous knowledge. The Afro-sensed perspective or approach was coined by Masoga (2017). The Afro-sensed approach argues that African contexts and spaces present unique opportunities for the discourse of knowledge development. While we admit the nomothetic (that is, the generalised use and analysis of knowledge in the community, country, or the world in a great measure to bring understanding) characteristics of knowledge, we must, at the same time, consider the idiographic (more localised, individualised, or specific knowledge) perspective of knowledge. The idiographic perspective is about focusing on the specifics of the Indigenous knowledge. Both nomothic and idiographic knowledge must be related in the global sense to bring more understanding of Indigenous knowledge. In this case, one has to strike the balance between universal and specifics of knowledge development. An Afro-sensed approach departs from Afrocentricity by emphasising the following: (1) acknowledgement of nomothetic trends of knowledge; (2) acknowledgement of specifics of knowledge; (3) a call to respect the competence of the African space for the development of knowledge and science; (4) a call for inclusion of African knowledge in the broader (mainstream) knowledge spaces; and (5) an admission that introducing exogenous knowledge into African knowledge spaces should make sense to African life orientations – in this case, one should avoid impositions. In general, the Afro-sensed approach calls for (a) acknowledgement, (b) respect, (c) admission, (d) fair play, (e) a balancing act; and (f) a back-to-basics approach. Afro-sensed responses and African Indigenous knowledge can be important tools for developing social work interventions for work with families and in the school community (Shokane and Masoga 2018).

Afro-sensed epistemology works from an African worldview that forms the foundation for understanding Africans' realities (Shokane and Masoga 2021). African beliefs, values, and traditions deserve to be recognised when social workers intervene with local Indigenous communities. Recognition, in this regard, will be done through the indigenised social work process, with an appreciation of the experiences of community spaces and the people being assisted by social workers. It is critical to note that people who are custodians of local Indigenous knowledge are creative and should be considered when research is undertaken in their communities. Indigenous knowledge systems are located in the context of utilitarian and creative forces, to ensure comprehensive well-being for both humans and other forms of life. Mongane Wally Masoga (2005) describes Indigenous knowledge systems that emanate "from the human spirit are life experiences organised and ordered into accumulated knowledge with the objective to utilise it to improve the quality of life and to create a liveable environment for both human and other forms of life" (personal interview with Serote by Masoga on 6 June 2004).

Indigenous Knowledge Systems in Social Work

Indigenous knowledge systems can be an important tool for supporting social work interventions intended to tackle various social ills. Consequently, utilising Indigenous knowledge practices as a starting point in social work can assist the profession to tackle some of the problems experienced by service users within the social services field and in Indigenous communities. It is against this backdrop that Indigenous knowledge intervention efforts can be utilised by social workers to enhance social functioning, in order to sustain the well-being of all local people. Furthermore, the majority of the African population that is served by the social work profession is striving to make a mark in society, through social service provision that addresses issues such as poverty, violence, climate change, unemployment, and other social ills, including those related to the recent COVID-19 pandemic. Therefore, social workers and other social and human service professionals are encouraged to adopt Indigenous models and frameworks that no longer rely on Western models and philosophies. Indigenous scholars, such as Lalonde (1991), Thabede (2008), Mwansa (2011), Masoga (2017), and Shava and Manyike (2018, p. 36) recommend that African Indigenous knowledge is recognised and allude to its prominence in development activities relevant to Africa and the world.

Endogenous practices grow from within a community and, so, form part of Indigenous knowledge systems. Indigenous knowledge systems involve unique webs of beliefs and practices within a specific ecological context and are usually associated with traditional ways of life of particular groups. Like all systems, Indigenous knowledge systems are adaptable and can be adapted to social work practice; for instance, storytelling, dancing, or singing can be applied as a social work intervention tool to enrich community social value systems. In addition, systems such as Indigenous proverbs and idioms can be utilised to promote community efforts to stimulate the development and growth of young people through, for instance, the proverb *"It takes a village to raise a child"*, implies that every member of a community is responsible for the upbringing of all the children in the community. In the case of issues faced by Indigenous communities, such as child-headed families that have resulted from, for instance, orphanhood, these issues can be dealt with in the community setting, whereby everybody contributes to the socialisation and upbringing of the children through the provision of care, food, and clothes. As an example, in Indigenous communities, the problem of neglected and 'street kids' do not exist. Though some children who do not have parents can be vulnerable and exposed to abuse, in Indigenous communities the whole community is responsible for caring and rearing of the children. At times these children, when sent on errands, are told that *"makhura a ngwana ke go rongwa"*: a child benefits in being sent by elders, the children can learn discipline, focus, and can be trusted. The Indigenous community upbringing and socialisations are a very important component in the bringing of the child for support, structure, and family guidance.

Indigenous Models of Social Work Practice

Indigenous social work models and practice can be applied to various areas and spheres, where it can influence government's social work policies and legislations. The authors are not advocating Indigenous knowledge systems as a panacea, as there is no single intervention method that can address all the social issues that confront social workers on a daily basis, including those related to vulnerable populations, such as children, women, youth, the elderly, and people living with disabilities.

The Indigenous practice of social work can encourage the development of specific skills and competencies through intervention efforts that attempt to understand the dynamics of traditional families and communities. In African traditional families, the family comprises of the extended family, and includes grandparents, parents, uncles and aunts, cousins and nieces, which means family members can support each other when they are confronted by social functioning challenges. An example is the case of a family dispute or conflict, which should be solved internally in the family before the services of a social work are sought. The extended family becomes integral in mediation or resolving family disputes, conflicts, or problems. It becomes integral as from the beginning of a marriage, through negotiations, families come together and agree on wedding procedures such as '*ilobolo or makgadi*' (Zulu and Sotho word for bride price). In the African context, if *ilobolo* has not been paid such a union is not recognised and frowned upon. It is believed that most family problems can be solved if *ilobolo* has been paid and both families have agreed on the marital union. In Indigenous ways of knowing, the extended family has authority, which is promoted as a support system to families to forge healthy communication, interaction, and decision-making between the couples.

In other words, social work in Africa should provide practical solutions to African problems that are pertinent to the people of the continent's social problems and are informed by prevailing conditions. Thus, there is a need for the social work profession to identify Indigenous and innovative approaches and call for the development of evidence-based models that could meet the contemporary needs and challenges of the continent's Indigenous people. Furthermore, Van Breda (2019) supports the call to generate social work knowledge and theory that owes its existence and practice to an African perspective; he argues that there is a need to decolonise social work. This can only be realised if Indigenous knowledge on which social work practice is based finds its roots in African philosophies, such as Ubuntu. In this case, Ubuntu is an African word for a universal concept (Shokane and Masoga 2018, p. 9), which advocates collective responsibility for one another as a value and philosophy to promote mutual coexistence and compassion. The viewpoint of Ubuntu resounds with the principles and values of the social work profession, especially the principle of recognition of humanity, caring for each other's well-being, and a spirit of mutual support, which is also recognised by the South African White Paper on Welfare (1997). Using Ubuntu to achieve this goal will require a strong ethic of commitment by the social work profession, so that it can remove historical divisions and othering, and inject enthusiasm into the promotion of unity in and across diversity, which is observed in natural and social qualities such as race, language, culture, religion, gender, sexuality, and age (Van Breda 2019).

Consequently, the practices of Indigenous knowledge in social work should be based on the philosophy and practices of Ubuntu, such as reciprocity, spirituality, and caring for others. The traditional beliefs of Ubuntu are explicated by Mbiti (1969, p. 106), as follows:

only in terms of other people does the individual become conscious of his own being, his own duties, his privileges and responsibilities towards himself and other people... Whatever happens to the individual happens to the whole group, and whatever happens to the whole group happens to the individual. The individual can only say: 'I am, because we are; and since we are, therefore I am.' This is a cardinal point in the understanding of the African view of man.

An Indigenous knowledge perspective, such as Ubuntu, advocates for a strong sense of communal capital, as opposed to individual wealth or poverty. Community resources are not exclusively 'for an individual', instead they form part of a pool that people may dip into, or give to, in cases of need. An example is se*bata kgomo* (a Sepedi expression meaning 'to call out for help'), which is a community practice of collective care and support, where often group of women who have organised themselves into different social groups participate in self-help activities, for saving money, buying groceries, supporting members during bereavement, and meeting other needs such as paying for school fees and health needs. Another example is *letsema*, a Sesotho expression implying community members coming together to work the soil – a way rendering social services to communities. As a result, *letsema* is essential for providing a sense of togetherness, belonging, and relatedness in the community. Both *sebata-kgomo* and *letsema* are practiced in most rural communities of South Africa's Limpopo province.

Twikirize and Spitzer (2019) contend that, when people are empowered, they can actively harness their available resources, potentials, and social networks and draw from the wealth of their long-held value system to address challenges in their communities and environments. We advocate for social policy planners in development, whether social or physical, to include local knowledge, through participation, and to do capacity building, in order to provide a sustainable society. The utilisation of Indigenous knowledge is significant for addressing most of Africa's social problems and is key to sustainable development (Breidlid 2009). For this reason, Indigenous knowledge can serve as the social capital of poor people. Thus, developmental programmes should be established to empower people to take control of their own situations and communities, and the practices of *sebata-kgomo* and *letsema* are cases in point of how Indigenous knowledge perspectives can be beneficial in community interventions. If there is a problem in the family, the whole community can rally behind each other and support one another. Social work practice that incorporates Indigenous knowledge is essential for rebuilding the moral fabric of society, through Ubuntu, to promote respect, empathy, and compassion for others.

Indigenous knowledge systems in social work can provide a community with a participatory decision-making process that will eliminate the current wave of community protests that are being experienced by some communities, and which result in the destruction of livelihoods and property. Integrating Indigenous knowledge practices in social work provides an opportunity to create a space for problem-solving and decision-making. Indigenous knowledge should place the emphasis on inclusion, interconnectivity, and holistic ways of being – one cannot include some

Indigenous knowledge in the academy without also including knowledge from other socially excluded groups (Dumbrill and Green 2008). Consequently, Indigenous knowledge practices can provide the social work profession with new models for intervention and development, which are locally, culturally, and socially relevant for Indigenous communities.

Conclusion

It is, thus, essential for social work practitioners to learn from the Indigenous systems and practices of the local people they are serving. It is imperative that these Indigenous knowledge systems, Indigenous structures, and Indigenous beliefs are part of social work interventions in problem-solving and decision-making systems. By Indigenous interventions we are referring to approaches that are locally developed and implemented. Reference here is on localised and contextualised thinking and practices. These Indigenous interventions can be applied by social work professionals in local communities and contexts. When all the Indigenous intervention options have been exhausted, other social work services, such as statutory interventions, are sought as a measure of last resort. Correspondingly, the use of Indigenous knowledge systems in social work can be beneficial for the preservation of families, which could contribute to better social functioning of society. Indigenous knowledge systems, skills and techniques can be used in social work casework problem-solving. An example of a case could be family problems that need family efforts of mediation and reconciliation, where family meetings or a *legotla* could be called as an intervention. These Indigenous mediation and reconciliation efforts can be utilised to solve family problems and can be expedited by Indigenous knowledge holders, or elders.

It is for these reasons that Masoga and Shokane (2019) encourage the recognition of traditional knowledge and innovations in working with communities. The authors recommend that social work practitioners and educators who are interested in the field of Indigenous knowledge should acquire adequate knowledge and learn from the Indigenous practice experiences of a community. Knowledge and understanding of Indigenous theoretical frameworks, such as Afro-sensed approaches, that can be used in social work, can be integral for interventions through Indigenous social work, specifically, considering the integral nature of the kinship system in relation to responsibilities for practice. What can be drawn from this chapter is that traditional knowledge is located in the community, which has its own unique culture and beliefs.

Social work practitioners should be able to deepen their knowledge and appreciation of people's cultures, and social workers should learn and understand local Indigenous languages that are spoken, and the cultural beliefs of that particular community. The provision of social work services from an Indigenous perspective should strive to achieve the collective good of all, much as the principle of Ubuntu – reciprocity, interconnectedness, interdependence, and community participation. The

Indigenous social work practices should respond to interventions that promote family preservation, community practices, and participation; such interaction could be essential for communities and families, and for the healing of the nation.

References

Breidlid A (2009) Culture, Indigenous knowledge systems and sustainable development: a critical view of education in an African context. Int J Educ Dev 29(2):140–148

Campbell R, Wasco SM (2000) Feminist approaches to social science: epistemological and methodological tenets. Am J Community Psychol 28(6):773–791

Dumbrill GC, Green J (2008) Indigenous knowledge in the social work academy. Soc Work Educ 27(5):489–503

Faruque CJ, Ahmed F (2013) Development of social work education and practice in an era of international collaboration and cooperation. J Int Soc Issues 2(1):61–70

Gray M, Coates J, Yellow Bird M, Hetherington T (2013) Introduction: scoping the terrain of decolonization. In: Gray M, Coates J, Yellow Bird M, Hetherington T (eds) Decolonizing social work. Ashgate, Burlington, pp 1–24

Hart MA (2009) Anti-colonial Indigenous social work: reflections on an Aboriginal approach. In: Sinclair R, Hart MA, Bruyere G (eds) Wicihitowin: Aboriginal social work in Canada. Fernwood Publishing, Halifax, pp 25–41

Isaacson M (2014) Clarifying concepts: cultural humility or competency. J Prof Nurs 30(3):251–258

Lalonde A (1991) African Indigenous knowledge and its relevance to environment and development activities. Paper presented at the Common Property Conference, Winnipeg, Manitoba, 26–29 September 1991

Masoga, MA (2005) South African research in Indigenous knowledge systems and challenges for change. Indilinga, 4(1):15–29

Masoga MA (2017) Critical reflections on selected local narratives of contextual South African Indigenous knowledge. In: Ngulube P (ed) Handbook of research on theoretical perspectives on Indigenous knowledge systems in developing countries. IGI Global, Hershey

Masoga MA, Shokane AL (2019) Indigenous knowledge systems and environmental social work education: towards environmental sustainability. S Afr J Environ Educ 35. https://doi.org/10.4314/sajee.v35i1.14

Mbiti J (1969) African religion and philosophy. London: Heinemann

Mwansa LJ (2010) Challenges facing social work education in Africa. Int Soc Work 53(1):129–136. https://doi.org/10.1177/0020872809348959

Mwansa LK (2011) Social work education in Africa: whence and whither? Soc Work Educ 30(1):4–16

Ngũgĩ wa Thiong'o (1986) Decolonising the mind. In: The politics of language and culture in African literature. Heinemann, Nairobi

Olaleye EL (2013) Indigenous cultural practices as precursors to social work education in Nigeria. IFE PsychologIA 21(2):106–112

Oliver E, Oliver WH (2017) The colonisation of South Africa: a unique case. HTS Teol Stud/Theol Stud 73(3):a4498

Osei-Hwedie BZ (1996) Environmental protection and economic development in Zambia. J Soc Dev Afr 11(2):57–72

Puckree T, Mkhize M, Mgobhozi Z, Lin J (2002) African traditional healers: what health care professionals need to know. Int J Rehabil Res 25(4):247–251

Republic of South Africa (1996) Constitution of the Republic of South Africa (Act No. 108 of 1996). https://www.gov.za/sites/default/files/images/a108-96.pdf

Republic of South Africa (1997) White paper on welfare, Department of Welfare. Government printer

Rugege S (2003) Traditional leadership and its future role in local governance. Law Gov Democr 7(2):171–200

Shava S (2013) The representation of Indigenous knowledges. In: Stevenson RB, Brody M, Dillon J, Wals A (eds) International handbook of research on environmental education. Routledge, New York

Shava S, Manyike TV (2018) Decolonial role of African Indigenous language. Ind Afr J Indig Knowl Syst 17(1):36–52

Shokane AL, Masoga MA (2018) African Indigenous knowledge and social work practice: towards an Afro-sensed perspective. S Afr J Soc Work Soc Dev 30(1):1–18

Shokane AL, Masoga MA (2021) An Afro-sensed perspective on decolonising research methodologies. In: Fouché CB, Strydom H, Roestenburg W (eds) Research at grass roots – for the social sciences and human services professions, 5th edn. Van Schaick Publishers

St-Denis N, Walsh CA (2017) Traditional healing in an urban Indigenous setting: an auto-ethnography. J Indig Soc Dev 6(2):50–64

Thabede DG (2008) The African worldview as the basis of practice in the helping professions. Soc Work/Maatskaplike Werk 44:233–245

Truter I (2007) African traditional healers: cultural and religious beliefs intertwined in a holistic way. S Afr Pharm J 74(8):56–60

Twikirize JM, Spitzer H (eds) (2019) Social work practice in Africa: Indigenous and innovative approaches. Fountain Publishers, Kampala

Van Breda A (2019) Developing the notion of Ubuntu as African theory for social work practice. Soc Work/Maatskaplike Werk 55(4). https://doi.org/10.15270/55-4-762

Environmental Social Work

14

Margaret Alston

Contents

Introduction	268
Climate Change and Environmental Disasters	269
Environmental Justice	271
Sustainability	271
Social Work and the Environment	272
Social Work's Theoretical Base	273
Awakening Understanding of the Social Impacts of Environmental Degradation	274
From Systems Theory to an Eco-Critical Perspective	275
Environmental Social Work	276
Ecological Social Work	276
Deep Ecology	277
Green Social Work	277
Ecosocial Transition?	278
Social Work Practice in the Context of a Growing Environmental Awareness	278
A New Paradigm	280
References	282

Abstract

There is growing recognition amongst social work researchers and practitioners of the significance of the physical environment to the health and well-being of people and communities. Traditionally social workers have placed significant attention on the 'person-in-environment' concept, a concept that has related largely to the social world ignoring the interaction between humans and nature. However, the physical environment is now widely recognised as a critical factor shaping well-being and as a factor worthy of its own justice. In this chapter I explore the nature of social work in the context of a prioritised physical

---

M. Alston (✉)
Social Work, University of Newcastle, Newcastle, NSW, Australia

Monash University, Melbourne, VIC, Australia
e-mail: Margaret.alston@newcastle.edu.au; margaret.alston@monash.edu

environment and explore the links between social work, the environment, environmental justice and sustainability. This analysis has become increasingly significant in the context of climate changes, climate-induced disasters, environmental degradation and burgeoning populations placing increasing pressure on eco-systems and ecological well-being. In this context social work researchers are recognising new environmental challenges – challenges that are exacerbated by levels of poverty, inequitable access to resources and uneven power relations. Environmental social work, and its corollary – disaster social work, are areas of increasing practice significance as social workers are challenged to work with people in damaged environments. These emerging areas of practice highlight an increasing need for social workers to challenge practices that enhance environmental degradation, to incorporate sustainability and environmental consciousness as critical areas of practice and to undertake disaster preparation, planning, response and adaptation strategies to assist communities to build capacity and responsiveness in the face of environmental threats.

Keywords

Environment · Ecosystems · Climate change · Environmental degradation · Adaptive capacity · Eco-anxiety · Solastagia · Person-in-environment

Introduction

For much of the twenty-first century widespread and increasing global concerns for the health of planet earth have been evident. Rarely is there a week without news reports of a major life-threatening weather event or environmental disaster of catastrophic proportions somewhere in the world. These increasingly frequent events have focused critical attention on the environment and, in particular, onto the unsustainable human practices that are a major catalyst for environmental disasters. The production of greenhouse gases resulting from unfettered industrial growth are causing erosion of the ozone layer and resultant increases in temperature and climate-induced disasters (IPCC 2021). What has become increasingly evident is that the earth's climate is changing irrevocably, and that urgent attention is needed to reduce greenhouse gases and environmental degradation before a tipping point is reached and temperatures will rise to levels that are unsustainable to human life (IPCC 2021). Already observable climate changes are leading to rising morbidity and mortality; to threatened global food and water security; to sea level rises; to mass migrations; and to widespread species eradication (IPCC 2021).

These concerns, and a renewed focus on the environment, have been sharpened by a change of government in the USA in 2021 and the immediate announcement by President Joe Biden of a recommitment to the 2015 Paris Climate agreement and to net zero carbon emissions by 2050 (McGrath 2020). The catalyst for these decisions has been the threat to people and the environment posed by climate changes and rising temperatures; the fear of reaching a tipping point where recovery is not possible; the increasing number of catastrophic weather events; the dwindling of non-renewable resources; the rising concerns of people across the globe about environmental health; and the failure of governments to adequately address these concerns. As a result climate activism is increasing across the world and is particularly evident amongst young people concerned about their futures. These young activists, ably led by committed figures such as Greta Thunberg, are asking hard questions about the future. There is no doubt that governments will be held to account in the coming decades by new generations and that the battle to address climate changes and environmental health will be protracted. To add to global environmental concerns, the Covid 19 flu epidemic has caused widespread deaths and community destabilisation throughout 2020 and into 2021 and this has added to the sense of threat hanging over the global population.

Why is this of relevance to social workers? Why should we be troubled beyond our role as concerned citizens? And how does environmental health affect the way we work? These issues form the basis of this chapter where I discuss the growing interest in environmental health as a critical part of social work practice; the development of environmental social work and its various nuances; the melding of private concerns about environmental health with public practice roles; and how this is leading researchers and practitioners to question the very nature of social work. In building this discussion I examine various theoretical ideas emerging across the discipline and across the several theories of social work linked to environment – including environmental social work, ecological social work and green social work. I discuss how theorists are canvassing ideas as to how social workers can broaden their understanding of the environment in the context of practice and how social workers can become central agents addressing environmental and climate challenges.

Climate Change and Environmental Disasters

Climate changes, resulting from the build-up of greenhouse gases, are resulting in fundamental environmental changes and causing rises in temperatures and changing weather patterns across the world. These changes are impacting on people and communities and, in some cases, reducing access to resources necessary for a sustainable life. For example, rises in temperatures interrupt cropping cycles resulting in food insecurity in many parts of the world and, in some cases to food riots (see, e.g., Brodzinsky 2016 in relation to Venezuela). Water security is also threatened in many areas, and the impact on livelihoods is affecting the health and welfare of those experiencing major events (IPCC 2021).

Climate changes are already evident in many parts of the world (see, e.g., Alston 2015 for a discussion of Bangladesh) and are leading to mass migrations of people seeking work elsewhere in order to support themselves and their families. These 'climate refugees' are moving in large numbers across Africa, South Asia and the Pacific, areas where sea and temperature level rises are already having a major impact on livelihoods (IPCC 2021; Lutsgarten 2020).

Lutsgarten (2020) notes that 20% of the world may be uninhabitable by 2070 because of rising temperatures, reductions in rainfall, problematic fresh water access, increased storm activity and more frequent major catastrophic disasters such as floods, bushfires and droughts. Lutsgarten (2020) notes also that more than eight million people have moved from south Asia to the Middle East, Europe and North America and millions more are moving from inland areas of Africa to the coasts and cities. Australia is impacted by the movement of climate refugees from across the Pacific where sea level rises and rising temperatures are reducing the capacity of Pacific Island Nations people to thrive in place. Of concern is that nationalist governments such as that currently in Australia have a punitive approach to refugees and are not necessarily preparing for the inevitable movements of people (see, e.g., Briskman et al. 2008). Migrations are also leading to conflict in areas where refugees are contained on the borders of countries and to destabilised refugee families (Paynter 2019).

It is little wonder that Reyes Mason and Rigg (2019, p. 3) describe climate change as not only an environmental issue but also "a profoundly social and political challenge". As such they argue that it affects 'the distribution of rights, resources, and opportunities that people need to live healthy, productive and meaningful lives'. Climate changes have resulted in major weather events including bushfires of an unprecedented scale in Australia and the USA, floods across South Asia, sea level rises in the Pacific Ocean, melting ice caps in the Himalayas and the Antarctic and Arctic regions, major droughts in Australia, Africa and Asia, water wars across borders in Asia and widespread cyclones to name but a few events (IDMC 2020). The Internal Displacement Monitoring Centre (IDMC) (2020) notes that there were 1900 major weather-related disasters in 2019 alone, resulting in 24.9 million newly displaced people across 140 countries, and the numbers of people fleeing climate-induced environmental disasters (climate refugees) is expected to continue to rise. Social workers such as Reyes Mason and Rigg understand the social challenges created by disasters and the way social workers are engaging in the environmental and disaster space. For example, in recent years social workers have become critical members of disaster response teams working across government and non-government organisations engaged in disaster relief (Alston et al. 2019). These disasters and displacement create and exacerbate social crises including homelessness, poverty, fractured livelihoods, grief and trauma, family breakdown, mental and physical health impacts and dislocation (Alston et al. 2019). It is therefore little wonder that social work researchers are building new theoretical knowledge relating to social work and the environment and providing frameworks for social work practice deeply anchored in social justice.

For much of the twentieth and twenty-first centuries, regardless of cultural differences, social workers have maintained a collaborative commitment to social justice and human rights as critical core concepts guiding practice decisions (IASSW et al. 2012). There is also a surprising global unity emerging amongst social workers relating to the need to work with a consciousness of the environment bringing care for the natural elements into a central position within practice models across continents and cultures. International groupings and special sessions are evident in international conferences, and edited books are emerging building collaborations of like-minded social workers across the world. It is in this diffusion of international ideas that environmental social work is taking shape – where ideas are being explored and the environmental blind spot in social work practice is being questioned and developed. Matthies and Narhi (2017, p. 1) note that "... the manifold interconnections between environmental crisis, economic cupidity, social catastrophes and cultural losses are becoming increasingly evident ..." They note that the environmental debate in social work is global – linking across all cultures and continents, languages and livelihoods. Before moving to a discussion of the significance of the environment to social work practice, two critical concepts are discussed below to build our understanding of environmental social work. These are environmental justice and sustainability.

Environmental Justice

The definition of environmental justice in the context of social work practice has been somewhat contentious tracing the path of social workers' awakening understanding of the significance of the environment (Erickson 2018). As Dominelli (2012) notes there are numerous anthropomorphic definitions that prioritise humans and call for equal treatment of all people in regard to the environment. What they fail to do is provide a definition that centralises the environment and, in particular, the nurturing and caring for environment as an obvious strategy in its own right regardless of the desires of humans. Dominelli (2012, p. 431) notes that "environmental justice relies on the equitable sharing of both the benefits and the burdens in maintaining the healthy and sustainable environments that all living things can enjoy". Yet the global obsession with globalisation, world markets and economic rationalisation has had devastating consequences for the natural environment. This has been viewed as a resource to exploit regardless of the consequences, while environmental disasters are often viewed as economic problems requiring scientific solutions.

Besthorn (2012, p. 255) notes that social workers must absorb the notion of environmental justice into our understanding of social justice to develop a form of "deep justice", a position that supports equity between humans and nature. Environmental justice therefore requires social workers to incorporate advocacy for the environment and attention to how environmental degradation impacts the poorest and most marginal. Critically it requires us to step away from an anthropomorphic approach that prioritises humans over nature and to centralise the environment irrespective of the demands of humans.

Sustainability

Sustainability on the other hand is a critical and contentious concept in relation to the framing of the environment. The global understanding of sustainability draws heavily on the 1987 Bruntland Report (WCED 1987, p. 40) which defines sustainable development as development "that meets the needs of the present without compromising the ability of future generations to meet their own needs". This broad definition gives space for complex interplay of social, economic and environmental elements that facilitate communities prioritising various aspects of sustainability depending on circumstances (Cocklin and Alston 2003; Alston et al. 2016).

International efforts to address sustainability have led to the development of the Sustainable Development Goals (SDGs), goals that have been ratified by UN-focused nations (UN 2015). These goals which address poverty, hunger, education, access to water, energy and a protected environment also address gender equality, peace and partnerships. The goals provide a global roadmap that can guide the development of environmentally anchored practice and have added impetus to social work's approach to the environment (Narhi and Matthies 2018; Alston 2018). The SDGs link equality, with social, economic and environmental goals into a blueprint for addressing our global future. The international recognition of sustainability through the SDGs and its linking with factors such as poverty, equality and education provide social work with an internationally sanctioned guide.

The Social Work profession has incorporated sustainability as a major pillar of practice thereby providing a link to the SDGs. A major turning point in social work's acknowledgement of sustainability occurred with the release of the Global Agenda for Social Work and Social Development in 2012 by the International Association of Schools of Social Work (IASSW), the International Council on Social Welfare (ICSW) and the International Federation of Social Workers (IFSW) (IFSW 2012). One of the agenda's four central pillars is "promoting sustainable communities and environmentally sensitive development" (IASSW et al. 2012). In Australia this has also resulted in an acknowledgement within the Australian Association of Social Workers (AASW) code of ethics and the inclusion of the need to ensure that social work "promotes the protection of the natural environment as inherent to social wellbeing" (AASW 2020, p. 9). There is then a critical recognition of sustainability and the environment emerging at both national and international levels.

Social Work and the Environment

How then do we interpret social work's move to environmental justice and sustainability? Are they marginal concepts in the context of practice driven by a small rump of social work activists? Or are they a guide to a new social work paradigm? Further, the adoption of sustainability through the Global Agenda gives an authoritative voice to social work's engagement in this area. Surprisingly, awareness of the critical nature of the physical environment has been a significant part of our history. Social workers have been variously engaged with environmental actions since the days of Jane Addams – recognised as a pioneer of social work. Working at the end of the nineteenth and the beginning of the twentieth centuries, Addams was conscious of the serious social consequences of the industrial revolution and its impact on the health and well-being of workers and their families (Bartlett 1970). She saw the need for social workers to move beyond the casework/charity model (that was dominant at the time) to include in their practice advocacy about housing, work hours, health consequences, and, in the context of this chapter, to advocate for better water quality, more open spaces and parks (McKinnon and Alston 2016). Mary Richmond, another pioneer of the social work profession, acknowledged the importance of the physical environment but only in relation to its impact on the social environment indicating an anthropocentric (or human-centred) approach (Richmond 1922).

This once dominant anthropomorphic positioning of humans as superior to the environment, and the environment being only important in its relationship to humans is the cause of much recent challenge amongst social work researchers (Alston and Besthorn 2012; Besthorn 2012, Gray and Coates 2015). For Coates (2003) this idea represented evidence that social work had become 'a domesticated profession' looking only to put the social system to rights and failing to question structural disadvantage or environmental destruction as part of its remit. Arguably this has changed as many social workers now view the lack of attention to the physical environment as short-sighted (Gray et al. 2012; McKinnon and Alston 2016; McKinnon 2008). Zapf (2010), for example, notes that from its early days the social work profession has viewed the environment through a socio-cultural lens and solely with regard to how it impacts on people. In more recent times this has been a subject of much contention as researchers (see, e.g., Dominelli 2012; Gray et al. 2013; Alston et al. 2016) argue for environmental justice to be a critical feature of environmental social work thereby acknowledging the uniqueness of nature.

Social Work's Theoretical Base

Nonetheless, social work theorising and its practice base have been bound by a number of conceptual constraints that have limited our attention to the physical environment. One of these has been the dominance of systems theory and of social work's prioritisation of the notion of 'person-in-environment'. This concept (person-in-environment) alerted social workers to move beyond their initial understanding of the issues presented in practice and to acknowledge the critical role of the factors shaping a person's experience and welfare, and the lens through which they understood the world. This primary idea was designed to ensure that social workers worked more critically with individuals and families and that there was acknowledgement of the elements in the social environment that facilitated or constrained a person's welfare. During this mid-twentieth century period, systems theory dominated with its emphasis on the social environment (Narhi and Matthies 2017; Germain and Gitterman 1980), and Narhi and Matthies (2017) note that the dominance of systems theory emerged as a way of binding social work to a common core of practice and therefore served a political purpose beyond its practice implications.

Perhaps surprisingly given the term, the 'person-in-environment' concept dealt almost exclusively with the social environment with little regard for the links to the natural environment and how this might impact. In more recent years, systems theory has been widely criticised for ignoring the natural environment (see, e.g., Coates and Gray 2012; Coates and Gray 2012; Besthorn 2012; Dominelli 2012), and

Narhi and Matties (2017) note that it presents as a neutral position, ignoring the political issues that shape a person's environment, including the natural environment. It is equally perplexing, given the understanding of the early pioneer social workers of the critical nature of the environment, that this has not featured more prominently in our understanding of the factors shaping health and well-being for much of the twentieth century. It is only in the last 40–50 years that social workers have begun to acknowledge the critical importance of the physical environment as a factor that is largely out of the control of the person to change, as in the event of a catastrophic environmental disaster, potentially rendering them powerless and traumatised.

Yet the now tentative embracing of an environmental consciousness does not mean that we can simply add the physical environment and stir. For very obvious reasons relating to the health and welfare of people and communities impacted by environmental pressures, social work researchers and practitioners across the world are now becoming aware of the link between people and the environment in which they live. Yet social work has been very much shaped by its commitment to, and grounding in, modernist principles (see, e.g., Boetto 2017; Dominelli 2012) and its desire to be viewed as a modernist profession with legitimacy and status. Yet this approach also inadvertently endorses pollution, unfettered growth and environmental degradation (Beck 1999). As a result for much of the twentieth century, social workers have feared that undertaking environmental activism within the structures of the professional identity might render the profession as an extremist group and on the fringes of acceptable professional practice. While there is some substance to these fears, Gray et al. (2013) argue that environmental realities will inevitably cause social workers to critique their modernist roots and the overwhelming focus on therapy and rehabilitation and to recognise the essential connection between humans and nature.

Awakening Understanding of the Social Impacts of Environmental Degradation

While the profession has gradually embraced the environment as having a major impact on health and well-being, the latter half of the twentieth century saw an explosion of major disasters that were both climate-induced and human-induced. For example, the increase in toxic gases and waste has caused major health crises and devastated waterways and other environmental assets. The 1984 tragedy in Bhopal, India, which killed 4000 people when gases were released from a pesticide plant overnight killing 4000 people, immediately and another 20,000 over time (Banerjee 2013) is but one example. Another, more recent event is the devastating oil spill off the coast of Mauritius which occurred in 2020 causing untold and irreparable damage to one of the most pristine reefs and wetlands in the world (Khadka 2020) This event and others like it cannot be ignored by the global community. They have awakened an awareness of the impact of toxic substances and other hazards on the well-being of people and communities, particularly those people whose livelihoods have been destroyed and/or who cannot afford to move away from a toxic disaster site.

What has become clear is that those who suffer the most in environmental disasters are those least able to take action. For reasons of poverty and socio-economic circumstances, environmental degradation and climate-induced disasters impact most particularly on the most vulnerable. Besthorn (2012, p. 248) terms this environmental racism – that is the disproportionate impact of environmental disasters on "people of colour and low-income neighbourhoods" a circumstance that particularly affects women and girls (Alston 2015). This link between the environment and the impact on the most vulnerable is becoming increasingly evident amongst social workers. John Coates (2003, p. 2) notes that

> A serious environmental crisis exists . . . . This crisis is of such magnitude that the human community can no longer rest solely on a faith that science and technology will discover new materials to replace exhausted resources, uncover methods to deal with toxic waste, and provide all the food and means for an adequate standard of living for the billions of people who are poor and underemployed. Humans must seek a new relation with our planet earth.

From Systems Theory to an Eco-Critical Perspective

The emerging critique of structural social work has focused attention on the need for a new awareness of the environment. Narhi and Matthies (2017, p. 26) describe the 1970s as a period when social work theorising moved from a focus on systems theory to an 'eco-critical' approach. This social work approach absorbed the impact of growing environmental movements and critiqued modern industrial society and its political dimensions. Social workers began to engage in environmental projects and to work with community groups addressing environmental challenges. Theorists such as Hoff and McNutt (1994) in their book, *The Global Environmental Crisis*, noted the link between environmental destruction and human well-being and Hoff and Polack (1993) were influential in querying the economic paradigm that drove relentless environmental vandalism.

In moving into environmental activism, it became impossible for social workers in this space to ignore not only the political dimensions, including the environmental challenges and 'environmental racism', but also the critical impact of neoliberal, capitalist, industrial focused modes of government, the social policies that emerged from such systems and their impact on the health and welfare of people. Narhi and Matthies (2017, p. 27) note that social workers were forced to question unfettered "economic growth and the exploitation of nature". In fact, Pennisi di Floristella (2016) questioned whether natural disasters could truly be referred to as natural given the human-induced interventions of people, governments and businesses that eroded and damaged environmental assets. Coates (2003) in his book, *Ecology and Social Work: Towards a New Paradigm*, moved social work theorising of the environment beyond a tabulation of the perils of capitalism towards a new theoretical discussion of social work's potential engagement with the environment. Coates called on social workers to view the environment as an entity separate from humans and deserving of its own justice moving the debate further from an anthropocentric view of the environment as only relevant as it relates to humans to an ecocentric view (Rambaree 2020). At the same time, Coates challenged social workers to not ignore the crucial interlinking of people and environment.

In the following years there was a groundswell of both activism and theoretical development. Both the *Journal of International Social Welfare* and the *Journal of Environmental Social Work* published special editions on social work and the environment in 2012, and several books emerged including Lena Dominelli's *Green Social Work* (2012) and Gray, Coates and Hetherington's *Environmental Social Work* (2013). This period saw the burgeoning development of social work theories incorporating the environment including those listed below.

Environmental Social Work

Environmental social work theorists acknowledge that global warming and climate changes will have impacts on the "sociopolitical, economic and physical environment in which social workers are engaged, but also on the type of work, both mitigating and adaptive, social workers will be called on to carry out" (Gray et al. 2013, p. 3). Environmental social work recognises the interconnections of humans and the environment and notes that social workers will be drawn into a greater consciousness of the interaction between these. They argue that social workers will be extending their work to include an understanding of the impacts of food and water insecurity, of a reliance on fossil fuels, and the destruction of natural resources.

Ecological Social Work

Ecological social work emerged in Europe in the latter part of the twentieth century and focuses on understanding ecological and social sustainability and the reciprocal relationships between humans and the natural environment (McKinnon and Alston 2016; Matthies et al. 2001). It drew from systems theory and from social work practice that addressed not only the issues presented by an individual, but also from elements of a person's social system. However, as has been discussed, systems theory not only lacked attention to the environment it also failed to acknowledge power relations. In addressing a more comprehensive theoretical model, Ungar (2002) noted that early developments in ecological social work incorporated an understanding of the environment but that it was rudimentary at best.

Germain and Gitterman's (1996) life model approach introduced the idea that the natural environment, pollution and the misuse of power were critical elements of a more comprehensive ecological approach to social work practice. Social ecology, or new ecology, emerged in response to these early criticisms of ecological theory and was more transparent in its focus on humans and the environment (Bookchin 1980; Ungar 2002). Bookchin (1980) clearly argued against a romanticised acceptance of the environment without a focus on the consequences of the commodification of environmental assets and the need for a non-hierarchical relationship between humans and the environment.

Deep Ecology

Deep ecology draws from the work of Arne Naess (1989) and was perhaps the first challenge to anthropomorphism within the profession. It represented a shift to an acknowledgement of the intrinsic value of the environment independent of its relationship to humans (Besthorn 2012). Proponents of Deep Ecology argue for the acknowledgement of a mutual interdependence between humans and nature, and for a more complex understanding of justice and of the intrinsic value of all part of the ecosystem. Besthorn (2012, p. 255) argues for a deeper link between social and environmental justice. Alarmingly he noted:

> The natural world will not care if social workers spend their time solely focused on insuring a degree of social justice for the human species. The earth system will collapse whether social workers are successful at those efforts or not.

The global environmental crisis spurred attention to the environment and its incorporation in practice. The link between environmental crises and the profound impact on people and communities could not be ignored. In addressing this issue in 2012 Besthorn (2012, p. 250) noted that 'the absence of social work's involvement in critical environmental issues was not only short-sighted and harmful to clients, but, at a deeper level constituted a breach of the profession's long-held commitment to social justice'. Besthorn was instrumental in developing the Global Alliance for a Deep Ecological Social Work, an alliance that supports the idea of all aspects of living things having their own intrinsic value. The Global Alliance for Deep Ecological Social Work includes leading theorists who are working to promote awareness of the physical environment. The ecospiritual perspective is closely related to deep ecology (McKinnon and Alston 2016) and likewise makes a strong link between humans and planetary well-being. The ecospiritual approach queries capitalist growth and its impact on people and the environment and incorporates a spiritual and Indigenous positioning.

Green Social Work

Lena Dominelli (2012) introduced the term *Green Social Work* to describe a more nuanced understanding of the significance of the environment and the interaction between humans and nature. Dominelli (2012, p. 3) takes others to task for ignoring the "power relations based on geo-political social structures that have a deleterious impact upon the quality of life of poor and marginalised populations and the earth's flora and fauna". Dominelli's approach moves beyond building social workers' awareness of the significance of the environment to embrace and address environmental and social justice issues in the context of structural inequalities and industrialisation that has favoured the few. She brings together the environment, social structures and marginalisation, with an analysis of social and environmental justice, to build well-being and to protect the environment Dominelli 2018).

Ecosocial Transition?

More recently the ecosocial approach is viewed as combining the various theoretical positions outlined above (Narhi and Matthies 2018) and highlighting the need for a global transition to a more eco-friendly future. Inevitably social work will be caught up in this as peoples everywhere struggle to ensure a more secure way of life. Boetto (2019, p. 141) notes that

> At the heart of eco-social work, therefore, is an understanding that the delicate balance of Earth's ecosystems sustains humanity, and alternatively the disruption of healthy ecosystems threatens life on Earth for all living organisms.

In highlighting the links between people and their environment, ecosocial work follows the radical tradition dominant in social work during the 1970s and 1980s when the profession followed the lead of radical activist campaigns. This view acknowledges critical social work and feminist approaches in highlighting structural disadvantage (Narhi and Matthies 2018). The ecosocial approach is deeply embedded in community at the same time as being globally responsive.

Social Work Practice in the Context of a Growing Environmental Awareness

The approaches outlined above draw attention to the increasing need for a paradigm shift to an environmentally conscious social work. How might this affect traditional social work practice? Will there be a tendency for acknowledgement of the environment in social work to be viewed as a choice and to be shunted to the side with other obscure traditions. This would be a mistake as the increasing significance of environmental degradation and disasters is going to ensure that social workers are increasingly drawn into working with people impacted by disasters. Nonetheless, Boetto and Bell (2015) note that it is insufficient to view ecosocial work as a specialist field of practice and one that is at best marginalised. The environment will become a critical feature of social work practice regardless. They argue that what in fact is required is a radical transformative approach to incorporate environmental consciousness in all forms of practice.

While there has been a significant focus on theorising environmental social work, there has been a more limited attention on practising social work from an environmental perspective. Alston et al. (2019) note that social workers engaged in post-disaster practice are using their existing skills nuanced to the changing milieu in which they find themselves and with a consciousness and understanding of environmental and global issues and understanding. This is sage advice for social workers engaged in environmentally conscious practice. Regardless of circumstances, social workers will undertake casework, community work, advocacy and their full range of skills with the added perspective that environmental awareness gives. It will require workers to be engaged in locally based practice but with a global perspective on environmental degradation and the need for a championing of both social and environmental justice. It will require a fundamental reappraisal of the impacts of environmental degradation on vulnerable groups and communities and it will require the courage to bring public attention to environmentally damaging practices.

While there are several points made by researchers on the types of practice frameworks social workers engaging in an environmentally conscious practice may adopt, two worthy of note include that of Ramsay and Boddy (2016) and Narhi and Matthies (2018). Ramsay and Boddy (2016) conducted a concept analysis of ecosocial work literature in order to inform the types of skills and knowledge necessary for social work practice. They identified the main social work attributes of particular relevance as: applying existing skills creatively; being open to different values and ways of doing things; adopting a different change focus; working across boundaries and places; and being continually aware of the vision and consequences of ecosocial work. In a more global view, Narhi and Matthies' (2018, p. 493) framework outlines four themes: (a) adopting a global perspective; (b) critically reflecting on the Western type of professionalism in social work; (c) making a connection to the cross-sectoral ecosocial transition of societies; and (d) incorporating environmental and ecological justice in practice.

I would also add Dominelli's (2012) point about the need to acknowledge and address the differential power relations between and across nations and between wealthy and marginalised groups most affected by environmental degradation. My own additional point is the need for the inclusion of a self-conscious attention to gender equality in the context of environmental and disaster practice, drawing on ecofeminist values of inclusion and growth.

Our understanding of issues in the local context must draw on a global perspective to understand the interlinking of factors such as poverty, water and food security, migration movements. As Narhi and Matthies (2017, p. 499) note "environmental issues are ever more substantially related to the core issues of social work concerning equality, justice and the coping of the most disadvantaged members of society". We cannot ignore the environment in our understanding of what it is to be a social work practitioner.

Meanwhile social workers working from an environmentally conscious perspective will become increasingly familiar with concepts such as solastagia and ecoanxiety, terms now used extensively to describe the impacts of the destruction of one's place (or environment) and health.

Solastagia is a concept adapted by Albrecht (2006) and defined as a fear of an environmental disaster, and is based on feelings of powerlessness and hopelessness about environmental change or climate change. Albrecht developed this concept in response to the impact of disasters such as droughts and floods on people and place.

Warsini et al. (2017) further describe solastagia as a form of nostalgia for the environment, home and surroundings that no longer resemble the home they knew and loved. These changes in the familiar environment disrupt one's sense of place and impact on the individual's sense of identity, belonging and control. Albrecht et al. (2007) further describes somaterratic disease as a form of mental illness caused by the severing of links between a person and their environment.

Similarly, *ecoanxiety* is a term describing the emotional impact of anxiety related to the trauma of environmental disaster. Ecoanxiety can result in an excessive fear about the future in the context of climate change (Pihkala 2018; McCarroll 2020). Ecoanxiety can impact both individuals and whole communities whose experience of declining resilience leads to increasing feelings of hopelessness in the face of significant environmental changes. These terms effectively describe the experiences and feelings of individuals and communities who have experienced a disaster. Social workers drawn into disaster practice will recognise these elements. Understanding how to address these factors with clients and support people through the trauma caused by the destruction of their 'place' is essential for environmentally conscious social work.

A New Paradigm

How do we summarise these ideas and bring them forward a new social work paradigm? Climate changes, the increasing frequency and intensity of major environmental disasters, wars, food and water insecurity and the impact of industrial encroachment on environmental assets will increasingly come to impact on the health and well-being of individuals and communities and have major repercussions for the most vulnerable. Resulting physical and mental health impacts are already evident and are likely to increase. If the global community is to address these major challenges, an ecosocial transition of societies would appear inevitable. By default, social workers will be required to understand the impacts of global issues, of climate changes, of environmental disasters and of the resulting people movements and their consequences at the local level. At the same time issues such as rainforest destruction, the co-option of fertile land, land-slides caused by over-clearing and chemical and oil spills are linked through global capitalism to resultant major environmental degradation. These factors are creating winners and losers and causing an increasing disparity between communities across the world. Many vulnerable communities are powerless to address climate disasters, or the encroachment of environmental destruction, and may indeed be dependent on harmful development projects for their livelihoods. These events are creating an existential crisis on planet earth that is moving us inexorably to a tipping point where the environmental damage will be irreversible and temperature rises will be uncontrollable.

As a result, social work will move inexorably towards an acknowledgement of the need for a paradigm shift – one that fosters environmental justice, sustainability and the embracing of an environmentally conscious practice. As Narhi and Matthies (2018, p. 496) note, what is required is a paradigm that is transformative – one that centralises environmental justice, fosters a reduction of in the consumption of natural resources, supports a more even distribution of wealth and creates a "new vision for the wellbeing of humanity and the planet". What is clear is that a move to environmental consciousness will be inevitable within social work in particular and other health professions more generally.

At the same time, social work may indeed return to its roots with a tilt towards radical activism brought about by the need to reconnect with vulnerable communities. Practitioners will be required to understand the links between local level issues and global issues such as the distribution of scarce resources and the consequences of water and food insecurity. Workers will need to unpick power relations, not only as experienced by individuals and families, but also in a global context. Particularly relevant will be the impact of unequal gender relations in a world where the distribution of environmental assets and goods and services will be closely guarded. They will also be more engaged in cross disciplinary practice and research and will be more attuned to, and conversant with, sustainable development and the SDGs. The profession's embracing of environmental issues will build on its commitment to equality, social justice and sustainability and will be more attuned to the structural elements that lead to disadvantage.

Yet progress towards this goal continues to be slow and disparate. Bowles et al. (2016) remind us that social work remains at the margins of the greatest crisis the world has experienced. A significant factor in this slow progress is that we appear reluctant to abandon our modernist professional principles. Contemporary researchers such as Boetto (2019) argue that a challenge to our modernist assumptions is necessary and indeed urgent if we are not to remain on the margins of environmental activism. Our current position fosters a professional approach, pushes us into managerialist positions and reduces our ability to address global issues. But it also diminishes the environment, fosters the separation of humans from the natural world and fails to view the environment as an entity demanding its own justice. Both Bell (2019) and Boetto (2019) argue that what is required is a transformation of our profession to embrace environmental social work. As part of this process of re-evaluating our professional status, the link between the environmental crisis and the professional crisis we find ourselves in, must be addressed. The profession appears to be experiencing a crisis of identity and yet our long climb to professionalism and our historical fostering of casework and community work based on the limited notion of person-in-environment is now dated.

Ethically social workers have walked a fine line between professionalism and our understanding of social and indeed environmental justice. Boetto and Bell (2015) note that the fact that social work is grounded and formulated in industrial capitalism will make changing this position a major undertaking. This is not helped by a dominance of neoliberal policy making and a lack of political will to address climate issues in the wider political sphere. A milieu of climate denialism in government circles does little to assist the countries requiring transition to a more carbon reduced future and is a worrying trend that suggests the drive for adequate climate policies will be hard won. In the process, attention to vulnerable groups and communities and the funding of mitigation efforts may well also be protracted.

Yet increasingly individual social workers and students are becoming more interested in climate and disaster work as they are drawn into post-disaster work. Social workers engaged in post-disaster practice see the impacts on people's lives, and witness feelings of ecoanxiety and solastagia in clients. Many see their role as social change agents working with people going through environmental transition. This suggests that our focus in social work education requires change. Rambaree's (2020, p. 557) suggestion that what is required is "a transformative and emancipatory pedagogy (TEP) in the teaching and learning of Environmental Social Work" is a good one. Meanwhile the increase in research and the prominence of Australian researchers amongst those developing this area of practice (see, e.g., Gray et al. 2013; McKinnon and Alston 2016; Boetto 2019; Bowles et al. 2016; Bell 2019; Ramsay and Boddy 2016) suggest that strategies and understanding may well be shaped by colleagues in the global South. This is not surprising given that Australia is very much viewed as the 'canary in the coalmine' in the context of climate change and climate-induced disasters. We are indeed at the pointy end and the world is watching. The disasters in the global South ensure that the issue of climate changes remains dominant, and that support for vulnerable communities impacted by drought, fires, floods and storms is an almost constant element of Australian social work practice. Increasingly, therefore, workers are recognising that the environment is a significant factor shaping social crises as people and communities go through such significant trauma and loss.

Yet undertaking a transformational paradigm shift and challenging social work's professional focus remains a barrier to social work being central to the critical developments required to address global climate panic. Developing this area of practice and ensuring that social workers understand the critical importance of environmental justice, its link to social and gender justice and the human rights of people across the world remains our challenge for the future.

References

Albrecht G (2006) Solastalgia. Alt J (AJ) Canadas Environ Voice 32(4/5):34–36. Retrieved from http://search.ebscohost.com/login.aspx?direct=true&db=ehh&AN=23737810&site=ehost-live

Albrecht G, Sartore G-M, Connor L, Higginbotham N, Freeman S, Kelly B et al (2007) Solastalgia: the distress caused by environmental change. Australas Psychiatry 15:S95–S98. https://doi.org/10.1080/10398560701701288

Alston M (2015) Women and climate change in Bangladesh. Routledge. Women in Asia series

Alston M (2018) Ecosocial work: reflections from the global South. In: Matthies A-L, Narhi K (eds) The Ecosocial transition of societies : the contribution of social work and social policy, Advances in social work. Routledge, London/New York, pp 91–104

Alston M, Besthorn F (2012) Environment and sustainability. In: Lyons K, Hokenstad T, Pawar M, Huegler N (eds) Handbook of international social work international social work. SAGE, London

Alston M, Whittenbury K, Western D (2016) Rural community sustainability. In: McKinnon J, Alston M (eds) Eco-social work. Palgrave Macmillan, pp 94–111

Alston M, Hazeleger T, Hargreaves D (2019) Social work and disasters. Routledge

Australian Association of Social Workers (2020) Australian association of social workers code of ethics. North Melbourne, Victoria. Data retrieved on February 11, 2021 from https://www.aasw.asn.au/document/item/1201

Banerjee D (2013) Writing the disaster: substance activism after Bhopal. Contemporary South Asia 21(3):230–242

Bartlett H (1970) The common base of social work practice. National Association of Social Workers, Washington, DC

Beck U (1999) World risk society. Polity, Cambridge

Bell K (2019) Transforming social work for environmental justice: theory, practice, and education. Aust Soc Work 72(2):242–244. https://doi.org/10.1080/0312407X.2019.1569080

Besthorn F (2012) Deep Ecology's contributions to social work: a ten-year retrospective. Int J Soc Welf 21:248–259

Boetto H (2019) Advancing transformative eco-social change: shifting from modernist to holistic foundations. Aust Soc Work 72(2):234–247

Boetto H, Bell K (2015) Environmental sustainability in social work education: an online initiative to encourage global citizenship. Int Soc Work 58(3):448–462. https://doi.org/10.1177/0020872815570073

Boetto H (2017) A transformative eco-social model: challenging modernist assumptions in social work. Br J Soc Work 47(1):48–67

Bookchin M (1980) Toward an ecological society. Black Rose, Montreal

Bowles W, Boetto H, Jones P, McKinnon J (2016) Is social work really greening? Exploring the place of sustainability and environment in social work codes of ethics. Int Soc Work 61(4):503–517. https://doi.org/10.1177/0020872816651695

Briskman L, Latham S, Goddard C (2008) Human rights overboard. Scribe Publications, Melbourne, Australia

Brodzinsky S (2016) We are like a bomb: food riots show Venezuela crisis has gone beyond politics. The Guardian. 21 May. Data retrieved on March 13, 2021 from https://www.theguardian.com/world/2016/may/20/venezuela-breaking-point-food-shortages-protests-maduro

Coates J (2003) Ecology and social work. Toward a new paradigm. Fernwood Publishing, Nova Scotia Canada

Coates J, Gray M (2012) *Guest editorial:* the environment and social work: an overview and introduction. Int J Soc Welf 21:230–238

Cocklin C, Alston M (2003) Introduction. In: Cocklin C, Alston M (eds) Community sustainability: a question of capital. Centre for Rural Social Research, Wagga Wagga

Dominelli L (2012) Green social work. From environmental crises to environmental justice. Polity Press, Cambridge

Dominelli L (2018) Green social work in theory and practice. In: Dominelli L (ed) The Routledge handbook of green social work. Routledge, New York, pp 9–20

Erickson CL (2018) Environmental justice as social work practice. Oxford University Press, New York

Germain CB, Gitterman A (1996) The life model of social work practice: advances in theory and practice. Columbia University Press, New York

Germain CB, Gitterman A (1980) The life world of social work practice. Columbia University Press, New York

Gray M, Coates J (2015) Changing gears: shifting to an environmental perspective in social work education. Soc Work Educ 34(5):502–5012. https://doi.org/10.1080/02615479.2015.1065807

Gray M, Coates J, Hetherington T (2012) Environmental social work. Taylor and Francis, UK

Gray M, Coates J, Hetherington T (eds) (2013) "Introduction", environmental social work. Routledge, Oxon, pp 1–29

Hoff M, Polack R (1993) Social dimensions of the environmental crisis: challenges for social work. Soc Work 38(2):204–211

Hoff MD, McNutt JG (eds) (1994) The global environmental crisis: implications for social welfare and social work. Ashgate, Aldershot

Intergovernmental Panel on Climate Change (IPCC) (2021) AR6 climate change 2021: Impacts, adaptation and vulnerability. 6th assessment report. Data retrieved on March 13, 2021 from https://www.ipcc.ch/report/sixth-assessment-report-working-group-ii/

Internal Displacement Monitoring Centre (IDMC) (2020) Global report on internal displacement. Data accessed on February 11, 2021 from https://www.internal-displacement.org/sites/default/files/publications/documents/2020-IDMC-GRID.pdf

International Association of Schools of Social Work (IASSW), International Council on Social Welfare (ICSW) and International Federation of Social Workers (IFSW) (2012) Global agenda for social work and social development. Data retrieved on February 11, 2021 from https://www.ifsw.org/wp-content/uploads/ifsw-cdn/assets/globalagenda2012.pdf

International Association of Schools of Social Work/International Federation of Social Workers/International Council on Social Welfare's 'Global Agenda for Social Work and Social Development' (IASSW, IFSW and ICSW, 2012)

Khadka NS (2020) Why the Muaritius Oil Spill is so serious. BBC News August 2020. Data retrieved on February 20, 2021 from www.BBC.Com/news/world-africa-53754751

Lutsgarten A (2020) The great climate migration. New York Times. 23/7/2020. Data retrieved on February 28, 2021 from https://www.nytimes.com/interactive/2020/07/23/magazine/climate-migration.html

Matthies AL, Nahri K, Ward D (eds) (2001) The eco-social approach in social work. Sophi, Jyvaskyla

Matthies A-L, Narhi K (2017) Introduction: it is the time for social work and social policy research on the ecosocial transition. In: Matthies, Narhi (eds) The Ecosocial transition of societies. Routledge/Taylor and Francis Group, New York/London, pp 1–14

McGrath M (2020) Joe Biden: how the president-elect plans to tackle climate change. BBC News 10 November. Data accessed on February 8, 2021 from https://www.bbc.com/news/science-environment-54858638

McCarroll PR (2020) Listening for the cries of the earth: practical theology in the Anthropocene. Int J Pract Theol 24(1):29–46. https://doi.org/10.1515/ijpt-2019-0013

McKinnon J (2008) Exploring the nexus between social work and the environment. Aust Soc Work 61(3):256–268

McKinnon J, Alston M (2016) Introducing ecological social work. In: McKinnon J, Alston M (eds) Eco-social work. Palgrave Macmillan, London, UK, pp 1–18

Naess A (1989) Ecology, community and lifestyle: outline of an Ecosophy, translated by David Rothenberg. Cambridge University Press, Cambridge

Narhi K, Matthies A-L (2018) The ecosocial approach in social work as a framework for structural social work. Int Soc Work 6(4):490–502

Narhi K, Matthies A-L (2017) The contribution of social work and social policy in the ecosocial transition of society. In: Matthies A-L, Narhi K (eds) The ecosocial transition of societies: the contribution of social work and social policy. Routledge, Advances in Social Work, London/New York, pp 319–326

Paynter E (2019) Europe's refugee crisis explains why border walls don't top migration. The Conversation. Data accessed on March 17, 2019 from https://theconversation.com/europes-refugee-crisis-explains-why-border-walls-dont-stop-migration-110414

Pennisi di Floristella A (2016) Dealing with natural disasters. Pac Rev 29(2):283–305. https://doi.org/10.1080/09512748.2015.1013498

Pihkala P (2018) Death, the environment, and theology. Dialog J Theol 57(4):287–294. https://doi.org/10.1111/dial.12437

Rambaree K (2020) Environmental social work implications for accelerating the implementation of sustainable development in social work curricula. Int J Sustain High Educ 21(3):557–574

Ramsay S, Boddy J (2016) Environmental social work: a concept analysis. Br J Soc Work 47(1):68–86. https://doi.org/10.1093/bjsw/bcw078

Reyes Mason L, Rigg J (2019) Climate change, social justice: making the case for community inclusion. In: Reyes Mason L, Rigg J (eds) People and climate change: vulnerability, adaptation and social justice. Oxford University Press, New York, pp 3–22

Richmond M (1922) What is social case work? An introductory description. Russel Sage Foundation, NewYork. Reprinted 1939

Ungar M (2002) A deeper, more social ecological social work practice. Soc Serv Rev 76(3):480–497

United Nations (UN) (2015) Sustainable development goals officially adopted by 193 nations. Data accessed on March 18, 2021 from http://www.un.org.cn/info/6/620.html

Warsini S, Mills J, Usher K (2017) Solastagia: living with the environmental damage caused by natural disasters. J Prehospital Disast Med 29(1):1–4. https://doi.org/10.1017/S1049023X13009266

World Commission on Environment and Development (WCED) (1987) Our common future. Oxford University Press, Oxford

Zapf MK (2010) Social work and the environment: understanding people and place. Crit Soc Work 11(3):30–46

Part IV

Social Work Values and Principles

Social Work, Human Rights, and Ethics

15

Sharlene Nipperess

Contents

Introduction	290
Understanding Human Rights	291
The Origins of Human Rights	291
The International Human Rights Regime	292
Three Generations of Human Rights	293
Contesting Human Rights	295
Defining Human Rights	297
A Fundamental Principle of Social Work	299
A Stated Commitment	299
Contemporary Global Commitments to Human Rights	300
National and Regional Interpretations	302
Toward a Decolonised Ethics	303
Social Work and Human Rights	304
Social Work as a Human Rights Profession	304
Putting Human Rights into Practice	304
Social Work, Human Rights, and Transformative Practice	305
Toward a Critical Human Rights–Based Approach in Social Work	306
A Challenge for a Critical Human Rights–Based Approach in Social Work	307
Conclusion	307
References	308

Abstract

Social work has embraced the idea of human rights. They are clearly positioned as foundational to ethical practice with many scholars arguing that social work is a human rights profession. This chapter provides an overview of human rights and its relationship with ethical social work practice. It explores the idea of human rights in depth before moving onto an examination of the position of human rights as a foundational principle for ethical practice. It concludes with an examination

S. Nipperess (✉)
School of Global Urban and Social Studies, RMIT University, Melbourne, VIC, Australia
e-mail: Sharlene.nipperess@rmit.edu.au

© Springer Nature Singapore Pte Ltd. 2023
D. Hölscher et al. (eds.), *Social Work Theory and Ethics*, Social Work,
https://doi.org/10.1007/978-981-19-1015-9_15

of human rights in the scholarly social work literature and proposes a critical human rights–based approach to practice. This chapter argues that despite the conceptual challenges associated with the idea of human rights and the human rights discourse, human rights nonetheless provide a strong foundation for ethical practice that challenges the inequality, exploitation, domination, and oppression experienced by people and communities around the world.

Keywords

Social work · Human rights · Ethics · Codes of ethics · Principles · Ethical practice · Critical human rights–based practice

Introduction

There is a long history of social workers being committed to the idea of human rights (Healy 2008). This commitment is demonstrated in the formal policy statements of the international social work associations and is reflected in many social work codes of ethics around the world. While there is evidence that social workers have been guided by human rights principles long before the publication of these documents, these documents clearly put human rights on the social work agenda. Since human rights principles first appeared in these international documents, there has been a proliferation of literature on social work and human rights. Numerous books have been published on human rights–based practice, a plethora of journal articles explore human rights in relation to a wide variety of issues, including in relation to direct practice, research, and social work education, and a journal dedicated to human rights and social work was launched in 2016. Human rights are clearly seen to be fundamental to social work with many arguing that social work is first and foremost a human rights profession.

While human rights as a concept and as a basis for practice is complex, contradictory and critiqued both within and outside the profession (Ife 2012), there is a risk that our commitment to human rights may be more rhetorical than it is real (Nipperess 2013). Despite these challenges the central argument of this chapter is that a critical approach to human rights provides a strong ethical foundation for transformative practice. The chapter begins with a detailed exploration of human rights. It then discusses the position of human rights as fundamental to the ethical basis of social work. This is followed by an account of human rights in social work scholarship. The chapter ends with an overview of the core elements of a critical human rights–based approach to social work and concludes with a challenge to social work to reconstruct our commitment to human rights in light of the current ecological crisis.

Understanding Human Rights

Commitments to human rights abound in social work yet research demonstrates that even when practitioners are highly committed to the idea of human rights, they often find human rights complex, conceptually challenging, and difficult to define (Nipperess 2013). This has implications for practice. In particular, there is a risk that the human rights discourse remains rhetorical (Cemlyn 2008), despite it being a core ethical principle of social work, with practitioners committing to the idea of human rights but unable to translate this ethical commitment into practice. Understanding the complexity and contradictions inherent in human rights is therefore pivotal before it is possible to discuss how human rights can be embedded into our everyday practice (Nipperess 2016).

The Origins of Human Rights

The term 'human rights' is relatively modern but some scholars argue that the idea of human rights has a much longer history than the formation of the United Nations (UN) in 1945 and the declaration of the *Universal Declaration of Human Rights* (UDHR) (UN 1948) would suggest. The origins of human rights can be found in numerous historical documents, in various religions and philosophies, and in social movements throughout the ages. Wronka (2017), for example, suggests that ideas about human rights can be traced from antiquity and are found in many religious and spiritual traditions such as Islam, Judaism, Christianity, Confucianism, and Hinduism. Ishay (1997) also argues that ideas about human rights can be traced back to antiquity and cites the early philosophical writings of Plato, Aristotle, Cicero and Epictetus, the Enlightenment writings of Thomas Hobbes, John Locke, Jean-Jacques Rosseau, Mary Wollstoncraft, and Immanuel Kant through to the Industrial Age writings of Proudhon, Marx, Engels, and Bebel to name but a few. There are also a number of significant documents that have been developed over time that have contained ideas that would now be called human rights such as the *Magna Carta* (1215), the *English Bill of Rights* (1689), the *United States Declaration of Independence* (1776), and the *French Declaration of the Rights of Man and Citizen* (1789).

The contemporary concept of human rights did not appear though, until the Second World War and the recognition of the atrocities committed by the Nazis in Europe. The UN was established in 1945 to replace the ineffective League of Nations. The UN Human Rights Commission was established and soon after, on 10 December 1948, the UDHR was proclaimed. Since then the concept of human rights has become one of the most powerful and pervasive ideas in social and political life (Freeman 2011; Ife 2012).

The International Human Rights Regime

One of the chief aims of the establishment of the UN was "to reaffirm faith in fundamental human rights, in the dignity and worth of the human person, in the equal rights of men and women and nations large and small" (UN 1945). The UN Charter paved the way for the declaration of the UDHR in 1948, and along with the *International Covenant of Civil and Political Rights* (ICCPR) (1966) and the *International Covenant on Economic, Social and Cultural Rights* (ICESCR) (1966), it has become the cornerstone of the international human rights regime.

The UDHR was adopted on 10 December 1948 by the UN General Assembly. It was the result of several years of work led by Eleanor Roosevelt, who was the Chair of the UN Human Rights Commission. When finally the vote was taken, 48 states voted for its adoption, none voted against it and eight abstained, which included six Communist states, Saudi Arabia, and South Africa. The significance of the UDHR to the contemporary understanding of human rights cannot be overstated. In the 30 articles of this Declaration a range of civil, political, social, cultural, economic, and collective/solidarity rights are articulated. It is a powerful statement; one that still has the power to inspire despite the passage of more than 70 years.

The UDHR is not a list of laws, rather it was meant to be a statement of principles to which member states should aspire. It is therefore not legally binding. Recognising this, at the same time that the UDHR was adopted and proclaimed, the Human Rights Commission was asked to develop a covenant that *would* become legally binding, and after many years of drafting and redrafting, two covenants were declared: The ICCPR (1966) and the ICESCR (1966). These two covenants (and the two Optional Protocols) along with the UDHR comprise the International Bill of Rights. After enough countries had signed and ratified them the two covenants were entered into force in 1976.

The ICCPR focuses on civil and political rights such as the right to life, right to liberty, equality before the law, right to privacy, freedom of religion, freedom of expression, the right to vote, and so on. The ICESCR focuses on economic, social, and cultural rights including the right to work, to join trade unions, to social security, an adequate standard of living including adequate food, clothing, and housing, the right to education, the right to health, and so on. Both of the covenants prohibit discrimination.

Countries that have ratified either of these covenants have committed themselves to protect human rights and to take the necessary steps to give effect to the rights outlined in the covenants. Carey et al. (2010, p. 31) state:

> In becoming a state party to an international human rights treaty, each state party is committing itself not only to protecting human rights within its own territorial borders, but also to helping to work towards the elimination of violations of human rights, no matter where these might take place. It is this aspect, more than anything else, that truly makes human rights so revolutionary.

As of May 2022, 173 state parties have ratified the ICCPR and 171 state parties have ratified the ICESCR (OHCHR 2022).

In addition to the ICCPR and the ICESCR there are seven other core international human rights instruments. They are as follows:

- ICERD – International Convention on the Elimination of All Forms of Racial Discrimination (1965)
- CEDAW – Convention on the Elimination of All Forms of Discrimination Against Women (1979)
- CAT – Convention Against Torture and Other Cruel, Inhuman, or Degrading Treatment or Punishment (1984)
- CRC – Convention on the Rights of the Child (1989)
- ICMW – International Convention on the Protection of the Rights of All Migrant Workers and Members of Their Families (1990)
- CPED – International Convention for the Protection of All Persons from Enforced Disappearance (2006)
- CRPD – Convention on the Rights of Persons with Disabilities (2006)

There are many more conventions and declarations that are of particular significance to social workers including: The *Convention Relating to the Status of Refugees* (1951), The *Declaration on the Right to Development* (1986), The *Declaration on the Rights of Indigenous Peoples* (2007), and the *Declaration on Sexual Orientation and Gender Identity* (2008) to name a few.

A number of international organisations have been established which focus on human rights, in particular the UN, and a number of bodies located within it, including the Human Rights Council, the Security Council, and various human rights monitoring bodies such as the Committee on the Rights of Persons with Disabilities. There are a number of highly visible positions, including the High Commissioner for Human Rights – currently Michelle Bachelet – and the Secretary General of the United Nations – currently António Guterres – as well as other international structures such as the International Court of Justice and the International Criminal Court. There are also regional structures including the European Convention on Human Rights, the American Convention on Human Rights, and the African Charter on Human and Peoples' Rights. Finally, there are various international nongovernment organisations that play a major role in human rights, including Médecins Sans Frontières (Doctors Without Borders), Human Rights Watch, Amnesty International, and Oxfam (Carey et al. 2010).

Three Generations of Human Rights

The three generations of human rights is a useful framework for understanding human rights, although it is not without its conceptual difficulties (Frezzo 2011; Ife 2012). The three generations of human rights framework was developed by Karel Vasak, a Czech jurist, in 1979, which reflects the three tenets of the French Revolution: liberty, equality, and fraternity (Frezzo 2011). The three generations are: civil and political rights; economic, social, and cultural rights; and collective or solidarity rights.

The first generation of rights – *civil and political rights* – are also referred to as negative rights because these are the rights that require protecting by the state (Ife 2012). These 'liberty' rights include the right of self-determination, the inherent right to life, the right to vote, the right to peaceful assembly, the right to freedom of expression, equality before the law, and freedom from discrimination. No one should be subjected to torture or to cruel, inhuman, or degrading treatment or punishment, which includes being subjected to medical or scientific experimentation without consent, and no one should be held in slavery or subjected to arbitrary arrest or detention. These are individual rights and align closely to the ICCPR (1966), are protected largely through legal mechanisms and have their origin in the Enlightenment and eighteenth-century ideas of liberal political philosophy (Ife 2012). Non-government organisations, such as Amnesty International, are actively involved in campaigns to prevent violations of these first-generation rights and much of their work is involved in calling out abuses and working to protect these rights, often on behalf of oppressed groups.

The second generation of rights – *economic, social, and cultural rights* – align closely to the ICESCR (1966). These 'equality' rights are those that enable people to live their life fully. They include the right to work, the right of everyone to social security, an adequate standard of living (including adequate food, clothing, and housing), the right of everyone to the enjoyment of the highest attainable standard of physical and mental health, the right to education, and the right of everyone to take part in cultural life. These rights have their origin in the social democracy or socialism of the nineteenth and twentieth centuries, though the collective foundations are not as widely accepted as the more individualist ideas underpinning the first-generation rights (Ife 2012). There is considerably more disagreement about the extent of state obligation in relation to second-generation rights and as such are also referred to as positive rights because a much more active role has to be taken by the state to ensure that these rights are realised. These rights require more resources, are more contentious as a result, and the legal and constitutional mechanisms surrounding these rights are weaker (Ife 2012).

The third generation of rights – *collective or solidarity rights* – do not align with a UN covenant. These rights emerged in the late twentieth century and developed in response to the criticism that the human rights discourse was overly individualistic and not reflective of more collective cultures and values (Ife 2012). These 'fraternity' rights are about whole groups and communities and include the rights to a healthy environment, peace, development, and self-determination (Freeman 2011). These rights are only just starting to be codified in treaties and conventions, see, for example, the *Declaration on the Right to Development* (UN 1986).

The three generations of human rights framework is helpful in understanding that there has been a dominance of first-generation views of human rights. It also helps to explains the dominance of lawyers and the legal profession in relation to human rights theorising and practice. Ife (2012) suggests that the three generations framework has the potential to broaden the discussion of human rights from the individual to the collective, to be more holistic, recognising the interconnectedness and indivisibility of human rights, and it opens up the business of human rights to numerous other disciplines and practitioners.

Even though the three generation framework has been widely used and its utility as a pedagogical device is clear, there are also some conceptual difficulties with the approach. Frezzo (2011, pp. 5–6) argues that the three-generation framework runs the risk of atomisation (reinforcing false dichotomies between the different generations), Eurocentrism (overemphasising the influence of the European Enlightenment), and historical imprecision (ignoring the historical contexts of rights). The creation of the third generation has inadvertently had the effect of implying that the first two generations are not collective, so in effect they are pitted against each other – individual versus collective. In addition, the language of generations suggest that each generation succeeds the other but this is not the case and has the unintended effect of implying that the first-generation rights are more fundamental than the others. This prevents the more holistic approach to human rights that is required.

Other frameworks have been developed in order to account for these conceptual difficulties. For example, Jim Ife (2012) argues for a seven-way classification of human rights: survival rights, social rights, economic rights, civil and political rights, cultural rights, environmental rights, and spiritual rights. Another example is proffered by Frezzo (2011, p. 3) who argues for three "bundles" of rights:

> 'longevity' (consisting of the rights to food, housing, healthcare, and a clean ecosystem); the 'full development of the person' (consisting of the rights to a nurturing milieu, an education, occupational training, leisure activities, and identity choices), and 'peace' (consisting of protections from interstate warfare, civil strife, crimes against humanity, and the structural violence stemming from racism, classism, sexism, homophobia, and xenophobia).

Other frameworks have been developed to conceptualise human rights, but if we consider that human rights are constructed there can be no definitive framework of rights because rights change over time and in different contexts. Working with people to understand what framework makes sense in their own context is the aim of a discursive understanding of human rights (Ife 2012). This will be explored in the next section.

Contesting Human Rights

The UDHR, which underpins the International Bill of Rights, and informs so much of our contemporary understanding of human rights, is an extraordinary achievement but it is also contested. Given this, as Ife notes (2012, p. 16), it should not "be reified and seen as expressing a universal and unchanging truth". Likewise it is important to understand that the idea of human rights itself is also contested. Some of the key criticisms of contemporary human rights revolve around the dominance of Western, legal, patriarchal, and privileged voices that some argue dominate the human rights discourse (Tascón and Ife 2008; Ife 2012). Each of these critiques will be briefly explored in turn.

One of the main critiques of human rights is that the discourse is dominated by *Western* voices and that as a result, human rights are a culturally imperialist construct. This criticism centres on the competing claims of 'universalism' and 'cultural relativism'. A universalist position argues that human rights apply to everyone equally, whereas the cultural relativist position argues that human rights are relative and are dependent on culture and context. In particular, it is argued that human rights are a Western construct and are based on Western values and are therefore not applicable to non-Western cultures, which are said to be based on collectivist rather than individualist (Western) values. Some of the arguments that have been used to counter this critique include the assertion that even though Western Enlightenment ideas are extremely influential in the modern conception of human rights, it does not necessarily follow that there is no value in the concept because of this. Ife (2012, p. 8) argues that the task "is to loosen them from the shackles of Western modernity and to reconstruct them in more dynamic, inclusive and cross-cultural terms".

The cultural relativist position has also been challenged. The counterargument is that human rights violations have been justified in the name of culture. Cultural relativists have been accused of essentialising culture – of suggesting that cultures are homogenous and unchanging. Whereas the opposite is true, argues Donnelly (2003, p. 86), who suggests that cultures are in fact "complex, variable, multivocal, and above all contested. Rather than being static things 'cultures' are fluid complexes of intersubjective meanings and practices". An intersectional approach helps us to appreciate that all cultures are inherently diverse and experienced differently on dimensions such as class, gender, race/ethnicity, sexuality, (dis)ability, age, and so on.

Conceptualising the debate as a dichotomy is not particularly helpful (Ife 2012; Sewpaul 2016). Ife (2012) argues that a "naïve" universalism can lead to colonialism and a "naïve" relativism can lead to the uncritical acceptance of all behaviour on the basis of culture therefore:

> The challenge is to develop an approach to the universalism of human rights that, while emphasizing our common 'humanity' and seeking to articulate what that humanity means, at the same time acknowledges different cultural traditions as providing different contexts within which that humanity is constructed (Ife 2007, p. 94).

Hugman (2013) argues that an ethically pluralist position can help us move beyond these binaries. It encourages a dialogue but also recognises that limits must be set – an important point for social workers who are required to make decisions in practice.

The domination of *legal* voices is another key critique of human rights. Freeman (2011, p. 8) contends "the field of human rights has become a technical, legal discourse, and lawyers dominate it because they are the technical experts". This is beginning to change though. Other disciplines such as sociology, anthropology, and political science are engaging with the human rights discourse and there is literature emerging from a wide range of professions including social work. Ife (2010, p. 88) argues that "the notion that human rights need to be protected by law and that, for a right to be justiciable, it has to be defended through legal processes" is an important characteristic of the human rights discourse. It is clear that some rights are not easily justiciable such as the right to work, for example. The rights that are not as easily justiciable – many second- and third-generation rights – are at risk of being marginalised as a result. Nevertheless, the fact that many nation-states have agreed to become a party to these international treaties means that they have agreed to ensure that their domestic legislation complies with the treaty. For many social workers, this means they are required by law to address human rights in their practice and the laws themselves provide a powerful mechanism to both promote and protect human rights. However, it is important to go beyond conservative law and use legislation and the various conventions in radical ways (Ife 2016) acknowledging the limitations of a purely legal response.

The domination of *patriarchal* voices is another critique of human rights. The UDHR privileges the male voice – male pronouns are used throughout – and the male experience. It does not refer to women's experience of violence at the hands of men or the vulnerability women experience particularly in relation to economic discrimination. While the UDHR was proclaimed for everyone, Reichert (2011) argues that the rights declared reflect a male-dominated view of the world. Despite the criticisms, feminist scholars in the main have not rejected the idea of human rights. They have continued to challenge the patriarchal domination of human rights and in 1979 the *Convention on the Elimination of All Forms of Discrimination Against Women* was proclaimed, which has become one of the core international human rights instruments.

The domination of *privileged* voices critique challenges us to recognise that the human rights discourse needs to be more inclusive. In relation to the various UN conventions and declarations, Tascón and Ife (2008, p. 319) note "these statements of rights, laudable in their intention, are drafted and enacted by a small privileged group: politicians, diplomats, academics, and a handful of people from NGOs such as Amnesty International". The solution according to Tascón and Ife (2008) is to construct human rights "from below", that is more inclusively, taking into account everyday practices and lived experiences.

These critiques are dynamic and constantly evolving and demonstrate the complexity inherent in the human rights discourse. Constructing human rights more inclusively and moving to a position that recognises that human rights are both universal and contextual provides a useful way forward through these debates.

Defining Human Rights

There are considerable conceptual difficulties in defining human rights. By themselves the two concepts 'human' and 'rights' are contested but used together 'human rights' as a concept that is both abstract and challenging (Freeman 2011; Ife 2012). In the literature human rights are often defined as those rights that appear in the

UDHR (1948) and the numerous treaties that are derived from it. These rights are specific and usually relate to a value or principle such as freedom or in relation to a particular group, for example, women or refugees.

Human rights are usually considered to be universal, indivisible, inalienable, and inabrogable (Freeman 2011; Ife 2012). Human rights are considered to be *universal* because they are said to belong to everyone regardless of their class, gender, ethnicity, age, religion, ability, sexuality, and so on. The universality of human rights provides a powerful moral foundation for practice but it is also contested, particularly the risk that difference and diversity are not taken into account in human rights formulations. Human rights are considered to be *indivisible* because they are all equally important; there is no hierarchy of rights that suggests that one right is more fundamental than another. Human rights are considered to be *inalienable* because another person, organisation, or government cannot take them away, without good reason or due process (e.g., the right to liberty may be taken away if a person has committed a crime but only if due process is followed). It is also important to note that just because human rights are considered to be inalienable does not mean that they cannot be violated. Indeed, there is significant evidence documented by numerous human rights organisations of human rights violations around the world. Finally human rights are also considered *inabrogable*, which means that rights cannot be given up or traded off for some other privilege. While these four dimensions are commonly cited as core to human rights, Ife (2010, p. 86) makes the point that these four key dimensions represent "an ideal to be worked towards, rather than a description of reality".

According to Ife (2012), three traditions of human rights can be found in the literature: the natural rights tradition; the legal or state obligations tradition; and the constructed rights tradition. In the natural rights tradition human rights exist 'naturally', they are attached to people simply on the basis of being human and it is the philosophers and theologians who are concerned with identifying what these rights are. The legal or state obligations tradition suggests that human rights "exist to the extent that they are protected, guaranteed or realised as a result of state action" (Ife 2012, p. 15). In this tradition, lawyers and legislators have the main role in defining human rights and human rights practice. The constructed rights tradition avoids the suggestion that human rights objectively exist and argues instead that human rights are constructed by people, whether individuals or communities.

Although recognising aspects of all traditions, Ife (2012, p. 16) argues that a constructed or discursive understanding of human rights offers the most promise for social workers. Such an approach means that it is difficult to construct a definitive list of rights because to do so would privilege the author of the list whereas a discursive understanding suggests that human rights are defined and constructed together. As Ife notes (2010, p. 77), this approach raises some difficult questions about the universality and contextuality of human rights but he argues that "it also has more potential for spreading the responsibility for human rights throughout the society, and for giving people a sense of agency when it comes to human rights protection and realisation".

The following definition of human rights focuses on the idea of rights, rather than listing a number of specific rights:

> Human rights recognise the inherent value of each person, regardless of background, where we live, what we look like, what we think or what we believe. They are based on principles of dignity, equality and mutual respect, which are shared across cultures, religions and philosophies. They are about being treated fairly, treating others fairly and having the ability to make genuine choices in our daily lives. Respect for human rights is the cornerstone of strong communities in which everyone can make a contribution and feel included (Australian Human Rights Commission (AHRC) 2022).

This definition provides a good starting point to enter into dialogue with others on what should constitute a common or shared humanity.

A Fundamental Principle of Social Work

The social work profession has embraced human rights. Evidence of this can be found in a number of key global policy documents which cite human rights as a fundamental principle of social work. It can also be found in many national associations' codes of ethics as well as the literature of social work which has grown exponentially since the 1980s, with many scholars arguing that social work is a human rights profession.

A Stated Commitment

There is a long history of social workers being committed to human rights (Healy 2008; Staub-Bernasconi 2016). For example, as early as 1967, Elery Hamilton-Smith – one of the first national presidents of the Australian Association of Social Workers (AASW) – discussed the profession's commitment to human rights and its connection with social action in the national newsletter of the AASW (which later became the *National Bulletin*). In relation to the 1967 Referendum, in which the Australian people were asked to vote for changes to the Constitution that would allow the government to make laws in relation to Aboriginal and Torres Strait Islander peoples and to include Aboriginal and Torres Strait Islanders in the Census, he said:

> I trust that our profession will accept over the coming years the fullest possible share of responsibility for positive social action in regards to human rights. This means we should give a positive vote as individuals at the coming referendum; it means we should, as a corporate body, promote any action to remove discrimination or any other issue adversely affecting humans, such as capital punishment. (Hamilton-Smith 1967, p. 3)

There have been other social workers who have referred to human rights in their speeches or writings but the first major international policy statement to reference human rights was the *International Policy on Human Rights* which was adopted by the International Federation of Social Workers (IFSW) in 1980 (Alexander 1984). The policy was published in 1988 at the same time as the International Commission on Human Rights was established. The most recent version states in part:

> The social work profession accepts its share of responsibility for working to oppose and eliminate all violations of human rights. Social workers must exercise this responsibility in their practice with individuals, groups and communities, in their roles as agency or organisational representatives and as citizens of a nation and the world. (IFSW 1996)

This policy documents the following human rights: life, freedom and liberty, equality and nondiscrimination, justice, solidarity, social responsibility, peace and nonviolence, and the environment, and locates human rights within the realm of the UN and the various conventions and declarations derived from the UDHR (UN 1948). Since the publication of this policy, commitments to human rights have gradually been included in other key policy documents and in national codes of ethics. As a case in point there was no mention of human rights in the 1981 version of Australia's *Code of Ethics*, which is the earliest version on record. Not long after the IFSW published its policy on human rights, the AASW included a clause from the policy in the 1989 review of the *Code of Ethics* and since then subsequent reviews in 1999, 2010, and 2020 have retained and expanded on this ethical commitment (see AASW 2020).

Contemporary Global Commitments to Human Rights

The two main international social work organisations – the IFSW which was established in 1956 and the International Association of Schools of Social Work (IASSW) which has a much longer history being established in 1928 – have worked together to develop three global joint statements which make clear the professions' commitment to human rights: the *Global definition of social work* (2014) (hereafter referred to as the Global definition), the *Global social work statement of ethical principles* (2018) (hereafter referred to as the Global principles), and the *Global standards for social work education and training* (2020) (hereafter referred to as the Global standards). These global documents have been developed over successive iterations and are the result of significant consultation and agreement on the nature and purpose of social work, the ethical principles of social work, and how social work should be taught (Sewpaul and Henrickson 2019).

The Global definition was approved by the IFSW General Meeting and the IASSW General Assembly in July 2014. It states:

> Social work is a practice-based profession and an academic discipline that promotes social change and development, social cohesion and the empowerment and liberation of people. Principles of social justice, human rights, collective responsibility and respect for diversities are central to social work. Underpinned by theories of social work, social sciences, humanities and Indigenous knowledges, social work engages people and structures to address life

challenges and enhance wellbeing. The above definition may be amplified at national and/or regional levels.

This definition was developed after extensive consultation and represented a revision of the earlier 1982 and 2000 definitions. Sewpaul and Henrickson (2019, p. 1470) argue that the revised Global definition recognises "that social work has become far more than a liberal humanist profession whose centre was located in a European-North American axis. Its practice, teaching and research are informed by a global array of philosophical positions and cultural values".

The principle of human rights is clearly proclaimed as being central to social work and this declaration is expanded on in the accompanying explanatory statements:

> Advocating and upholding human rights and social justice is the motivation and justification for social work. The social work profession recognizes that human rights need to coexist alongside collective responsibility. The idea of collective responsibility highlights the reality that individual human rights can only be realized on a day-to-day basis if people take responsibility for each other and the environment, and the importance of creating reciprocal relationships within communities. Therefore a major focus of social work is to advocate for the rights of people at all levels, and to facilitate outcomes where people take responsibility for each other's wellbeing, realise and respect the inter-dependence among people and between people and the environment. (IFSW and IASSW 2014)

Notably the Global definition suggests that this is but a starting point and that it may be amplified at the local level.

The Global principles statement was jointly agreed to by the IFSW and IASSW at their General Meetings in 2018. It too was based on an earlier (2004) iteration and again was based on significant consultation and "embraces a decolonization agenda" (Sewpaul and Henrickson 2019, p. 1479). Of the nine core principles, the second is promoting human rights:

> Social workers embrace and promote the fundamental and inalienable rights of all human beings. Social work is based on respect for the inherent worth, dignity of all people and the individual and social/civil rights that follow from this. Social workers often work with people to find an appropriate balance between competing human rights. (IFSW and IASSW 2018)

The IAASW (2020) subsequently endorsed a longer version of this statement and expanded on this principle with six specific clauses which provide considerably more detail. These clauses explore social workers commitment to embracing, respecting, promoting, and defending all human rights as reflected in the human rights instruments, recognising the complex role of culture and human rights, understanding that human rights coexist alongside collective responsibility, the importance of information provision to enable access of human rights, and recognition of the state as a key actor in the defence, promotion, and fulfilment of human rights. Sewpaul and Henrickson (2019, p. 1477) argue that the Global principles statement:

disarticulates human dignity and human rights from their constraints of autonomy and independence, as constructed by liberal theory, to recognise the inter-subjectivity and interdependence of human dignity and human rights; it reconceptualizes 'person' beyond the individual and problematizes principles such as self-determination and confidentiality to reflect diverse contextual realities.

The Global principles also make clear the foundational position on human rights and the accompanying explanatory material acknowledges the contested nature of the principles that are listed. The Global principles move beyond a simplistic understanding of human rights that is evident in much of the literature to a much more nuanced approach that engages with the complexity and contradictions inherent in the discourse.

The final global document jointly agreed to by the IFSW and IASSW is the Global standards. This too represents the updating of an earlier document (2004), is based on significant consultation, and reflects the changes that occurred in the Global definition and the Global principles. Like the two previous documents, the Global standards (IAASW 2020) clearly states the profession's commitment to human rights. This includes the commitment that "schools should always *aspire* to develop curricular that ... are based on human rights principles and the pursuit of justice" (2020, p. 11) (italics in original). In relation to the context of social work, core curricula must include knowledge of human rights (2020, p. 12) and in relation to the practice of social work, core curricula must prepare students to critically analyse how social policies and programs promote or violate human rights and use human rights–based advocacy alongside peace building and nonviolent activism as key intervention methods (2020, p. 13). In relation to equity and diversity, schools of social work must ensure that programs have clear learning objectives in relation to respect for cultural and ethnic diversity, gender equity, and human rights (2020, p. 19) and aspire toward the "recognition and development of Indigenous or locally specific social work education and practice" within a human rights context (2020, p. 19). Finally, the document states that all schools must "prepare students to be able to apply human rights principles (as articulated in the International Bill of Rights and core international human rights treaties) to frame their understanding of how current social issues affect social, economic and environmental justice" (2020, p. 19). Again this document, reflecting the position of human rights in the other two documents, clearly identifies the importance of human rights to social work and moves beyond rhetorical commitments to human rights to specific guidance in relation to how human rights should be included in the social work curriculum.

National and Regional Interpretations

Sewpaul and Henrickson (2019, p. 1479) argue that "social work, as a profession and an academic discipline, must be in agreement about some core set of ethical principles that unite us across countries and international associations". At the same time, they also acknowledge "that no set of principles, let alone a code of ethics or code of conduct, can of itself comprehend every context or make every social worker an ethical practitioner. Social work education, research and practice are fraught with ethical complexities, and there are no formulaic answers to these" (2019, p. 1479). As such both the Global definition and the Global principles recognise that they may need to be 'amplified' at national or regional levels. This encourages a localised approach which takes into account differing cultural contexts.

A number of national associations of social work have committed to promoting and protecting human rights. In research that was conducted in 2014 most codes of ethics that were uploaded on the IFSW website at the time the study was conducted mentioned human rights, nearly half-referenced the UDHR, with only five not making any reference to human rights in their code (Keeney et al. 2014). In later research, Keeney et al. (2019, p. 13) focused their research on five national social work organisations that did not explicitly reference the UDHR and suggested that "explicitly referencing the UDHR in social work codes of ethics is one way for the international social work community to align globally and clearly assert that social work is, at its core, a human rights profession". Since both of these studies were completed the number of IFSW national social work organisation members has increased from 90 to 135 and of this number the IFSW has provided links to the codes of ethics of 31 national social work organisations an increase of nine codes of ethics since the two studies were completed. The limitation of both these studies, as the authors note, is that only the codes of ethics on the IFSW website were examined which is only one indication of whether human rights is supported by the national organisation or not (e.g., human rights could appear in other policy and ethics statements, websites, and so on). Nevertheless, it would appear increasing numbers of national social work associations are incorporating the principles of human rights into their own codes (Reichert 2016) indicating the primacy of human rights to social work at the national and international level.

Toward a Decolonised Ethics

These three documents clearly articulate the social work profession's commitment to human rights. Human rights are fundamental principles that guide social work practice, education, and research. The commitment to human rights that appears in these documents references the UDHR and the conventions and treaties that are derived from the UDHR. Unlike earlier iterations of these documents which present human rights unproblematically and in taken-for-granted ways, these latest iterations draw attention to the contested nature of human rights and, in relation to the Global standards, highlight the need for social work training to include knowledge on human rights, which ensures that the complexity and contradictions inherent in human rights is well understood by students in preparation for practice. These documents go some way toward a decolonised ethics. However, as Weaver (2016, p. 136) notes "it is unclear, however, how these words may or may not translate into meaningful action". This is a key challenge for social work – how to ensure that human rights is moved from the rhetorical shelf of global statements to the reality of the complex world of social work practice, research, and education (Cemlyn 2008; Nipperess 2013). The next section will take this challenge up and explore how human rights have been translated into practice.

Social Work and Human Rights

While there is evidence that social workers have been committed to human rights long before such commitments appeared in our national and international policy documents, it is only relatively recently that social work scholars have examined what such a commitment to human rights actually means in relation social work practice, research, and education.

Social Work as a Human Rights Profession

The recent Global statements make it very clear that human rights are at the heart of the profession. Sewpaul and Kreitzer (2021, p. 12) go further and argue that "from its inception social work has been regarded as a human rights profession". This claim is echoed by a number of scholars (e.g., Healy 2008; Ife 2012; Staub-Bernasconi 2016; van Wormer and Link 2018; Mapp et al. 2019). What this claim means, according to Banks (2021, p. 145), is that:

> social work exists because of a societal commitment to enhancing and protecting the rights of all people to a dignified life, protection from discrimination, and provision of adequate physical and social resources. Furthermore, social work is conducted according to human rights principles – treating people with dignity and respect, promoting equality and so on.

This is a perspective that goes beyond a legalistic top-down approach of human rights–based practice and draws on key values and principles including dignity, respect, participation, accountability, nondiscrimination, and equality.

Putting Human Rights into Practice

Since the late 1980s, accompanying the policy declarations at the global level, the social work literature on social work and human rights has gradually increased. The commitment to human rights is evident in the literature and a number of human rights–based approaches to social work have been developed (e.g., Connolly and Ward 2008; Lundy 2011; Reichert 2011; Ife 2012; Briskman 2014; Androff 2015; Berthold 2015; Gatenio Gabel 2016; Maschi 2016; Nipperess 2016; Wronka 2017; Mapp 2020). Ife (2010, pp. 210–211) makes the point though:

> There can never be simple 'how to do it' prescriptions about human rights practice... Rather than seeing the human rights worker as a technician, following a set of prescribed

procedures, it is more useful to think of the human rights worker as a street-level intellectual who will bring a wide range of understandings, conceptual tools, frames of reference and resources to be applied in a particular and unique way.

Nevertheless, there is substantial agreement that a human rights–based social work, particularly that which is informed by a critical perspective, is valuable for transformative practice (e.g., Turbett 2014).

Despite the significant increase in literature exploring human rights in social work practice, there is rather less evidence of how human rights have been put in practice. Cubillos-Vega (2017) conducted a review of the literature from 2000–2015 and concluded that while the scholarly output on human rights and social work has increased, much of what has been published is theoretical in nature. This is beginning to be addressed with an increasing number of empirical studies conducted in the last decade which explore how human rights are being explored in social work practice, research, and education (e.g., Martínez Herrero and Charnley 2019; Nipperess 2013; McPherson 2015; Gatenio Gabel and Mapp 2020; McPherson and Abell 2020; Reynaert et al. 2022). These studies help to move human rights from "the rhetorical shelf" of commitments within global statements (Cemlyn 2008, p. 237) and show how human rights can be translated into everyday practice, research, and education.

Human rights practice can be deductive or inductive (Ife 2012). Deductive approaches start with the key human rights statements and derive practice from them. For example, disability workers might start with the CRPD and build practice around the articles identified in the Convention. The critiques of human rights highlight some of the challenges with this approach. However, as Ife (2012) notes, these documents carry a strong moral force, they can be used with service users to engage in conversations about human rights and many of the rights outlined in these statements are legally enforceable. Inductive approaches on the other hand start "with the grounded and 'real' world of practice, identifying issues, needs or problems, and then seeing what human rights issues lie behind them" (Ife 2012, p. 211). Effectively social workers will use both approaches in practice.

Social Work, Human Rights, and Transformative Practice

The human rights discourse begins with the idea that everyone has human rights. However, the reality is that many do not (Offord et al. 2021; Zembylas 2021). There are examples all over the world of people's rights being trampled, with neoliberalism and continuing forms of imperialism implicated (Sewpaul 2016), resulting in vast numbers of the world's population experiencing inequality, exploitation, domination, and oppression. The world is facing unprecedented environmental challenges with dire impacts on the human and more-than-human world. Arguably, a human rights–based approach to social work has never been more important. This chapter argues that a human rights approach which engages with the critiques, challenges and complexity of human rights, provides a strong basis for transformative practice.

Toward a Critical Human Rights–Based Approach in Social Work

A critical human rights–based approach in social work is underpinned by critical social work; it is committed to the concept of human rights; it is enacted across the various domains of practice; and it is performed at the personal, cultural, and structural levels (Nipperess 2013). Critical social work is the foundation of this approach and from this perspective, drawing on a range of critical theories including green theories, postcolonialism, and feminism, a critical approach engages with the critiques and complexities inherent in human rights and engages in discussion and debate to reconstruct human rights from the bottom-up. A commitment to human rights is the ethical standpoint of this approach. It is informed by a critical understanding of the UDHR and the commitments to human rights that appear in the Global statements. Working across the domains of social work is another key element of this approach. This means human rights practice can occur in all domains of practice including: work with individuals; work with families and partnerships; groupwork; community work; social policy practice; research and evaluation; organisational practice, management, and leadership; and education and training (Chenoweth and McAuliffe 2020). Finally, a critical human rights–based approach to social work requires practice at the personal, cultural, and structural levels.

A critical human rights–based approach in social work begins with the lived experiences of the people with whom we work, whether it be service users or students. It also invites social workers to critically reflect on their own lived experiences and to co-construct and codesign practice with service users and students with principles of human rights at the centre of the relationship (Nipperess 2016). A critical ethics of care offers much to human rights–based practice (Nipperess 2018). Practice which is informed by a critical ethics of care acknowledges the importance of human rights but does so alongside an equal focus on care and the relationship. It also emphasises the importance of intersectionality, critically reflective practice, and self-care, which is not to remove organisations and governments responsibilities to provide safe working environments. However, it acknowledges that social work often means caring in uncaring and downright dangerous places. A critical human rights–based practice requires exploring the ethical, legal, historical, political, organisational, theoretical, and practice contexts of practice (Nipperess 2016). Ife (2012, p. 305) argues that:

> Human rights are seldom given; they have to be seized. The struggle, inevitably, will continue. Human rights are not simply defined; they have to be struggled for and are hard won. Then once they are won, there is a continuing struggle to protect them. The human rights struggle is one that will never end, and human rights will always be a work in progress. However, defining social work as a human rights profession locates social work practice firmly within that ongoing struggle to assert the values of a shared humanity.

This framework avoids a narrow prescription of 'how to do' human rights–based social work. Rather, it provides general principles to consider, recognising that a critical human rights–based approach in social work is contextual.

A Challenge for a Critical Human Rights–Based Approach in Social Work

In recent years, the critical posthumanities have begun to critique the moral superiority of humanism and the human exceptionalism that underpins the human rights discourse (Ife 2016; Braidotti 2019; Bozalek and Pease 2020; Woods and Hölscher 2020; Zembylas 2021). A critical human rights perspective needs to engage with these debates especially that which is posed by post-anthropocentrism. Certainly there are human rights imperatives related to climate change and the ecological crisis which we are experiencing (Boddy and Nipperess 2022). Is it possible though to be committed to human rights while at the same time shifting to a more ecocentric perspective that values the entire ecosystem – human, nonhuman, and more than human? Jim Ife (2016) argues that while "human rights represent a very powerful narrative of a just and fair world for humans", it does not currently do the same for nonhumans or the more-than-human world. He concludes that "if the idea of human rights is to retain its potency, it will need a reconfigured discourse, to take account of these challenges" (2016, p. 8). Social workers are in a good position to do this – to take into account these challenges and engage with the posthumanist and post-anthropocentric critiques in order to reconstruct human rights (Zembylas 2021) to protect and promote not only the rights of humans but also nonhumans and the more-than-human world.

Conclusion

While the term human rights is relatively recent, the idea of human rights has a much longer history that can be traced back to antiquity. It owes its intellectual origins to religious humanism, stoicism, liberalism, and indeed socialism. Ideas of human rights can be found in documents as diverse as the Code of Hammurabi, the Magna Carta, and the French Declaration of the Rights of Man and Citizen. It was not until 1945 though, with the establishment of the UN and the subsequent proclamation of the UDHR on 10 December 1948, that it emerged as one of the most powerful and pervasive social and political concepts. Human rights are not without critique, but despite the complex and contested nature of human rights they provide a powerful moral basis for practice in social work.

Respecting the inherent dignity of all the people with whom we work is the cornerstone of human rights–based practice. Human rights practice requires us to work in ways that are participatory, accountable, nondiscriminatory, and empowering. It also means recognising that human rights are protected by the law, though there are limitations to envisaging human rights practice in a purely legalistic way, as there are numerous human rights that are not protected well, if at all, by legislation. A critical human rights approach to social work engages with the critiques, contestations, and complexity of human rights and, in light of the ecological crisis that the world faces, is challenged to reconstruct human rights in a way that recognises and protects as well as promotes the rights of humans, nonhumans, and the more-than-human world.

References

Alexander C (1984) Social work in the 80s: issues and strategies. https://www.ifsw.org/about-ifsw/archives/. Accessed 1 May 2022

Androff D (2015) Practicing rights: human rights-based approaches to social work practice. Routledge, London

Australian Association of Social Workers (AASW) (2020) Code of ethics. https://www.aasw.asn.au/practitioner-resources/code-of-ethics. Accessed 1 May 2022

Australian Human Rights Commission (AHRC) (2022) What are human rights? https://humanrights.gov.au/about/what-are-human-rights. Accessed 1 May 2022

Banks S (2021) Ethics and values in social work, 5th edn. Red Globe Press, London

Berthold S (2015) Human rights-based approaches to clinical social work. Springer, Cham

Boddy J, Nipperess S (2022) Green social work and social justice. In: Webb S (ed) Routledge handbook on critical and radical social work, 2nd edn. Routledge, London. (in press)

Bozalek V, Pease B (2020) Towards post-anthropocentric social work. In: Bozalek V, Pease B (eds) Post-anthropocentric social work: critical post-human and new materialist perspectives. Routledge, London, pp 1–15

Braidotti R (2019) A theoretical framework for the critical posthumanities. Theory Cult Soc 36(6):31–61

Briskman L (2014) Social work with Indigenous communities: a human rights approach, 2nd edn. The Federation Press, Annandale

Carey S, Gibney M, Poe S (2010) The politics of human rights: the quest for dignity. Cambridge University Press, Cambridge

Cemlyn S (2008) Human rights practice: possibilities and pitfalls for developing emancipatory social work. Ethics Soc Welfare 2(3):222–242

Chenoweth L, McAuliffe D (2020) The road to social work and human services practice, 6th edn. Cengage, South Melbourne

Connolly M, Ward T (2008) Morals, rights and practice in the human services. Jessica Kingsley, London

Cubillos-Vega C (2017) Análisis de la producción científica sobre derechos humanos en trabajo social: Perspectiva internacional (2000–2015) [Analysis of the scientific output on human rights within social work: an international perspective]. Revista Española De Documentación Científica 40(1):1–10. https://doi.org/10.3989/redc.2017.1.1387

Donnelly J (2003) Universal human rights in theory and practice, 2nd edn. Cornell University Press, Ithaca

Freeman M (2011) Human rights: an interdisciplinary approach, 2nd edn. Polity Press, Cambridge

Frezzo M (2011) Sociology and human rights education: beyond the three generations? Societies Without Bord 6(2):3–22. https://scholarlycommons.law.case.edu/swb/vol6/iss2/1/

Gatenio GS (2016) A rights-based approach to social policy analysis. Springer, Cham

Gatenio Gabel S, Mapp S (2020) Teaching human rights and social justice in social work education. J Soc Work Educ 56(3):428–441

Hamilton-Smith E (1967) From the President AASW Federal Newsletter 3:3

Healy L (2008) Exploring the history of social work as a human rights profession. Int Soc Work 51(6):735–748. https://doi.org/10.1177/0020872808095247

Hugman R (2013) Culture, values and ethics in social work: embracing diversity. Routledge, Abingdon

IAASW (2020) Global social work statement of ethical principles. https://www.iassw-aiets.org/archive/ethics-in-social-work-statement-of-principles/. Accessed 1 May 2022

Ife J (2007) Cultural relativism and community activism. In: Reichert E (ed) Challenges in human rights: a social work perspective. Colombia University Press, New York, pp 76–96

Ife J (2010) Human rights from below: achieving rights through community development. Cambridge University Press, Port Melbourne

Ife J (2012) Human rights and social work: towards rights-based practice, 3rd edn. Cambridge University Press, Port Melbourne

Ife J (2016) Human rights and social work: beyond conservative law. J Hum Rights Soc Work 1(3): 3–8. https://doi.org/10.1007/s41134-016-0001-4

IFSW, IASSW (2014) Global definition of social work. https://www.ifsw.org/what-is-social-work/global-definition-of-social-work/. Accessed 1 May 2022

IFSW, IASSW (2018) Global social work statement of ethical principles. https://www.ifsw.org/global-social-work-statement-of-ethical-principles/. Accessed 1 May 2022

International Association of Schools of Social Work (IAASW) (2020) Global standards for social work education and training. https://www.iassw-aiets.org/featured/5867-announcement-of-the-updated-global-standards-for-social-work-education-and-training-the-new-chapter-in-social-work-profession/. Accessed 1 May 2022

International Federation of Social Workers (IFSW) (1996) International policy on human rights. https://www.ifsw.org/human-rights-policy/#:~:text=Policy%20statement&text=The%20social%20work%20profession%2C%20through,survival%20of%20the%20human%20race. Accessed 1 May 2022

Ishay M (ed) (1997) The human rights reader: major political essays, speeches and documents from the Bible to the present. Routledge, New York

Keeney AJ, Smart AM, Richards R, Harrison S, Carrillo M, Valentine D (2014) Human rights and social work codes of ethics: an international analysis. J Soc Welfare Human Rights 2(2):1–16

Keeney AJ, Albrithen A, Harrison S, Briskman L, Androff D (2019) International analysis of human rights and social work ethics. In: Marson SM, JRE MK (eds) The Routledge handbook of social work ethics and values. Routledge, Abingdon, pp 7–14

Lundy C (2011) Social work, social justice and human rights: a structural approach to practice. University of Toronto Press, Ontario

Mapp S (2020) Human rights and social justice in a global perspective: an introduction to international social work, 3rd edn. Oxford University Press, New York

Mapp S, McPherson J, Androff D, Gatenio Gabel S (2019) Social work is a human rights profession. Soc Work 64(3):259–269. https://doi.org/10.1093/sw/swz023

Martínez MI, Charnley H (2019) Human rights and social justice in social work education: a critical realist comparative study of England and Spain. Eur J Soc Work 22(2):225–237

Maschi T (2016) Applying a human rights approach to social work research and evaluation: a rights research manifesto. Springer, Cham

McPherson J (2015) Human rights practice in social work: a rights-based framework and two new measures. Dissertation, Florida State University

McPherson J, Abell N (2020) Measuring rights-based practice: introducing the human rights methods in social work scales. Br J Soc Work 50:222–242

Nipperess S (2013) Human rights: a challenge to critical social work practice and education. Dissertation, Curtin University of Technology

Nipperess S (2016) Towards a critical human rights-based approach to social work practice. In: Pease B, Goldingay S, Hosken N, Nipperess S (eds) Doing critical social work: transformative practices for social justice. Routledge, Abingdon, pp 73–88

Nipperess S (2018) Caring in an uncaring context: towards a critical ethics of care in social with people seeking asylum. In: Pease B, Vreugdenhil A, Stanford S (eds) Critical ethics of care in social work: transforming the politics and practices of caring. Routledge, Abingdon, pp 105–115

Office of the High Commissioner for Human Rights (OHCHR) (2022) Status of ratification: interactive dashboard. https://indicators.ohchr.org/. Accessed 1 May 2022

Offord B, Fleay C, Hartley L, Woldeyes YG, Chan D (2021) The pedagogies of human rights: in truthfulness, what should be done? In: Offord B, Fleay C, Hartley L, Woldeyes YG, Chan D (eds) Activating cultural and social change: the pedagogies of human rights. Routledge, Abingdon, pp 1–12

Reichert E (2011) Social work and human rights: a foundation for policy and practice, 2nd edn. Columbia University Press, New York

Reichert E (2016) Human rights and ethics. In: Hugman R, Carter J (eds) Rethinking values and ethics in social work. Palgrave, London, pp 16–32

Reynaert D, Nachtergaele S, De Stercke N, Gobeyn H, Roose R (2022) Social work as a human rights profession: an action framework. Br J Soc Work 52:928–945. https://doi.org/10.1093/bjsw/bcab083

Sewpaul V (2016) The west and the rest divide: human rights, culture and social work. J Hum Rights Soc Work 1:30–39

Sewpaul V, Henrickson M (2019) The (r)evolution and decolonization of social work ethics: the global social work statement of ethical principles. Int Soc Work 62(6):1469–1481

Sewpaul V, Kreitzer L (2021) Culture, human rights and social work: colonialism, eurocentrism and Afrocentricity. In: Sewpaul V, Kreitzer L, Raniga T (eds) The tensions between culture and human rights: emancipatory social work and Afrocentricity in a global world. University of Calgary Press, Calgary, pp 1–24

Staub-Bernasconi S (2016) Social work and human rights: linking two traditions of human rights in social work. J Hum Rights Soc Work 1:40–49. https://doi.org/10.1007/s41134-016-0005-0

Tascón S, Ife J (2008) Human rights and critical whiteness: whose humanity? Int J Human Rights 12(3):307–327. https://doi.org/10.1080/13642980802069609

Turbett C (2014) Doing radical social work. Palgrave Macmillan, London

UN (1945) United Nations charter. https://www.un.org/en/about-us/un-charter. Accessed May 1 2022

UN (1948) Universal declaration of human rights. https://www.un.org/en/about-us/universal-declaration-of-human-rights. Accessed 1 May 2022

UN (1966) International covenant on economic, social and cultural rights. https://www.ohchr.org/en/instruments-mechanisms/instruments/international-covenant-economic-social-and-cultural-rights. Accessed 1 May 2022

United Nations (UN) (1966) International covenant on civil and political rights. https://www.ohchr.org/en/instruments-mechanisms/instruments/international-covenant-civil-and-political-rights. Accessed 1 May 2022

United Nations (UN) (1986) Declaration on the right to development. https://www.ohchr.org/en/instruments-mechanisms/instruments/declaration-right-development. Accessed 1 May 2022

Van Wormer K, Link RJ (2018) Social work and social welfare: a human rights foundation. Oxford University Press, New York

Weaver H (2016) Ethics and settler societies: reflections on social work and Indigenous peoples. In: Hugman R, Carter J (eds) Rethinking values and ethics in social work. Palgrave, London, pp 129–145

Woods G, Hölscher D (2020) Return of the post-human: developing Indigenist perspectives of social work at a time of environmental crisis. In: Bozalek V, Pease B (eds) Post-anthropocentric social work: critical post-human and new materialist perspectives. Routledge, Abingdon, pp 121–133

Wronka J (2017) Human rights and social justice: social action and service for the helping and health professions, 2nd edn. SAGE, Thousand Oaks

Zembylas M (2021) A posthumanist critique of human rights: towards an agonistic account of rights in inclusive education. In: Thomas MKE, Heng L, Walker P (eds) Inclusive education is a right, right? Brill, Rotterdam, pp 9–20

Social Justice and Social Work

16

Neil Thompson and Paul Stepney

Contents

Introduction	312
Social Justice in International Codes of Ethics	313
Competing Definitions and Theories of Social Justice	314
Social Justice and the Development of the Welfare State	316
Social Movements and Social Justice	319
Feminist Ideas on Social Justice	320
Social Justice in the Global South	320
Conceptualizing Social Justice: The Practitioner Speaks	321
Power and Empowerment	323
PCS Analysis	325
Critically Reflective Practice	327
Conclusion	328
References	329

Abstract

Social work has long been associated with social justice. In this chapter we explore the relationship between the two with a view to clarifying the importance of social justice as part of the social work value base. We achieve this by first reviewing the place of social justice in codes of ethics and other such value statements before considering the contested status of social justice as a theoretical concept. This is followed by an exploration of the part a commitment to social justice has played in the development of the welfare state. Next comes an examination of the role of social movements in promoting social justice. This leads into a discussion of the significance of power and empowerment as key

N. Thompson (✉)
Avenue Consulting and visiting professor at the Open University, Wrexham, UK
e-mail: neil@avenueconsulting.co.uk

P. Stepney
Tampere University, Tampere, Finland
e-mail: paul.stepney@tuni.fi

© Springer Nature Singapore Pte Ltd. 2023
D. Hölscher et al. (eds.), *Social Work Theory and Ethics*, Social Work,
https://doi.org/10.1007/978-981-19-1015-9_16

concepts that can be used to make connections between social justice at a philosophical level and its role as a guide to ethical, effective and safe practice. This sets the scene for a discussion of the potential use of PCS analysis as an analytical tool for making sense of the discrimination and oppression that stand in the way of social justice and, indeed, for making sense of social justice itself. Finally, the importance of a critically reflective approach to practice is highlighted. Without critically reflective practice there is a danger that a commitment to social justice remains at a rhetorical level and is not reflected in actual practice, making such practice not only hypocritical, but also potentially dangerous.

Keywords

Social justice · Social policy · Social work · Power · Empowerment · PCS analysis · Critically reflective practice

Social inequality within rich countries persists because of a continued belief in the tenets of injustice. (Danny Dorling 2015, p. 15)

To be truly radical is to make hope possible, rather than despair. (Raymond Williams 1989, p. 118)

Introduction

One Saturday morning some years ago both authors, who were at the time part-time Open University tutors for the undergraduate course *Social Problems and Social Welfare,* attended a day school in Manchester. Unfortunately, the main speaker for the morning's programme was delayed on a train, and the 150 students in the lecture hall soon realized there was a problem and became restless. One tutor came to the rescue by coming to the rostrum and announcing some enforced changes to the scheduled program. The main lecture would now be put back to the afternoon, and he asked students to go into their tutor groups during the morning for an exercise on social justice before coming back together for a plenary session at midday. The assembled group of tutors hurriedly conferred and agreed to ask students to identify social problems and injustices from their own work or life experience and feed back the implications for social welfare at the plenary. At the end of the day school when students were asked to give feedback they highlighted the morning exercise on social justice as the most rewarding part of the day. Several students said it had helped to make the course themes and underpinning theory 'come alive' by revealing the connections between real-life social problems, issues of justice and social welfare.

The day school exercise not only offered a crucial lesson on how adults learn best, learning by enquiry addressing issues felt to be real and compelling – andragogy, rather than pedagogy – but captured something rather important about the role of social justice in social work. As we shall discover, social justice is a contested concept and one that has a long history of being referred to rather imprecisely and inconsistently in our practice. In this chapter we want to critically examine this concept and explain how the principle and goal of social justice are manifested in social work practice. In doing so, we will draw on Thompson's (2018) PCS analysis, explore the significance of power and empowerment and propose critically reflective practice as a foundation for social interventions that are consistent with a commitment to social justice.

There is clearly a close relationship between social problems and social justice within the context of social welfare. In other words, they are inextricably connected and exert considerable influence on each other. Neil Thompson (2017) is no doubt correct in saying that: "social problems reinforce social injustices and social injustices reinforce social problems" (p. 56). These are the practice realities that social workers frequently face every day and reflect a central dilemma that is as relevant today as when it was first posed by Geoffrey Pearson over 45 years ago: "whether social work is an agency which enlarges human freedom or restricts it, and whether it is relevant to the problems it confronts or irrelevant" (Pearson 1975, cited in Thompson and Stepney 2018, p. 27). In addition, as we shall note later, there is also the possibility of ill-informed or unduly narrow approaches to practice actually doing more harm than good (e.g., by failing to recognize – or address – discrimination in people's lives and thereby reinforce its insidious effects).

Although it is clearly difficult to resolve such dilemmas, one response has been to develop codes of ethics that set out the profession's fundamental guiding principles for practice. While such codes are not in any way definitive responses to the intellectual challenges involved in defining and promoting social justice, they do give us a useful starting point to engage with the issues.

Social Justice in International Codes of Ethics

Principles of social justice are enshrined in social work's international Code of Ethics. The global definition of social work, agreed by the IASSW General Assembly and IFSW General Meeting in July 2014 states that:

> Social work is a practice-based profession and an academic discipline that promotes social change and development, social cohesion, and the empowerment and liberation of people. Principles of social justice, human rights, collective responsibility and respect for diversities are central to social work. Underpinned by theories of social work, social sciences, humanities and indigenous knowledges, social work engages people and structures to address life challenges and enhance well-being. (IFSW 2014)

The above definition has been adopted with minor adaptation by many National Associations and now informs national codes in the UK, the USA, Canada, Australia and in many European countries. They all share a common narrative that advocates for social change and social justice, encompassing a crucial role for social work in driving this forward (Hugman 2005; Reisch 2019). However, although it would be difficult to find a practitioner who does not subscribe to this imperative, the voice of the practitioner has nonetheless rarely been heard (Reisch 2011). We suspect that this is because the social justice principle is sometimes viewed as somewhat controversial and political, and in the USA the term may be conflated with socialism or even communism (Morgaine 2014). Further, the goal of social justice alongside a commitment to equality, empowerment and inclusion may be viewed as rather general, contextual and policy driven – something that offers a good ethical framework, but somewhat distant from everyday practice realities. This inevitably creates a degree of ambiguity and inconsistency about how such principles should be interpreted and applied (Reisch 2008). This raises the question of whether social justice can be defined more precisely, particularly in ways that can help shape frontline practice.

Competing Definitions and Theories of Social Justice

Defining social justice has proved to be a challenge for theorists, policy makers and practitioners alike. Social justice has become a popular yet contested term that has attracted adherents from across the theoretical and ideological spectrum, thus making it a rather slippery concept capable of different interpretations (Reisch 2019). In the USA the National Association of Social Workers (NASW) Code of Ethics, mindful of earlier criticism about institutional racism and discrimination against women, defined social justice as "an ideal condition in which all members of society have the same basic rights, protections, obligations and social benefits" (NASW 2012, p. 242). This confirms the development of a more rights-based approach to empowerment and social justice (Stepney 2019a) and the rejection of explanations derived from individual and/or cultural pathology.

Similar debates have evolved in the UK and Europe where, according to Neil Thompson (2017), social justice is seen as comprised of three main elements: equality and diversity, rights and responsibilities, and merit. In relation to equality: "social justice can be seen to apply when an individual, group or category of people is discriminated against … or treated unfairly in one or more ways" (p. 42). Promoting equality also involves respecting people from different cultures and recognizing the importance of diversity and inclusion, as Practice Focus 1 reveals.

Practice Focus 1
Adnan and Farid were two Syrian refugees that one of the authors stopped to speak with one spring day in Helsinki. They were standing near the Central railway station carrying a poster with the Finnish words 'OIKUS ELÄÄ' (which means right to live) and were organizing a petition. We went across to a nearby cafe to talk in the warm over coffee. In a smattering of different languages, English supplemented with Arabic, German and Finnish they told their harrowing story of fleeing from war and global conflict, and concerns about their wives and children stuck in a refugee camp in Lesbos. They were living in a reception centre and had applied for asylum in

Finland. However, they were worried because the political climate had recently changed due to the activities of far-right protest groups telling refugees to go home.

Adnam's and Farid's stories are not unique, but highlight what global inequality, dispossession and discrimination look like living on the margins of life in one of Europe's rich cities. We discussed how social work could help, guided by principles of social justice and respect for their culture. Social work could organize counselling for the trauma they had suffered back in Syria and on the journey across Europe, plus practical support with their asylum applications. In the face of such injustice, it seemed inadequate, but the least a social worker could do.

The second element of rights and responsibilities means promoting social justice by "recognising people's rights and respecting them, thereby enabling people to carry out their civic responsibilities" (op cit, p. 42). The third dimension concerns the notion of merit and what people are fairly entitled to and "raises questions about what we attribute value to, what we reward and conversely what is disapproved of" (p. 43). The advantage of this definition is that it helps to connect the micro with the macro, a theme taken up by John Solas from Australia who explored what kind of justice social work seeks.

In a telling contribution to the social justice debate, Solas (2008a) draws upon the experience of Aboriginal people where average life expectancy in the Northern Territories is still a little over 55 years, some 20 or so years less than non-Indigenous males (Graham 2006). It follows, in Solas's terms, that a convincing theory of social justice is urgently needed because of poverty and increasing inequality and injustice (pp. 814–815). Theories of justice, as noted by other writers (Reisch 2019; Thompson 2017), have traditionally been based on merit and rights, as well as social contract (Rawls 1999). More recently, utilitarian ideas have influenced the debate to suggest that a society is just when its institutions achieve the greatest good for the greatest number. As we shall see below, utilitarian principles have been influential in social policy since the beginning of the welfare state and were utilized during the modernization reforms of the 1990s (Stepney 2009, 2018). One of the central issues raised by utilitarian theories of justice is that they are based on equity, rather than equality, and therefore, as Solas (2008a) points out, bring questions of fairness and distribution into play, but not as absolute aims to achieve full equality. This has clear implications for social work. An equitable utilitarian-based system of rights would, for example, allow inequalities to continue, including poverty in the midst of affluence (Nussbaum 2006).

Solas (2008b) extended his critique and directed it towards the Australian Association of Social Workers (AASW) Code of Ethics, in particular for not making social justice the primary value. Solas called for social work to embrace a more radical and egalitarian form of social justice. This would extend the commitment to cultural diversity by going further and recognize the inequalities that exist between different social groups. Radical egalitarianism, if implemented, would constitute an approach that aimed to eliminate inequality and promote a fair distribution of benefits, rights, utilities and capabilities (Solas 2008b). It involves securing 'equal means' to the resources of life. This refers to something more than wealth or capital and income but a whole range of life chances – what the American philosopher Martha Nussbaum (2006) refers to as capabilities. She has identified ten capabilities which are central to a dignified life, including health, bodily integrity, senses, emotions, reason, affiliation, other species, play and finally control over one's environment. This is quite a list and where the confusion arises concerns which capabilities should be prioritized, who decides and whether access to all can be equalized.

Solas's article in the *Australian Social Work* journal provoked, in the same edition, responses from both Jim Ife and Richard Hugman. While broadly sympathetic to Solas, both Ife and Hugman highlighted a number of caveats and made some pertinent observations. Ife (2008) noted that social work has long been associated with the uncritical use of concepts that required a more nuanced treatment and argued that: "justice cannot be constructed in a historical and cultural vacuum" (p. 139). He also queried whether the profession had the necessary moral courage and political skills to push for radical equality, given the prevailing political climate. If the situation in Australia, as elsewhere, in 2008 was unsympathetic to a more radical approach to social justice, then it has certainly become even more difficult since that time. The welfare state has come under sustained threat from politicians on the political right and is increasingly shaped by global markets and neoliberal ideology (Mullaly 2010; Stepney 2018, 2019b; Thompson and McGowan 2020).

Hugman (2008) welcomed Solas's critical contribution to the social justice debate but pointed out that the values in the AASW's code were not ranked in order of importance and therefore social justice was not subordinate to other values. He acknowledged the advantages of adopting the capabilities approach, because it broadened the focus from purely material resources (Nussbaum 2006). A focus on capabilities can take account of the plurality of values that people from diverse cultures hold, while recognizing common humanities. In this important sense, social justice becomes a moral good. Hugman (2008) introduced an element of realism by suggesting that, while utilitarianism leaves room for unequal outcomes to emerge, it has the advantage of recognizing that resources for public welfare services are always likely to be finite. This means that social workers, along with other welfare professionals, are required to make difficult decisions about how such resources are to be distributed and do this by trying to meet need in the most equitable way for the greatest number of people. In such a scenario a narrower, rights-based form of egalitarianism may be all that is possible or justifiable. The centrality of welfare resources in the social justice debate means that we must look more closely at the role of social policy in the development of the post-war welfare state.

Social Justice and the Development of the Welfare State

Once the welfare state had been established as a necessary part of post-war reconstruction in the developed world, built upon the Beveridge/Keynes foundational pillars and consensus, it became subject to opposition and critical appraisal. The welfare consensus was viewed as being outmoded by commentators across the political spectrum. Those on the political left had become disillusioned by the rediscovery of poverty, rising inequalities and injustices in life chances – reflective of the growing gap between rich and poor. Those on the right disagreed and pointed to increasing bureaucracy, the high cost of public services and claimed that welfare created dependency among people living in poverty. They insisted that an overemphasis on justice only confirmed that a 'welfare society' was a step too far, as it undermined incentives to work. The collectivist welfare order could therefore not be sustained and the only consensus to emerge was that reform of the welfare state was urgently required (see Stepney 2019b).

The welfare consensus had been constructed on principles of equality, universalism and social justice which, it was hoped, would promote social solidarity. However, these principles were put under pressure by the growing political hostility from the political right and growing social divisions. This was intensified by the rise of economic globalization which marked out the parameters for welfare reform (Midgley 2007). The search for greater efficiency, effectiveness and economy in public services dictated by the need to compete in global markets overlaid and ultimately undermined concerns about equality and social justice. Globalization has contributed to the rise of market fundamentalism informed by neoliberal ideology – a new common-sense approach to welfare reform where the role of the state is broadly to help citizens help themselves by meeting their own social needs. It is only those assessed as high risk, dangerous to themselves or others, plus citizens who clearly cannot help themselves who will have access to protection-oriented state services (Thompson and Stepney 2018). This has set a new more sceptical agenda for social justice and social welfare everywhere.

The contrasting response from different welfare states across the globe concerning the imperative for social justice has been analysed very differently at the local level, reflecting cultural priorities and alternative systems of social protection. This links to contrasting welfare state typologies and the seminal work of Esping-Andersen (1990). It is worth identifying the most divergent and significant trends, as these have established the framework for much subsequent comparative social policy research. These trends have importantly set a benchmark for how much priority should be given to the goal of social justice.

First, there are the liberal welfare states in the UK and the USA, characterized by modest contributions from national insurance and federal tax, leading to basic levels of social benefits, backed up by means-tested 'safety nets' and targeted support for the working poor (Stepney 2018). This UK-American approach situates social justice within a more general commitment to individual freedom and liberty, alongside the protection of property rights. One of the problems with this approach is that it operates within a system of limited state intervention in the workings of largely deregulated markets. In the UK, the welfare state is more extensive than in the USA, but under recent governments, both Conservative and Labour, has become subject to increasing marketization and privatization which have undermined universal commitments to equality and justice. In the USA the expansion of social welfare during the latter half of the twentieth century sought to reduce inequalities but, according to Reisch (2019), "the patchwork system that emerged, however, reinforced gender and racial inequalities, although it purported to advance the ideal of social justice" (p. 126).

This liberal approach to policy making in the UK and the USA is in stark contrast to much of mainland Europe, where a more *Dirigiste* model has evolved (control by the state in economic and social affairs) and regulation is extensive. The European Union (EU) now performs this regulatory function. Although important differences exist in policy-making priorities, for example, between the Nordic welfare states, such as Sweden and Finland, continental regimes like France and Germany and Mediterranean countries epitomized by Spain and Greece, the EU promotes a common approach. The aim is to enhance citizens' rights, enforced, if necessary, through the European Court of Justice. It follows that, from a European perspective, social justice is generally interpreted as an essential component of social policy for promoting social inclusion and solidarity alongside tackling discrimination. With democratic trends highlighting concerns about the long-term care of Europe's growing older population (European Commission 2018), in the social justice debate the rights of older people come into play, as Practice Focus 2 reveals.

Practice Focus 2

Anna was a frail older woman who was waiting to be discharged from the city hospital after recovering from a bad fall which had damaged her hip joint. An assessment of her health and care needs revealed that she had a number of health and mobility problems and was still grieving for her late husband who died the previous year. The assessment concluded that Anna was on the borderline between remaining independent and requiring residential care. The hospital consultant suggested the latter due to Anna's age and general frailty, while Anna herself said she wanted to go back home to her small flat. At a team meeting Anna's case was discussed. Staff had recently attended a training course about discrimination and how certain problems, including ageism, can be associated with social justice. The trainer had also said that ageism is a factor that contributes to older people's experiences of grief. Consequently, Lars, the social worker, and Greta, the occupational therapist, agreed to work together to devise a post-discharge rehabilitation support programme with grief counselling and home care to help Anna remain independent at home. The care package would be reviewed monthly.

The implications for social work are significant, but quite difficult to unpack due to the differences in policy making noted above – in particular, cultural differences, contrasting priorities, different systems of social protection and the proportion of GDP devoted to supporting those at risk of poverty (Stepney 2018). In a global world, a business model, budgets and the search for best value have increasingly shaped what social workers can now do and have influenced practice, even in the more progressive Nordic countries. Good practice from skilled staff is always possible, as the case of providing high-quality support for Anna in the practice focus above reveals. However, with increasing pressure on public resources, there is a constant struggle in many social work agencies to maintain the imperative for social justice. Unless this is done, the commitment to justice may become little more than a mission statement. In this ongoing project the role of social movements has been quite significant.

Social Movements and Social Justice

The development of social work practice has been subject to a number of internal and external influences. According to Thompson (2002), the role of social movements represents a significant example of the latter. This influence has given the profession a more sociological orientation and strengthened the focus on social justice. It also signifies that the age of pressure group politics and community action had arrived and would expand into what we witness across the globe today.

In general, social movements can be seen as community-based pressure groups that take up particular causes around specific issues and organize for social change. According to Stepney and Popple (2008), with declining membership of traditional political parties, "people have become engaged in identity politics, the 'counterculture' and decentralised non-hierarchal grass-root activity" (pp. 48–49). As these new forms of community action evolve and grow over time, attracting more people, they develop into social movements. Since the rise of the American Civil Rights movement in the 1960s, personified by Martin Luther King's march to freedom in 1963, a number of new social movements have emerged across the globe. They have taken up a range of social issues, including women's rights, anti-racist struggles, disability rights, anti-psychiatry, to name but a few social causes amongst many. Recently the Me Too and Black Lives Matter movements have exemplified efforts to raise awareness of the continued inbuilt discrimination and the need for change. According to Thompson (2002), "what united these diverse struggles was the pursuit of social justice through attempts to challenge oppression" (p. 714).

Many of these new social movements can be linked to social work and have contributed to the growth of emancipatory practice. In addition, the citizen empowerment movement has become influential both in the policy arena and by calling for more holistic and participatory services. Mullaly (2010) suggests that new social movements that champion client interests have contributed to progressive models of practice that challenge oppression and promote social justice. This has helped to counteract the legacy of professional elitism and patronizing approaches that the 'social worker knows best'. The net result is that the influence of social movements has led to a more partnership approach with practitioners having a clearer focus on citizen rights and social justice. However, clearly there is a need to carry out practice-based research, specifically to establish the extent to which practitioners incorporate social justice values in their work, a point to which we shall return later.

Feminist Ideas on Social Justice

While women have gained new opportunities in the labour market and freedoms in leisure and public services, Feminist writers such as Angela McRobbie (2009) argue that these have been achieved at a significant social cost that undermines the cause of social justice. She argues that women are subject to competing pressures, moral scrutiny and contradictions concerning looking and behaving in particular ways. Failure to live up to dominant social norms and ideas creates many losses – identity loss, loss of self, loss of control and when this becomes problematic women's mental health suffers.

At the same time, McRobbie (2009) suggests that young women are consistently subject to a celebratory discourse of equal opportunity which, it is argued, liberates them from the domestic sphere. In western society women are consistently told that 'they have achieved justice in the workplace and home, and never had it so good'. However, while there is now more sharing of domestic work women still take responsibility for the majority of chores in the home.

McRobbie (2009) drawing on the work of Judith Butler suggests that current female freedoms are in fact marked by associated political costs and losses, in particular, a radical sexual politics and a loss of feminism. She argues that this manifests in both individual and collective melancholia which is expressed through things like binge drinking, self-harm, self-regulation including eating disorders and body dysmorphia, all of which have been normalized as 'female complaints'. In other words, according to Melissa Stepney, such 'female problems' signal a privatization or 'internalization of discontent', with the prospect of possible long-term psycho-social trauma and harm (Stepney 2015). For McRobbie (2009) this is in the absence of a feminist rebellion that would challenge the heterosexual and patriarchal matrix and question female identity and male orientated consumer culture.

Social Justice in the Global South

The need for a more radical and empowering social work approach to promoting social justice in the global South could not be more necessary and urgent, as in working with people affected by HIV/AIDS. The work of Vishanthie Sewpaul in South Africa provides an authoritative and compelling account of social work in the global South and offers a beacon of hope in this field. It represents a fitting example of the very best in social work and gives a very powerful voice to a client, Princess Nkosi Ndlovu, who is living with HIV, and has become an HIV/AIDS counsellor. Her story is extremely moving and has important implications for developing empowering community-based social work committed to promoting social justice. The article calls for a shift away from neoliberal, new managerial and positivist paradigms to participatory and democratic ways of working with local people and disadvantaged groups. In so doing it demonstrates the power of small groups in the townships supporting the transition from adversity to hope, activism and emancipatory development. The article makes a groundbreaking contribution, particularly in the area of HIV/AIDS, to the international social work literature.

Social work in the global South reflects worldviews influenced by notions of poverty, injustice and restricted life chances, a legacy from the high tide of colonialism. This is highlighted in the Global Social Work Statement of Ethical Principles (GSWSEP; IASSW, 2018), principles 4.7 and 4.8:

> Social workers recognize that dominant sociopolitical and cultural discourses and practices contribute to many taken-for-granted assumptions and entrapments of thinking, which manifest in the normalization and naturalization of a range of prejudices, oppressions, marginalizations, exploitation, violence and exclusions.

According to Vishanthie Sewpaul (2015), social workers in the global South are facing issues in the community every day related to social justice. In a more recent article, she writes that they recognize:

> the urgent need for developing strategies to heighten critical consciousness that challenge and change taken-for-granted assumptions for ourselves and the people whom we engage with. This forms the basis of everyday ethical, anti-oppressive practice. At the heart of emancipatory social work is understanding multiple sources of oppression and/or privilege and working towards more just societies. (Sewpaul and Ndlovu 2020, p. 110)

Conceptualizing Social Justice: The Practitioner Speaks

We have already noted that, while social justice is a fundamental value in social work, it has become a contested term with multiple meanings (Reisch 2019). This is confusing and creates a lack of clarity about what the term means and how it can be used in practice. Three research studies are cited, two from the USA and one from New Zealand.

The first study is from Karen Morgaine (2014) at California State University. The stimulus for her research derived from when she proposed a name change, to include the term 'social justice', in the title of one of her taught programmes on social welfare. The proposed change provoked a mixed response. Faculty members questioned whether it might be viewed with suspicion and have a negative impact in local welfare agencies. Consequently, the first part of Morgaine's research was to ask practitioners in local agencies what they thought of the proposed name change. She found that, while the majority were quite relaxed about it and viewed the change positively, a significant minority (25%) felt that the term social justice was "too political".

On the surface this was quite a surprising finding, given that California is generally perceived to be one of the most progressive states in the USA. Also, a number of practitioners were known to work in partnership with various local social movements, including women's groups, civil rights and LGBTQQI groups. The initial evaluation of this finding was that, as the political landscape in California changes and the meanings attached to social justice become more complex and contested, practitioners become ambivalent, and some may withdraw support. This led to the second part of Morgaine's research.

The second part of the research was a more substantial qualitative study with local practitioners from different welfare agencies. The research was carried out in five focus groups ($n = 16$) over an 18-month period. The participants ($n = 16$, ages: 22–58; gender: 9 Female, 5 male and 1 trans; identity: 9 identified as white, 5 Latino, 1 bi-racial, 1 multi-racial) had a range of qualifications, including half with MSW degrees, and varied practice experience. Morgaine (2014) asked participants in each group a series of prompt questions which focused on "how they defined social justice; how they believed service users and the general public might define social justice; where they saw social justice intersect with social work; and if/how they saw their work as enacting principles of social justice" (p. 8).

As a preliminary observation, Morgaine (2014) noted that "the primary focal point in most, if not all, focus groups was the response to the initial question about how participants defined social justice, which typically ended up being the heart of the discussions" (p. 8). What stood out most clearly was that, while social justice had multiple meanings, it was primarily seen by practitioners as an individual rights-based concept designed to achieve fair treatment. A number of participants saw it as value led and culture laden, so that it defied a universal definition. A minority saw social justice as a macro system issue requiring a cultural shift to enhance civil rights.

When asked about how clients and the general public might view social justice, one practitioner dryly observed: "they don't have time to think about the bigger picture, look ... they're struggling to survive". Others were more positive and said that: "they're certainly aware of the injustices they face". The 'political' nature of the term social justice was duly noted in every focus group, which reflected, as one participant put it, "the influence of our rather conservative media". It was also associated with those seeking social change that made some participants feel uncomfortable. Hence, the feeling of ambivalence that emerged concerning the proposed name change from stage one of the research.

Regarding how social workers used the principle of social justice in their practice, some participants argued that the best way of doing this was to incorporate the justice value in micro-level work. Such practitioners saw social services work essentially as a "band aid". Other participants said it helped to bring equity and fairness into play. A third group saw social justice as an "umbrella" concept under which we all work, while a fourth group said that it was a "building block, hopefully to a better more caring and forgiving world".

Morgaine (2014) concluded her interesting research by arguing that: "positioning social work in a social justice framework is a hollow exercise if applied with no critical reflection about what social justice means – particularly for those most intimately affected by injustice and for social workers engaging in daily practice with groups that have been marginalized and disenfranchised" (p. 16). We shall return to the importance of critically reflective practice below.

Two further studies found broadly comparable and consistent results. Simon Funge (2011) from the University of California researched the term with a group of experienced social work educators. He found that they unanimously agreed that they had a duty to teach students about social justice and felt confident about doing this. So far so good. However, only a third believed that they should go further and actively encourage a social justice perspective in modules on the MSW program. A number of staff members urged caution by identifying some of the constraints students were likely to find once they went out in practice.

In another study Michael O'Brien (2010) from Massey University, New Zealand, undertook a substantial quantitative study by surveying social workers ($n = 191$) from a variety of welfare agencies across both the North and South islands. He asked a number of questions to ascertain how practitioners defined and utilized the concept of social justice in their work. The findings were quite similar to what Karen Morgaine (2014) was to discover some 4 years later and commented on above in some detail. The only notable additional observation was that O'Brien found that a majority of practitioners used the term social justice to include a commitment to equality, fairness and rights specifically at the micro level.

Overall, the three studies confirmed that social justice is a highly contested concept with multiple meanings. There is clearly a danger that it can become a meaningless 'feel good' statement if used in a too vague and imprecise way. Moreover, there is the added concern that it may be used as rhetoric which "masks the social control function of channelling clients' needs within existing parameters" (Reisch 2011, p. 7). Critically reflective practice is clearly required to ensure the term does not lose its emancipatory potential. This raises the important issue of whether social justice can promote critically reflective models of practice which we will discuss later. First, though, we turn our attention to the significance of power and empowerment in relation to social justice.

Power and Empowerment

Dobratz, Waldner and Buzzell (2019) make the point that: "Power is everywhere, in every social interaction between individuals, groups, and global actors" (p. 1). It is, of course, particularly salient in relation to social justice. Indeed, it could be argued that social justice is primarily about the operation of power in terms of whether such power is used to oppress, marginalize and exclude or to support, protect and empower. For example, power can be used to deny people their rights or to ensure that such rights are upheld.

In a social work context, this takes us back to the longstanding recognition that while social work is promoted as a force for good, it can also have the effect of oppressing certain groups or categories of people by allowing discrimination to occur (Thompson 2021). As we shall note below, most incidences of discrimination are unintentional. This therefore raises the question of how power is used in social work: Is it used in a controlling, potentially oppressive way or is it used as a basis of empowerment (i.e., of helping people gain greater control over their lives)? The potential for practice to go either way has long been established, as we noted earlier by drawing on the classic work of Geoffrey Pearson (1975).

One of the reasons professions have a value base is to ensure, as far as reasonably possible, that professional power is used ethically. Social work is no exception. Given the prominent role of social justice in the social work value base, it is essential that power is used in positive ways for legitimate professional purposes. Thompson (2018) distinguishes between the abuse and misuse of power. The former refers to the deliberate use of power for illegitimate reasons (e.g., for personal gain and/or the oppressive treatment of one or more people). Of course, there is no guarantee that social workers will never indulge in that sort of behaviour, but we feel it is safe to assume that it is not a common occurrence.

The misuse of power, by contrast, refers to situations in which the consequences of the use of power are detrimental to one or more individuals, but not as a result of an intention to cause such harm. Examples would include a social worker disadvantaging a female client by relying on sexist assumptions or social work actions reinforcing racism by failing to be suitably ethnically sensitive or culturally competent. This type of problem is, of course, likely to be far more common. It is for this reason that there has been a strong emphasis on *anti*-discriminatory practice, rather than *non*-discriminatory practice. Without suitable education, there is a very strong danger that caring professionals who are genuinely trying to be helpful will unwittingly contribute to oppressive outcomes. The fact that discriminatory outcomes are often unintentional does not mean that they are any less problematic or in any less need of eradication. Efforts to promote social justice therefore need to be evaluated in terms of the outcomes they give rise to, rather than intentions, however good. This is part of the rationale behind the argument that social justice should be a central feature of social work education and not simply a separate part of the curriculum disconnected from everything else.

A commitment to social justice therefore requires an awareness of how power operates, a level of understanding above and beyond the so-called common sense that will often be rife with discriminatory assumptions and stereotypes. Power, even in caring hands, can do harm if it is not accompanied by a sufficiently sophisticated understanding of power dynamics.

We would also want to go a step further in arguing that a robust understanding of empowerment is also called for. Unfortunately, empowerment has become a buzzword that is much more widely used than it is understood (Stepney 2019a). As educators, we have come across examples of it being used in a narrow sense of 'enabling' without any recognition of the wider context; used as a reason for not getting involved; and featured in essays, assignments and reports in ways that suggest its significance has not been grasped. This is a great pity, as the role of empowerment, in our view, should be central to social justice, anti-racism and social work practice.

Just as the term social work begins with the word 'social' for a reason, it is not simply an accident of history that the term social justice also begins with the word 'social'. Social justice is much more than a simple sense of fairness. It encapsulates a recognition that injustices arise not simply as a result of the actions and attitudes of individuals but also as a result of cultural and structural forces In other words, it is a *sociological* phenomenon (Thompson 2019).

The extent to which sociology features in social work education programmes appears to vary significantly from institution to institution, a major focus in some, quite marginal in others. Without an awareness of the 'sociological imagination' the complexities of power and empowerment (and, indeed, of social justice more broadly) may not be appreciated, and so the level of analysis is unlikely to rise above that of the individual. This then leaves scope for the misuse of power, as discussed earlier – discriminatory acts (and omissions) arising from a failure to appreciate the complexities involved.

Practice Focus 3
Alex had read about empowerment while at university, but it was only when out on placement that it started to make sense to her. She became involved in a project for young offenders. The basic idea behind the scheme was that the team's efforts should be devoted to helping young people at risk of (re-offending) develop new interests, new ways of building self-esteem and winning peer approval. What struck her about the project was that the manager had a very broad focus and was keen to make sure that the empowerment work they were doing did not just consider individual issues – he was constantly reminding people to think more holistically and to take account of poverty, racism and other socio-political factors. Alex could see how all this fitted together and how simply focusing on 'enabling' people at an individual level – although important in its own right – was not enough, as it left so many important issues untouched. She started to see how what she had been taught at university could come to life in practice and she was grateful that the project manager was sufficiently well tuned in to make sure that team members did not lose sight of the bigger picture.

PCS analysis is a framework that has been developed to help make sense of the subtle intricacies of power, empowerment, discrimination and oppression. How this framework fits with the promotion of social justice is what we turn to next.

PCS Analysis

Introduced in 1993 in the first edition of Thompson (2021), PCS analysis is a framework developed to highlight the complex interactions of discrimination. It was proposed as a counterbalance to much of the simplistic literature available at that time that accounted for discrimination in either individualistic terms (i.e., the result simply of personal prejudice) or as deterministic structural forces like capitalism, patriarchy and imperialism 'causing' discrimination. It was recognized that a more nuanced approach was needed in order to appreciate the subtleties that much of the thinking at that time obscured.

The basis of PCS analysis is the proposition that: (i) trying to explain discrimination purely as an individual phenomenon (the Personal or P level) fails to do justice to the wider Cultural (C) and Structural (S) factors that are an important part of the dynamic; (ii) presenting structural formations as direct causal factors is deterministic and fails to recognize the role of human agency (P) and the role of shared meanings or discourses (C). Some aspects of sociology took us forward – for example, in terms of Giddens's structuration theory which emphasized the importance of understanding the *interaction* of personal agency (P) and social structures (S) (Stones 2005), as did the work of poststructuralist thinkers, such as Foucault (Faubion 2000), which emphasized the role of the discourses that form the shared meanings at the cultural level (C). However, there was no bringing of these elements together holistically to give a theoretical framework that does justice to the complex interplay of various elements or the dangers of focusing on one aspect without appreciating the need for an encompassing overview that shows how the different levels work together to produce the reality of the discrimination and oppression that blight so many people's lives.

PCS analysis locates discriminatory actions, attitudes, assumptions and language use (the P level) within the broader context of norms, expectations, taken-for-granted assumptions, stereotypes, discourses and language patterns (the C level). In turn, the C level is located within the broader framework of social structures, social divisions and institutions (the S level). But, this is not a static model. The three levels constantly interact within a "double dialectic" (Thompson 2018). That is, the personal interacts with the cultural, each level playing a part in shaping the other over time. Simultaneously, the cultural and the structural levels interact in a similar way, producing a complex set of dynamics. For example, sexism at a personal level does not operate in a vacuum. To a large extent it will be a reflection of a wider culture characterized by patriarchal discourses. In turn, it is, of course, no coincidence that the C level operates on the basis of patriarchal assumptions: it, in turn, is a reflection of patriarchal structures within a male-dominated society. Social practices at a personal level that reflect the dominant cultural discourses also then reinforce and perpetuate those discourses. Likewise, the persistence of such discourses serves to play a part in sustaining the patriarchal structures they both reflect and reinforce.

PCS analysis also highlights two other features of this multidimensional picture. First, it acknowledges the central role of power at all three levels. Second, it counsels against focusing on each area of discrimination separately and thus failing to appreciate the common themes, processes and dynamics. It highlights the importance of understanding the various forms of discrimination as different dimensions of human experience. For example, an older black woman does not experience, racism, sexism and ageism as separate entities, but as dimensions of her experience that enter into complex dynamics. Today, we would talk in terms of "intersectionality" (May 2015) and the need to move away from single-issue approaches that neglect the interplay of a variety of discriminatory processes, discourses and institutions.

This is not to say that each form of discrimination cannot be studied, critiqued or fought against in its own right, but it does mean that, say, developing anti-racist policies that do not take account of how racism interacts with sexism, ageism and so on is to fail to see the big picture and therefore likely to lead to the fragmented approaches common in the 1980s and beyond. Amina Mama's (1989) plea for an "anti-oppressive alliance" is as valid now as it was then.

Critically Reflective Practice

Han (2019) argues that:

> Power achieves a high degree of stability when it appears as a 'they', when it inscribes itself into 'everydayness'. What makes power more effective is not coercion but the autonomism of habit. An absolute power would be one that never became apparent, never pointed to itself, one that rather blended completely into what goes without saying. *Power shines in its own absence.* (p. 40)

This is a significant passage for three main reasons. First, it reflects the C level of PCS analysis – power operates very effectively through established discourses, taken-for-granted assumptions and the other factors that make up the cultural level. In this way, it connects the personal with the structural.

Second, 'autonomism' is a key term. As PCS analysis highlights, discrimination – and the oppression it gives rise to – is not simply a matter of personal prejudice. For every act of overt, deliberate discrimination, there will be many others that are 'institutionalized' – that is, historically established in patterns of thought, action and language. They become the unquestioned norm. For example, for every deliberate act that seeks to preserve male privilege, there will be many others that have this effect purely through the force of habit ('autonomism'), such as sexist forms of language and stereotypical assumptions about gender roles.

Third, the discriminatory potential of the power in this autonomism gives rise to a need for critically reflective practice (Thompson and Thompson 2018). The need for reflective practice has long been recognized in social work education, largely informed by the work of Schön (1983) and others. A key focus of this work has been the need to avoid operating on automatic pilot and addressing work challenges in an unthinking routinized or habitualized way. Although Schön's work does not specifically address discrimination and oppression, his point is particularly pertinent to attempts to promote social justice, in so far as such unthinking approaches to practice are likely to lose sight of the subtle ways in which power and discrimination operate.

Consequently, there is a need to incorporate an element of critical thinking – that is, to make sure that practice is not only reflective, but also *critically* reflective. This fits well with the argument put forward by Thompson and Thompson (2018) that practice needs to incorporate both critical depth and critical breadth. The former refers to not taking situations at face value, being prepared to look beneath the surface. This echoes the traditional social work principle of distinguishing between presenting problems and underlying problems.

Critical breadth, as the term implies, involves looking holistically at situations, taking account of wider socio-political factors (power, social divisions, social expectations and so on), thereby going beyond the limitations of an individualistic approach that fails to address wider influences and constraints on people's lives. There is, therefore, a clear alignment between critically reflective practice and PCS analysis. The latter can inform the former and the former can bring the latter to life as a practically useful analytical tool, and not simply a descriptive theoretical model.

Without critically reflective practice there is a danger that attempts to promote social justice will prove of little value, as the key issues involved are likely to be either not addressed at all or addressed in a superficial way that does not do justice to the complexities involved. These matters are far too important for us to allow them to be treated in this far from satisfactory manner.

Conclusion

As we have seen, social justice is in some ways a difficult concept to pin down, but we should not let this 'slipperiness' distract us from recognizing its central role in the social work value base. If we consider a parallel, defining music is an exceptionally difficult thing to do, but that in no way distracts from its significance in people's lives, its role as a cultural resource or a matter of social and economic significance.

We have outlined a number of social policy issues that have been part of the debate around, and development of, social justice. This showed both the contested nature of social justice, but also its importance as a feature of a genuinely humanitarian social work.

From this we moved on to highlight the central role of power in relation to social justice and, indeed, to social work in general and wider society. We argued that any authentic commitment to promoting social justice needs to be based on a fairly sophisticated understanding of power if it is to be effective. Likewise, the related concept of empowerment needs to be understood at a level of complexity far above the common tendency for it to serve as an oversimplified buzzword.

Having highlighted some of the many complexities that relate to the discrimination and oppression that stand in the way of social justice, we offered a theoretical framework that provides a way of understanding the complex dynamics that operate at personal, cultural and structural levels. PCS analysis can be used as a means of engaging with the complexities and thereby avoiding much of the reductionism and oversimplification that have sadly proven common in many circumstances.

This led us into a discussion of critically reflective practice centred around Han's (2019) notion of 'autonomism' – that is, for power to operate largely unseen based on habituation. Critically reflective practice is therefore offered as a basis for ensuring that such autonomism does not lead practitioners into practising in ways that are discriminatory or oppressive (or failing to recognize when others are doing so or when institutionalized discrimination is operating).

The notion of critical breadth put forward by Thompson and Thompson (2018) is seen as particularly important in highlighting the role of critically reflective practice as a foundation for promoting social justice.

Clearly, there are no simple, straightforward ways of responding to the challenges of promoting social justice. However, we hope that our comments here will serve to provide important food for thought and highlight the importance of continuing to wrestle with the many challenges of trying to make social justice a reality in both our practice and in wider society.

References

Dobratz BA, Waldner AK, Buzzell T (2019) Power, politics and society: an introduction to political sociology, 2nd edn. Routledge, New York
Dorling D (2015) Injustice: why inequality still persists. Policy Press, Bristol
Esping-Andersen G (1990) The three worlds of welfare capitalism. Polity Press, Cambridge
European Commission (2018) European Commission ageing report. European Commission, Luxembourg. www.europa.eu.int/comm/
Faubion JD (ed) (2000) Essential works of Foucault 1954–1984: volume 3: power. Penguin, London
Funge SP (2011) Promoting the social justice orientation of students: the role of the educator. J Soc Work Educ 47(1):73–90
Graham C (2006) Billion dollar question – Indigenous disadvantage. Impact (Autumn):5–7
Han B-C (2019) What is power? Polity, Cambridge
Hugman R (2005) New approaches in ethics for the caring professions. Palgrave Macmillan, Basingstoke
Hugman R (2008) Social work values: equity or equality: response to Solas. Aust Soc Work 61(2):141–146
Ife J (2008) Comment on John Solas. Aust Soc Work 61(2):137–140
International Federation of Social Workers (IFSW) (2014) Definitions of social work. Retrieved March 2021 from: http://ifsw.org/policies/definition-of-social-work
Mama A (1989) The hidden struggle. LRHRU/Runnymede Trust, London
May VM (2015) Pursuing intersectionality: unsettling dominant imaginaries. Routledge, New York
McRobbie A (2009) The aftermath of feminism: gender, culture and social change. Sage, London
Midgley J (2007) Perspectives on globalization, social justice and welfare. J Sociol Soc Welf 34(2):17–36
Morgaine K (2014) Conceptualising social justice in social work: are social workers 'too bogged down in the trees?'. J Soc Justice 4:1–18. ISSN: 2164-7100
Mullaly B (2010) Challenging oppression and confronting privilege. Oxford University Press, Toronto
National Association of Social Workers (NASW) (2012) Social work speaks: National Association of Social Workers policy statements 2012–2014, 9th edn. National Association of Social Workers, Washington, DC
Nussbaum M (2006) Frontiers of justice. Harvard University Press, Cambridge, MA
O'Brien M (2010) Social justice: alive and well (partly) in social work practice? Int Soc Work 54(2):174–190
Pearson G (1975) The deviant imagination. Macmillan, London
Rawls J (1999) A theory of justice, revised edn. Harvard University Press, Cambridge, MA
Reisch M (2008) From melting pot to multiculturalism: the impact of racial and ethnic diversity on social work and social justice in the USA. Br J Soc Work 38:788–804
Reisch M (2011) Being a radical social worker in reactionary times. Keynote address to the 25th anniversary conference of the social welfare action alliance, Washington, DC. Retrieved on June 10, 2012 from http://www.socialwelfareactionalliance.org/reisch_keynote_110610.pdf
Reisch M (2019) The interpretation of social justice, equality and inequality in social work: a view from the US. In: Payne M, Reith-Hall E (eds) The Routledge handbook of social work theory. Routledge, New York
Schön D (1983) The reflective practitioner. Ashgate, Aldershot
Sewpaul V, Ndlovu N (2020) Emancipatory, relationship-based and deliberative collective action: the power of the small group in shifting from adversity to hope, activism and development. Czech Slovak Soc Work J 20(1):108–122
Sewpaul V, Ntini T, Mkhize Z, Zandamela S (2015) Emancipatory social work education and community empowerment. Int J Soc Work Hum Serv Pract, Horizon Research Publishing 3(2):51–58

Solas J (2008a) What kind of social justice does social work seek? Int Soc Work 51(6):813–822

Solas J (2008b) Social work and social justice: what are we fighting for? Aust Soc Work 61(2):124–136

Stepney P (2009) English social work at the crossroads: a critical review. Aust Soc Work 62(1):10–27

Stepney M (2015) The challenge of hyper-sexual femininity and binge drinking: a feminist psychoanalytic response. Subjectivity 8:57–73. https://doi.org/10.1057/sub.2014.21

Stepney P (2018) Theory and methods in a policy and organisational context. In: Thompson N, Stepney P (eds) Social work theory and methods: the essentials. Routledge, New York

Stepney P (2019a) Empowerment ideas in social work. In: Payne M, Reith-Hall E (eds) The Routledge handbook of social work theory. Routledge, New York

Stepney P (2019b) The rise of the global state paradigm: implications for social work. In: Webb S (ed) The Routledge handbook of critical social work. Routledge, London

Stepney P, Popple K (2008) Social work and the community: a critical context for practice. Palgrave Macmillan, Basingstoke

Stones R (2005) Structuration theory. Palgrave Macmillan, Basingstoke

Thompson N (2002) Social movements, social justice and social work. Br J Soc Work 32:711–722

Thompson N (2017) Social problems and social justice. Red Globe Press, London

Thompson N (2018) Promoting equality: working with diversity and difference, 4th edn. Red Globe Press, London

Thompson N (2019) Applied sociology. Routledge, New York

Thompson N (2021) Anti-discriminatory practice: equality, diversity and social justice, 7th edn. Red Globe Press, London

Thompson N, McGowan J (2020) How to survive in social work. Avenue Media Solutions, Wrexham

Thompson N, Stepney P (eds) (2018) Social work theory and methods: the essentials. Routledge, New York

Thompson S, Thompson N (2018) The critically reflective practitioner, 2nd edn. Red Globe Press, London

Williams R (1989) Resources of hope. Verso, London

Virtues, Social Work and Social Service Organizations

Virtue Ethics in Social Work Practice

Eleni Papouli

Contents

Introduction	332
Virtue in Virtue Ethics	334
Typology of Virtues	336
Social Workers and Organizations as Virtuous Agents	338
Virtues as Bedrock of Organization	340
Virtues, Vulnerability and Organizations	341
External Factors	341
Internal Factors	342
Social Workers, Virtues and Ethical Culture in the Organization	343
Examples of Virtue Ethics Case Studies	344
Conclusion: What Might Be Next?	345
References	346

Abstract

Virtues are an integral part of human flourishing, both personal and professional. In the professional field, particularly social work, virtues are fully compatible with the role of the social worker as a good person and a good professional. On that account, the notion of virtue is thought to be related only to individual professionals as moral agents. But it is certainly true that as individual professionals need virtues to flourish, organizations need virtues to flourish as well. In accordance with this idea, this chapter takes the discussion to another level, arguing that organizations, like individuals, that lack virtues or neglect them in any way are in danger of unethical practices. In this context, the chapter explores the role of virtues in social service organizations and their impact on ethical practice of social workers and other stakeholders. Finally, it suggests ways to have virtuous social service organizations so that social workers and other

E. Papouli (✉)
University of West Attica, Athens, Greece
e-mail: epapouli@uniwa.gr

© Springer Nature Singapore Pte Ltd. 2023
D. Hölscher et al. (eds.), *Social Work Theory and Ethics*, Social Work,
https://doi.org/10.1007/978-981-19-1015-9_17

professionals are encouraged and empowered to foster ethical decision-making and embrace shared values and beliefs to support ethical practice in the workplace.

Keywords

Virtue · Virtue ethics · Social work · Social service organizations

Introduction

Social work is often described as an 'ethical-based' profession, which has its own values, ethical principles and ethical standards binding social worker conduct. These general components are part of what is called 'professional ethics' and are at the core of social work. For many years, as Hugman, Pawar, Anscombe and Wheeler (2021) point out, research practice and debates about professional ethics in social work were dominated by references to ethical principles and values such as 'dignity', 'human rights' or 'social justice', without taking into account the notion of virtue as it is used in virtue ethics. As a result, virtue ethics had long been neglected in the social work literature, as will be discussed later, although as a concept it is embedded within values and principles of the profession according to Pawar, Hugman, Anscombe and Alexandra (2020). Fortunately, today, virtue ethics, which is also an important pillar of professional ethics, has become a more common topic of discussion in the social work profession due to the growing recognition of the important role that virtues play in the ethical practice of social workers. Thanks to this change, in recent years, there is indeed a small yet growing body of research around the world exploring virtues in social work from different perspectives (practice, education, research) (see, for example, Banks and Gallagher 2009; Donaldson and Mayer 2014; Garlington et al. 2020; Kasseri 2019; Papouli et al. 2022; Pawar et al. 2018, 2020; Pekkarinen 2020). Certainly, the recognition of virtues as an equally essential guide to the professional practice of social workers is by no means accidental. As has been shown, virtues in professional life are about performing good and ethical actions that contribute to the wellbeing and flourishing of all parties concerned including clients as receivers of social work services. As such, they are an important prerequisite for social workers in order to be able to act ethically and professionally. Arguably, virtues are important pathways to professional flourishing and have been traditionally associated with personal qualities that define, for example, social workers as individual moral agents. According to recent literature, the qualities social workers carry within them, can be cultivated and put into practice, thereby helping them to perform well in their professional roles (Banks and Gallagher 2009; Pawar et al. 2018; Hugman et al. 2021; Papouli 2019).

Considering the above, it is not surprising that when we think or talk about virtues in social work, we have in mind the virtuous (or moral) character of the individual professional carrying out an action. This is particularly evident in the social work literature of virtues, which is all about individual agents and their virtue. Yet, recent trends in the literature of ethics – derived mostly from the organizational studies – show that the idea of virtuous character is not only used to consider individuals as moral agents, but, mutatis mutandis, also collective agents such as groups, communities and organizations. As Garlington et al. (2020) aptly put it, "virtue and character can be understood in any form of collective action, whether individual, organizational, community action, or parameters for action such as social policy" (p. 198). Thus, this reasoning concurs that the concept of virtue does not only regard the individual's character as moral subject, but also applies to organizations, where, for example, social workers and other professionals work together towards a common mission. Specifically, with regard to organizations, Moore and Beadle (2006) write that "it seems perfectly possible, by way of analogy.... to speak of the institution as having a virtuous or vicious character, or a character that is somewhere between these two extremes" (p. 374). In social work, the organizations are often referred to as social service organizations and may belong to the public, private and non-profit or social movement sector. But why are virtues so important to social service organizations and why do social workers need to be aware of this topic? How are social workers related to virtues in social service organizations? These questions provide basis for exploring new ways of looking at virtues into professional practice of social workers, which have not been explored by social work ethicists, scholars and researchers so far.

Following the Aristotelian ethics, in this chapter, we contend that virtues are inseparable from the environment where they may or may not be placed and as such, are associated with the ways organizations as "moral communities" (Milley 2002) provide their services to clients and treat their employees, such as social workers. This view is of particular importance for social workers working in social service organizations because it highlights the interdependent and relational nature of organizational life; as individuals cannot flourish alone, nor can organizations. In addition, it considers the organization as an ethical entity and prioritizes the role of virtues at the organizational level for achieving successful outcomes for clients.

In view of the foregoing and drawing on the idea that like individuals, organizations develop their own virtues, this chapter discusses the role of virtues at organizational level and their impact on ethical practice for social workers and other professionals at work, without, however, ignoring their value at an individual level. In this chapter, we discuss the challenges that social workers as individual moral agents face in applying values and virtues to organizational practice due to their commitment to professional ethics, and then, we explore the reasons why organizations should, first and foremost, and regardless of their employees, act in a virtuous manner and possess a virtuous character through corporate culture, setting the ethical tone for the way the social workers and other employees behave. Moreover, we focus on the relations between virtues and ethical culture in the organization and suggest some models that could help social workers have a concrete view of which virtues and elements constitute ethical organizations. Finally, we present two examples of ethics case studies to identify virtues-based topics and reflect on the advantages that virtue ethics can offer to social service organizations. Given that there is no available social work literature that would shed light on this topic, we need to draw on the material of other professions and disciplines such as business and management, and apply that knowledge to the field of social service organizations. The chapter hopes to enrich existing social work literature on virtue ethics in social service organizations through interdisciplinary knowledge.

But to understand virtues and their role in any given social service organization, we first need to clarify what they encompass and give a brief overview of their history and evolution, as well as to look at the typology of virtues regarding both individuals and organizations.

Virtue in Virtue Ethics

The concept of virtue is over two thousand years old. It traces its origins back to ancient Greek philosophy in the West (virtue ethics) and the ancient Chinese philosophy (Confucian ethics) in the East. Such a diachronic interest in virtues makes evident their timeless nature and meaning and demonstrates the important role they play in human fulfilment so far. But although the concept of virtue has survived from generation to generation because of the timeless truth behind it, it has never been static or unchanging, nor in any part of the world nor at any point of history, as will be discussed below.

By and large, the pursuit of virtue as essential to eudaimonic living, had been the subject of debate and a major source of division in philosophy and theology for a long period of history. Since ancient times, philosophers and religious thinkers around the globe, attempted to identify the meaning of living a virtuous and good life in a moral sense. In doing so, they suggested ways to go about developing and keeping the practice of virtues in daily life following different interpretive approaches and applications. Thus, with the passage of time, a variety of approaches about human virtues have been developed based on different ethical schools of thought. Especially in the western world, virtue ethics approaches have been, to a considerable extent, influenced by Aristotle and other ancient Greek philosophers (Plato, Socrates and the Stoics), who paved the way for the major ethical theories of the western philosophy.

For many centuries in Western societies, virtues would influence the prevailing religions and related socio-political systems and would be tied to their moral beliefs and values. Thus, the concept of virtue was defined in relation to religion and dogmatic moral perspectives and therefore, was closely linked to religious practices and social conservative ideas and policies (Chapman and Galston 1992; MacIntyre 2007). This is the main reason why virtues were on the decline as a subject of philosophical inquiry until the second half of the twentieth century (Papouli 2019). Since then, there has been a modern revival of interest in virtue ethics as a normative ethical theory, taking inspiration from the Aristotelian ethics, as stated earlier. This revival gave new life to the notion of virtue and modern philosophers (the so-called neo-Aristotelians) began to talk about virtue again and to examine its content from a secular perspective rather than a religious point of view. Since the beginning of 2000, the concept of virtue has also begun to attract the attention of social work scholars (see, for example, McBeath and Webb 2002; Houston 2003; Clark 2006; Banks 2008; Banks and Gallagher 2009; Grey 2010; Pullen-Sansfacon 2010) in terms of the individual social worker's moral responsibility and accountability within various circumstances, as mentioned earlier (Hugman et al. 2021; Parrott 2010; Pawar et al. 2018), much of their work has drawn on Aristotelian or neo-Aristotelian virtue ethics (Papouli 2019).

Throughout the literature, the term 'virtue' is often used synonymously with other terms such as values, strengths, qualities, traits and dispositions (Harrison et al. 2016, p. 19). (The word itself comes from the Greek word 'aretê', which means 'excellence or goodness of any kind'.) It is often used as a synonym for integrity in the social work literature as well (e.g. professional integrity) (Hugman et al. 2021). The terms listed above may be similar (e.g. the word 'values') or have a related meaning (e.g. 'qualities' or 'strengths'). Yet, virtue is the term preferred by several scholars due to its philosophical underpinnings and the fact that it has a wider, more substantial meaning and clout and clarity (Harrison et al. 2016). Moreover, as happens with definitions, the term 'virtue' has been defined in different, often related ways. The Ancient Greek philosophers like Plato and Socrates, for example, described virtue as a sort of knowledge (the knowledge of good and evil) through which people have the power to reach the ultimate good, i.e. to produce flourishing or eudaimonia (from daimon – true nature). Of interest for the present section is Aristotle's view on the definition of virtue.

Aristotle, one of the most influential philosophers of all time, put his own twist on the concept, identifying virtue as a habit of choosing and performing right actions. Aristotle (2004) held that a virtue lay in the middle of two contrary vices and described it as the mean by reference to two vices: the one of excess and the other of deficiency. Courage, for example, lies between cowardice and recklessness. Compassion lies between callousness and indulgence. For him, virtues help achieve 'eudaimonia', by which the Greeks meant 'flourishing' or 'the good life' (MacIntyre 2007). Aristotle, more so than Plato and Socrates, discussed the significance of external goods in the context of achieving the good life and emphasized the fact that virtues cannot exist in isolation from broader social environment, as already mentioned. Putting this into social work practice, it is argued that virtuous professional living is strongly connected with the way societies or organizations are organized around power structures, groups and individuals.

A review of the current literature reveals that although there are various definitions of virtue, they all share some common characteristics. They describe virtues as both knowledge (what is, for example, courageous, honest or just) and habits (or stable dispositions) that enable individuals to do the right think, at the right time and place, and in the right way. As Aristotle pointed out long ago, virtues presuppose a teachable knowledge of the good and the use of logic and deliberate decision, in order to develop and apply the beneficial habits of righteous living. In the Aristotelian view, 'people are neither praised nor blamed for their passions, but they are praised or blamed for their virtues or vices'. For this reason, virtues (like vices) can be acquired only through continuous learning and practice, either individually or collectively (organizational). This way of virtues acquisition echoes the idea of habituation, i.e. "the acquisition of virtuous character traits through the repeated practice of corresponding virtuous actions" which allows individuals to exercise their virtues until they become automatic ways of living (Banks and Gallagher 2009; Hugman et al. 2021; Papouli 2019; Pawar et al. 2018; Sanderse 2020, p. 98). Obviously, Aristotle placed great emphasis on repetition of virtuous actions as necessary for personal ethical improvement; this view is clearly reflected in his famous phrase "we are what we repeatedly do. Excellence, then, is not really an act, but a habit". Therefore, to be a virtuous social worker or a virtuous organization, you have to be dedicated to your pursuit and be more disciplined for staying committed to challenging goals and tasks.

Unlike Kantians and utilitarians, who assess an action's ethics based on the rules system or the consequences of the action, according to Alzola (2015), "virtue ethicists do endorse so-called be-rules ('be honest', 'be generous', 'be loyal', etc.) and Hursthouse's 'v-rules,' which can be formulated by employing virtue and vice terms ('do what is honest'; 'do not do what is dishonest', etc.)" (p. 291). Moreover, virtue ethicists consider ethical behavior as inseparable from the notion of ethical action and deal with morality outside of religious beliefs (Papouli 2019). The latter illustrates the secular nature of virtues as applied morals-actions according to which, virtues are universal across cultures and nations and accordingly, can be applied to anyone regardless of religious faith, socio-economic status, ethnicity, etc. (Peterson and Seligman 2004). As a secular proposal, virtues are opposed to values which may not be universally accepted and differ between individuals and cultures. Furthermore, virtues are usually more concrete than values and as such, they may often be conveyed well (van Oudenhoven et al. 2014). In the literature of professional ethics, however, the word 'moral values' is often used to denote virtues and for this reason, today, virtues can also be understood as moral (or ethical) values.

Typology of Virtues

For some years now, there is an ongoing debate about the typology of virtues, as well as the preferred virtues for exercising good and ethical judgment in organizations and social work practice. As a result, some scholars agree with the idea of differentiated virtue by reference to professional roles, while others are opposed to any particular set of virtues in the human professions and organizations alike. Yet, most scholars of virtue ethics seem to agree with the significance of profession-specific virtues, the so-called role-differentiated virtues (Morris and Morris 2016) and present their own set of virtues (or virtue frameworks) that provide guidance to professionals or/and organizations about ethical decision-making and behaviour. In this respect, for example, the social work ethics literature provides valuable information about the types of virtues which might be appropriate in professional practice, and why (Adams 2009; Banks and Gallagher 2009; Donaldson and Mayer 2014; Garlington et al. 2020; Hugman et al. 2021; Papouli 2019). Due to the large number of these lists, they cannot all be included here, but a few of the more notable ones have been included as examples. The following lists derived from the literature of virtue ethics in general can be helpful for understanding the overall landscape of preferred virtues in professional practice of social workers, but in reality, none of them is comprehensive by any means.

Aristotle (2004) developed the first typology system of virtues in the history of ethics. In his book Nicomachean Ethics, particularly, he described set of virtues (good habits) and their opposite vices (bad habits) that are vital for a flourishing life. According to him, there are two types of virtues – intellectual and moral (Table 1). Intellectual virtues concern the qualities of mind and are required for good thinking and learning. Instead, moral (or ethical) virtues, as already said, are considered the means to perform good and ethical actions. By and large, Aristotle identified four virtues (the so-called cardinal virtues) that are placed above all others and play a vital role in making justifiable and just decisions, i.e. courage, justice, practical wisdom or phronesis (the original Greek word) and temperance (Papouli 2019).

Lastly, Aristotle considered intellectual virtues superior to the moral virtues. But although intellectual virtues lay out the strong foundation for moral virtues, they are not sufficient in themselves for consciousness. Currently, it is commonly accepted that both types of virtues are equally important for ethical practice at the individual and organizational level.

An alternative typology of virtues is based on character traits and their relations to human flourishing. Drawing on ideas from philosophy and psychology, as well as their studies, Peterson and Seligman, pioneers of positive psychology, identified six core virtues that are considered as universal across cultures and religions over the last three millennia. These virtues include: wisdom, courage, humanity, justice, temperance and transcendence. The 6 classes of virtues are made up of 24-character strengths (Table 2).

More recently, the Jubilee Centre for Character and Virtues in the UK distinguished four different categories of virtues (moral, performance, civic, intellectual) plus an intellectual meta-virtue called practical wisdom (Table 3). The Jubilee Centre considers all four virtue clusters as important for life success, but by far it prioritizes the moral virtues as the most important for enabling individuals and societies to flourish (Jubilee Centre 2013, p. 3). Finally, the Jubilee Centre's typology puts practical wisdom at the top of the virtues list because it helps people to make the best possible choices in life and work. Practical wisdom is vital for the continuing professional development of social workers and "can be learned and developed with conscious attention" (Hugman et al. 2021, p. 15) "through the intersubjective encounter between the practitioner and service user" (Cheung 2017, p. 619).

As we can notice from the examples above, there are many different types of virtues that are also found in social work practice and typically, they are categorized by their characteristics or underlying objectives, some of which are unique to each list. Also, some virtues may depend on reciprocity, while others may originate from the individual without regard to the existence of reciprocity. Based on this reasoning, it is argued that some virtues are related to social workers as individuals or organizations separately depending on the context and social circumstances, while others may apply to social workers or other employees and organizations as shared virtues in the service of common good. What is more, certain virtues like 'social justice' are seen as an overarching virtue of both individuals and organizations in modern societies. So, from this perspective, social justice within the organization is both an individual and

Table 1 Aristotelian Virtues

Intellectual virtues	Moral (ethical) virtues
Scientific knowledge (episteme), artistic or technical knowledge (techne), intuitive reason (nous), practical wisdom (phronesis) and philosophic wisdom (sophia)	Courage, temperance, self-discipline, moderation, modesty, humility, generosity, friendliness, truthfulness, honesty, justice

Table 2 The six core virtues and their associated character strengths

Wisdom: Creativity, Curiosity, Judgement, Love of learning, Perspective	**Courage**: Honesty, Bravery, Perseverance, Zest	**Humanity**: Kindness, Love, Social intelligence
Justice: Fairness, Leadership, Teamwork	**Temperance**: Forgiveness, Humility, Prudence, Self-regulation	**Transcendence**: Appreciation of beauty and excellence, Gratitude, Hope, Humour, Spirituality

Table 3 The Jubilee Centre's typology of virtues

Moral: virtues that enable us to respond well to situations in any area of experience. **Examples**: courage, honesty, compassion, justice, humility, gratitude	**Performance**: virtues that might also be considered psychological capacities, that can be used for both good and bad ends and which enable us to put moral virtues into practice. **Examples**: resilience, grit, teamwork, determination
Civic: virtues and skills that are necessary for engaged and responsible citizenship. **Examples**: service, volunteering, citizenship	**Intellectual: virtues** that support learning, as well as to critically reflect on our own as well as other people's characters. **Examples**: practical wisdom, critical thinking, integrity, open-mindedness, resourcefulness, curiosity
Practical wisdom (or phronesis): A meta-virtue that moderates and enables all the others.	

Adapted from Jubilee Centre 2013, p. 4

team-level phenomenon and social workers need to be aware of the challenges that might arise for addressing justice issues at work. Taking into account the above, as a final comment, one should point out that the variety of virtues lists highlights the diversity and plurality of virtues that underlie individual or organizational practices. At the same time, it shows the contextual character of particular virtues that are desirable in order for moral agents (individuals, organizations) to flourish.

Social Workers and Organizations as Virtuous Agents

> One swallow does not make a summer

As stated earlier, social workers are employees in social service organizations that provide welfare and advocacy services to individuals, families and communities. In such organizations, social workers may work alone or in groups closely with other professionals, often referred to as 'interprofessional working'. Empirical evidence shows that social work practitioners are among the employees who have an increased sense of responsibility for ethics-related actions in the workplace, due to their professional roles; as is well known the social work profession is strongly committed to ethical responsibilities based on the virtues and values contained in international and national codes of ethics (see for example, the International Association of Schools of Social Work's (IASSW) and the International Federation of Social Workers' (IFSW) 2018 'Global Social Work Statement of Ethical Principles'). Due to their commitment to professional ethics, social workers are often expected to have high ethical expectations for themselves, while acting as exemplars (or role models) for ethical behaviour at work. At times, they may also appear as the only specialty within the workplace holding ethical responsibilities and accountability. Not infrequently, such role expectations and situations make social workers see themselves as personal exponents of virtuous actions within organizations. But this might make them feel like they carry ethical responsibility upon their shoulders for matters that, originally, do not fall within their remit or for which they may be personally blamed such as the ethical failures or mistakes of others in the organization. In cases like these, social workers, especially neophyte practitioners in the field, do often feel stressed and may even be disappointed with themselves because they are not able to meet their own ethical standards easily or at all.

Weinberg (2010) observes that "social work practitioners often see ethics as being primarily a personal rather than a communal responsibility, supported by codes that place the blame for inadequacies squarely on the shoulders of individuals as independent actors" (p. 36). In the same way, Hughes (2016) argues that "there is a danger that discussing social workers' ethical responsibilities in organizations may drift towards an individualized notion of ethics" (p. 192). Authors' concerns seem perfectly reasonable, because they reflect the neo-liberal 'responsibilisation' agenda of ethics matters which, in turn, reminds us of the 'individualistic approach' to ethical responsibility. According to this approach, individual practitioners are considered morally responsible for the decisions they make, regardless of the context and associated determinants (Juhila et al. 2017). The individualistic approach is a perspective common to ethical stances according to which all are considered from the moral perspective of the agent. From this perspective, for example, when the social workers and other employees are acting ethically, then we talk of having an ethically virtuous organization. Yet, this is a simplified view of understanding ethical practice and responsibility within an organization, which essentially reinforces the idea that virtues and their defence are a personal, individual matter, which is exclusively associated with the professional autonomy in social work practice. However, as many studies have shown, social workers' professional autonomy of action and ethical orientation are largely constrained and circumscribed by the organizational procedures and conditions of employment, as well as managerial practices (Parrott 2010; Preston-Shoot and Hojer 2012; Papadaki and Papadaki 2008; Weiss-Gal and Welbourne 2008). Of course, this in no way means that social workers' have no control and influence over what they ethically do, but that their choices and decisions are likely limited under the above-mentioned conditions.

However, just as there are two sides to a coin, there are two sides to ethics approaches in organizations.

Given the above, the other side of the coin refers to the 'communal approach', according to which, individuals and their actions are viewed not in isolation, but as members of the communities, i.e. the organizations to which they belong. On this basis, as Brown (1989) argues, if we want to change 'individual's behavior we need to understand and try to change the communities to which they belong'. Such an approach is in agreement with the view that it must be social service organizations that primarily take responsibility for functioning as virtuous agents with specific qualities, thus dispelling the frequently held notion that virtue is only related to the quality of individual employee as moral agent.

Virtues as Bedrock of Organization

Undoubtedly, social service organizations have primary ethical responsibilities to protect workers' well-being, create workplaces that enable their employees to flourish, and enhance clients' outcomes. Hasenfeld (2010, p. 4) describes organizations as "conveyers and enactors of moral systems". Such moral systems are often reflected on the codes of ethics that articulate the mission of the organization and set minimum standards of ethical behaviour, including personal traits such as honesty, kindness and integrity. However, it is well known that rules and standards may not always anticipate every situation at work, thus helping employees to find the answers they need in the code and deal with challenges and problems in a virtuous and effective way. Even in cases where professionals, like social workers, have their own code of ethics, tensions do exist between professional and organizational commitment (Hughes 2016). Thus, without neglecting the significance of codes of ethics, virtues as an ethics practical system can play a key role in ensuring organizational ethos that emerges as organization ethical culture, and which, in turn, permeates the workforce.

At the aggregate level, the establishment of solid virtues provides not only internal, but also external advantages to the organization. According to Cameron (2003), the advantages of virtues in organizations are as follows:

1. Virtues foster a sense of meaning, well-being and ennoblement in human beings.
2. Virtues are experienced cognitively, emotionally and behaviorally.
3. Virtues foster harmony in relationships.
4. Virtues are self-reinforcing and positively deviates amplifying.
5. Virtues serve a buffering function and foster resilience.

As noted above, virtues are essential requirements for the flourishing of social workers, other employees and organizations. MacIntyre (2007), a follower of Aristotle's virtue ethics, points out that virtues are associated with practices, which form a solid basis for ethical action. As he put it, "Without them, without justice, courage and truthfulness, practices could not resist the corrupting power of institutions" (p. 194). But putting the virtues in practice is not always an easy task; it is often said that it seems easier to apply rules and guidelines than virtues. This is because a virtue is not just about following ethics standards or laws, but is mostly about building and fostering an ethical culture in the organization as stated earlier; it is only within this ethical context that virtues can be cultivated and flourish.

Virtues, Vulnerability and Organizations

Virtues are particularly vulnerable to environmental changes. Such changes may due to external factors (e.g. economy, government policies) that occur outside the organization or internal factors that occur inside the organization and are associated with the organization's internal environment (e.g. people, structures, conditions). This distinction is important for social workers in their understanding of the role and vulnerability of virtues in social service organizations. In the discussion which follows, external factors refer to neoliberal policies and managerialism practices implemented by social service organizations all over the world in recent years, while internal factors refer to the internal environment of the organization.

External Factors

Most countries in Europe and the globalized world have undergone dramatic welfare changes over the course of recent decades, due to the dominance of neoliberal policies and managerial practices in the provision of public services (Juhila et al. 2017; Hasenfeld 2010; Rogowski 2011; Weinberg and Banks 2019). As a consequence, social service organizations have been forced to change themselves too, in order to survive under the new regime of uncertainty and austerity, while causing many negative effects on the quality of social services provided. At the same time, employees, like social workers, are struggling to act ethically in what Weinberg and Banks (2019) characterize as the "unethical climate" of neoliberalism (p. 361).

Faced with the reality of managerialism as "de-personalizing practice" (Weinberg and Banks 2019), many social service organizations today tend to have more task-oriented work procedures, than people-oriented focusing on satisfaction, motivation and well-being of workers. As a result, they focus more on rules and bureaucratic procedures, as well as on ongoing performance measurement and feedback and less on the virtues and values underlying their mission statements such as 'justice', 'integrity', 'caring' or 'wisdom', which make the professional environments more humane in the age of sustainability. Typically, large organizations (e.g. hospitals) are examples of such elements, as they have complex rules and bureaucratic procedures that should be strictly followed. Social workers working in such organizations, often, report bureaucracy as a major problem with serious ramifications to their work lives. For this reason, there is a general concern about the potential for a bureaucratic welfare organization to promote virtuous ethical practice. As Bauman (1994) points out, this form of organization tends to encourage the phenomena of 'free-floating responsibility' and ethical indifference among its employees. In such a working environment, thus, as many scholars agree, there is always the risk for social work to be transformed from an ethical and practical profession to a rational technical activity with unpleasant consequences for the profession itself (Parrott 2010; Parton and O'Byrne 2000; Weinberg and Banks 2019).

Internal Factors

As it has been well documented, virtues as forms of human capital are the main drivers that can help both social workers as employees and the organization as well to flourish. Nevertheless, many organizations adapting to today's challenges by having virtues (or values) statements, do not follow them, fully or partially, for different reasons, one of which has already been mentioned earlier. Another reason is related to unethical behaviours or potentially harmful practice in the working environment. Unethical behaviour (e.g. fraud, corruption, conflicts of interest policies, discrimination and sexual harassment) has numerous negative effects within and outside the organization and voices significant scepticism about the organization's virtuousness and ethical orientation. Here, it is important to highlight the crucial role of whistleblowing by social workers in disclosing wrongdoing in the workplace. But unfortunately, international literature shows that the number of those making disclosures (internal or external) remains low, due to fear of retaliation at work and lack or inadequate legal protection mechanisms in most countries of the world (Preston-Shoot 2011; Preston-Shoot and Hojer 2012; Raymond et al. 2017).

Moreover, recent high-profile scandals and crises in the non-profit social sector around the world have made it clear that many organizations are not able to communicate in an open and constructive manner their values statement (DiGangi 2016). In regard to this, studies have also shown that ethical transgressions trigger more negative reactions from consumers when committed by non-profits rather than business sector (Hornsey et al. 2020). This kind of negative reaction is due to the fact that non-profit organizations such as social service organizations are naturally involved "in moral work, upholding and reinforcing moral values about 'desirable' human behavior and the 'good' society" (Hasenfeld 2010, p. 90).

Thus, supporting virtuously sound behaviour, social service organizations are committed to maintaining high quality standards, ethical reputation, trust and corporate accountability to stakeholders (Hornsey et al. 2020). Such characteristics are significant contributors towards the organization's success, i.e. to fulfil its social goals, as well as to guarantee effective social work innervations within it. Evidence from studies of practice suggests that the most effective social work takes place in environments which balance respect for professional values and standards with organizational accountabilities (International Federation of Social Workers 2012). This person-organizational ethical fit is also known as 'value congruence' (or value fit) and is particularly reflected in the ethical culture of the organization as will be discussed below (Edwards and Cable 2009).

Social Workers, Virtues and Ethical Culture in the Organization

As seen above, all too often, social workers today find themselves working in difficult conditions, characterized by neoliberal, managerial and (post) bureaucratic practices. With that in mind, promoting ethical culture in organizations is important in conveying virtues in a meaningful way to social workers and other employees and establishing ethical climates within them. But how can a social service organization create a virtue-based ethical culture for their members? And what can be measured, if anything, in order to guarantee the ethos of the organization and benefit all stakeholders? In reality, there are no single 'right' answers to these questions, simply, because virtues are context-specific and therefore, there is no 'one-size fits-all set up that works for every organization (Johnson 2021; Taylor 2017). In other words, how to measure ethical culture remains a complex question given that each organization has different interests and goals, as well as it includes formal and informal systems that influence its ethics functionality. It is perhaps for this reason that there are also different ideas and models in the literature about building and maintaining a virtuous organization. Nevertheless, here are some suggested virtue-based models, which appear in organizational studies and could be helpful to social workers as frontline workers or managers, to have a concrete view of which virtues and elements constitute ethical organizations. For example, Johnson (2021) identifies five markers of highly ethical organizations, i.e. inclusion, trust, justice, integrity, structural reinforcement and organizational citizenship. Likewise, Kaptein (2008) has developed the Corporate Ethical Virtues (CEV) model, which motivates employees to ethical conduct. It includes seven virtues as follows: clarity, congruency, feasibility, supportability, transparency, discussability, sanctionability. Finally, Taylor (2017) suggests a multilevel approach at which organizations should build a virtuous ethical culture. Taylor's model of ethical culture includes five levels (individual, interpersonal, group, intergroup, inter-organizational), each of which examines specific topics within organizational behaviour or broader fields.

As seen above, the two first models include a set of different types of virtues -from individual to collective virtues- including ethical virtues. These one or the other appear suitable for small social service organizations, with few or no levels of management. However, Taylor's model is more complicated compared to other approaches, while it appears to fit well with medium to large organizations, which are inherently more complex because ethical decisions involve more stakeholders. Despite this, it must be pointed out that all the models described above, emphasize the role of managers or leaders in the organizational hierarchy as key to virtues alignment as they model and reinforce virtues and hold members accountable for following them. As managers, social workers are cognizant of their dual ethical responsibility to clients and to the organization and the need to balance virtuous practices and organizational performance.

Examples of Virtue Ethics Case Studies

To highlight the practical challenges and value of the virtue-driven environment, we provide two case study examples below to assist with the understanding of virtue issues in the workplace of social workers. Both examples have to do with conflicts of interest, which are one of the most pervasive issues facing modern social workers across the globe.

Case Study 1
George is a social worker, who works as an executive director of a children's autism organization. This is a non-profit organization that seeks to protect its clients through advocacy as well as action-based and educational initiatives. George is responsible for the overall management, and operations of the organization according to the strategic direction, and policies set by the Board of Directors. Due to the reduction of government funding for non-profits, the organization decided to add fundraising events throughout social media campaigns to attract new donors. George was asked by the Board of Directors to involve their clients (children and families) in the advertising campaigns, showing their faces on the Internet in order to enable more donors to make donations to the organization. George feels the pressure of the Board to follow the decision to help his organization increase donations and generate revenue. But at the same time, he has an ethical responsibility that flows from his mission as a social worker to protect the image of their clients, their privacy and their self-determination. George is most concerned about his reputation as an ethical manager towards their clients and colleagues.

> Questions for discussion:
> What are the issues of virtues, ethics and law posed in the case study? What options does the organization and outreach team have, and what should they do and why? What factors will influence their ethical decisions?

Case Study 2
Maria is an experienced social work practitioner, who has worked for many years in services with homeless people. She recently found a new job at a community-based organization that provides services for homeless individuals and families. Maria is a member of a mobile team that aims to identify and engage the homeless population in the community. The team works with area shelters as well as seeks out homeless individuals on the streets, under bridges, in alleys, on railroad tracks, park benches and other places. Due to high demand, it may take a few days for the outreach team to consider the request for intervention homeless services. Maria and her colleagues accepted a request for urgent intervention and despite the difficulties, they were able to provide immediate services to a homeless person on the street after the request of a neighbour. However, the organization was accused by journalists working for a local online newspaper, of lacking immediate intervention. In order to prove the opposite, the top manager of the organization decided to take a photo of the homeless person

without his permission and uploaded it on the Facebook page of the organization to show that the homeless person did actually get the care he needed.

> Questions for discussion:
> What are the issues of virtues, ethics and law posed in the case study? What options does the organization and outreach team have, and what should they do and why? What factors will influence their ethical decisions?

Conclusion: What Might Be Next?

This chapter discussed the role of virtues in social service organizations, the visibility of virtues' importance and the acceptance, proper measurement and monitoring of them by all social workers and other employees. However, as has been indicated, virtue setting and application are a tough business; virtues are embodied in the ethical culture of the organization, which, as is well known, does not imply normalcy for oneself. Hofstede (2011) and Taylor (2017) point out that organizations, like societies, are more than the sum of their parts. For social workers, either as frontline professionals or managers and leaders, this is especially important to understand so that they are able to look at the practice of virtues within organizations from a holistic perspective in order to prevent ecological fallacy. But to be realistic, this demands constant effort on the part of all those involved in the organization from the manager to the employee. To this effect, a lot of research needs to be done to illuminate the various aspects of virtues' applicability in social service organizations and their impact on the ethical performance of organization members including social workers.

Drawing on the literature, it is concluded that virtuous social service organizations have the ethical culture they need to compromise their ethical practices, using a range of specific measures such as ethical training, virtues measurement (visible and invisible dimensions of them), rewards for ethical behaviour and continuous improvement and consistent enforcement. Of particular importance is the implementation of a safety system for reporting unethical behaviour as it is critical for all parts involved to have an effective way to report their concerns (inside or outside the organization) where they observe instances of poor ethical practice or wrongdoing. In the non-profits, such organizational measures can help social workers and other stakeholders to understand the boundaries between ethical and unethical behaviours and address ethical issues at work. Still, the above measures should be consistent, but flexible in order to facilitate the establishment of virtuous practices within the organization by enabling employees to take ownership over their work. In a virtue-based organization, it is certain that social workers are morally courageous rather than morally distressed to help others during difficult dilemmas, despite the adversity they may face in doing so; employees who are virtuously safe and cared for by their organization feel more comfortable speaking up about misconduct (Papouli 2019a).

Due to the nature of their profession, social workers are well-educated professionals to promote virtues and values, as well as lead by example in the workplace. This position enables them to make a positive contribution by developing the bottom-up approach management of virtues practices that could improve the recognition of a holistic spectrum and make possible the ethics of resistance in organizations, where ethical violations are observed. Nevertheless, as already suggested, it would be wrong to infer that such initiatives would be defined only as an individual duty.

In view of the above, and taking into consideration that regulatory agencies such as professional social work associations across the countries and world, operate as collective moral entities, it is necessary for them to be actively involved in the development and implementation of policies, promotion and observance of virtues-based organizations for social workers, other employees and stakeholders. To this direction, professional associations can play a vital role as forums for the discussion of virtuous practices within organizations. Given that many professional associations are often external monitoring mechanisms, ultimately, they can create or develop appropriate networks to support their members and amplify their voices to monitor an organization's ethical practices in order to prevent or tackle systemic ethical lapses. With these initiatives, social workers can better understand that the pursuit of virtue can equally be a collective process, which, however, requires monitoring and adherence to collective activities in order to be truly applicable to any organization.

References

Adams P (2009) Ethics with character: virtues and the ethical social worker. J Sociol Soc Welf 36(5):83–105. https://scholarworks.wmich.edu/jssw/vol36/iss3/5

Alzola M (2015) Virtuous persons and virtuous actions in business ethics and organizational research. Bus Ethics Q 25(3):287–318. https://doi.org/10.1017/beq.2015.24

Aristotle (2004) Aristotle: the Nicomachean ethics (Further revised edn) (trans: Thomson JAK, rev: Tredennick H, intro: Barnes J). Penguin Books, London

Banks S (2008) Critical commentary: social work ethics. Br J Soc Work 38(6):1238–1249. https://doi.org/10.1093/bjsw/bcn099

Banks S, Gallagher A (2009) Ethics in professional life: virtues for health and social care. Palgrave, Basingstoke

Bauman Z (1994) Alone again: ethics after certainty. Demos, London

Brown M (1989) Ethics in organizations. Issues Ethics 2(1). Retrieved from http://www.scu.edu/ethics/publications/iie/v2n1/homepage.html

Cameron KS (2003) Organizational virtuousness and performance. In: Cameron KS, Dutton JE, Quinn RE (eds) Positive organizational scholarship: foundations of a new discipline. Berrett-Koehler, San Francisco, pp 48–65

Chapman WJ, Galston AW (1992) Virtue: nomos XXXIV. New York University Press, New York

Cheung JCS (2017) Practice wisdom in social work: an uncommon sense in the intersubjective encounter. Eur J Soc Work 20(5):619–629. https://doi.org/10.1080/13691457.2016.1255592

Clark C (2006) Moral character in social work. Br J Soc Work 36(1):75–89. http://www.jstor.org/stable/23720867

DiGangi C (2016, January) 7 scandals from the nonprofit world. MSN Money. Retrieved from https://finance.yahoo.com/news/7-scandals-nonprofit-world-120046834.html

Donaldson LP, Mayer LM (2014) Justice as a core virtue for social work practice. Soc Work Christ 41(2/3):207–231. 25p

Edwards JR, Cable DM (2009) The value of value congruence. J Appl Psychol 94(3):654–677. https://doi.org/10.1037/a0014891

Garlington SB, Collins ME, Bossaller MRD (2020) An ethical foundation for social good: virtue theory and solidarity. Res Soc Work Pract 30(2):196–204. https://doi.org/10.1177/1049731519863487

Grey M (2010) Moral sources and emergent ethical theories in social work. Br J Soc Work 40(6):1794–1811

Harrison T, Morris I, Ryan J (2016) Teaching character in the primary classroom. Sage, London

Hasenfeld Y (2010) Human services as complex organizations, 2nd edn. Sage, Thousand Oaks

Hofstede G (2011) National cultures, organizational cultures, and the role of management. In: Values and ethics for the 21st century. BBVA, Madrid, pp 459–481

Hornsey MJ, Chapman CM, Mangan H, La Macchia S, Gillespie N (2020) The moral disillusionment model of organizational transgressions: ethical transgressions trigger more negative reactions from consumers when committed by nonprofits. J Bus Ethics. https://doi.org/10.1007/s10551-020-04492-7

Houston S (2003) Establishing the virtue in social work: a response to McBeath and Webb. Br J Soc Work 33:819–824

Hughes M (2016) Ethics in organizations. In: Hugman R, Carter J (eds) Rethinking values and ethics in social work. Palgrave, London, pp 180–194

Hugman R, Pawar M, Anscombe B, Wheeler A (2021) Virtue ethics in social work practice. Routledge, Abington

International Association of Schools of Social Work (IASSW), International Federation of Social Workers (IFSW) (2018) Global social work statement of ethical principles. Available online at: https://www.iassw-aiets.org/2018/04/18/global-social-work-statement-of-ethical-principles-iassw/

International Federation of Social Workers (IFSW) (2012) Effective and ethical working environments for social work: the responsibilities of employers of social workers. Available online at: https://www.ifsw.org/effective-and-ethical-working-environments-for-social-work-the-responsibilities-of-employers-of-social-workers-2/

Johnson CE (2021) Meeting the ethical challenges of leadership: casting light or shadow, 7th edn. Sage, Thousand Oaks

Jubilee Centre for Character and Virtues (2013) A framework for Character Education in Schools, Birmingham: University of Birmingham, Jubilee Centre for Character and Virtues, [Online]. Retrieved from www.jubileecentre.ac.uk/userfiles/jubileecentre/pdf/character-education/Framework%20for%20Character%20Education1.pdf

Juhila K, Raitakari S, Hall C (2017) Introduction. In: Juhila K, Raitakari S, Hall C (eds) Responsibilisation at the margins of welfare services. Routledge, Abington/New York, pp 1–8

Kaptein M (2008) Developing and testing a measure for the ethical culture of organizations: the corporate ethical virtues model. J Organ Behav 29(7):923–947. https://doi.org/10.1002/job.520

Kasseri Z (2019) Social work in the field of addiction: in a search of an ethical practice based on virtues. Soc Work (Greek J) 134:3–29

MacIntyre A (2007) After virtue: a study in moral theory, 3rd edn. University of Notre Dame Press

McBeath G, Webb SA (2002) Virtue ethics and social work: being lucky, realistic, and not doing one's duty. Br J Soc Work 32:1015–1036

Milley P (2002) Imagining good organizations: moral orders or moral communities? Educ Manag Adm 30(1):47–64. https://doi.org/10.1177/0263211X020301007

Moore G, Beadle R (2006) In search of organizational virtue in business: agents, goods, practices, institutions and environments. Organ Stud 27(3):369–389. https://doi.org/10.1177/0170840606062427

Morris MC, Morris JZ (2016) The importance of virtue ethics in the IRB. Res Ethics 12(4):201–216. https://doi.org/10.1177/1747016116656023

Papadaki E, Papadaki V (2008) Ethically difficult situations related to organizational conditions: social workers' experiences in Crete, Greece. J Soc Work 8(2):163–180. https://doi.org/10.1177/1468017307088497

Papouli E (2019) Aristotle's virtue ethics as a conceptual framework for the study and practice of social work in modern times. Eur J Soc Work 22(6):921–934. https://doi.org/10.1080/13691457.2018.1461072

Papouli E (2019a) Moral courage and moral distress in social work education and practice: a literature review. In: Marson SM, McKinney RE (eds) The Routledge handbook of social work ethics and values. Routledge, Abingdon

Papouli E, Chatzifotiou S, Tsairidis C (2022) Character strengths and virtues for competent fieldwork education: Perspectives of undergraduate students from two university departments of social work in Greece. In: Baikady R, Sajid SM, Varoshini N, Rezaul Islam M (eds) The Routledge international handbook of field work education in social work. Routledge, New York

Parrott L (2010) Values and ethics in social work practice, 2nd edn. Learning Matters, Exeter

Parton N, O'Byrne P (2000) Constructive social work: towards a new practice. Palgrave Macmillan, Basingstoke

Pawar M, Hugman R, Alexandra A, Anscombe A (2018) Virtue-led social work practice. In: Pawar M, Bowles W, Bell K (eds) Social work: innovations and insights. Australian Scholarly Publishing, pp 47–60

Pawar M, Hugman R, Anscombe B, Alexandra A (2020) Searching for virtue ethics: a survey of social work ethics curriculum and educators. Br J Soc Work 50(6):1816–1833

Pekkarinen A (2020) Virtues in social work research with children and families: the ethical accounts of Finnish PhD theses. J Soc Work Values Ethics 17:2

Peterson C, Seligman MEP (2004) Character strengths and virtues: a handbook and classification. American Psychological Association, Washington, DC

Preston-Shoot M (2011) On administrative evil-doing within social work policy and services: law, ethics and practice. Eur J Soc Work 14(2):177–194

Preston-Shoot M, Hojer S (2012) Social work, social justice and protection: a reflective review. In: Lyons K, Hokenstad T, Pawar M (eds) The SAGE handbook of international social work. Sage, pp 249–264

Pullen-Sansfacon A (2010) Virtue ethics for social work: a new pedagogy for practical reasoning. Soc Work Educ 29(4):402–415. https://doi.org/10.1080/02615470902991734

Raymond S, Beddoe L, Staniforth B (2017) Social workers' experiences with whistleblowing: to speak or not to speak? Aotearoa N Z Soc Work 29(3):13–29. https://doi.org/10.11157/anzswj-vol29iss3id305

Rogowski S (2011) Managers, managerialism and social work with children and families: the deformation of a profession? Practice 23(3):157–167. https://doi.org/10.1080/09503153.2011.569970

Sanderse W (2020) Does Aristotle believe that habituation is only for children? J Moral Educ 49(1):98–110. https://doi.org/10.1080/03057240.2018.1497952

Taylor A (2017) The five levels of ethical culture. Working paper, BSR, San Francisco. Retrieved from https://www.bsr.org/reports/BSR_Ethical_Corporate_Culture_Five_Levels.pdf

van Oudenhoven JP, de Raad B, Timmerman ME et al (2014) Are virtues national, supranational, or universal? Springer Plus 3(223). https://doi.org/10.1186/2193-1801-3-223

Weinberg M (2010) The social construction of social work ethics: politicizing and broadening the lens. J Progress Hum Serv 21(1):32–44

Weinberg M, Banks S (2019) Practising ethically in unethical times: everyday resistance in social work. Ethics Soc Welf 13(4):361–376. https://doi.org/10.1080/17496535.2019.1597141

Weiss-Gal I, Welbourne P (2008) The professionalisation of social work: a cross-national exploration. Int J Soc Welf 17:281–290. https://doi.org/10.1111/j.1468-2397.2008.00574.x

An Ethic of Care: Contributions to Social Work Practice

18

Donna McAuliffe

Contents

Introduction	350
Establishing Feminist Theory and an Ethic of Care as Theory for Social Work Practice	351
An Ethic of Care: Early Developments	352
The Ethic of Care as Political Activity	355
Moving to a Critical Ethic of Care and the Contributions of Social Work to a Neoliberal Pushback	359
Locating the Ethic of Care Within Social Work Practice	360
Conclusion	363
References	364

Abstract

The definition of the term philosophy is 'love of wisdom'. From the earliest of times, in all cultures and traditions, the search for meaning and knowledge has been accompanied by a passing on through generations of ways that meaning can be made and connections drawn or discarded. The oral histories steeped in ancient ancestry of Indigenous peoples, and the written tomes that have influenced many a religious, spiritual, and belief system, all have their place in establishing a moral philosophy and body of ethical theory that provides rich fodder for those who seek explanations and answers to the compelling questions of life. This chapter focuses on tracing the history, defining and understanding the central tenets of what has become known as an Ethic of Care. This relational ethical theory had its roots in feminist thinking in the mid-twentieth century providing a critical understanding of the importance of interdependence and relationship while maintaining focus on the situational, structural, and political factors of importance to the individual. While ethics of justice highlight obligations, rights, and fairness, an Ethic of Care focuses on reciprocity, relationships, connections, and

D. McAuliffe (✉)
School of Health Sciences and Social Work, Griffith University, Logan, QLD, Australia
e-mail: d.mcauliffe@griffith.edu.au

© Springer Nature Singapore Pte Ltd. 2023
D. Hölscher et al. (eds.), *Social Work Theory and Ethics*, Social Work,
https://doi.org/10.1007/978-981-19-1015-9_18

context. This chapter positions an Ethic of Care as a central ethical theory for social work practice and provides examples of how questions about what a compassionate response requires can shift what ought to be done from a focus on rational-objective to the relational-emotional dimension. In doing so, social workers have a foundation for decision-making that holds them on firm footing when exploring moral obligations, deservedness, and the expectations about how social relations play out on all levels. A critical Ethic of Care will also be explored as a more recent development of this perspective that provides further application to the socio-political context of human relationships. The chapter concludes with two case studies of how an Ethic of Care approach can be applied in social work-related contexts, drawing on recent research and global events.

Keywords

Ethic of Care · Feminist ethics · Care-giving · Interdependence · Relational ethics · Social work practice

Introduction

From ancient times, people have sought to find ways to organise and construct boundaries around activities that are required to keep those within their sphere of responsibility safe, well, and productive. People who live in close proximity to each other have so-called moral obligations to ensure that those closest to them do not succumb to conditions that will cause difficulty for the immediate unit, thus avoiding impact on their capacity to maintain a stable environment where basic needs of food, shelter, and safety can be met. The family unit is the functional collective of people who share relational ties through kinship or ancestry, and it is within this micro context that obligations to provide care, and to receive it, are strongest. The connection of families within a geographic space creates a village, a community, or a group who share common needs, and the drawing together of these communities results in a society that develops rules around who should provide services, how these should be distributed on what basis, and how people who need different types of care should be treated. This concept of 'care' has long been debated in literature spanning back to the earliest philosophers and explored in ancient religious texts. What do we mean by the idea of 'care'? Do people have moral obligations to care for others regardless of the nature of their relationship? Under what circumstances does this moral obligation to care for another cease? Who should determine what levels of care should be provided under what criteria? Do people by their actions and behaviours nullify the responsibility of others to care for them? Do those in positions of power and authority inherit a moral or legal obligation to provide care to those who need it, and what are the sanctions if such care is not provided?

These questions, and many more, lie at the heart of the professions that have a role in 'caring', that is those professions who have as their mandate a duty to respond to situations that prevent people from living their optimal life characterised by health, happiness, safety, and stability. Hugman (2005, p. 1) furthers this definition of 'caring professions' as "those occupations that, on the basis of a high level of training in specific knowledge and skills, undertake work in which the human person is both the object and subject, whether physically, mentally, emotionally or spiritually". Social work is one of a number of professional disciplines that claim legitimacy in the space of 'caring' or 'helping' professions (Meagher and Parton 2004; Hugman 2005; Chenoweth and McAuliffe 2020). Clarifying the obligations and responsibilities of the role that social workers play in the caregiving workforce requires navigation of many layers of understanding of what constitutes care, and what 'lack of care' or neglect looks like in practice which is often more the focus of research and reflection. Theory and practice become entwined in these debates making the requirement to establish theory *for* practice an important starting point.

Establishing Feminist Theory and an Ethic of Care as Theory for Social Work Practice

As with any body of theory, ideology, perspective, model, or paradigm, there are figures through history that become associated with ways of articulating and defining core concepts, generally in published form, that are then accepted or critiqued, extended, and reformulated. The Ethic of Care has its own clear trajectory characterised by central ideas based in a thread that has woven its way across time alongside the historical developments of the waves of feminist theory. It is not the intention of this chapter to cover feminism in depth, although the purported waves of feminism, four well established and the fifth perhaps gaining traction, are commonly known.

As a brief recap, the first wave of feminism had as its primary goal the achievement of the vote for women, previously denied until 1920 for white women, but not for another 45 years for women of colour. The Suffragettes, as they were known, included Mary Wollstonecraft (1759–1797), a young English writer and philosopher, who wrote *A Vindication of the Rights of Woman* in 1792, not long before her death at the age of 38. As a staunch advocate of women, Wollstonecraft sowed seeds of a more unconventional view of femininity and posited the idea that if women could be as educated as men have been, they would not necessarily be viewed as inferior to men, rather their equals. Prominent first wave feminists active in both the USA and Britain included Susan B. Anthony, Alice Stone Blackwell, Elizabeth Cady Stanton, Emeline Pankhurst, and Sojourner Truth, all of whom championed women's rights to vote, education, and freedom from slavery. Simone de Beauvoir, a French feminist activist and philosopher, explored the oppression of women in her book *The Second Sex* (1948) that set the foundations for modern feminism. The day in 1955 that an indignant Rosa Parkes refused to give up her seat on a bus for a white man saw racial segregation become an issue more explicitly entwined with the feminist cause.

As feminist ideals began to take hold, and debates around reproductive rights and the fight for women to be seen as more than property unfolded, the second wave of feminism swept through the 1960s–1970s alongside civil rights movements and social activism. Traditional roles of women in the family and home were questioned, and social structures that were seen to hold women back from engagement in work and education were challenged. Liberal (mainstream) feminists focused on gender discrimination, seeking equality for men and women. Radical feminism resisted the idea of men and women being the same, focusing on the patriarchal system and its downfall. Cultural feminism focused on differences between men and women being the result of cultural construction rather than innate biology. The catchcry of the second wave was 'the personal is political', and notable feminist writers such as Betty Friedan (*the Feminine Mystique* 1963), Germaine Greer (*The Female Eunuch* 1970), and Gloria Steinam (*Women's Action Alliance* 1972) paved the way for new ways of thinking about sex and gender, the role of women, gender stereotypes, and women's participation in the workforce.

The third wave of feminism in the 1990s defied previous traditions and proclaimed that women should make their own choices and live lives of freedom from socially constructed norms. Women like Kimberle Crenshaw (1989, 2017), an American civil rights advocate and critical race scholar, devised the term "intersectionality" that turned the focus to the intersections of race, gender, sexuality, disability, class, and the multiplied oppressions that happen as a result of these intersections. The connections to feminist theory were clear and contributed to a new knowledge base about gender and critical race relations. The fourth wave of feminism, characterised by the #MeToo movement begun in 2006 by activist Tarana Burke, emphasised transgender inclusivity, body-positivity, and largely online activism gaining momentum against a backdrop of conservative political forces in many countries that have continued to stand in the way of full representation of women at the tables of power. Challenging those social structures that continue to marginalise women is a primary focus of fourth wave feminism, with gender equality back in the centre and empowerment of women to stand up and collectively agitate for change a core message. It is often argued that the waves of feminism continue in conflict with each other, as 'fourth wavers' (granddaughters) come head to head with 'second wavers' (grandmothers).

The fifth wave of feminism is under construction, and likely with global events to become a tsunami as some of the hard-fought rights of women (like rights to legalised abortion and challenges to landmark legal precedent like Roe vs Wade) are challenged by forces of conservatism. The fifth wave is founded on activism, building on fourth-wave achievements but recognising the enormity of the task still ahead albeit with ideologies of antiwork, abolition of carceral systems, and distrust of anything related to government. The vibrancy of feminist history with all of its activism and achievements to elevate the status of women created an ideal context for the development of a moral philosophy based on ideals of connectedness, relationships, inclusivity, reciprocity, and interdependence. The Ethic of Care had fertile ground on which to seed and grow, as will be seen in the following section.

An Ethic of Care: Early Developments

In 1982, a book was released titled *In a Different Voice*, authored by an American psychologist who had been part of the second wave feminist movement and actively

18 An Ethic of Care: Contributions to Social Work Practice

involved in women's rights activities. Carol Gilligan had been researching the development of girls from a moral psychology perspective, which brought her into academic conflict with her teacher and friend Laurence Kohlberg whose research with boys concluded that they were able to reach a higher level of moral development than girls. In conducting her own research, Gilligan argued that differences in moral reasoning meant that while boys focused primarily on fairness and logic, girls were more focused on human relationships. Her conclusion was that boys experience relationship separations differently at a younger age than girls, moving toward autonomy more quickly, so girls have a deeper propensity to guard and nurture relationships with the additional years of emotional maturity. Gilligan's theorising about the moral development of girls and hypotheses about caring relationships resulted in the first articulations of the Ethic of Care, attributed to her and then a series of others who followed in her path (Gilligan 1982). In an interview in 2011, Carol Gilligan provided her thoughts on how the Ethic of Care had crystallised in her own mind with the following quote:

> A feminist ethic of care is an ethic of resistance to the injustices inherent in patriarchy (the association of care and caring with women rather than with humans, the feminization of care work, the rendering of care as subsidiary to justice—a matter of special obligations or interpersonal relationships). A feminist ethic of care guides the historic struggle to free democracy from patriarchy; it is the ethic of a democratic society, it transcends the gender binaries and hierarchies that structure patriarchal institutions and cultures. An ethics of care is key to human survival and also to the realization of a global society. https://ethicsofcare.org/carol-gilligan/

While Carol Gilligan paved the way for scholarship on the Ethic of Care to move forward in the discipline of psychology, others within the feminist movement focused on the concept of 'care' by exploring different applications. Nel Noddings, an American educator and mother of 10, with a background in mathematics became interested in moral education and published her book *Caring: A Feminine Approach to Ethics and Moral Education* in 1984. Noddings largely agreed with Gilligan on many points about moral development, but took the treatise to a new level with her ideas about what has become known as relational ethics. Essentially, Noddings held the position that an Ethic of Care is founded on an understanding of the position of the 'one-caring' and the 'one cared for'. This relational commitment is complex and not without many inherent problems as the 'one-caring' may at times feel resentment and burden, while the one 'cared for' may feel that the one-caring has not gone far enough in providing what is needed. The caring relationship will be inevitably different if it is within a family, to the relationship with one not so familiar or a more distant relative. If the one-caring is a paid worker, the relationship takes on a different dimension again.

There is also a distinction between natural caring and ethical caring. Natural caring is based on love whereas ethical caring is based on duty and obligation. Noddings (1984, p. 8) states: "An ethic built on caring is, I think, characteristically and essentially feminine – which is not to say, of course, that it cannot be shared by men, any more than we should care to say that traditional moral systems cannot be embraced by women. But an ethic of caring arises, I believe, out of our experience as women, just as the traditional logical approach to ethical problems arises more obviously from masculine experience". Noddings drew much criticism from second wave feminists for her views on differences between female and male morality, particularly as she was seen as promoting women as better suited to unpaid caring responsibilities. Some other feminist thinkers of the time such as Virginia Held took the position that care is both a practice and a value, but not necessarily a virtue. Care is something to be worked at, developed, and exists in relation to others, not as purely an internal disposition. There is a responsibility involved in the work and practice of caring, that makes it an ethical matter because there is a moral dimension underlying relationships and the nature of those relationships defines how care is then actualised. In her book *The Ethics of Care: Personal, Political, Global* (2006), Held draws the distinction between the ethics of care and virtue ethics, focusing on this relational dimension as the primary point of difference between action and character.

Another prominent philosopher, Eva Feder Kittay, aligned with Virginia Held's views on the criticality of relationships in the Ethic of Care, shifted the debates further with her unravelling of the role of 'dependence' in caring relationships, particularly in the field of disability. Kittay argues that the relationality of humans to humans, (which she says also extends to relationality to human to non-human where responsibility is part of that relationship) means that violation of the terms of that relationality is morally unacceptable. She uses her experiences of mothering her daughter who has multiple disabilities as a way of exploring concepts of dependency, interdependency and independence, and argues convincingly that 'care' needs to be much better understood as a way of meeting needs well, particularly for people who cannot meet their own needs themselves. Kittay has extended her thinking about what constitutes an Ethic of Care from disability into fields of ageing, and responses to people seeking refugee status and asylum. Her premise is that caregiving is labour, and should be compensated as such and given value as a skill that can be developed so that it is done well. This conceptualisation of care as labour resonates with feminist ideology and extends it further into the political realm (Kittay 1999, 2021).

Social work, as a discipline committed to human rights and anti-oppressive practice upholds the connections between the personal and the political as this is well aligned with a critical social work approach (Pease et al. 2016). Furthermore, when social workers view individuals within their social spheres in accordance with a person-in-environment approach, workforce engagement should be non-discriminatory and anti-oppressive in terms of gender. When women take on caring roles as paid work, this work should be appropriately remunerated, and when women take the primary share of unpaid caring work, this should also be recognised and compensated. Feminist social work practice has a long history of promoting the rights of women in work and in unpaid labour, and this sits comfortably with the Ethic of Care as a moral philosophical position, alongside Virtue Ethics (Wendt and Moulding 2016). The following section takes the Ethic of Care into the political sphere which is also where social work situates itself in its alignment with critical theory, structural and radical positions that take a broader societal and power-based view of care relations.

The Ethic of Care as Political Activity

While the early development of an Ethic of Care arose within the domain of psychology and moral development, with the focus on gender relations and roles, it was inevitable that it would shift, along with the waves of feminist thought, into the political sphere. One of the most influential women who took the Ethic of Care into her analysis of political systems is Joan Tronto, an American professor of political science. Tronto has become one of the most cited writers on the Ethic of Care making an impact in this field with her 1993 book *Moral Boundaries: A Political Argument for an Ethic of Care*, drawing on the previous work of Carol Gilligan and Virginia Held. In this book, Tronto put forward the argument that there are four essentially linear phases of care: 1. caring about; 2. taking care of; 3. care-giving; and 4. care-receiving. Many years later, she added a fifth phase, caring-with. Each of these phases corresponds to a particular ethical dimension, or virtue, which makes care an action rather than an emotion. The four virtues are attentiveness, responsibility, competence, and responsiveness. The associated virtues that connect to 'caring-with' are solidarity and trust. These phases and virtues provide explanation for interdependent relationships between care-providers and those requiring care that move across the cultural, economic, and social spheres (Tronto 1993).

If a person is caring *about* someone else, they bring to the relationship qualities including nurturing, well wishes, curiosity about potential needs, and an awareness of what the other may not be making explicit in words or actions. When a person is 'taking care of' another, they display a willingness to meet expressed needs through some form of action designed to address, alleviate, or promote something that is of relevance to the person requiring care. The willingness to meet needs may be promulgated by financial or material gain, and be a contracted arrangement, but this does not negate the actions of responsibility. Care-giving is an activity that requires competence and the capacity to engage in tasks that do not cause harm. The requirement for competence ties care-giving into a more formalised arrangement than 'taking care of' that may be much more informal with different relational reciprocity. Care-receiving requires a responsiveness to the care offered by another, with an implicit understanding that there will be protection and safety in the relationship that will help bridge the vulnerability of the power dynamics between the one cared-for, and the one caring. When this protection and safety are not present, or are violated, the potential for abuse has deep ramifications for the one receiving care. Unfortunately, this scenario plays out all too often in aged, disability, mental health services, and child protection.

Tronto expanded her ideas about the Ethic of Care in a substantial body of literature that continues to have currency in the contemporary global situation. Of significance over the past two decades is her contribution to exploring what makes a caring or a noncaring institution (Tronto 2010), followed by her work on caring democracy (Tronto 2013, 2015). It is worth tracking back to look at how Tronto and her colleague Berenice Fisher originally defined 'care', this being "on the most general level we suggest that caring be viewed as a species activity that includes everything that we do to maintain, continue and repair our 'world' so that we can live in it as well as possible. That world includes our bodies, our selves, and our environment, all of which we seek to interweave in a complex life-sustaining web" (Tronto 1993, p. 40). Such language is familiar to social work with its focus on person-in-environment, making it entirely reasonable that social workers should be concerned with the institutions that provide care for vulnerable people, as well as the individual care that is provided. Tronto (2010) raises some pertinent points in her discussion of caring institutions as places that need to have a purpose for caring, a good analysis of the power relations both internal and external to the institution, and a capacity to provide particular care tailored to the expressed needs of care-receivers. Inclusion of the voices of those being cared for within institutions is one indicator of 'good care'. This is something that is well within the social work scope of practice, as social workers are particularly skilled in empowerment approaches that encourage those with marginalised status to actively engage in decisions about issues that affect them. Social workers will often be the member of the care team who draws in support from family or significant others, who reminds others that the person being cared for may have an opinion about a treatment or a decision being considered, and who raises questions about the person's place in their immediate living environment and perhaps their broader community.

There is substantial evidence that when people are invited to be a part of decision-making about their environment and services that they are receiving, they are more likely to benefit from those services and are more committed to finding workable solutions to problems (Barnes and Bennett 1998, Barnes et al. 2015). The literature about inclusion of service users in design and evaluation of programmes, the moves to increase service user voice in decision-making, and promotion of peer workers in fields such as mental health, alcohol and other drugs, disability, and community work align well with an Ethic of Care and are very compatible with Tronto's framework and points made about caring institutions. In social work language, this is all about the valuing of lived experience and the recognition that people are experts of their own lives and experiences. Enabling people who require some form of care to share their experiences is a powerful way of respecting their human dignity and worth, guarding against a slide into paternalism that Tronto and others who write about the Ethic of Care highlight as a risk to 'good care'.

The activities of care that Tronto put forward have formed the basis of a number of explorations of the giving and receipt of care in different fields in social work, health, and human services. Some of these fields will be explored further here to illustrate how an Ethic of Care might be used to understand injustice that comes into stark form when exposed through research. For example, Dorothee Hölscher explored participatory parity in a South African higher education context using a combination of Tronto's Ethic of Care (1993, 2010) and Nancy Fraser's work on social justice (2008) to conclude that the violations and lack of care experienced by students entangled in a neoliberal University could only be shifted if there were an "expansion of spaces in which good care becomes possible" (Hölscher 2018, p. 45). Students needed the solidarity of their lecturers to give voice to practices that were harmful to them, for example, the expectations of men working in university administration that poor female students would trade sex for accommodation security. To shift to a space of caring for vulnerable students who voiced these experiences, lecturers would have to "engage with their own experiences of lacking care, apply the strategies suggested by the students in their own spheres, and re-articulate their own demands for voice" (p. 46). Hölscher uses this example to engage with the complexity of the caring for justice debates in highlighting the enormous pressures that exist in neoliberal contexts that prioritise money over care.

In another example, disability rights activist and author Tom Shakespeare (2013) has drawn on Ethic of Care work to explore how constructions of people living with disabilities can be reframed to position them not as people who place burden on society, but who offer society different and useful vantage points from which to observe institutional structures and accessibility. Shakespeare (2000), who in earlier writing preferred the term 'help' to 'care' because of the connotations of dependency, often refers to feminist Ethic of Care writers like Tronto and Kittay as setting out a theoretical alternative for disability studies. This point was also made in the Australian Royal Commission Report into Violence, Abuse, Neglect and Exploitation of People with Disability. In this report, a recommendation is made that "understanding theoretical debates about independence, dependence and interdependence helps us to balance systems that elevate care and those that empower autonomy (the dignity of risk)" (Clifton 2020, p. 35). Shuttleworth (2018) sets out a convincing argument that of all the fields of practice that social workers are employed within, disability is the area that is most contested when it comes to defining care. Strong advocacy movements and critical disability studies have resulted in system change that have seen growth of user-directed models of care in many countries, and people living with disabilities afforded much greater levels of control and autonomy over engagement with services that broker and provide care.

In the field of child protection, the Ethic of Care and relational practice has also had an increasing impact on exploration of systems that have traditionally not focused on this way of viewing complex social issues. Child protection work falls under the justice banner more so than care because of its requirements for evidence to support actions (such as removal of children from families) and its statutory foundations which place processes within legal systems that are punitive and rife with power. The inherent tension between 'care and control' has for decades been one of the most challenging parts of social work practice (Day 1979). On the one hand, a social worker will 'care' about the best interests of a child who is at risk of abuse or neglect, but then exert 'control' by using statutory authority to take action against the wishes of the family in order to protect that child.

Holland (2010) conducted research with 'looked after' young people leaving foster arrangements and found that the most important signifiers of 'care' for them were longevity (lasting relationships), fairness, partiality, reliability, and everyday acts. Many examples given of perceptions of care were actually more about 'lack of care' and what this felt like from a position of powerlessness and vulnerability. Again, the ideas about care of writers such as Gilligan, Held, Noddings, and Tronto are commonly used in literature to assist practitioners to work from a more relational and care-focused ethical framework in carrying out their responsibilities with families and children (Lonne et al. 2015). There have been slow but steady changes in many child protection and juvenile justice systems as the pendulum swings toward a better understanding that care-based interventions, at least in tandem with justice, are likely to secure better long-term outcomes for children, young people, their families, and communities (Featherstone et al. 2014; Harries 2018).

There have been many other influential feminist political scientists such as Selma Sevenhuijsen (1998), Fiona Robinson (1999), and Fiona Williams (2001) who have both supported and critiqued Joan Tronto and each other in the attempts to apply the Ethic of Care to a range of global scenarios such as world poverty, concepts of citizenship, human security, the dilemmas of institutional care of the aged, those with disabilities, children, and refugees. As these prominent academics craft their ideas into books, articles, conferences, and websites, the growing literature on the Ethic of Care continues to expand and the applications to global events such as the COVID-19 pandemic are drawn forth. Tronto and other feminists have had much to contribute to analysis of the political management of the pandemic in the USA and other countries, highlighting the gross inequities in responses that have seen 'essential workers', predominantly women, forced to hold the front line of the crisis while most at risk of contracting the virus themselves due to poor provision of PPE in many settings (Fine and Tronto 2020; Hamilton 2020). As economies collapsed and people shifted from workplaces to home-based work, it was again women who predominantly shouldered the tasks of caring for children and educating them at home during lengthy periods of lockdown. The most vulnerable citizens, those in aged care and disability facilities, were segregated and separated from families, and the care workforce, again mainly women on very low rates of pay, were expected to continue their caring responsibilities despite high risk and little compensation.

In an article about crisis management in the context of COVID-19, Branicki (2020, p. 880) used the feminist Ethic of Care to propose a new way of managing work, lockdowns, and education, concluding that "feminist crisis management would see crises as multiple and contextualized, as enduring and overlapping phenomena that are enmeshed and embedded within each other to a significant extent. Crises compound and confound each other within webs of relationships informed by care". Kabeer et al. (2021) concluded that marginalised and low-income women bore the brunt of the COVID-19 crisis across a large part of the world and, of interest, also found that countries with women leaders fared better in maintaining systems of care than those led by men. From a feminist perspective, the implications for women who needed to spend more time mobile outside the home to get to and from work, or travel between more than one job, while continuing to provide care-giving to older family members and children placed them at high risk of care overload. As essential workers, these women were generally not entitled to any benefits, and many lost their jobs due to the competing demands of work and family care. There has also been evidence that family and domestic violence has steadily increased through and following periods of stay-at-home orders and lockdown, placing women at even more risk, and disrupting precarious care-giving responsibilities (Piquero et al. 2021). Rauhaus et al. (2020) have also explored responses to the problems caused by the pandemic where lockdowns increased incidents of violence but also made it very difficult for women to reach out for help, arguing that an Ethic of Care response combined with empathy and care-based social policies was urgently needed.

The examples provided indicate clearly that the contributions of the political scientists, economists, and feminist philosophers have been usefully drawn across to assist the understanding of alternate ways of constructing care systems in a range of diverse areas. There is great benefit to social work in having the Ethic of Care perspectives from these sources of expertise applied to some of the challenges facing the profession. As social work had already claimed feminist theory as aligned with its mission and mandate, the development of the Ethic of Care has proved compatible with ways of working that support collective action, anti-oppressive and empowerment approaches, and relational practice. Over time, the language surrounding the Ethic of Care as it applies to social work has firmed up, as seen in the use of these terms to describe it in the context of neoliberal social work: "Indeed, ethical perspectives concerned with inter-dependence, embodiment, relationality, proximity, mutuality and trust typically characterize post-liberal ethics and are therefore especially relevant to contemporary social work theory and practice" (Shaw 2018, p. 422).

Moving to a Critical Ethic of Care and the Contributions of Social Work to a Neoliberal Pushback

Koggel and Orme (2010, p. 109) made a statement in an editorial for a special issue on Care Ethics for the journal *Ethics and Social Welfare* that "There is an ongoing need for a critical analysis of any policy initiative from the perspective of the ethic of care, a need that makes this a significant area for further development". While this statement is now over a decade old, it would be true to claim that the perspective of care has moved more deeply into social policy practice in the domains of the helping professions and human services work. In social work, the term now more commonly embraced in social work literature is a 'Critical Ethic of Care' which shows the alignment with critical social theory, anti-oppressive practice, and empowerment approaches, all of which align closely with feminist theory. More recent literature and research showcase how a Critical Ethic of Care can shift and challenge common issues within social work settings, with the aim of pushing back on neoliberalism and managerialism that have continued a stranglehold on social work in the contemporary era (Pease et al. 2016). Neoliberalism in this context is the shifting of care from the responsibility of public institutions into the private sphere where such care is either unpaid and under-resourced within families or positioned within for-profit organisations. The underlying premise of neoliberalism is that individuals are autonomous beings with free will to make their own decisions and choices about their care needs within a market that will provide for those needs for those able to pay and contribute. Neoliberalism is therefore problematic for people who are more marginalised or disadvantaged, which is where the Critical Ethic of Care has its most weight.

A Critical Ethic of Care will not draw assumptions that women are more natural care-givers than men but will address the power imbalances in societal structures and institutions that privilege men in the world of work, relegating care responsibilities largely to women. In this way, a Critical Ethic of Care is at odds with some of the earlier writings of feminist moral philosophers such as Carol Gilligan. A Critical Ethic of Care will also take a position aligned with intersectionality, mentioned earlier in this chapter as championed by Kimberle Crenshaw. The intersections of race, class, gender, ethnicity, sexuality, disability, and age, when analysed in relation to care-givers and care-receivers, show up the dominance of unequal distributions particularly around class, gender, and race (Hankivsky 2014).

Locating the Ethic of Care Within Social Work Practice

Case Studies: Ethic of Care in Action

The Impacts of Climate Change and the Case for an Ethic of Care in Responses to Natural Disasters

For decades, social work has been one of the professional disciplines that has supported climate justice and environmental responsibility. Drawing in the environment to a central space in social work education has been much more recent, and there has been substantial criticism that green social work, or eco-social work, has not had a more prominent place.

There is scientific consensus that weather patterns and shifts in natural environments on land and sea have been changing on a global scale for many decades. Social work practice focuses on understanding people within their unique contexts – social, cultural, economic, legal, religious and spiritual, and environmental – and what happens with unanticipated climate events can have significant impacts on lives, livelihoods, and psychological well-being. The purpose of social work is to intervene and "respond with passion, hope and care, to human, social and environmental need wherever and however it is manifested" (Chenoweth and McAuliffe 2020, p. 17). In recent years, parts of Australia have seen devastation by fires, floods, and cyclones, leaving an aftermath of destruction and despair as human and non-human species battle the elements. Whole communities have been razed to the ground by flames, or completely inundated with relentless rising floodwaters. While community action is swift in these situations, typically government action in response to disasters moves frustratingly slowly. There is an undertone of the 'deserving vs undeserving' in the provision of financial relief, particularly if an impacted household or community has been through the same horrific scenario more than once. For those without insurance, there is a subtle blaming that pushes responsibility back onto those who 'should have been better prepared', even if the cost of insurance or relocation to higher ground or a more fire-proof space was out of their reach. Emergency evacuation centres and community hubs spring into action in times of natural disasters, with policies and processes ready and waiting for those who need to make urgent claims for assistance. And then the reality hits. To get government assistance, documents are required as proof of identity, income, expenditure, assets, and liabilities. Those documents, however, have been burnt to a cinder in fire, or destroyed in muddy waters. Donna Orange (2011), a psychoanalyst and philosopher, writes about the 'school of suspicion' where the focus lies on questioning the ulterior motive in seeking help, the suspicion of someone (the suffering stranger) trying to gain something to which they are not entitled. Tying financial relief up in bureaucratic red tape seems to buy into this suspicion and is completely antithetical to a 'hermeneutic of trust' which requires the one from whom help is sought to suspend suspicion and acknowledge that defensiveness may well be a survival strategy. While Orange does not explicitly describe the hermeneutic of trust as an Ethic of Care strategy, this is essentially what is being proposed.

The catchcry of the Ethic of Care is 'what does a compassionate response require?' The action following on from this question would, under an Ethic of Care response, be to observe and acknowledge the loss of all worldly possessions, moving immediately to provide financial assistance to the level required to reinstate families and communities to a position where relationships can be rebuilt and regenerated. An Ethic of Care response would not be that people are forced to wait in insecure housing, with compromised safety, separated from their community and important relationships. Unfortunately, the Ethic of Care response is incompatible, it seems, with the machinations of policy that operate under a model that privileges those who have resources to work their way through complicated systems. An Ethic of Care response, in which social workers should be front and centre in times of disaster, would use the skill of observation to determine who needs care, who is vulnerable, who lacks the support and resources to navigate bureaucratic mazes, and who is at risk of personal and family breakdown. Under an Ethic of Care, this observational evidence gained from relational practice would be enough to secure immediate financial assistance that is always in abundance from donations and charitable organisations. There was little justification from a position of moral obligation, let alone a position of care, for the Australian Federal Government to hold back an Emergency Response Fund of 4.8 billion dollars while families were sleeping in cars, tents, and emergency caravans in the 2022 floods. There should be no waiting time, no immediately required documentation, no delayed insurance payouts, and no families falling victim to bureaucratic lack of care. Insurance companies should operate on provision of insurance cover for those most in need, not those most able to pay. This would be a response based on an Ethic of Care at the level of the individual, family, group, and community.

As Jenny Boddy points out in her analysis of the impacts of climate change and the usefulness of an Ethic of Care response, "some people are disproportionately affected by climate change, and bear the brunt of environmental disasters, particularly when they are at the intersection of multiple oppressions" (2018, p. 225). In taking the example to the macro level where an Ethic of Care draws in a political response, a systematic review of ethics and flood management identified a number of important themes (Mitrovic et al. 2019). Of interest was the finding in this analysis that 'virtue ethics' was prominent, that being the acknowledgment that in dealing with flood preparation and response, a high level of trust was required at all levels, from politicians providing funds for flood relief, to contractors engaged to rebuild and repair, to services negotiating interventions and crisis management. Virtue ethics and the Ethic of Care share many commonalities and have been described as the "character and relationship-based ethics" (Pullen Sansfacon 2016). On this basis, political interventions and policies to address climate change need to show honesty, impartiality, humility, moral courage, compassion, respect for others, and transparency. Again, this is the language enshrined in the Ethic of Care through all of its literary history.

Case Study: Immersive Virtual Reality in Aged Care

It would not be possible for those writing in the field of ethics of care to neglect exploration of the largely privatised industry that has developed to manage aged care, inclusive of care within the home, residential care, retirement villages, and nursing homes. The aged care sector has come under intense scrutiny in recent times in Australia with a Royal Commission into Aged Care Quality and Safety (2021) describing it as a "national shame" and handing down recommendations about problematic and substandard physical conditions, understaffing and incompetence of staff to carry out basic care needs, poor pay rates of employees, below standard hygiene and food, and restrictive environments that do little to uphold autonomy or human dignity. Social work has been slow to infiltrate the aged care system, but where social work does find entry points, there is a significant amount of work that can be done to promote environments that are based on care and justice (Lloyd 2006; Ward and Barnes 2016). While reports such as the one released following the Royal Commission set out ways in which systemic failures should be addressed by government, how regulatory authorities should deal with breaches of standards, how the aged care workforce should be overhauled, and how the industry should monitor governance and measure performance, there are small micro level actions that can make a real difference in the lives of older people and those caring for them. It is perhaps the balance between the macro and the micro that provides the space for realisation of an Ethic of Care in facilities for frail older people who are moving toward end of life.

A recently published research paper explores an innovative programme where older people across seven aged care facilities were provided with immersive Virtual Reality technology designed to assist them to visit different places and spaces through an individualised experience facilitated and supported by care-givers in the facility (Waycott et al. 2022). This research was founded on an Ethic of Care premise, using the four phases of caring as defined by Tronto (1993) to guide and assess the VR experience. First, 'caring about' meant that managers in charge of the facilities took active steps to purchase VR technology and provided training for staff in the use of this technology. The second phase 'taking care of' resulted in staff of the facilities understanding that older people need and deserve enrichment in their lives, beyond the standardised activities of the larger group, and tailored to their own individual past experiences. This led into the third phase of 'care-giving' where aged care residents were purposefully assessed by care-giver staff for their capacity to engage with the technology in a positive way. In this phase, staff made decisions based on careful observation and assessment, about residents who may not have had the physical capability to manage the headset or controls, or who may have had other cognitive issues (like dementia) that could have made the VR experience frightening or traumatic. The final phase of 'care-receiving' focused on the experiences that the aged care residents had through virtual travel, relaxation imagery, VR games, and personalised engagements.

For some, the experiences brought undeniable joy as they visited places that held memories for them, and relived past experiences that held value. In the research, staff described noticeable positive experiences such as a resident dancing and singing while watching a VR animation. The importance of taking an Ethic of Care approach was highlighted by the fact that for some residents, VR experiences could be distressing, hence the need for individualised preparation before proceeding. An example was provided of a resident who visited the Grand Canyon on an immersive VR experience, only to panic when he found himself standing on the edge of the canyon. The fear of heights he experienced in VR was not immediately picked up by the staff because of the difficulty in gauging reactions of the resident due to the heavy VR headset covering the eyes. The research was important in understanding how staff observed responses and reactions, and how they assessed older people's capacity to engage with the VR experience in a positive way. Gentle touch was noted as an important care-giver skill used by staff to reassure and comfort. This example goes some way to illustrating how an approach based on an Ethic of Care can shift social activities in an aged care facility to engender a positive experience that older people deserve to have created for them by those who are in the care-giver role. It brings care down to the personal level which is where the bedrock for a caring institution, and then a caring system, must be laid for an Ethic of Care to have its place to seed and grow.

Conclusion

It is well established that feminist perspectives and theoretical frames are aligned to the mission and purpose of social work because of the attention to questions of gender, power, relationality, and connectedness within a context of the personal inextricably entwined with the political (Featherstone and Morris 2012; Pullen Sansfacon 2016; Bozaleck 2019). The early feminist writers paved a way forward for consideration of the role and place of women in society, gender differences and the challenges posed to such claims, and discriminatory factors that continue to hold women back from equal participation in home and work. More contemporary feminist political scientists and economists have expanded the arguments into the spheres of democracy, citizenship, and caring institutions, building momentum for the understanding of interdependence as this relates to humans, nonhumans, and the environment. A critical Ethic of Care has gained momentum in the analysis of intersectionality and how this plays out in global events like COVID-19, posing questions about why 'care' as an 'essential service' has not been given the support that it deserves.

The 'caring professions' are not in the highest income brackets, and women shoulder the bulk of unpaid caring within the home in most countries. How the work of caring is valued depends largely on how the institutions of care are constructed. The Ethic of Care stands as a perspective that gives a unique reframe to justice, moulding the edges of what is required by law and policy to incorporate the importance of relationships, connectivity, and trust. Gray (2010, p. 1809) phrased the care/justice dichotomy well: "Neither justice nor care, by itself, is sufficient. Justice says everyone is entitled to the same treatment but an ethics of care may lead to differential treatment, as it may dictate that some people are needier of care than others based on situational and often subjective judgements. Thus, an ethics of care is not necessarily just and a just system is not necessarily caring". At the end of the day as so many writers have pointed out, we are all carers, and we are all cared for. Care is complex and multifaceted. Social work needs the Ethic of Care, so it can hold a steady position within neoliberal organisations that operate from a very different position, one based on individualism and self-reliance rather than collectivism and solidarity. If social workers can continue to pose the question 'what does a compassionate response require?' then the answers may move more toward a response that values care as much as it values justice and rights.

References

Barnes M, Bennett G (1998) Frail bodies, courageous voices: older people influencing community care. Health Social Care Commun 6(2):102–111

Barnes M, Brannelly T, Ward L, Ward N (eds) (2015) Ethics of care: critical advances in international perspective. Bristol University Press, London

Boddy J (2018) The politics of climate change. In: Pease B, Vreugdenhil A, Stanford S (eds) Critical ethics of care in social work. Routledge, London

Bozaleck V (2019) Towards response-able social work: diffracting care through justice. In: Marson S, McKinney R (eds) The Routledge handbook of social work ethics and values. Routledge, New York, pp 215–222

Branicki L (2020) Covid-19, ethics of care, and feminist crisis management. Feminist Frontiers. https://doi.org/10.1111/gwao.12491

Chenoweth L, McAuliffe D (2020) The road to social work and human service practice, 6th edn. Cengage, Melbourne

Clifton S (2020) Hierarchies of power: disability theories and models and their implications for violence against, and abuse, neglect and exploitation of, people with disabilities. Royal Commission into Violence, Abuse, Neglect and Exploitation of People with Disabilities. Research Report

Crenshaw K (1989) Demarginalizing the intersection of race and sex: a black feminist critique of antidiscrimination doctrine, feminist theory and antiracist politics. Univ Chic Leg Forum 1(8):139–167

Crenshaw K (2017) On intersectionality: essential writings. Faculty Books:255. https://scholarship.law.columbia.edu/books/255

Day P (1979) Care and control: a social work dilemma. Soc Policy Adm 18(3):206–209

Featherstone B, Morris K (2012) Feminist ethics of care. In: Gray M, Midgley J, Webb S (eds) The sage handbook of social work. Sage, London

Featherstone B, White S, Morris K (2014) Reimagining child protection: towards humane social work with families. Policy Press, Bristol

Fine M, Tronto J (2020) Care goes viral: care theory and research confront the global COVID-19 pandemic. Int J Care Caring 4(3):301–309

Fraser N (2008) Scales of justice: reimagining political space in a globalizing world. Polity Press, Cambridge

Gilligan C (1982) In a different voice: Psychological theory and women's development. Harvard University Press

Gray M (2010) Moral sources and emergent ethical theories in social work. Br J Soc Work 40(6): 1794–1811

Hamilton M (2020) Carers need respite from care: COVID-19's limiting the options and pushing many to breaking point, Women's Agenda. https://womensagenda.com.au/latest/soapbox/carers-need-respite-from-care-covid-19slimiting-the-options-pushing-many-to-breaking-point/

Hankivsky O (2014) Rethinking care ethics: on the promise and potential of an intersectional analysis. Am Polit Sci Rev 108(2):252–264

Harries M (2018) Protecting children within a relationship -based feminist ethic of care. In: Pease B, Vreugdenhil A, Stanford S (eds) Critical ethics of care in social work. Routledge, London

Held V (2006) The ethics of care: personal, political, global. Oxford University Press, London

Holland S (2010) Looked after children and the ethic of care. Br J Soc Work 40(6):1664–1680

Hölscher D (2018) Caring for justice in a neo-liberal university. South Afr J Higher Educ 32:31–48

Hugman R (2005) New approaches to ethics in the caring professions. Palgrave, London

Kabeer N, Razavi S, Rodgers Y (2021) Feminist economic perspectives on the COVID-19 pandemic. Fem Econ 27:1–29. https://doi.org/10.1080/13545701.2021.1876906

Kittay EF (1999) Love's labour: essays on women, equality and dependency. Routledge, London

Kittay EF (2021) Precarity, precariousness and disability. J Soc Philos 52(3):292–309

Koggel C, Orme J (2010) Care ethics: new theories and applications. Ethics Soc Welfare 4(2):109–114

Lloyd L (2006) A caring profession? The ethics of care and social work with older people. Br J Soc Work 36:1171–1185

Lonne B, Harries M, Featherstone B, Gray M (2015) Working ethically in child protection. Routledge, London

Meagher G, Parton N (2004) Modernising social work and the ethics of care. Soc Work Society 2 (1):28–39

Mitrovic VL, O'Matuna DP, Nola IA (2019) Ethics and floods: a systematic review. Disast Med Public Health Preparedness 13(4):817–828

Orange D (2011) The suffering stranger: hermeneutics for everyday clinical practice. Routledge, London

Pease B, Goldingay S, Hosken N, Nipperess S (2016) Doing critical social work: transformative practices for social justice. Allen & Unwin, Melbourne

Pease B, Vreugenhil A, Stanford S (2018) Critical ethics of care in social work: transforming the politics and practices of caring. Taylor & Francis, London

Piquero AR, Jennings WG, Knaul FM, Jemison E, Kaukinen C (2021) Domestic violence during the COVID-19 pandemic: Evidence from a systematic review and meta-analysis, J Crim Just, 74, https://doi.org/10.1016/j.jcrimjus.2021.101806

Pullen Sansfacon A (2016) Ethics and feminist social work. In: Wendt S, Moulding N (eds) Contemporary feminisms in social work practice. Taylor and Francis, London, pp 40–51

Rauhaus BM, Sibila D, Johnson A (2020) Addressing the increase of domestic violence and abuse during the COVID-19 pandemic: a need for empathy, care, and social equity in collaborative planning and responses. Am Rev Public Adm 50(6–7):668–674

Robinson F (1999) Globalising care: ethics, feminist theory and international relations. Westview Press, Boulder

Royal Commission into Aged Care, Quality and Safety (2021) Final report. https://agedcare.royalcommission.gov.au/publications/final-report

Sevenhuijsen S (1998) Citizenship and the ethics of care: feminist considerations on justice, morality and politics. Routledge, London

Shakespeare T (2000) Help. Venture Press, Birmingham

Shakespeare T (2013) Disability rights and wrongs revisited. Routledge, London

Shaw J (2018) Introducing post-secular social work: towards a post-liberal ethics of care. Br J Soc Work 48(2):412–429

Shuttleworth R (2018) Critical engagements with the politics of care and disability. In: Pease B, Vreugdenhil A, Stanford S (eds) Critical ethics of care in social work. Routledge, London

Tronto JC (1993) Moral boundaries: a political argument for an ethic of care. Routledge, New York

Tronto JC (2010) Creating caring institutions: politics, plurality and purpose. Ethics Soc Welfare 4(2):158–171

Tronto JC (2013) Caring democracy: markets, equality, and justice. New York University Press, New York

Tronto JC (2015) Who cares?: how to reshape a democratic politics. Cornell University Press, New York

Ward L, Barnes M (2016) Transforming practice with older people through an ethic of care. Br J Soc Work 46(4):906–922

Waycott J, Kelly R, Baker S, Neves B, Thach K, Lederman R (2022) The role of staff in facilitating immersive virtual reality for enrichment in aged care: an ethic of care perspective. In: CHI conference on human factors in computing systems (CHI '22), April 29–May 5, 2022, New Orleans. ACM, New York, 17 pages. https://doi.org/10.1145/3491102.3501956

Wendt S, Moulding N (2016) Contemporary feminisms in social work practice. Taylor and Francis, London

Williams F (2001) In and beyond new labour: towards a new political ethics of care. Crit Soc Policy 21(4):467–493

Reconfiguring Social Work Ethics with Posthuman and Post-anthropocentric Imaginaries

19

Vivienne Bozalek and Dorothee Hölscher

Contents

Introduction	368
Towards a Posthuman and Post-anthropocentric Turn in Social Work Ethics	371
Figuration: *Becoming-Octopus*, and a Justice-to-Come	374
Octopus	377
Octopus Sensibilities for an Ethical Social Work	382
Being of the World Rather than in the World	382
Attuning to Situations	383
Beyond Subject/Object	385
Being Curious	388
Being Attentive	388
Rendering Each Other Capable and Response-Able	390
Conclusion	391
References	393

Abstract

This chapter provides provocations for reconfiguring social work ethics by engaging with posthuman and post-anthropocentric imaginaries. It uses the figuration of becoming-octopus to consider what a posthuman, post-anthropocentric ethics might look, be, and feel like, and how it might matter in relation to the complex afflictions social workers are at once entangled with and

---

V. Bozalek (✉)
Women's and Gender Studies, University of the Western Cape, Cape Town, South Africa

Centre for Higher Education Research, Teaching and Learning (CHERTL), Rhodes University, Eastern Cape, South Africa

D. Hölscher
School of Nursing, Midwifery & Social Work, The University of Queensland, St Lucia Brisbane, QLD, Australia

Department of Social Work & Criminology, University of Pretoria, Pretoria, South Africa
e-mail: d.holscher@uq.edu.au

© Springer Nature Singapore Pte Ltd. 2023
D. Hölscher et al. (eds.), *Social Work Theory and Ethics*, Social Work,
https://doi.org/10.1007/978-981-19-1015-9_20

called to respond to, in the twenty-first century. Like much of posthuman and post-anthropocentric scholarship, making multispecies encounters and entanglements the basis of a reconfiguration of social work ethics is a complex undertaking. This chapter is informed by multispecies encounters with an octopus's modes of being and becoming and the ways in which it crafts and responds to whatever it encounters. A highly attentive creature, octopuses use their sensory capacities to deeply attune to their surrounds. This chapter shows how by *becoming-octopus*, social work ethics might be reconfigured as sensibilities – those of being of the world rather than in the world, attunement, beyond subject/object, curiosity, attentiveness, and response-ability. Such sensibilities might prove useful for social work to creatively tune in to arts of living that matter on a disturbed and damaged planet.

Keywords

Posthuman · Post-anthropocentric · Becoming-octopus · Sensibilities · Attunement · Curiosity · Attentiveness · Response-ability

Introduction

How can social work, as "a practice that thinks" (Manning 2016, p. 27), creatively tune in to the world? How might it reconsider – and reconfigure – the ways in which it seeks to matter, ethically, on a disturbed and damaged planet? Historically, social work has treated the human as central to its ethical deliberations and concern. This outlook is epitomised in the general pre-eminence of principle ethics in social work's self-understanding (Weinberger 2022) and, more specifically, in social work's commitment to human rights (see for example, Ife 2012; Nipperess 2016; Staub-Bernasconi 2016). Both traditions gained pre-eminence by being formalised, between the late 1980s and early 2000s, into a network of national, and successive international, codes of ethics (Banks 2021; Hölscher and Nipperess 2021). This commitment remains core to social work's conception of who we are and what we do, with many calls to see social work as "a human rights profession" (Keeney et al. 2019, p. 13). However, at the present conjuncture of intersecting ecological, social, cultural, and political crises, the authors of this chapter are among a growing number of writers who have expressed concerns about the conceptual viability of conflating social work's self-identification with the idea of human rights as an ethical principle, and who have articulated a sense of urgency for critical engagement with the notions of both *human* and *rights* (see for example, Bell 2012, 2021; Bozalek and Pease 2021; Ife 2016; Wilson 2021; Woods and Hölscher 2021).

Social work's foundation in principle ethics and its commitment to human rights are rooted in the philosophical tradition of liberal humanism, which, at its core, assumes that modern societies consist of individuals of equal moral worth. It is not accidental that the term 'individual' is derived from the Latin word, *individuus*, meaning indivisible. Neither is it coincidental that humans reserve the term 'individual' to denote themselves, but generally not to denote other species (with the exception of domesticated companions such as, for example, pet dogs). In this tradition, humans are conceived of as "determined", to a considerable extent, "by characteristics of internal attributions" (Webb 2021a, b, p. 2976), who ideally function as "[e]ssential, autonomous, rational, [and] singular" agents and are deemed to be "perfectible" (Wilson 2021, p. 37). As a short-hand, Braidotti (2013) refers to the ideal-type human as *Human*.

Measured against this idealised Human are all Others: Raced, classed, sexed, or gendered humans, humans categorised as disabled or aged, are just some of the groups who have been deemed 'less than ideal' and, thus, requiring intervention. Moreover, enduring systems of patriarchal violence and coloniality, the holocaust and, indeed, the frequent recurrence of modern genocides are grim examples of how humans, once categorised as 'less than' can have their humanity questioned altogether. Finally, modern economies' apparent dependence on growth with their attendant disregard for the costs thereof for the multispecies world, and humans' apparent difficulties in reconsidering their underlying ideologies even at the current conjuncture of global heating and mass extinction, are illustrative of the harmful and often deadly effects of defining Humanness in opposition to the 'lesser' and the 'non'-human. Thus, for all its emancipatory potential, always implicit in this understanding of the equal moral worth of each and every individual is the presence of a binary opposite – those excluded human Others regarded as 'less-than' and 'non'-human Others – and since the onset of modernity, scientific knowledge of Others has served both discursive and material functions, providing a normative justification and the technological means for conquest, subjugation, colonisation, and control (Barad 2019; Bozalek and Hölscher 2022; Braidotti 2013; Gosh 2021; Hölscher et al. 2020a; Mignolo 2011).

Under the wide umbrella of social work, of course, there are also those traditions that form part of those interdisciplinary and multifaceted movements which critique the assumptions underlying liberal humanism, helping to expose them as flawed, harmful, and indeed deadly, while exploring and proposing critical, conceptual and practical, alternatives (see, as a selection from myriad examples, Alston et al. 2018; Masson and Harms Smith 2019; Ruspini et al. 2011; Weinberger 2022). It is this self-understanding, which is placed further into question by a posthuman and post-anthropocentric turn in the social and human sciences, and which has now also begun to be considered in earnest in terms of its implications for social work theorising, ethics, and practice (see, as a selection from a fast-growing body of scholarship, Bell 2012, 2021; Bozalek and Pease 2021; Hölscher et al. 2020b; Pease 2021; Webb 2021a; Wilson 2021). This chapter is concerned with the ethical implications of this turn. It uses the conceptual persona of *becoming-octopus* (Roberts 2020) to propose one of the ways in which social work ethics might be reconfigured through posthuman and post-anthropocentric imaginaries. The authors alighted on the octopus because one of them (Vivienne) encounters octopuses in her daily sea-swimming and freediving (Shefer and Bozalek 2022). Through "passionate immersion", that is, "becoming curious and so entangled, 'learning to be affected' and so perhaps to understand and care a little differently" (van Dooren et al. 2016,

p. 6), it has been possible to provide 'thick' accounts of octopuses' modes of being, and of the ways in which they craft their worlds – and these accounts are offered below.

The section "Towards a Posthuman and Post-anthropocentric Turn in Social Work Ethics" below presents a selection of ideas, which, the authors contend, are pivotal for a posthuman and post-anthropocentric reconfiguration of social work ethics. To this end, becoming-octopus is employed as a conceptual, practical, and material means of decentring the Human. Becoming-octopus is, thus, a figuration, and this concept is explained in the section "Figuration: *Becoming-Octopus*, and a Justice-to-Come". Braidotti (2022, p. 212) explains that figurations are "thinking aids", which can "help us work through complex issues". Referring to them as "theoretical fictions", Braidotti (2022) contends that figurations "work to dismantle the posture of scientific objectivity, academic hierarchies and lethal binary oppositions" and "gesture towards worlds where being different-from is not an indictment and thinking differently-from does not necessarily mean being worth less than the standard norm set by Man/Anthropos" (212–213). As such, the section "Figuration: *Becoming-Octopus*, and a Justice-to-Come", delves more deeply into the reasons why, and how, becoming-octopus constitutes but one of the possibilities, which are brought to the fore by the noted posthuman and post-anthropocentric turn. The octopus and its manifold capabilities are detailed in the section "Octopus". Section "Octopus Sensibilities for an Ethical Social Work", finally, pulls together the arguments presented across the sections "Towards a Posthuman and Post-anthropocentric Turn in Social Work Ethics", "Figuration: *Becoming-Octopus*, and a Justice-to-Come", and "Octopus" into a set of six octopus sensibilities, which, it is proposed, may be helpful for a social work that seeks to matter ethically, at the current juncture.

Importantly, this chapter is not intended to propose a new, let alone fully-fledged, normative ethics for social work. Instead, it proposes a curious, playful, non-linear and tentacular, yet attentive, and hopefully generative, multispecies thought experiment. It does not pretend to have ready-to-apply answers to any of the questions raised, nor to any of the questions it might prompt a reader to raise. Instead, it hopes to matter, it hopes to provoke, and it just might affect some readers in as-yet unthought-of ways (Manning 2020). None of this is to say that the authors are lacking a sense of urgency about what has prompted this engagement. Accelerating wildfires, pandemics, extreme weather events, desertification, and ensuing sociopolitical crises necessitate new ways of thinking and doing, which "refuse to take refuge" within discourses that are no longer tenable in a "world of rapid anthropogenic alterations" (Alaimo 2016, p. 188). Forms of more-than-human noticing and encounters have never been more urgent and necessary. Unless we find ways of breaking clear from the discourses that separate idealised types of humans from those marked out as 'lesser than' and separate humans from the Earth's multiple others, human extinction may very well be possible alongside that of everyone and everything else (Rose 2017).

Towards a Posthuman and Post-anthropocentric Turn in Social Work Ethics

The terms posthumanism and post-anthropocentrism signify a "qualitative shift in our thinking about ... the basic unit of common reference for our species, our polity and our relationship to the other inhabitants of this planet" (Braidotti 2013, p. 2). They mark out what Tina Wilson (2021) aptly describes as "a third wave ... of critical social theory", following on the "structural (functionalism and conflict)" and, thereafter, the "poststructural (postmodern, postcolonial and some identity knowledge)" waves (p. 32). As such, they are not "discrete traditions", in that the preceding theoretical waves are not "over" (Wilson 2021, p. 32). However, the two concepts do denote paradigmatic changes in our understandings of the world, both ontologically (in terms of being and becoming) and epistemologically (in terms of knowing and who can be knowers), and the purpose of this section is to explicate some of these shifts, with reference to social work.

The gist of the posthuman and post-anthropocentric turn is that the idea of being human as an individual and discrete entity is considered to be no longer sustainable, and, correspondingly, that being in, thinking about, and acting within the world can no longer place the idea of the human at the centre. Instead, posthuman and post-anthropocentric authors such as Karen Barad, Rosi Braidotti, Vinciane Despret, Donna Haraway, and Isabelle Stengers decentre the human by foregrounding entanglements of humans with other species and phenomena. As such, posthuman and post-anthropocentric scholarship centres on a relational ontology, however extending the idea of relationality (as embraced especially by social workers within feminist relational traditions, such as the ethics of care). Posthuman and post-anthropocentric thought also draws attention to the entanglement of other phenomena, which modern thought has tended to treat as binary opposites: discourse and matter; nature and culture; knowing and acting; human and non-human forms of being and becoming; politics and ethics. Thus, posthuman and post-anthropocentric thought enjoys important commonalities with decolonial and Indigenist scholarship (Rosiek et al. 2019), something which is increasingly recognised in social work discourse (see for example, Bell 2021; Wilson 2021; Woods and Hölscher 2021).

As posthuman and post-anthropocentric philosophies disrupt well-established and generally accepted humanist ideas around individuality and identity (Braidotti 2022; Manning 2016, 2020), they eschew the kinds of identity politics that infuse some contemporary understandings of critical social work (Fenton and Smith 2019). Wilson (2021) explains how often, social workers in the critical tradition action their ethical commitments to human rights and social justice by leveraging –

> the contradictions between liberal humanist ideals and actual practices to make the case that marginalised peoples should also be 'included, have 'access' and be 'participants' in the developmental potential and perfectibility that universalising European humanism imagines. This interpretive work to include a perceived margin within a perceived centre is institutionally structured by established strategies of legal advocacy in which an essential rights-bearing subject demands recognition and repair for harm done. Gayatri Spivak's term

'strategic essentialism' is often used to describe this kind of intentional group-based and group-making work (p. 34).

Posthumanist and post-anthropocentric thought complicates such endeavours considerably (Wilson 2021), and this is due to its roots in Baruch Spinoza's philosophy of monism. Spinozist monism, simply put, holds that "everything constitutes everything else", that "things do not have inherently determinate boundaries or properties", that "words do not have inherently determinate meanings" (Webb 2021a, p. 2967), and that "the individuality of specific people and things" is the result of, rather than preceding, their "intra-actions". The idea of intra-action is pivotal here, and Barad (2007) explains it as follows:

> The neologism 'intra-action' signifies the mutual constitution of entangled agencies. That is, in contrast to the usual 'interaction,' which assumes that there are separate individual agencies that precede their interaction, the notion of intra-action recognizes that distinct agencies do not precede, but rather emerge through their intra-action. It is important to note that the 'distinct' agencies are only distinct in a relational, not an absolute, sense, that is, agencies are only distinct in relation to their mutual entanglement; they don't exist as individual elements (p. 33).

To the extent, then, that the difference between the Ones and the Others are treated as phenomena within which all actors are entangled, the strategy of making essentialised identities the base of strategies to overcome the harmful effects of historical, political, economic, and cultural forms of subjugation, marginalisation and exclusion can be shown to be conceptually fraught. Instead, social work's focus is turned on "processes of formation", that is, with relations between the Ones and the Others seen not as opposites but as "a meshwork of interwoven lines of growth, decay, and movement", and "instead of reaching for attributional understandings . . . we find . . . partial and situated results" (Webb 2021a, p. 2977). At its most general, therefore (and without denying the importance of well-being and the reality of structural injustice and the oppression experienced by so many of its service users), posthuman and post-anthropocentric thought provides social work with alternatives to those theoretical and methodological traditions, which take the well-being of individuals (that is, singular, indivisible beings) as central: while concerned with issues of justice, this is not some "teleological endpoint" but instead is continuously "reworked and reconfigured" (Juelskaer et al. 2021, p. 134). This chapter seeks to demonstrate how this can be imagined.

Moreover, the paradigmatic shift heralded by these traditions also places in question social work's tradition of treating the well-being of *anthropos* (that is, humans) as central (Bell 2021; Boulet 2021; Bozalek and Pease 2021; Webb 2021b; Wilson 2021). Thus, both notions – the individuality and centrality of humans – are contested in posthumanist and post-anthropocentric thought. In their place is a vitalist conception of the world, which considers that which exists outside human consciousness to be vital; regards matter not as inert but as having its own life force or vibrancy (Bennett 2009; Braidotti 2013); and recognises all entities as coming into being first and foremost through relationships. While it is impossible to distinguish neatly between the two, Braidotti (2019) contends that, "the *posthuman knowing subject* has to be understood as a relational embodied and embedded, affective and accountable entity and not only as a transcendental consciousness" (p. 31, highlights added), whereas *post-anthropocentrists* contest any worldview, which places human beings at its apex, or centre. Consequently, humans, as all other beings, are seen as "subjects-in-process", *becoming-with* human and non-human others in cycles of "perpetual motion" (Braidotti 2019, p. 6). This also has implications for the binary oppositions of "nature" versus "culture", and "human" versus "animal", which critical posthumanism and post-anthropocentrism have sought to rethink. Conventional social work discourse has tended to reify and reproduce binary categories such as public/private, mind/body, nature/culture, whereas Spinozist monism, as the premise upon which posthumanism and post-anthropocentrism are built, rejects such dualisms (Braidotti 2013), and multispecies alliances and a relational ontology annihilate such divides (Haraway 2008). Instead, it sees the material world as vital, proposing a "radical immanence" (Braidotti 2013, p. 56). Barad puts it thus: "[m]atter feels, converses, suffers, desires, yearns and remembers" (Dolphijn and van der Tuin 2012, p. 59).

It follows that social work's posthuman and post-anthropocentric turn also has an inherently ethical dimension: Ethics, too, is situated and relational, and involves a recognition of *entanglement* – rather than the Human – as central to mattering. To "mark [this] inseparability of ontology, epistemology, and ethics" and to signify the profoundness of the paradigmatic change at stake, Karen Barad devised the neologism, "ethico-onto-epistemology" (Barad 2007, p. 409). Viewed from this perspective, social work practice emerges as inextricably co-imbricated with the wider contextual conditions and dynamics that give rise to the very problems to which the profession is then employed to respond. Consequently, to speak of a posthuman and post-anthropocentric turn in social work ethics is to suggest that there is a need to reconsider the requirements of ethical theorising and practice:

> Entanglements between species mean that predetermined humanist frameworks such as 'human good is more important' and appeals to 'inviolable animal rights' are both unworkable and undesirable (Haraway 2008, p. 87). This then lays the foundation for Haraway's core argument about what should replace longstanding ethical frameworks: care generated from entangled and embodied encounters. (Hollin et al. 2017, p. 934)

Much can be learned for social work ethics from considering diverse multispecies encounters such as those within which this chapter is grounded (that is, Vivienne's daily encounters and passionate immersions with octopuses in her daily sea swimming and free diving), and the recognition that humans are intimately entangled with multispecies relations. Such an ethical sensibility has been termed a cosmopolitical one, which includes non-human actors being able to place their own requirements on humans (see Despret and Meuret 2016; Stengers 2010, 2011 for more on cosmopolitics). Making multispecies encounters and human-nonhuman entanglements the basis of a reconsideration – and propositions for a reconfiguration – of social work ethics is, like much of posthuman and post-anthropocentric scholarship, a complex undertaking. To this end, scholars have developed a number of conceptual tools, of which figuration is an important one. This concept is explained and discussed further in the following section, with reference to Neimanis' (2013) *body of water* and to *becoming-octopus*, the figuration at the heart of this chapter.

Figuration: *Becoming-Octopus*, and a Justice-to-Come

This chapter employs UK artist and founding member of Orphan Drift (see https://www.orphandriftarchive.com/), Maggie Roberts' (2020) *becoming-octopus* as a figuration for what a posthuman, post-anthropocentric ethics might look, be, and feel like, and how it might matter in relation to the complex afflictions social workers are at once entangled with and called to respond to, in the twenty-first century. As stated on its website, https://imagemusictext.com/maggie-roberts-becoming-octopus-meditations/, *Becoming Octopus* is an eight-session guided meditation experience, the aim of which is to transport the meditator into the body, perception and liquid environment of a Common Octopus. Figurations, according to Braidotti (2022), are conceptual personae, which we can use as to figure out what to do about "our material life conditions and the complexities of the present" (p. 212). Over the past 40 years, writers on posthuman and post-anthropocentric ethics have employed a range of figurations. These include the *companion species* (Haraway 2003) and *cyborg* (Haraway 1985), created as a mode of engagement with new ethical concerns and possibilities arising from changes in trans-species relationships in a context of gene- and biotechnological advances, environmental degradation and depletion and destruction of habitats. Other examples are the *world-traveller* (Lugones 2987) and *nomadic subject* (Braidotti 2002, 2006, 2011a, b) which have helped to conceptualise and explore questions of being and modes of relating within contexts of global mobility. Particularly relevant for the purposes of this chapter is Neimanis' (2013) *body of water*, which denotes and explores humans' ontological condition of being constituted largely by and interdependent with water, and its attendant the "ethico-political implications" (p. 27). Indeed, the *posthuman* is itself a conceptual persona, while the figuration of *becoming-octopus*, proposed in this chapter to explore ethical sensibilities for contemporary social work theorising and practice, may be considered just one of the range of imaginaries that are thinkable within a posthuman and post-anthropocentric frame.

Figurations are imaginative responses to particular historical and material conditions, within which their creators are embedded, and of which they are trying to make sense. This sense-making includes figuring out, literally, what these conditions' ethical and political implications might be. Thus emerging from something that is "already there *and* waiting to be tapped", figurations are neither ethically neutral descriptors nor mere metaphors (Neimanis 2013, p. 26; highlights in original). Instead, they mark "concretely situated historical positions" (Braidotti 2006, p. 90) and contain aspirational statements in relation to them. Yet for all their situatedness, and no matter how "intimately local" figurations are, Neimanis (2013) emphasises that figurations are, by definition, "always ... plugged into the global" (p. 26). This matters, given the generalised terms in which the ethical sensibilities arising from *becoming-octopus* are articulated below. With their imaginative power, crisscrossing as they do the binary of the real versus the imagined, resonating as they do with other terms and imaginings, figurations dramatise "processes of becoming", yet "without referring to a normative model of subjectivity, let alone a universal one" (Braidotti 2019, p. 34).

So if figurations *are* more than just metaphor or description, but constitute aspirational statements and dramatisations of sorts, what do they actually *do*? Firstly, to say that figurations are created by someone is actually a misapprehension, as it implies the passivity of objects, which, in order to exist, require the pre-existence of their creators, as a result of whose imaginings they become. Talking about her own conceptual journey in relation to the figuration, *body of water*, Neimanis (2013) alludes instead to a deep and complex entanglement:

> [W]e *are* bodies of water, but we also *reside within* ... a fragile global hydrocommons where ... water's capacity to sustain life is seriously imperilled. *It is this ... context in which I am inextricably embedded that draws me* with a heightened sense of urgency *to ... [this] figuration ... right now* (pp. 27–28; emphases added).

Precisely this pull is what enables figurations to express "grounded complex singularities, not universal claims" (Braidotti 2019, p. 34), attending instead to "the materiality" from which they receive their "metaphorical heft" (Neimanis 2013, p. 27). This attention to materiality, in turn, gives rise to particular sensibilities and facilitates the making of "ontological proposition[s]" rather than principles or injunctions. In other words, figurations make "somewhat banal statement[s] of fact", but with "epistemological and ethico-political implications" that can be challenging indeed (Neimanis 2013, p. 27). Thus, in proposing below that *becoming-octopus* is a figuration of use for ethical theorising and practice in contemporary social work, the following section begins by outlining how an octopus *becomes* as part of the world, what octopuses *do*, and *how* they do what they do. It is only consequently that ethical sensibilities will "flash up" (Barad 2017, p. 38; see also Bozalek and Hölscher 2021). Enacting "political" and ethical "fictions" (Braidotti, cited in Neimanis 2013, p. 26), then, figurations amplify what already is. It is in this way that they enable better attunement to possibilities that are, in fact, always already present. This is the dynamic by which figurations open up "imaginative spaces" without risking "overdetermination ... as a utopian ideal" (Neimanis 2013, p. 26).

The idea of figurations as imaginative, aspirational responses to particular historical and material conditions inevitably raises the question as to what kind of conditions evoke what kind of aspirations. It makes for a good match with social work writers in the critical posthuman and post-anthropocentric traditions, who are concerned with justice. The manner in which this concern manifests departs from social justice discourses, specifically its conceptualisation as an ethical principle, as mainstreamed in social work to date: instead, it might be better conceived of in terms of Derrida's (1994) *justice-to-come*. This term denotes the idea that in the pursuit of justice, there is no endpoint, no fixed ideal, and no one right state to be reached: "*No issue is ever resolved, finally. No past is ever finished finally*" (Barad and Gandorfer 2021, p. 33 emphases in original), but just because it is infinite and will never arrive, it doesn't follow that we mustn't engage with it. In other words, justice is always in the making; it is an open-ended, never-to-be-finished task that must be strived for infinitely and continually in an ongoing, intra-active ethical process (Barad 2010, 2019). This ethical process is rooted in the condensation of the "thick-now" (Barad 2017, p. 21) of *this* moment, which includes the past, the present, and the future in *particular* constellations, and it necessarily entails paying attention to one's material entanglements in all their specificity (Barad in Juelskaer et al. 2021). And, because all life forms – including social life – are regarded first and foremost as relational, as entanglements, and because the differences between the Ones and the Others are, in fact, a product of *intra*-actions rather than interactions, exclusions *can* be undone *without* taking away difference: In this view, justice is a responsive ethical relationality, an inseverable responsibility – with no opt-out clause – towards the entangled Other (Barad 2010):

> Justice is the lived possibility of difference ... without exclusion, a differencing that undoes exclusions through the dynamism by which that which is constitutively excluded becomes a constitutive part of the self, precisely in an undoing of Self/Other (as well as the Self). (Barad and Gandorfer 2021, p. 46)

Accordingly, knowing, being, relating and doing ethically is an ongoing, never-to-be-completed undertaking to participate in the enactment of a justice-to-come.

As with Neimanis' (2013, 2017, 2021) *body of water*, one of the key contributions of *becoming-octopus* to social work's searching for such sensibilities as might contribute to a justice-to-come is what it has to offer for reconsidering the ideas of identity and subjectivity. Both figurations of body of water and becoming-octopus are, in fact, reconfigurations of what in social work are often taken-for-granted understandings of where a self ends, and its Other begins, and both draw on the idea that many presumed *inter*-actions are in fact *intra*-actions, with the difference between self and Other being altogether unsettled (Barad 2007; Webb 2021a, b). The notion of intra-action is centrally important: In dissolving the generally taken-for-granted understanding that self and Other are separate first, and relata only thereafter, both *body of water* and *becoming-octopus* join the tradition of feminist approaches to social work theory and ethics, such as for example the ethics of care, however extending the idea of relationality into the post-human and post-anthropocentric realm. As such, they seek to invite our attention, generate better attunement, rekindle our curiosity, and enable different kinds of responsiveness alongside accountability – all as a result of our deepening consciousness in relation to that which is "too often relegated to the passive backdrop of our lives" (Neimanis 2013, p. 28). It is this which helps to cultivate "a knowing-*with* and knowing-*alongside*, instead of a colonial drive to mastery" (Neimanis 2013, p. 37). Against this background, the next section presents some key features of octopuses, together with an explication of how these open up possibilities for a reconfiguration of ethical sensibilities that is responsive to some of the key challenges social work is facing at the present.

Octopus

Why out of all possibilities settle on *becoming-octopus* as a figuration to help re-imagine ethical sensibilities for a posthumanist and post-anthropocentric social work? Why should there be any detailed focus on, and attention towards, the figure of the octopus? What can be learnt from such a cross-species engagement, from a close and careful observation of fluid octopuses in their watery spaces, and from delving deeply into their capabilities (Fig. 1)?

Octopuses are unusual. As part of the cephalopod family (which also includes squids and nautiluses), they are considered to be highly intelligent, have large brains, and are capable of high-order cognitive functioning such as problem-solving. They are not only aware of their surrounds – they actively engage with it, play with it, recognise it, and change it, figuring and reconfiguring themselves as part of the world. Octopuses have complex nervous systems where the neurons extend through the whole body – including their tentacles, where three fifths of their neurons are located, which have a sense of taste and touch, and which can operate both individually and together (Godfrey-Smith 2017). Importantly, while octopuses

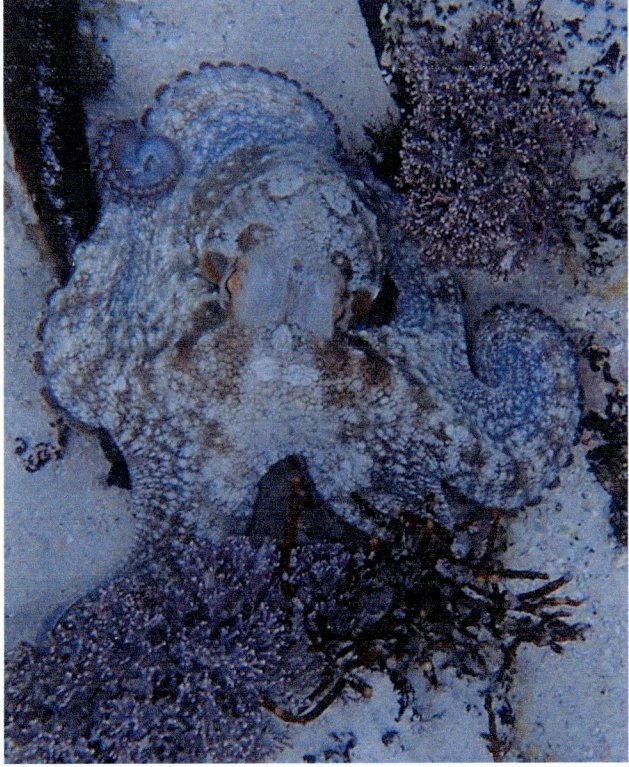

Fig. 1 Octopus vulgaris [Windmill beach, Cape Town]

Fig. 2 Attentive octopus [St James tidal pool]

have a hard beak (similar to a parrot's) which they can use to bite, and they do not have a shell. This renders them vulnerable to predators – for example, seals, pyjama sharks and humans – but it also provides them with unique capabilities by which to protect itself, as well as predating on others (Fig. 2).

Octopuses are highly attentive creatures, using their sensory capacities in deep attunement to their surrounds, while concentrating deeply on particular phenomena. Female octopuses caress their eggs with exquisite diligence, using their suckers "and blow[ing] water through them with ... [their] syphon[s]" (Montgomery 2015, p. 98). Octopuses also explore touch and taste, playing with other creatures through unfurling, stretching, and reaching different tentacles in different directions at once. They are curious, embrace novelty, and want to know about everything around them, intra-acting in exploratory ways with the world. Barad (2007) notes about another sea creature, the brittlestar, that its "survival depends on its capacity to discern the reality of its changing and relational nature", showing the entangled practices of knowing, being and doing-which are all material practices (Barad 2007, p. 376). The same is true for octopuses (Fig. 3).

What is most notable and impressive are octopuses' skilled abilities to change their colour, posture, and shape. Shapes and colours are played out across the whole body. Octopuses are extremely sensitive and can speedily change to become part of their surroundings – as Montgomery (2015) observes, they "can change colour, pattern, and texture in seven tenths of a second" (p. 45) from being red (excited), white (calm, dreaming) and bumpy, to grey and smooth, to looking like a rock or seaweed, all in relation to – intra-acting with – whatever the environment happens to be.

Fig. 3 Unfurling tentacles, becoming-with sand and rock [Windmill Beach, Simon's Town, Cape Town]

> To blend with its surroundings, or to confuse predators or prey, an octopus can produce spots, strips, and blotches of colour anywhere on its body except its suckers and the lining of its funnel and mantle openings. It can create a light show on its skin. (Montgomery 2015, p. 45)

This light show happens through using mechanisms and activating chromatophores in the next layer of skin, which reflects back incoming light. One of the several moving patterns an octopus can create is called "'Passing Cloud', because it's like a dark cloud passing over the landscape – making the octopus look like it's moving when it's not" (Montgomery 2015, p. 46). In addition to their shapeshifting and colour-changing capabilities, octopuses are able to use shells and rocks to cover themselves and their dens, while shooting ink to outwit predators. They can squeeze into tiny places and are excellent at navigation. These are the means by which they can hoodwink other species of animals, escaping, hunting, and attacking them when they are not looking (see for example Craig Foster's film documenting an octopus riding on a pyjama shark's back) (https://en.wikipedia.org/wiki/My_Octopus_Teacher) (Figs. 4 and 5).

Moreover, to escape dangerous predators in the surrounds, an octopus can even lose its limbs - only to regrow it again later (see again, Craig Foster's documentary, My octopus teacher), with

> The regrown arm of an octopus ... [being] as good as new, complete with nerves, muscles, chromatophores, and perfect, virgin suckers. Even the specialised arm of the male, the ligula, can be re-grown (though this reportedly takes a while longer). (Montgomery 2015, pp. 103–104)

With this, octopuses materialise the idea of intra-action beautifully:

Fig. 4 Changing colours, becoming-sea wall [St James tidal pool, Cape Town]

Fig. 5 Becoming-sand, octopus at dawn [Windmill beach, Simon's Town, Cape Town]

> There is no absolute inside or absolute outside. There is only exteriority within, that is, agential separability. Embodiment is a matter not of being specifically situated in the world, but rather of being of the world in its dynamic specificity. (Barad 2007, p. 377)

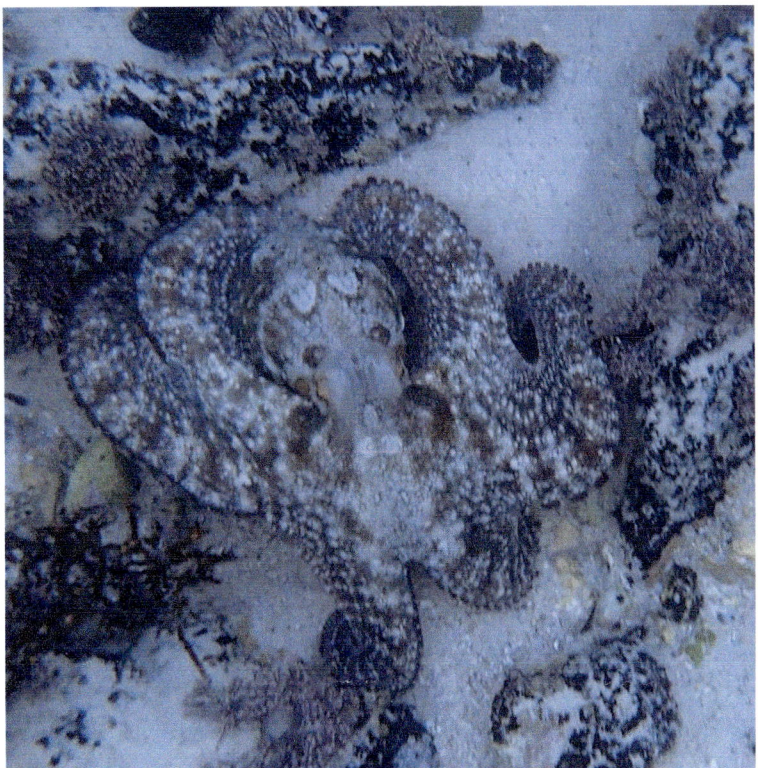

Fig. 6 Octopus, becoming-rock [Windmill beach, Simon's Town, Cape Town]

Indeed, few animals can help humans comprehend the idea of intra-action better than octopuses, with their ability to change colour and shape to merge with the environment and to lose limbs in acts of survival, although Barad (2007) makes similar observations about brittlestars. Octopuses constantly make and unmake, draw and redraw boundaries between themselves and the environments with which they intra-act through practices which matter to their continued existence. Like the shells with which an octopus covers itself, its dismembered tentacle can be seen as part of the octopus or part of the environment, where distinctions of self and other are blurred. The ability to change colour and shape to blend in – if not merge – with whatever environment they find themselves in, to be at once alert and fugitive and relaxed in oceanic hybridity – all this shows that octopuses are agentive beings, which are always already entangled with other phenomena. They, like other phenomena, are not *in* the world, but rather part *of* the world (Barad 2007) (Fig. 6).

In sum, then, octopuses are creatures, which engage curiously and experiment, as they intra-act with their surrounds, becoming-with whatever they alight on. This fine-tuned sensibility serves to trouble and interrupt normative ethical thinking in social work, by cultivating an awareness of what we are doing and how we are connected to and share life with other human, non-human and more-than-human others and the planet more generally. If social work could attend to non-innocent experimentation and risky encounters, it might be better placed to be committed and accountable to what is required to live and die better on our damaged planet. Reconfiguring social work with becoming-octopus is a stark reminder that we as humans do not reside outside of Nature but are part of it.

Octopus Sensibilities for an Ethical Social Work

Different ethical sensibilities "flashed up" (Barad 2017) for the authors of this chapter, as they passionately immersed themselves, and allowed themselves to become entangled, with octopuses – both through direct encounters through sea-swimming and freediving, and through online intra-actions over weeks and months of sharing images, sharing conversations, shared writing, *becoming-octopus*. These are presented below. Other sensibilities may yet emerge, for readers of this chapter, or through other encounters, also with other species, and hopefully, these will be shared elsewhere.

Being of the World Rather than in the World

Recognising the entanglement of octopuses with their surrounds – its ability to "[drop] into resonance with whatever it is in contact with" (Roberts 2020, n.p.) might encourage social workers to move beyond the notion of individuals as separate entities with discrete boundaries, and to see the act of *being* as *being part of* the world, unfolding and reconfiguring within the events or the phenomena within which they, too, are entangled. *Becoming-octopus*, thus, means recognising that the self and the not-self intra-actively co-constitute each other. Such sensitivity to composing-with the surrounds – becoming imperceptible through drawing that which *surrounds* the self *into* the self – opens the self up, continuously moving towards what might yet be, what might yet come or appear. Observing octopuses bring into focus their liveliness both in flux, in moving fluidly, and in resting as part of the world, dissolving separation or boundaries through reinventing its size, shape, colour, and texture, through losing a sense of individuated being, instead reinforcing a sense of indeterminacy, a dynamic, ongoing becoming. As Barad (2007) notes:

> Bodies do not simply take their places in the world. They are not simply situated in, or located in, particular environments. Rather, 'environments' and 'bodies' are intra-actively co-constituted. Bodies ('human,' 'environmental,' or otherwise) are integral 'parts' of, or dynamic reconfigurings of, what is (p. 170).

What would being *of* the world, rather than *in* the world, mean for social work ethics? Firstly, it eschews the idea that the world is made up of individual entities. This metaphysics of individualism lies at the core of principle ethics and of human rights approaches in social work and, as such, is almost taken for granted. This includes a belief that the world consists of independent entities with their own properties and characteristics. Changing this viewpoint to one of entanglement in the world requires significant effort to move away from the idea that individuals pre-exist their relations. Secondly, social work would need to recognise that the human is no longer the centre of relations and existence but is part of an enfolded and entangled articulation of the universe. Responsibilities and ethics do not reside in individual humans but are part of entangled relations of which we are a part. Thirdly, contrary to essentialist accounts of the human, agency is not located in the individual human but is part of the intra-action through which phenomena come into being. Furthermore, intentions are not "pre-existing determinate mental states of individual human beings" (Barad 2007, pp. 22–23). Rather, it is important to understand intentionality as an entangled agency within the complexity of phenomena, which include the human and the non-human. Fourthly, the yearning for a justice-to-come is larger than any one human but pertains to an ongoing concern for living and dying across species on our damaged planet. In this way, becoming-octopus invites a radical rethinking of some of social work's taken-for granted ethical claims as were outlined in the introductory section of this chapter.

Citing Barad, Webb (2021a, p. 2977) suggests that "our current individualistic assumptions, that certain events out in the world follow as a consequence of human actions, choices, intentions and presuppositions, need to be radically re-thought as 'after-the-fact attributions we make in relation to the outcomes' of . . . intra-active events . . .". The implications of conceptualising "being" as a matter of being *of*, rather than *in* the world are, thus, considerable: within a posthuman and post-anthropocentric frame of reference, social workers can no longer be satisfied with thinking about ethical practice in deontological or consequentialist terms (Fig. 7).

Attuning to Situations

Octopuses attune themselves in form, texture and colour, resonating, self-contouring and shifting in quality, absorbing and reflecting light to become indistinguishable from its surrounds, becoming-rock, becoming-kelp, becoming-sea sand. This helps, among other things, to protect itself from predators. Watching octopuses becoming whatever they alight on, in their material sensitivity, one realises that they are endlessly attuned through subtle shifts rather than grand gestures, alternating forms of stillness with tremulous, quick movements. Leading humans through her octopus meditations, Roberts (2020) notes that the focal point for an octopus is both somewhere and everywhere, and it is *not* at the centre of its vision (Fig. 8):

> The octopus drops into resonance with whatever it is in contact with… translates and replicates texture. All of [it] touch[es] through suckers. Subjectivity is in the touching, and [an octopus] become[s] the thing [it] match[es] … dropping into the exact frequency of a thing, a sort of quantum pattern recognition. There is no sense of a separate state.

Fig. 7 Becoming-with seaweed [Windmill beach, Simon's Town, Cape Town]

Fig. 8 Dropping into resonance with surrounds [St James tidal pool, Cape Town]

Another form of attunement to its surrounds is its ability to change its forms of mobility – it can crawl, walk, flow, move all tentacles at the same time or individually. It is highly attuned to vibration and touch: a "force of form" rather than the "form itself" (Manning 2016, p. x). Developing such capacity for attunement can help social work enhance its sense that nothing is fixed in advance; being attuned to whatever happens in events means that we might be "composing at the edges of the as-yet unthought" (Manning 2016, p. 7). From this perspective, predetermined notions of value are of limited use, and an ongoing attunement to what-is-not-yet-but-might-yet-be is a more fruitful way of being in the world.

Moreover, attunement to difference is a crucial sensibility for social work. Not to assume the neurotypical, able-bodied, white, heteronormative, middle-class human as the standard against which to judge, and not to pathologise those who deviate from this norm, remains a work-in-progress. This work-in-progress includes, further, the need to unsettle social work's human-centeredness, founded as it is on a particular imagery of the ideal Human as an independent, self-sufficient, and rational agent, and its traditional disregard for all matters other than, or 'lesser than' that ideal type. Moving beyond such normative positions will facilitate better attunement to what difference can offer social work in thinking and doing otherwise. Some important examples of attunement to difference in social work are those of LeFrançois and Voronka (2022) and their contributions to mad methodologies, Fraser and Taylor's (2021) challenges to humanist social work through a review of domestic violence to animals, and Ross et al. (2021) trans-species ethics of ecological justice, non-violence, and love. These examples demonstrate how attunement may contribute to social workers imagining more affirmative, response-able alternatives to the "problem→intervention→outcome structure" that is so "common in social work" (Wilson 2021, p. 41).

Beyond Subject/Object

Traditional social work, which focuses on reflection and reflexivity, involves a distance between subject and object. In order to see a reflection of yourself in the mirror, there necessarily has to be a distance between you and the mirror (Interview with Barad, in Dolphijn and van der Tuin 2012). From this perspective then, there is a separation between subject and object, whereas from a posthuman and post-anthropocentric position, subject and object are inextricably entangled and only come into being through agential cuts (what Karen Barad refers to as "cutting together-apart") (Barad 2014, p. 168). Agential cuts are enacted through intra-actions and as such, they are different from Cartesian cuts, which denote the presumption, foundational to modern thought, of an inherent, pre-existing distinction between a phenomenon and its binary opposite (like subject/object, but also: human/non-human; observer/observed; knower/known; expert/client; service provider/service user). Agential cuts cut together/apart, in that they both separate and entangle at the same time. In a relational ontology one can never really sever one part or component of a phenomenon from another, thus an agential cut is a

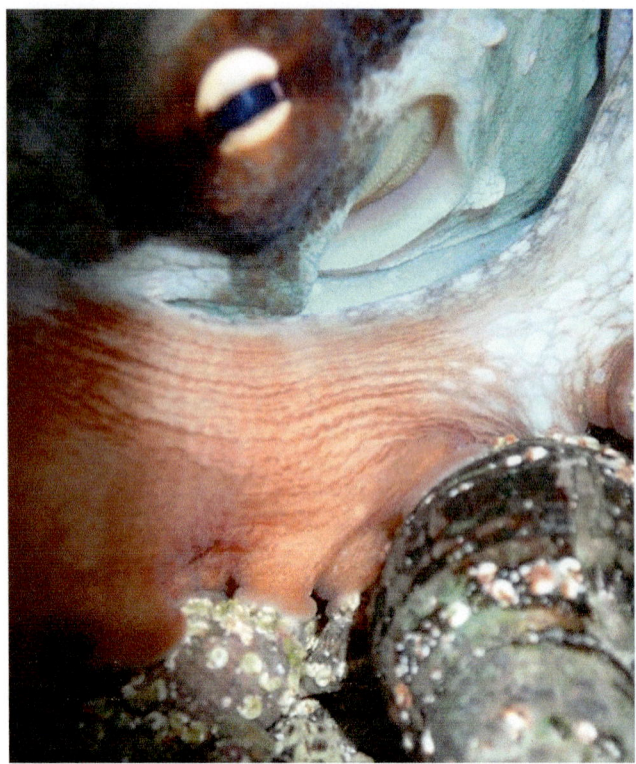

Fig. 9 Octopus shell entanglement [St James tidal pool, Cape Town]

contingent cut: it enacts a provisional separation between subject and object within phenomena. In so doing, it makes the subject and object co-determinate within the phenomenon. In short: rather than regarding independent entities or individuals as pre-existing, according to posthuman and post-anthropocentric thought, it is rather through intra-actions that subject and object emerge from their entangled relations (Fig. 9).

One way of understanding the posthuman enlarged sensibility of relationality, of intra-actively moving beyond subject and object, is by queering the beginning and end of a body, which attuning to octopuses allows us to do. It is difficult to pin something down as a body when its affective tonality makes it at once part of its surrounds, and part of the self (if, as Barad alerts us, there is ever a 'self' to begin with). Octopuses are ultimate shapeshifters, performing a multidimensional openness to indeterminable beings and becomings. Such a sense of indeterminacy can help social workers overcome any sense of complacency or paralysis about what is happening on our damaged planet and what this may mean for our work. Swanson et al. (2017, p. M2) alert us that, "[i]n the indeterminate conditions of environmental damage, nature is suddenly unfamiliar again", and ask, "How shall we find our way?" Able to fit into tiny cracks or holes (which is useful because of their extreme precarity, not having a shell to protect themselves), octopuses give us a sense of the ineffable. That an octopus, moreover, only lives for about 2 years reminds us that life is short and precarious. Octopus also are a forward-force, becoming whatever they alight on or are near to. This is a tangible reminder of how the world's relationality is endless indeed (Roberts 2000). It also opens up new ways of knowing, of becoming in the making, becoming as part of a process or an event (Manning 2016, p. 24). This process can be seen as a making-with, as what Haraway (2016) refers to as *sympoiesis*.

From a posthuman and post-anthropocentric perspective, then, what matters are not the predetermined ends to which the One (social worker) intervenes in the life of the Other (service user) to help them 'develop', 'improve', or 'problem-solve'. Instead, attention is drawn to the manner in which social work processes lead to particular subjectivities. This will, in turn, afford better sight of how social work becomes entangled in the kinds of violences that remain, far too often, embedded in everyday social work practice. Because there is no pre-given or constituted subject and object, social work happens in the midst or middle of relations. This means that neither social worker nor service user can be situated in advance of the event's coming-into-being and the affective tonality of the experience (Manning 2016, p. 28). Ethical practice, then, becomes a matter of relating well: "Rather than conceiving of the service user as the follower of a direction mapped by social work, it is more profitable to consider the relation as 'togethering'" (Webb 2021a, p. 2977; but see also Bozalek and Pease 2021; Bozalek 2020; Webb 2021b) (Fig. 10).

Fig. 10 Octopus, forward-force [Windmill beach, Simon's Town, Cape Town]

Being Curious

An octopus' curiosity and its manner of attentiveness are closely related. It uses its tentacles and suckers to explore its environment in a tactile way. The tentacles are sensitive to light and can also taste as well as touch. In their curiosity towards all situations and creatures and openness to flux and movement, octopuses remind social work of the importance of developing, sustaining, and nurturing an expansive consciousness. Not rigidly nor even closely adhering to rules and regulations but protecting and preserving our sense of mobility and fluidity are what generates and enlarges our ability to feel, perceive, and relate well: what matters is the willingness to take our imagination for a walk (Haraway 2016) – or a swim (Shefer and Bozalek 2022) – or better still, allowing others to take our imagination for a walk (or a swim). Rather than social work relying on its power to assess its Other – its service user, voluntary or involuntary, individual group or community – rather than devising interventions to improve its Other, to make it fit better *into* the environment, becoming-octopus invites social work to be curious in a manner of being engaged and entangled *with its* Other, thus *watering down* the distinction – the opposition – between the One and the Other. It is on the basis of curiosity perceived as a fluid enlargement of being, thinking, engaging, and connecting – on the basis of curiosity as a way of being *part of* the world – that becoming-octopus also encourages attentiveness. Curiosity, then, is not founded on surveillance, control or regulation; instead, this is a curiosity of connection and care. The social work that emerges in the process may well be one that is guided by an ethics of not-knowing, of humility, and of being-with (Fig. 11).

Being Attentive

Attention originates from the Latin word *attendere*, which refers to waiting and overlooking, and which octopuses perfect with its mindful presence. Barad (2007) defines attentiveness as "the ongoing practice of being open and alive to each meeting, each intra-action, so that we might use our ability to respond, our responsibility, to help

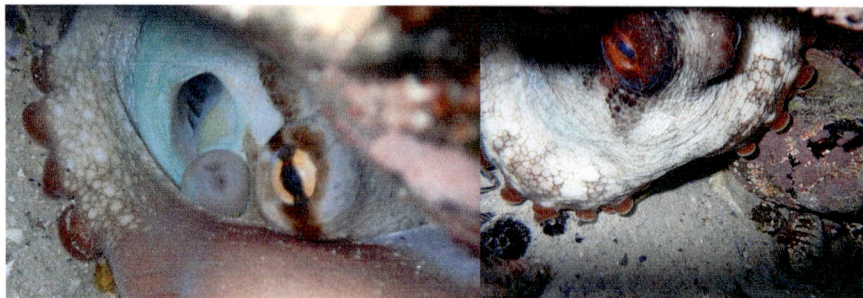

Fig. 11 Octopuses, curious [St James tidal pool, Cape Town]

awaken, to breathe life into ever new possibilities for living justly" (p. x). Generally, an octopus pays careful attention, acting and adjusting its being and becoming, showing both patience and precision in its engagement with the field. The attentiveness of octopuses are evident in their tentacles, which explore the environs through their coiling, unfurling, and stretching in their sensitive and explorative touch.

Perhaps its most loving and meticulous display of attentiveness is to its eggs, which the female defends against predators, through which she blows water to keep them oxygenated and clean, which she never leaves, even while depriving herself of food while caring for them. During the time that she is caring for her eggs, her whole effort is to create conditions for their flourishing, being truly present in her surrounds, in deep awareness of the dangers that predators pose for herself and her eggs. It is true that when the eggs hatch, the mother octopus dies. To be sure, the point here is hardly to propose self-sacrifice as an ethical sensibility for social work practice; instead, the purpose is to highlight the sheer expanse of attentiveness that becoming-octopus denotes and to consider why expanding social work's attentiveness is so important. Often located at the bottom and the margins of large institutions, yet also often positioned such as to profoundly affect the lives of Others, social work practice is deeply entangled in contemporary formations of power, with many social workers at once able to subject others *and* being subjected to power which others hold over them. Foucault's insight into power as constituting both restrictive and productive forces (Braidotti 2013) are centrally important for a posthuman and post-anthropocentric ethics in that the types of power formations within which contemporary social work is entangled and within which it must respond to the world, "are neither coherent, nor rational". Instead,

> The awareness of the instability and lack of coherence of the narratives that compose social structures and relations, far from resulting in a suspension of political and moral action, becomes the starting point to elaborate new forms of resistance suited to the polycentric and dynamic structures of contemporary power. (Braidotti 2013, pp. 26–27)

Given the inevitability of its complex entanglements, learning to be truly present is a critical sensibility: it is a foundation for discerning ways of responding justly to one another; or, more precisely, it is a precondition for discerning ways of subverting and overcoming social works foundational Self/Other divide. As Haraway (2008, p. 88) puts it, "meeting the look of the other, and in so doing facing oneself" is what being present is all about.

Moreover, becoming-octopus in an attentive social work would involve activating the "sensibility of all our embodied faculties" (Lenz Taguchi 2012, p. 272), with a radical openness, so that we are alert and truly present to the multispecies needs within which human needs are entangled, and indeed, in relation to which human needs are foregrounded at the peril of a damaged planet. Finally, with such refined sensibilities of being open and alive to all meetings, becoming-octopus would mean being rigorously attentive to temporality; that is, to how the violences of the past continue to haunt us in the present and will always affect the future – while at the same time retaining a radical openness to, and working actively towards, a justice-to-

Fig. 12 Octopus, attending to its surrounds [St James tidal pool, Cape Town]

come. With its rich, exquisite sensory capacities, becoming-octopus can help address any paucity of imagination in social work (Fig. 12).

Rendering Each Other Capable and Response-Able

As noted before, octopuses have an uncanny ability for responding to, and syncing with the frequencies of other life forms. In doing so, they are a prime example of the ability to open the self to being affected by an other, as well as opening to the Other in the self and its affects on the self, an exteriority-within as Barad (2014) puts it. Haraway (2016) foregrounds learning to pay attention to each other across species. Unlike empathy – which is about trying to identify with an Other to understand what they are thinking and feeling – learning to pay attention denotes a desire for relations of reciprocity and exchange (Despret 2016). This cultivation of attentiveness across difference leads to becoming-with, thus changing who and what the partners become.

With its body ever ready to experiment, deeply immersed in the medium around it, an octopus is able to read difference in the oscillating flow of water movement, ever alert to prey and to predators (Roberts 2020). With their colour-, texture-, and shape-shifting abilities, octopuses have one of the most versatile bodies as far as the ability to respond is concerned: It is well and truly response-*able*. Becoming-octopus is an invitation to help re/configure an ethical social work as an entangled part of the world, a social work that is response-able towards the flourishing of the world. As Karen Barad (2007) aptly expresses it:

> Intra-acting responsibly as part of the world means taking account of the entangled phenomena that are intrinsic to the world's vitality and being responsive to the possibilities that might help us and it flourish. Meeting each moment, being alive to the possibilities of becoming, is an ethical call, an invitation that is written into the very matter of all being and becoming (p. 396).

The implications for a reconfigured social work ethics are that, as against a foregrounding of responsibility (always with the attendant risk of slipping into patronage over individuals in the name of the larger human 'good'), response-ability emerges where social workers and their service users alike are entangled in, implicated in, and responsible for, a justice-to-come.

Conclusion

This chapter cautioned at the onset that what would be presented was not intended as the formulation of a new normative ethics for social work, but rather as a multispecies thought experiment. As such, for some readers, it may have raised more questions than it was able to answer. Potentially, the most burning question is how to account for the considerable constraints placed upon social work by the current neoliberal constraints on practice. To what extent is it – even thinkable to try and realise posthuman and post-anthropocentric modes of being under the weight of current, everyday realities? What would remain of what has been heretofore known as social work? The impression might have been generated that the ethics envisaged by the authors of this chapter places the burden yet again on social workers to make, things different – better – thus taking responsibility for overcoming these constraints. Much rather, the authors wished to make a start at exploring, as part of wider processes of intra-action, how social workers might think differently about the current predicament, within which they are deeply entangled, and about what sorts of ethical sensibilities might thus emerge.

As a creature that is highly transformable and ever-changing, octopuses are full of potential for a figuration of embodied sensibility and flourishing for a social work that matters. This flourishing, as noted earlier, includes living and dying well on our damaged planet. Becoming-octopus alerts us to the importance of moving beyond the volitional, intentional social worker as a human agent and a key determinant of what comes to be. Rather, it demands of social work a cultivation of attentiveness to the details of practices for becoming-with human and more-than-human others, who, too, are consequential. In the words of van Dooren et al. (2016, p. 6), "[t]ransforming noticing into attentiveness—into the cultivation of skills for both paying attention to others and meaningfully responding" is what is needed for social work to begin recrafting its place in a world that we share with what is still a rich variety of other species.

Becoming-octopus is a way of eschewing such normative standards as are typical of conventional social work human rights and principle ethics positions. Honouring different sorts of bodies like octopuses and observing how they are able to exceed the bounds of their bodies through attunement allows us to think otherwise about social work ethics. Octopuses often go unnoticed because through their assimilation to their surrounds, they are able to make themselves imperceptible and unrecognisable. For social work, these subtle acts of resonance and attunement to the wildness of the surrounds provide the potential for reorientation and a move into new directions. With different relational fields forming all the time, new modes of existence can come into being. Here, the knower is not the human social worker but the relationships that create subjects and objects in the first place; it is the relations themselves which create ethics, which create the "ecology where knowledge occurs" (Manning 2016, p. 30). Accordingly, becoming-octopus is one of the many possibilities by which a posthuman and post-anthropocentric approach to social work might create new modes of thinking, new processes of life-living (which are focused not only on human life) on a damaged planet.

For octopuses, forms and identities are dependent on relations, events, and context. Thus, the figuration, *becoming-octopus* alerts social work practitioners to experimental forces and tendencies, which unsettle and shift the field into new modes of existence of what it might yet come to be – the force of the 'what else?' This is a necessary shift from the kinds of practices that social work finds itself habitually engaging in without thinking about the shapes and forms in the surrounds which it might become composed with. It also impresses the importance of moving beyond identity politics as static states, framing "our idea of which lives are worth fighting for, which lives are worth educating, which lives are worth living, and which lives are worth saving" (Manning 2016, p. 3). Rather, social work needs to incorporate difference and otherness within, and allow itself to come into being through encounters with forms and forces of lives beyond humans.

An octopus has a short life span and can fail to thrive by being hunted and eaten at any time by its predators. Living and dying well on the damaged planet is a crucial concern, as Donna Haraway (2016), Anna Tsing et al. (2017), and Thom van Dooren (2019) keep reminding us: "[o]ur task is to make trouble, stir up potent response to devastating events, as well as to settle troubled waters and rebuild quiet places" (Haraway 2016, p. 134). Octopuses show us the impossibility of separating life's ethical, ontological, and epistemological dimensions. If we are entangled with the other – with the other and self threaded through, bound to, and inseparable from one another in their enfolded tracings – then we are always already responsible for the other, indebted to the other. *Becoming-octopus* with its different sensibilities of being of the world rather than in it, attunement, curiosity, attentiveness, and response-ability is generative for reconfiguring social work, as "a practice that thinks" (Manning 2016, p. 27), and as an art of living to creatively respond to the world in ways that matter on a disturbed and damaged planet.

Acknowledgments This work is based on the research supported by the National Research Foundation of South Africa (Grant Numbers: 120845) Doing Academia Differently.

References

Alaimo S (2016) Exposed: environmental politics and pleasures in posthuman times. University of Minnesota Press, Minneapolis

Alston M, Hargreaves D, Hazeleger T (2018) Postdisaster social work: reflections on the nature of place and loss. Aust Soc Work 71(4):405–416. https://doi.org/10.1080/0312407X.2017.1409776

Banks S (2021) Ethics and values in social work, 5th edn. Red Globe Press, London

Barad K (2007) Meeting the universe halfway: quantum physics and the entanglement of matter and meaning. Duke University Press, Durham/London

Barad K (2010) Quantum entanglements and hauntological relations of inheritance: dis/continuities, space time enfoldings, and justice-to-come. Derrida Today 3(2):240–268

Barad K (2014) Diffracting diffraction: cutting together-apart. Parallax 20(3):168–187

Barad K (2017) What flashes up: theological-political-scientific fragments. In: Keller C, Rubenstein M-J (eds) Entangled worlds: religion, science and new materialisms. Fordham University Press, New York, pp 21–88

Barad K (2019) After the end of the world: entangled nuclear colonialisms, matters of force, and the material force of justice. Theory Event 22(3):524–550

Barad K, Gandorfer D (2021) Political desirings: yearnings for mattering (,) differently. Theory Event 24(1):14–66

Bell K (2012) Towards a post-conventional philosophical base for social work. Br J Soc Work 42(3):408–423

Bell K (2021) A philosophy of social work beyond the anthropocene. In: Bozalek V, Pease B (eds) Post-anthropocentric social work: critical posthuman and new materialist perspectives. Routledge, London/New York, pp 58–67

Bennett J (2009) Vibrant matter: a political ecology of things. Duke University Press, Durham/London

Boulet J (2021) Restorative and regenerative relational praxis must include the non-human. In: Bozalek V, Pease B (eds) Post-anthropocentric social work: critical posthuman and new materialist perspectives. Routledge, London/New York, pp 46–57

Bozalek V (2020) Agential realism for social work. In: Webb S (ed) The Routledge handbook of critical social work. Routledge, Abingdon

Bozalek V, Hölscher D (2021) Higher education hauntologies and spacetimemattering: response-ability and non-innocence in times of pandemic. In: Bozalek V, Zembylas M, Motala S, Hölscher D (eds) New materialist hauntologies in higher education: living with ghosts for a justice-to-come. Routledge, Abington/New York

Bozalek V, Hölscher D (2022) From imperialism to radical hospitality: propositions for reconfiguring social work towards a justice-to-come. South Afr J Soc Work Soc Dev 34(1):1–20

Bozalek V, Pease B (2021) Towards a post-anthropocentric social work. In: Bozalek V, Pease B (eds) Post-anthropocentric social work: critical posthuman and new materialist perspectives. Routledge, London/New York, pp 1–15

Braidotti R (2002) Metamorphoses: towards a materialist theory of becoming. Blackwell, London

Braidotti R (2006) Transpositions: on nomadic ethics. Polity Press, Cambridge

Braidotti R (2011a) Nomadic subjects: embodiment and sexual difference in contemporary feminist theory. Columbia University Press, New York

Braidotti R (2011b) Nomadic theory: the portable Rosi Braidotti. Columbia University Press, New York

Braidotti R (2013) The posthuman. Polity Press, Cambridge

Braidotti R (2019) A theoretical framework for the critical posthumanities. Theory Cult Soc 36(6):31–61

Braidotti R (2022) Posthuman feminism. Polity Press, Cambridge

Derrida J (1994) The spectre of Marx: the state of the debt, the work of mourning and the new international (trans: Kamuf P). Routledge, London

Despret V (2016) What would animals say if we asked the right questions? Minneapolis: University of Minnesota Press

Despret V, Meuret M (2016) Cosmoecological sheep and the arts of living on a damaged planet. Environ Humanit 8(1):24–36

Dolphijn R, van der Tuin I (2012) New materialism: interviews & cartographies. Open Humanities Press, University of Michigan Library, Maidenhead and Berkshire

Fenton J, Smith M (2019) You can't say that!': critical thinking, identity politics, and the social work academy. Societies 9(4):1–14

Fraser H, Taylor N (2021) Animals as domestic violence victims: a challenge to humanist social work. In: Bozalek V, Pease B (eds) Post-anthropocentric social work: critical posthuman and new materialist perspectives. Routledge, London/New York, pp 161–174

Godfrey-Smith P (2017) Other minds: the octopus, the sea, and the deep origins of consciousness. Harper Collins Publishers, New York

Gosh A (2021) The nutmeg's curse: parables for a planet in crisis. The University of Chicago Press, New York

Haraway J (1985) A manifesto for cyborgs: science, technology, and socialist feminism in the 1980s. Socialist Review, no. 80:65–108

Haraway D (1988) Situated knowledges: the science question in feminism and the privilege of partial perspective. Feminist Studies 14:575–599

Haraway D (2008) When species meet. University of Minnesota, Minneapolis

Haraway D (2003) The companion species manifesto: dogs, people, and significant otherness. Chicago: Prickly Paradigm Press

Haraway D (2016) Staying with the trouble: making kin in the chthulucene. Durham & London: Duke University Press

Hollin G, Forsyth I, Giraud E, Potts T (2017) (Dis)entangling barad: materialisms and ethics. Soc Stud Sci 47(6):918–941

Hölscher D, Nipperess S (2021) Reconsidering human rights in the context of mass-displacement and refugee encampment. Conference presentation. The 26th Asia-Pacific Regional Social Work Conference, Australia

Hölscher D, Bozalek V, Zembylas M (2020a) Coloniality, injustice, and Nancy Fraser's contribution to a decolonisation of higher education in South Africa: concluding thoughts. In: Bozalek V, Hölscher D, Zembylas M (eds) Nancy Fraser and participatory parity: reframing social justice in South African higher education. Routledge, Abington/New York

Hölscher D, Kanamugire C, Udah H (2020b) A matter of lies and death: necropolitics and the question of engagement with the aftermath of Rwanda's genocide. J Gend Stud 29(1):34–48

Ife J (2012) Human rights and social work: towards rights-based practice, 3rd edn. Cambridge University Press, Port Melbourne

Ife J (2016) Human rights and social work: beyond conservative law. J Hum Rights Soc Work 1(3):3–8

Juelskaer M, Plauborg H, Adrian SW (2021) Dialogues on agential realism: engaging in worldings through research practice. Routledge, London/New York

Keeney AJ, Albrithen A, Harrison S, Briskman L, Androff D (2019) International analysis of human rights and social work ethics. In: Marson SM, McKinney JRE (eds) The Routledge handbook of social work ethics and values. Routledge, London and New York, pp 7–14

LeFrançois BA, Voronka J (2022) Mad epistemologies and maddening the ethics of knowledge production. In: Macias T (ed) Un/ethical un/knowing: ethical reflections on methodology and politics in social science research. Canadian Scholars Press, Toronto, pp 105–130

Lenz Taguchi H (2012) A diffractive and Deleuzian approach to analysing interview data. Feminist Theory 13(3):265–281

Manning E (2016) The minor gesture. Duke University Press, Durham/London

Manning E (2020) For a pragmatics of the useless. Duke University Press, Durham/London

Masson F, Harms Smith L (2019) Colonisation as collective trauma: fundamental perspectives for social work. In: Kleibl T, Lutz R, Noyoo N, Bunk B, Dittmann A, Seepamore B (eds) The Routledge handbook of postcolonial social work. Routledge, Abington, pp 13–26

Mignolo WD (2011) The darker side of Western modernity: global futures, decolonial options. Duke University Press, Durham

Montgomery S (2015) The soul of an octopus. A surprising exploration of one of the world's most intriguing creatures. London: Simon & Schuster

Neimanis A (2013) Feminist subjectivity, watered. Fem Rev 103:23–41

Neimanis A (2017) Bodies of water: posthuman feminist phenomenology. Bloomsbury Academic, London/New York

Neimanis A (2021) We are all bodies of water. Rivus 23rd biennale of Sydney. A glossary of water. Institute for Culture and Society. University of Western Sydney. https://www.westernsydney.edu.au/ics/events/past_events/a_glossary_of_water. Accessed 30 May 2022

Nipperess S (2016) Towards a critical human rights-based approach to social work practice. In: Pease B, Goldingay S, Holsken N, Nipperess S (eds) Doing critical social work: transformative practice for social justice. Routledge, Abington, pp 73–88

Pease B (2021) Fostering non-anthropocentric vulnerability in men: challenging the autonomous masculine subject in social work. In: Bozalek V, Pease B (eds) Post-anthropocentric social work: critical posthuman and new materialist perspectives. Routledge, London/New York, pp 108–120

Roberts MM (2020) 'Becoming octopus' meditations. https://www.orphandriftarchive.com/if-ai/becoming-octopus-meditations/. Accessed 30 May 2022

Rose DB (2017) Shimmer: when all you love is being trashed. In: Tsing A, Swanson H, Gan E, Bubandt N (eds) Arts of living on a damaged planet: ghosts. University of Minnesota Press, Minneapolis, pp 51–64

Rosiek JE, Snyder J, Pratt SL (2019) The new materialisms and Indigenous theories of non-human agency: making the case for respectful anti-colonial engagement. Qual Inq 26(3–4):331–346

Ross D, Bennett B, Menyweather N (2021) Towards a critical posthumanist social work: transspecies ethics of ecological justice, nonviolence and love. In: Bozalek V, Pease B (eds) Post-anthropocentric social work: critical posthuman and new materialist perspectives. Routledge, London/New York, pp 175–186

Ruspini E, Hearn J, Pease B, Pringle K (2011) Men and masculinities around the world: transforming men's practices. Palgrave Macmillan, Houndmills

Shefer T, Bozalek V (2022) Wild swimming methodologies for decolonial feminist justice-to-come scholarship. Fem Rev 130:26–43

Staub-Bernasconi S (2016) Social work and human rights: linking two traditions of human rights in social work. J Hum Rights Soc Work 1:40–49

Stengers I (2010) Cosmopolitics I. University of Minnesota Press, Minneapolis

Stengers I (2011) Cosmopolitics II. University of Minnesota Press, Minneapolis

Swanson H, Tsing A, Bubant N, Gan E (2017) Introduction: bodies tumbled into bodies. In: Tsing A, Swanson H, Gan E, Bubant N (eds) Arts of living on a damaged planet: monsters and the arts of living. University of Minnesota Press, Minneapolis, pp M1–M12

Tsing A, Swanson H, Gan E, Bubandt N (Eds) (2017) Arts of living on a damaged planet. Minneapolis: University of Minnesota Press

van Dooren T (2019) The wake of crows: living and dying in shared worlds. Columbia University Press, New York

van Dooren T, Kirksey E, Münster U (2016) Multispecies studies: cultivating the arts of attentiveness. Environ Stud 8(1):1–23

Webb SA (2021a) Why agential realism matters to social work. Br J Soc Work 51(8):2964–2981. https://doi.org/10.1093/bjsw/bcaa106

Webb SA (2021b) What comes after the subject? Towards a critical posthumanist social work. In: Bozalek V, Pease B (eds) Post-anthropocentric social work: critical posthuman and new materialist perspectives. Routledge, London/New York, pp 19–31

Weinberger M (2022) The supremacy of whiteness in social work ethics. Ethics Soc Welf. https://doi.org/10.1080/17496535.2022.2058579

Wilson T (2021) An invitation into the trouble with humanism in social work. In: Bozalek V, Pease B (eds) Post-anthropocentric social work: critical posthuman and new materialist perspectives. Routledge, London/New York, pp 32–45

Woods G, Hölscher D (2021) Return of the posthuman: developing Indigenist perspectives for social work at a time of environmental crisis. In: Bozalek V, Pease B (eds) Post-anthropocentric social work: critical posthuman and new materialist perspectives. Routledge, London/New York, pp 121–133

Ethical Pluralism and Social Work

Richard Hugman

Contents

Introduction 398
Ethical Pluralism: Ideas from Moral Philosophy 399
Challenging Ethics in Social Work 403
    Ethical Monism 404
    Ethical Relativism 405
    Pluralism 407
    Codes and Other Formal Ethical Statements 410
Understanding Ethical Pluralism in Social Work 411
    Example 1: Social Justice in Everyday Practice 411
    Example 2: Ethics in Situations of Conflict 412
    Example 3: The Idea of an 'Ethical Dilemma' 412
Conclusion 413
References 414

Abstract

This chapter considers the position of ethical pluralism. It addresses this as a position that is distinct from both 'absolutism' (or 'monism') and relativism. Having considered these distinctions from the perspective of moral philosophy, the chapter then addresses the challenges that such a position presents for social work ethics. In particular, it is noted that while ethical monism is possible in social work (for example, when either human rights or social justice is treated as the most important principle), in practice an implicit pluralism usually occurs because these two principles are held together in many debates and discussions. Ethical relativism is considered to be a position that is sometimes adopted in relation to issues of culture and ethnicity and the challenges of this are identified. Ethical pluralism is then explored as a flexible but critically realistic position that if adopted explicitly enables the tensions and paradoxes of everyday practice to be

R. Hugman (✉)
School of Social Sciences, University of New South Wales, Sydney, NSW, Australia
e-mail: r.hugman@unsw.edu.au

grasped. Examples are examined from the areas of social justice, social work in situations of conflict and the idea of an 'ethical dilemma'. In conclusion, the chapter argues that the position of ethical pluralism enables social work to engage with uncertainty and to reconcile the challenges of balancing difference and particularity with clear, solid ethical foundations that reflect commonality and solidarity.

Keywords

Social work ethics · Pluralism · Absolutism – ethical monism · Relativism · Human rights · Social justice · Virtue · Ethics of care

Introduction

In the introductory chapter to this volume it was noted that there has been considerable growth in attention to the role of ethics in social work through the last 50 years (Banks 2012; Reamer 2018; Hardy 2019). Over this period several ethical approaches have come to be regarded as defining the values of the profession, reflecting both the goals that social work pursues and the means by which social work is undertaken. The preceding chapters of this part of the book identify key approaches to ethics that have become key in the formulation of a distinctive social work ethics: human rights; social justice; virtue; care; postcolonial; and other contemporary critical approaches (compare with IFSW/IASSW 2018a, b).

These ethical approaches are significant in understanding the identity and purpose of social work. For example, we might say that social work pursues human rights and the practice of social work is conducted within a human rights framework. Similarly, it can be asserted that social work seeks to promote social justice and social workers endeavour to act justly to achieve these ends. Again, social work can be seen as pursuing professional virtues and expressing care, while in espousing these goals social workers are expected to practice in ways that are consistent with them. A great deal of attention is given particularly to human rights and social justice, while some commentators argue that social work has not given sufficient thought to other approaches (McBeath and Webb 2002; Banks 2016; Papouli 2018). Nevertheless, all of these approaches are reflected in social work ethics, whether in formal documents such as codes of ethics or in the everyday conversations and debates of social workers.

However, if we look closely at the debates in moral philosophy, they reveal that these different approaches are built on quite diverse foundations (Hugman 2005). The assumptions and the logic of each approach are quite distinctive. This can be seen, for instance, if we compare human rights and social justice. A human rights approach is grounded in the assumption of the unique and absolute moral worth of each human being, so that attention to the rights claims of an individual or group should be considered in and of themselves. In contrast, a social justice approach is built on the balance of moral claims between people, whether as individuals or groups, so that everyone must be considered fairly even if their moral claims are in competition with each other. Frequently we can find that discussions of one or the other approach assume attention to one of these values in itself leads to attainment of the other as well, or else that together these are the defining characteristics of social work (Lundy 2011; Mapp 2021). For example, Bonnycastle (2011) identifies human rights as a dimension of social justice in social work practice. Explorations of a connection between care and social justice have also been developed (Orme 2002; Hölscher 2018). In contrast, other social workers focus on one approach and ignore the others, or even become advocates for the superiority of one approach over the others. For example, Solas (2008) argues for the primacy of social justice, while Ife (2012) suggests that human rights is the paramount social work value.

This chapter argues that although this process of bringing together different ethical approaches is a reasonable aspiration for social work, even desirable, if it is not addressed explicitly problems arise in the way social workers understand ethics. These can take the form of internal conflicts between parts of the profession, or in confusion and inconsistency in ethical statements such as codes. In those situations where a complete understanding or agreement may not be reached, it should at least be possible to acknowledge the basis of a lack of comprehension or of disagreement and to continue to think and debate in ways that leave open future resolution of these challenges. Doing so seeks to recognise the importance of each of the key ethical values and approaches, so that even where the fit between them is uneasy it is still accepted as a goal that should be pursued.

In moral philosophy the approach that has developed which expresses this understanding of competing ethical values and approaches is that of 'ethical pluralism'. In order to examine how this approach can assist social workers to grasp ethical complexity, this chapter first considers the distinctive nature of ethical pluralism and the contributions of significant moral philosophers in developing it. Then the chapter begins to connect this approach to the processes of ethical thought in social work by using the central debates about ethical pluralism to examine in greater depth the way in which social work ethics fails to address the plurality of values in professional ethics. The following sections of the chapter then explore how ethical pluralism might be developed for social work and the benefits for social work ethics in having an explicit grasp of ethical pluralism and applying this critically to all aspects of ethics in the profession.

Ethical Pluralism: Ideas from Moral Philosophy

Hinman (2013) argues that although the major approaches to ethics are often considered separately, or even advanced by their proponents as the most effective way of thinking, each has something to tell us about how we can live well and achieve what is good. Moreover, for Hinman, it is possible to have a comparative conversation about different approaches to ethics without first having to accept one as superior; rather it is more effective not to have such a prior commitment to one perspective.

Hinman is concerned that a very clear distinction must be made between ethical pluralism and ethical relativism. The difference can be seen clearly by looking critically at the claims made by the latter. According to Hinman (2013, pp. 29–31) ethical relativism asserts the following:

1. The importance of understanding and tolerance – to live well we must all seek to listen carefully to the moral values of others and accept the differences.
2. The fact of moral diversity – it simply is the case that values differ between people, especially on the basis of culture.
3. The lack of a plausible alternative – there is no single overarching set of values that everyone accepts in all circumstances.
4. The relativity of all understanding – all truth is provisional and partial, no-one can see the whole picture and ideas change with new evidence.
5. The lack of a right to cast moral judgement on others – to be critical of a different moral position assumes a superior vantage position, which no-one has.

The overall sense of these ideas is one of ethical humility – that is, they convey a sense that ethical relativists do not set themselves above others. Rather, ethical relativism leads to an avoidance of judgement about varying positions. Often this takes the form of cultural relativism, in which values can only be judged in relation to the norms of a given culture. At the extreme it may become subjectivism, in which each person's values are appropriate for that person and no-one else may reasonably say that they are wrong.

However, Hinman argues (pp. 38–41), ethical relativism presents us with serious problems for normative thinking. This can be seen in the problems that ethical relativism presents in its assertions:

1. What if there is a limit to tolerance? – Speaking out against atrocity is not possible from an ethically relative perspective.
2. Moral diversity may be an empirical fact but that does not of itself commit us to moral relativism – The question of the diversity of moral norms may also be a fact but we cannot actually derive norms from facts as such (simply because something is the case does not of itself say it should be the case).
3. The possibility that there are alternatives to ethical relativism other than a rigid ethical absolutism – Put simply, there may be values that can be agreed between cultures without having to agree that one value is superior in every situation.
4. The logical conclusion of the relativity of all understanding is that it is self-defeating – For example, if we say 'there is no such thing as truth' then that statement itself cannot be taken as being true.
5. The possibility of moral isolation – Ethical relativism can become a 'conversation stopper', in that it asserts people simply have different values and that's all there is to be said.

Hinman reasons that the conclusion of ethical relativism leads to ethical immobilisation, in that if we cannot say that someone else is bad or is wrong then we also cannot say that they are good or right. Ultimately judgement becomes delegitimised. As Bauman (1994) puts it, this leaves each of us alone in a world of uncertainty and subject only to the choices of those who possess power.

For Kekes (1993), the question of ethical pluralism as a third position between absolutism and relativism requires more than just standing between the two, partially agreeing with each on every aspect. Instead, it necessitates a distinct position that addresses ethical problems and challenges. Kekes refers to ethical 'monism' rather than 'absolutism', in that in his analysis it is not solely a matter of asserting something absolutely but of such positions usually being grounded in one value alone, whether that is rights or justice for example, and that view excluding attention to all other values. (The term 'monism' is used in different ways in different strands of philosophy. The usage here, to mean a single overarching ethical value or principle, contrasts with the usage associated with the work of Spinoza in which it refers to an ontological concept that all matter is of the same substance.) Against ethical monism, drawing on the philosophy of Berlin (1992), Williams (1981) and others, Kekes argues that values are inevitably open to review (they may change over time), contradictory (equally important values may clash and be incompatible) and even incommensurable (not able to be compared). This is the case whether we think of the values of an individual person or an entire society. So to be able to reason carefully about ethical values we need the widest stock of ideas that can be considered. Thus, respect and dignity, human rights, social justice, virtue, care and other values ought to remain open for consideration. That there may be instances where they are in conflict or even unable to be compared does not limit the importance of this breadth of vision. In summary, ethical pluralism states that while there are limits to what is good or right, it also asserts that there is no one overriding value that supersedes all others.

In response to the problems inherent in ethical relativism, Kekes suggests that we might consider the difference between those values that can be seen as basic to views about human life across cultural and historical values and which can be grasped on grounds independent of a particular context. These Kekes calls 'primary values' (1993, p. 38). They are the minimum requirements of a human life and as such may be moral, such as whether a person is degraded as in a relationship of slavery, or they may be non-moral goods, such as a minimum level of nutrition. Those values that a pluralist perspective can accept as relative to context (such as culture) Kekes refers to as 'secondary values'. The moral examples he uses here are that of whether social arrangements are expressive of religious beliefs and of non-moral values such as the form that food might take to be regarded as good, for example whether carbohydrate in a normal diet takes the form of bread or rice.

Both Hinman and Kekes draw on ideas that were developed by European moral philosophers in the middle of the twentieth century. Berlin (1997) strongly argued that values that are equally important may conflict with each other, such as rights sometimes being in conflict with justice, or loyalty with truth, or be incommensurable such as when we try to compare beauty with family relationships. Although he is widely regarded as never proposing a particular ethical framework, Williams (1981) articulated another key pluralist idea in that the way in which a person or group might rank values can reasonably shift in relation to circumstances, so the same person might prioritise human rights (for example) over social justice in one situation and reverse that priority in another without this being a confusion or a contradiction. Williams (1993) also proposed the notion of 'moral luck', to express the way in which circumstances may not be in the control of the person who has to choose between values. In other words, it is simply that sometimes the way events proceed can make it easier or more difficult to be respectful, or just, or to care. However, this does not remove the responsibility that each of us has for our ethical choices even if we cannot be sure of the outcomes of our decisions. Williams' answer to the challenge of moral luck is to engage with ethics. In other words, if we are conscious of making moral choices and the basis on which we make them, then we are in a better position to address those life events over which we have no control. For Williams, therefore, ethics becomes an intentional activity: it is deliberate (intentional) because it requires us to deliberate (to think consciously).

Nagel (1979) similarly argues that the ordering of values in ethical pluralism is not fixed but can be regarded as contingent on context and on which values are being compared. However, he asserts a more clear definition of the values that he considers are central to ethics in the contemporary world. These are: obligations; rights; utility; perfectionist ends (inherent value); pursuit of personal projects. The pluralist challenge comes from the ways in which the ordering of these values can differ between the various circumstances faced by an individual person and also vary between people who are faced with the same circumstances. It is rarely the case, Nagel suggests, that a person or a group will always value obligations over rights or utility, for example. In debate with Williams (1993), Nagel (1993) proposes that the way in which our ordering of values is seen by others is a form of moral luck in that whether we are regarded by others as good is in many ways dependent as much on luck as judgement. What happens as a result of our moral choices, which is contingent on things we have no control over, then provides a basis for ascribing moral qualities.

As with Williams' argument, Nagel's treatment of the idea of moral luck could be said to rely on consequences rather than rationality and intention, making these claims much closer to consequentialist arguments than the deontological approach that underpins ideas of respect or rights. Yet, this is not what either intends, as both are primarily concerned to assert that there is a range of plausible moral values that can be used by people to make sense of their choices and actions. Their concerns with the problems of moral luck stem from the problems that they both see in asserting one primary value or moral position.

From a somewhat different starting point, Nussbaum (2000, pp. 78–80) has proposed a list of 'human capabilities', which are those socially arranged capacities that people may enjoy that enable them to live what they regard as a good human life. Nussbaum regards these capacities (such as bodily health and integrity, exercising practical reason and choosing affiliations) as common to human life in diverse circumstances, while the balance between them and the expression of each may differ between individuals and cultures in any given situation as well as varying over time. They may be considered as values in the sense that these aspects of life are qualities that a person may have a reason to choose as the basis for thinking about whether their life is good or not. As with the ordering of values in the views of Williams and Nagel, the capabilities Nussbaum defines constitute the goals that people pursue in order to live well. Similarly, each person orders these capabilities differently according to their social and cultural context and their personal preferences.

The difference between this approach and that of Kekes or Nagel is that Nussbaum's suggested values each represent the structural connections between the individual and their society. That is, to be achieved it is not only necessary that the person must direct their own actions towards their achievement but at the same time the society in which the person lives must be structured in such a way as to make their achievement possible. For example, it is very difficult for a woman to exercise practical reason if she lives in a context where culture and law combine to allocate decision making about her life to another person, such as her husband or her father. This difference comes from the foundations Nussbaum uses in her approach, which draws on a wide range of sources, including Aristotle, Marx, Kant and Mill (Nussbaum 2002, pp. 129–135). However, as each of these philosophers is a central figure in the major approaches that have shaped ethics in the early twenty-first century, Nussbaum's concept is clearly pluralist, which is a claim that she makes herself in later discussions of the idea (Nussbaum 2006).

Each of the arguments presented by Kekes, Nagel and Nussbaum contributes something to the development of an alternative to both ethical absolutism or monism and ethical relativism. The relevance of this perspective for social work can be seen in considering issues of moral judgement and moral progress. First, social work ethics in recent years has begun to address important differences between people in various parts of the world. Although questions of the connections between culture and ethics remain relatively under-explored, questions of culture and ethnicity, 'race' and of colonisation are all now seen as important challenges for social work theory and practice (Gray 2005; Hugman 2013; Ravulo et al. 2019). Second, at the same time, social work continues to place great emphasis on ethical values such as respect and dignity, human rights, social justice, virtue (often in form of professional integrity) or care. Given that we can often have differences of opinion about whether these values are ordered, and if so in what way, and at the same time assent to some or all of them, it is vital that social work ethics enable us to be able to say "when different is just different and when different is wrong" (Healy 2007, p. 23). Without the capacity to do this, to take one example, social workers cannot speak out against the atrocity of interpersonal violence; and there are many other such concerns that are shared across cultures.

Challenging Ethics in Social Work

The social work profession internationally builds its ethics on a form of pluralism. In the *Global Social Work Statement of Ethical Principles* that is shared by the International federation of Social Workers and the International Association of Schools of Social Work (IFSW/IASSW 2018b), the opening sections address respect for human worth and dignity, human rights and social justice and the document concludes by addressing professional integrity. Thus, this statement brings together the major ethical approaches that have shaped professional ethics in the modern world. However, as the present chapter has already begun to identify, there remain some very important debates and disagreements that must also be taken into account in an analysis of social work ethics and values.

The terms of these debates can be summarised as follows:

- Implicit and unaddressed monism
- Implicit and unaddressed relativism (especially in relation to culture)
- Implicit and unaddressed pluralism (especially in the conflation of human rights and social justice)

To understand the nature of each of these issues it is necessary to look at each in turn before then considering how together they present a challenge to a more thorough grasp of ethics for social work practice. The argument here is not that debate and disagreement is unhelpful, or even avoidable, but rather that it is necessary to be able to develop a wider ethical fluency on the part of social workers in the wide range of settings where they practice, so that they can use ethics as part of their repertoire to be more able to engage with the struggles faced by service users in these diverse contexts.

Ethical Monism

The challenge of monism (or absolutism) in social work ethics is encountered when one specific value is asserted against all other possible values as primary in all circumstances. As identified above, there are two different forms of monism that occur in social work ethics. The first is seen in arguments that assume when one particular value is pursued, this automatically ensures that other important values will be sought as well. The second occurs when it is claimed that one specific value overrides all others, so that when there is a potential incompatibility of values that one value always 'trumps' alternative points of view.

Assumptions that attending to one value automatically addresses another at the same time can be seen widely in social work in discussions of human rights and social justice. So, we see for example, that many discussions of these values bring them together without considering the very different logics on which each rests. Solas (2008) argues that social justice is at the heart of social work's goals. The focus of this analysis is that of the approach taken to social justice by social workers. It is not that Solas argues against attention to rights, virtues, care or other conceptions of the good, but rather that he does not address them except in passing. However, to this limited extent, when Solas refers to these other values and principles he subsumes them in terms of social justice as the paramount goal of social work. For instance, he allows that the conditions that enable social justice to be achieved require a defined set of rights, but explains these as requirements of justice not in their own terms

(p. 135). Likewise, in discussing Nussbaum's concept of capabilities his reference to care is subsumed as a means for the achievement of social justice (p. 134). Again, (social) justice as a virtue is considered as a way of thinking about the type of society that enables the achievement of social justice, so here too it is a means (p. 126). Finally, Solas invokes Kant's deontological principle that people ought not to be used as means but only as ends in themselves to support the argument against a particularly harsh form of Utilitarianism (p. 127).

The other approach to the question of the relationship between values resolves possible incompatibilities by asserting the primacy of a specific principle. This can be seen in Ife's (2012) discussion of the relationship between human rights and questions of justice or of need. For Ife, when questions of justice or need are considered, they are embodying a concern with what people must have in order to live a human life. This argument is very similar to Nussbaum's claim that the 'capabilities' she identifies 'exert a moral claim that they should be developed' (2002, p. 131). In other words, that unless people are able to achieve these capabilities they are being denied the possibility of living a life that is fully human. However, while for Nussbaum such a view enables us to avoid contested definitions of 'rights', for Ife that such claims *should* be met actually constitutes them as a right. This is summed up when he writes "[s]statements of need within social work are [...] statements about rights" (Ife 2012, p. 136). The conclusion is that it is only by pursuing the value of human rights that social work can have a truly moral core. This leads him to assert that social work is 'the core human rights profession' (Ife 2012, p. 315).

Taken together, these two arguments demonstrate forms of monism in social work ethics. The issue here is not what either says about their focus (social justice, human rights) but rather that these accounts subsume other approaches, either implicitly (as in Solas' discussion) or explicitly (as in Ife's analysis). Both these discussions are incisive and make considerable contributions to ethical debates in social work. However, that both have much to offer does not obscure the monist approach that both embody. Unless this is recognised and addressed, we are left with accounts that are partial and prevent us from hearing alternative ethical voices.

Ethical Relativism

The limitations of monism may appear to be addressed by ethical relativism. However, as argued about, this is also an approach with clear limitations. In social work ethics, relativism most usually takes the form of valuing cultural difference and asserting that because values develop and are held within particular cultural and historical contexts it is not possible to separate such values from their origins. Therefore, criticism of values from other contexts is illegitimate because it represents a form of discrimination based on culture. In turn, this is seen as occurring to the advantage of those cultures that historically have gained power over others and so is both racist and colonialist (Gray 2005).

Gray's concern is to question unrecognised universalism, in which the strong voices from social work in the global North might generate an uncritical expression of key values in professional ethics. Certainly, movements towards the indigenisation of social work emerging in post-colonial societies have challenged assumptions that were embedded in the international documents, including past iterations of ethical principles as well as in material used in social work education (Osei-Hwedie 1993; Yip 2004; Yellow Bird and Gray 2008). From the perspective of Indigenous peoples and also more generally from global Southern standpoints universal application of values is highly problematic. For example, the principles that are embodied in the *Universal Declaration of Human Rights* (UN 1948) are written in terms that it is argued reflect global Northern values (for example, Yip 2004). Indeed, a central aspect of the cultural relativist argument about ethics and values in social work focuses specifically on human rights.

Arguments for the formulation of social work ethics and values relative to varying cultural contexts have been advanced in many areas of the global South. For example, Osei-Hwedie et al. (2006) state that a more communitarian approach is required in Africa compared to the individualism of existing ethics that are seen as inherently based on global Northern culture. Similarly, Reamer and Nimmagadda (2015) propose a distinct ethical framework for social work in India that is grounded in the traditional world-views of that country compared to the world-views that predominate in Europe and North America. Again, Yip (2004) argues for a distinctive Chinese social work ethics. That each of these arguments is distinct reflects the diversity between global Southern cultures and countries. For example, they vary from a strong communalism in Africa to an emphasis on the family in Asia, as well as between parts of Asia in terms of the influence of major religious and philosophical traditions. The commonality lies in asserting the importance of the difference between global Southern and Northern values.

A notably common area of criticism from these global Southern perspectives is the centrality of human rights as a key aspect of social work ethics. This in turn derives from differing cultural views about the nature of individuality and communality. Thus, a shared criticism is the way in which the international ethical documents of social work in previous iterations have been couched solely in individualistic terms (compare Sewpaul and Henrickson 2019 with IFSW/IASSW 2018).

Yet there are a number of points at which the relativist critique of universalism the recent version of the core *Statement of Ethical Principles* (IFSW/IASSW 2018), which was produced with leadership from the global South, has taken a counterintuitive direction. For example, section 4 of the Statement, 'Promoting the right to self-determination', raises 'self determination' to the level of a principle compared to its inclusion as one aspect of the principle of human dignity and worth in the previous version (dated 2004). This is contradicted by Reamer and Nimmagadda's analysis of contemporary Indian social work, in which the emphasis is on the family as the primary focus of moral concern and individual self-determination is somewhat limited (compare with Yip 2004 discussing China). Sewpaul and Henrickson (2019, p. 1475) argue that the inclusion of self-determination as a distinct principle is necessary to bridge the divides between different parts of the world on individualism and collectivism, while acknowledging that it remains highly contested.

This argument contrasts with the widespread acceptance of the *Convention on the Rights of the Child* (CRC) (UN 1989) by national governments in the global South. Costello et al. (2019) demonstrate that using the CRC enabled social workers in Palestine to develop complex and effective models for child protection. This model integrated respect for the family while also being grounded in children' rights. Similarly, Jayasooria (2019) argues that achievement of the *Sustainable Development Goals* (SDGs) in Malaysian social work necessitates a human rights perspective, while Noyori-Corbett and Moxley (2019) provide an account of how human rights informed practice benefitted refugees from Myanmar living in the USA.

The problems of the relativistic critique based on culture is perhaps best summed up by Sewpaul (2016, p. 34) in her caution that a dichotomy of individual and collective values attached to the global North and South respectively does a great disservice to the diversity within them, between regions as well as within cultural communities. This is an incisive observation, as values do not only differ in terms of cultures, but within them in terms of sex and gender, ethnicity, (dis)ability, sexuality, socio-economic class, age and so on. When considering the claims to cultural difference as a reason to diminish human rights as a social work value we ought always to consider who is doing so and for what reason. For example, claims to the primacy of family can implicitly favour the interests of older generations over the young, embody patriarchy in normalising men's social control of women or justify ethnic or caste-based oppression. The present author has noted that global Northern cultures can also embody many value expressions that social work has worked against, such as the norms of family violence, homophobia and so on (Hugman 2008). In this sense social work values can at times be experienced as a critique within one's own cultural context and are not always simply a matter of 'the West against the Rest' (Scwpaul 2016), although this often may be so. Social work has and continues to be critical of the societies in which it first developed as well as those in which it is now developing.

Where respect for culture does play an essential part of how we understand and respond to social work ethics and values lies in the ways in which we practice. That is, we do not have to accept the arguments of relativism in order to be sensitive to culture. What is required is that social workers grasp the difficult task of making sense of when difference is to be respected and celebrated and 'when difference is wrong' (see above). In turn, this necessitates the integration of diverse values, each of which has something to say for our ethics: this is the task of ethical pluralism.

Pluralism

One apparent form of ethical pluralism that has developed in social work is the dual claim to human rights and social justice together as core values. Lundy (2011) provides a particular example of this in her analysis of structural social work. For Lundy, human rights and social justice together define both the goals of social work and the means by which social workers seek to achieve them. Lundy's argument is grounded in concrete examples from North America, in which context particular human rights are enshrined in law but where, as she demonstrates, often limited by being confined within those laws, such that they can be restricted to the extent that major causes of human need such as basic income or housing are not considered as rights (Lundy 2011, p. 41).

Lundy's argument can be understood as a form of ethical pluralism because it brings together two major principles that have quite different philosophical foundations. Indeed, this conjunction is widespread in social work and reflected in the international definition of the profession (IFSW/IASSW 2014). Yet, it is a nascent pluralism in that Lundy does not explicitly address the ethical arguments that connect the two ethical approaches. Indeed, it appears from the way they are discussed that these values are, in effect, extensions of each other. At one point, quoting Shewell (2010), Lundy (2011, p. 41) notes that social work addresses social needs, which in turn constitute social rights (compare with Ife 2013). In effect, this is a similar position to that reached by Nussbaum (2000, 2002) but whereas she presents the concept of 'capabilities' as a way of moving beyond debates about particular rights claims, Lundy follows the arguments set out by Shewell, which are similar also to those of Wronka (1998) on distinguishing political, social and economic, and cultural rights. The set of social rights identified in this approach include some that appear in the *Universal Declaration of Human Rights* (UN 1948), such as the right to health, housing or education (Articles 25 and 26). These are also human needs that are met more easily by some members of the community than others. So in achieving these rights it is also necessary to address the distribution of the means to access required resources. While the claim to rights is universal, in that all people hold the property of being absolutely and uniquely morally valuable and worthy of respect solely on those grounds, the argument for justice is that only some people are able to achieve this humanity because of inequalities, whether these are natural or socially created. This is an ethically pluralist position for social work.

The legitimacy of social work's values in the period of global neoliberalism can be regarded as fragile, precisely because of this pluralist position. Arguments for rights hinge around those aspects of society that can be agreed as essential to a truly human life. The debate occurs between those who wish to be as parsimonious as possible, offering a restricted view, and those who seek to achieve an expansive vision of what it is to be human. For example, the global COVID-19 pandemic has revealed a stark difference between those who want to prioritise the economy and those who seek to protect human health (Banks et al. 2020; Truell and Crompton 2020). In political terms, this division broadly follows those who would restrict or expand definitions of human rights. The extent of spread of COVID-19 infection points to the power of the economic over the health goals in social policy and practice.

So far this discussion has focused on the relationship between human rights and social justice, reflecting the predominant ethical frameworks of social work. Yet, as this chapter has already identified above, ethics of care, virtue and emerging ethical debates such as post-humanism all have something potentially to say to us about the values of the profession. There have been some examples of how these different ideas may work together for the field, including examinations of the relationship between social justice and the ethics of care (Orme 2002), between virtue and care (Banks 2016; Featherstone and Gupta 2020), debates about humanism (Garrett 2020), recognition, respect and postmodern ethics (Niemi 2020), as well as others. Taking the connections between the ethics of care, justice and virtue as a key example, we can see that these developments represent a shift from engaging with ethics in terms of abstract principles to a concern with the ethics of human relationships. The work that seeks to integrate these different approaches begins from critiquing the more traditional view that each is a distinct way of grasping ethics and values. Through an examination of what occurs in practice the difficult task to look for the connections between these different ideas is undertaken, both in terms of their underlying logics and in the way that they assist in understanding and acting in the world.

For example, Orme's early analysis of the relationship between the ethics of care and justice focuses particularly on the problem of social power within care relations: that care may be a constraint on women or that care may take the form of surveillance (2002, pp. 803–806). It is by integrating care with a relational understanding of justice (and, to an extent, of rights) that care can be just, and that justice can be caring (that is, related to the reality of people and not confined to being abstract). Extending this view, Featherstone and Gupta (2020) argue that it is only by seeing the use of ethics as a response to social injustice in terms of a dialogical understanding of the particular (historical individual lives) and the general (laws, policies and so on) that we can relate ethical theory to practice. This can only occur if social workers are able to engage with the ethics of their work and the competing approaches and frameworks that are available. Niemi's (2020) argument for the development of connections between recognition and the postmodern concept of 'being for the Other' similarly informs a way of bringing apparently different sets of ideas together to enable social workers to connect the particular and the general – in other words, to integrate the person and the political.

Houston (2012) provides a very clear and succinct articulation of the way in which ethical pluralism offers a way to think about social work ethics that is both relevant theoretically and helpful in practice. His argument accepts that the competing ethical perspectives on which social work can draw may be incompatible, but at the same time he asserts that we must engage with this difficult task in a world in which decisions must be made and actions taken. For Houston, the metaphor of 'head, heart, hands and feet' encompasses the range of considerations that have to be brought to ethical decision-making processes (2012, p. 658). This enables social workers to explore rational thought, principle, emotion, relationship, personal qualities (virtue) and situational factors. In doing so, Houston argues that social workers should not seek to answer ethical challenges by reference to one overarching or absolute value. This does not negate established key principles, such as 'above all else do no harm', but as Houston (2012, p. 661) observes these are ideas that are found across cultures and which meet the requirements of many ethical approaches (in this case, of deontology, consequentialism, virtue, care and postmodern ethics). Rather, Houston (2012, p. 667) refers to Berlin's (1992) image of humanity as 'crooked timber', which points to the way in which our lives simply do not fit a predetermined mould, so acting on such principles requires that social workers relate them to context.

Banks (2016) supports this understanding of ethics as an active part of the practice of social work. It is not simply a set of standards that can be taken and applied from outside the circumstances of that practice. Banks refers to 'ethics work', by which she means the active engagement of social workers in examining all aspects of their practice. There are seven dimensions to this process:

- Framing – defining key issues and aspects of a situation
- Role – developing an approach to people in the situation
- Emotion – engaging one's own subjective qualities and responding to others
- Identity – developing one's ethical self and integrity
- Reason – forming and justifying moral judgments and evaluations
- Relationship – engaging in dialogue with others
- Performance – making ethics visible and being accountable (Banks 2016, p. 37)

Banks is clear that these are not stages to be worked through in a neat order, but elements which may overlap. The experienced and ethically skilled social worker may find that they are developed as moral habits, although subject to conscious review. Most importantly, these are not stages of an ethical decision making framework to be applied in advance of acting, but are interwoven with practice. Indeed, some dimensions can only be realised through interaction with service users, colleagues and others. For Banks (2016, p. 45), ethics is what we 'do' not just what we 'think': it is accomplished in 'ethics work'.

Elsewhere, Banks (2012) has established a basis for ethical pluralism in social work. Her concept of 'ethics work' follows from this as the concrete expression of how social workers can make practical sense of the messy nature of ethics and address the diversity of human life while still being accountable and sharing a sufficiently common basis for ethical decision making. Before proceeding to look at some examples of ethical pluralism in practice, this chapter will briefly explore why codes and other ethical statements are not in themselves sufficient to achieve this.

Codes and Other Formal Ethical Statements

Codes of ethics are often referred to as a basis for ensuring morally acceptable and accountable practice. They have become the hallmark of professions, including social work (Banks 2012; Reamer 2014, 2018). Ethical codes are written within a particular social and legal context and usually serve both as guidelines to make clear to practitioners what their profession regards as good practice and when problems are alleged (such as malpractice) they serve as the rules by which such issues can be judged. In countries where social workers are legally registered or licensed codes of ethics form one major way in which someone can be excluded from practising.

The *Global Social Work Statement of Ethical Principles* (IFSW/IASSW 2018b) likewise provides guidance at a great level of abstraction. As this chapter has already noted, there are questions of how responsive such a statement can be to social and cultural diversity, but nonetheless this document serves as a basis for social workers in all countries to consider professional ethics (Sewpaul and Henrickson 2019).

In most cases codes of ethics and the international statement of principles can be seen as inherently pluralist. There is a widespread commonality to the inclusion of values such as human dignity, respect, human rights, social justice and professional integrity. However, these documents do not provide a basis for social workers to engage with the messiness that has been described above. Indeed, empirical research suggests that very many social workers do not refer to the relevant code of ethics (or the global statement of principles) when making decisions or explaining their practice (Congress and McAuliffe 2006; Weinberg and Campbell 2014; Banks 2016). Yet the same studies and others (such as Featherstone and Gupta 2020) also demonstrate the ways in which social workers do ethics work often use the same range of values and principles.

From this perspective, to strengthen ethics in social work, collectively and individually, requires that a wider conversation is encouraged and enabled. For social workers to avoid the problem of seeking the 'one right answer' implied by the idea of a code and to be able to live with the uncertainty that ethics demands requires that social workers develop ethical skills and knowledge alongside other forms of skills and knowledge.

Understanding Ethical Pluralism in Social Work

To illustrate how 'ethics work' embodies ethical pluralism, the following three brief vignettes of practice are offered to provide specific examples. These are intended to be the basis for further thought and are not written as definitive statements on the values or principles involved.

Example 1: Social Justice in Everyday Practice

Several social workers have identified that although the value of social justice refers to structural social arrangements, it is often encountered in micro-level practice as well as macro-level work (O'Brien 2010; Lundy 2011; Wamara and Karvalho 2021). It is as relevant in work with individuals and families as it is with community practice or social policy. Indeed, the impacts of social injustice are frequently encountered in the issues faced by service users in inadequate income, poor housing, problems in access to education and health and so on.

O'Brien (2010) argues that social justice is pursued by social workers who are primarily engaged in micro-level practices. He conducted a study of social workers in Aotearoa New Zealand that demonstrated participants identified questions of social justice as central to their thinking about both the goals and the methods of their work. This was reflected also in the terms they used to give an account of the issues faced by service users, including equality, fairness, opportunities and discrimination (O'Brien 2010, p. 179). It was also seen in the centrality accorded to the practice of advocacy with individuals and families. O'Brien calls this "the daily micro practice of social justice" (p. 180). At the same time, social justice was also seen by participants to involve human rights, where denial of rights occurred because of social justice issues (compare with Lundy 2011).

Similarly, Warmara and Karvalho (2019) identified discrimination and injustice being experienced by older people in Uganda as a major issue for social work. However, they also relate the failure of Ugandan social workers to address such problems to the large number of under-qualified or untrained social service workers who lack awareness of social work ethics and values. For Warmara and Karvahlo (2019, p. 8), individual advocacy and community development are both practices to challenge injustice. Like other studies, they too see an integration of human rights concerns with social justice as a means to strengthen social work's responses (p. 10). Although such rights formally exist in Uganda, achieving them requires social justice practice.

Example 2: Ethics in Situations of Conflict

Maglajlic (2011) describes several types of social work practice in the post-conflict context of the Balkans in which she was involved between 1999 and 2007. These include practice with a local non-government organisation undertaking the development of a community-based mental health service and with UNICEF Croatia to provide activities for children during a break in hostilities that UNICEF had negotiated. Underlying Maglajlic's account are ethical questions about the relationships between international social workers and local populations. Maglajlic observes that where international social workers engage collaboratively with local people 'a truly relevant reform process' can develop (p. 110). However, she concludes that too often agendas set in other parts of the world by external powerful agencies come to dominate and to be imposed irrespective of the needs and interest of local people (p. 111).

This account and Maglajlic's analysis implicitly raise questions of the ethics of care. Practice of this kind can quite easily become 'careless' in that it fails to recognise or respond to the reality of people's lives and treats them as passive recipients rather than active participants. Here we see the intersection of a political ethics of care with questions of social justice. Maglajlic's decision to stop undertaking this work represents a form of ethical virtue, in that it placed the longer term needs and interest of the community to forge their own solutions ahead of her own need and interest in paid professional work (compare with Hugman et al. 2021). Thus, we can see this account as one informed by ethical pluralism, weaving together concerns that are grounded in several perspectives.

Example 3: The Idea of an 'Ethical Dilemma'

The third example of ethical pluralism from practice offered here is that of a concern that is encountered by many social workers, rather than a specific instance: the idea of the 'ethical dilemma'. This phenomenon is often perceived by social workers when faced with ethically difficult decisions. Strictly, an ethical dilemma occurs when there are two or more possible choices that can be made, while the ethically desirable or undesirable aspects of each are equally compelling. These can be conflicts between ethics and policy or between competing ethics and values (Okkonen and Takala 2019). For Juujävi and her colleagues (2020) dilemmas may be also encountered in both dimensions together, that is of 'doing ethics work' in the context of an organisation. Their research identified a conflict between the ethics of care and ethics of justice in public welfare agencies as the key area of such struggles. They conclude that further work needs to be done to integrate care and justice to create more ethically responsive practice.

Hyde (2012) examines the ethical decision making of social work mangers in a variety of human service and social change organisations. She concludes that ethical dilemmas mainly arise from conflicts between social work values and agency or government policies. She states that participants followed various forms of value ranking, although none used a formal ethical decision making framework. Hyde also notes that none expressed any sense of 'getting it right' (p. 362), but rather that they were responding as best they could. As a consequence, the resolution of ethical dilemmas was achieved on a case-by-case basis (p. 363). Hyde argues for efforts to increase training to create common standards. However, it is also possible to see these data as revealing the inherent messiness of ethics in practice. Greater awareness and explicit understanding of plural values does not have to lead to external creation of a single value ranking.

Ethics can be viewed as a continuous conversation, one that has stretched over a very long period of time (Hinman 2013, p. 3). In social work, ethics has been discussed since the earliest days in the nineteenth century, but the ideas that form the basis of the conversation go back centuries (even in the case of virtue ethics for millennia). The challenge of pluralism is to develop the capacity of each social worker to be part of this conversation and to relate it to their commitment to social work. This can be seen as 'moral fluency' (Sellman 1996; Hugman 2005) or as 'ethical literacy' (Kline and Preston-Shoot 2012). Although this is not the same thing as 'ethics work' (Banks 2016, p. 37), it is a necessary prerequisite (Houston 2012, p. 666). Ethical pluralism offers a way to achieve this without creating constraints on the moral dimension of social work or removing ethical accountability (compare with Bauman 1994).

Conclusion

This chapter has examined the challenges posed to social work ethics from the debates in moral philosophy between different approaches that are often expressed as conflicts. It has then explored the alternatives of ethical relativism and ethical pluralism. Ethical relativism was seen as inadequate because it fails to address problems of the limit to tolerance (for example, of interpersonal abuse or systemic inequalities), the possibility of intercultural agreement on primary values or even in silencing moral debate (as in 'it's just different, that's all'). In contrast, ethical pluralism accepts that values may be incompatible or incommensurable, but at the same time it provides a basis for engaging in dialogue between the various possible value positions that are relevant.

From this, there are practical gains in explicitly recognising ethical pluralism as the way in which many social workers actually address ethical challenges in their day-to-day work. This not only reflects the diversity of values that are held by individual social workers, but also that policies, laws and so on are also created from a range of ethical positions. Developing form this understanding, it can be seen that there are benefits for the growth of social work in recognising ethical pluralism.

First, from this perspective social work may not only accept but celebrate the 'crooked timber' of humanity (Houston 2012), in that no one rationale suits all people or circumstances. This is the basis of embracing diversity and responding to the particularity of each situation without giving up on the key ethical commitments that social work affirms and which we share across contexts. Second, ethical pluralism enables us to affirm responsibility in ethical decision making, without seeking to constrain our moral impulse within a rigid framework. Third, these two benefits in turn equip social workers to live with uncertainty. Rather than seeing indeterminacy as a problem to be overcome, it enables us to grasp the unfinished nature of practice (Banks 2012). It is not that social workers should be complacent about the possibility of there not always being a single right answer, but instead accept that achieving what is good enough is a reasonable goal precisely because ethics is always contested.

Reamer (2014, 2018) has argued that highly developed ethical frameworks are the mark of professional maturity. In so far as these documents are discursive and provide guidelines to assist people in their struggles with ethical challenges we may agree. However, if they are allowed to become definitive sets of rules that obscure the unsettled and unfinished nature of social work, then they do not assist the growth of the profession. Indeed, it may be that the limited use made of codes of ethics by practitioners comes from this way of understanding codes and other ethical documents. It is only by seeking to understand the different claims of the various ethical approaches that can inform social work and by being more critically aware of our own values that social workers can achieve ethical practice.

References

Banks S (2012) Ethics and values in social work, 4th edn. Palgrave, Basingstoke
Banks S (2016) Everyday ethics in professional life. Ethics Soc Welf 10:35–52. https://doi.org/10.1080/17496535.2015.1126623
Banks S, Cai T, de Jonge E, Shears J, Shum M, Sobocan AM, Strom K, Truell R, Uriz MJ, Weinberg M (2020) Practising ethically during COVID-19: social work challenges and responses. Int Soc Work 63:569–583. https://doi.org/10.1177/0020872820949614
Bauman Z (1994) Alone again: ethics after certainty. Demos, London
Berlin I (1992) The crooked timber of humanity: chapters in the history of ideas. Edited by Hardy H. Vintage Books, New York

Berlin I (1997) The proper study of mankind. Edited by Hardy H, Hausheer R. Chatto & Windus, London

Bonnycastle C (2011) Social justice along a continuum: a relational illustrative model. Soc Serv Rev 85:267–295. https://doi.org/10.1086/660703

Congress E, McAuliffe D (2006) Social work ethics: professional codes in Australia and the United States. Int Soc Work 49:151–164

Costello S, Kanyi T, Dalling M (2019) Child protection and family group conferencing curriculum for social workers in Palestine. Crit Radic Soc Work 7:173–188

Featherstone B, Gupta A (2020) Social workers' reflections on ethics in relation to adoption in the UK: everywhere but nowhere? Br J Soc Work 50:833–849. https://doi.org/10.1093/bjsw/bcz033

Garrett PM (2020) Against stultifying classifications for a 'new humanism'. Br J Soc Work, Advance online publication. https://doi.org/10.1093/bjsw/bcaa134

Gray M (2005) Dilemmas of international social work: paradoxical processes of indigenization, universalism and imperialism. Int J Soc Welf 14:231–238

Hardy T (2019) Then and now: the history and development of social work ethics. In: Marson SM, McKinney RE (eds) The Routledge handbook of social work ethics and values. Routledge, Abingdon

Healy L (2007) Universalism and cultural relativism in social work ethics. Int Soc Work 50:11–26. https://doi.org/10.1177/002087.28070711479

Hinman LM (2013) Ethics: a pluralistic approach to moral theory, 5th edn. Wadsworth, Boston

Hölscher D (2018) Caring for justice in a neo-liberal university. S Afr J High Educ 32:31–48. https://doi.org/10.20853/32-6-2676

Houston S (2012) Engaging with the crooked timber of humanity: value pluralism and social work. Br J Soc Work 42:652–668. https://doi.org/10.1093/bjsw/bcr092

Hugman R (2005) New approaches in ethics for the caring professions. Palgrave Macmillan, Basingstoke

Hugman R (2008) Ethics in a world of difference. Ethics Soc Welf 2:118–132

Hugman R (2013) Culture, values and ethics in social work. Routledge, London

Hugman R (2014) A-Z of professional ethics. Palgrave, Basingstoke

Hugman R, Pawar M, Anscombe AW, Wheeler A (2021) Virtue ethics in social work practice. Routledge, London

Hyde CA (2012) Ethical dilemmas in human service management: identifying and resolving the challenges. Ethics Soc Welf 6:351–367. https://doi.org/10.1080/17496535.2011.615753

Ife J (2012) Human rights and social work: towards rights-based practice, 3rd edn. Cambridge University Press, South Melbourne

International Federation of Social Workers & International Association of Schools of Social Work [IFSW/IASSW] (2018a) Global definition of the social work profession, electronic document downloaded 19 January 2021 from https://www.ifsw.org/what-is-social-work/global-definition-of-social-work/

International Federation of Social Workers & International Association of Schools of Social Work [IFSW/IASSW] (2018b) Global social work statement of ethical principles, electronic document downloaded 19 January 2021 from https://www.ifsw.org/global-social-work-statement-of-ethical-principles/

Jayasooria D (2019) Sustainable development goals and social work: opportunities and challenges for social work practice in Malaysia. J Hum Rights Soc Work 1:19–29. https://doi.org/10.1007/s41134-016-0007-y

Juujävi S, Kalunki E, Luostari H (2020) Ethical decision making of social welfare workers in the transition of services: the ethics of care and justice perspectives. Ethics Soc Welf 14:65–83. https://doi.org/10.1080/17496535.2019.1710546

Kekes J (1993) The morality of pluralism. Princeton University Press, Princeton

Kline R, Preston-Shoot M (2012) Professional accountability in social care and health. Learning Matters/Sage, London

Lundy C (2011) Social work, social justice and human rights: a structural approach to practice, 2nd edn. University of Toronto Press, North York
Maglajlic AM (2011) International organisations, social work and war: a 'frog's perspective' reflection on the bird's eye view. In: Lavalette M, Ioakimidis V (eds) Social work in extremis: lessons for social work internationally. The Policy Press, Bristol
Mapp SC (2021) Human rights and social justice in a global perspective: an introduction to international social work, 3rd edn. Oxford University Press, New York
McBeath G, Webb SA (2002) Virtue ethics and social work: being lucky, realistic, and not doing your duty. Br J Soc Work 32:1015–1036
Nagel (1979) Mortal questions. Cambridge University Press, Cambridge
Nagel T (1993) Moral luck. In: Statman D (ed) Moral luck. State University of New York Press, Albany, pp 57–71
Niemi P (2020) Recognition and the other in social work. Br J Soc Work Advanced online publication. https://doi.org/10.1093/bjsw/bcaa023
Noyori-Corbett C, Moxley DP (2019) Staging developmental research with Myanmar refugee women in the design of a community resettlement center: advancing the interpersonal dimension of human rights. Soc Dev Issues 41:63–79
Nussbaum M (2000) Women and human development. Cambridge University Press, New York
Nussbaum M (2002) Capabilities and social justice. Int Stud Rev 4:123–135
Nussbaum M (2006) Frontiers of justice. Harvard University Press, Cambridge
O'Brien M (2010) Social justice: alive and well (partly) in social work practice? Int Soc Work 54:174–190. https://doi.org/10.1177/0020872810382682
Okkonen I, Takala T (2019) Managers' moral struggle: a case study on ethical dilemmas and ethical decision-making in the context of immigration. Ethics Soc Welf 13:392–408. https://doi.org/10.1080/17496535.2019.1604784
Orme J (2002) Social work: gender, care and justice. Br J Soc Work 32:799–814
Osei-Hwedie K (1993) The challenge of social work in Africa: starting the indigenization process. J Soc Dev Afr 8:19–30
Osei-Hwedie K, Ntseane D, Jacques G (2006) Searching for appropriateness in social work education in Botswana. Soc Work Educ 25:569–590
Papouli E (2018) Aristotle's virtue ethics as a conceptual framework for the study and practice of social work in modern times. Eur J Soc Work 22:921–934. https://doi.org/10.1080/13691457.2018.1461072
Ravulo J, Mafile'o T, Yeates DB (eds) (2019) Pacific social work: navigating practice, policy and research. Routledge, Abingdon
Reamer FG (2014) Risk management in social work: preventing professional malpractice, liability and disciplinary action. Columbia University Press, New York
Reamer FG (2018) Social work values and ethics, 5th edn. Columbia University Press, New York
Reamer FG, Nimmagadda J (2015) Social work ethics in India: a call for the development of indigenized ethical standards. Int Soc Work 60:182–195
Sellman D (1996) Why teach ethics to nurses? Nurs Ed Today 16:44–48
Shewell H (2010) Social rights are human rights. In: Pulkingham J (ed) Human welfare, rights and social activism: rethinking the legacy of J. S. Woodsworth. University of Toronto Press, Toronto
Sewpaul V (2016) The west and the rest divide: human rights, culture and social work. J Hum Rights Soc Work 1:30–39
Sewpaul V, Henrickson M (2019) The (r)evolution and decolonization of social work ethics: The Global Social Work Statement of Ethical Principles. Int Soc Work 62:1469–1481
Solas J (2008) Social justice and social work: what are we fighting for? Aust Soc Work 61:124–136
Truell R, Crompton S (2020) To the top of the cliff: how social work changed with COVID-19. International Federation of Social Workers, Rheinfelden
United Nations [UN] (1948) The universal declaration of human rights. United Nations, New York
United Nations [UN] (1989) Convention on the rights of the child. United Nations, New York

Wamara CK, Carvalho MI (2021) Discrimination and injustice against older people in Uganda: implications for social work practice. Int Soc Work 64:1022–1034

Weinberg M, Campbell C (2014) From codes to contextual collaborations: shifting the thinking about ethics in social work. J Progress Hum Serv 49:25–37

Williams B (1981) Moral luck: philosophical papers 1973–1980. Cambridge University Press, Cambridge

Williams B (1993) Moral luck. In: Statman D (ed) Moral luck. State University of New York Press, Albany, pp 35–55

Wronka J (1998) Human rights and social policy in the 21st century, revised edn. University Press of America, Lanham

Yellow Bird M, Gray M (2008) Indigenous people and the language of social work. In: Gray M, Coates J, Yellow Bird M (eds) Indigenous social work around the world: towards culturally relevant education and practice

Yip K-S (2004) A Chinese cultural critique of the global qualifying standards for social work education. Soc Work Educ 23:597–612

Part V

Ethical Issues and Challenges in Social Work

The Ethical Challenge of Populism in Social Work

21

Dorothee Hölscher and Derek Clifford

Contents

Introduction	422
Populism: Concepts and Key Debates	423
Contemporary Populism: Definition and Examples	424
Contextual Conditions and Points of Divergence between Contemporary Populism and Social Work	426
Populism, Social Work, and Social Work Values: A Complex Dynamic	428
Challenges of Populism in Everyday Social Work Practice: Four Case Studies	430
Challenges in Context	432
The Ethical Dimension	434
Concerning Responses	434
Justice, Care, and Democracy: The Relevance of Iris Marion Young for Responding Ethically to Populism	436
Conclusion	439
References	441

Abstract

This chapter explores the ethical implications of populism – a form of politics focusing on the opposition of 'the people' to 'the elite'. Populism is compatible with a variety of political perspectives but emphasizes the alleged homogeneous nature of 'the real people', with limited acknowledgment of difference and social division. This can place populism at odds with social work's traditional embrace of universalist values such as respect for persons, human rights, and justice, and its commitment to care. The chapter considers in what ways the recent increase in populist movements presents ethical challenges for social work. This is done in

D. Hölscher
School of Nursing, Midwifery and Social Work, The University of Queensland, Brisbane, Australia

Department of Social Work & Criminology, University of Pretoria, Pretoria, South Africa
e-mail: d.holscher@uq.edu.au

D. Clifford (✉)
Formally, Liverpool John Moores University, Liverpool, UK

© Springer Nature Singapore Pte Ltd. 2023
D. Hölscher et al. (eds.), *Social Work Theory and Ethics*, Social Work,
https://doi.org/10.1007/978-981-19-1015-9_25

relation to four case vignettes, based on both first-hand and social media accounts. The chapter draws on the philosophy of Iris Marion Young to consider how social work might respond to populism in a manner that upholds its key ethical commitments. It is argued that such a response must take seriously *both* some of the underlying concerns that draw people to populist values and movements *and* the need to challenge inhumane or unjust ideas and movements, so that vulnerable and oppressed members of society have their stories told, their voices heard, and are protected from the harms that populism can cause. The chapter concludes that populism requires considerable ethical and political competence among social workers to protect and expand the caring capacity of the institutions within which they work.

Keywords

Social work · Populism · Ethics · Justice · Care · Iris Marion Young

Introduction

Social work has a long tradition of defining itself in relation to universalistic values about equal respect for all human beings and their needs, including their right to equal participation in politics and society, and by its commitment to the advancement of human rights and social justice (Hugman 2013). However, many people do not hold those views or do so only partially. Resultant challenges have been brought to the fore by an increase in populism in the last 50 years (Kaltwasser et al. 2017). Populism is diverse and has a variety of forms (Mudde 2017), some of which conflict with traditional social work values and self-understanding. This is apparent in wider public discourses and within politics and public service, where social and economic policies are made. However, social work practitioners, students, and service users, too, may hold concerning populist views (see, for example, Fazzi and Nothdurfter 2021). Accordingly, Fazzi and Nothdurfter (2021) propose that the profession treat populism not just as an external problem, calling instead for "situated" ethical approach, which "starts from the challenges social workers encounter... in difficult ethical circumstances" (p. 650), and which regards "responsibility in a wider, more relational sense" (Banks 2016, p. 36). This chapter responds to their call.

The chapter differs from much of the growing body of social work literature on the challenge of populism for social work, which focuses predominantly on *right-wing* populism due to the direct threat it poses for social work's self-understanding and prospects for acting in solidarity with some of its most vulnerable service users (see, for example, Fazzi and Nothdurfter 2021; Noble and Ottman 2021). Without negating the urgency of that project, we start from the position that limiting the debate to only one side of the spectrum risks being parochial in that it does injustice to the complexity of the phenomenon: populism of the left and center can also be problematic (see, for example, Forde 2011). In other words, our purpose is to help insert another layer of considerations into the debate. Doubtlessly, there will be tensions between the different manners of framing the problem and different priorities and approaches on offer (Banks 2016). We propose that these tensions will need to be held, not negated.

The section "Populism: Concepts and Key Debates" begins with an overview of different perspectives on populism, which are as uncontroversial as possible to introduce the subject clearly. The basic problem of definition of these debated concepts – problems widely recognized in the social sciences – is that concepts are contested, changing, and context-dependent: they do not admit of 'scientific' definition, and reflect differing perspectives and purposes. The way this chapter attempts to define terms is not exempt. Readers always need to use their own judgment – even more so in this contentious area. However, recent literature suggests that there are *some* basic areas of commonality or at least overlap, upon which we can base a broad concept of populism, and thus be as clear as we can be. Thereafter, some *contested* perspectives are signaled, indicating where social workers need to be thinking carefully about the controversies, and the positions they themselves hold. These points of contestation are exemplified via presentation and discussion of four vignettes (in section "Challenges of Populism in Everyday Social Work Practice: Four Case Studies"), followed by an exploration of political philosopher, Iris Marion Young's, relevance for an ethical response in contexts that are shaped by contemporary forms of populism (in section "Justice, Care and Democracy: The Relevance of Iris Marion Young for Responding Ethically to Populism").

Echoing Fazzi (2015) and Fazzi and Nothdurfter (2021), we conclude by advocating the importance of political *and* ethical competence in analyzing current politics and social policy, however extending their call in the face of the complex politics of populism at large. We propose that populism always needs to be assessed both in the context of specific societies *and* with respect to the global impact of social and other media. Social work's practice requirements include making time and space to listen to those with different life experiences, working towards the identification of grievances underlying populist politics, and inclusion of the aggrieved and oppressed within discussion and decision-making. The aims should include working across *all* social divisions and flattening hierarchies to reduce the top-down flows of power, and increasing the potential influence of the marginalized, thereby challenging the varied sources of oppression.

Populism: Concepts and Key Debates

In this section, we explain some of the key concepts associated with populism and refer to recent literature where their dimensions have been debated. Often, populists are seen as right-wing, associated with abhorrent views inconsistent with social work's universalistic values. This may sometimes be the case, but it is important to consider that such a narrow account may be wholly or partially mistaken. The section begins with a broad definition of populism, which is exemplified through a wide range of examples, before discussing specific formations of particular concern for social work.

Contemporary Populism: Definition and Examples

In order to accommodate an inclusive definition, it is important to recognize that the most common components in accounts of 'populism' are, firstly, that it includes an appeal to 'the people', with "... the idea that 'the people' can authoritatively recover power from the government to reconstitute institutions, or wrestle power from corrupt or self-serving elites" (Kaltwasser et al. 2017, p. 3). Secondly, populism entails identification of an 'elite' of some specific description, who are 'opposed' to 'the people'. This 'elite' may be *within* a given society or nation, external to it, or a combination of both. In other words, both 'the people', 'the elite' and hence, populism itself, are significantly context-dependent in meaning and thus, always require identification of a specific geographical and historical context. It follows that identification of exactly who is being referred to as 'the people', and how inclusive (or not) this term appears in a specific context, is essential. Likewise, careful contextual analysis of why certain groups are identified as 'elite', and to what end, is pivotal to making meaningful inferences for social workers.

Historically, the term populism denotes the idea of a democratic system where political authority is supposed to be invested in the 'demos' – originally, the common people of an ancient Greek state. Some who are disparagingly described as populist may therefore retort they are simply being democratic (Rummens 2017). However, a distinguishing feature of democratic as against populist politics is the extent to which democrats accept the existence of many diverse social groups that make up a 'people' who *all* must be represented in politically accountable institutions. Moreover, classic representative democracy requires shared institutions whose members are freely elected, based on their promise to promote the interests of disparate individuals and social groups, whose legitimate disagreements are managed by compromise and voting procedures. Populists reduce the importance of these institutions by direct appeal to the 'people', often with significant implications for who are (or are not) included in 'the people'.

When defining 'the people' in narrow homogeneous terms, the usual default position for populists is to use a form of nationalism to demarcate the 'real' people against those people who are not. However, although narrow definitions of 'the people' as a homogenous national group is typical, it is possible to be 'nationalist' without being populist. For example, the liberation of nations from foreign control – especially in the context of decolonization – has been done in the name of 'all' the varied people within a nation (see, for example, Mabandla and Deumert 2020). Populism can also embrace left-wing movements and their leaders, but it *cannot* usually be stretched to include the pluralism typical of liberal democratic states where it is accepted that numerous social groups with competing interests are 'free' to contest for the votes of the populace, and where homogeneity is neither required nor desirable. Of course, such distinctions are matters of degree, and real politics is not always so clear.

Academic commentators often refer to populism as a 'thin' ideology (Mudde and Kaltwasser 2013) precisely because this term does not have a 'thick' content with which it is associated but instead can be assigned a range of meanings to suit someone's political purpose, depending on the situation: "Thin-centred ideologies such as... populism habitually appear in combination with very different concepts and ideological traditions" (Mudde and Kaltwasser 2013, p. 150). As such, populism is often opportunistic – making use of available causes to increase voter appeal. This will likely include criticism of established institutions and cultural norms, feeding on popular sentiments of disappointment, anger, and resentment about social injustices, as well as appealing to popular prejudice against groups and/or individuals designated as scapegoats for the experienced afflictions. Furthermore, recent research has emphasized that populism is not just a system of ideas designed to maximize the political interests of one group over another (Mudde 2017) and can include strategies (Weyland 2017) and styles (Ostiguy 2017) that leaders may use to enhance their access to power. Emphasis on (often) charismatic leadership is one of the common features of populist politics, and leaders typically employ a range of styles to attract the popular vote. This includes the use of "common" or "vulgar" language; the adoption of popular music and cultural images, and notoriously the spread of "... 'post-truth' communication depend[ing] not only on... disinformation but on vagueness as well" (Knoblock 2020, p. 140).

A few examples of the variety of people and politics that have been called 'populist' may help to appreciate the range of interpretations currently in circulation. A recent obvious case in point is that of Donald Trump, who has famously appealed to 'the people' of America, rallying them, at once, against the alleged 'elites' of the Washington political and media 'swamp', against refugees and irregular migrants seeking to enter the US territory via the Mexican border, and against racialized citizens belonging to visibly distinct ethnic and religious minorities. Yet, there has been a very different kind of populism in South American countries, such as Ecuador and Bolivia, recently described as (respectively) "republican populism and Marxist populism" (Cadalen 2020). The late Hugo Chavez, former president of Venezuela, was also widely regarded as a left-wing populist (De La Torre 2017), as have been groups in Europe such as the Spanish Podemos (Issel-Dombert 2020), and in the UK and USA, left-wing politicians such as Bernie Sanders and Jeremy Corbyn (Demata 2020). South African populist Julius Malema has been characterized as both a socialist revolutionary and a neo-nationalist (Forde 2011). Nevertheless, right-wing figures across the globe such as Pauline Hansen in Australia (Fenton-Smith 2020), Victor Orbán in Hungary, or Vladimir Putin in Russia are more usually seen as populists (Müller 2017, p. 597). In other words, 'populism' has been attributed to a wide range of people and parties, holding a variety of political positions. The commonalities between such disparate figures are very 'thin', but the opposition between an internal and/or foreign 'elite' that exploits 'the people' is a basic element in their thinking and a basis upon which people who are resentful about their lot can unite and mobilize. The lesson is to be very careful about what someone means when using these terms, especially what they imply by 'people' and 'elite' – and what evidence is offered to justify that usage – without jumping to conclusions about where they sit on a political spectrum.

The following diagram offers a visual approximation of basic ideas about the relationship between populist and other kinds of politics. It shows that both liberal democracy and populism claim to avoid the tyranny of elites. It also shows that both might still be swerved towards the elitist authoritarian pole or more towards popular participation. Other differences will vary according to local context.

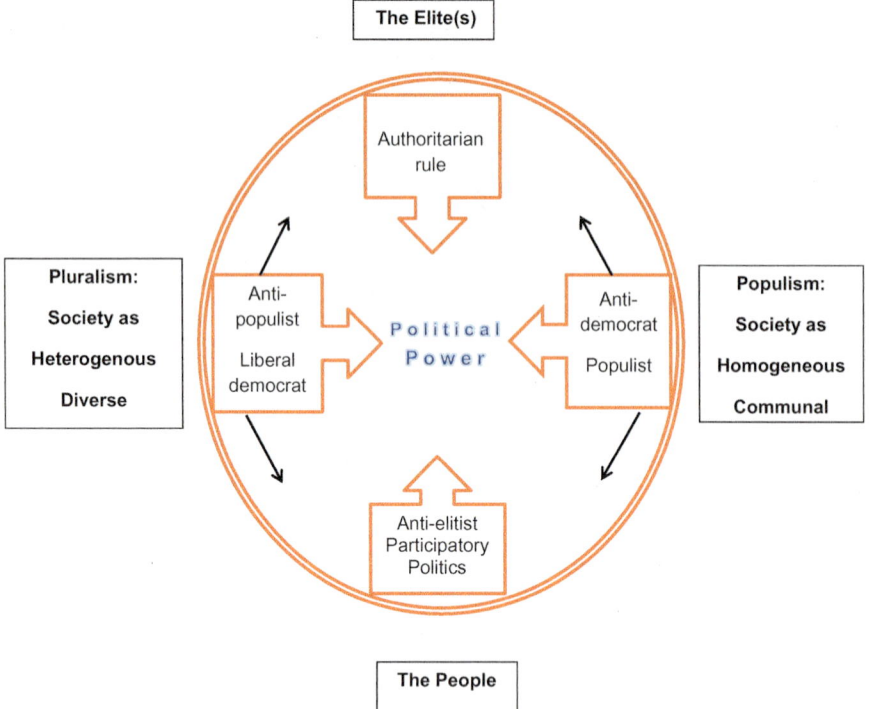

Diagram: Relationships between populism and other politics

Contextual Conditions and Points of Divergence between Contemporary Populism and Social Work

Several regimes in the last century are regarded as populist, although recent research has illuminated the increase in populism in the past 50 years (Kaltwasser et al. 2017). Why now? Given the contested nature of the term, contested explanations of the causes of populism are inevitable. However, a common theme is that it is associated with crises of modernization, globalization, and, more recently, internet technology (Hawkins et al. 2017; Ife 2021). Yet more precisely, the contemporary emergence of populisms ought to be seen in relation to the advent of 'market fundamentalism' – the neoliberal economics boosted by Ronald Reagan and Margaret Thatcher and since imposed elsewhere across the globe (Ferguson 2021). Sayer (2016) provides evidence of the "return of the rich" over the last four decades, closely associated with the rise of neoliberalism (see also Fraser and Jaeggi 2018). The political and cultural shift towards seeing ourselves as competing individuals with no responsibility for anyone else is connected to this shift in the economic class structure towards the creation of powerful, wealthy elites. Sayer (2016) and others document the way neoliberal economics has exacerbated inequalities of wealth and power. The new elites commonly get most of their income "...from control of existing assets that yield rent, interest or capital gains, including gains from speculation on financial products" (Sayer 2016, p. 18). This development has been associated, especially since the subprime lending crisis and subsequent economic crash of 2008, with growing levels of poverty and insecurity – so it is unsurprising that some of those locked out from such opportunities will respond positively to appeals to 'the people' against those elites (Fraser and Jaeggi 2018).

While in this context populist appeals can be made from the right *or* from the left, traditional conservative thinking emphasizes the status of the individual citizen, as 'striver', entrepreneur, source of wealth and legitimacy – often implicitly male in orientation. The populist angle on this is to place the individual citizen in opposition to bureaucracies and alleged political and cultural elites. Missing from current global conservative populism is any recognition of the reality of social structures, especially ones that involve social injustice, and their changing – and continuing – histories. On the contrary, a characteristic feature of populism is to propose a homogeneous society composed of individuals and families where social structures are conspicuous by their absence. There is little or no understanding that inequalities are mediated through macro-social arrangements, which in turn are rooted in sociohistorical and economic processes such as colonialism, industrial capitalism, patriarchy, or global corporatism. For example, at a global internet level, there is powerful opposition by populist "dark web" figures against any hint of concern about structural disadvantage by "radical leftist", "social justice warriors", and "political correctness" movements (Kelsy 2020, p. 179).

In this context, populists can reinterpret all structural forms of oppression as individual aberrations, which afflicted groups and individuals can and should deal with and overcome. For example, part of the "culture wars" associated with populist politics in some parts of the world includes the downplaying of structural racism, and the celebration of individual minority ethnic 'achievers'. The populist Toryism of Johnson in the UK included ethnic minority politicians, who have actively campaigned against any reference to structural racism, producing a widely criticized report (Sewell 2021), which suggested that black children are less in need than poor white children. Such moves served to deliberately discount historical injustice and manipulate voters accordingly, thereby avoiding having to attend to the stark, if complex and intersecting, inequalities that continue to harm *both* poor white and black children.

A related concern pertains to the frequent conflation of populism and nationalism, referred to above. In the context of modern territorial states, the 'real' people are often denoted by means of recourse to racist or ethnocentric tropes such that the ones who turn out to be included are those who match the self-image and stereotypes dominant within a specific national border (Anand et al. 2021; Fazzi 2015). This then tends to exclude anyone seen as 'foreign'; anyone seen as physically or culturally different from the traditional majority population; anyone with an ancestry outside the nation state borders; and certainly, anyone without legal right to be resident. At its extreme, it leads to the institutionalization of anti-foreigner racism – "xeno-racism" (Fekete 2018), or even more radically, fascism.

The recent global upswing towards populist ideas also raises the specter of sexual and gender injustice, including the role and experience of women in society, and the distribution of caring responsibilities (Noble 2021). Populist approaches to the family and community – like populist accounts of racism and poverty – tend to ignore historic structural injustices suffered by women and sexual minorities. Recent research shows that as populism reflects local culture in relation to gender, some iterations *may* "...advocate for gender equality and sympathize with gender struggles" (Abi-hassan 2017, p. 440). However, it is striking that even where women are included in leadership roles, most types of populism, right or left wing, maintain "... a rather traditional-conservative approach to societal dynamics (family, work, political participation, etc.)" with "... feminist movements that advocate for women's individual rights and autonomy ... constructed as corrupt and elitist" (Abi-hassan 2017, p. 441).

This anti-feminism is not surprising in view of the connection between populism and religious fundamentalism. Populism sometimes lends itself to a quasi-religious belief in 'the people' (Zúquete 2017), with traditional religions frequently contributing to the identity of 'the people', thereby reinforcing conventionally negative attitudes towards the rights of women and sexual minorities. Thus, the rise of populism has coincided with a rise of fundamentalist versions of religion across the world and associated with conservative views on matters of gender and sexuality: fundamentalist Christians have been a source of support for populism in the USA and Brazil; fundamentalist versions of Buddhism have influence in Myanmar; fundamentalist anti-Muslim Hinduism has supported populists in India; and fundamentalist versions of Islam are well-known for their antipathy to the rights of women and sexual minorities across the Muslim world (Zúquete 2017).

An uncritical approach to conventional 'family' values has become part of a populist platform in some countries, as, for example, in the marriage referendum in Croatia, where changes that might benefit women and sexual minorities have been resisted (Kahlina 2020). It is also apparent in global internet and social media sources. Leading figures on the "intellectual dark web", for example, tend to oppose feminism (Kelsey 2020, p. 192). In a recent interview, a popular academic "...was using psychological and neurobiological arguments as a clinician to counter some of the social theories of gender inequality" (Kelsey 2020, p. 181), suggesting that such lead figures are keen to support common conservative themes such as: "... fundamental biological differences between men and women" (Kelsey 2020, p. 180), while finding a ready market for their ideas. Thus, traditional beliefs of allegedly 'homogeneous' societies take precedence over the structural injustices that are such frequent concerns for women and men working in social services.

Populism, Social Work, and Social Work Values: A Complex Dynamic

Social work's well-established commitment to human rights and social justice alongside its longstanding concern with ethics and care could loosely be termed a form of humanism, inasmuch as it is often associated with 'soft' women's issues. Historically, the profession has been dominated by women, especially at the frontline, and it has been frequently scapegoated for apparent failures and criticized for maintaining 'dependency' on the state. Against this background, many social workers have embraced a feminist 'ethics of care', which has powerfully argued for the importance of relational concepts that rest upon an understanding of interdependency as inherent to human existence (Tronto 1993; Mackenzie and Stoljar 2000; Robinson 2011), including interdependency with nonhuman species (Bozalek et al. 2020; Fraser and Taylor 2021). Such relational understandings of the world not only assert care as basic to life but also include structural explanations of historic and continuing social injustice towards women and other dominated social groups and remain highly relevant to social work (Clifford 2013).

Social work's value base, its predominant gender profile and professional positioning, all make it a natural target for right-wing politics, populist or not. The right in politics is significantly about preserving and advancing dominant cultural and economic interests, usually by defending traditional forms of life, such as patriarchal family structures, existing private ownership of land and industry, and disparities of wealth and power. There is a range of political possibilities for those interested in social welfare that are compatible with certain conservative positions. However, insofar as social work stresses the importance of social welfare being equitably available for all persons, with a special interest in the most vulnerable, it is always going to be under attack. This will be even more the case where social workers are actively arguing for a reduction of gross inequalities of wealth and power, for such positions place the profession in direct opposition to those for whom: "... upholding universal human rights... would negatively affect their wealth, life-style choices, and cohesion of an imagined national 'community'" (Noble and Ottmann 2021, p. 8). Social workers thus need to be wary about the apparent discriminatory implications of populism – even (especially) when those same populist leaders are expressing their views in apparently anti-elite language (Ife 2021). Yet, they do need to attend to the underlying grievances of those whom populists may aim to manipulate.

The above characterization of global populism's orientation on key issues of structural injustice illustrates the level of dialogue that, we contend, social workers need to have with populists. While some social work academics claim that such dialogue is impossible (see, for example, Ife 2021), a suggested liberal democratic response is that it is necessary, and it must: "... show why the solutions they [populists] propose are usually not adequate while acknowledging that the problems they detect are real" (Kaltwasser 2017, p. 503). In the following, we argue that pragmatic solutions to problems do have some uses, but social workers also need to challenge assumptions about the nature of the issues, questioning their own thinking at the same time as challenging populist ideas. This task is complicated by the fact that social workers themselves, as well as their service users, may be attracted to populism of the right, left, or center, and need to assess critically both the limitations and the alleged benefits of both populist and representative democratic politics. Our position, as shown in the section "Justice, Care and Democracy: The Relevance of Iris Marion Young for Responding Ethically to Populism" below, is that dialogue *is* achievable, but that it *does* require a more robust basis than what Kaltwasser (2017) suggests. First, however, we offer some examples of social work where populism has been either directly or indirectly influential. We also include some commentary on these examples highlighting their ethical dimension and illustrating how the people involved might have handled things differently or what they could or should have considered.

Challenges of Populism in Everyday Social Work Practice: Four Case Studies

This section explicates the reasons why contemporary forms of populism may be considered a concern in everyday social work practice by exploring how they can give rise to particular ethical challenges. Our explorations are grounded in four vignettes. Of these, vignettes 1, 2, and 3 are based upon first-hand accounts from social work education and practice, while vignette 4 retells a video that has been widely circulated on social media. All four vignettes have been fictionalized and decontextualized to the extent necessary to ensure anonymity and with the view to constructing an argument of relevance to a global readership. There is a tension inherent in considering the global significance of a phenomenon without at the same time negating its contextual specificity, which remains no matter how carefully such an argument is constructed and how tentative its conclusions are drawn, and readers are asked to bear this in mind as they proceed through this section.

Vignette 1: Janet was the course lecturer of a popular equity and diversity module with almost 300 enrolled students from social work and related degrees. Due to the COVID-19 pandemic, this year's course was rendered entirely online. This might have exacerbated certain challenges Janet had previously encountered, but not to such a degree. For example, despite an agreed-upon code of practice, which in all of Janet's experience should have been apt to support a safe-enough learning environment for the class to discuss difficult topics, a small group of students appeared to repeatedly provoke others with deliberately racist and sexist comments. At one point, Matt, a social work student, made such a disparaging remark about the transgender community that Janet decided to initiate a disciplinary process by reporting him to the program lead. In part, her response was prompted by a prior disclosure by one of the trans students that they were experiencing a heightened sense of vulnerability. Now, the program lead informed Janet that, in following-up on her report, Matt had been "counselled", had undertaken not to repeat his offensive behavior, but Janet would need to "keep an eye on him" to ensure that he stuck to this commitment.

Vignette 2: Paul was the founding member of a community initiative, a nonprofit organization by and for First Nations peoples. He had been chairing a meeting to review and advise the municipality on a priority list for social housing allocations. Ella, a senior social worker, had also been in attendance. Towards the end of the meeting, Ella spoke up, saying that she was "increasingly concerned" about the committee's "continued disregard" for "white poverty". Why was it that First Nations families were constantly being prioritized? Were not housing shortages a problem for everyone? She was concerned that "this process" risked becoming "a case of reverse racism", proposing that instead, resources should be allocated "according to need". There was a stunned silence, followed by a heated debate. Eventually, Ella was asked to leave the meeting. After further discussion, the committee tasked Paul to lodge a complaint against her with the Social Work Association, based on, most committee members agreed, her blatantly racist remarks. Paul understood Ella's position to be linked to her own upbringing, which he knew had been harsh. He would have preferred to relay the committee's concerns in private, urging her to be more cautious around what kinds of issues she raised in public, and how. Yet, he did feel that what had happened really had gone too far.

Vignette 3: John was supporting Kaylee, a woman in a refuge, who, having problems caring for a child with health issues and having suffered domestic abuse, needed him to retrieve some of her and her child's belongings. Kaylee's husband and mother-in-law let him into the house politely enough, but their anger surfaced soon: they criticized social services as an "interfering bureaucracy", and their staff as middle-class "do-gooders" and "busybodies", who were "breaking up families" and allowing their child to be kept in the "poor conditions" of a women's refuge. The grandmother was adamant that the child had been well until the mother took her away and skeptical about the alleged violence perpetrated by her son, expressing fervent belief in the values of marriage and the privacy of family life. John should do whatever he could to return the child to their care and to encourage the mother to come home. As John tried to explain why his role simply did not allow him to do what they asked, he was also struck by the genuineness of their convictions. He had considered this visit to be an opportunity to start assessing how best to manage this case, and started wondering: to what extent, in what way, and to what end did his role require him to engage with their hostile views?

Vignette 4: Blessing was employed as a community development officer in the local government office. Two hours ago, Blessing had been in the foyer, when some ten members of the Convention for National Democracy had walked in. One of them, a recent high school graduate, had been screaming at him with the others cheering and filming the entire incident: "Why are you here? What is it that you can do that our people cannot also do? Don't we have our own graduates? Documented, undocumented or whatever, you are stealing jobs. Why can't you go home?" For Blessing, the last question was pivotal, but the group seemed hardly keen on his response. This tirade went on for a while until Blessing's office manager succeeded in dispersing the crowd by threatening to call the police, and by agreeing to receive a memo outlining the community's grievances about the local government's continued employment of foreigners. Later, the office manager approached Blessing, asking if he wanted to talk about the incident, as well as offering to contact the municipality's well-being unit on his behalf as he felt that some counselling would be essential following this traumatic event. Blessing was not ready to talk. He understood that his manager had needed to de-escalate the situation, yet he could not help feeling betrayed, exposed, and unprotected.

Service users, volunteers, social workers, and other professionals always occupy overlapping social positions, which are unlikely to ever fully harmonize. They bring to their roles a range of additional identities, including those ascribed to them by others. They perform these roles and duties with recourse not only to professional knowledge but also to their general life experiences, and to the social histories and systems within which these are embedded (Clifford and Burke 2009) – including news reports and political commentary, and the views held by people around them, all which are increasingly shaped by social media and other forms of virtual reality (Kelsey 2020). Moreover, most social workers are located at the interface of service users and their employing organizations, often serving at the lower rungs of the institutional hierarchies, while their actions are both enabled and constrained by codes of conduct and, in most countries, professional codes of ethics (Banks 2021). These complex configurations can render social workers at once participants in, targets of, and witnesses to, populisms and the harms (and sometimes benefits) they may generate. The following discussion unpacks these complexities by considering the four vignettes, in conjunction, along three lines: the nature of the challenges and the contextual conditions within which they had emerged; the ethical dimension of these challenges; and ethical concerns regarding what, the vignettes suggest, may be typical responses to the kinds of populism social workers have to confront in their everyday practice.

Challenges in Context

The protagonists in vignettes 2 and 4 are all embroiled in the aftermath of colonial conquest and exploitation, as well as contemporary forms of inequality, albeit positioned very differently in relation to one another. Vignette 2 is set within a policy and practice context where insufficient resources appear to be available to cater for all of those who need shelter yet are unable to access it on the 'free' housing market. It is against this background that Ella decides to speak on behalf of an aggrieved social group – economically disadvantaged descendants of white settlers, and she does so by taking recourse to populist tropes such as "white poverty" and "reverse racism" (compare Fazzi and Nothdurfter 2021). Her arguments insinuate the presence of a political elite, which expediently favors descendants of the colonized. Missing from her account is a historical understanding of *both* the intergenerational injustices afflicting colonized peoples *and* the ways in which neoliberal economies worldwide have placed affordable housing beyond the reach of many (Walia 2021). With social provision and welfare nets cut substantially in regions of the global North and never having reached comprehensive coverage in much of the global South, social workers are often placed in positions where they must define needs and serve as gatekeepers to resources in ways that provide for some groups but leave out others (Weinberg and Banks 2019; Ferguson 2021). Unsurprisingly, it appears not to be the brief of the committee to problematize this.

In vignette 4, a group of postcolonial citizens organized themselves to give voice to their grievances. While their protest is targeting Blessing as a foreign national, their actual addressee is their government, which they appear to view as having failed "the community" – possibly on account of a political elite who are seen to no longer care for 'the people', instead recklessly favoring strangers, who probably should have never come in the first place. In the face of widespread unemployment, including youth unemployment, the vignette exemplifies how xeno-racism is able to draw on colonial borders to justify calls for the expulsion of Others (Fekete 2018). There is no regard for how socioeconomic problems such as unemployment are, like much of contemporary migration itself, a function of neoliberal globalization, which, while especially afflicting economies of the global South, have gravely exacerbated socioeconomic problems worldwide (Fraser 2016; Fraser and Jaeggi 2018; Sayer 2016). Across the globe therefore, nationalist discourses are working to diminish the complexities of contemporary and historical geopolitical and economic relations (see, for example, Brøgge 2020). This, then, is the context of vignette 4, where a conservative populist discourse has served to embroil colonized people in a complex reenactment of preexisting social, economic, and power relations, with borders, established during colonial conquest and rule, continuing to subjugate and divide colonized peoples to date (Walia 2021). Yet again, this is hardly a global South problem alone, as worldwide, colonial, civil, and international wars have resulted – and continue to result – in the turbulent creation of modern nation states. Consequent appeals to ill-informed nationalist and xeno-racist forms of conservative populism are a worldwide scourge and will likely remain a deep ethical and political concern for international social work for a long time to come (Noble and Ottman 2018).

Vignettes 1 and 3 could also have been situated in a range of possible contexts, given the global prominence of populist discourses surrounding gender and sexuality (Noble 2021). In vignette 3, John is faced with conflicting perspectives on what is really in the child's best interest, with Kaylee's husband and mother-in-law expressing hostility towards the department for which he works and suspicion about the role he is playing – not an entirely unreasonable view given the neoliberal welfare context within which their interaction is placed (Weinberg and Banks 2019; Ferguson 2021). Akin to the views apparent in vignette 4 therefore, they seem to regard their relationship with 'the government' and its administration in *Us*-versus-*Them* terms. Kaylee's partner and his mother appear to believe that a government agency, which bases its assessment on 'dubious' claims about family violence and then supports a woman in her decision to bring up a child "in the poor conditions of a... refuge", thereby "breaking up families", is – if nothing else – at least morally "corrupt" (Abi-hassan 2017, p. 441). The grandmother in particular may well have had a bond with her grandchild, consequently resenting both her daughter-in-law's spirit of independence and anyone who is helping to sever that tie. She is also reflecting one of the common themes of conservative populist movements: despite the progressive advances made by women across the world, there remains a strong current in favor of traditional family values in many societies, and in some cases, a backlash against women (Kahlina 2020).

Gender is also at stake in vignette 1, where Janet has to confront transphobic comments – and their potential to cause harm to transgender students – as one of several issues she must deal with in a virtual classroom. Importantly, the recent move in higher education towards online teaching provides opportunity for some class members to employ trolling tactics that have come to be associated with populist internet-based groups seeking to intimidate and silence outspoken advocates of gender, sexual, and racial justice. Indeed, the fact that certain student groups – in the case at hand, transgender students – are treated by some of their peers as fair game is reminiscent of the "dark web" campaigns against "radical leftist", "social justice warriors", and "political correctness" movements discussed in the section "Populism: Concepts and Key Debates" (Kelsy 2020, p. 179). That all this is occurring during live classes in a course on equity and diversity underscores the point made above: social work's concern with ethics, care, and social justice renders it a prime target for global right-wing populist wrath – and this wrath may well be felt by members of the profession itself – in this case, by social work students.

The Ethical Dimension

A "situated ethics", like any ethical approach, requires the identification, analysis, and dis-embedding of what renders a given challenge, an *ethical* one (Banks 2016, p. 36). Here, we argue that the challenges raised by contemporary forms of populism – as articulated in the four vignettes – have a distinctly ethical dimension in that they constitute, firstly, "matters of harm and benefit" and, secondly, the subject of "rights and responsibilities" (Banks 2016, p. 36). To begin with, in all four instances, persons – by virtue of their group membership – are exposed to discriminatory and/or abusive treatment. Raced, sexualized, and transgender students of social work are subject to verbal abuse and online trolling by fellow students in vignette 1. In vignette 2, a social worker presents arguments that pit descendants of colonized peoples against the victims of an increasingly polarized economic system: who, according to this understanding, should be denied their basic needs – the victims of historical injustice or those of an unjust economic dispensation? In vignette 3, a woman seeking shelter from alleged family violence finds her concerns questioned and rendered irrelevant by the very family from whom she sought refuge; whereas in vignette 4, a social worker becomes the direct target of a xenophobic protest, intimidation, and threat. Thus, far from being a mere set of political views and discourses, then, populism can be shown in each case to be the potential cause of direct harm to very real people, to which social workers are directly connected – either as witnesses (vignettes 1 and 3), as implicated in historical wrongs (vignette 2), or as victim (vignette 4). Iris Marion Young posits that responsibilities for justice derive "for all of us who – through our social positioning, relationships, daily practices, and assumptions on which our practices are based – are woven into ... processes of injustice" (Hölscher et al. 2014, p. 188). Precisely this applies in all four vignettes, and this is the second ground rendering populism an ethical concern.

Concerning Responses

Accepting that responsibilities exist, however, does not yet answer the question of what is to be done. In all four vignettes, it is individuals, who are either targeted for intervention or tasked to intervene, with little to no regard being paid to any of the broader discourses, practices, and other contextual conditions within which the actions concerned are embedded. According to authors such as Weinberg and Banks (2019, p. 363), this is a hallmark of neoliberal and managerialist welfare regimes, which across a wide range of contexts, put "ethical practice under serious threat" by creating "contradictory demands": on the one hand, social work is reduced to "a rational technical" rather than a "moral... activity", while on the other, social work continues to define itself by its commitment to upholding and advancing human rights and social justice. The resultant "ethical tension" turns "everyday practice" into "a landmine of conflicting loyalties and pressures" (Weinberg and Banks 2019, p. 363), and this is played out in different ways across the four cases at hand.

In vignette 1, an entire group of students are said to "repeatedly provoke others with deliberately racist and sexist comments", deploying right-wing populist language against them, with such behavior being normalized in social media. Despite this, and despite the evident relevance of other factors such as the size of the class and its online environment, a managerial intervention is devised, which targets one single student for correction. While this does seem necessary, the underlying problems are left to fester. Likewise in vignette 2, Ella is being singled out by the committee for punitive action on account of her "blatantly racist remarks", while Paul, in appreciation of Ella's socioeconomic background, is considering alternatives such as simply advising her to stop publicly exposing her contentious views. In both these propositions, superficiality is at play. None of the protagonists – and this includes Paul and the other committee members – display the required depth of awareness about the complex intersections between differing types of injustices and therefore, of how different groups also have important organizational and economic needs in common. Instead, narrowly focusing on Ella's speech, an opportunity for constructive engagement around *both* her problematic views *and* her legitimate concerns about class-based injustices is being missed.

Similarly individualistic, and in seeming disregard of the underlying complexities, are the office manager's actions in the face of the xenophobic attack on Blessing in vignette 4. Placating protesting community members by agreeing to receive their memo, threatening a law-and-order response, and offering debriefing and counselling support to Blessing may all be necessary parts of an immediate crisis intervention. However, none of this does justice to the potential genuineness of the grievances underlying the protest, nor to the fact that Blessing has been marked and targeted for expulsion by virtue of his group membership. Finally in vignette 3, John could have chosen to be satisfied with completing the task of retrieving some of Kaylee's and her child's belongings, for which he had called at her family home. Yet, concerns around how to respond ethically arise directly from the outpouring of her husband's and mother-in-law's frustrations and the populist values which this revealed. There are many occasions when there is not too much evidence for social workers to go by, with one party's words against another's – so how do they assess? How much should they take account of 'traditional family values' when people explicitly support them, and how far do they assume that structural injustice matters always trump them, especially when it's 'our' (social work) values as against 'their' (lay) 'prejudice'? Where *would* a child be best placed?

In sum, then, the vignettes presented and discussed in this section illustrate how populism is at once a political process and concern of global scale and is fed by particular individual and community grievances and concerns, giving rise to distinct ethical challenges in everyday social work practice. They also depict what we consider currently to be quite typical responses to this complex dynamic: responses tend to be reactive and symptomatic, tending to individualize, manage, penalize, and appease, with wider concerns and underlying dynamics being either placated or disregarded altogether. We propose that instead, an ethical response to populism should stretch from the discursive to the practical, from the in-principle to the everyday, and from cultural and structural to the (inter-)personal. To unpack this proposition is the purpose of the following section.

Justice, Care, and Democracy: The Relevance of Iris Marion Young for Responding Ethically to Populism

This section sketches out some concepts drawn from social philosophy and ethics that help to situate the argument we are making about populism and its implications for social work, both at the levels of policy and practice. It draws on the ethics of care and the writing of Iris Marion Young (among others), who passed away in 2006, but whose incisive and engaging analysis of political and ethical concepts remains valuable to social work (see, for example, Clifford 2013; Hölscher et al. 2014; Pease 2020). While Young is not the only theorist who has engaged with the issues discussed in the following, we contend that the value of her work extends to informing an ethical response to the challenge of populism.

As noted in the section "Populism: Concepts and Key Debates", populist ideas do not usually embrace a structural account of power and social difference. Populists' opposition to 'identity politics' misses the mark here: since her landmark publication on *Justice and the politics of difference*, Young (1990) has emphasized that injustices arise from structural social division. In this way, she differs substantively from a cultural politics of identity, arguing instead that although cultural and structural factors overlap, they should be distinguished: "differentiations of gender, race or ability... like class... concern structural relations of power, resource allocation, and discursive hegemony" (Young 2000, pp. 82–83). Young was also very clear about the complexities of social difference: "Most people have multiple group identifications... every group has group differences cutting across it" (Young 2006a, p. 254). Accordingly, we argue that social workers need to operate from a conceptualization of difference, which, rather than identity per se, is about how the unequal structured relationships of social groups interact to condition the situations in which people live their lives.

Ife (2021) argues with specific reference to "right wing populist politicians and their followers", that "dialogue... represents a worldview and way of being – an ontology – that they simply cannot embrace or validate. It is a waste of effort to even try to persuade them otherwise" (pp. 23–24). Young's (1997) observations about the possibility of dialogue across unequal structures and relationships suggests otherwise. Hence, they are important for any consideration of populism's challenge for social work. Young has demonstrated that ordinary assumptions about the possibility of dialogue are questionable: reciprocity is a basic premise of respectful dialogue, but it cannot easily be equal or symmetrical: "...even though there may be much I do understand... there is also always a remainder, much that I do not understand, about the other person's experience and perspective" (Young 1997, p. 53). Appreciating the generally "asymmetrical" nature of reciprocity is critical where social positions of privilege and oppression are involved, as these positions are not simply reversible: "One person cannot adopt another person's perspective because he or she cannot live another person's history" (Young 1997, p. 51). The only appropriate consequence of this understanding is moral humility: "... one starts with the assumption that one cannot see things from the other person's perspective and waits to learn by listening to the other person" (Young 1997, p. 49).

Accordingly, the appropriate response to anyone whose views and life experiences are (inescapably) different from one' own (especially whose experience of life encompasses oppression and discrimination) must be to give the space to tell their story and to have their perspective listened to. For social workers, this may include 'populists' whose views may appear to clash with the profession's values – as John found in vignette 3 where he needed to listen with care to the grievances being expressed, including the grandmother's life experience, an older woman in the local community with loyalty to 'family' as a haven in an unequal society, and with a potentially close bond with the child involved. But he needed to do this without either jettisoning social work values regarding domestic violence or neglecting the perspectives of Kaylee and other women at the refuge, for populist pressure to deny space to others who do not fit into their definition of 'the people' has to be resisted and challenged in order for these others to offer *their* perspectives. Social workers have a responsibility to make space for all marginalized voices: to challenge denial of space and voice, and to consider involving available institutional or other collective policies and procedures to consistently support marginalized voices as well as halting those responsible for diminishing or harassing minority and oppressed groups. An apt case in point for this is vignette 1, where such practices needed to be arrested – but as a continuing strategy rather than superficial reactions to specific events. These are simultaneously ethical and political decisions.

Young's understanding of the structural nature of social difference also underlies her "social connection model" of responsibility for justice (Young 2006b, 2007, 2011), which further politicizes our understanding of ethical relationships. Embedded in the need to listen to marginalized stories is the question of how to promote care and justice when professionals endeavor to assess situations in respectful but unavoidably imperfect dialogue. Responsibility for justice in caring cannot fall on the shoulders of social workers alone, even on the most cursory estimate. Instead, they share responsibility with professional colleagues in the context of organizations whose remit, resources, and policies are also implicated. In addition, they work within nation-state boundaries, where political powers are exercised in ways that obviously also bear responsibility for justice and care.

Populist assumptions about responsibility for justice tend to target individuals and their organizations for retribution and blame. 'The elite' is said to operate against the interests of 'the people', so individuals in political leadership and the bureaucracies (including social services) that carry out their policies are the ones alleged to be the causes of injustice, and this can inspire protests by populist movements, whether right, left, or center. Against this, Young rightly insists that justice must be seen in the context of *structural* inequalities. The historic injustices that persist in most societies against working people, women, ethnic minorities, and other social groups are "... a kind of moral wrong distinct from the wrongful action of an individual agent or the wilfully repressive policies of a state" (Young 2007, p. 170). This does not mean that individuals and politicians are not to blame for specific policies and practices for which they *are* directly and intentionally responsible. It *does* mean, however, that because accepted norms and institutional rules habitually construct societies in which repeated and widespread actions lead to enduring social injustice: "All the persons who participate by their actions in the ongoing schemes of cooperation that constitute these structures are responsible for them, in the sense that they are part of the process that causes them" – but *not* in the sense of "having directed the process or intended its outcomes" (Young 2007, p. 170). This clearly applies to all persons within a given society, including social workers holding positions within an institution charged with underpinning the accepted norms and policies of that society.

It follows that when regarding structural injustice through the lens of Young's social connection model, several responsibilities become apparent: *In addition* to the need to call out wrongdoing and assigning culpability where evidence demonstrates reprehensible policy or practice, "...others whose actions contribute to the outcomes" are not absolved "from bearing responsibility" (Young 2007, p. 176). Moreover, besides accountability for *past* misdeeds, the collective nature of structural injustice requires responsibility for thinking *forward* towards possibilities for change. And rather than constituting mere individual responsibilities, such change necessarily demands collective action – "political" in the broadest sense – involving effort across networks and organizations as well as political parties to work for different outcomes. Such an effort was needed for example in vignette 2 where all the participants – Ella, Paul, and the other committee members – could have been networking *already* to develop and advocate for mutually acceptable and just policies.

Several aspects of this model have direct implications for social work. These are to do with Young's (2007) contention that notwithstanding the collective nature of responsibility for structural injustices, "[d]ifferent agents have different kinds of responsibilities in relation to particular issues" (p. 183). Possibilities for working collectively to change social outcomes will vary. Being positioned differently within social structures means that individuals and groups have different opportunities and constraints in contributing to change. This indicates fluctuating responsibilities based on, for example, the relative ease with which people can organize collective action, and the relative power that individuals and organizations have, their location and accessibility. People "... should focus on issues where they have more capacity to influence structural processes", and it is important to engage in decision-making dialogue with victims of social injustice whose interests and insight into possibilities of change make their contribution particularly significant (Young 2007, pp. 183–185).

When populists challenge the values and practices of social work, different responses may be appropriate as to what justice and care might mean in any given situation. It is always necessary to examine the claims to justice of both the defender of a given social services practice or policy, and of any challenge to it, requiring attention to the key aspects of social difference that we have seen emerging from the vignettes, and upon which Young throws additional light. The questions that arise in social work about who or what is responsible for justice thus need to be considered both at the level of *intentional* policies and practices and with regard to the *taken-for-granted* unjust "background conditions" (Young 2006b, p. 120) of popular ideas and movements around which populist politics appear to mobilize. In vignette 4, the office manager had to *de-escalate* a tense situation and offer individual support, but also needed to *escalate* the issue as a matter of ethical policy and politics, raising the issue within his own hierarchy and involving other organizations.

Supporters of populist politics should have to answer the same questions. It would be foolish to assume the possibility of easy mutual understanding – dialogue, while not impossible, certainly *is* difficult – but the ideas of populists vary, as indicated already, and their underlying grievances may themselves reflect the injustices of background conditions within which social services work. The task is to try to identify valid issues of injustice and needs for care and to clarify where privileged groups are insidiously (by means of unquestioned background conditions) or openly (through intentional policies) promoting their own vested interests to the detriment of vulnerable others. Required are both ethical and political competence in understanding a populist political position and respecting the different histories and experience of its supporters, while simultaneously critically analyzing and acting upon the implications for justice and care.

Conclusion

Contemporary social work literature on populism has tended to focus on right-wing populism, juxtaposed this with social work's value base, and called on the profession to respond urgently and decisively. Our starting point has been somewhat different. Firstly, rather than regarding populism as external to social work and purely as a threat, it has framed the profession instead as entangled with it. Secondly, taking a situated ethics approach, this chapter has shown the complexity and shifting nature of populism, which cannot be assumed to have stable political objectives but must be examined within a particular geographical and historical context. Furthermore, any assessment of an instance of populism cannot expect to remain valid indefinitely, given the likelihood that it will respond quickly to social and political change. For social workers, this demands political and ethical competence in analyzing current politics, policy directions, and possible ethical implications.

Social workers need to be aware of *both* the dangers *and* of the possible openings for justice that inhere in populist ideas and movements. The recent global preponderance of populist movements has been right wing, with some versions being close to (or identical with) fascist ideologies that are completely incompatible with respectful treatment of human beings and thus, with serious negative implications for social work's commitments to justice and care. Understandably therefore, Ife (2021) has warned that "...social work must be careful not to be seduced into joining forces with right-wing nationalist populism in its attack on neo-liberalism" (p. 24). Yet as this chapter has shown, a republican or left-wing populism is possible, with strong progressive elements in opposing domination by external powers, or by local elite politicians. As such, there is no simple choice to be had between a right- and a left-wing populism. Whether on account of deliberate strategy by populist leaders to maximize votes or of aggrieved people voting 'with their feet' when feeling – rightly or wrongly – neglected by established parties, populisms may include elements that are progressive *or* regressive, but they will always favor *some* of 'the people' at the expense of others.

Social workers need to bear these complexities in mind when responding to populist challenges and ideas, taking into account their own social positions and how these might be seen by populists of differing persuasions. Sound political judgment of contemporary developments in a given society then needs to be connected to an ethics of care and social justice agenda towards decision-making and action. Accordingly, responses may stretch from support for progressive aspects of a forward-thinking populism on the one hand, and the need for social workers to act when they find themselves either implicated in, or confronted with, unjust, uncaring policies and practices that cause suffering on the other – as was the case in all four vignettes considered in this chapter. In between these two poles are vexed questions about situations where real people are at risk of actual harm, which may well leave social workers with ethical dilemmas about whether to resign, or whether to stay and try to ameliorate the harm, and if so, how to counteract uncaring policies and procedures. In all cases, developing networks and relationships with allies both internal and external to employing agencies are essential, exploring possibilities for change, taking both political and moral responsibility for justice and care.

The question of how needs should be defined and whose needs should be met is simultaneously moral and political. Populists of different hues challenge established institutions on these issues, including social services. In democratic societies that are based on respect for the rights of all, institutions should reflect this key value. Tronto (2010, 2013) has argued that no caring institution in a democratic society can function well without having formal and informal spaces for everyone involved to contribute to discussion and resolution of issues about whose needs are being met, and how to meet them – implying that institutional hierarchies must be flattened to allow and facilitate this involvement. Such built-in networking serves to make space for grievances underlying populist challenges to be aired and properly considered, while at the same time protecting vulnerable groups from being scapegoated and enabling all voices to be heard and taken seriously. Social workers should work towards such democratic and inclusive ways of engagement.

References

Abi-hassan S (2017) Populism and gender. In: Kaltwasser CR, Taggart P, Espejo PO, Ostiguy P (eds) The Oxford handbook of populism. Oxford University Press, Oxford, pp 426–444

Anand J, Borrmann S, Das C (2021) Resisting the rise of right-wing populism: European social work examples. In: Noble C, Ottmann G (eds) The challenge of right-wing nationalist populism for social work: a human rights approach. Routledge, New York, pp 168–182

Banks S (2016) Everyday ethics in professional life: social work as ethics work. Ethics Soc Welfare 10(1):35–52

Banks S (2021) Ethics and values in social work. Red Globe Press, London

Bozalek V, Zembylas M, Tronto JC (2020) Introduction. In: Bozalek V, Zembylas M, Tronto JC (eds) Posthumanism and political care ethics for reconfiguring higher education pedagogies. Routledge, Abington/New York, pp 1–12

Brøgge K (2020) A specter is haunting European higher education – the specter of nationalism. In: Bozalek V, Zembylas M, Motala S, Hölscher D (eds) Higher education hauntologies: speaking with ghosts for a justice-to-come. Routledge, Abington/New York, pp 63–75

Cadalen P-Y (2020) Republican populism and marxist populism: perspectives from Ecuador and Bolivia. In: Kranert M (ed) Discursive approaches to populism across disciplines: the return of populists and the people. Palgrave Macmillan, London, pp 313–338

Clifford DJ (2013) Ethics, politics and the social professions: reading Iris Marion Young. Ethics Soc Welfare 7:36–53

Clifford D, Burke B (2009) Anti-oppressive Ethics and Values in Social Work, Palgrave Macmillan, Basingstoke.

De La Torre C (2017) Populism in Latin America. In: Kaltwasser CR, Taggart P, Espejo PO, Ostiguy P (eds) The Oxford handbook of populism. Oxford University Press, Oxford, pp 195–213

Demata M (2020) Populism and nationalism in Jeremy Corbyn's discourse. In: Kranert M (ed) Discursive approaches to populism across disciplines: the return of populists and the people. Palgrave Macmillan, London, pp 253–284

Fazzi L (2015) Social work, exclusionary populism and xenophobia in Italy. Int J Soc Work 58(4): 595–605

Fazzi L, Nothdurfter U (2021) Why are you backing such positions? Types and trajectories of social workers' right-wing populist support. Br J Soc Work 51:636–654

Fekete L (2018) Europe's fault lines: racism and the rise of the right. Verso, London

Fenton-Smith B (2020) The (re) birth of far-right populism in Australia: the appeal of Pauline Hanson's persuasive definitions. In: Kranert M (ed) Discursive approaches to populism across disciplines: the return of populists and the people. Palgrave Macmillan, London, pp 339–365

Ferguson (2021) 'A roar of defiance against the elites': Brexit, populism and social work. In: Noble C, Ottmann G (eds) The challenge of right-wing nationalist populism for social work: a human rights approach. Routledge, New York, pp 99–110

Forde F (2011) An inconvenient youth: Julius Malema and the 'new' ANC. Picador Africa, Johannesburg

Fraser N (2016) Expropriation and exploitation in racialized capitalism: a reply to Michael Dawson, critical historical studies. Spring 2016:163–178

Fraser N, Jaeggi R (2018) Capitalism: a conversation in critical theory. In: Milstein B (ed) . Polity Press, Cambridge

Fraser H, Taylor N (2021) Animals as domestic violence victims: a challenge to humanist social work. In: Bozalek V, Pease B (eds) Post-anthropocentric social work. Routledge, Abington/New York, pp 161–174

Hawkins KA, Read M, Pauwels T (2017) Populism and its causes. In: Kaltwasser CR, Taggart P, Espejo PO, Ostiguy P (eds) The Oxford handbook of populism. Oxford University Press, Oxford, pp 267–286

Hölscher D, Bozalek VG, Zembylas M (2014) Assuming responsibility for justice in the context of South Africa's refugee receiving regime. Ethics and Social Welfare 8(2):187–204

Hugman R (2013) Culture, values and ethics in social work: embracing diversity. Routledge, London and New York

Ife J. (2021) Social work, modernity and right-wing nationalist populism. In: Noble C, Ottmann G (eds) The challenge of right-wing nationalist populism for social work: a human rights approach. Routledge, New York, p15–29

Issel-Dombert S (2020) Using mass and pop culture to dominate political discourse: how the left-wing party Podemos conquered Spanish living-rooms with IKEA. In: Kranert M (ed) Discursive approaches to populism across disciplines: the return of populists and the people. Palgrave Macmillan, London, pp 285–312

Kahlina K (2020) On behalf of the family and the people: the right-wing populist repertoire in Croatia. In: Kranert M (ed) Discursive approaches to populism across disciplines: the return of populists and the people. Palgrave Macmillan, London, pp 227–250

Kaltwasser C R (2017) Populism and the question of how to respond to it. In: Kaltwasser C R, Taggart P, Espejo P O, Ostiguy P (eds) The Oxford handbook of populism, Oxford University Press Oxford, p489–507

Kaltwasser CR, Taggart P, Espejo PO, Ostiguy P (2017) Populism: an overview of the concept and the state of the art. In: Kaltwasser CR, Taggart P, Espejo PO, Ostiguy P (eds) The Oxford handbook of populism. Oxford University Press, Oxford, pp 1–24

Kelsy D (2020) Archetypal populism: the "intellectual dark web" and the "Peterson paradox". In: Kranert M (ed) Discursive approaches to populism across disciplines: the return of populists and the people. Palgrave Macmillan, London, pp 171–198

Knoblock N (2020) Trump's text appeal: vague language in post-truth politics. In: Kranert M (ed) Discursive approaches to populism across disciplines: the return of populists and the people. Palgrave Macmillan, London, pp 119–144

Mabandla N, Deumert A (2020) Another populism is possible: popular politics and the anticolonial struggle. In: Kranert M (ed) Discursive approaches to populism across disciplines: the return of populists and the people. Palgrave Macmillan, London, pp 433–460

Mackenzie C, Stoljar N (eds) (2000) Relational autonomy, feminist perspectives on autonomy, agency and the social self. Oxford University Press, Oxford

Mudde C (2017) Populism: an ideational approach. In: Kaltwasser CR, Taggart P, Espejo PO, Ostiguy P (eds) The Oxford handbook of populism. Oxford University Press, Oxford, pp 27–47

Mudde C, Kaltwasser CR (2013) Exclusionary vs. inclusionary populism: comparing contemporary Europe and Latin America. Gov Oppos 48(2):147–174

Müller J-WM (2017) Populism and constitutionalism. In: Kaltwasser CR, Taggart P, Espejo PO, Ostiguy P (eds) The Oxford handbook of populism. Oxford University Press, Oxford, pp 590–606

Noble C (2021) Right-wing populism and a feminist social work response. In: Noble C, Ottmann G (eds) The challenge of right-wing nationalist populism for social work: a human rights approach. Routledge, New York, pp 69–83

Noble C, Ottmann G (2018) Nationalist populism and social work. J Hum Rights Soc Work 3:112–120

Noble C, Ottmann G (2021) Right-wing nationalist populism and social work: some defining features. In: Noble C, Ottmann G (eds) The challenge of right-wing nationalist populism for social work: a human rights approach. Routledge, New York, pp 1–14

Ostiguy P (2017) Populism: a socio-cultural approach. In: Kaltwasser CR, Taggart P, Espejo PO, Ostiguy P (eds) The Oxford handbook of populism. Oxford University Press, Oxford, pp 73–97

Pease B (2020) From privileged irresponsibility to shared responsibility for social injustice: the contributions of Joan Tronto and Iris Marion Young to critical pedagogies of privilege. In: Morley C, Ablett P, Noble C, Cowden S (eds) The Routledge handbook of critical pedagogies for social work. Routledge, Abington/New York, pp 165–175

Robinson F (2011) The ethics of care: a feminist approach to human security. Temple University Press, Philadelphia

Rummens S (2017) Populism as a threat to liberal democracy. In: Kaltwasser CR, Taggart P, Espejo PO, Ostiguy P (eds) The Oxford handbook of populism. Oxford University Press, Oxford, pp 554–570

Sayer A (2016) Why we can't afford the rich. Policy Press, Bristol

Sewell Report, The (2021) The report of the commission on race and ethnic disparities. HMSO, London

Tronto JC (1993) Moral boundaries: a political argument for an ethic of care. Routledge, New York

Tronto JC (2010) Creating caring institutions. Ethics Soc Welfare. 4(2):158–171

Tronto JC (2013) Caring democracy: markets, equality, and justice. New York University Press, New York

Walia H (2021) Border and rule: global migration capitalism and the rise of racist nationalism. Haymarket Books, Chicago

Weinberg M, Banks S (2019) Practicing ethically in unethical times: everyday resistance in social work. Ethics Soc Welfare 13(4):361–376

Weyland K (2017) Populism: a political-strategic approach. In: Kaltwasser CR, Taggart P, Espejo PO, Ostiguy P (eds) The Oxford handbook of populism. Oxford University Press, Oxford, pp 267–286

Young IM (1997) Intersecting voices: dilemmas of gender, political philosophy and policy. Princeton University Press, Princeton

Young IM (2000) Inclusion and democracy. Oxford University Press, Oxford

Young IM (2006a) Polity and group difference: a critique of the ideal of universal citizenship. In: Goodin RE, Pettit R (eds) Contemporary political philosophy: an anthology, 2nd edn. Blackwell, Oxford, pp 248–263

Young IM (2006b) Responsibility and global justice: a social connection model. Soc Philos Policy 23(1):102–130

Young IM (2007) Global challenges: war, self determination and responsibility for justice. Polity Press, Cambridge

Young IM (1990) Justice and the politics of difference. Princeton University Press, Princeton

Young IM (2011) Responsibility for justice. Oxford University Press, Oxford

Zúquete JP (2017) Populism and religion. In: Kaltwasser CR, Taggart P, Espejo PO, Ostiguy P (eds) The Oxford handbook of populism. Oxford University Press, Oxford, pp 455–466

Critical Social Work and Ethics: Working with Asylum Seekers in Australia

22

Kim Robinson

Contents

Introduction	446
Background to International Forced Migration	447
Forced Migration in Australia	448
Settlement of Refugees	450
Asylum Seekers	450
Asylum Seekers Lived Experience	451
Behrouz Boochani	452
Abbas Nazari	452
Ethics, Critical Social Work and Working with Displaced People	453
Social Work Practice: Ways Forward?	457
Conclusion	460
Conclusions: Ethical Social Work Practice in Displacement	460
References	460

Abstract

This chapter explores the ethical challenges facing social work with marginalised, excluded, and displaced humans subject to forced migration, and highlights working with asylum seekers in Australia. Presenting a background to forced migration internationally it describes the humanitarian refugee programme, and the challenges facing asylum seekers claiming protection. For the latter group the evidence is of human rights abuses and a failure to deliver socially just outcomes, particularly for people in immigration detention. Social workers engage with diverse communities including those who have been formally approved as refugees, or lived in detention, and who may continue to live on temporary protection visas. This presents tensions between meeting the aims of the ethical codes of practice and the reality facing their clients of having limited access to resources

K. Robinson (✉)
School of Health & Social Development, Faculty of Health, Deakin University, Geelong, VIC, Australia
e-mail: kim.robinson@deakin.edu.au

© Springer Nature Singapore Pte Ltd. 2023
D. Hölscher et al. (eds.), *Social Work Theory and Ethics*, Social Work,
https://doi.org/10.1007/978-981-19-1015-9_23

and social justice. It presents the lived experience of two prominent refugees who have written about their experiences of unsuccessful claims for protection in Australia. The chapter addresses how, in the face of silencing refugee and asylum seeker voices, critical social work can identify sites of resistance, hope and compassion.

Keywords

Refugees · Asylum seekers · Ethics · Critical social work · Immigration detention

Introduction

> The year 2020 will be remembered like no other. The COVID-19 pandemic has disrupted all facets of life, causing millions of deaths around the world and leading to human suffering, economic recession, restrictions on human mobility and severe limitations on daily life (United Nations High Commission for Refugees [UNHCR] 2021, p. 5).

After 2 years of the international COVID-19 pandemic, the world faces unprecedented challenges and change. The differentials between the global South and North in relation to access to vaccines and health care have further highlighted deep social inequalities. For those living in uncertainty and subject to war, persecution, and climate change, the options for safety and international protection are limited. There are now 84 million people in the world who are forcibly displaced (UNHCR 2021, p. 9). There has been a dramatic decrease in asylum applications in 2020 and 2021 due to travel restrictions and the closure of borders and asylum institutions. In 2020, refugee resettlement plummeted to its lowest level in almost two decades with only 34,400 people resettled to 21 countries (see UNHCR 2021). The COVID-19 public health emergency has increased the risk to health and social care and seen a deterioration of conditions in many countries of origin (UNHCR 2021, p. 36). Opportunities for resettlement present for only a tiny fraction of durable solutions, and millions of refugees have been unable to relocate to safety.

This chapter aims to explore the ethical challenges faced in social work with marginalised, excluded, and displaced humans, particularly when working with asylum seekers in Australia. Social workers engage with diverse communities including those who have been approved by UNHCR as refugees, or who have lived in immigration detention, and those who live in the community on temporary protection visas. Contemporary critical social work engages with debates about racism, xenophobia, and nationalism along with dominant discourses of 'othering' of refugees and asylum seekers. There is a considerable literature on the regulation and guidance of ethical practice, and this chapter will be addressing how, in the face of silencing refugee and asylum seeker voices, critical social work's understanding of power can highlight sites of resistance, hope and compassion.

Social work is committed to social justice and human rights and has an ethical responsibility to be both informed and proactive when working with newly arrived communities and those experiencing violations of their human rights. The chapter examines some of the background issues comprising forced migration internationally and in Australia. It then highlights the lived experience of two prominent refugees who have written about their experiences of claiming protection: the Kurdish-Iranian writer Behrouz Boochani, who was detained for 7 years in off-shore detention on Manus Island, Papua New Guinea, and Abbas Nazari who was a child when rescued by the Tampa after fleeing Afghanistan with his family in 2001.

The ethics and the role of critical social work in practice with displaced persons will be discussed particularly in the context of the insider/outsider status, where social workers are positioned in both Government agencies, and in Non-Government Organisations (NGOs) such as Save the Children, Amnesty International, and specialist torture and trauma services. Returning to the lived experience of the two asylum seekers, the chapter will identify how critical social work can move forward to navigate these ethical challenges to support our direct practice, policy, research, and advocacy.

Background to International Forced Migration

The 1948 Universal Declaration of Human Rights [UDHR] states that "everyone has the right to seek and enjoy in other countries asylum from persecution" (Article 14, United Nations [UN]). The word 'asylum' is not defined in international law, but the 1967 UN Declaration on Territorial Asylum noted the granting of asylum is a humanitarian and apolitical act. The quasi-legal understanding of claiming asylum is the process of obtaining protection through the legally endorsed processes of states party to the 1951 Convention Relating to the Status of Refugees and/or the 1967 Protocol. For this chapter, the term 'asylum seeker' will be used to refer to someone who is in the process of or has applied for asylum and is awaiting an outcome on their claim. The United Nations Convention on Refugees guarantees the right to seek asylum from persecution, and if successful, the Convention states that refugees are entitled to the same protection and benefits as all other citizens of that country. 'Refugee' will refer to someone who has successfully obtained permanent secure immigration status according to the UN Convention grounds. It is important to acknowledge that the language and usage of these terms is highly contested and critiqued in the literature particularly across disciplines (Fiske and Briskman 2020). The author uses the more generic term of 'service user' to apply to both asylum seekers and refugees in the context of those using or participating in services.

Displacement is one of the defining characteristics of the twenty-first century. There are more people forcibly displaced from their homes now than at almost any time in human history, estimated at more than 84 million (UNHCR 2021) and 85% are hosted by developing countries. Recent wars, coups, and other events in countries such as Syria, Myanmar, Afghanistan, and the Ukraine illustrate the extent of human suffering and displacement with the limited options offered for safety. In 2020 6.8 million Syrians were listed as displaced people, followed by Venezuelans with 4.9 million; and Afghans and South Sudanese with 2.8 and 2.2 million respectively (UNHCR 2021). Since the release of those data the UNHCR estimates increasing number of individuals and families have fled their home due to conflict in Afghanistan and the return of the Taliban to power (UNCHR 2021). This number is very likely to be higher as news of atrocities emerge from the humanitarian disaster and is in addition to the 2.9 million people internally displaced and the 2.2. million refugees registered in Iran and Pakistan (UNHCR 2021, p.18). The current situation in the Ukraine with Russian forces threatening a sovereign nation is creating a humanitarian disaster with an estimated 100,000 people leaving the country.

Migration and refugee studies are interdisciplinary, and acknowledge the contribution of anthropologists, sociologists, political scientists, historians, economists, and many others in attempting to understand the complexity in relation to the movement of people between the source and destination countries. No one discipline can adequately describe and analyse migration, and social work can benefit from this breadth of knowledge, theory, and research expertise as noted here by migration scholar Castles:

> A sociology of forced migration cannot exist in isolation: it has to understand itself as part of an interdisciplinary and transnational project, informed by reflection on the social, cultural and political dimensions of forced migration (Castles 2003, p. 14).

The implications for social workers who are engaged in services, including health and social care, human rights protection, legal advice, and other human centred practice, places them in a unique position to work across and with a range of disciplines.

Forced Migration in Australia

Australia has a complex history of settling refugees and asylum seekers which has been shaped by two key dynamics – the dispossession of First Nations people and immigration (Neumann 2015, p. 4). While this chapter is about marginalisation and exclusion of refugees, it is important to acknowledge the profound dispossession and displacement of Aboriginal and Torres Strait Islander peoples on their land. The colonisation of Australia has led to brutal treatment and living conditions of Aboriginal people, and with no Treaty in place, Australians continue to live on unceded land often ignorant of the atrocities committed by settler communities. Contemporary Australia has 30% of its current population comprised of people born overseas with most migrants settled in capital cities (Australian Bureau of Statistics [ABS] 2020). Approximately 800,000 of these migrants have been refugees and asylum seekers and are people who have been determined to meet the criteria of refugee and who needed permanent resettlement for their protection.

This history of migration has seen hostility and an attitude of othering towards refugees and asylum seekers. Australians have labelled new arrivals as "reffos", "wogs", "Balts", and asylum seekers as "boat people", "queue jumpers", blaming them for being "illegal" for having no visa, having "bogus claims", and for perpetuating people smugglers to facilitate their journey (Neumann 2015; Green 2020, p. 914). While Australia has a history of supporting humanitarian refugees and asylum seekers many argue that the deterrence policies of the past 20 years have perpetuated discrimination and racism (Fiske and Briskman 2020). Asylum seekers have been vilified and subject to intense criticism and relegated to the margins of society, literally and figuratively. We will see this in the lived experience of the two authors presented in this chapter. Australia's implementation of strict legislation and a range of measures to deter asylum seekers following the 'Pacific Solution' in the 2000s means that people arriving by boat are prevented from landing on the mainland and are detained in offshore detention centres on Christmas Island, Manus Island, in Papua New Guinea, or Nauru. For those arriving by plane they are detained in immigration centres, often located in capital cities. Previous centres operational in remote areas of the country such as Woomera or Baxter are now closed. Detention centres are a key feature of current policy, including the use of hotels on the mainland of Australia when people are transferred for medical treatment (Medevac). The topic of offshore detention and processing of those arriving by "boat" in the last two decades has contributed to heated debates within government and in the community (Kaldor Centre 2020). Advocates, many of whom are social workers, bear witness to the ways in which asylum seekers and refugees are relegated to a status of being dehumanised and invisible to the public eye.

The hardship facing people living in detention centres has been well documented, and Amnesty International (2017) has highlighted unethical practices of corporate profit-driven complicity in the provision of the detention centre facilities. This includes the hiring of guards with little or no understanding of immigration including the previous torture and trauma of refugees, or the impact of detention on the health and wellbeing of the detainees. The Australian Human Rights Commission (AHRC) has consistently and repeatedly challenged and exposed the myths perpetuated against those seeking sanctuary from war and persecution, particularly in relation to the detention of children (see the report by AHRC 2014). UNHCR (2021, p. 3) estimates show that almost one million children were born as refugees between 2018 and 2020. Many children are at risk of remaining in exile for years to come, some potentially for the rest of their lives. It is especially challenging for social workers to ensure the best interests and safety of children who are at risk, and who are unaccompanied or separated from their families, and find themselves in detention facilities designed for adults.

There are two distinctive areas of social work practice working with refugees and asylum seekers which are specifically about the context and legal status of those people who are in the process of securing humanitarian protection. Social workers are used to applying a strength based and anti-oppressive theoretical approach when working with all people, irrespective of legal status, so this can create ethical tensions for practitioners. Essentially this distinction builds a 'two tier' system. For social workers working in settlement services, there are opportunities for supporting people to establish themselves in a new home and build their social and economic capital. In contrast, for social workers advocating for asylum seekers, particularly while they are in detention and on temporary protection visas, the same resources are not available. The following section of the chapter identifies these two different areas of practice.

Settlement of Refugees

The aim of Australian humanitarian settlement services is to support the arrival of refugees in collaboration with the aims of UNHCR at an international level to ameliorate the displacement of refugees. The Department of Home Affairs is responsible for the Refugee and Humanitarian Program including immigration and settlement outcomes (Australian Government 2020). Key to successful settlement is economic participation (labor-force outcomes, occupational status, sources and level of income, and housing); social participation and well-being (English proficiency, satisfaction with life and Australian citizenship); and physical and mental well-being. The Federal Government of Australia allocated 13,750 places to the Refugee and Humanitarian Program for 2021–22 (Australian Government 2020). Australia also has an extensive network of services for torture and trauma survivors that work closely with families, adults, and children, and is funded by state and federal governments, and philanthropic donations and grants (see the Forum of Australian Services for Survivors of Torture and Trauma [FASSTT] report 2018).

Research highlights how humanitarian entrants experience both positive and negative outcomes in their settlement depending on their location and country of origin, their accessibility to education and employment, their mental health and wellbeing, and dealing with cultural and social changes such as newly defined gender roles (Higgins 2020, p. 361). Humanitarian entrants often have high levels of determination to succeed, and a strong work ethic coupled with a sense of community, bringing many skills and diverse knowledges (Marlowe 2017). However, research indicates people from refugee backgrounds also face poverty and barriers to gaining meaningful employment (Fozdar and Banki 2017). The legal restrictions on refugee rights for family reunion and fears for family overseas are also prominent concerns. For example, the return in 2021 of Afghanistan to the rule of the Taliban has created specific risks for minority groups and women and girls who face persecution, causing alarm for the diaspora (Ahmad et al. 2021). Settlement services funded by government employ social workers and work with communities to facilitate and advocate for support, rights, and access to services available to all citizens in Australia.

Asylum Seekers

The current policy for those claiming asylum in Australia is dependent on the type of arrival, whether by plane or boat, and proof of persecution. People arriving by boat are processed offshore and prevented from ever securing permanent residency in Australia (Kaldor Centre 2020). Hugman and Carter note that there is a "lucrative new industry in the detention of refugees" (2016, p. vii). Asylum seekers are subjected to secrecy and human rights abuses when confined to both onshore and offshore detention centres (Nethery and Holman 2016). There is an extensive academic and grey literature documenting the negative impact of indefinite detention on the mental health of adults and children, along with additional crimes including the sexual assault of women (see Briskman and Doe 2016; Green 2020; Fleay et al. 2021).

Early research identified social workers experiencing a range of positions including presenting a lack of resistance to work practices that condoned marginalisation and victimisation, collusion in abusive practice, and in contrast those who advocated and challenged oppressive systems (Hayes and Humphries 2004). Social workers frequently acknowledge that they are trying to ameliorate structural and systemic problems and ease the stress and isolation facing service users, but they also note that they can come to be identified as part of an abusive and inhumane system (Robinson 2014; Briskman and Doe 2016). There is an inherent contradiction of both being part of and actively challenging 'the system'.

Social workers often find themselves in tension when they are working in restrictive contexts and institutions that are in violation of the human rights and social justice aims that underpin ethical critical social work practice (Morley et al. 2020). This is particularly acute in this practice area of forced migration where social workers can feel exploited and complicit in poor and dehumanising practice, and this has contributed to discussions about being insider/outsiders. Many argue that it is important to be located *inside* institutions to bear witness to oppressive practice, and to work *outside* to agitate for change and build capacity for the sector to improve outcomes for refugees and asylum seekers (Robinson 2014, p. 1604). Despite this dilemma social work has contributed significantly to advocacy with asylum seekers and in 2005 the Australian Council of Heads of Social Work was the auspicing body for the People's Inquiry into Detention (Briskman et al. 2008). The Inquiry documented the accounts of human rights abuses in Australia, with a focus on asylum seekers and social work advocates. Participants spoke about disrupting systems and finding ways to manage to work in compassionate ways that upheld the dignity of asylum seekers.

Central to the narratives of participants to the Inquiry was the importance of acting towards asylum seekers with compassion and decency, and not repeating the practices that have brutalised so many people (Briskman et al. 2008, p. 390). Documenting the voices of marginalised people is a profound and radical tool, and truth telling is one of the only ways we can learn and heal the damage that has been inflicted on innocent people. Two of the experiences of asylum seekers are the focus of the next section of this chapter.

Asylum Seekers Lived Experience

The following two narratives are from asylum seekers escaping persecution who were prevented from arriving in mainland Australia to claim protection under international law. The first is Behrouz Boochani, author, poet and journalist, a vocal critic of the Australian system of offshore detention who has written extensively on his experience of attempting to claim asylum. The second is by a young man Abbas Nazari, a Hazari

Afghan, who left Afghanistan as a child and was rescued by the Tampa in 2001 and wrote a book 20 years later reflecting on his experiences.

Behrouz Boochani

Kurdish journalist and writer Behrouz Boochani was detained by Australian authorities when trying to reach the country by boat as he fled from persecution in his homeland. Boochani was forcibly transferred to Manus Island, Papua New Guinea, for an indefinite period which turned out to be 7 years. In *No Friend but the Mountains* (Picador, 2018), Boochani vividly tells his story of escape from Iran and how he was imprisoned in Australia's "Manus Island Regional Offshore Processing Centre", what he calls "The Kyriarchal System". Reminiscent of Foucault's description of prisons (1991), the Manus Prison represents torture and control, and a form of governmentality that is oppressive and all encompassing. He wrote the book on a mobile phone in Farsi and it was translated into English by Omid Tofighian. It presents ethnographic descriptions of various forms of oppression and torture, and meditations on the meaning of self-identity and displacement. He writes:

> Groups of men are up against the wall/
> Groups of men are embedded into the wall/
> The spectacle of the prison queue is a raw and palpable reinforcement of torture (Boochani 2018, p. 193).

Following an invitation to the Auckland Writers Festival in New Zealand in 2019 and the provision of a month-long visa, he successfully claimed asylum there and now is a resident and political journalist.

Abbas Nazari

Abbas Nazari was 7 years old when he and his family escaped Afghanistan and sought refuge in Indonesia before heading towards Australia. When their boat was about to sink, he saw the faint 'upside-down triangle' on the horizon – that triangle was the MV Tampa, a Norwegian freighter that would sail to his and his family's rescue, along with 426 other asylum seekers, mostly from Afghanistan. He was weak from dehydration and illness, and the small boat carrying him, and hundreds of others was severely battered by the terrifying storm. Nazari remembers staring over the sea at the ship that would rescue them.

> I cannot find the words to describe the feeling that washed over me at that moment. Twelve hours earlier we had been huddled together awaiting the cold embrace of death. Now, our would-be coffin was in a watery grave and we were floating in the sky (Nazari 2021, p. 146).

The Tampa would become the central player in an extraordinary legal battle, and shorthand for the genesis of a new generation of hard-line border policies in

Australia that prevented the arrival of those seeking protection, effectively contravening the UN Refugee Convention. Abbas was accepted into New Zealand with his family as a refugee after a brief period in offshore detention.

Ethics, Critical Social Work and Working with Displaced People

The International Federation of Social Work (IFSW 2018) and the Australian Association of Social Workers (AASW 2020) have clearly stated positions on the values and ethics that underpin the principles which support and respect the people with whom we work. Specifically, the AASW *Code of Ethics* (2020) identifies three core principles: respect for persons, social justice, and professional integrity. In relation to social justice, it states that the social work profession "promotes justice and social fairness, by acting to reduce barriers and to expand choice and potential for all persons, with special regard for those who are disadvantaged, vulnerable, oppressed or have exceptional needs" (AASW 2020, p. 9). Social work scholars have written extensively about values and ethics, examining changing political contexts, specific service areas, research and policy, and direct service delivery (see Pullen-Sansfacon and Cowden 2012; Hugman and Carter 2016; Chenoweth and McAuliffe 2020; Banks 2020). This literature informs students and newly qualified social workers, but also experienced practitioners who work with increasing demands and complexity.

Critical social work scholars argue that ethical issues in social work practice are contextualised and situated in power relationships and require "conscious" ethical practice that challenges dominant assumptions and discourses of oppression (Pullen-Sansfacon and Cowden 2012; Banks 2016a). In their summary of the literature Morley et al. (2019, pp. 143–150) argue that a critical approach to ethics in social work has revolved around the following key areas:

- Raising questions about what one ought to do or how one should live, personally and professionally.
- Awareness of the contextual nature of ethical behaviour, rather than a futile attempt at "objectivity".
- Questioning the assumption that social work should be "neutral".
- Awareness of one's own potential complicity with oppressive discourse and developing strategies to challenge and resist this.
- Engaging in critical reflection regarding implicit assumptions in working with 'others'.
- Taking a dialogical approach to ethical decision-making.
- Aiming to create more emancipatory and socially just outcomes for service users.

Addressing critical multi-cultural social work practice Nipperess and Williams (2019) describe three key principles: human rights, recognition of diversities and social justice – all of which are underpinned by international and national ethical conventions and declarations. The extensive work by Banks advocates for "ethics work" which "encompasses reasoning, but also includes work on emotion, identity, roles and responsibilities" (2016a, p. 36). This connects also to her work about integrity as literally meaning wholeness, and that social workers enact moral integrity by remaining focused on the purpose, values and ethics that underpins their work (2016b, p. 50). This requires interrogation of one's positionality, reflexivity, and moral courage. Hölscher also argues that reflexivity must inform practice and the interaction of contextual complexities facing social workers who are engaged with people who have experienced "discrimination, stigmatization, subjugation, marginalisation, exclusion and inadequate and unfairly distributed resources" (2016, p. 106). Working with social injustice requires hope and empathy, and an understanding of what the limitations are for social workers.

Critical social work focuses on equalising relationships, but also considers that there are genuine power differentials between service users and service providers. Importantly, this work requires that social and human services workers challenge the deficit model and negative tropes which suggest that refugees and asylum seekers are a liability. Research has identified the benefits to society that asylum seekers and refugees contribute, particularly in relation to employment and revitalising communities which promotes social justice for a range of marginalised groups via Welcome Zones, Cities of Sanctuary and other community based initiatives (see Marlowe 2017; Kaplan 2020; Robinson 2020).

Hugman and Carter (2016, p. viii) preface their book on re-thinking values and ethics with the cautionary tale about ethical practice for social workers working in contemporary organisations, particularly those working with refugees detained or 'trapped' in offshore detention centres. A body of research has emerged in the past 20 years from social work scholars and people working in services highly critical of the politicised treatment of asylum seekers and refugees and highlighting the tensions in the role of social work in this space (Hayes and Humphries 2004; Marlowe 2017; Morley et al. 2020). Additional research has focused on the impact of torture and trauma, and the lived experience of forced migrants in resettlement and detention settings particularly in relation to mental health and recovery from the effects of trauma (see Kaplan 2020). Nipperess and Clark (2016) specifically focus on anti-oppressive practice with people seeking asylum in Australia, and note the complexity of working across micro, meso, and macro levels and recommend several practice principles which we will return to in the final section of this chapter.

In 2014, the federal parliament passed the Australian Border Force Act and Part 6 of the Act is titled "Secrecy and disclosure provisions". It included section 42, which makes it a criminal offence, punishable by up to 2 years prison, if a person who works in the immigration system discloses any fact they learned while working in the immigration system – including evidence of abuse to children and adults. Social workers, often employed by NGOs supporting victim/survivors of torture and trauma have been witness to crimes committed in detention. In raising these crimes to authorities, social workers found that *they* were targeted for *inciting* violence by "encouraging the refugees to commit acts of self-harm, to protest at their poor conditions and to concoct assault allegations including child sexual abuse" (Hugman and Carter 2016, p. viii) and their contracts terminated. There is increasing evidence that government is preventing social workers in third sector and non-government organisations (NGOs) from speaking out about human rights abuses and terminating contracts when they do (Marks 2021). This highlights the precarity of working in this sector. Cruel and inhuman treatment by guards employed by government and private firms toward refugees, witnessed by social workers was covered up but subsequently verified by an independent expert review (Moss 2015). This occurred at the detention centre where Behrouz Boochani was held. Supporting social workers and preparing them for working conditions that conflict with IFSW and AASW ethical principles and values remains an essential area of social work education and practice.

Social workers are often placed in impossible situations where they are prevented from speaking out, with no resources, and witness to poor practice which is often the result of unachievable contract aims and budgets. Shifting work away from statutory services to the third sector and NGOs under 'new public management' over the past 20 years has put social workers into the invidious position of being reliant on government grants for their service users and organisational survival and being reluctant or unable to be critical of government policy for fear of losing their funding. For NGOs receiving contracts to work in offshore detention centres, this debate about being insider/outsider was subjected to scrutiny, particularly when responding to the needs of survivors of torture and trauma (FASSTT 2018, p. 13). The report from Amnesty International (2017, p. 14) tables the extensive reports of child abuse and sexual assault from the "Nauru Files" that occurred *inside* the detention centre by staff allegedly there to protect them on behalf of the Australian Government. Behrouz Boochani refers to these violent incidents in his book (2018).

Social workers are directly exposed to the lived experience of people subject to displacement and separation from their home and family. The cruelty shown to asylum seekers with the implementation of policies including off-shore detention and "boat turn backs" has raised questions about whether social work can engage in an ethical manner in detention settings and what options are available (Briskman and Doe 2016). Researchers have argued that social workers have opportunities to push back against implementing social policies that are denigrating and inhuman towards asylum seekers and refugees (Green 2020). Critical social workers working for social justice are in conditions and circumstances that promote human rights abuses, must both resist and subvert the dominant narratives, and engage in a range of social work including research, policy reform and advocacy. The descriptions offered by Boochani and Nazari about their treatment, and that of others around them illustrates how dehumanising detention centres are, and the lack of accountability of staff. The ethical parameters must be raised and critically reviewed at all stages of service delivery in health, social care, and other settings.

Outside of detention centres, the issues of surveillance and the racial targeting of asylum seekers and refugees are controversial and raise ideological and political debates about the role of both the nation state and the welfare state in the provision of care. Some academics are highly critical of any surveillance role by health and social care workers and argue that social workers must actively resist any attempts to collude with government against the needs of asylum seekers and refugees. Hugman and Carter (2016, p. xii) argue that it is no longer plausible to assume the way in which human rights, social justice and professional integrity were understood previously are currently fit for practice. The complexity of organisations and the context within which social workers practice highlight the need for professional integrity to be more nuanced. Banks (2016b, p. 50) argues that integrity has three aspects: conduct, commitment, and capacity and that all of these are impacted by context. The intersection of these elements, for example a commitment to principles of human rights, is both a personal decision but is also constrained by the circumstances and location of the social worker. It is also relative to positions of power, and critical social work that draws on Foucauldian theory might be a formative way of understanding this further.

Foucault (1991) describes mechanisms of power, which are embedded in language, relationships, and practice, and then facilitated by a macro-structure such as the state. The Foucauldian concept of governmentality is described as the convergence of power and knowledge, with both positive and negative connotations, a central dimension of which is the role of the expert who regulates and controls the 'body' of society. Boochani (2018, p. 124) describes Australia's "Manus Island Regional Offshore Processing Centre", what he calls "The Kyriarchal System", as a form of governmentality, the regulation of the body and the narrative about asylum seekers which is a central feature of Foucault's description of prisons (1991). He notes "that the principle of The Kyriarchal System governing the prison is to turn the prisoners against each other and to ingrain even deeper power to keep people in line" (2018, p. 124). The role of social work as an instrument of governmentality has been identified as one that reproduces dominant state discourses as illustrated here:

> Social policy, enacted via a range of institutions (schools, universities, hospitals, workplaces) aims to act on the 'well-being' of the population as a whole promoting social cohesion while simultaneously acting on the innumerable decisions taken by individuals in their everyday lives thus managing their conduct (Gilbert and Powell 2010, p. 5).

Behrouz Boochani observed the health professionals and social workers situated inside the oppressive and restrictive detention centre and was also aware of the advocacy occurring in the outside world and by visitors who visited. Social workers are often caught between the discourses of care and control experiencing what Briskman and Zion (2014) call a "dual loyalty" between the organisation they work for (employer) and the service user (client) or person with whom they are in contact. Services are increasingly dominated by neoliberal discourses and a political context which determines whether people are eligible or denied access to resources. Listening to the voices of those who are excluded, such as Boochani and Nazari is an act of solidarity and empowerment that social workers can take into their organisations and activism with refugees. Challenging discriminatory and oppressive policy and practice is difficult for social workers in the neoliberal context and requires strategising for and with service users. While social workers may align with critical social work practice that promotes structural change and advocacy, many are working in organisations that uphold a dominant view of neoliberalism and austerity measures that restrict opportunities for real change. Navigating these tensions form part of the agenda to critically examine our practice for the future in the forced migration space.

Social Work Practice: Ways Forward?

Social workers are positioned between being controlling agents of the state *and* promoting a philosophy of self-determination and empowerment to reduce the effects of social inequality. Research has illustrated how both national and international legislative immigration and refugee frameworks often conflict with human rights and social welfare models, and that this leaves social workers feeling like the service user/client – powerless and outside of any supportive mainstream structures. Frontline social workers have identified working to change systemic problems and barriers in their practice and are aware of the inherent contradiction of both being part of and actively challenging 'the system'. They know that some service users are suspicious of them, and that they are often seen by asylum seekers to be aligned (or indeed working) with government immigration services, despite explaining otherwise (Robinson 2014). The experiences of Boochani and Nazari shows that despite being unable to claim asylum they were able to tell their stories, illustrating the dehumanising and marginalising experiences they faced with immigration officials. One of the challenges facing critical social work is to actively hold both perspectives or discourses, of the asylum seeker and refugee as both resilient and vulnerable. This tension in micro level dynamics is one that mirrors society's attitudes and views towards refugees and asylum seekers and is reflected in the macro level dimensions of society and policy.

In writing about social work with cross-border migrants, Hölscher (2016) argues that the "field is characterized by significant degrees of collusion and complicity in prevailing regimes of social injustice". While global definitions and ethical principles in codes of practice define and prescribe practices, it is the knowing and doing of social work that continues to be ambivalent and uncertain. Hölscher highlights how social workers are engaged or "entangled" in multiple structures and in practices that may be contributing to the binary of moral prescription and moral condemnation (2016, p. 102). For practitioners working with marginalised and displaced people, they often experience the very same feelings of powerlessness and loss of hope which are due to the conditions of structural injustice. Hölscher argues that social justice is not something "out there" but rather that "Social justice is better seen as a relational concept and contextual practice, in which effect is appreciated both as constitutive and indicative of relations and processes of social (in)justice" (2016, p. 110). Reminding ourselves of the lived experiences of those claiming asylum, such as Boochani and Nazari, and other refugees is just one way of doing this.

Nipperess argues that social work practice needs to move towards a 'critical ethics of care' in the context of Australia's cruelty to people seeking asylum (2018, p. 105). She argues for a twin focus on rights and care, and that this is informed by five key principles in practice. These include a knowledge of international human rights and Australia's engagement, the primacy of relationships with refugees, intersectionality, critical reflective practice, and self-care (2018, pp. 112–13). Displacement can feel profound and alienating and critical reflection on this aspect of work with newly arrived communities is key to understanding and adopting a compassionate positionality.

In developing ethical practice and research with refugee populations, the impact of oppression, including the misuse of power and processes of objectification, needs to be acknowledged. Critical social work aims to address human rights and social justice issues and works to both challenge and implement the instruments of law and protection to advocate for change. The advocacy for and with service users is informed by an understanding of the structural factors that create the barriers for genuine resettlement and ongoing marginalisation (Marlowe 2017). These barriers include those settlement conditions such as the limited access to employment, with poor pay and conditions; limited access to housing; and inadequate healthcare that impacts on wellbeing and mental health, and no rights to family reunion. Working with those who are in detention or have been released from detention continues to be a major challenge for new arrivals and their advocates and requires ongoing interrogation. Ensuring the voices of those who have told their story, like Boochani and Nazari, is included in teaching, research and policy making is essential to ensuring services are responsive to the needs of diverse communities.

Organisations that support human rights and social justice frameworks, face increasing demands and pressures. Critical social work offers a way forward to explore the ethical issues in social and human services work practice that are contextualised and situated in contradictory power relationships. These power differentials require conscious ethical practice that challenge dominant assumptions and discourses of oppression, particularly in the lived experience of those who have faced forced migration (Pullen-Sansfacon and Cowden 2012; Banks 2016a). Banks identifies several ways forward to engage in an "ethics of resistance" and describes the importance of engaging with networks, peers, and mentors to guide this development of practice, and to have courage not to collude but to call out bad behaviour and practice (2016b, pp. 61–62). Incorporating anti-oppressive practice underpins the model developed by Williams and Graham (2016) which identifies four value principles that commit social work to critical multicultural policy and practice: responsiveness, critical reflexive interrogation, co-production, and rights-based advocacy. Green (2020, p. 918) summarises a range of practice models that identify social justice frameworks, and a questioning of colonising practices, power, privilege, and political competency. These build on existing frameworks developed that specifically identify measures where there are opportunities to build respectful diverse communities (Nipperess and Clarke 2016; Fleay et al. 2021) The narratives from refugees who define successful settlement are about building new industries, creating opportunities and success in all areas of their lives.

Further research is required that captures the experiences of critical social workers who struggle to change structural barriers in their work with asylum seekers and refugees. This can support the earlier request made by Castles that we need practice that contributes to a "global social transformation" and an interdisciplinary and transnational project (Castles 2003, p. 14). Forced migration research must be grounded in the structural dimensions, not only the cultural and social, and engage in some degree of resistance against the policies and procedures formulated by immigration departments that vilify asylum seekers and refugees. In the settlement context strategies that promote inclusion and minimise exclusion tend to have key defining features that work towards securing social capital, such as networks, norms, and trust that enables individuals and groups to participate meaningfully in society and to work together toward shared goals.

Another key issue in moving forward for social work in forced migration is building hope. Freire, whose views were grounded in humanism and critical theory, argues that hope is radical and emancipatory, and in the new preface of *The Pedagogy of Hope* Giroux notes that the "intersecting crises of economics, health, climate change, politics, racism, and democracy can appear overpowering at times" (Freire 2021, p. 1). These are precisely the challenges facing social work, and forced migration is a distillation of all of them. Boddy et al. (2018) identify a range of areas in social work where hope is key to recovery and envisaging a healthy future for both service users and social workers. In their paper they describe a model embedded in strengths based and relational work and argue "social workers must 'walk' with others to revisit their context, reframe their issues, rediscover their strengths and revitalise their life with hope in the life journey. If social workers want to make a difference to the world, social work must be a profession of hope" (Boddy et al. 2018, p. 595).

In the lived experience of Behrouz Boochani and Abbas Nazari described above, neither of them were able to successfully claim asylum or access the Australian mainland. Their inclusion here highlights the fundamental tenant in the *Code of Ethics* (2020) noted above to support social justice and human rights and illustrates how social work can be seen to be outside the structural systems to challenge and change those exclusionary practices. Their stories highlight the impact of how policies have contributed to the criminalization of asylum seekers and the perception of them as dangerous and violent, or punished for not following formal migration processes. Their experiences illustrate what Fraser and Bedford (2008) call the "misframing" of social injustice, a process of state-territorial structures that are imposed on transnational sources of injustice, where the poor and disenfranchised are not able to claim support under international agreements. They note "What I mean by the 'who' question is simply: who counts as a subject of justice? Whose needs and interests deserve consideration?" (Fraser and Bedford 2008, p. 231). These are indeed the very questions pertinent to ethical critical social work, including the education of social work students. Morley et al. (2020, p. 403) argue that social work needs to "find ways to transgress and resist neoliberal imperatives that contradict espoused social work values and ethics". Drawing on the models and theoretical frameworks described can inform this practice and assist in navigating the complexities of those subjected to forced migration.

Finally, problematising power and control in the role of social workers in their relations with refugees and asylum seekers is an area for future research. Examining the work of social workers in terms of how they engage with and resist practices of the misuse of power and surveillance in their own interactions with refugees and asylum seekers, alongside the state apparatus continues to be central to this work. Critical social work needs to build on existing ethical principles about a dialogical approach to decision making, that value inclusive practices and community development work to transform working relations with asylum seekers and refugees.

Conclusion

Conclusions: Ethical Social Work Practice in Displacement

This chapter has highlighted the experiences and tensions facing social workers who struggle to change structural barriers in their work with asylum seekers and refugees. Forced migration research and practice must be grounded in the structural dimensions, along with the cultural and social. While social work has engaged to some degree of resistance against the policies and procedures formulated by immigration departments that vilify asylum seekers and refugees, there needs to be ongoing examination of how to move forward with increasingly restrictive policies and practices. Validating the voices of people like Boochani and Nazari and highlighting their experiences as survivors of punitive policy and practices is central changing and challenging the dominant narratives of them not being worthy of protection. Social workers have a key role in working towards change and challenging systemic problems and barriers in their practice and critically reflecting on the contradictory roles of both being part of and actively challenging 'the system'. Questioning the role of social work in administering services and working in contexts and settings that are contradictory and oppressive must inform critical social work education.

It is essential for social workers to commit to and sustain ethical practice in this area of practice by continuing to interrogate policies that undermine global commitments to human rights and social justice. Social workers are using creative and positive ways to engage with the wider community and counteract 'othering' by promoting the narrative of asylum seekers as human beings with agency and providing hope for the future. Part of sustaining and enabling critical frontline social workers to be effective is to be involved in political campaigns, writing for journals and news media, providing training and education, and social activities with asylum seekers refugee communities to support them in their activities. This chapter has highlighted how keeping the lived experience of asylum seekers and refugees front of mind can counter dehumanising and politicized discourses and keep social work true to the aims of a critical approach to ethics.

References

Ahmad A, Rassa N, Orcutt M, Blanchet K, Haqmal M (2021) Urgent health and humanitarian needs of the afghan population under the Taliban. Lancet 398(10303):822–825

Amnesty International (2017) Treasure Island: how companies are profiting from Australia's abuse of refugees on Nauru. Available via https://www.amnesty.org/en/documents/asa12/5942/2017/en/. Accessed 27 Feb 2022

Australian Association of Social Workers (2020) Code of Ethics. Available via https://www.aasw.asn.au/practitioner-resources/code-of-ethics. Accessed 27 Feb 2022

Australian Bureau of Statistics (2020) Australia's Population by Country of Birth. Released 23/04/2021 Available via https://www.abs.gov.au/ausstats/abs@.nsf/Latestproducts/3412.0Main%20Features32018-19?opendocumentandtabname=Summaryandprodno=3412.0andissue=2018-19andnum=andview=. Accessed 27 Feb 2022

Australian Government (2020) Refugee and Humanitarian Program. Available via https://immi.homeaffairs.gov.au/what-we-do/refugee-and-humanitarian-program. Accessed 27 Feb 2022

Australian Human Rights Commission (AHRC) (2014) The forgotten children: national inquiry into children in immigration detention. Available via https://www.humanrights.gov.au/our-work/asylum-seekers-and-refugees/national-inquiry-children-immigration-detention-2014. Accessed 27 Feb 2022

Banks S (2016a) Everyday ethics in professional life: social work as ethics work. Ethics Soc Welf 10(1):35–52

Banks S (2016b) Professional integrity: from conformity to commitment. In: Hugman R, Carter J (eds) Rethinking values and ethics in social work. Palgrave, London, pp 49–63

Banks S (2020) Ethics and values in social work. Bloomsbury Publishing

Boddy J, O'Leary P, Tsui MS, Pak CM, Wang DC (2018) Inspiring hope through social work practice. Int Soc Work 61(4):587–599

Boochani B (2018) No friend but the mountains: writing from Manus prison. Picador

Briskman L, Doe J (2016) Social work in dark places: clash of values in offshore immigration detention. Soc Altern 35(4):73–79

Briskman L, Zion D (2014) Dual loyalties and impossible dilemmas: health care in immigration detention. Public Health Ethics 7(3):277–286.

Briskman L, Latham S, Goddard C (2008) Human rights overboard: seeking asylum in Australia. Scribe Publications Carlton Australia

Castles S (2003) Towards a sociology of forced migration and social transformation. Sociology 37(1):13–34

Chenoweth L, McAuliffe D (2020) In: Cengage AU (ed) The road to social work and human service practice, 6th edn

Fiske L, Briskman L (2020) Chapter 5. Transcending racism in asylum politics: quest for social workers. In: Singh G, Masocha S (eds) Anti-racist social work: international perspectives. Red Globe Press, pp 95–113

Fleay C, Kenny MA, Andaveh A, Askari S, Hassani R, Leaney K, Lee T (2021) Doing something for the future: building relationships and hope through refugee and asylum seeker advocacy in Australia. In: Weber L, Tazreiter C (eds) Handbook of migration and global justice. Edward Elgar Publishing

Forum of Australian Services for Survivors of Torture and Trauma (FASSTT) (2018) Never turning away Australia's world leading program of Assistance for Survivors of Torture and Trauma (FASTT). Available via https://fasstt.org.au/wordpress/wp-content/uploads/2018/12/FASSTT_BOOKLET_2017_A4_FA_web.pdf. Accessed 27 Feb 2022

Foucault M (1991) The Foucault effect: studies in governmentality. University of Chicago Press

Fozdar F, Banki S (2017) Settling refugees in Australia: achievements and challenges. Int J Migr Border Stud 3(43):43–66

Fraser N, Bedford K (2008) Social rights and gender justice in the neoliberal movement: a conversation about welfare and transnational politics. Fem Theory 9:225–245

Freire P (2021) Pedagogy of hope: reliving pedagogy of the oppressed. Bloomsbury Publishing

Gilbert T, Powell JL (2010) Power and social work in the United Kingdom: a Foucauldian excursion. J Soc Work 10(1):3–22

Green BA (2020) Drowning in neoliberal lies: state responses towards people seeking asylum. Br J Soc Work 50(3):908–925

Hayes D, Humphries B (eds) (2004) Social work, immigration and asylum: debates, dilemmas and ethical issues for social work and social care practice. Jessica Kingsley, London

Higgins M (2020) Social work with refugees and migrants. In: Ow R, Poon AWC (eds) Mental health and social work. Springer Publishing, pp 353–374

Hölscher D (2016) The political is personal: on being, knowing, and doing something about social justice. In: Hugman R, Carter J (eds) Rethinking values and ethics in social work. Palgrave, London, pp 97–113

Hugman R, Carter J (2016) Rethinking values and ethics in social work. Palgrave, London

International Federation of Social Work (2018) Statement of ethical principles. Available via https://www.ifsw.org/global-social-work-statement-of-ethical-principles/. Accessed 27 Feb 2022

Kaldor Centre (The) (2020) Australia's refugee policy: an overview. [Fact sheet:] Available via https://www.kaldorcentre.unsw.edu.au/publication/australias-refugee-policy-overview. Accessed 27 Feb 2022

Kaplan I (2020) Rebuilding shattered lives. Integrated trauma recovery for people from refugee backgrounds, 2nd edn. Victorian Foundation for Survivors of Torture

Marks R (2021) The Silence of the Lambs. The Monthly November. Available via https://www.themonthly.com.au/issue/2021/november/1635685200/russell-marks/silence-lambs. Accessed 27 Feb 2022

Marlowe J (2017) Belonging and transnational refugee settlement: unsettling the everyday and the extraordinary. Routledge

Morley C, Ablett P, Macfarlane S (2019) Engaging with social work. A Critical Introduction. Cambridge University Press

Morley C, Le C, Briskman L (2020) The role of critical social work education in improving ethical practice with refugees and asylum seekers. Soc Work Educ 39(4):403–416. https://doi.org/10.1080/02615479.2019.1663812

Moss P (2015) Review into recent allegations relating to conditions and circumstances at the regional processing Centre in Nauru. Commonwealth of Australia, Canberra

Nazari A (2021) After the Tampa. From Afghanistan to New Zealand. Allan and Unwin

Nethery A, Holman R (2016) Secrecy and human rights abuse in Australia's offshore immigration detention centres. Int J Hum Rights 20(7):1018–1038

Neumann K (2015) Across the seas: Australia's response to refugees: a history. Black Inc

Nipperess S (2018) Caring in an uncaring context: towards a critical ethics of care in social work with people seeking asylum. In: Pease B, Vreugdenhil A, Stanford S (eds) Critical ethics of care in social work. Routledge, pp 105–115

Nipperess S, Clark S (2016) Anti-oppressive practice with people seeking asylum in Australia: reflections from the field. In: Pease B, Goldingay S, Hosken N, Nipperess S (eds) Doing critical social work. Routledge, pp 195–210

Nipperess S, Williams C (2019) The ethical, legal and policy context of critical multicultural practice. In: Nipperess S, Williams C (eds) Critical multicultural practice in social work. New perspectives and practices. (50–65). Allan and Unwin, Crows Nest, pp 50–66

Pullen-Sansfacon A, Cowden S (2012) The ethical foundations of social work. Pearson Education Limited

Robinson K (2014) Voices from the front line: social work with refugees and asylum seekers in Australia and the UK. Br J Soc Work 44(6):1602–1620

Robinson K (2020) A 'good news' story of social inclusion. Refugee resettlement in Australia. In: Crisp B, Taket A (eds) Sustaining social inclusion: ensuring an implementation legacy. Routledge, Oxon, pp 231–245

UNHCR (2021) Global trends: forced displacement 2020 published 18 June 2021. Available via https://www.unhcr.org/flagship-reports/globaltrends/. Accessed 27 Feb 2022

United Nations. Universal Declaration of Human Rights (1948) Available via https://www.un.org/en/about-us/universal-declaration-of-human-rights. Accessed 27 Feb 2022

Williams C, Graham MJ (2016) Building transformative practice. In: Williams C, Graham MJ (eds) Social work in a diverse society: transformative practice with black and minority ethnic individuals and communities. Policy Press, pp 3–19

Emerging Ethical Voices in Social Work

23

Ming-Sum Tsui, Ruby Chien-Ju Pai, Peace Yuh Ju Wong, and Cheong-Hay Chu

Contents

Introduction	464
Culture: Definitions and Differentiation	466
The Cultural Characteristics of Confucian Societies in East Asia	467
Traditional Roots of Ethics and Values in East Asian Confucian Societies	469
Life Principles in Confucian Culture	470
The Influence of Confucian Ways of Thinking in East Asia	471
The Cultural Characteristics of Confucian Societies in East Asia	471
Emphasis on Kinship and Relationship	472
Human Relationships and Relational Obligations	472
Life Philosophy and Problem-Solving Orientation Harmony and Doctrine of Mean	472
Comparison Between the East and the West	473
The Base of Social Work: Relationship-Based, Client-Based, Evidence-Based or Values-Based?	474

M.-S. Tsui (✉)
Felizberta Lo Padilla Tong School of Social Sciences, Caritas Institute of Higher Education, Hong Kong, Hong Kong
e-mail: mstsui@cihe.edu.hk

R. C.-J. Pai
Department of Guidance and Counselling, National Changhua University of Education, Changhua, Taiwan
e-mail: rubywhite@cc.ncue.edu.tw

P. Y. J. Wong
Department of Social Work, National University of Singapore, Singapore, Singapore
e-mail: swkwyi@nus.edu.sg

C.-H. Chu
Felizberta Lo Padilla Tong School of Social Sciences, Caritas Institute of Higher Education, Hong Kong, Hong Kong
e-mail: chchu@cihe.edu.hk

© Springer Nature Singapore Pte Ltd. 2023
D. Hölscher et al. (eds.), *Social Work Theory and Ethics*, Social Work,
https://doi.org/10.1007/978-981-19-1015-9_24

Conclusion: Integration and Transformation – The Dialectic and the Way Forward
for Professional Ethical Practice in the Social Work Profession 476
References 477

Abstract

This chapter aims to: (1) define the nature of culture, (2) identify the characteristics of East Asian societies with a Confucian heritage, (3) compare these with Western ethics and culture and (4) examine the impact of culture on social work practice in East Asia. As this is an ambitious attempt, the chapter focuses on how ethical development influences social work practice in specific cultural contexts. With these constraints and limitations, the authors thus highlight how Eastern culture differs from its Western counterparts. In addition, the authors illustrate the differences between Western culture and Confucian heritage. In conclusion, the authors explain why incompatibilities arise when social workers transplant Western social work practice into East Asian societies, and explore and explain how this emerging ethical voice is shaping social work practice.

Keywords

Confucian heritage societies · Social work · Culture · Ethics · Values · East Asia

Introduction

When examining the idea of ethical development in social work, it is natural to focus discussion on values and culture (Hugman 2013). Values are not just personal beliefs that are significant and important to an individual in daily decision making, they also serve as principles and action guidelines for the daily behaviour of members in a specific social group. Similarly, culture is something that is easy to distinguish and discuss but difficult to define and differentiate. Usually, culture is perceived as the shared values, attitudes, behavioural patterns, symbols, social norms and mutual expectations among people who identify as members of the same social group. In this sense, culture can also be perceived as the characteristics for classifying members by distinguishing them from other social groups. Thus, for all of the authors, both as members of a specific society (citizens) and a profession (social workers), culture often has a strong impact on their social work practice within specific cultural contexts (Hugman 2013).

This assertion is also supported by Tsui (2001, 2005) in his studies of social work supervision. He found that culture can be simultaneously explicit and implicit, and there may be different meanings for different people in different times and contexts. Therefore, there are constant debates on the meanings and definitions of culture. As suggested by Tsui (2001, 2005), until culture can be identifiable through a set of specific characteristics, it remains very difficult to have a meaningful discussion and derive consensus on it.

The process of social work practice is to actualize the concepts and components of social work intervention with professional values in specific cultural and institutional contexts. Therefore, it is important and interesting to examine how culture in non-Western societies influences the ethics and values of social work practice in particular societies. Social work, as a global profession with local practice (International Federation of Social Workers & International Association of Schools of Social Work 2014), shares common core values, for example, (1) social justice, (2) human rights, (3) collective responsibility and (4) respect for diversity. This explains why there must be common or at least similar practice, even though social workers are conducting their practice with people in different cultures in different parts of the world. In this chapter, the authors will focus on the distinction, diversities and differences between Western and non-Western societies with an East Asian Confucian heritage culture (Leung 1998) and how they influence daily social work practice in various service settings.

Since World War II, the Western (i.e., the United Kingdom, the United States and Europe) notion of professional ethics of social work has been the key reference framework for teaching and practicing social work in East Asian societies. Although respect for multiculturalism is sometimes regarded as a core ethical principle in social work, the indigenization of the social work profession and the ethical dilemmas in transplanting, translating and transforming Western professional practice to East Asian practice have been concerns for practitioners in non-Western societies. Consequently, much effort has been placed on transferring both Western ideas and ideals into their professional practice.

In these circumstances, 'West is best' is always used as the hidden guiding principle for social work education and practice. However, in many service settings, from the young to the elderly, from the family to the community and from the sick to the rehabilitated, this imported approach is incompatible and inappropriate for East Asian societal cultures. This may explain why social workers trying to do good deeds may not be well received and accepted by ordinary people in the local communities. For example, O'Leary, Tsui and Ruch (2013) illustrated that the professional boundaries of social work relationships transferred from the Western medical model do not receive wide acceptance from clients in rural villages and cultures in Asia that emphasize personal kinship and friendship during the helping process.

The term 'non-Western' societies is rather general and vague. According to Huntington's (1996) classification of civilizations, Western civilizations come from Europe, America or the North Atlantic, while the non-Western ones cover six major civilizations, including those of China, Japan, India, Islam, Latin America and Africa. Based on the common characteristics of these cultures, it is possible to classify non-Western civilization as Confucian, Islamic and Indian. If geographical area and political entity are adopted as the criteria for this classification, the most frequently discussed entities are East Asian Confucian societies which refer to those East Asian societies that share the Confucian culture and its behavioural patterns, including the Chinese Mainland, Hong Kong, Macau, Taiwan and Singapore as well as non-Chinese societies that share Confucian culture but where Chinese people do not comprise the major ethnic group, such as Vietnam, Thailand, Malaysia, Philippines and Indonesia. Due to its unique culture and socio-political characteristics, this chapter focuses on shared Confucianism among these East Asian societies as the basis for discussing the non-Western cultural perspective as an alternative and emerging one.

Culture: Definitions and Differentiation

Culture is a complex entity consisting of knowledge, beliefs, art, norms, laws, customs, habits, symbols and rituals owned by a specific social group (Tylor 1871). There are more than 200 definitions identified by Kroeber and Kluckhohn (1952) who created a typology to allow understanding of the essence of these cultural concepts. First is merely descriptive, simply listing the features of various cultures without exploring the essence in a deeper manner. Second is the historical perspective, which highlights the heritage of the social group by illustrating the origin and development of a specific culture. Third is normative culture, which refers to the shared rules and social norms followed by the people belonging to the same group. Fourth is psychological culture, which emphasizes the process of adaption and socialization to culture and learning the essence of culture, which is more interactive and dynamic. Fifth is the structural definition of culture, which focuses on social organizations and their structural patterns, for example, hierarchy, duties and positions. Last is genetic definitions, which emphasize the origin and succession of specific culture. Unfortunately, after examining all these definitions, no consensus can be achieved. Instead, there have been continual debates. This journey of exploration forms the base of cultural studies as an academic discipline.

Other scholars (Ingold 1994; Jenks 1993) tried to define culture through a fourfold typology. First, culture is a general state of mind set or world view. It refers to the mission or common goal of a social group. Second, culture can be a set of intellectual achievement and moral norms of a society. Third, culture is a descriptive and concrete category. It can refer to the collective body of artistic and intellectual works in a society. This can be likened to the collections of antiques seen in museums in various cities. This is also the way 'culture' is used in our daily language. Fourth, culture is a social category, the entire way of living for a group of people. This is the pluralist use of culture often used in social sciences, especially anthropology and cultural studies (Jenks 1993).

Instead of defining culture, D'Andrade (1984) identified three major views in the nature of culture. Whenever culture is taken as knowledge, it can be taught systematically as a transmission of cultural heritage. In this sense, culture can be accumulated and disseminated from one generation to another. Second, culture consists of conceptual structures for people to form their world view. Based on this perception of the natural and social environment, people can live in a physical and social environment that they can understand, adapt, survive and develop. Third, culture can be viewed as all kinds of social institutions such as the family, the Church, the Government and business firms, etc.

In the following sections, the authors will identify the cultural traits of East Asian societies with a Confucian heritage and discuss how these characteristics influence social work practice in different service settings.

The Cultural Characteristics of Confucian Societies in East Asia

Contemporary professional ethics in social work originated from individualism based on Western ethical principles and values. There are many differences in terms of social life when such an orientation is contrasted to one based on East Asian Confucianism.

In East Asia, the traditional value of 'reciprocity' is the guiding principle for handling human relationships and interpersonal interactions. Reciprocity entails a two-way interaction involving a dynamic exchange of emotional and resource support. This reveals the most distinctive feature of the relationship between social workers and clients in the cultural context. The relationship has a dual perspective, similar to the two sides of a coin, both personal and professional. This explains why people in East Asian societies sometimes have psychological transference. For example, they may take the social worker as a personal friend or a member of their nuclear or extended family (e.g., father, mother, uncle, aunt, brother or sister). This supports the notion that the family is the fundamental social unit of East Asian Confucian societies.

Many scholars have revisited the influence of Confucian thoughts in East Asia. Yang (1981) divided Chinese people's relationships into three categories: (1) family members, (2) insiders (relatives, friends, neighbours, classmates and colleagues) and (3) strangers. Hwang (1988) further found that Chinese people deal with each category in a very distinct manner. First, they use excessive ties that emphasize the needs of the individual when they deal with people they consider to be family members. Second, with insiders, they have mixed ties in which equality is the norm in the process of exchange. Third, with strangers, Chinese people have instrumental ties in which equity (a balance in terms of give and take) will act as the guiding principle. In mixed ties, *qing* and *face* greatly influence the behaviour of the parties involved. Between the two involved parties, there is a balancing of *qing* (which refers to a primary relationship involving exchange of feelings, information and resources). In Chinese culture, both parties are expected to maintain equilibrium, to prevent one becoming inferior in front of the other resulting in them avoiding contact with, or even removing themselves from the social network.

In East Asian societies, *qing*, *yuan* and *face* help to release tensions in interpersonal relationships and improve harmony. *Qing,* without an exact equivalent term in English, is a long-lasting and close primary relationship. *Qing* can facilitate the continuity of harmonious relationships even between individuals in different roles or of different ranks, for example, the social worker and their client in the service setting. When *qing* is properly used it can be very effective in reducing the tension arising from different personalities, social roles and social classes.

Qing can enhance mutual trust and help even when the parties are not members of the same social group. There is an expectation that the relationship will be a more reliable one. To a certain extent, it looks like 'love' in Western culture but is more implicit, relatively subtle and less passionate. Whenever this mutual expectation is established, both parties will be more patient and inclusive, they will not demand the other to settle the imbalance right away. However, *qing* can be abused by either party as a subtle form of 'emotional blackmail' or for obtaining inappropriate advantages. For example, the social worker may abuse the relationship to intrude on the privacy of the client. Alternatively, the client may request an inappropriate favour from the social worker for personal benefit. This explains the need for professional bodies to establish a comprehensive and systematic code of ethics as guiding principles for professional social work practitioners.

Yuan refers to the relationship pre-arranged by God. In reality, there is no free will or choice for either party. This facilitates the worker-client relationship as they believe that the relationship is predetermined by God, making people passively accept the existing status as a natural arrangement. In addition, *yuan* can arise from the perception of compatibility of appearance, personalities, hobbies, preferences and working styles. In this sense, *yuan* can be generated from first impressions. Once both parties believe that there is a component of *yuan* in their relationship, communication and interaction will be much smoother.

Finally, *face* is also a very effective way to reduce interpersonal conflicts and preserve social norms in the existing power structure of the social network. *Face* refers to the status of a person in the social network. *Face* demands appropriate social behaviour and recognition from other members in the same social network, especially in public. 'Loss of face' is the inability to follow the social norm, which will lead to devaluation of their significance and existence in the social network. Thus, *face* is one of the components integral to reciprocity in the relationship: whenever someone gives you *face*, they expect you to give *face* in return. Of course, 'facework' is not only limited to East Asian Confucian societies. The custom of giving *face* to others is also common in the Western world. However, the concept in Chinese culture has more dimensions and complicated meaning than its counterpart in the West.

As Hu (1944) pointed out, there are two basic features of *face* in Chinese culture: *lian* and *mianzi*. *Lian* can be preserved by faithful compliance through rituals and social norms. It represents the confidence of a society in the integrity of an individual's moral character. The loss of *lian* makes it difficult for a member of the society to function well in the social network. In contrast, *mianzi* refers to the aspect of face that is emphasized in the Western world: a social reputation achieved through effort and social interactions. Hu (1944) noted that the Western concept of *face* corresponds to the Chinese *mianzi* but entirely lacks the connotations of *lian*. In addition, the sensitivity of Chinese people to *face* is much stronger than that of other ethnic groups (King 1990a, 1990b, 1994). A loss of *face* is very serious for Chinese people. In short, the dual perspective (personal and professional) and the value of reciprocity in the worker-client relationship (*qing, yuan* and *face*) are the two distinctive and crucial features of social work practice in East Asian Confucian societies.

To summarize, in East Asian Confucian societies the worker-client relationship needs to accommodate reciprocity in a harmonious but tactful manner regardless of the intricate nature of personal and professional relationships. This is because the tension created by this mixed relationship is mitigated by *qing*, *yuan* and *face*. As illustrated by Tsui (2001, 2003, 2005), *Qing* increases their level of mutual tolerance, *yuan* enhances their mutual acceptance and *face* maintains their mutual respect. This helps to significantly reduce or resolve the potential tension arising from crossing personal and professional boundaries.

Traditional Roots of Ethics and Values in East Asian Confucian Societies

As asserted by Chan and Tsui (1997), the legacy of traditional Chinese values and beliefs is a mixture of Confucianism, Taoism and Buddhism. First, the notion of Confucian welfare places more emphasis on the informal sector and voluntary contributions instead of social policy and government intervention. The notion of the 'ideal state' is similar but not identical to the welfare state in the Western world (Blau 1989; Chow 1987). In this sense, the Confucian concept of the ideal welfare state seems utopian and the extent of provision has been questioned; there have been a number of concrete measures in the history of China that adhered to Confucian ways of thinking in social planning and welfare programmes. As a fundamental philosophy in East Asian Confucian societies, the doctrine may be summarized as 'individual responsibility for collective good'. Confucian thought emphasizes hierarchy in terms of seniority, social norms, family roles and collective responsibility. It has thus been adopted by the Empire and the power elites as a guiding principle in governing the state and regulating the components of society. This explains why Confucian thoughts are always perceived as the dominant cultural values in East Asia.

Second, the value base and wisdom in East Asian societies is Taoism. *Tao* is the law of nature (the 'Way') that governs regulations in the universe. Humans should not violate *Tao* but instead follow the law of nature. This principle is universally applied to interpersonal relationships as well as the relationship between the natural environment and humans. The essence of *Tao* is a spirit of 'becoming' (Chan and Tsui 1997); people do not think that they can change the environment but rather maintain a harmonious relationship with it, both natural and social. *Tao* has two features in terms of its practice. It can be a common religion in villages and also the practice in everyday life. Although it is low-profile, subtle and implicit, it has great influence on the customs and behaviour of ordinary people, instead of the governing elite.

Third, the teachings of Buddhism emphasize helping behaviour while expecting nothing in return. Buddhists perceive the life process in four stages: (1) birth (2) old age (3) sickness and (4) death. It is as natural as the sunrise and the sunset. Throughout the stages in this process, pain is a part of life that cannot be avoided. With wisdom, it is possible to reduce pain by reframing the mind set to a minimum demand for material resources. The Buddhist way of thinking helps people deal with natural disasters and trauma; as long as they do not gain they have nothing to lose. Buddhist monasteries were major sources of charity activities in many East Asian societies. Indeed, many temples became the service stations of NGOs in East Asia, from food banks to family service centres. These became the bases and mainstay of the voluntary sector of social welfare.

Life Principles in Confucian Culture

According to Pai (2020), in Confucian heritage societies interaction among different individuals is based on the strategies of being a member of the social group. Understanding social norms, *qing* and giving *face* to everyone is crucial. *Qing*, relationships, *face* and reciprocity all emphasize harmony, reliance and trust. These can be summarized into six perspectives.

- *Principle of Face*: *Face* is the self-respect and social status in the social network. When one receives respect from another person, they must show respect or give advantages in return to achieve the balance of face-work. Then neither party will feel that they are losing *face*. This matches the characteristics of the 'shame culture' in Confucianism. However, the shortcoming of this behavioural pattern is that there will be a lack of sincerity as well as superficial behaviour whenever *face* is overemphasized.
- *Qing and Rationality Balance Principle*: Members of Confucian societies have to consider their position in the multi-layered social and kinship networks in which interpersonal relationships have become important and valuable social capital. Human behaviour in the networks is expected to simultaneously achieve both *qing* and reason. Although affective and rational are two sides of the same coin, people need to achieve both. This is the main difference from Western ethics in that *qing* and reason can be handled separately.
- *Reciprocity Principle*: This refers to the obligation to return favours received from others in the social network, even though they may not be appropriate or ethical. This differs from the contractual principle in the West where legal rights and obligations are clearly defined, agreed and executed.
- *Seniority Principle*: As well as social circles, there is also hierarchy in the social network. As such, every member has to understand their position and status as well as their relationships with others. Junior members have to respect the authority of their seniors, regardless of the interactions in their family or work organization. Seniors enjoy autonomy and authority. At the same time, there is expectation from juniors for protection and provision of resources. For example, the junior employees will expect their bosses will pay their lunch bill.
- *Contingency Principle*: Although there are explicit social bonds and implicit social norms, handling of interpersonal relationships is still an art in the social network. Members are expected to be flexible and accommodating. There may be different versions of presentations in front of different figures with various social status and

power. Members try to be nice to everyone; however, this may violate the principle of honesty and justice.

Harmony Principle: Members in the social network try to be nice to everyone and complete tasks in a harmonious manner. Sometimes however, this attitude will lead to members making compromises instead of maintaining their life principles. Consensus has become the optimal alternative instead of seeking the best solution.

The Influence of Confucian Ways of Thinking in East Asia

There are several characteristics in Confucian ways of thinking: First, every person is located in a well-structured network of human relationships. Here, everyone is assigned specific duties and responsibilities. The obligation to help others is based on the individual's assigned social roles with obligations in the social network. Second, the guiding principle in resolving conflict is consensus and the most valuable norms are harmony and interdependence, instead of fair competition and independence as in the West. Third, care and concern do not come from the Government but from the people themselves as they are members of the intricate social network. In this social network, the individual has a specific position and relationships with others on many different levels with social bonds. The hierarchy is clear and rigid. The major social bond is kinship, explaining why family, both nuclear and extended, is the core social unit for major social and economic activities. Another is friends, which includes classmates, peers and colleagues. Fourth, redistribution of income and wealth for achieving social equity is not the major goal. Instead, care and concern are given on a voluntary basis. Being helped is not a right or a shame but helping others is a responsibility and an honour that can earn a person *face* in the social network.

The Cultural Characteristics of Confucian Societies in East Asia

Predominant approaches to the discussion of ethics emerged from Western Europe in the medieval period (Hugman 2013). Interestingly, according to Hugman (2013) ideas of democracy that are seemingly 'Western' do not have their origins in traditional Western European cultures. Yet, the strong influence of individualism based on Western ethical principles and values has impacted on social work professional ethics. The creation of a code of ethics for the social work profession serves to guide the professional conduct of social workers across different contexts. Given the need to contextualize practice in different countries, there is a clear need to consider if the influence of Confucianism impacts on social work practice. This is especially so since Western culture stresses independence and individualism, whereas Confucian philosophy emphasizes integration and harmony (Leung 1998). It is unclear how the attempt by the social work profession to promote social change through emphasizing the principles of human rights and social justice (International Federation of Social Workers & International Association of Schools of Social Work

2014) can be reconciled in Confucian-influenced countries/communities. The following highlights some of the concepts that influence people and social work practice in Confucian-influenced East Asian countries.

Emphasis on Kinship and Relationship

The core component of East Asian Confucian society is centred around family blood kinship. The relationship extends to relatives, kinship, acquainted people and then to strangers forming the relationship (*Guanxi*) network. Yang (1981) used the term 'social orientation' as opposed to individual orientation to label this aspect of culture. According to Yang (1981), social orientation is defined as a tendency of an individual according to external social norms rather than internal wishes or personal integrity.

Within this view, the concept of the individual self is different from the independent self in the West. Family origins are very significant for individuals, and it is hard for them to ignore the opinions of family members concerning major life events, such as marriage, jobs, career arrangement and even house purchases.

Human Relationships and Relational Obligations

In general, East Asian Confucian societies consider that individuals have the obligation to help their family members. Individuals are required to share the collective responsibility to support their family members when they encounter various kinds of difficulty in life. Therefore, instead of requesting society to invest more resources in disadvantaged members, they would feel embarrassed for burdening society. For example, the Civil Law of Taiwan still requires individuals to take care of their family members who live with them. In addition, those who cannot afford to take care of their family members are required to appeal to the court to reduce the level of support or to relieve them of their obligation to take care of those family members. However, even if they were to be granted financial relief by the court, they would still face social pressure and self-blame due to their sense of filial piety.

Children are taught the importance of obedience and respect from childhood, and this has also influenced their tendency to comply with rules or orders more than Westerners (Leung 1998). Indirectly, this gives rise to a stronger tendency for uniformity and even conformity (Bond and Hwang 1986). This need to conform and promote collectivism is contrary to Western individualistic ideals.

Life Philosophy and Problem-Solving Orientation Harmony and Doctrine of Mean

The Doctrine of Mean suggests that an individual must adhere to moderation in their actions and thinking. In doing so, this results in harmony in action and leads to a more harmonious society. Additionally, there is the Confucian idea of man: "A man should discipline himself first, after that he could regulate his family then govern the state, and finally lead the world into peace" (Analetcs, trans. James Legg 1930). In adopting this idea to attain personal virtue individuals need to be progressively disciplined at different levels, starting with themselves, family, the State and then the world. These concepts influence their values such that individuals in Confucian-influenced countries strive towards achieving harmony with others and to prove their worth in their personal virtues and in their families (Leung 1998).

Comparison Between the East and the West

As suggested by Tsui and Chan (1995), four different characteristics can be identified between East Asian Confucian societies and the West in terms of ethics and values in social work and related social welfare programmes.

First, in East Asia the Confucian idea of the 'ideal state' is more than the Western notion of the welfare state. It is like the notion of 'welfare society'. In this welfare society, protection, care and concern can originate from various charitable organizations that require no state assistance or government intervention. People are ready to provide help to others on a voluntary basis. There is less need for social legislation as the well-being of people can be automatically addressed through mutual care and concern based on social norms and expectations.

Second, in the West the welfare state is a collective effort to ensure the protection of all members of a given society, which is rights-based and demand-based. In contrast, in East Asian Confucian societies the core concept of the 'ideal state' is 'individual responsibility for the collective good'. It is everyone's duty to make the community better, and the role of the Government is not that significant. Indeed, the role of the Government is rather passive. The principle is 'to get what you need' after you have contributed wholeheartedly to the collective community. One of the goals of social work in the West is to eliminate social dependence. In Western culture the opposite of dependence is always independence. This explains why social workers often use various approaches to help their clients to help themselves to become more independent. However, in Confucian societies the emphasis is on achieving interdependence. The spirit of mutual trust and mutual care are greatly valued. It is not taboo for someone to depend on others when they encounter trauma or difficulties as it is perceived as natural as the sun rising. Thus, it can be perceived as 'need-based'.

Third, the Western notion of the welfare state is founded upon the concepts of citizenship (as a member of the society) and civil rights. The emphasis is more on individual rights to own private property (land, money, knowledge and information). This constitutes an economic and political counterweight to the State's authority. As a result, the debates on welfare provision in the West are debates between different concepts of rights. Social work in the West is mainly based on the concept of rights, stressing a contractual relationship between the provider and the recipient. In East Asian Confucian societies helping behaviour is largely a voluntary action expressed via the natural helping network. There is a minimum level of intervention from the Government via social legislation or public policy. The collective ownership of the means of production strengthens the spirit of mutual support. The relationship between the helper and recipient is a type of kinship, friendship, fellowship or brotherhood/sisterhood but not a professional relationship or a legal contract. In this sense, social work can be taken as a type of voluntary mutual help.

Fourth, the welfare state in the West is a product of modernity, it is a product of the thinking of 'being'. That is, to do something good. In this sense, it has a progressive implication. Advocates for the welfare state in the West believe that they can achieve social justice and equality in redistribution of resources by social planning and engineering. In East Asian Confucian societies, people do not think that they can overcome natural adversities, such as typhoons or earthquakes. What they can do is to live with the fate and the natural environment in a harmonious way. This is essentially post-modernist thinking for handling change in terms of time and space with the notion of 'becoming'. Developing resilience in dealing with the misfortunes instead of changing it enables people to survive natural disasters and life traumas.

The above differences explain why social work practice and social welfare provision transferred from the West cannot fully address the needs of clients in East Asian societies. This is because they come from different value bases. We should not depend on theories and knowledge from the West and transplant them for practice in different cultural contexts. This situation is like serving green tea to French people and wine to Japanese people.

The Base of Social Work: Relationship-Based, Client-Based, Evidence-Based or Values-Based?

As O'Leary and Tsui (2019) asserted in their editorial in *International Social Work*, the base of social work practice can be classified into four categories: (1) relationship-based, (2) client-based, (3) evidence-based and (4) values-based. By making use of this typology, it is possible to revisit social work practice in East Asian Confucian societies to discover the following points.

First, social work practice builds on the professional relationship between the social worker and the client as well as significant others, such as informal caregivers. In the process of social work intervention, the professional relationship will be the main medium for communication and exchange of ideas and emotional support. Relationships are fluid but concrete. Clearly, the personal relationship also has a significant role in determining the orientation of social work intervention in East Asian Confucian societies. In addition, it is important to fully understand the roles and position of the client as well as how they relate to significant others in the social network. This explains why social workers who try to follow the rational official code of professional practice will be perceived by their clients as too cold and official.

Second, in client-based social work it is essential to understand that the client, not the social worker, is the major target for social work practice. Without clients there is no need to do such a thing as social work. The process of social work intervention includes eight steps: (1) *enter* the physical, social and cultural world of a client, (2) *engage* the client in a meaningful problem-solving relationship, (3) *enable* the client to identify, recognize and face their problem(s), (4) *enhance* the capability and capacity of the client to deal with this particular problem, (5) *educate* the client about knowledge and skills in dealing with the problem, (6) *empower* the client with awareness and insight about their rights and related strategies in achieving them, (7) *evaluate* the effectiveness, efficiency and outcome of the intervention and (8) *exchange* the ideas and share the ideal with professional peers. It is essential that social workers understand the '*qing*' of clients, which includes their emotional state, interpersonal relationships as well as their social environment. "What we need to do is to transform the client from the state of *helpless* to *asking help*, from *receiving help* to *self-help*, as well as from *mutual help* to *helping others*" (O'Leary and Tsui 2019, p. 1327; italics in original).

Third, the social worker as a professional practitioner, by nature, should be rational. This shows the scientific perspective of social work as a social and behavioural science. It refers to fact-finding, logical thinking and problem solving. Social work has an evidence-based nature in its needs assessments, evaluative research and decision making. However, the scope and kind of evidence should not be limited to measurement and numbers. Evidence should go beyond research evidence. Just like the practice of Chinese medicine, there is a need to observe, listen, ask and care. The client's demographic characteristics, nature of practice context, practice expertise and experience of the social worker, and the client's experience and choices should also be taken into consideration. Evidence should also include the client's background, identity, self-image, life history and context. Evidence-based practice in this sense could be transformed into 'evidence-informed practice'. This means, evidence is a major factor for consideration but not the entirety for decision making. Both internal evidence (e.g., the client's feeling) and external evidence (the cultural environment of the community) should be explored, understood and considered.

Fourth, social work originates from and is guided by values and then develops related knowledge and skills. As values determine decisions, they are always more important than knowledge and skills. Thus, it is important to understand the social values of people before entering into the community to practice with professional values, otherwise incompatibilities will arise. This explains why value dilemmas persist when social work practice is directly transferred from the West to the East, as illustrated by Chu, Tsui and Yan (2009). Social work practice always involves decision making with ethical dilemmas and power issues. It is easy to understand, but difficult to resolve.

As O'Leary and Tsui (2019) suggest, social work practice is complicated and dynamic; thus, social workers cannot simply adopt a 'stand-alone' approach. The four specific bases of social work practice need to be combined with care. Self-awareness, common sense and uncommon sense (wisdom) are all needed to pursue the truth, the good and the beautiful in a humanistic manner.

Conclusion: Integration and Transformation – The Dialectic and the Way Forward for Professional Ethical Practice in the Social Work Profession

Although the core values of the social work profession – human rights and social justice – have been universally recognized in East Asian Confucian societies, they are exemplified as a theoretical concept, legal obligation and social policy documents. The basic values, social life and human behaviour of local people are still deeply influenced by Confucian culture. The life of ordinary people is built around their core social network of family relationships. The resolution of important life events and difficulties still relies heavily on the core social network of their family rather than government intervention or social welfare provisions from public funding.

The established cultural norms exercise considerable influence over the professional values of social work, the ethical codes and the ethical decisions made by the social worker during the helping process. The professional virtues mentioned by Banks and Gallagher (2008) such as care, respect, trust, justice, courage and integrity in Western culture are not the same, albeit similar to, the notions of benevolence, righteousness, reason, wisdom and courage in Confucian culture. When social workers rely excessively on Western professional codes of ethics and ethical decision-making principles, they may neglect the existing social culture as well as emerging ethics, and then may run the risk of 'saying one thing and doing another' to avoid the accusation of being 'unprofessional and unethical'. In this circumstance, it would be rather difficult for social workers to tackle the situation as they have become a 'marginal person' between Western professional ethics and Confucian cultural values. Although it is no easy task, a bridge has to be built over the troubled water.

At present, the history and the focus of social work differ in different East Asian societies. While the incorporation of the social and cultural characteristics of each society may have transformed the professional core spirit of safeguarding and assisting the socially disadvantaged, the professional core values remain unchanged. For example, coffee and tea mixed together is served in Hong Kong but in Taiwan milk tea is served with 'pearls'.

Faced with this dilemma, it is proposed here to identify the differences through a dialectic approach. For instance, try to contextualize it with an Indigenous approach and then try to be as inclusive and culturally sensitive as possible. This 'dialectic transformation' approach involves two stages. First, the social worker has to actively integrate contextual ethics and moral ethics to develop the core principles of the local social work professional code of practice. Second, as illustrations of dilemmas, cases should be documented as reference material for both social work practitioners and social work students in fieldwork settings.

References

Banks S, Gallagher A (2008) Ethics in professional life: virtues in health and social care. Palgrave Macmillan, Basingstoke
Blau J (1989) Theories of the welfare state. Soc Serv Rev 63(1):26–38. https://doi.org/10.1086/603676
Bond MH, Huang KK (1986) The social psychology of Chinese people. In: Bond MH (ed) The psychology of the Chinese people. Oxford University Press, Hong Kong, pp 213–266
Chan RKH, Tsui MS (1997) Notions of the welfare state in China revisited. Int Soc Work 52:177–189. https://doi.org/10.1177/002087289704000205
Chow NWS (1987) Western and Chinese ideas of social welfare. Int Soc Work 30:31–41. https://doi.org/10.1177/002087288703000105
Chu WCK, Tsui MS, Yan MC (2009) Social work as a moral and political practice. Int Soc Work 52(3):287–298. https://doi.org/10.1177/0020872808102064
D'Andrade RG (1984) Cultural meaning systems. In: Shweder RA, LeVine R (eds) Cultural theory: essays on mind, self, and emotion. Cambridge University Press, Cambridge, UK, pp 88–119
Hu HC (1944) The Chinese concepts of face. Am Anthropol 46(1):45–64. https://doi.org/10.1525/aa.1944.46.1.02a00040
Hugman R (2013) Culture, values and ethics in social work. Routledge, New York
Huntington SP (1996) The clash of civilizations and the remaking of world order. Simon & Schuster, New York
Hwang KK (1988) Jen Qing and face: the power of Chinese people. In: Hwang KK (ed) The power game of Chinese people. Great Trend Publishing Company, Taipei (in Chinese), pp 7–56
Ingold T (ed) (1994) Comparison encyclopedia of anthropology: humanity, culture and social life. Routledge, London
International Federation of Social Workers, International Association of Schools of Social Work (2014) Global definition of social work. https://www.ifsw.org/what-is-social-work/global-definition-of-social-work/
Jenks C (1993) Culture: key ideas. Routledge, London
King AYC (1990a) An analysis of 'Jen Qing' in interpersonal relationship. In: Yang KS (ed) The psychology of Chinese. Gui Guan Publishing Company, Taipei (in Chinese), pp 75–104
King AYC (1990b) An analysis of 'Jen Qing' in interpersonal relationship. In: Yang KS (ed) The psychology of Chinese. Gui Guan Publishing Company, Taipei (in Chinese), pp 319–346
King AYC (1994) 'Kuan-his' and network building: a sociological interpretation. In: Tu WM (ed) The living tree: the changing meaning of being Chinese today. Stanford University Press, Stanford, pp 109–126
Kroeber AL, Kluckhohn C (1952) Culture: a critical review of concepts and definitions. Peabody Museum, Cambridge, MA
Leung FKS (1998) The implications of Confucianism for education today. J Thought 33(2):25–36
O'Leary P, Tsui MS (2013) The boundary of the social work relationship revisited: towards a connected, inclusive and dynamic conceptualisation. Br J Soc Work 43:135–153. https://doi.org/10.1093/bjsw/bcr181
O'Leary P, Tsui MS (2019) The base of social work: relationship, client, evidence or values? Int Soc Work 62(5):1327–1328. https://doi.org/10.1177/0020872819875006
Pai CJ (2020) Jen Qing society and ethics for social work practice: dilemmas and alternatives. Hung Yeh Publications, Taipei

Tsui MS (2001) Towards a culturally sensitive model of social work supervision in Hong Kong. Unpublished PhD thesis, Faculty of Social Work, University of Toronto, Toronto

Tsui MS (2003) The supervisory relationship of Chinese social workers in Hong Kong. Clin Superv 22(2):99–120. https://doi.org/10.1300/J001v22n02_07

Tsui MS (2005) Social work supervision: contexts and concepts. Sage, Thousand Oaks

Tsui MS, Chan RKH (1995) Divergence and convergence: in search of a common base of the notion of the welfare state in China and in the West. J Int Comp Soc Welf 11(1):42–55. https://doi.org/10.1080/17486839508412586

Tylor EB (1871) Primitive culture. Murray, London

Yang KS (1981) Social orientation and individual modernity among Chinese students in Taiwan. J Soc Psychol 113:159–170. https://doi.org/10.1080/00224545.1981.9924368

Social Work in Extremis: Human Rights, Necropolitics, and Post-human Onto-ethics

24

Goetz Ottmann and Iris Silva Brito

Contents

Introduction	480
Social Work and Post-humanism	482
The Problem with Western Humanism	483
Post-humanism and Universal Human Rights	485
Reconstructing Universal Principles: A Bottom-Up Approach	486
Value Plurality and Collaborative Normative Neutrality	487
Post-humanism, Ethics, and International Social Work	488
Conclusion	494
References	495

Abstract

International social workers inserted into crises contexts in the global South need concepts and theories in order to make sense of local circumstances and conditions and to inform their practice. This chapter applies a critical posthumanist lens to such conflict situations. Post-humanism, as shall emerge, deconstructs the term 'human' and its associated socio-political significance viewing 'human' as a contested hierarchical category (Braidotti, 2013) at the core of a biopolitics involving "life itself" (Agamben, 1998). Employing a critical post-humanist lens could expose decisions such as ending the Western military intervention in Afghanistan as acts of necropolitics, Mbembe's term denoting policies that decide over life and death (Mbembe, 2019). A post-humanist analysis could be used to highlight the fragility of supposedly inalienable human rights. The question

---

G. Ottmann (✉)
School of Social Work, Federation University Australia, Berwick, VIC, Australia
e-mail: g.ottmann@federation.edu.au

I. S. Brito
Australian College of Applied Professions (ACAP), Discipline of Social Work, Melbourne, Australia
e-mail: iris.brito@acap.edu.au

raised in this chapter is whether this kind of deconstruction of humanist universals that brings to light ethno-centric arrogance as well as brutality and cruelty can assist social workers to make sense of the events unleashed by militants in Afghanistan or Mozambique's Cabo Delgado province and ultimately lead to better social work practice.

Keywords

International social work · Critique of western modernity · Onto-ethics · Human rights · Post-colonialism · Post-humanism

Introduction

While writing this chapter, troops of a United States (US)-led Western alliance were withdrawn from Afghanistan in a bewilderingly uncoordinated fashion; the Taliban were overrunning Afghan government troops supported by the West; and Taliban leaders formed a new government. In little more than a week, a 20 year-long experiment aimed at installing a moderate Islamic, democratic government based on a template derived from European enlightenment was brought to a rather abrupt halt. Afghan government troops that were supposed, in US President Biden's terms, to step up and fight for their liberal democratic freedom failed to do so. Their refusal to fight in defence of Western ideals administered by a corrupt local elite saw the crumbling of human rights and the rule of law. At the blink of an eye, the liberal freedom of exploitative global capitalist commodification was replaced by very different patriarchal social norms, laws, and exploitative economic systems justified by Islamist beliefs benefiting the victor. Within the space of a week, the human rights and the protection they afforded vanished – resulting in the displacement of thousands of citizens at risk of violent retributions. Those who were left behind faced the prospects of testing their entitlements under the new Islamist colonising power equipped with the latest biopolitical administrative technologies and military hardware – placed in the hands of the previous pro-Western Afghan government to ensure peace and fair and democratic elections.

Another conflict that attracted less international media attention was the insurgency in Mozambique's Cabo Delgado province that started around 2017 but has roots that reach back decades. Here a local Muslim majority eventually radicalised by Jihadist fighters from Tanzania and further afield overran a weak national army killing thousands of mainly Christian civilians forcing hundreds of thousands (around 800,000 in November 2021) to seek security in bulging refugee camps further south that lacked security alongside basic sanitation and health facilities. While this local uprising had Islamist tinges, local commentators largely agreed that the rank and file of the insurrection consisted of poor farmers, fishers, and labourers that joined the movement locally known as Al Shabab (not linked to the Somali group with a similar name) in order to further their financial prospects (Almeida dos Santos 2020). Joining the insurrection gave them access to a wide range of privileges and resources that can be appropriated at gunpoint. The Mozambique government and its – at the time – US allies, while initially referring to the group as criminals, increasingly saw Al Shabab as a product of Global Jihad and thus a form of terrorism with foreign roots – despite the fact that links to ISIS and other Jihadist movements were forged much later in the uprising. While there are numerous similarities with the Afghan conflict including the poorly paid, porous, and undisciplined nature of the national armed forces that allegedly formed one of the sources of Al Shabab's supply of military hardware, the unequal distribution of resources along the lines of ethnic groups, the growing importance of mineral and hydrocarbon deposits exploited by foreign multinationals largely benefitting national elites, and the dissatisfaction with the national leadership (Almeida dos Santos 2020), there are also decisive differences. Al Shabab has become known for its extreme brutality (perhaps more so than the Taliban) using the physical dismemberment, maiming of children, sexual violence, abductions, and pillaging to terrorise and traumatise local ethnic and religious minorities to dislodge them, forcing them give up their livelihoods.

International social workers inserted into contexts such as the above need concepts and theories in order to make sense of local circumstances and conditions and to inform their practice. This chapter applies a critical post-humanist lens to the above conflicts. Post-humanism, as shall emerge, deconstructs the term 'human' and its associated sociopolitical significance, viewing 'human' as a contested hierarchical category (Braidotti 2013) at the core of a biopolitics involving 'life itself' (Agamben 1998). Employing a critical post-humanist lens could expose decisions such as ending the Western military intervention in Afghanistan as acts of necropolitics, Mbembe's term denoting policies that decide over life and death (Mbembe 2019). A post-humanist analysis could be used to highlight the fragility of supposedly inalienable human rights. The question raised in this chapter is whether this kind of deconstruction of humanist universals that brings to light ethnocentric arrogance as well as brutality and cruelty can assist social workers to make sense of the events unleashed by militants in Afghanistan or Mozambique's Cabo Delgado province and ultimately lead to better social work practice.

The authors argue that at an ontological and epistemological level, such a reconceptualisation has a number of important implications that could strengthen international social work (ISW) practice. The post-humanist critique can bring to the fore a Western-centrism that still permeates contemporary ISW, community development, and Western humanitarian interventions. And while the professional bodies associated with ISW have taken considerable steps to address these – in Braidotti's words – 'bad habits' (i.e., the tendency to see some designated people as 'lesser' or the 'Other' of Western modernity) (Braidotti 2013), this deconstruction has started only recently and its outcome is, as yet, undetermined (Bormann 2021; Heilmann and Rosskopf 2021). It is important to point out that critical post-humanism harbours a risk. It has the potential to undermine the human rights fabric anchored in international laws providing very little to replace it. Given this, its critical lens has to be applied with care and with respect for universal principles. This chapter will provide an introduction to the work of Rosi Braidotti, Achille Mbembe, and Giorgio Agamben as three very different instalments in critical post-humanist scholarship and hereafter perhaps too loosely referred to as "critical post-humanism" (Braidotti 2016), in order to explore how and to what extent their oeuvre can be applied to social work *in extremis*. (An attempt was made to 'translate' the at times extremely dense and complex writings of these three thinkers into simpler terminology in order to make their work more accessible to a wider audience. As a result, some of the intricacies and complexities of the arguments and the performativity of the language used in the original are lost. The term "social work *in extremis*" is borrowed from Michael Lavalette and Vasilios Ioakimidis (2011) Social work in extremis: Lessons for social work internationally. Polity Press.) The chapter illustrates how social work and its underpinning onto-ethics is fundamentally shaped by discussions of a political philosophical nature as the post-humanism of these three authors disrupts the flow of ethics and the ethical flow of culture from the global North to the global South (Blaut 1993).

We should point out at the outset that the kind of ethics we are primarily discussing in this chapter is not that of morality answering questions such as 'what should be done'. Rather, it is an ethics that is tied up with the way we define and think about the world, how we structure it, the kind of role and status we assign ourselves within it, and, above all, how we imagine how the world might change and what it/we might become. This onto-ethics, as Elizabeth Grosz calls it, is intensely political inasmuch as it deconstructs the assumptions that underpin our social, cultural, and economic fabric, the sociocultural hierarchies they generate, and the possibilities for change that flow from them (Grosz 2017). Because of its focus on the link between the way we conceptualise and imagine the world and how this shapes our future, this has been termed an 'ethics of becoming'. In the work of Braidotti, Mbembe, and Agamgen, this ethics is used to bring into view how the way Western humanism has been deployed often resulted in devastating consequences for vulnerable people in the global South exposed to social, economic, or political crises – often resulting from the extremely brutal, exploitative capitalism that forms the neocolonial underbelly of Western modernity. Their work calls for a much more reflective and accountable humanism that carefully considers its impact not only in relation to people but also to the wider environment. This chapter outlines how this 'ethics of becoming' within the work of the three critical post-humanists gives rise to major questions as to what it is to be human reflecting on the utility of this approach for social work *in extremis*.

Social Work and Post-humanism

Social work is a product of the eighteenth-century Enlightenment with its social imaginary based on the teleology of a civilising process (Elias 1994) driven by rational thought gradually overcoming "faith, superstition or revelation" (Moffatt and Irving 2002). While the relational 'art' of social work is often mentioned or even celebrated in social work literature, social work has been largely consolidated and professionalised on the basis of a modern canon of Western philosophy, academic theories, and empirical research (Healy 2007). Mbembe, Braidotti, and Agamben, the three thinkers this chapter is focused on, take critical post-humanist approaches that seeks to break with Euro-centric humanism in order to move beyond and redefine it. To be sure, these authors are at odds with some of the key tenets of ISW. And readers who approach them with an expectation to glean from them pearls of wisdom that might advance their human rights-based practice will walk away perplexed if not frustrated. Post-humanists are deeply sceptical about the power of humanism, modernity, and Western articulations of universal human rights. They attempt to develop a new ethics that is not grounded in humanism's core concept of 'the human' and her moral rights and duties to others but in life itself – "bare life" as Agamben (1998) calls it. The strength of critical post-humanist thought and its relevance for international social work, we will argue, is the deconstruction, suspension, and peeling back of humanist layers of taken-for-granted assumptions to arrive at new insights and new possibilities. Having said this, it is also true that the critique resonates strongly with a societal moral fabric which has implications for social work practice. It should be also pointed out that, while Braidotti and Agamben declare affinities with anti-humanism, their writings are clearly informed by progressive ideals and values that crystallised during the Enlightenment, such as "freedom, social justice, anti-racism, openness to others, respect and human decency and diversity and the affirmation of the positivity of difference" (Braidotti 2013). Indeed, Braidotti states that she has "no difficulty in recognizing that her ideals are perfectly compatible with the best humanist values" (Braidotti 2013). For Braidotti, critical post-humanist theory is a "tool to help us re-think the basic unit of reference for the human" to develop an all-inclusive community based on an "ethics of becoming" (Braidotti 2013).

The Problem with Western Humanism

The rationale for the critical post-humanist projects advanced by these three thinkers is encapsulated in the argument that Western humanism has been "complicit in a long tradition of marginalization and violence" (Cloyes 2010) that defined certain human beings as 'Other'. For critical post-humanists, the term 'human' is a label that has hierarchical, normative, and ultimately ethical connotations. Braidotti and Mbembe take issue with the fact that for too long the label and its associated rights were the "almost exclusive prerogative of white, secularly religious, heteronormative men, speaking a standard language, and that were full citizens of a well-functioning polity" (Braidotti 2016). The remainder of humanity (in the global North and South) is viewed as 'lesser than' or as 'Other' and is left struggling to be recognised as human.

Braidotti, Agamben, and also Mbembe aim to alter the foundational concepts underpinning Western modernity. By doing so, they seek to reweave our cognitive fabric to prompt us to think and act differently. Braidotti argues that Western humanism has become interwoven with Western foundation myths that turn Western culture into the pinnacle of human development rendering opaque the many failings of the Western humanist legacy (Braidotti 2013). Agamben highlights that the institutions produced by Western humanism enable the creation of spaces where the rule of law is suspended and where citizens are stripped of their rights and social significance reducing them to life itself. Agamben calls such spaces "zones of exception" (Agamben 1998). There are parallels between Agamben's 'zones of exception' and Stuart Rees' (following a humanist trajectory) "cruelty as policy" suggesting applying Rees' insights that zones of exception are created by omission (i.e., choosing to ignore Greek border guards' cruel treatment of asylum seekers), by design (i.e., the creation of spaces such as the Guantanamo Bay detention centre designed to actively circumnavigate humanitarian law and human rights legislation), by collusion (i.e., supporting regimes or institutions that fail to uphold human rights), by pragmatism (i.e., the decision not to fund humanitarian activities in some regions that are of lesser strategic or geopolitical significance), or by deception (e.g., the Tuskergee Syphilis study) (Rees 2020, p. 82). The upshot of this is that in these zones of exception, public servants or administrators (e.g., of humanitarian agencies in the mentioned cases) decide who is and who is not human based on factors (e.g., funding priorities, geo-political considerations) that routinely curb the universality of human rights. Those exposed to this dehumanising process have their social significance taken potentially reducing them to mere biological facts without social meaning. As a result, they can be disposed of or left to perish without social or legal consequence (Agamben 1998; Braidotti 2013). Critical post-humanists seek to uncover and rally against these exclusionary, authoritarian tendencies that have survived in or are actively fostered by the global North. For this reason, critical post-humanists such as Braidotti and Agamben argue that Western humanism is no longer fit for purpose. And that rather than focusing on the human whose rights are supposedly universal but are in fact tied to one's position within a well-functioning political economy, it is time to rebuild political philosophy starting with life itself (Agamben 1998; Braidotti 2013).

Applying this argument to the refugees in the above cases would prompt social workers to recognise that most of the structures and systems of meaning that ordered (and protected) their lives have been stripped away leaving them utterly vulnerable. However, employing an ethics of becoming would also encourage them to see the potential for change as it potentially encourages social workers to reflect on the myriad of ways in which events may be lived. This thinking ethics (as opposed to a religious ethics that establishes behavioural norms) seeks to reshape Western civilization, to give life to new possibilities by creating new theoretical lenses through which to view the world. For Mbembe, this opens "... the way to an investigation of the possibility of a *politics of fellowship* [italics in the original]" (Mbembe 2019, p. 73) where people are afforded equality of dignity.

It is the deconstruction of old and the crafting of new lenses that links Braidotti's project with that of Mbembe and, more generally, that of decolonisation and post-colonialism. For Mbembe, decolonisation articulates the hope in the coming of a universal and fraternal community of equals once colonialism and racism have been abolished. In other words, Mbembe and also Braidotti focus on the individualism, parochial nationalism, racism, ethnocentrism, and imperialist ambitions that have warped and perverted humanist values. Clearly, this has implications for ISW in contexts such as Afghanistan and Mozambique, countries that through the prism of the West (including some humanitarian aid organisations) are still seen as 'inferior' in terms of human and cultural development. In the case of Afghanistan, this hierarchy at the core of the Western worldview is audible in the way members of the US Committee of Foreign Affairs explained the failure of the US-led intervention in Afghanistan, namely in terms of a failure to appreciate the level of cultural underdevelopment of a 'primitive' people simply not ready for modern democracy (Committee on Foreign Affairs 2020). Mbembe's and Braidotti's critical posthumanist critique brings to light how the globalisation of Western modernity, in Afghanistan's case advanced through the US-led intervention, devalues and in places extinguishes local forms of knowledge and thinking (see also Escobar 1995; Grosfoguel 2013; Quijano and Ennis 2000; Sousa Santos de 2014).

Post-humanism and Universal Human Rights

At the core of the post-human critique of universal human rights is the argument that human rights thinking and rhetoric have come to the end of their 'use-by' date as they are simply another manifestation of colonising governmental power used to condone a wide range of atrocities (Agamben 1998; Braidotti 2013; Mbembe 2019). Agamben argues that the political rights and entitlements of citizens are defined by politico-legal thresholds. On one side of the threshold, the law potentially maintains the rights of citizens, on the other, people are mere bodies that have no political persona and, as a result, have no rights. Biopolitics suspends sociopolitical rights, treating humans as mere biological bodies at the mercy of those who decide on the value or non-value of life as such (Agamben 1998 [1995], p. 91). Mbembe calls this generalised reduction of human beings to biological existence that can be extinguished without political or legal consequences "necropolitics" (Mbembe 2006, p. 19). Similarly, Braidotti argues that the implications of necropolitics are that the structuration of the exercise of power issuing from law and universal values and morals are no longer in existence thereby unleashing an unrestricted "right to kill, maim, rape and destroy the life of others" (Braidotti 2013, p. 123). For critical post-humanists, the kind of universalism advanced by Western powers in the global South serves as a smokescreen to mask the fact that people all too often are unable to summon the protection of any right and are at the mercy of individuals or administrative processes that decide who is to live and who is not. This line of argument resonates with the countless human rights abuses witnessed by social workers *in extremis* and the sense that people living in a 'state of exception' are vulnerable, traumatised, and often without any rights (Heilmann and Rosskopf 2021; Hölscher et al. 2020). While this line of thinking can shed some light on social work *in extremis*, it is easy to overstretch this thesis. For example, in the late 1990s, there were moments in the Afghan war when locals (and to a lesser degree humanitarian workers) were stripped of their rights and when the bodies of dead fighters were lining the main streets of provincial capitals. However, these liminal moments of transition occurred during a transition period when the Taliban (with almost complete disregard for the Geneva Convention) stamped their authority on existing allegiances and regional power structures turning a region into a zone of exception allowing for a moment of murderous excesses, retribution, and vengeance before imposing new rules, obligations, and (non-Western) rights.

Braidotti posits that one's 'humanity' and by extension human rights are determined by a political economy that produces different degrees of humanity in line with a "value assigned to human life in a particular given context following a more instrumental logic of opportunistic exploitation of life itself" (Braidotti 2013, p. 123). This interpretation is transforming politics into a machinery of cold instrumental rationality (Agamben 1998; Mbembe 2019) and warfare into economically and emotionally efficient deployment of intelligent, technological weaponry delivered from the constraints of international treaties and conventions (Braidotti 2013, pp. 122–3). The drone strike that was launched on 29 August 2021 to destroy an ISIS safe house in retribution for the bomb attack at Kabul airport that left American soldiers dead and a nation's pride wounded serves a case in point. Killing 10 Afghan civilians including women and children instead, the rocket brings to light the rawness and econometrics of this kind of necropolitics. The fact that the United Kingdom's Ministry of Defence paid an average of £2380 and as little as £104.17 in compensation for the lives of Afghan civilians its forces killed in error – a value determined by legal principles including past and future losses and local customs – speaks to Braidotti's assessment that the value of a 'human' is the product of a very uneven political economy. It signals that even if on the 'right side' of Agamben's politico-legal threshold, people are not equal and that there is a gradation of human worth that is, as in the West, largely determined by actuarial and legal arguments. Also, comparing the cost of Afghan lives with the average per unit cost of Air-to-Ground AGM -114 Hellfire rocket of US$70,000 (Trevithick 2020) brings into focus the stupendous economic asymmetry that underpins necropolitical interventions and that makes the killing of civilians (i.e., the collateral damage) economically viable. It is this asymmetry that further undermines notions of universal human rights.

Reconstructing Universal Principles: A Bottom-Up Approach

An important issue that emerges within Mbembe's and Braidotti's work is the question of what local or Indigenous epistemologies and models of practice look like that international social workers need to know and respect. How should we define in the global South notions of fairness, justice, reciprocity, and associated rights and obligations that guide and regulate communal life? In many parts of the global South, the ardent critique of anti-colonial scholarship and the re-appreciation of local culture and traditions has given rise to a lively, celebrated counterculture grounded in the knowledge, art, and artisanal practices of local and Indigenous communities (Ife 2001; Silva-Brito and Ottmann 2020; Tascon 2020). Interestingly, Mbembe dismisses such epistemological developments arguing that after more than half a century, "we still do not have a precise idea of what a 'truly decolonized knowledge' might look like. Nor do we have a theory of knowledge as such that might compellingly underpin the African injunction to decolonize" (Mbembe 2019, p. 56). For Mbembe, the recognition of local knowledge formations is a mere 'compensatory act' geared to rehabilitate a denigrated and defeated 'Other'. Here, Mbembe's theorising succumbs to a negative ontology as it forecloses the possibility to escape the ontological and epistemological enclosure of the colonising West. Yet an ethics of becoming would affirm that constantly shifting, interdependent constellations of ideas, processes, and systems always generate the possibility of change, intensive experimentation, and 'becoming' and, ultimately, the emergence of new hybrid forms of being (Deleuze and Guttary 1987). In other words, even in contexts epistemologically profoundly disrupted by colonialism, such as Afghanistan and Mozambique, there are always possibilities for new, hybrid forms of local knowledge to emerge – despite (or perhaps because) of ontological and epistemological limitations imposed by the colonisers.

That being said, Mbembe has a point. After half a millennium of colonisation and globalisation, there is not much knowledge left that could be termed 'authentically' local, Indigenous, African, or Persian for that matter. Knowledge formations that emerge more or less in isolation are, some exceptions notwithstanding, a thing of a pre-Columbian past. What survives are hybrid cultures that have adapted to modern global systems of domination and exploitation while defending some cultural reference points and meaning. However, through this process of forced adaptation, many communities have developed social alternatives to the globalising Western modernity that, although they may not be grounded in a discrete epistemology, are nevertheless important local forms of 'knowledge in practice' that international social workers need to understand and appreciate (Ife 2001; Silva-Brito and Ottmann 2020; Tascon 2020). And while it may be difficult to find an epistemological framework that has successfully uncoupled itself from Western Modernity, local life worlds, forms of knowledge, culture, identities, and strategies do matter. Yet they are easily disparaged by Western-centric social work and its truth claims rooted in a worldview that sees the global South as inferior. This has led to discussions whether ISW needs to relinquish Western humanism and its associated universal ethico-legal frameworks and reconstruct itself following critical post-humanists in order to be compatible with local conceptualisations of reciprocity, dignity, and justice in the zones of exception of the Global South (see, for example, Bell 2011; Hölscher et al. 2020).

Value Plurality and Collaborative Normative Neutrality

The decentring of Western ethics with the aim to produce a more pluralistic reflexive ethics has given rise to two distinct approaches that try to translate the onto-ethics into a moral fabric that is not based on Western philosophy. Latin American de-colonial scholars, rather than producing an anti-European fundamentalism, call for a radical universalism based on the notion that there are many truths arrived at from a variety of perspectives that, however, coincide in important ways (Grosfoguel 2013, Sousa Santos de 2014). This position is largely grounded in widely shared notions of common sense, norms, and values produced by communities in the margins of society elevating notions such as human dignity to universally principles.

Braidotti takes a different approach. She derives new norms from a collective deliberative process based on normatively neutral, all-inclusive structures. She asserts that this will result in the "[e]laboration of new normative frameworks ..." (Braidotti 2013, p. 92) and the production of a new 'ethics of becoming' that is collectively enacted and produced through experimentation directed at "becoming the best we are capable of" (Braidotti 2013, p. 93). In other words, Braidotti's approach creates the possibility of deriving ethical principles through experimental deliberation from the ground up. This should allow for the inclusion of non-Western (e.g., Islamic, Indigenous) ethical frameworks and could possibly circumvent the 'clash of cultures' that seemed to undermine interventions in Afghanistan and Mozambique's Cabo Delgado conflict. However, the outcome of this process would depend on whether normatively neutral relational positions can be achieved at the outset of the process. It is also important to note that the left-libertarian principles the process is based on can be easily subverted by vocal minorities that use the process to take control to impose illiberal, authoritarian values, potentially leading to very brutal outcomes. Braidotti argues that self-reflection, dialogue, and compromise, processes that social workers should be thoroughly familiar with, can help us to overcome anthropocentrism, racism, ethno-centrism, parochialism, homophobia, xenophobia, and sexism, along with other 'bad habits'. It is not easy to see how this could be implemented into practice with people and communities whose 'bad habits' are deeply ingrained in their identity and self-understanding. Clearly highlighting the limits of the above cultural relativist approaches are the calls from a minority of Ugandan social workers during the deliberations leading up to the 2014 Global Ethical Principle statement (see section below) who in the name of 'African culture' supported the vicious anti-gay legislation introduced (but later repealed) by the Museveni government in 2013/2014 to make homosexuality a crime punishable by death. Indeed, as history should have taught us by now, communities are not all inclusive by default. Indeed, this insight generated the post-WWII consensus that ultimately led to the drafting of the Universal Declaration of Human Rights.

Post-humanism, Ethics, and International Social Work

International social work (ISW) has become the focus of an intense critique that probes the degree to which (a) the Western liberal worldview that permeates its core assumptions and values is compatible with the values of communities in the global South and, more radically still, (b) whether the concept of a 'human' at the core of universal human rights and her way of knowing ought to form the basis of ISW (see, for example, Bell 2011; Healy 2007; Hölscher et al. 2020; Sewpaul and Henrickson 2019; Tascon 2020). The critique highlights how Western modernity not only exploits the global South economically, it also justifies this exploitation by assigning people of the global South a lower stage of human development thus entrapping them in an ontological web (and its political implications) whose rules are made by and that exculpate the global North. It posits that the global North consciously or semi-consciously imposes multilayered and complex relations of power onto the global South, colonizing its way of knowing, culture, life worlds, and life itself.

Epistemological strands of this critique have been taken on board by numerous social work academics alerting us that the imposition of universal standards in ISW education is unlikely to empower the people it is supposed to serve if it replicates an epistemological hierarchy that places a Western-centric body of knowledge at the top of a developmental hierarchy (Bormann 2021; Gray and Webb 2008). Indeed, commentators have argued that ISW exponents run the risk of perpetuating "cultural and intellectual imperialism" and "discouraging development or valuing of Indigenous models by promoting dominant western social imaginaries and practices" (Hokenstad [2014, pp. 172–173] in Bormann 2021, p. 49). This raises the question whether and how international social workers of the global North can be taught to feel, think, and act beyond their cultural and experiential horizon. And while critical whiteness, privilege, racism, and epistemic violence are increasingly being discussed in social work programmes of the global North in an attempt to sensitise social work students to potential asymmetries of power in social work and to change their perspectives on the people they will be working with (Heilmann and Rosskopf 2021), a number of authors have highlighted gaps in the translation of decolonising scholarship into practice (Hölscher et al. 2020; Melter 2018; Schmelz 2021).

ISW has also become the focus of a critique from within. For some social workers, the framework contained within the Global Statement of Ethical Principles (disseminated with slightly different content both by the International Federation of Social Workers [IFSW] and the International Association of Social Workers [IASSW]), with its ethical grounding in universal human rights, social justice, and democracy (see, for example, Staub-Bernasconi 2014) can ring hollow in conflict zones they find themselves in. Indeed, some have questioned the philosophical and ethical premises that underpin the deployment of international social workers querying whether an ethics grounded in Western values should be imposed on the global South (Hugman 2008). Others have extended this critique to the role and purpose of ISW (see, for example, Hölscher et al. 2020; Mupedziswa and Sinkamba 2014). Such criticism from within has amplified questions whether ISW is suffering from an ethnocentric 'blind spot' and whether a de-colonial or post-human deconstruction could assist social workers to make better sense of people and the processes that shape their life worlds (Hölscher et al. 2020).

The Global Social Work Statement of Ethical Principles promoted by IASSW and IFSW, albeit with slightly different commentaries, could be regarded as a case in point. Although an introductory statement asserts that the current version was the result of an extensive consultation in an attempt to counter Western hegemony in social work practice, education and research, and an effort to work towards a decolonising agenda (IASSW n.d.), it is very much framed in the language of universal human rights. Traces of value pluralism, ethical reflexivity, and a decolonisation of social work can be found in the preamble asserting, with Nussbaum and Sen (Nussbaum 2000; Sen 2001), that vulnerability is a universal human condition and that people are "always embedded in societies and dependent on their socio-political, economic and cultural structures and conventions" (IASSW n.d.). Furthermore, the IASSW version of the Global Ethical Principles instructs that the statement should be regarded as layered and that they, not unlike UN charters, "may be amplified and/or adapted at national and/or regional levels" (IASSW n.d.). In this sense, the Global Ethical Principles asserts a grounding in Western philosophy and human rights legislation but encourages a culturally sensitive interpretation. As highlighted by Jane Orme, this insistence on a Western humanist framework can become problematic when Western practitioners find themselves in situation where they have to rely on codified principles as they are likely to interpret these in the context of the country of their origin rather than in the context of the global South (Banks 2012). In other words, this approach faces the danger that it will be interpreted as a humanism that originates in the global North with all its trappings of cultural superiority – rather than starting in the global South as Mbembe quietly hoped.

By contrast, the goals promoted under the Global Agenda for Social Work and Social Development (GASWSD) (The 2014 definition promoted by IASSW and IFSW reads: "Social work is a practice-based profession and an academic discipline that promotes social change and development, social cohesion, and the empowerment and liberation of people. Principles of social justice, human rights, collective responsibility, and respect for diversities are central to social work. Underpinned by theories of social work, social sciences, humanities and Indigenous knowledges, social work engages people and structures to address life challenges and enhance wellbeing". The next iteration of the Global Agenda for Social Work gave rise to the following five statements that are currently being discussed with the peak organisations of ISW: (1) Valuing Social Work as an Essential Service; (2) Co-building Inclusive Social Transformation; (3) Ubuntu: 'I am because we are'; (4) Transforming Social Protections Systems; and (5) Promoting Diversity and the Power of Joint Social Action) has been shaped much more profoundly by social workers seeking to decolonise ISW. Indeed, a growing number of social work scholars and practitioners argue that a post-colonial paradigm of rights and global collaboration should be based on extensive consultations arriving at concepts that are more respectful of the ways of knowing of local and/or Indigenous communities (Sewpaul and Henrickson 2019), thus creating the possibility to recreate the idea of social development in a way that is no longer captured by a hierarchical understanding of human development with the West and particularly Europe at its apex. Such a rendering can potentially give rise to the kind of political fellowship of equals Mbembe is dreaming of. Indeed, the IFSW's 2-year consultation process culminating in the publication of a Global Agenda in 2020 differs substantially from its predecessor both in presentation and language. Whereas the previous version was much more aligned with Western ideas of development and rights, the current version focuses on interdependence and cooperation and the codesign of collaborations to further human dignity and rights of all people (see footnote 2). In this sense, the most recent rendition of the Global Agenda is based on a compromise. The core of the new Global Agenda is decidedly and self-consciously more culturally pluralist making use of a transcultural language, and there is a much stronger emphasis that processes should be based on a collaborative, all-inclusive, bottom-up approach that Braidotti would probably endorse. Still, some of its aims strongly resonate with the United Nations' Sustainable Development Goals, such as "social transformation" promoting participatory democracy, gender equality, economic sustainability, and climate justice alongside anti-racist action and a commitment to promote Indigenous knowledge and the decolonisation of social work. Indeed, the most recent Global Agenda statements would suggest that the formation of a global consensus arriving at universally endorsed onto-ethical principles is possible.

However, upon a closer reading, one might gain the impression that the current version no longer encapsulates the 'progressive' content (i.e., social justice has been translated into climate justice) treasured in parts of the global North and South. Also, its call for "a greater acceptance of diversity" seems to be more elusive in terms of the recognition of LGBTIQ and other minority communities, and the fairly well-defined human rights have been replaced with the much more intangible "rights of all people" (see also Ife 2001). Thus, the accommodation of a more reflexive value plurality in the current Global Statement introduces ambiguities. In light of the above, one wonders whether in the context of social work *in extremis* the new, value diverse Global Agenda will ultimately fail to serve those who need our support the most (see also Ife 2001). This leads us to a dilemma discussed at length in the social work literature (Banks 2012; Gray 2005; Gray and Webb 2008; Healy 2007; Hugman 2008; Ife 2001).

Human rights were a fairly radical and ambitious proposition that has challenged the core values of communities in the global North and South since their inception. They are still controversial today precisely for the fact that they enabled persons or groups ostracised or regarded as inferior or worthless by other more powerful groups to claim full humanity. It should not come as a surprise that human rights are not particularly popular among conservative elites. Human rights form the bedrock of the claims of many minorities and disadvantaged majorities for recognition and equal opportunity. Progressive Western humanism with all its faults, has been used by Indigenous communities to mount a defence against the murderous encroachment of the *latifundium* and consolidating agrobusiness. Human rights enable activists to showcase the inhumane treatment Indigenous people are subjected to. And while communal values may diverge from the Western liberal ethics packaged in the charters of the United Nations (UN), universal human rights are nevertheless strategically deployed to voice grievances and demands at a national and international level. Furthermore, observers have pointed out that human rights are being creatively adapted and re-elaborated to fit local contexts in much the same way as the Global Statement of Ethical Principles asks us to (see, for example, Ife 2001; Tascon 2016). More importantly still, in conflict zones where the rule of law is suspended, universal human rights supported by a massive humanitarian infrastructure are often the only hope to find some relief and protection from lawless brutality. Clearly, that hope is all too often disappointed highlighting an increasing gap between normative human rights claims and their ability to impact on social realities *in extremis* (see, for example, Eberlei 2018). Still, the concept of human rights allows communities to bring to light this gap and to transform it into an entitlement.

Within the operational context of social work *in extremis*, universal human rights are not something that ought to be dispensed with lightly. With all their shortcomings, human rights promote a powerful social imaginary that permeates most aspects of ISW (Hugman 2008). In extremis, human rights provide an aspirational goal, benchmark, source of empowerment, organisational vision, and a practice framework (Staub-Bernasconi 2014). In conjunction with the wider fabric of international conventions, they form an important legal and political reference point. Humanitarian ideals have spawned a sizeable network of organisations that collaborate across geographical, religious, and political divides. These networks still manage to attract considerable resources that are often used to strengthen local civil society. More importantly still, human rights inspire hope.

Post-colonial scholars have unmasked important deficiencies of a human rights-based ISW and have contributed to the emergence of a more reflexive approach that increasingly informs the vision, mission, and mandate of ISW (Sewpaul and Henrickson 2019). They have contributed to an emergent profession that is perhaps less dogmatic and more able to valorise local socioeconomic and cultural contexts (Bormann 2021). This new reflective ISW is increasingly able to recognise that the global North might be, in all sorts of ways, the aggressor – not the good guy as the human rights discourse it promotes would suggest. However, this value pluralistic approach offer little in the way of a viable alternative to an ethico-legal fabric that informs conventions and legislation (see also Ife 2001). Furthermore, while a post-humanist approach can help to make analytical sense of certain conflict situations by urging us to reflect on our subject location and to peel back some of the metaphysical assumptions and cultural layers that underpin universal claims of Euro-centric enlightenment, it gives less rise to a positive, nourishing vision. Furthermore, several commentators have argued that post-humanist deconstruction has a tendency toward a negative ontology, which leads to a very dark place indeed (Deranty 2007; Negri 2011; Prozorov 2014; Ziarek 2008). For example, the only escape from repressive structures Agamben or Braidotti are able to offer is their suspension, the rendering inoperative of the apparatus of power, to step out of the logics of law and sovereignty (Agamben 1998 [1995]). In other words, the power to lead out of injustice is vested in nomadic life operating outside the confines of stratified society and the state. Many commentators doubt that this theoretical approach can be fruitfully translated into practice and argue that it results in political paralysis (Deranty 2007; Deutscher 2008; Prozorov 2014; Ziarek 2008).

In his more recent work, Mbembe argues that we are witnessing the end of democracy as democracies are turned into fortresses fighting a continued war on terror due to the spectacular escalation of destruction driven by market forces and war (Mbembe 2017 [2016]). The case of Mozambique's Cabo Delgado highlights that these forces unleash a raw and deadly brutality associated with the political turmoil that is often the hallmark of 'failed states'. In Mozambique's case, the failure of the state to protect its citizens is associated with a great number of factors, key amongst which is a case of corrupt, predatory global capitalism that depleted state resources to a point where it affected all state-run services – particularly those outside the capital. Mozambique's fiscal meltdown was the result of a US$2.2 billion secret deal to develop a fishery industry signed by the Mozambique government in 2013. Financial improprieties, the alleged misallocation of funds to buy arms, and the alleged payment of massive 'kick-backs' of at least $136 m to influential individuals (i.e., members of the Guebuza and Nyusi governments and Credit Suisse employees) caused the International Monetary Fund to cancel loans, which contributed to the collapse of Mozambique's currency (Almeida dos Santos 2020; Holmey 2021). Other factors included an alliance between illicit business and Islamic militants, the influence of ISIS stirring a Muslim uprising against the political domination of clans located in the south, the attempt of local 'big men' to gain control over the resource-rich north, political wrangling between the two main power-brokers, and the Nyusi government's attempt to use of Russian and South African mercenaries to fight insurgents (Almeida dos Santos 2020), not to mention the economic displacement of low-income communities due to global warming. The result was the emergence of a 'new war' of extraordinary brutality. Braidotti's work needs to be adapted to theorise these 'new wars' that form within failed states. Mbembe's more recent work argues that they are the product of an inversion of colonial violence where the identification of a common enemy has replaced other social bonds resulting in a relentless and obsessive search for the enemy that is right in our midst (Mbembe 2017 [2016]). While this interpretation is thought provoking, it tends to gloss over complexities that social workers deployed in these contexts may find better explained in the work of Kalyvas (2006) or Staniland (2014).

The work of critical post-humanists does not provide a ready-made platform for emancipatory collective action that is organised along the lines of a clearly demarked ethics, praxis, and identity (Deutscher 2008; Ziarek 2008). There is no easily identifiable agent in their work that could take control of historicity. To be sure, Braidotti offers an escape route from the negative ontology that plagues the work of Agamben but also the more recent work of Mbembe. Her philosophical turn to neo-Spinozan monadic ontology and her embrace of an 'ethics of becoming' grounded in an all-inclusive, relationally normatively neutral community of 'self-constituting matter' embarked on a journey of discovery of what it might mean to be 'the best we can possibly be' opens new possibilities – and risks (i.e., what do we do if a well-organised illiberal minority hijacks the process to supplant inclusive collective with authoritarian structures?). More perplexing still, because in Braidotti's work, the basic unit is 'self-constituting matter', we would first need to make sure we understand what is meant by 'we'.

ISW education tries to balance universal and local claims of human dignity, worth, and justice. On the one hand, its vision and mandate states that every human being has the same inalienable rights. Cultural distinctions can be acknowledged but ultimately will not alter the relevance and authority of these rights (Healy 2007). On the other, the critical post-humanists discussed above argue that ethnic, sociocultural, and other distinctions are of crucial importance and that universal norms of morality are only possible if some groups are excluded. However, there is an alternative to this dichotomous reading. It is possible to view the break of critical post-humanists with Western modernity as merely a critical distancing that ultimately affirms the values of progressive humanism. This is the perspective employed in this chapter. To be sure, this is not an easy, immediate solution but one of constant negotiation that traverses the kind of intellectual territory outlined in this chapter.

In early-October 2021, the Mozambique government in alliance with Rwandan and South African armed forces gained the upper hand over the insurgents in Cabo Delgado encouraging displaced families to return to their homes. Rather than embarking on an intervention with the US forces, which would have symbolised a continuation of the 'war against terror' and the significance of 9/11, it sought an 'African solution'. As it turned out, this enforced peace did not endure and the outcome of the conflict is as yet uncertain (at the time of writing this chapter, the insurgents regrouped and the war continued). Mozambique civil society organisations are sceptical about the outcome of armed intervention. They have long argued against the use of military force in favor of an approach that involves the co-creation of economic and community development strategies (Almeida dos Santos 2020). International social workers may have a role to play in advocating for a peaceful solution and in facilitating deliberations that can accommodate value diversity, perhaps testing out Braidotti's version of an ethics of becoming.

In Afghanistan, the Taliban, once one of the key protagonists within the 'Axis of Evil', look like an increasingly acceptable real political choice as it becomes clear that they form a bulwark against more extreme Islamic forces and the influx of yet more refugees into Europe. Are these early signs of an emergence of a new human in the global South freed from ethno-centrism, racism, and parochialism by the transformative power of 'bare life' (i.e., in the form of the refugee) in the way envisaged by critical post-humanists? Probably not. However, there is a faint possibility that we might be moving out of the shadow of 9/11 and that the dehumanising rhetoric that formed the core of US-led Western geopolitics will give way to new challenges, possibilities, and imaginable solutions with yet uncertain outcomes.

Conclusion

The work of Braidotti, Mbembe, and Agamben has given rise to theories geared to challenge established *doxa* and associated ontological and epistemological divisions; it encourages us to experiment with new ways of 'conceptualising' the world. While these three thinkers claim to break from the normative and hierarchical metaphysical premises associated with Western Enlightenment, they largely tend to do so as part of a critique that reaffirms progressive humanist values. As such, their critique is arguably rooted in strands of progressive, critical thought produced by the Enlightenment (see, for example, Braidotti 2013). Their oeuvre brings into sharp focus some of the dehumanising processes that strip humans of their rights and social significance turning them into mere biological facts – 'bare life'. The concept of necropolitics enables us to recognise that this process is an all-too-common policy 'solutions' of supposedly 'civilised' polities. It enables us to peel back claims embedded in terms such as 'democracy', 'welfare', and 'social wellbeing' that linguistically distort the (un-)ethical principles of murderous pragmatic politics that expose some of us to life-threatening danger. The insight that necropolitics and, by extension, social injustice 'in extremis', is hiding in plain sight (we can recognise its brutal premises in many 'welfare', health, and social care policies not to mention geopolitical interventions) in the global North and South should serve as a call to action, turning the struggle against necropolitics into a concern that is central to social work.

In this sense, their work engenders theoretical approaches, questions, and concepts that can be used to shed new light on situations and contexts that seemed familiar but are actually a discursive mirage generated by claims and expectations of a civilising process rooted in the enlightenment. It has the capacity to shift the focus of social work *in extremis* and can entice us to imagine new solutions based on deliberation and the development of principles endorsed by all parties. The juncture with decolonisation has reinforced post-colonial endeavours to reconceptualise ISW generating widely endorsed (quasi-universal) principles from an extensive and inclusive deliberation process no longer predetermined by a Euro-centric humanist worldview. Thus, this onto-ethics of becoming has the potential to include non-Western civilising processes reducing the danger of a 'clash of cultures'.

This chapter attempted to outline some of the strength and limitations of the work of Braidotti, Agamben, and Mbembe in terms of their application for social work *in extremis*. It illustrated how the onto-ethical strands of their work potentially disrupt social work ethics and practice. The authors argued that the intellectual tenet of critical post-humanism can lead to more a reflexive ethics and potentially a more inclusive practice. However, their radical critique of modernity creates a conundrum as it is less suited to generate firm thresholds that are anchored in internationally ratified conventions that delineate clear benchmarks that can be translated into entitlements that are recognised at least notionally by an international community. In this chapter, we argued that critical post-humanism forms very much part of an enlightenment tradition and as such, it is likely that its tenets will, over time, generate more inclusive principles. What is more, at the onset of the Anthropocene, it is not too difficult to see that the construction of rights rooted in 'life itself' could become a source of hope that nurtures the social imaginary of humanity. However, it is important to bear in mind that critical post-humanism is vulnerable to an infiltration of a socially conservative, illiberal, anti-humanism that has the potential to lead us to very dark places indeed. Still critical post-humanists have developed an important critique that will continue to reshape ISW education; its critical distancing from Euro-centric humanism has created a number of theoretical approaches that will render social work more reflective and inclusive.

References

Agamben G (1998) Homo Saccer: sovereign power and bare life. Stanford University Press
Almeida dos Santos F (2020) War in resource-rich northern Mozambique – six scenarios (CMI). Insight, Issue. www.cmi.no
Banks S (2012) Ethics and values in social work. Macmillan International Higher Education

Bell K (2011) Towards a post-conventional philosophical base for social work. British J Soc Work 42(3):408–423. https://doi.org/10.1093/bjsw/bcr073

Blaut J (1993) The colonizer's model of the world. Geographical diffusionism and Eurocentric history. Guilford Press

Bormann S (2021) Personal and structural prerequisites for international social work education. In: Rosskopf R, Heilman K (eds) International social work and forced migration: developments in African, Arab and European countries. Barbara Budrich

Braidotti R (2013) The posthuman. Polity Press

Braidotti R (2016) Posthuman critical theory. In: Banerji D, Parnjape MR (eds) Critical posthumanism and planetary futures. Springer

Cloyes K (2010) Rethinking biopower: posthumanism, bare life, and emancipatory work. ANS Adv Nurs Sci 33(3):5–43. https://doi.org/10.1097/ANS.0b013e3181eb4200

Deleuze G, Guttary F (1987) A thousand plateaus. University of Minnesota Press, Minneapolis

Deranty JP (2007) Witnessing the in human: Agamben or Merleau-Ponty. South Atl Q 107(1):165–186

Deutscher P (2008) The inversion of exceptionality: foucault, Agamben, and 'Reproductive Rights'. South Atl Q 107(1):55–70

Eberlei, Walter/Neuhoff, Katja/Riekenbrauk, Klaus (2018), 'Soziale Arbeit mit geflüchteten Menschen', in 'Menschenrechte. Kompass für die Soziale Arbeit'. Stuttgart: Kohlhammer, 109–120

Elias N (1994) The civilising process. Blackwell

Escobar A (1995) Development: the making and unmaking of the Third World. Princeton University Press

Gray M (2005) Dilemmas of international social work: paradoxical processes in indigenisation, universalism and imperialism. Int J Soc Welf 14(3):231–238

Gray M, Webb SA (2008) The myth of global social work: double standards and the local-global divide. J Prog Hum Serv 19(1):61–66

Grosfoguel R (2013) The structure of knowledge in westernized universities epistemic racism/sexism and the four genocides/epistemocides of the long 16th century. Hum Arch: J Soc Self-Knowl 11(1):73–90

Grosz E (2017) The incorporeal: ontology, ethics, and the limits of materialism. Columbia University Press

Healy LM (2007) Universalism and cultural relativism in social work ethics. Int Soc Work 50(1):11–26

Heilmann K, Rosskopf R (2021) Reflections on international social work in contexts of forced migration. In: Rosskopf R, Heilman K (eds) International social work and forced migration: developments in African, Arab and European countries. Barbara Budrich

Holmey O (2021) Mozambique's $2 bn scandal with shipping company Privinvest and Credit Suisse. The Africa Report. www.theafricareport.com/80841/mozambiques-2bn-scandal-with-shipping-company-privinvest-and-credit-suisse

Hölscher D, Kanamugire C, Udah H (2020) A matter of lies and death – necropolitics and the question of engagement with the aftermoth of Rwanda's genocide. J Gender Stud 29(1):34–48. https://doi.org/10.1080/09589236.2019.1691982

Hugman R (2008) Ethics in a world of difference. Ethics Soc Welf 2(2):118–132

IASSW (n.d.) Social work statement of ethical principles. International association of social workers. https://www.iassw-aiets.org/wp-content/uploads/2018/04/SWSEP-2018-final.pdf

Ife J (2001) Human rights and social work. Cambridge University Press

Kalyvas SN (2006) The logic of violence in civil wars. Cambridge University Press

Mbembe A (2017 [2016]) Politik der Feindschaft. Suhrkamp

Mbembe, A (2006) Necropolitics. Public Culture 15:11–40

Mbembe A (2019) Out of the dark night: essays on decolonization. Columbia University Press

Melter C (2018) Soziale arbeit zwischen zuschreibender Kulturalisierung und einer diskriminierungs- und rassismuskritischen Migrationspaedagogik sowie der Orientierung an de Integritaet jedes Menschen. In: Prasad N (ed) Sociale arbeit mit gefluechteten. Rassismuskritisch, professionell, menschenrechtsorientiert. Barbara Budrich

Moffatt K, Irving A (2002) 'Living for the Brethren': idealism, social work's lost enlightenment strain. British J Soc Work 32(4):415–427

Mupedziswa R, Sinkamba RP (2014) Social work education and training in the southern and east Africa: yesterday, today and tomorrow. In: Noble C, Helle S (eds) Global social work: crossing borders, blurring boundaries. Sydney University Press

Negri A (2011) Art and multitude: nine letters on the arts. Polity

Nussbaum M (2000) Women and human development: the capabilities approach. Cambridge University Press

Prozorov S (2014) Agamben and politics: a critical introduction. Edinburgh University Press

Quijano A, Ennis M (2000) Coloniality of power, eurocentrism, and Latin America. Nepantla: Views South 1(3):533–580

Rees S (2020) Cruelty or humanity. Policy Press

Schmelz A (2021) Social work as a human rights profession in the context of refuge and migration: global perspectives. In: Rosskopf R, Heilman K (eds) International social work and forced migration: developments in African, Arab and European countries. Barbara Budrich

Sen AK (2001) Development as freedom. Oxford University Press

Sewpaul V, Henrickson M (2019) The (r)evolution and decolonization of social work ethics: the global social work statement of ethical principles. Int Soc Work 62(6):1469–1481. https://doi.org/10.1177/0020872819846238

Silva-Brito I, Ottmann G (2020) Refractory interventions: the incubation of rival epistemologies in the margins of Brazilian social work. In: Tascon S, Ife J (eds) Disrupting whiteness in social work. Routledge

Sousa Santos de B (2014) Epistemologies of the South: justice against epistemicide. Routledge

Staniland P (2014) Networks of rebellion: explaining insurgent cohesion and collapse. Cornell University Press

Staub-Bernasconi S (2014) Transcending disciplinary, professional and national borders in social work education. In: Noble C, Strauss H, Littlechild B (eds) Global social work: crossing borders, blurring boundaries. Sydney University Press

Tascon S (2016) Human rights, film, and social change: screening rights film festival, Birmingham Centre for film studies. Eur J Med Stud 5(1):S255–S263. https://doi.org/10.25969/mediarep/3337

Tascon S (2020) Disrupting white epistemologies: de-binarising social work. In: Tascon S, Ife J (eds) Disrupting whiteness in social work. Routledge

Trevithick J (2020) Here is what each of the Pentagon's Air-Launched Missiles and bombs actually cost. The Drive. thedrive.com/the-war-zone/32277-here-is-what-each-of-the-pentagons-air-launched-missiles-and-bombs-cost

U.S. Lessons Learned in Afghanistan, House of Representatives (2020) (15 January 2020). govinfo.gov/content/pkg/CHRG-116hhrg38915/html/CHRG-116hhrg38915.htm

Ziarek EP (2008) Bare life on strike: notes on the biopolitics of race and gender. South Atl Q 107(1):89–106

Emerging Futures and Technology Ethics

25

Melanie Sage and Gina Griffin

Contents

Introduction	500
Risk Management for Direct Service Delivery with Technology	500
Learning Technology-Related Lessons from Covid-19	503
The Ethical Mistake of Not Using Technology	503
Ethical Issues and Emerging in Macro Social Work with Technology	504
Algorithms	504
Data Ownership	506
Technology Ethics and Social Work	507
Service	507
Social Justice	508
Dignity & Worth of the Person	509
Competence	510
Collaboration	510
Harnessing Technology for Social Good	511
Conclusion	512
References	513

Abstract

Ethical standards in social work as they relate to technology have given much focus to issues of boundaries, confidentiality, and practicing within one's area of expertise. This offers a temptation for social workers to claim that technology is not in their expertise, and thus avoid technology-mediated practice tools. Yet, as technology becomes more prominent in the lives of people served by social workers, it becomes more vital that social workers are conversant in ethical issues

M. Sage (✉)
University at Buffalo School of Social Work, New York, NY, USA
e-mail: msage@buffalo.edu

G. Griffin
James A Haley Veterans Administration, Tampa, FL, USA

beyond online boundaries between social worker and client, as social workers may possess important roles related to helping clients navigate their technology-mediated lives. The global Covid-19 pandemic brought to light the ways that technology served as a first-line service for many clients, whether or not the social workers were ready for technology-mediated practice. This experience is likely to change our future practice. Ideally, it helps us move toward deeper discussions about the impact of technology on social service delivery, including present and near-future ethical issues related to the use of data, machine learning, and other emerging practices.

Keywords

Technology · Algorithms · Racism · Pandemic

Introduction

In the decade beginning in 2010, nearly 10 years after Facebook appeared on our internet screens, social work associations internationally began improving their guidance to social workers who practice with technology. The guidance came in part to address the increasing ubiquity of technology in the lives of practitioners, along with the increasing number of ethical dilemmas they faced. For instance, the United States National Association of Social Workers published a Technology Standards for Social Workers (National Association of Social Workers 2017b) alongside other social work organizations. The 64-page booklet offered values and ethics principles alongside practice standards. Perhaps already overly-rigid given the pace of change of technology, they faced true challenges in the face of Covid-19, which reached international pandemic status in early 2019, driving practitioners and those they serve online. Other regions of the world are only beginning to grapple with the ethical implications of technology in social work; for instance, the South African Council for Social Service Professions issued emergency guidelines for ethical technology use in 2020 in the face of Covid-19. This chapter addresses contemporary ethical dilemmas faced by social workers regarding technology, and the implications for policy and practice in a world that is increasingly and seemingly irrevocably integrates more and more technology. It extends present-day conceptualizations of tech ethics and explores the next generation of ethical issues in technology.

Risk Management for Direct Service Delivery with Technology

The first wave of practice guidance about social workers who use technology, and indeed the primary focus of the aforementioned 2017 NASW technology standards, was risk management. Published scholarship in this area focused on data management and data breaches, authentication of users, the security of passwords, and the security of any transmission that included client information (Barsky 2017; Mattison 2012; Reamer 2013, 2015; Rock and Congress 1999). Yet even these early ideas about digital landscapes in our modern office environments often did not permeate social work education programmes. Without good guidance for the typical social worker on how to practice without technology, it is no surprise that many social workers felt incompetent in this space. In this knowledge vacuum, it is little surprise that Reamer's (2018) article described "emerging consensus" about the technical issues in social work as those related to practice standards, ethical standards, and licensing standards. The standards place emphasis on not practicing outside of our areas of expertise, and technology fit that area for many. As a result, the messaging from this body of research has left social workers contemplating outcomes that focused on risks and liability for social workers who use technology, and technical and legalistic principles about engaging with technology use.

Then social media dilemmas began to raise red flags in the social work practice community. These included concerns about ways social workers represent themselves online, what clients might see about them, what they might see about clients, and the boundary crossings and dual relationships risks faced by social workers who used social media and other digital tools (Boddy and Dominelli 2017; Byrne et al. 2019; Ricciardelli et al. 2020). In response, social work ethicists began covering the topic. Dr. Frederic Reamer, a NASW Pioneer for his extensive writing on social work ethics, offered a series of commentary and counsel in over a dozen publications, including his 2013 paper *Social Work in a Digital Age: Ethical and Risk Management Challenge* published in the journal *Social Work*, now cited by nearly 300 other papers. Yet, these articles primarily provided anecdotal evidence and trends in the news rather than original research and statistics about practicing social workers. They focused primarily on ways social workers should attune themselves to privacy and boundaries online, highlighting again, risk management issues. The articles posed stories about social workers losing their jobs and professional licenses, and even being sued due to their social media use. Some guidance presented in these early academic journal articles suggested that use of social work services that are mediated by technology "require a great deal of technical mastery in addition to awareness of, and compliance with, rapidly developing standards of care and ethical guidelines" (Reamer 2015, p. 127). Reamer went on to co-author the Technology Standards published by the NASW in 2019. At the same time, NASW updated their code of ethics to include new guidance about technology (National Association of Social Workers 2017a). The Code of Ethics was clear: social workers should not introduce tools that do not meet all the privacy standards of electronic medical records held by hospitals and other large institutions, or those in which they do not hold professional expertise, despite the fact that online therapy has been demonstrated efficacious in systematic literature reviews across many populations, and is favoured by many clients (Kruse et al. 2017; Langarizadeh et al. 2017; McCarty and Clancy 2002; Monaghesh and Hajizadeh 2020).

The warnings of the ethical dilemmas posed about delivering web-based video consultations or therapy with clients may have accounted for the rapid emergence of psychologists and counsellors as leaders in online therapy services, given their professional bodies were earlier to adopt guidelines that supported ways of practicing online instead of the risk-management lens posed by social work boards. For instance, the American Psychological Association (APA) gathered a taskforce on telepsychology in 2012, issuing standards of care for web-based therapy that included ethical expectations, encouraging psychologists to consider "the unique benefits of delivering telepsychology services (e.g., access to care, access to consulting services, client convenience, accommodating client special needs, etc.) relative to the unique risks (e.g., information security, emergency management, etc.)" alongside the needs and comfort of both parties. The guidance recommended reasonable steps related to data security, informed consent, and compliance with interjurisdictional guidelines given their licensure, like social workers, is issued by the state that the therapist practices within. The APA document referenced a 2006 document issued by the Canadian Psychological Association that provided very few legalistic terms, and instead focused on respect, responsible care, and integrity when using technology-mediated services (American Psychological Association 2012). Other international guidelines, such as the British Association for Social Work, offers guidance in the form of Digital Capabilities: Ethical Considerations. This document is just a few pages and is less directive, asking social workers to consider the implications of technology use and align them with social work values. As a result, their guidance is more flexible.

In February of 2019, Covid-19 caused a worldwide shift in service delivery, in which social workers and other care providers were forced to rely on technology for much of their service delivery. Many social workers found themselves unequipped for technology-based practice, and without the digital tools to support online practice, but also obligated to offer services to clients in the face of agency closures, social distancing mandates, and lacking the personal protective equipment needed to support face-to-face encounters during this international crisis (Archer-Kuhn et al. 2020; Giwa et al. 2020; Monaghesh and Hajizadeh 2020; Papouli et al. 2020). This meant that social workers had to forego much of the ethical guidance provided by agencies in order to meet the needs of those they served. Social workers proceeded with practice using personally owned devices while agencies struggled to create policies, practice guidelines, and secure the equipment to support service delivery during this emergency. The lack of preparation for emergencies such as this left workers using non-secure equipment, holding zoom meetings from their dining rooms, and certainly operating outside of their practice expertise as outlined by restrictive technology ethical advice that suggested they should be knowledgeable about best practices for web-based service delivery before embarking on it. It was so clear that providers were operating technology in ways that defied best practices in security that the United States Health and Human Services Administration publicly announced that they would practice "enforcement discretion" regarding services mediated by technology, saying that the federal expectations of data security would be waived due to the national emergency, including sanctions and fines normally associated with disclosures of protected health information (COVID-19 & HIPAA Bulletin, March 2020).

Initially expected to last weeks, after a year of remote technology-facilitated service delivery agencies adopted strategies, and in many cases policies, regarding remote social work. Today, the field of social work is adjusting to a new normal as it relates to technology-mediated practice. Social work researchers have begun exploring best practices for service delivery in digital settings with new vigour.

Health organizations expect that technology-mediated practice is here to stay. Accordingly, the aforementioned ad hoc jumble of agency policies now needs to be revisited to evaluate their merit as an enduring structure. The field of social work needs to reconvene in light of what it has experienced. With this in mind, the field of social work must accommodate a new set of ethical principles and new ways of conceptualizing online dilemmas. Although technology started out as an ethics issue, Covid-19 has inspired us to think about service delivery in new ways, forcing us to reckon with our technology phobia and meet the future (Nissen 2020).

Learning Technology-Related Lessons from Covid-19

Covid-19 exasperated poor mental health for many who were already vulnerable. Yet, it also provided some insights that are very relevant to our practice with technology.

- Social workers need training and access to tools for remote work, which requires investment by agencies in technology and training (Neely-Barnes et al. 2021). As exception policies lift post Covid-19, they will need to be replaced by enduring policies that support our changing relationships with technology-mediated practice.
- Emergencies expose and perpetuate inequity, and technology access is among many inequities heightened by Covid-19 (Abrams and Dettlaff 2020). In social work we have justified technology avoidance due to unequal distribution of technology, and we must think about ways that technology serves as an important lifeline to services.
- Technology may improve access to care. In large patient samples, late-cancellations and no-shows for technology-mediated mental health services significantly decreased (Thakkar and Tarshis 2021). Social workers who care about client access to care will need to rethink client preferences, who is effectively served online, the best practices for remote delivery of mental health and other services, and what that means for their offerings.
- A risk-avoidance approach to social work ethics will not sustain our profession. During Covid-19 we operated within a set of exceptions to the code of ethics (Barsky 2020). Yet, to face our new practice realities, professional organizations will need to update codes to adapt to, and perhaps even embrace, core competencies of technology that all social workers need.

The Ethical Mistake of Not Using Technology

Many ethical mistakes and dilemmas are acts of omission: the failure to use best practice is less about what people do, but more often about what they do not do. These omission errors can include but are not limited to not adequately securing online data, or not consulting with a colleague or supervisor in ethical dilemmas more broadly. We rarely consider not attending to best practices in technology-mediated social work as an omission that leads to an ethical violation. For instance, the ethical negligence of not offering technology-mediated services when they are the most effective, economical, or client-preferred method of treatment, may also be considered an ethical violation. The decline in missed mental health appointments during Covid-19 (Thakkar and Tarshis 2021) is a signal that digital social work meets a client need.

Ethical Issues and Emerging in Macro Social Work with Technology

This section offers current considerations and rapidly-emerging issues related to the use of technology in macro social work services, including policy development, practice innovations, and tools that fall broadly within categories of machine learning and artificial intelligence. Despite the goals of many of these tools to make our lives easier, their designs have significant impact on the equitable use of technology and the ethical issues that social workers and policy makers will need to confront in the next years. While some hope that the promise of tools such as algorithms or artificial intelligence may replace the must burdensome parts of our work, or even fear that they will replace social work all together, we are not close to this reality. In fact, emergence of these tools necessitates interventions by ethical social workers who are highly skilled in clinical decision making and ethical nuance. Another fast-moving development that has a significant impact on our profession is data ownership. As those who work within systems and understand how social systems impact client services, data is of major consequence to the lives of those we serve. Whether we are attending to human relationships facilitated by technology, or are working in systems that increasingly use electronic records to data-mine and predict trends, a social worker's knowledge about the ramifications of technology used within their agencies is critical.

Algorithms

Algorithms may be one of the most rapidly emerging innovations that promise to make our lives easier; and in many ways, they do. We may get better book recommendations based on prior purchases, and they may help route the closest taxi to us and save time. They are wildly seductive in their promises to help to predict outcomes, identify patterns, and take much of the effort out of tasks that would otherwise prove to be very time-consuming. Social workers, and moreover resource-limited agency administrators, want to make less biased decisions more quickly, and to get resources to those who most need them. Algorithms were once touted as a technology that would remove bias from difficult decisions and provide impartial decision support. This has not been the case (Cuccaro-Alamin et al. 2017; Garcia 2016; Rodriguez et al. 2019; Wexler 2018).

Much of the problem with algorithms is that they often rely on historical data that is used to train the next logical decision in the case. That training data can reflect and replicate the implicit biases of the people who entered the data. A famous example of this is the use of algorithms to predict criminal recidivism. While these tools were intended to provide an impartial prediction of human behaviour, they have proven to be biased, and more often predict that people from marginalized communities are a greater risk for recidivism, even if all other factors in their records are equal to their white counterparts (O'Neil 2017). Even when stripped of data about client race, there are many proxies for race in datasets, such as geographic codes or highest grade of school completion. Since these data are also correlated with race, predictors using these data might inadvertently and indirectly point to race as a cause of recidivism or another poor outcome. The result is that the predictors that align with negative outcomes in algorithms may correlate with race, and the causes of those poor outcomes (such as rate of arrest, zip code, or school completion) may be related to oversurveillance, systemic oppression, or other types of marginalization.

Algorithms are also designed, inherently, to replicate the historical features of a system. For instance, child welfare agencies can use client characteristics alongside case outcomes to determine which characteristics are most aligned with child removal. A formula can be built from this data. If this formula is used, the predictive algorithm would suggest a set of characteristics that identify the highest risk cases. However, this ignores many facts: child welfare workers often have a very short tenure, and their decisions to remove or not are often inconsistent, which draws correlated characteristics into question (Keddell 2017; Moore et al. 2016); the field of social work counts on families changing over time due to interventions and personal growth, thereby improving their circumstances, but algorithmic data often relies on unchangeable characteristics such as a history of child welfare interactions which do not account for progress. Social workers may over-rely on data, and lose trust for their own clinical decision making. Finally, outcomes that appear infrequently, such as child death, are very hard to predict even though they are the most consequential outcomes and the data used to build algorithms was rarely created for this purpose, leading to the use of data that may be incomplete, poorly matched, or otherwise insufficient for sound decision-making.

Algorithms have also been known to present problems in fair and equal hiring practices. Women and people of colour are underrepresented in fields such as computer science (Dastin 2018). The training data touts the current employees as the most successful types of employees, so if the current employee body already represents hiring bias, factors associated with that bias may be replicated in their recommendations. For instance, in a male-dominated workplace, attendance at a women's college may be an indication of poor fit.

Additionally, algorithms complicate the lives of social users on a regular basis. Applicants and users may be denied services based on sealed records, data from other agencies, or data input incorrectly (Eubanks 2012). Participants often have no say in how that data is used, or with whom the data is shared. There is little accountability for social services systems when they implicate the algorithm in decision-making, and the use of an algorithm, which is often described as a probability formula, gives the false impression of impartiality. People impacted by the algorithm often have little recourse; agency employees where algorithms are used may not even know how the risk scores are calculated. The abuse and misuse of data in social services has become so concerning that countries such as the Netherlands and the United Kingdom have banned the use of data in these areas for the foreseeable future (Goldkind et al. 2021).

Many algorithms are sold by private and for-profit agencies to social services agencies because the in-house expertise is unavailable. When this is the case, the algorithm builders may refuse to disclose their algorithm because it is proprietary. Thus, agencies never know what data is used to calculate the risk scores, leaving them with no space to correct or address bias. Other times, even when the data sources are clear, formulas are used that maximize the predictive power of the algorithm in unclear ways. Both these types of cases are referred to as Black Box algorithms, which describe a type of algorithm where the formula is unclear or hidden (Diakopoulos 2017; Gillingham 2016; Weerts et al. 2019). Although typical algorithms at least add the benefit of improving transparency in the ways decisions are made, the use of these types of Black Box algorithms decrease accountability and transparency in decision-making.

Yet, the use of and demand for algorithms is likely to continue to grow throughout the world, including in social services systems. Social workers who work in these systems, or alongside other systems that use algorithmic decision-making, can better respond to ethical issues when they are aware of the inherent risks and biases. Likewise, ways of counteracting some kinds of algorithmic bias may emerge. Social workers must stay current about these issues to best advocate for ethical and efficient service delivery.

Data Ownership

Social services systems, and especially public and government services, increasingly link data across systems. In Alleghany County, Pennsylvania, multiple agencies from hospitals and prison systems to child welfare and financial assistance have linked records to better predict risks to those served (Chouldechova et al. 2018; Dare and Gambrill 2017). Often, clients have not given permission for these systems to 'talk to' each other. Again, those who use systems for survival, or are over-surveilled already by systems, are more likely to show up in these datasets. Thus, those who are poor or minoritized are at increased risk to show up in these datasets, justifying the need for more surveillance. In these ways, instead of data sharing meeting its goal of promoting connected service delivery, it instead creates a system of keeping people who are system-involved stuck in these systems.

As machine learning tools become more sophisticated, it is not only quantitative data that ends up in algorithms. Natural Language Processing is a method of machine learning that takes qualitative data, such as case notes, or even recordings, and draws themes. Case notes entered today, for the purposes of recording client struggles and progress, may later be used unbeknownst to the original social worker, for purposes such as deciding who is the best match for services. Many would record their case notes differently if they knew this was a possible future outcome.

Government service recipients, hospital patients, and other types of consumers of social services often have no explicit right to purge their records or not have their data fed into algorithms. Their personal information is not their own and can be used to make future decisions about whether they, or others, get services. This runs counter to core values of social workers across the globe, such as informed consent, self-determination, and confidentiality. Even in anonymized data sets where names and birthdays are stripped, researchers can easily discover how to link identities to data based on user habits (Crețu et al. 2022). Thus, social workers must know that even removing key identifying information such as names, birthdays, and locations often does not protect client confidentiality, especially in a world where sophisticated technology can link data points.

Data ownership is not only related to confidential data held in protected systems. Even social media data is sometimes used by service providers to learn information about clients (Sage et al. 2017) or conduct large-scale research (Guntuku et al. 2019). Computer scientists and others who use social media data to make decisions have debated the ethics of such use (Reijers et al. 2018). Social work researchers have not yet been very involved in these discussions, although their unique lens related to ethical considerations that centre the most vulnerable have the potential to add a unique contribution to these discussions.

Technology Ethics and Social Work

Social workers have an obligation to become technologically literate given the increasing importance that technology plays in the lives of those served. Sometimes the role of the social worker may be to provide equitable access to technology that may be helpful, and sometimes it is to help shield vulnerable people from the negative impacts of technology. Below, some considerations and examples are offered that highlight the unique intersections of social work values and technological issues.

Service

Many questions arise about the use of technology-mediated client services. A primary example is that many clients do not have the appropriate skills or equipment to adapt to services that use telehealth. Reasons may be because of digital literacy skills, or access to an adequate phone, tablet, or laptop, or even reliable internet service. This can leave clients without the services that they need in order to thrive (Barsky 2017). Client safety also needs to be considered. When working remotely, social workers need to be able to appropriately assess for the safety of the client, and to have a reliable plan in place if the client requires assistance. If a client is deemed unsafe or suicidal, the social worker needs to be able to send help via an emergency service, which requires making sure that the provider has established the location of the client at the beginning of the session so that help can be dispatched. This raises issues of self-determination, informed consent, and confidentiality, as sometimes a client does not consent to an emergency intervention and providers use technology to trace the users' location. Even well-meaning interventions related to safety lead to dilemmas in which social workers must choose between competing ethical principles, and professional discussions about these issues are vital as new technologies emerge that allow for increasing surveillance of consumers.

Privacy is also a service concern. The equipment and the software used by the provider should guarantee the privacy of the client (Barsky 2017). Any storage of client information should also be secure, whether using personal equipment, or equipment provided by the agency. It is also important to work with the client to provide a safe environment for online sessions. Working through the pandemic, clients realized that they could use phones and tablets to meet at locations such as their jobsite, or from the privacy of their automobiles. While this improved accessibility, it also created questions regarding client confidentiality. When attending meetings from home, either the social worker or the client may also find themselves surrounded by family members. Minor children may be present when discussing stressful or age-inappropriate subjects. A client may also be in an unsafe relationship, in which an abusive partner may want to monitor their partner's words and actions. A remote session may leave a client open to abuse or manipulation. In these situations, the provider is responsible for helping the client to think through risks in providing an online session. Neil (2020) offers a framework for physicians conducting telehealth sessions, which includes confirming the patient is alone and safe to talk, use of a safety word, safety planning, and safe follow-up.

Even when providing face-to-face services, clients may present with technology-related concerns or needs for psychoeducation. This may be related to cyberstalking, finding online support groups, troubles in online relationships, or risks related to vulnerabilities online such as trafficking. In any of these cases, social workers should be prepared to learn and support clients to resolve these issues that interfere with their well-being or are the subject of service delivery.

Social Justice

Technology works in the service of, as well as against the interests of, social justice. Those who find themselves organizing for social change now have multiple tools at their disposal. Social media is commonly used to organize protests or rallies. Additionally, bystanders and protesters use the cameras on their cell phones to record the police, as a form of countersurveillance (Canella 2018). This allows evidence against false reports by the police, or can document abuse by authority. Some apps provide assistance to those at risk of law enforcement abuse; for instance, an app called Hands Up 4 Justice allows the user to record a video which is sent to the cloud so that it cannot be deleted by police. The app I'm Getting Arrested allows users to push a single button to alert a list of friends about the arrest and their GPS application.

Conversely, law enforcement agencies often use technology in ways that violate the rights and privacy of protestors. They have used social media accounts and cell phone data to track the location and movements of protestors and community organizers (Canella 2018). Law enforcement also utilizes technology that combines web scraping of social media accounts and facial recognition to identify protestors that are perceived as threats (Miyamoto 2020). Part of the intention of these types of technologies may be to instil fear and to reduce the occurrence of protests. Recently, police in the United States played copyrighted music loudly from their cars so that if a bystander attempted to load the video of an arrest to a video site like YouTube, the video is taken down immediately for copyright violation (Sung 2021). Social workers committed to social justice should work to understand the ways that technology can facilitate and create barriers in this domain.

Dignity & Worth of the Person

Social workers recognize the dignity and worth of all they serve, including those who are impoverished and otherwise marginalized. Poverty, itself, is not a crime. However, technology is used in ways that often disproportionately affect poor communities and clients. Practices such as over-policing and predatory lending negatively impact low-income communities and are often facilitated by technology (Gilman and Green 2018). These practices lead to poorer outcomes in mental health, access to fewer resources, and other decreased well-being (Sheehy 2020).

Social work, as a profession, should become more aware of ways in which unjust practices related to technology affect communities and clients. Social workers who are unaware of the negative impacts of technology may unwittingly become guilty of using technology in ways that harm clients, or further rob clients and communities of their dignity and worth. An example of this is the use of information in public assistance. Applicants for social services in the US essentially sign away their rights to privacy; the refusal to do so can result in the denial of services that lead to food and housing (Eubanks 2012). In these ways, technology can rob service users of their basic human dignity.

On the other hand, despite the increasing ways that people use technology to get their basic needs met, technology and internet services is generally not seen as a human right. Internet access is not distributed equally across the world or in any given community. Despite growing access to smartphones, penetration is still less than 70% in countries such as China and India (Statista.com), and according to Pew Research Center, rural and urban divides persist even in North America, where broadband and cell service may be limited or absent. Yet, some employers only accept online applications, websites expedite social services applications, and grade schools ask students to complete work online. People who cannot afford these services are not provided access to them as a human right. The lack of access to technology denies people as worthy of basic access to tools that improve living.

Competence

Many social workers had to adjust to frequent use of technology to deliver services during the global pandemic. Goldkind notes that social workers have not traditionally adjusted well to technological advances, and that they have often been resistant to new skills in this area (2016). While other fields such as nursing have incorporated a focus on specific technical skills as part of standard training (Collins et al. 2017), social work has yet to do so.

While NASW drafted new technology standards in 2018, they require only that social workers are competent with the tools they use, and do not require social workers to have basic computer competency (Parker-Oliver and Demiris 2006; Goldkind et al. 2016). Research suggests that the ability of the social worker to competently and effectively use technology is an important part of successful telehealth practice (Barsky 2017). Providers who were surveyed regarding their use of telehealth delivery reported that they needed appropriate time and training to develop new skills, team-based learning, and assistance from a manager who possesses good technical skills and who can provide adequate guidance in order to be successful (Venville et al. 2021).

In order to maintain relevance as a helping profession, social work needs to develop more and better curricula, and ongoing professional development, to assure that social workers graduate with the skills they need in order to competently make use of technology in the workplace, in order to provide quality services to clients.

Collaboration

Learning to work as part of an interdisciplinary team, and across disciplines, is an important part of social work education. While social work and engineering initially seem disparate, they share similar values such as problem-solving, flexibility, and professional standards (Miller et al. 2019). While Miller notes that there are currently few collaborations between social work and engineering, it is the differences in these two disciplines that make potential collaborations novel.

In an international service learning (ISL) project that lasted from 2009 to 2015, a team of civil engineering students, social work students, and local project managers worked together to install and monitor water filtration systems in communities across Guatemala. Matthew et al. (2016) notes that social workers helped to address reasons that the filters were not used consistently, as the engineering team could not understand why this would occur. Social workers discovered that the engineering teams did not adequately explain to the community what they were doing, which bred mistrust. To further complicate the problem, previous research abuses in the country stirred up fears. Additionally, the engineering team had been unable to communicate effectively with frontline Guatemalan project managers. A social work student was able to work with the team to bring these things to light. The team then learned to communicate the outcomes of the water testing so that the entire community could understand that the water had been tested, and was safe to use. Lenore noted that this successful collaboration required all of the skills of engineering, social work, the local project managers, and the community to make things work. However, social work values such as dignity, respect, and self-determination are evident in these processes; the absence of these are the places where communication and collaboration initially failed.

In another project, Miller et al. (2019) detail the collaboration of students in civil engineering, computer science, and social work to build an app that would gather research data on transportation disadvantage in local communities. Lack of transportation often affects underserved communities, and the data gathered would help the team to study these effects. Social work students focused on providing suggestions on the end-user experience to the engineering and computer science students to develop an application that would be more understandable and easier to use.

The American Academy of Social Work and Social Welfare noted that social work does not often engage in these types of integrative research projects (2014), and that in failing to do so, the problems of the elderly, socially isolated, and underserved populations are left unmet.

Harnessing Technology for Social Good

In 2013, the American Academy of Social Work & Social Welfare (AASWSW) brought together leaders from across the field of social work as a volunteer panel with a goal to focus the field toward a vision for solving some of the most pressing problems affecting marginalized communities. The group elicited feedback from a national audience of stakeholders and received dozens of suggestions about problems in need of focus, which they synthesized into ten grand challenges. Among the list of ten, the challenge to 'Harness Technology for Social Good' was chosen as a timely goal. Unlike the other Grand Challenges for Social Work, which are problems to be solved, this challenge focuses on the opportunities of technology to improve our field through practice innovation and the use of big data.

The idea of 'Grand Challenges' comes from an early 1900s list of unsolved mathematical puzzles that required collective community problem-solving due to complexity, and since then has come to represent a way for disciplines, foundations, agencies, and so on to conceptualize unsolved problems in their fields. During the official Grand Challenges launch in 2015, HTSG produced concept papers that provided a scan of the current state of innovation in the social work field related to the grand challenges, which included policy recommendations related to issues including technology access for vulnerable populations.

Although *Harnessing Technology for Social Good* has been defined as one of the *Social Work Grand Challenges*, the definition of 'social good' has proven to be slightly more elusive. Mor Barak has suggested a definition in which technology figures prominently, and where it is used in the pursuit of social justice, and overall well-being (2018).

Rapid advances in technology have often left poor and disenfranchised communities on the wrong side of the digital divide. Families in disadvantaged or rural communities often find themselves without access to common technologies such as laptops or tablets. These communities also often find themselves without appropriate access to the internet. This makes it increasingly difficult to apply for jobs and services, and to keep up in school. This disadvantage was poignantly demonstrated during the early days of the pandemic, when many schools shifted to online and remote models. As a result, many first-generation students from marginalized communities were forced to drop out of college, as they no longer had free access to the internet or the technological tools for success.

The Grand Challenge movement is one of many that describes efforts to improve social justice in technology. Movements such as Data Justice seek to protect vulnerable individuals and communities from the harmful effects of big data, to move towards the ownership of and access to one's individual data, and to foster empowerment against abuse and misrepresentation in the digital age (Goldkind et al. 2021). These principles are closely aligned with social work values such as self-determination.

Grassroots efforts sprung up around the United States in which data and data science are used to help communities to fight back against social injustice. San Francisco's housing crisis has left many without housing. People in these communities are frequently forced out of their neighbourhoods by gentrification, and at the mercy of dishonest landlords. Projects such as the Anti-Eviction Mapping Project (AEMP), established in 2013, brought together activists across disciplines to help disenfranchised communities to identify bad actors in the housing community (Goldkind et al. 2021). This provided the community with a way to resist the effects of gentrification.

Another organization that rose to the challenge is *Data for Black Lives*. Their mission statement reads, "Data as protest. Data as accountability. Data as collective action" (2021). This organization recognized that Black communities are often underrepresented, even as data is collected on the Covid-19 infection and vaccination. *Data for Black Lives* has responded by advocating that existing data is made public, and by compiling their own data on ways in which Black communities have been affected by the pandemic (Data for Black Lives 2021).

Conclusion

Social workers have many future opportunities to shape the scope of ethical work at the intersection of technology and social work. Because this work is increasingly led by the private sector, social workers may find themselves returning to the subfield of occupational and industrial social work. They may answer questions such as how wearable monitoring technologies (step tracking watches, heart rate monitors, sleep sensors, etc.) should be used by employers, for instance, addressing complex issues about who is advantaged and disadvantaged by sharing employee data with employers. They may work with industry on the design of wearables or machine learning to ensure fairness, or they may write state policy that governs the fair use of face recognition software, considering what marginalized groups might be disadvantaged by its use. Although some fear that technology will replace social workers, it may actually be more likely that there are more roles for social workers than ever, and especially social workers who are equipped to work ethically alongside technology, advocate in ways that highlight the risks and benefits of technology, and in supporting people with both access to and protection from technology, informed by research from our field about who is served and who is harmed by our growing reliance on these tools.

It is not enough for social workers to rely on others to learn to effectively employ technology in the service of wellbeing (Goldkind et al. 2018), this is increasingly the job of ethical social workers. Although our profession may be amongst late adopters of emerging technology, there is no good reason for us to hide from it. It touches those we serve in ways that are both troubling and heartening. Without attuning ourselves to implications, both positive and negative, we risk violating our values and ethical standards, and denying our responsibilities to those we serve.

References

Abrams LS, Dettlaff AJ (2020) Voices from the frontlines: social workers confront the Covid-19 pandemic. Soc Work 65(3):302–305. https://doi.org/10.1093/sw/swaa030

American Psychological Association (2012) Guidelines for the practice of telepsychology. https://www.apa.org/practice/guidelines/telepsychology

Archer-Kuhn B, Ayala J, Hewson J, Letkemann L (2020) Canadian reflections on the Covid-19 pandemic in social work education: from tsunami to innovation. Soc Work Educ 39(8):1010–1018

Barsky AE (2017) Social work practice and technology: ethical issues and policy responses. J Technol Hum Serv 35(1):8–19

Barsky A (2020) Ethical exceptions for social workers in light of the COVID-19 pandemic and physical distancing. The New Social Worker 27(2). https://www.socialworker.com/feature-articles/ethics-articles/ethical-exceptions-social-workers-in-light-of-covid-19-pandemic-physical-distancing/

Boddy J, Dominelli L (2017) Social media and social work: the challenges of a new ethical space. Aust Soc Work 70(2):172–184

Byrne J, Kirwan G, Mc Guckin C (2019) Social media surveillance in social work: practice realities and ethical implications. J Technol Hum Serv 37(2–3):142–158

Canella G (2018) Racialized surveillance: activist media and the policing of Black bodies. Commun Cult Critique 11(3):378–398. https://doi.org/10.1093/ccc/tcy013

Chouldechova A, Benavides-Prado D, Fialko O, Vaithianathan R (2018) A case study of algorithm-assisted decision making in child maltreatment hotline screening decisions. In: Conference on fairness, accountability and transparency, pp 134–148. http://proceedings.mlr.press/v81/chouldechova18a.html

Collins S, Yen P-Y, Phillips A, Kennedy MK (2017) Nursing informatics competency assessment for the nurse leader. JONA J Nurs Adm 47(4):212–218. https://doi.org/10.1097/nna.0000000000000467

Crețu AM, Monti F, Marrone S, Dong X, Bronstein M, de Montjoye YA (2022) Interaction data are identifiable even across long periods of time. Nat Commun 13(1):1–11

Cuccaro-Alamin S, Foust R, Vaithianathan R, Putnam-Hornstein E (2017) Risk assessment and decision making in child protective services: predictive risk modeling in context. Child Youth Serv Rev 79:291–298. https://doi.org/10.1016/j.childyouth.2017.06.027

Dare T, Gambrill E (2017) Ethical analysis: predictive risk models at call screening for allegheny county [Ethical analysis]. The Allegheny County Department of Human Services, Allegheny County Analytics. https://www.alleghenycountyanalytics.us/wp-content/uploads/2019/05/Ethical-Analysis-16-ACDHS-26_PredictiveRisk_Package_050119_FINAL-2.pdf

Dastin J (2018) Amazon scraps secret AI recruiting tool that showed bias against women. Reuters. https://www.reuters.com/article/us-amazon-com-jobs-automation-insight-idUSKCN1MK08G

Data for Black Lives (2021) Programs. Data for Black Lives https://d4bl.org/programs.html

Diakopoulos N (2017) Algorithmic accountability reporting: on the investigation of black boxes. Tow Center for Digital Journalism, Columbia University; Columbia Academic Commons. https://doi.org/10.7916/D8ZK5TW2

Eubanks V (2012) Digital dead end: fighting for social justice in the information age. MIT, Cambridge, MA

Garcia M (2016) Racist in the machine: the disturbing implications of algorithmic bias. World Policy J 33(4):111–117. https://doi.org/10.1215/07402775-3813015

Gillingham P (2016) Predictive risk modelling to prevent child maltreatment and other adverse outcomes for service users: inside the 'black box' of machine learning. Br J Soc Work 46(4): 1044–1058. https://doi.org/10.1093/bjsw/bcv031

Gilman ME, Green R (2018) The surveillance gap: The harms of extreme privacy and data marginalization. NYU Review of Law and Social Change (42):253. Available at SSRN: https://ssrn.com/abstract=3172948

Giwa S, Mullings DV, Karki KK (2020) Virtual social work care with older black adults: a culturally relevant technology-based intervention to reduce social isolation and loneliness in a time of pandemic. J Gerontol Soc Work 63(6–7):679–681

Goldkind L, Wolf L, Jones J (2016) Late adapters? How social workers acquire knowledge and skills about technology tools. J Technol Hum Serv 34(4):338–358. https://doi.org/10.1080/15228835.2016.1250027

Goldkind L, Thinyane M, Choi M (2018) Small data, big justice: The intersection of data Science, Social Good, and Social Services. Journal of Technology in Human Services 36(4):175–178. https://doi.org/10.1080/15228835.2018.1539369

Goldkind L, Wolf L, LaMendola W (2021) Data justice: social work and a more just future. J Community Pract 29(3):237–256. https://doi.org/10.1080/10705422.2021.1984354

Guntuku SC, Preotiuc-Pietro D, Eichstaedt JC, Ungar LH (2019) What twitter profile and posted images reveal about depression and anxiety. In: Proceedings of the International AAAI conference on web and social media, vol 13, pp 236–246. https://www.aaai.org/ojs/index.php/ICWSM/article/download/3225/3093

Keddell DE (2017) Comparing risk-averse and risk-friendly practitioners in child welfare decision-making: a mixed methods study. J Soc Work Pract 31(4):411–429. https://doi.org/10.1080/02650533.2017.1394822

Kruse CS, Krowski N, Rodriguez B, Tran L, Vela J, Brooks M (2017) Telehealth and patient satisfaction: a systematic review and narrative analysis. BMJ Open 7(8):e016242

Langarizadeh M, Tabatabaei MS, Tavakol K, Naghipour M, Rostami A, Moghbeli F (2017) Telemental health care, an effective alternative to conventional mental care: a systematic review. Acta Informatica Medica 25(4):240

Matthew LE, Piedra LM, Wu C-F, Kramer Diaz A, Wang H, Straub AP, Nguyen TH (2016) Social work and engineering: lessons from a water filtration project in Guatemala. Int Soc Work 60(6): 1–13. https://doi.org/10.1177/0020872816655869

Mattison M (2012) Social work practice in the digital age: therapeutic e-mail as a direct practice methodology. Soc Work 57(3):249–258

McCarty D, Clancy C (2002) Telehealth: implications for social work practice. Soc Work 47(2): 153–161

Miller VJ, Murphy ER, Cronley C, Fields NL, Keaton C (2019) Student experiences engaging in interdisciplinary research collaborations: a case study for social work education. J Soc Work Educ. https://doi.org/10.1080/10437797.2019.1627260

Miyamoto I (2020) Surveillance technology challenges political culture of democratic states. In: Vuving AL (ed) Hindsight, insight, foresight: thinking about security in the Indo-Pacific. Daniel K. Inouye Asia-Pacific Center for Security Studies, Honolulu, pp 49–66. Retrieved November 13, 2021, from https://apcss.org/wp-content/uploads/2020/09/04-miyamoto-25thA.pdf

Monaghesh E, Hajizadeh A (2020) The role of telehealth during COVID-19 outbreak: a systematic review based on current evidence. BMC Public Health 20(1):1–9

Moore TD, McDonald TP, Cronbaugh-Auld K (2016) Assessing risk of placement instability to aid foster care placement decision making. J Publ Child Welfare 10(2):117–131. https://doi.org/10.1080/15548732.2016.1140697

Mor Barak ME (2018) The practice and science of social good: emerging paths to positive social impact. Res Soc Work Pract 30(2):139–150. https://doi.org/10.1177/1049731517745600

National Association of Social Workers (2017a) Code of ethics of the National Association of Social Workers. NASW Press https://www.socialworkers.org/About/Ethics/Code-of-Ethics/Code-of-Ethics-English

National Association of Social Workers (2017b) NASW, ASWB, CSWE, & CSWA standards for technology in social work practice. https://www.socialworkers.org/includes/newIncludes/homepage/PRA-BRO-33617.TechStandards_FINAL_POSTING.pdf

Neely-Barnes S, Hunter A, Meiman J, Malone C, Hirschi M, Delavega E (2021) Leaning into the crisis: Managing COVID-19 in social services and behavioral health agencies. Human Service Organizations: Management, Leadership & Governance 45(4):293–306

Neil J (2020) Domestic violence and COVID 19. Aust J Gen Pract

Nissen L (2020) Social work and the future in a post-Covid 19 world: a foresight lens and a call to action for the profession. J Technol Hum Serv 38(4):309–330

O'Neil C (2017) Weapons of math destruction. Penguin Books

Papouli E, Chatzifotiou S, Tsairidis C (2020) The use of digital technology at home during the COVID-19 outbreak: views of social work students in Greece. Soc Work Educ 39(8):1107–1115

Parker-Oliver D, Demiris G (2006) Social work informatics: a new specialty. Soc Work 51(2):127–134. http://www.jstor.org/stable/23721277

Reamer FG (2013) Social work in a digital age: ethical and risk management challenges. Soc Work 58(2):163–172

Reamer FG (2015) Clinical social work in a digital environment: ethical and risk-management challenges. Clin Soc Work J 43(2):120–132

Reamer FG (2018) Ethical standards for social workers' use of technology: emerging consensus. J Soc Work Values Ethics 15(2):71–80

Reijers W, Wright D, Brey P, Weber K, Rodrigues R, O'Sullivan D, Gordijn B (2018) Methods for practising ethics in research and innovation: a literature review, critical analysis and recommendations. Sci Eng Ethics 24(5):1437–1481

Ricciardelli LA, Nackerud L, Quinn AE, Sewell M, Casiano B (2020) Social media use, attitudes, and knowledge among social work students: ethical implications for the social work profession. Soc Sci Humanit Open 2(1):100008

Rock B, Congress E (1999) The new confidentiality for the 21st century in a managed care environment. Soc Work 44(3):253–262

Rodriguez MY, DePanfilis D, Lanier P (2019) Bridging the gap: social work insights for ethical algorithmic decision-making in human services. IBM J Res Dev 63(4/5):8:1-8:8. https://doi.org/10.1147/JRD.2019.2934047

Sage M, Wells M, Sage T, Devlin M (2017) Supervisor and policy roles in social media use as a new technology in child welfare. Child Youth Serv Rev 78:1–8. https://doi.org/10/gbknpn

Sheehy B (2020) Ethics beyond transparency: Techné: Research in Philosophy and Technology 24(3):256–281

Sung M (2021, July 1) Cops are playing music during filmed encounters to game YouTube's copyright striking. Mashable. https://mashable.com/article/police-playing-music-copyright-youtube-recording

Thakkar S, Tarshis T (2021) The impact of the covid-19 pandemic and telehealth on clinic no-shows in a multidisciplinary mental health agency. J Am Acad Child Adolesc Psychiatry 60(10):S244. https://doi.org/10.1016/j.jaac.2021.09.363

Venville A, O'Connor S, Roeschlein H, Ennals P, McLoughlan G, Thomas N (2021) Mental Health Service user and worker experiences of psychosocial support via telehealth through the COVID-19 pandemic: qualitative study (preprint). https://doi.org/10.2196/preprints.29671

Weerts HJ, van Ipenburg W, Pechenizkiy M (2019) Case-based reasoning for assisting domain experts in processing fraud alerts of black-box machine learning models. ArXiv Preprint ArXiv:1907.03334

Wexler R (2018) The odds of justice: code of silence: how private companies hide flaws in the software that governments use to decide who goes to prison and who gets out. Chance 31(3): 67–72

Part VI
Conclusion

The Ideas of Social Work Practice

Dorothee Hölscher, Donna McAuliffe, and Richard Hugman

Contents

Social Work Ideas in Practice: Conceptual Arcs 520
    Arc 1: The Human at the Centre 522
    Arc 2: The Person/Structure Interface 524
    Arc 3: Against Dehumanising the Human – Colonialism and Its Aftermath 526
    Arc 4: Decentring the Human 527
Conclusion 529
References 530

Abstract

This chapter presents the concluding arguments of the edited collection, *Social work theory and ethics: Ideas in practice.* It contextualises the 24 substantive chapters contained in this volume in relation to some of the major recent developments in social work theorising and ethics. This volume has brought together 36 authors from 5 continents, tackling an exceptionally wide range of issues, drawing on over a thousand citations, across decades of social work theorising and ethics in practice. Their works are brought together in conversation across four arcs, which cut across the four parts into which this volume had been grouped. It is concluded that social work is eminently well-placed to continue its

---

D. Hölscher (✉)
School of Nursing, Midwifery and Social Work, The University of Queensland, Brisbane, QLD, Australia

Department of Social Work & Criminology, University of Pretoria, Pretoria, South Africa
e-mail: d.holscher@uq.edu.au

D. McAuliffe
School of Health Sciences and Social Work, Griffith University, Logan, QLD, Australia
e-mail: d.mcauliffe@griffith.edu.au

R. Hugman
School of Social Sciences, University of New South Wales, Sydney, NSW, Australia
e-mail: r.hugman@unsw.edu.au

mission of responding to the complex challenges, and to the profound and intersecting crises, to which human activity has given rise, but which always also contain openings and possibilities for a more just and caring world.

> **Keywords**
>
> Social work theory · Social work ethics · Social work practice · Social work research

Social Work Ideas in Practice: Conceptual Arcs

Social work as a professional discipline, a science, and an art has a long and chequered history that stretches across time, place, fields, and methods. The dynamic nature of social work has given rise to a body of literature that has experienced continued growth as practitioners and academics research and report on their work in both conceptual and empirical pieces designed to challenge dominant thinking with new ideas. From the onset, it has been argued that those seeking professional status are required to have a foundation of knowledge that defines theory of, and theory for practice, in their nominated field of expertise. In addition, it has been understood that claiming professional status would entail being able to define what is appropriate and inappropriate conduct, often set out in codes of ethics or some other standards that connect to a defined value base (Greenwood 1957; McAuliffe 2021).

Social work draws from a multitude of other disciplines to ensure the growth and development of discipline-specific theories, while new innovations push traditional boundaries into sometimes uncharted territory. Knowledge from disciplines such as sociology, psychology, anthropology, and cultural studies provides valuable ways of viewing the world through understandings of human development, learning, problem-solving, socialisation, social processes, discrimination, and social stratification. Indigenous worldviews have begun to merge into dominant discourses to probe different ways of exploring such topics as (de)colonisation, relationships, connectivity, and reciprocity. Other disciplines such as humanities, education, and law provide knowledge about history, legal and judicial processes, pedagogy, and philosophy, while business and economic disciplines provide insights into globalisation, distribution and trade, and international finance. Life sciences add knowledge about genetics, ecology, neuroscience, and environmentalism (Chenoweth and McAuliffe 2020). Finally, theoretical developments that put human and social sciences into conversation with natural sciences, such as physics, chemistry, and earth sciences, are beginning to be recognised as valuable to social work as well. As these areas of knowledge and theoretical developments continue to be embedded, a rich ontological and epistemological environment emerges within which social work can expand and evolve its self-understanding, continuously reconsidering and refining its own unique definitional and purposive vantage point.

Most practitioners and academics will agree that social work's knowledge, practice, and ethical base are inextricably entwined (Banks 2020). Thus, the introductory chapter to this collection highlighted that, when it comes to ethics, too, social work is a profession that does not stand still. The empirical research and the wisdom gleaned from philosophy and practice across time, place, and a wide range of traditions paint a picture of responsiveness to local and global events that are well illustrated in the many examples provided by the contributing authors to this volume. Moreover, the complexities inherent in a profession that has always had a mandate to care and sometimes the responsibility to control highlight deep tensions that require social workers to critically and reflexively engage with their own roles and positionings in relation to issues of power, discrimination, oppression, and structural disadvantage at multiple levels. Add to this the historical injustices that continue to reverberate across regions of the global South and North, which in this volume have been taken up by authors with a particular interest in decolonisation and the indigenisation of social work. Despite all the ways in which some humans treat other humans and the non-human environment, and notwithstanding the often-complex and hard-to-address reasons that lie behind such treatment, there remains a hope within the value position of social work that the principles of social justice and human rights are more than just aspirations.

There is great value in bringing together multiple voices, as seen in the proliferation of edited volumes published in the last decade about topics as diverse as religion and spirituality (Crisp 2019); art in social work practice (Huss and Bos 2018); social work practice in health (Petrakis 2020); theories for post- and decolonial practice (van Breda and Sekudu 2019; Kleibl et al. 2020); ethics and values in social work (Marson and McKinnon 2019); green social work (Dominelli 2018); social work supervision (O'Donoghue and Englebrecht 2023); social work practice research (Joubert and Webber 2022); financial social work (Callahan et al. 2021); social work theory (Payne and Reith-Hall 2019); and post-anthropocentric social work (Bozalek and Pease 2021). Drawing together global perspectives provides an opportunity to open the lens and challenge practices that may have become complacent, consider new viewpoints, and better understand cultural differences through case examples from unfamiliar situations. The more voices that are welcomed into discussions of complex and controversial topics, the more consideration can be given to alternate constructions of ideas. The more voices that are given space, the louder the cumulative voice about the relevance of social work becomes.

There is also an ever-evolving range of generalist texts that focus on theories for social work practice (for example, Healy 2022, Thompson and Stepney 2017, Watts and Hodgson 2019, Payne 2022) upon which students, practitioners, and scholars can draw to orient, position, and ground themselves within this diverse and expanding profession. Likewise, there is an expansion of texts that focus on specific theoretical perspectives such as feminist theory for practice (Cocker and Hafford-Letchfield 2022), the eco-social approach to social work theory (Wendt 2021), narrative theory in clinical social work (McTighe 2018), to name just a few. In addition, there are texts in the field of social work ethics that also cover the generic application of ethical theory to social work practice (Hugman and Carter 2016; Reamer 2018; Banks 2020) and those that focus on more specific ethical theories such as a critical ethic of care (Pease et al. 2019), virtue ethics (Hugman et al. 2021), or ways of conceptualising ethics as an interprofessional activity (McAuliffe 2021).

This collection stands in its own space given the connections between theory and ethics, and there is intentional synergy and balance across the vertical and horizontal dimensions of the chapters. At its core, it has aimed to explore – within the framework of a single volume – theories for practice; practice theories; well-established, evolving, and newly emerging debates around values and principles; and contemporary ethical issues in social work, and to do so from a wide range of author positions. This – horizontal – organisation was set out in the introductory chapter (Part I) and provided the volume's overarching structure across four substantive parts. Theories for social work formed Part II; social work practice theory constituted Part III; social work values and principles comprised Part IV; and ethical issues and challenges in social work were explored in a dedicated section on applied ethics (Part V).

This current chapter (Part VI) concludes the volume by traversing the vertical paths that run across the volume's four substantive sections. There are, firstly, those chapters that continue in the vein of placing the human at the centre of social work's (ethical) theorising and practice. Then, there is that group of chapters, which, while not decentring the human as such, shift their gaze to the person/structure interface; and these are writings that are generally rooted in social work's critical traditions. Related but not reducible to this are those chapters that are concerned, specifically, with colonialism and its aftermath, and with ways of mainstreaming traditions, marginalised as a result, within the social work canon. Inevitably, decolonial writings are concerned with decentring particular and problematic ideas of what it means to be human. This is an agenda strongly pursued by a type of scholarship that is only beginning to make inroads into social work theorising and practice, that is, post-humanism and post-anthropocentrism. Of course, many of this volume's chapters pursue several of these conceptual arcs.

Arc 1: The Human at the Centre

Several chapters in this collection started with the premise that human beings and their interactions with others across the lifespan will engage in ways that represent theories of human development, moral development, and responses to stressful or crisis situations that disrupt harmonious relations within systems. In Part II, Herman Lo (▶ Chap. 2, "Psychological and Clinical Theories") provided a critical review of psychological and clinical theories – one of social work's key sources of knowledge, which continue to inform professional practice around the globe. Using mindfulness as a case in point for the unceasing relevance of this body of knowledge, Lo demonstrated its versatility as it is applied to advance other contemporary agendas such as empowerment and trauma-informed practice. The profession will do well, he concluded, to persist in reflecting upon and adapting psychological and clinical theories in a fast-changing world. Time-honoured is also the influence of systems theory in social work, as argued in ▶ Chap. 3, "Systems Theory and Social Work", by Jan Wirth and Heiko Kleve. Taking Niklas Luhmann's seminal work as their starting point, Wirth and Kleve contended that social work is concerned with the question of *Lebensführung* – conduct of life. Professional practice, thus, is aided by practitioners' appreciative and constructive engagement with people's unfolding efforts to navigate the contradictions, ambivalences, and paradoxes of their everyday lives. For a profession in which ecosystems perspectives have had a long-standing and considerable influence, the significance of this contribution rests in its foregrounding of a systems theoretical tradition that has taken a rather different and refreshing trajectory indeed.

Adrian van Breda's chapter (▶ Chap. 8, "Person-Centred Approaches to Social Work Practice") opened Part III with a comprehensive overview of the wide variety of person-centred traditions in social work, attending, moreover, to their considerable evolution and development over time. Writing from South Africa – where following centuries of (neo-)colonial rule and influence, clinical services are something that few people can afford – van Breda expressed concern regarding person-centred approaches' propensity for prioritising individual change over environmental, or systemic, change. This then formed the yardstick by which he evaluated these rich traditions, concluding that social workers should be sure to embed any person-*centred* practices within attention to the required structural changes in the environments *surrounding* the persons with whom they work. Of course, few would dispute that human beings do have problems, which they can and do resolve – especially when provided with the requisite scaffolding and supports – and social workers continue to assume pivotal roles in this regard. Against the background of van Breda's critique, therefore, it is noteworthy how, in ▶ Chap. 9, "Problem-Solving Theory: The Task-Centred Model", Bianca Ramos and Randall Stetson demonstrated not only the unceasing relevance of one such tradition – problem-solving theory and task-centred practice – but also how its contemporary uses are now much wider than initially imagined: Social workers have proven its successful application at organisational and community levels where challenges emanating, for example, from cultural diversity, racism, and coloniality need to be addressed, often in the face of high staff turnover and under considerable financial constraints. Problem-solving theory and task-centred practice, thus, remain essential in social workers' theoretical and methodological arsenal for practice.

Arguably, all but two of the values, principles, issues, and challenges discussed in Parts IV and V of this volume placed the well-being of humans at their centre. Here, however, the focus shall be on the following: Eleni Papouli's chapter on virtues, social work, and social services (▶ Chap. 17, "Virtues, Social Work and Social Service Organizations") unsettled a common (mis)conception that virtues were solely individual properties. While agreeing that indeed, virtues are essential for human flourishing and that the idea of virtues is entirely consistent with that of social workers as good persons and good professionals, Papouli argued that organisations, too, require virtues to flourish, while a lack of organisational virtues risks giving rise to unethical practices within them. She thus set forth how social service organisations may become ethical workplaces that foster shared values and beliefs, uphold ethical decision-making, and support ethical practice. Such virtues are congruent with an ethic of care, as outlined by Donna McAuliffe in ▶ Chap. 18, "An Ethic of Care: Contributions to Social Work Practice". Here, McAuliffe made the point that attention to individual care needs is just as critical as attention paid to organisational structures, which again serves to promote the well-being of humans within systems at multiple levels.

A long-standing debate affecting social work's ability to hold together its increasingly diverse professional body with a shared sense of identity and purpose across the globe pertains to the tension between ethical absolutism and ethical relativism. The former denotes positions that treat one of social work's guiding principles – for example, either human rights or social justice – as more important than all others, while the latter denotes positions that can hold attraction especially when apparently irreconcilable cross-cultural differences appear to clash. Richard Hugman addressed this debate in ▶ Chap. 20, "Ethical Pluralism and Social Work". Following an examination of a variety of examples, Hugman proposed ethical pluralism as a theoretically and practically sound alternative that can support the profession as it engages with uncertainty and attempts to balance respect for difference and particularity with its need for a clear, solid ethical foundation that reflects commonality and enables solidarity.

Arc 2: The Person/Structure Interface

Located at the person/structure interface were writers in the critical theory tradition, where social work has displayed a sustained concern with historical and structural injustices. Often on account of their membership in devalued social groups alone, people have been – and continue to be – categorised, silenced, made invisible, rendered powerless, exploited, marginalised, and violated and – to add insult to injury – habitually blamed for the effects of the hardships suffered as a result. Responding to these injustices has necessarily required attention, at once, to these structural processes, the harms they do in people's lives, the manner in which both social workers and service users can be implicated in them, and what they can do about them.

In Part II: ▶ Chap. 4, "Revisiting Critical Theory", Edgar Marthinsen discussed the enduring relevance of critical theory for contemporary social work practice. There were two corresponding chapters in Part III of this book. In ▶ Chap. 11, "Caring Justice: *The Global Rise of Feminist Practice Theory*", Tina Maschi, Smita Dewan, Sandra Turner, and Padma Christie provided an in-depth exploration of feminist practice theory, at once tracing feminism's diverse roots, political leanings, and applications, while drawing particular attention to its connections with, and relevance for, anti-oppressive theorising and practice. Donna Baines and Hannah Kia's chapter on anti-oppressive social work practice theory (▶ Chap. 10, "Anti-oppressive Social Work Practice Theory") reviewed this by now well-established and growing body of scholarship on anti-oppressive social work theorising and practice, providing an overview of its core knowledge, ethics, and skills base and considering how social work can do better to avoid its – unfortunately far too frequent – complicity historical and contemporary injustices and to strengthen its contribution to wider social justice agendas. The authors extended these themes by drawing on synergies with other, equally relevant traditions, concepts, developments, and movements in social work, such as critical social analysis, advocacy, capacity-building to mobilise colleagues and service users around positive and progressive action, critical allyship, critical attunement, and cultural humility and cultural safety, as well as identifying key areas where further development is still required.

Two chapters in Part IV exemplified social work's long-standing commitment to human rights and social justice. In ▶ Chap. 15, "Social Work, Human Rights, and Ethics", Sharlene Nipperess' starting point was the by now widely shared understanding of social work as a human rights profession. Acknowledging that conceptual challenges do attach to the idea of and dominant discourses around human rights, this author maintained that they continued to provide an important foundation for social work's ability to challenge the inequality, exploitation, domination, and oppression experienced by people and communities around the world, advocating, in conclusion, for a *critical* human rights-based approach to practice. A comparable approach was taken by Neil Thompson and Paul Stepney in their chapter on social justice and social work (▶ Chap. 16, "Social Justice and Social Work"): Noting that social work has long been associated with social justice, the authors proceeded by drawing attention to both the prominent place of social justice in social work codes of ethics and other values statements and to the contested status of social justice as a theoretical concept. Considering a range of historical and contemporary applications, Thompson and Stepney concluded by advocating for a critically reflective approach to practice in order to protect the profession from the danger of committing to social justice at a rhetorical level only. Also located in Part IV was Donna McAuliffe's chapter on the ethic of care (▶ Chap. 18, "An Ethic of Care: Contributions to Social Work Practice"), which draws on several traditions. Thus, while profoundly shaped by the critical theory tradition, the ethic of care can also be credited with articulating a feminist value base in a manner that is pivotal for the profession's ethical understandings. At the same time, as McAuliffe explained, the ethic of care betrays an inherently relational ontology, and this creates important cross-cultural and cross-disciplinary affinities with decolonial, posthuman, and post-anthropocentric theories (see below).

In the field of applied ethics (Part V of this volume), Dorothee Hölscher and Derek Clifford considered the ethical implications of populism for social work (▶ Chap. 21, "The Ethical Challenge of Populism in Social Work"). To this end, they explored the relevance of political philosopher Iris Marion Young for an ethics of justice and care, thus picking up the theme of feminism's relational ontology while highlighting some of the complexities and dilemmas surrounding critical social work's long-standing concern with political voice and social inclusion. Focusing on the Australian context, finally, Kim Robinson's focus was on social work with marginalised, excluded, and displaced humans subject to forced migration (Part V: ▶ Chap. 22, "Critical Social Work and Ethics: Working with Asylum Seekers in Australia"). Engaging with the, sadly, well-known tension facing social workers, who are at once committed to their profession's ethical principles and expected to adhere to their employers' codes of conduct within increasingly hostile socio-political environments, while trying to address the realities of deprivation, marginalisation, and voicelessness among so many of their service users, Robinson reassessed – and readdressed – how critical social work can go about identifying – and using – sites of hope, compassion, and resistance. In so doing, Robinson of course argued strongly against dehumanising humans thus categorised, and this she shared with writers with a special interest in (de)coloniality.

Arc 3: Against Dehumanising the Human – Colonialism and Its Aftermath

Other authors, while certainly sympathetic to the critical theory traditions in social work, are accurately located within a tradition that may loosely be referred to with reference to colonialism and its aftermath. Their chapters were particularly concerned with taking a stand against – and providing solutions to – established traditions in the global North that deeply and habitually dehumanise *other* humans. Importantly, they drew on non-Western knowledge systems, which cannot, and should not, be subsumed under the umbrella of critical theory. In Part II, Sue Green grappled with the concepts and history of colonialism, post-colonialism, and decolonisation (▶ Chap. 6, "Colonisation, Post-colonialism and Decolonisation"). Green noted that the profession's commitment towards decolonising its ethical, theory, and practice base is by now clearly articulated, but that without the depth and detail of historical and geopolitical understandings – of how colonial conquest, subjugation and rule continue to reverberate in the lives of colonised peoples across the world – social work cannot but be found wanting by its own standards. Not only do social workers have a responsibility to know and seek to understand, said Green, but they are also called upon to work respectfully with and alongside Indigenous peoples to learn how the structures that continue to create spiralling inequalities today might be undone and replaced. Across this volume, several chapters demonstrated further what this means.

For example, in Part III, Maschi, Dewan, Turner, and Christie reminded us that our understanding of feminist theory and practice would be incomplete without an appreciation of the impact of Indigenous feminism (▶ Chap. 11, "Caring Justice: *The Global Rise of Feminist Practice Theory*"). Going further, it was Janestic Twikirize's and Allucia Shokane and Mogomme Masoga's chapters (▶ Chaps. 12, "Developmental and Community-Based Social Work", and ▶ 13, "Indigenous Knowledge and Social Work Crossing the Paths for Intervention", respectively), which provided particularly detailed accounts of what it is that social workers around the world can learn about, and alongside whom they might work, to the benefit of the profession and its service users worldwide. Drawing on the rich social work traditions of East Africa and the global South more generally, Twikirize traced the conceptual evolution of developmental social work, and its links with the traditions of developmental social welfare, social and community development, to (re-)assert the significance of macropractice and a commitment to sustainable social change for any attempt to respond meaningfully to the range of historical and contemporary social injustices afflicting also the global North. Writing from South Africa, Shokane and Masoga enlisted the concepts of (de-)colonisation and employed an Afro-sensed perspective to critique contemporary social work and to demonstrate how Indigenous worldviews and knowledges, ethical principles, values, traditions, and practices can be drawn upon to correct, enrich, and enhance the profession's research, education, and practice. Indeed, as advocated by Baines and Kia, there is great scope for dialogue and for synergy between anti-oppressive, feminist, decolonial, and Indigenous social work theorising and practice (see also Hölscher and Chiumbu 2020).

Two chapters draw the decolonial arc into the ethical sections of this volume: In Part V, Ming-Sum Tsui, Ruby Chien-Ju Pai, Peace Yuh Ju Wong, and Cheong-Hai Chu explored the differences – and incompatibilities – between Western culture and the Confucian heritage of East Asian societies (▶ Chap. 23, "Emerging Ethical Voices in Social Work"), arguing that, as voices representing the latter tradition become more audible in social work discourse, they are also reshaping what the profession may consider to be ethical practice. Finally, in ▶ Chap. 24, "Social Work in Extremis: Human Rights, Necropolitics, and Post-human Onto-ethics", Goetz Ottman and Iris Silva Brito critically engaged with how the "darker side of modernity" (Mignolo 2012) reverberates across locations of the global South and embroils the profession, as practitioners are time and again called upon to help respond to massive humanitarian crises, practicing in extremis while struggling to work out the kinds of ethical conundrum to which such positionings give rise. Thus attempting to come to terms with colonialism's continued legacy of destruction, the authors interrogate several seminal contributions in this disturbing yet pivotal realm: Considering Rosi Braidotti's version of critical posthumanism, Achille Mbembe's *necropolitics*, and Giogio Agamben's *homo sacer* through a decolonial lens, they reaffirm social work's humanist tradition, particularly its commitment to human rights in education and practice, however advocating a humbler, more critically reflexive, and inclusive approach.

Arc 4: Decentring the Human

As such, Ottman and Silva Brito's contribution also grappled with a type of scholarship that unsettles many established canons about the relationship between humans and the non-human world, which, while not new, is certainly gaining momentum across the human and social sciences and increasingly recognised as something that social work should not ignore (Webb 2020). Among those who have placed into question the centrality of the human, as conceptualised in dominant European thought, are certainly its own postmodern and social constructionist thinkers. The relevance of this scholarship for social work theorising and practice was well-explained by Catrina Brown in Part II: ▶ Chap. 5, "Postmodern Theory in Practice: Narrative Practice in Social Work". One of the key insights of postmodernism and post-structuralism is that power is not something that humans have and use but is a force in and of itself, which is "complex, scattered and productive", and which transcends humans (Braidotti 2013, p. 27). As Brown reminded her readers, these processes are helpfully understood in relation to discursive processes, the construction of narratives and counternarratives, and meaning making. As importantly, however, Brown's chapter convincingly demonstrated social work's expanding and deepening understanding of just how these insights can be put to work in ways that close the divide between clinical work and social justice.

But once humans question the centrality of their own perspective on the world, how would they establish or confirm what it means to be human, or what it means to live well in this world? Consequently, what do these fast-evolving theoretical insights and provocations mean for a profession that has for the entirety of its existence placed the idea of human well-being at its centre? And how might these sorts of questions work to reconfigure social work's self-understandings at this point in their development? Across this volume's different sections, contributors have drawn on a wide range of knowledge systems and understandings to grapple with this kind of question. In Part II, Sue Green wrote from within Australia's Wiradyuri cosmology to highlight the primacy of relationships, which denote not just what occurs between humans but also humans' connections with place, including all that lives and exists in specific places, and their intricate embeddedness in relationships past, present, and emerging. Responsibility for, and the ability to respond to, the economic, social, cultural, political, and environmental crises humans face in the present emanate and must be conceptualised from there. Equally mindful of contemporary intersecting crises, Karen Bell engaged in ▶ Chap. 7, "Post-anthropocentric Social Work", with posthuman and post-anthropocentric scholarship to consider possibilities for social work to respond to persistent global inequities and injustices in affirmative, creative, hopeful, and transformative ways, and to re-imagine its future under what for many are rapidly deteriorating contextual conditions indeed. This idea was developed further by Vivienne Bozalek and Dorothee Hölscher in their chapter on how posthuman and post-anthropocentric thought might serve to reconfigure social work ethics (Part IV, ▶ Chap. 19, "Reconfiguring Social Work Ethics with Posthuman and Post-anthropocentric Imaginaries"). Employing the conceptual persona of the *becoming-octopus* to explore what might be learned from multispecies encounters, theirs might possibly be considered this volume's most provocative response to the question: What are the implications of a decentring of the human for social work?

However, humans' relationships and entanglements with their non-human *others* are not mere matters of thought experiment, and two sets of authors took on the challenge of exploring the relevance of our evolving understandings for practice: Margaret Alston's chapter on environmental social work (Part III: ▶ Chap. 14, "Environmental Social Work") and Melanie Sage and Gina Griffin's chapter on emerging futures and technology ethics (Part V: ▶ Chap. 25, "Emerging Futures and Technology Ethics"). Noting that social work's traditional person-in-environment perspective has tended to ignore the human/nature interface, Alston's chapter explored the interconnection between environmental degradation, global heating and thus-induced disasters on the one hand, and the eco-systemic pressures emanating from still-growing populations, growing levels of poverty, inequitable access to resources, and uneven power relations within and across societies on the other. Against this background, Alston challenged practitioners in the burgeoning fields of environmental social work, disaster social work, and beyond to better appreciate the inseparability of environmental justice and sustainability to make sustainable contribution to enhancing communities' responsiveness and capacities in the face of environmental threats on a damaged planet. While Alston's are clearly also ethical concerns, ethical questions are foregrounded explicitly in Sage and Griffin's engagement with the human/technology interface. Not accepting any contention that technology might fall outside social workers' expertise, Sage and Griffin referred readers to the Global COVID-19 pandemic as a case in point to demonstrate that not only is everyday practice increasingly technology-mediated, but service users, too, lead increasingly technology-infused lives, a fact which social workers ought not – actually cannot – ignore. The authors called thus for the profession to proactively and deeply engage with the ethical issues to which the evolving human/technology interface in social services is giving rise, including questions concerning electronic data use, the impact of artificial intelligence, and newly emerging forms of practice.

Doubtlessly, the ideas of posthumanism and post-anthropocentrism denote a fast-evolving, cross-disciplinary field, and the challenges emerging in that shifting realm where human and non-human worlds intersect and interact were taken up by contributors to this volume via a diverse, creative, and innovative set of discourses and debates, which impress with their future-orientation, open-endedness, and willingness to hold the resultant ambiguities. However, in terms of criticality, critical reflexivity, willingness to confront the ways in which past injustices reverberate in the present, and openness to reconsider established themes and concerns about how the profession would best contribute to the makings of a just world in which *all* can flourish, they simply meet the standards set by the chapters spanning this volume's other conceptual arcs.

Conclusion

This book was conceptualised from long-standing and diverse active engagement in social work research, education, and practice across several continents and informed by widespread collegial collaborations and networks. The contributions to this volume have grappled with the complexities to which social work must respond and which, as the authors have demonstrated, have not abated. If anything, they have deepened, with socio-economic and political contradictions increasingly palpable across the world. These complexities and contradictions are evident in the themes the authors have tackled, including the challenges of climate change and threats to the environment, unprecedented events like global pandemics, the continued effects of historical atrocities and injustices, ever-deepening levels of inequality, and rising (geo-)political polarisation and tensions.

As, moreover, the advent of the Fourth Industrial Revolution (4IR) heralds significant changes in work and business, the bar is raised considerably. Against this background, the World Economic Forum (2016) contends that the ten skills that will make up the jobs of the future include critical thinking, creativity, complex problem-solving, people management, co-ordinating with others, emotional intelligence, judgement and decision-making, service orientation, negotiation, and cognitive flexibility. Social work is called on to develop new responses and exercise flexibility in uncertain situations. Its strength as a relational discipline lies in its capacity to hold the human experience at the focal point, while the communication skills and ability of social workers to engage constructively and respond with empathy and care continue to be required to support those who experience vulnerability in societies worldwide. At the conclusion of this volume, we are confident that social work will hold its place.

Early on in its development, the profession has organised to put systems in place for democratic governance and engagement, including the International Association of Schools of Social Work (IASSW) in 1928, the International Federation of Social Workers (IFSW) in 1956, and its professional member associations across many countries. While certainly not without flaws, these bodies have brought to the fore consistent leadership and steady guidance including definitions, policies, and standards, including statements on ethical principles and formal codes of ethics, as well as spaces for vigorous debates that assist navigation of complexities in both written and oral formats. That many authors in this volume used these organisations, their documentation, and the spaces they continue to provide as reference points for their arguments speaks volumes about the continued cohesiveness of an ambitious and increasingly diversified profession. The wealth of knowledge that sits behind every chapter is evident, and it is hoped that these contributions have opened new lines of thinking in a continued and enduring global professional conversation.

References

Banks S (2020) Ethics and values in social work, 5th edn. Bloomsbury, London
Bozalek V, Pease B (2021) Post-anthropocentric social work: critical posthuman and new materialist perspectives. Routledge, London
Braidotti R (2013) The posthuman. Wiley, Chichester
Callahan C, Frey JJ, Imboden R (2021) The Routledge handbook on financial social work: direct practice with vulnerable populations. Routledge, New York
Chenoweth L, McAuliffe D (2020) The road to social work and human service practice. Cengage, South Melbourne
Cocker, C, Hafford-Letchfield, T (2022) Rethinking feminist theories for social work practice. Palgrave Macmillan, Houndmills Basingstoke, Hampshire, UK
Crisp B (2019) The Routledge handbook of religion, spirituality and social work. Routledge, London
Dominelli L (2018) The Routledge handbook of green social work. Routledge, Abingdon
Greenwood E (1957) Attributes of a profession. Soc Work 2:44–55
Healy K (2022) Social work theories in context, 3rd edn. Bloomsbury Academic, New York
Hölscher D, Chiumbu S (2020) Anti-oppressive community work practice and the decolonisation debate: a contribution from the global South. In: Todd S, Drolet J (eds) Community practice and social development in social work. Singapore, Springer Nature
Hugman R, Carter J (2016) Rethinking values and ethics in social work. Palgrave Macmillan, London
Hugman R, Pawar M, Anscombe A, Wheeler A (2021) Virtue ethics in social work practice. Routledge, Abingdon
Huss E, Bos E (2018) Art in social work practice: theory and practice. Routledge, London
Joubert L, Webber M (2022) The Routledge handbook of social work practice research. Routledge, Abingdon

Kleibl T, Lutz R, Noyoo N, Bunk B, Dittmann A, Seepamore B (2020) The Routledge handbook of postcolonial social work. Routledge, Abingdon

Marson S, McKinnon R (2019) The Routledge handbook of social work ethics and values. Routledge, London

McAuliffe D (2021) Interprofessional ethics: collaboration in the social, health and human services. Cambridge University Press, Port Melbourne

McTighe JP (2018) Narrative theory in clinical social work practice. Springer, Cham

Mignolo WD (2012) The darker side of western modernity: global futures, decolonial options. Duke University Press, Durham

O'Donoghue K, Englebrecht L (2023) The Routledge international handbook of social work supervision. Routledge, New York

Payne M (2022) Modern social work theory, 5th ed, Red Globe Press and MacMillan Education. London

Payne M, Reith-Hall E (2019) The Routledge handbook of social work theories. Routledge, Milton Park, Abington, Oxon and New York

Pease B, Vreugdenhil A, Stanford S (2019) Critical ethics of care in social work: transforming the policies and practices of caring. Routledge, United Kingdom

Petrakis M (2020) Social work practice in health. Routledge, Abingdon

Reamer F (2018) Social work values and ethics. Columbia University Press, New York

Thompson N, Stepney P (2017) Social work theory and methods: The essentials. Routledge. London

Van Breda A, Sekudu J (2019) Theories for decolonial social work practice in South Africa. Oxford University Press, Cape

Watts L, Hodgson D (2019) Social justice theory and practice for social work: critical and philosophical perspectives. Springer, Singapore

Webb SA (2020) Why agential realism matters to social work. Br J Social Work 51:2694–2981

Wendt WR (2021) Ecology of common care: the ecosocial approach as a theory of social work. Springer International Publishing, Cham

World Economic Forum (2016) The future of jobs: employment, skills and workforce strategy for the Fourth Industrial Revolution. WEF_Future_of_Jobs.pdf (weforum.org)

Index

A
ABCDEF model, 23
Absolutism, 400, 401, 403, 404
Adaptation, 28–30
Advocacy, 198
Affirmative relationships, 130
Africa, 232, 245, 246, 256, 260, 261
Afrocentricity, 259
Afro-sensed approach, 258, 259
Aged care system, 362, 363
Algorithms, 504–506
Al Shabab, 480, 481
Ambivalences, 49
American Civil Rights, 319
Ancient wisdom, 135
Anthropocene, 122, 124, 125, 131, 135–137
Anthropocentric paradigm, 122, 126
Anthropocentrism, 124
Anticolonial social work approach, 253
Anti-Eviction Mapping Project (AEMP), 512
Anti-feminism, 428
Anti-oppressive practice (AOP), 190
    BLM, defunding the police, 203–204
    capacity to advocate, 198–199
    critical ally-ship, 199–200
    critical attunement, 200–201
    critical clinical approach, 195
    cultural safety and cultural humility, 201–202
    intersectionality, 192
    LGBTQI+ social work, 202–203
    macro-level social relations, 194
    meso-level social relations, 194
    micro-level social relations, 194
    mobilization, 199
    mutual, reflexive dialogue, Indigenous social work, 202
    participatory approaches, practitioners and service users, 196–197
    self-reflexive practice and ongoing social analysis, 196
    social change and transformation, 195
    strategic, pragmatic, heterodox social justice theory and practice, 192–194
    theoretical and practical development, 197–198
Anti-racism, 193
Apartheid, 256
Aristotelian ethics, 333
Aristotelian virtues, 338
Aristotle, 335, 336
Assets-based community development, 241
Association for Social Work Education in Africa (ASWEA), 232
Asylum seekers, 450–451
    Boochani, Behrouz, 452
    Nazari, Abbas, 452–453
Asymmetrical, 437
Attentiveness, 388–390
Attentive octopus, 378
Australia, 105
Australian Association of Social Workers (AASW), 299, 300, 453
    Code of Ethics, 315
Australian Border Force Act, 454
Australian Human Rights Commission (AHRC), 449
A Vindication of the Rights of Woman, 351

B
Becoming Octopus, 374
Being of the world, 382–384
Beliefs, 253, 255–257, 259–261, 263
Binary, 124, 129
Bio-medical model, 88
Biosphere, 135
Black feminism, 213, 217
Black Lives Matter movement, 213

BLM, 203–204
Boochani, Behrouz, 452, 456, 459
Both-and approach, 6
Buddhism, 469
Burnout, 34
Business, 133

C

Canadian Association for Social Work Education, 212
Capability approach, 49, 150, 236, 241, 315–316, 402–405, 408
Capitalism, 67, 69, 72, 129
Carceral social work, 204
Cardinal virtues, 337
Care, 135
Care-giving, 351, 354, 355, 358, 359, 363
Caring institution, 440
Caring justice framework, 221–226
Case work, 144
Child protection services, 20
Chinese culture, 467
Chinese medicine, 475
Chinese social work ethics, 406
Civil rights, 473
Civil rights movements, 351
Client-based social work, 475
Climate activism, 269
Climate change, 269, 270, 276, 279, 280, 282, 361
Climate resilient futures, 131
Codes of ethics, 290, 299, 300, 303, 340, 410, 411, 476
Co-existence, 128
Cognitive behavioral therapy (CBT), 7, 23–24, 145, 158, 172
Coherent theory-building for practice, 128
Collaboration, 219, 220
Collaborative normative neutrality, 487
Collective paradigmatic shift, 126
Collective professional shift, 126
Collective/solidarity rights, 294
Collectivist principles, 131
Colonialism, 253, 255, 256, 526
Colonization, 104–106, 253, 255, 256
Communal approach, 340
Communitarian approaches, 128
Community-based interventions, 236, 238
Community development, 237–238
Complexity theory, 47, 62
Composting, 131
Confucian heritage societies, 470
Confucian welfare, 469
Constructivism, 43

Contemporary professional ethics, 467
Contemporary social work, 122, 127, 128, 130–132
Contradictions, 49
Convention on the Elimination of All Forms of Discrimination against Women (CEDAW), 293
Convention on the Rights of Persons with Disabilities (CRPD), 293
Convention on the Rights of the Child (CRC), 293, 407
Convention Relating to the Status of Refugees (1951), 293
Corporate Ethical Virtues (CEV) model, 343
2017 Council on Social Work Education (CSWE) Report, 212
Counter narratives, 192
COVID-19 pandemic, 123, 408, 446
Criminal recidivism, 505
Crisis intervention model, 171–173
Critical ally-ship, 191, 198–200
Critical analysis, 67
Critical attunement, 191, 198, 200–201
Critical clinical approach, 195
Critical ethic of care, 359, 360, 457
Critical human rights-based approach, 306
Critical human rights-based practice, 306
Critically reflective practice, 73, 74, 313, 322, 323, 327–328
Critical post-humanism, 128, 481–485, 487, 493–495
Critical postmodernism, 64
Critical realism, 62
Critical reflexivity, 196, 200, 202, 203
Critical self-awareness, 219, 220
Critical social theory, 62
Critical social work, 75, 446, 447, 451, 453, 454, 456–460
Critical theory, 62, 64, 70–72, 75
　mind and language, 64–68
　negative dialectic to symbolic power, 68–70
　and social work practice, 73–74
Critical thinking, 73
Cultural-relational awareness, 219
Culture, 252, 255, 257, 263, 464–466
　beliefs, 263
　capital, 72, 75
　definitions and differentiation, 466
　feminism, 352
　humility, 255
　relativism, 400
　safety and cultural humility, 201–202
　wars, 427
Curiosity, 388

D

Dark web, 427
Data ownership, 507
Declaration of Helsinki, 9
Declaration on Sexual Orientation and Gender Identity (2008), 293
Declaration on the Rights of Indigenous Peoples (2007), 293
Declaration on the Right to Development (1986), 293
Decolonization, 109–111, 191, 253, 256
Decolonized ethics, 303
Decolonize, 126
Deconstruction, 131
Deep ecology, 277
Demilitarize and defund the police, 204
Democratic socialism, 69, 72
Demos, 424
Depersonalization of clients, 34
Developmental social welfare, 234
Developmental social work, 144, 230
  assets-based community development, 241
  challenges, 244–246
  and community development, 237–238
  community level interventions, 233
  conceptual evolution, 231–234
  consultation and partnership development, 241
  definition, 233
  developmental social welfare, 234
  eco-systems approach, 234
  human rights, equality and social justice, 240
  isolation and institutionalisation, 240
  nature and purpose, 242–244
  notions of strengths, empowerment and capacity building, 239–240
  participation and self-determination, 240
  political participation and activism, 241
  skills, 242
  social development, 234–237
  social investment strategies, 239
Dialogue, 429
Dichotomies, 125
Dirigiste, 318
Disasters, 122
Discourses, 146
Discrimination, 135, 412
Discursive analysis, 83
Discursive resistance, 88
Distributive justice, 131
Diversity, 131
Doctrine of Mean, 472
Dominance, 124
Dominant discourse, 126
Double listening, 91
Dualisms, 125

E

East Asian Confucian societies
  cultural characteristics, 467–469
  ethics and values, 469–470
  face, 468
  human relationships and relational obligations, 472
  kinship and relationship, 472
  lian, 468
  life philosophy and problem-solving orientation harmony and Doctrine of Mean, 472–473
  mianzi, 468
  qing, 467, 468
  yuan, 468
Eclecticism, 177
Ecoanxiety, 280
Eco-feminism, 128, 213, 217
Ecological democracy, 128
Ecological justice, 135
Ecological social work, 276–277
Ecological thinking, 129
Economic(s), 133
  development, 236
  globalization, 317
  social and cultural rights, 294
Ecosocial contract, 130
Ecosocial lens, 127
Ecosocial transition, 278
Ecosocial work, 128–130
Eco-systems approach, 234
Ecosystems framework, 180
Educational initiatives, 344
Educational Policy and Accreditation Standards (EPAS), 212
Ego psychology, 172
Emancipatory aims, 122, 136
Embodied, 128
Embodiment, 128
Emotion, 85–86
Empowerment, 25, 178, 210, 211, 213, 219–221, 226, 313, 314, 319, 323–325, 328
Entanglement, 127, 373
Entitlement, 125
Environment, 133
  activism, 275
  awareness, 278–280

Environment (*cont.*)
   degradation, 268, 271, 274, 275, 278–280
   disasters, 270, 271, 274, 275, 279, 280
   justice, 213, 271
Environmental social work, 276
   climate change and environmental disasters, 269–271
   eco-critical perspective, 275–276
   environmental awareness, 278–280
   environmental degradation, social impacts of, 274–275
   environmental justice, 271
   sustainability, 271–272
Epistemic agency, 129
Epistemology, 125
Epistemology and ontology, 193
Equality, 239, 240, 317
Equity, 130
Ethical and political competence, 439
Ethical decision making processes, 336, 409
Ethical issues, and trauma-informed practice, 32
Ethical monism, 401, 404–405
Ethical pluralism and social work
   codes and formal ethical statements, 410–411
   ethical dilemma, 412–413
   ethical monism, 404–405
   ethical relativism, 405–407
   situations of conflict, 412
   social justice, 411–412
Ethical relativism, 400, 401, 403, 405–407
Ethical transgressions, 342
Ethic of care
   aged care system, 363
   approach, 363
   climate change, 361
   immersive virtual reality, 362
   natural disasters, 361
Ethico-onto-epistemology, 373
Ethics, 4, 8–13, 134, 290, 299, 300, 303, 306, 447, 453, 454, 459, 482–484, 487, 489, 493–495
   of care, 408, 409, 412, 413, 429
   decolonized ethics, 303
Euro-Western social work, 124, 136
Evidence-based practice, 475
Evidence-based social work practice, 174
Exceptional, 127
Exceptionalism, 128
Experiential knowledge, 136
Exploitative colonization, 104

F
False dichotomy, 135
Family' values, 428
Fascism, 428
Feminism, 70, 74, 128, 193
Feminist environmental justice theory, 217–218
Feminist ethic(s), 10, 11, 353, 357, 358
Feminist ethic of care
   critical ethic of care, 360
   early developments, 352, 355
   fifth wave of feminism, 352
   first wave of feminism, 351
   fourth wave of feminism, 352
   political activity, 355–359
   second wave of feminism, 351
   third wave of feminism, 352
Feminist narrative therapy, 89
   coping with trauma, 94–95
   counterstory creation, 96
   counterviewing the dangers of trauma talk and coping, 90–92
   scaffolding questions, 92–94
   therapeutic alliance, 90
   trauma case history, 89
Feminist practice theory
   Black feminism, 217
   caring justice framework, 221–226
   feminist environmental justice theory, 217–218
   feminist relational social work practice, 219–221
   indigenous feminist theory, 218–219
   intersectionality theory, 216–217
   migrant women and feminist theory, 218
   social workers and empowerment, 212–213
Feminist studies of science, 129
Feminist theory, 11, 12
Feminist values, 211
Figuration, 370
Five-stage program adaptation model, 29
Forced migration, in Australia, 448–449
   asylum seekers, 450–451
   settlement of refugees, 450
Foucault's analysis, 81
Frankfurt school, 63–64
Future social work, 124

G
Gender and intersectional oppression, 212
Gender inequality, 74
Gender justice, 213
Gender oppression, 130

Generic language, 64
Global Agenda for Social Work and Social Development (GASWSD), 490
Global challenges, 122, 127
Global citizenship, 133
Global COVID-19 pandemic, 408
Global environmental crisis, 277
Global Ethical Principles, 490
Globalization, 72, 126, 317, 426
Global neo-liberalism, 408
Global populism, 429
Global profession, 132
Global Social Work Statement of Ethical Principles, 321, 410
Government poverty reduction, 238
Grand Challenge movement, 512
Green social work, 277–278
Group dynamics, 19

H

Healing practices, 257
Health, 123
Hegemonic heterosexual masculine ideals, 125
Hermeneutics, 63, 64
Heterodox approach, 193
Heteropatriarchal capitalist status quo, 123
Hierarchical dichotomies, 125
Hierarchical dualisms, 125
Hierarchical patriarchal strategies, 211
Hierarchy, 125
High Commissioner for Human Rights, 293
Historical injustice, 427
Historical trauma, 217
Holistic practice, 131
Homeless people, 344
Human capital, 233
Human capital investments, 239
Humanism, 124
Humanistic theories, and social work practice, 22–23
Human oppression, 218
Human rights, 9–11, 135, 240, 398, 399, 401–408, 411, 412, 428, 480, 481, 483–486, 488–492
    civil and political right, 294
    collective or solidarity rights, 294
    critical human rights-based approach in social work, 306
    definition, 297, 299
    economic, social and cultural rights, 294
    origins, 291
Human rights-based practice, 290, 304, 306, 307

I

Ice cube exercise, 31
Identity politics, 371
Ideology, 69, 424
Idiographic perspective of knowledge, 258
Immersive virtual reality, 362
Immigration detention, 446
Indigenous, 123
    cultures, 256
    feminist theory, 218–219
    models of social work practice, 260–263
    people, 112
    social work practice, 253–255
    worldviews, 135
Indigenous knowledge, 113, 126
    Afro-sensed approach, 258
    context, 257
    definition, 255
    knowledge, 257
    language, 257
    people, 257
    in social work, 259, 260
    socio-cultural and religious motifs, 257
    space, 257
    traditional Indigenous and healing practices, 257
Indigenous social work and AOP, 202
Individual client systems, task-centered practice
    initial phase, 180–181
    middle phase, 181–182
    termination phase, 182
Individualized practice, 126
Individual rights, 473
Inequality, 216, 427
Inequity, 253
Innovation, 124
Institutional building, 234
Institutional hierarchies, 440
Integrative body–mind–spirit social work, 22
Intellectual virtues, 337
Interconnectedness, 124, 127
Interdependence, 352, 357, 363
Interdisciplinary scholarship, 134
Intergovernmental Panel on Climate Change, 123
Internal Displacement Monitoring Centre (IDMC), 270
International Association of Schools of Social Workers (IASSW), 254, 272, 300–302
International Association of Social Workers (IASSW), 489, 490
International Bill of Rights, 302

International Convention on the Elimination of All Forms of Racial Discrimination (ICERD), 293
International Council on Social Welfare (ICSW), 272
International Covenant of Civil and Political Rights (ICCPR), 292–294
International Covenant on Economic, Social and Cultural Rights (ICESCR), 292–294
International Federation of Social Workers (IFSW), 123, 211, 254, 272, 453, 489, 490
International forced migration, 447–448
International service learning (ISL) project, 510
International Social Work (ISW), 481, 483, 484, 486–490, 492–495
Intersecting systems of oppression, 125
Intersectionality, 129, 192, 193
  theory, 216–217
Interspecies ecojustice, 128
Intra-action, 372

J
Jubilee Centre for Character and Virtues, 337
Justice, 123, 126, 130
Justice-to-come, 375

K
Kinship, 471, 472
Knowledge-production, 129

L
Law enforcement agencies, 509
Letsema, 262
4-level model of oppression model, 211
LGBTQI+ social work, 202–203
Liberal approach, 318
Liberal democratic response, 429
Liberal humanism, 124
Life conduct, 50
Life principles, in Confucian culture
  contingency principle, 470
  harmony principle, 471
  principle of face, 470
  qing and rationality balance principle, 470
  reciprocity principle, 470
  seniority principle, 470
Lifespan psychology, 20
Lobola or makgadi, 261
Luhmann's systems theory, 41

M
Macro-level social relations, 194
Macro social work services, 504–506
Mainstream social work, 124
Managerialism, 341
Marginalized people, 129
Market fundamentalism, 426
Market mechanism, 72
Marxism, 66, 69, 193
Masculinist, 125
Merit, 129
Meso-level social relations, 194
#MeToo movement, 216, 352
Micro-level social relations, 194
Migrant feminism, 213
Militarism, 129
Mind and language, 64–68
Mindful eating, 31
Mindfulness
  definition, 26
  ethical issues and trauma-informed practice, 32–33
  family social work practice, 30–31
  social workers' professional practice and development, 33–34
  social work objectives, 27–28
Mindfulness-based cognitive therapy (MBCT), 26–29, 32
Mindfulness-based interventions, 158–159
Mindfulness-based programs (MBPs), 26, 30, 31
  adaptation, 28–30
Mindfulness-based stress reduction (MBSR), 26, 28, 29, 32, 34
Mindful parenting, 28
Mobilization, 199
Modernist, 124
Modernity, 63, 64
Monism, 372, 401, 403–405
Moral humility, 437
Moral obligations, 350, 361
Moral philosophy, 399
Moral relativism, 400
Moral virtues, 337
Motifs, 257
Motivational interviewing, 159–160
Multidisciplinary alliances, 131
Multidisciplinary efforts, 123
Multilevel action, 127
Multispecies, 128
  eco-justice, 135
  encounters, 373
Mutuality, 219–221

Index

N

Narrative theory, 24–25
Narrative therapy, 80, 154–156
    counternarratives as resistance, 87–89
    emotion, 85–86
    epistemology of, 80
    experience, 85
    feminist (*see* Feminist narrative therapy)
    knowledge, power and discourse, 81–84
    mental health, addiction policy and, 96–97
    postmodern influence on, 80
    stories, 86–87
    subject, 84–85
National Association of Social Workers (NASW) Code of Ethics, 211, 314
Nationalism, 133, 424
Natural disasters, 111, 361
Natural language processing, 506
Nazari, Abbas, 452–453, 459
Nazism, 63
Necropolitics, 481, 485, 486, 494, 495
Negative dialectic, 63
Neimanis' body of water, 376
Neo-Aristotelian philosophy, 64
Neo-Aristotelian virtue ethics, 335
Neoliberal and managerialist welfare regimes, 435
Neoliberal discourse, 124
Neo-liberalism, 359, 408, 426
Neoliberalization, 69, 72
New public management, 69
Non-governmental organisations (NGOs), 238
Non-Indigenous social workers, 254
Non-moral values, 401
Nonprofit organization, 344
Nonprofit social sector, 342
Nuclearization, 129

O

Objectives of social work, 25–26
Octopus vulgaris, 377
Official colonization, 253
Omnicrisis, 123
Onto-ethics, 482, 487, 495
Ontology, 124
Operative constructivism, 40
Oppression, 127, 427
Organizational commitment, 340
Organizational efforts, 234
Over-simplified dichotomies, 132

P

Paradigm, 124
Participatory approaches, 196–197
Partnership-building, 134
Patriarchal order, 125
Patriarchal power, 128
Patriarchy, 128
PCS analysis, 313, 325–328
Peace, 126
Personal relationship, 474
Personal social services, 234
Person-centred social work practice
    approaches, 160–162
    narrative therapy, 154–156
    relational social work, 152–154
    strengths-based social work, 149–151
    task-centred social work, 148–149
Person-centred therapy, 157–158
Person-in-environment (PiE), 146, 152, 244, 273, 281
Phenomenology, 63, 64
Philosophical foundations, 126
Philosophy, 125, 126
Planetary wellbeing, 129
Plato, 335
Pluralism, 407–410
Political activism, 241
Political participation, 241
Populism and social work, 426–428
    challenges, 430–434
    ethical dimension, 434
    justice, care and democracy, 436–439
    and social work values, 428–430
Positivism, 64
Positivist, 132
Post anthropocentric change, 127
Post-anthropocentric ethics, 11
Post-anthropocentric philosophy, 130
Post-anthropocentric social work, 124
Post-anthropocentric theory, 122
Post-anthropocentric transformation, 122, 127, 130, 132, 135
Post-anthropocentric turn, 369
Post-anthropocentrism, 127, 130, 135
Post-binary, 135
Postcolonial approach, 253
Post colonialism, 193
Post-colonial theory, 106–109
Post-dualist, 135
Post-humanism, 128, 369, 481, 482
    and social work, 482
    and universal human rights, 485, 486
Post-humanist ethics, 11

Post modernism, 64, 193
Postmodern theories, 24–25
Post-structuralism, 193
Poverty, 317
　eradication, 236
　reduction, 238
Power, 313, 323–328
　relations, 195
Practical wisdom, 337
Practice theory, 5–7, 12
Primary values, 401
Private and public concerns, 135
Privileges, 125
Problem-solving approach, 30
Problem-solving theory, and social work, 170–171
Problem specification, 180
Procedural justice, 131
Profession, 4, 5, 8, 9, 12
　ethics, 32, 332
　identity, 132
　practice, 132
　relationship, 474
　virtues, 476
Psychical systems, 46
Psychoanalysis, 67, 152
Psychodynamic approach, 152
Psychodynamic theory, 7, 20–22
Psychodynamic therapy, 159
Psychological theories, 18
　cognitive behavioral theories and social work practice, 23–24
　humanistic theories and social work practice, 22–23
　individuals' mental health, 19
　mindfulness (*see* Mindfulness)
　objectives of social work practice, 25–26
　postmodern theories and social work practice, 24–25
　psychodynamic theory and social work practice, 20–22
　self-knowledge and interpersonal communication for helping, 19
Psychosocial approach, 175
Public welfare services, 126

Q
Queer theory, 193

R
Racial injustice, 130
Radical constructivism, 40
Radical feminism, 352
Radical imagination, 130
Radical immanence, 373
Reciprocity, 337, 437, 467, 470
Reflexive professional practice, 132
Reflexive value plurality, 491
Refugees, 446–451, 454–460
Relational ethics, 353
Relationality, 124
Relational ontologies, 128
Relational social work, 151–154
Relationship to the state, 191, 197, 202–204
Relativism, 400, 401, 403, 404
Reminders, 33
Research and Development (R&D), 174
Resistance, 196
Responsibility for justice, 437
Re-storying, 192
Risk-avoidance approach, 503
Role-differentiated virtues, 336

S
Sebata-kgomo, 262
Secondary values, 401
Self-awareness, 19, 476
Self-care, 19, 33
Self-knowledge, 19
Self-understanding, 19
Sensibilities, 382
Service provision, 124
Settler-colonialist construction, 135
Settler colonies, 108
Settler colonization, 104
Sexual and gender injustice, 428
Sexual minorities, 428
Shame resilience theory, 23
Shape contradictions, 51
Situated ethics, 434
Social action, 199
Social activism, 351
Social care, 72
　adaptation of mindfulness-based programs, 28–30
Social case work, 144
Social change, 26, 42
Social connection model, 437
Social constructionism, 63, 67
Social constructionist epistemology, 83
Social contract, 125
Social control, 126
Social democracy, 72
Social development, 235–237
Social difference, 436

Social economy, 68
Social histories, 432
Social inequality, 231
Social investment strategies, 239
Socialism, 66, 67, 69
Socialization, 63
Social justice, 10, 11, 239, 240, 313, 337, 398, 399, 401–405, 407, 408, 411–412, 422, 428, 459, 474, 508
　critically reflective practice, 326–328
　definitions and theories, 314–316
　development of welfare state, 316–319
　feminist ideas, 320
　global south, 320–321
　in international codes of ethics, 313–314
　PCS analysis, 325–326
　power and empowerment, 323–325
　practitioner, 321–323
　and social movements, 319
　and social problems, 313
Social media, 428
Social movements, 319
Social philosophy, 436
Social policy, 41, 315–318, 328, 423
Social positions, 431
Social psychology, 41
Social relations, 194
　macro-level, 194
　meso-level, 194
　micro-level, 194
Social science, 63
Social service organizations, 333, 334, 338, 340–343, 345
Social structures, 427
Social struggles, 71
Social values, 475
Social welfare, 234
　approach, 146
Social work, 40, 48, 63, 67, 195, 196, 332, 354, 398, 422, 464, 476, 520–523, 525, 528
　agency, 67
　client-based, 475
　colonialism, 526, 527
　contemporary ethical issues, 522
　curriculum, 7
　decentring the human, 527–529
　decolonization, 521
　definition, 4
　domain, 123, 130, 134
　development of theory in, 6
　dynamic nature, 520
　education and training, 113
　evidence-based practice, 475
　in extremis, 482, 485, 491, 492, 495
　global definition, 300
　growth and relevance of ethics in, 9
　human at the centre, 522–524
　as human rights profession, 304
　implications for, 111–114
　indigenisation, 521
　LGBTQI+, 203
　mutual, reflexive dialogue, Indigenous social work, 202
　person/structure interface, 524, 525
　personal relationship, 474
　practice, 114
　and problem-solving theory, 170–171
　profession, 252–255, 257, 259, 261, 263
　professional relationship, 474
　religion and spirituality, 521
　theory and ethics, 11
　theory and practice, 133
　values, 475
Social Work Action Network (SWAN), 243
Social workers, 5, 7, 8, 10, 11, 290, 293, 296, 299, 301, 305–307, 344, 481, 484–490, 493, 494
　and organizations, 338–340
　virtues and ethical culture, in organization, 343
Social work ethics, 336, 398, 399, 403–407, 409, 412, 413
　attentiveness, 388–390
　attuning to situations, 383–385
　being of the world, 382–384
　beyond subject/object, 385–387
　curiosity, 388
　octopus sensibilities, 382–391
　posthumanism and post-anthropocentrism, 371–374
　re/configure, 390
Social work practice, 351, 356, 357, 359, 360, 362, 364, 457–459, 465
　and CBT, 23–24
　and critical theory, 72–74
　and humanistic theories, 22–23
　and postmodern theories, 24–25
　and psychodynamic theory, 20–22
Socio-analysis, 67, 68
Socio-cultural and religious motifs, 257
Socio-cultural beliefs, 255
Sociology, 41, 63
Socrates, 335
Solastagia, 279, 282
Solution-focused brief therapy (SFBT), 24, 155
South Africa, 256, 257

Species hierarchy, 131
State coercion and control, 190
State responsibility, 133
Status quo, 123
Stories, 86–87
Strategic essentialism, 372
Strengths-based model, 24
Strengths-based social work, 149–151, 161
Strengths perspective, 149
Structural disadvantage, 427
Structural oppression, 253, 255
Structural racism, 427
Suffragettes, 351
Supreme ontological entitlement, 125
Sustainability, 126, 271–272
Sustainable development, 272
Sustainable Development Goals (SDGs), 123, 272, 407
Symbiosis, 128
Symmetrical, 437
Systematically eclectic approach, 128
Systemic change, 130
Systems theory, 40
System-theoretical constructivism, 43

T
Tao, 469
Taoism, 469
Task-centered intervention, 176
Task-centered model, 170, 173, 176, 184
    application procedures and techniques, 179–184
    client empowerment, 177
    diversity, social justice, multiculturalism, 178–179
    eclecticism, 177
    effectiveness, 175
    egalitarian client-practitioner relationship, 177
    empirically based, 177
    empirical orientation, 174, 177
    generalist practice framework, 177–178
    multisystemic application, 177
    origins and historical context, 174
    planned brevity, 177
    problem solving actions, 177
    short term, 175
Task-centered practice
    family systems, 182–183
    groups, 183–184
    with individual client systems, 180–182

Task-centered social work, 145, 148–149
Task Planning and Implementation Sequence (TPIS), 181, 182
Task simulation, 181
Technology
    collaboration, social work education, 510–511
    competence, social worker, 510
    dignity and worth of person, 509–510
    ethical futures of social work and, 512–513
    ethical mistakes of not using, 503–504
    ethics and social work, 507–512
    Harness Technology for Social Good, 511–512
    issues in macro social work services, 504–506
    lessons from Covid-19, 503
    risk management for direct service delivery with, 500–503
    social justice, 508
Telehealth, 507
Telepsychology, 502
Tentacular thinking, 131
The elite, 424
The Global Environmental Crisis, 275
Theory-building, 128, 132
Theory for practice, 5, 6
Theory for social work, 7
The people, 424
Therapeutic alliance, 90
Transdisciplinary approach, 130
Transformative and emancipatory pedagogy (TEP), 282
Transformative approaches, 127
Transformative change, 127
Transformative social work, 122
Trauma-focused CBT (TF-CBT), 158
Trauma-informed practice, 32–33

U
Ubuntology, 128
Ubuntu, 258, 261–263
UN Human Rights Commission, 291, 292
United Nations Convention on Refugees, 447
Universal Declaration of Human Rights (UDHR), 291, 406, 408, 447, 488
Universal human rights, 135, 485, 486
Universalistic values, 423
Unofficial colonization, 253
Unsustainable practices, 126

V

Value plurality, 491
Virtue(s), 332, 334, 398, 401, 403–405, 408, 409, 412, 413
 advantages, 340
 ethical culture, in organization, 343
 ethics, 10, 332–336, 340, 354, 362
 external factors, 341–342
 internal factors, 342–343
 typology of, 336–338
 vulnerability and organizations, 341–343
Vitalist conception of the world, 372

W

Welfare consensus, 317
Welfare provision, 473
Welfare service systems, 124
Welfare state, 316–319, 473, 474
Western civilizations, 465
Western culture, 473, 476
Western humanism, 482–484, 487, 491
Western positivist science, 129
Western psychology, 26
Wiradyuri Cosmology, 115–117
Work, 133
1995 World Summit on Social Development, 236

X

Xeno-racism, 428

Z

Zones of exception, 484

Printed by Printforce, United Kingdom